EDUCATION OF THE GIFTED AND TALENTED

Second Edition

Gary A. Davis
University of Wisconsin

Sylvia B. Rimm
Family Achievement Clinic, Oconomowoc, Wisconsin

Prentice Hall, Englewood Cliffs, New Jersey 07632

LIBRARY OF CONGRESS
Library of Congress Cataloging-in-Publication Data

Davis, Gary A.,
    Education of the gifted and talented / Gary A. Davis and Sylvia B.
Rimm.
        p.   cm.
    Bibliography: p.
    Includes index.
    ISBN 0-13-236605-3
    1. Gifted children--Education--United States.   I. Rimm, Sylvia
B.,   . II. Title.
LC3993.9.D38 1989
371.95'0973--dc19   88-24343
                                                                CIP

Editorial/production supervision
  and interior design: Cyndy Lyle Rymer
Cover design: Wanda Lubelska
Manufacturing buyer: Peter Havens

© 1989, 1985 by Prentice-Hall, Inc.
A Division of Simon & Schuster
Englewood Cliffs, New Jersey 07632

Printed in the United States of America
10 9 8 7 6 5 4 3 2 1

ISBN 0-13-236605-3

Prentice-Hall International (UK) Limited, *London*
Prentice-Hall of Australia Pty. Limited, *Sydney*
Prentice-Hall Canada Inc., *Toronto*
Prentice-Hall Hispanoamericana, S.A., *Mexico*
Prentice-Hall of India Private Limited, *New Delhi*
Prentice-Hall of Japan, Inc., *Tokyo*
Simon & Schuster Asia Pte. Ltd., *Singapore*
Editora Prentice-Hall do Brasil, Ltda., *Rio de Janeiro*

To our families

Cathy, Kirsten, Ingrid, and Sonja
Buck, Ilonna, David, Eric, and Sara

Contents

chapter three

Program Planning   38

chapter four

Identifying Gifted and Talented Students   67

chapter five

Acceleration   102

chapter six

Grouping and Counseling   121

chapter ten

Creativity I: The Creative Person, Creative Process, and Creative Dramatics   205

chapter eleven

Creativity II: Teaching for Creative Growth   224

chapter twelve

Teaching Thinking Skills   249

chapter thirteen

Culturally Different and Economically Disadvantaged Children: The Invisible Gifted 277

chapter fourteen

Underachievement: Diagnosis and Treatment 303

chapter fifteen

The Cultural Underachievement of Females 336

chapter sixteen

The Handicapped Gifted Child 369

chapter seventeen

Parenting the Gifted Child   387

chapter eighteen

Program Evaluation   416

Preface

To provide programs designed to help meet the psychological, social, educational, and career needs of gifted and talented students.

To assist students in becoming individuals who are able to take self-initiated action . . . and who are capable of intelligent choice, independent learning, and problem solving.

To develop problem solving abilities and creative thinking skills; develop research skills; strengthen individual interests; develop independent study skills; strengthen communication skills; receive intellectual stimulation from contact with other highly motivated students; and expand their learning activities to include resources available in the entire community.

To maximize learning and individual development and to minimize boredom, confusion, and frustration.

To enable them to realize their contributions to self and society.

These are the goals of educational programs for gifted and talented students, and these are the purposes of this book. Gifted and talented students have special needs and special problems; they also have special, sometimes immense, talent to lend to society. We owe it to them to help cultivate their abilities; we owe it to society to help prepare tomorrow's leaders and professional talent. Gifted and talented students are a tremendous natural resource, one that cannot be squandered.

It is no secret that since the mid-1970s interest in special educational services for the gifted and talented has climbed to a higher level and with greater public awareness than ever before. Federal statements, definitions, funds, and professional staff now exist. States have been passing legislation that formalizes the existence and needs of gifted children and provides funds for directors, teachers, and programs. Cities and districts are hiring program directors and teacher-coordinators who design and implement specific identification, acceleration, and enrichment plans. And in those schools and classrooms where help from the outside does not appear, enthusiastic teachers plan challenging and worthwhile projects and activities for the one or two most gifted children in each of their classes.

While the ball is indeed rolling, it is also no secret that as with every other social or technological change, (a) mistakes are being made, some elementary ones and some major ones; and (b) there is resistance—from those who believe that providing special services to gifted students is like donating money to the Rockefellers. This book may or may not change the minds of critics who feel that special education for the gifted is unfair, undemocratic, or elitist. The list of virtues at the beginning of this preface, plus the argument that a true democracy includes full individual opportunity, may not make a dent in their well-intentioned defenses.

However, this book can help minimize the mistakes that plague so many thoughtfully planned G/T programs. Mistakes are made at every step, from selecting program goals and student participants to evaluating program success. There are many issues to consider, and many alternatives to choose from. This book should help the reader make better, more informed decisions. There are few absolutely right answers for G/T program plans, since their "rightness" depends upon the specific student needs and the particular educational circumstances. However, there are many absolutely wrong answers and methods. This book should help the reader decide which is which.

This text was prepared as an introduction to the exciting field of gifted education.* It is suitable for college undergraduate and graduate readers, for in-service teachers in elementary or secondary schools, for school psychologists, counselors, and administrators, and for parents of those bright but often bored and ignored gifted children and adolescents. The text provides an introduction—sometimes an in-depth one—to virtually all aspects of program planning and development, from (a) formalizing a statement of philosophy, rationale, goals, and objectives, to (b) identifying students, (c) outlining theory-based acceleration and enrichment activities, and (d) evaluating the ongoing or completed program. Often, specific rating forms and questionnaires for identification or evaluation are

---

*The authors are aware that "gifted education" is not grammatically correct, because it is not education but *students* who are gifted. However, "education of the gifted and talented" is so unwieldy that *gifted education* has become a widely used and fully accepted abbreviation.

presented as models that may inspire the creation of specific, program-relevant instruments. Also, lists of philosophy and goal statements, enrichment strategies, acceleration plans, strategies for teaching creative and critical thinking, and other central matters are described. Curriculum models that direct program planning and models that guide program evaluation also are reviewed. In most cases, an underlying theory, or at least a good rationale, accompanies the strategies and suggestions.

Importantly, the book does not ignore the special identification and programming needs of *female* gifted students or *culturally different, economically disadvantaged, handicapped,* or *underachieving* gifted students. Many existing programs do not adequately accommodate the needs and problems of these children.

Much has happened since the publication of the first edition of *Education of the Gifted and Talented.* All fifty states have adopted definitions of "giftedness," most states have legislated that gifted students receive special services, and many states have allocated funds for gifted programs. Professional and parent organizations, particularly the National Association for Gifted Children, continue to grow. Program planning models and strategies for teaching gifted students have become more sophisticated and more sound.

This second edition of *Education of the Gifted and Talented* includes many of these changes. All chapters have been expanded and updated. For example, gifted leader Joseph Renzulli's new Multiple Menu Model, a model for guiding curriculum planning, appears in Chapter 8. Also in Chapter 8 is June Cox's similarly new Pyramid Project, which describes what to do with students of different levels of giftedness. Another new and exciting development is John Feldhusen's high school program for teaching leadership (Chapter 9). Also, the special problems of gifted children in nontraditional families—single-parent families and multiple-parent families—are addressed in our revised parenting chapter (Chapter 17). We are especially pleased to announce an entirely new chapter on teaching thinking skills (Chapter 12). This chapter outlines the types of skills that are included under the heading "thinking skills," and describes exercises and commercial programs designed to foster their growth.

The authors wish to thank secretaries Marian Carlson and Barbara Ruder for their efficient and ever-helpful contributions, and Prentice-Hall staff members Susan Willig and Cyndy Rymer for their encouragement and assistance with the manuscript. Finally, we are grateful to our families for their encouragement, support, and real-life experiences that helped enrich our text.

GAD
SBR

chapter one

Giftedness
An Introduction

Parents and educators alike are becoming more and more "gifted conscious," and for very good reasons. Tens of thousands of gifted and talented children and adolescents are sitting in their classrooms—their abilities unrecognized, their needs unmet. Some are bored, patiently waiting for peers to learn skills and concepts that they had mastered two years earlier. Some find school intolerable, feigning illness or creating other excuses to avoid the trivia. Some feel pressured to hide their keen talents and skills from uninterested and unsympathetic peers. Some give up on school entirely, dropping out as soon as they are legally able.

Other gifted students tolerate school but satisfy their intellectual, creative, or artistic needs outside of the formal system. The lucky ones have parents who will sponsor their dance or music lessons, chemistry kits and telescopes, art supplies, frequent trips to the library, and home computers. The less fortunate ones make do as best they can, silently paying a price for a predicament that they may not understand, and that others choose to ignore. That price is lost academic growth, lost creative potential, and sometimes lost enthusiasm for educational success and eventual professional achievement.

Some educators—and many parents of nongifted students—are not swayed by the proposition that unrecognized and unsupported talent is wasted talent. A common reaction is, "Those kids will make it on their own," or "Give the extra help to kids who really need it!" The argument is that providing special services for highly able or talented students is "elitist"—giving to the "haves" and ignoring the "have-nots"—and therefore unfair and undemocratic.

Certainly, there are many students who need special help, and every state and school district in the United States has allocated funds for special-education programs. These programs include the "special ed" teachers, speech, reading, and language specialists and school psychologists, along with special equipment, materials, tests, and so forth. The rights of learning disabled, physically disabled, and retarded students are vehemently defended, and they should be.

However, a good argument can be made that gifted students have rights too, and that these rights are often ignored. Just as with other exceptional students, students with gifts and talents also deserve an education commensurate with their capabilities. It is unfair to them to ignore or, worse, to prevent the development of their special skills and abilities and to depress their educational aspirations and eventual career achievements. Our democratic system promises each person—regardless of racial, cultural, or economic background and regardless of sex or handicapping condition—the opportunity to develop as an individual as far as that person's talents and motivation will permit. This guarantee seems to promise intrinsically that opportunities and training will be provided to help gifted and talented students realize their innate potential.

To those who argue that gifted students will "make it on their own," sensible replies are that (a) they should not be held back and required to succeed in spite of a frustrating educational system, and (b) some do not make in on their own. Nyquist (1973), for example, reported that a full 19 percent of high school dropouts in New York State would be classed as "gifted." Almost invariably, gifted dropouts are underachievers, talented students who are unguided, uncounseled, and unchallenged (Rimm, 1986b; Whitmore, 1980). The widely cited *A Nation at Risk* report by the National Commission on Excellence in Education (1983) reported that ". . . over half the population of gifted students do not match their tested ability with comparable achievement in school."

It is not only the gifted students themselves who benefit from specific programs that recognize and cultivate their talents. Teachers involved with gifted students learn to stimulate creative, artistic, and scientific thinking, and they learn to help students understand themselves, develop good self-concepts, and value educational and career accomplishments. In short, teachers of the gifted become better teachers, and their skills benefit "regular" students as well. Society also reaps a profit. Realistically, it is only today's gifted and talented students who will become tomorrow's political leaders, medical researchers, artists, writers, innovative engineers, and business entrepreneurs. Indeed, it is difficult to propose that this essential talent be left to fend for itself—if it can—instead of being valued, identified, and cultivated. Tomorrow's promise is in today's schools, and it must not be ignored.

HISTORY OF GIFTEDNESS AND GIFTED EDUCATION

Giftedness over the Centuries

A capsule survey of the history of efforts to cultivate the abilities of gifted and talented children around the world might include the following.

In ancient Sparta, military skills were so exclusively valued that all boys beginning at age seven received schooling and training in the arts of combat and warfare. Giftedness was defined in terms of fighting skills and leadership. The process of selecting candidates for military education took place at birth—babies with physical defects or who were otherwise of questionable value were flung off a cliff (Meyer, 1965).

In Athens, upper-class free Greeks sent their boys (not girls) to private schools that taught reading, writing, arithmetic, history, literature, the arts, and physical fitness (Warmington, 1961). Higher education also was restricted to the upper crust. Sophists (professional teachers) were hired to teach young men mathematics, logic, rhetoric, politics, grammar, general culture, and "disputation." Apparently, only Plato's Academy charged no fees and selected both young men and women based on intelligence and physical stamina, not social position.

Across the Adriatic Sea, Roman education emphasized architecture, engineering, law, and administration. With more liberal attitudes, both boys and girls attended first level (elementary) schools and some girls attended second level (grammar) schools, but higher education was not permitted for females. According to Good (1960) Rome valued mother and family, and some gifted women emerged who greatly affected Roman society, for example, Cornelius, Roman matron and famous mother of statesmen Gaius and Tiberius Gracchus.

The Renaissance period in Europe (1300–1700) produced remarkable art, architecture, and literature. Strong and wealthy governments rewarded their creatively gifted with wealth and honor. Such aesthetically able persons as Michelangelo, da Vinci, Boccacio, Bernini, and Dante were sought out and supported well.

Moving back a thousand years, early China, beginning with the Tang Dynasty in A.D. 618, placed high value on gifted children and youth. For example, child prodigies were sent to the imperial court where their gifts were recognized and cultivated.

Said Tsuin-Chen (1961), China historically anticipated four principles of modern G/T education. First, they embraced a multiple-talent concept of giftedness. They valued literary ability, leadership, imagination, and originality, and such intellectual and perceptual abilities as reading speed, memory capacity, reasoning, and perceptual sensitivity. A second interesting notion was their recognition of (a) apparently precocious youth who grow up to be average adults, (b) seemingly average youth whose gifts emerge later, and (c) true child prodigies whose gifts and talents are apparent throughout their lives. Third, the early Chinese recognized that abilities of even the most gifted children would not fully develop without special training. Support was considered especially important because of the belief that these children were weak and unhealthy and would not live long. Finally, a fourth notion, attributed to Confucius about 500 B.C., was his nail-on-the-head belief that while education should be available to children of all social classes, they should be educated differently according to their abilities.

In Japan, during the Tokugawa Society period (1604–1868), schools of each clan tracked children of Japanese Samurai differently than children of commoners (Anderson, 1975). Children of Samurai nobility received training in Confucian classics, martial arts, history, composition, calligraphy, moral values, and etiquette. Poor village children were taught to value loyalty, obedience, humility, and diligence. However, a few individual scholars established private academies for the intellectually gifted, including children of both Samurai and commoners.

In early America, concern for the education of gifted and talented children was not great. According to Newland (1976), some gifted youth were accommodated in the sense that attending secondary school and college was based both on academic achievement and the ability to pay the fees.

With compulsory attendance laws schooling became available to all, but few provisions existed for gifted children. As noteworthy exceptions, some schools in Elizabeth, New Jersey, began tracking gifted and slow learners in 1866; St. Louis initiated tracking in 1871. Special classes for gifted children were initiated in Los Angeles and Cincinnati in 1916; Urbana, Illinois, in 1919; and Manhattan and Cleveland in 1922.

CONTEMPORARY HISTORY OF GIFTED EDUCATION

Recent history underlying and influencing today's strong interest in the education of the gifted and talented is not a long one. In fact, five events—four people and one Russian satellite—will bring us quite up to date.

Hereditary Genius: Sir Francis Galton

The English scientist Sir Francis Galton (1822–1911), a younger cousin of Charles Darwin, is credited with the earliest significant research and writing devoted to intelligence (or genius) and intelligence testing. Galton believed that intelligence was related to the keenness of one's senses; for example, vision, audition, smell, touch, and reaction time. His efforts to measure intelligence therefore involved such tests as those of visual and auditory acuity, tactile sensitivity, and reaction time. Highly impressed by cousin Charles's *Origin of the Species,* Galton reasoned that evolution would favor persons with keen senses—persons who could more easily detect food sources or sense approaching danger. Therefore, he concluded that one's sensory ability—that is, intelligence—is due to natural selection and heredity. The hereditary basis of intelligence seemed to be confirmed by his observations—reported in his most famous book *Hereditary Genius* (Galton, 1869)—that distinguished persons seemed to come from succeeding generations of distinguished families. Galton initially overlooked the fact that members of distinguished, aristocratic families also inherit a superior environment, wealth, privilege, and opportunity—incidentals that make it much easier to become distinguished.

Galton's emphasis on the high heritability of intelligence is today shared by some psychologists. Gage and Berliner (1984), for example, drawing upon Jensen's (1969) twin studies, estimate that intelligence is 80 percent inherited and 20 percent due to environment. Other psychologists and educators argue that environment and learning play a much larger role.

Roots of Modern Intelligence Tests: Alfred Binet

Modern intelligence tests have their roots in France, in the 1890s. Alfred Binet, aided by T. Simon, was hired by government officials in Paris to devise a test to identify which (dull) children would not benefit from regular classes and therefore would be placed in special classes to receive special training. Someone had perceptively noticed that teachers' judgments of student ability were biased by such traits as docility, neatness, and social skills. Some children were placed in schools for the retarded because they were too quiet, too aggressive, or had problems with speech, hearing, or vision. A direct test of intelligence was badly needed.

Binet tried a number of tests that failed. It seemed that normal students and dull students were not particularly different in (a) hand-squeezing strength, (b) hand speed in moving 50 cm (almost 20 in.), (c) the amount of pressure on the forehead that causes pain, (d) detecting differences in hand-held weights, or (e) reaction time to sounds or in naming colors. When he measured the ability to pay attention, memory, judgment, reasoning, and comprehension, he began to obtain results. The tests would separate children judged by teachers to differ in intelligence (Binet and Simon, 1905a, 1905b).

One of Binet's significant contributions was the notion of *mental age*— the concept that children grow in intelligence, and that any given child may be at the proper stage intellectually for his or her years, or else measurably ahead or behind. A related notion is that at any given age level, children who learn the most do so partly because of greater intelligence.

In 1890, noted American psychologist James McKeen Cattell had called for the development of tests that would measure mental ability (Stanley, 1978); his request was at least partly responsible for the immediate favorable reception to Binet's tests in America. In 1910 Goddard described the use of Binet's methods to measure the intelligence of 400 "feebleminded" New Jersey children, and in 1911 summarized his evaluation of two thousand normal children. The transition from using the Binet tests with below-average children to employing them with normal and above-average children thus was complete and successful.

Lewis Terman: The Stanford-Binet Test, His Gifted Children Studies

Stanford psychologist Lewis Terman made two historically significant contributions to gifted education. First, Terman supervised the modification and Americanization of the Binet-Simon tests, producing in 1916 the progenitor of all American intelligence tests, the *Stanford-Binet Intelligence Scale*. The test was revised in 1937, 1960 and again in 1986.

Terman's second contribution was his identification and long study of 1,500 gifted children—800 boys and 700 girls. These people were, and still are, the most studied group of gifted individuals in the world. In the 1920s, Terman and Melita Oden (1925) administered the Stanford-Binet test to students initially identified by teachers as highly intelligent. The final sample consisted almost entirely of those who scored 140 or higher, the upper 1 percent. The ensuing field studies in 1927–1928, 1939–1940, and the late 1950s, interspersed with occasional mailings, traced the personal and professional activities of the subjects for over half a century.

Leta Hollingworth: "Nurturant Mother" of Gifted Education

According to Stanley (1978), Galton was the grandfather of the gifted-child movement, Binet the midwife, Terman the father, and Columbia University's Leta Hollingworth the nurturant mother. Her pioneering contributions to gifted education consisted of personal efforts supporting gifted education and gifted students in the New York City area, until her death in 1939, and the publication of two books, *Gifted Children: Their Nature and Nurture* (Hollingworth, 1926) and *Children Above 180 IQ Stanford-Binet: Origin and Development* (Hollingworth, 1942). One noteworthy 1931 quote is: "It is the business of education to consider all forms of giftedness in pupils in reference to how unusual individuals may be trained for their own welfare and that of society at large" (Passow, 1981).

Sputnik: The Russians Are Gaining!
The Russians Are Gaining!

Our last significant historical event to predate the 1970s resurgence of interest in gifted education is the launching in 1957 of the Russian satellite Sputnik. To many, the launch of Sputnik was a glaring and shocking technological defeat—Russia's scientific minds had outperformed ours (Tannenbaum, 1979). Suddenly, reports criticizing American education and, particularly, its ignoring of gifted children became very popular. For example, a 1950 Educational Policies Commission had noted that mentally superior children were being neglected, which would produce losses in the arts, sciences, and professions. In a book entitled *Educational Wastelands,* Bestor (1953) charged that "know-nothing educationists" had created schools that provided "meager intellectual nourishment or inspiration," particularly for bored gifted students.

Following the 1957 launch, more reports compared the quality and quantity of American versus Russian education, and especially the numbers of American versus Russian children being trained in defense-related professions. America lost hands down. A report by the First Official U.S. Education Mission to the USSR (1959), entitled *Soviet Commitment to Education,* claimed that the typical Russian high school graduate had completed ten years of math, five years of physics, four years of chemistry, one year of astronomy, five years of biology, and five years of a foreign language.

Tannenbaum (1979) referred to the aftermath of Sputnik as a "total talent mobilization." Academic coursework was telescoped (condensed) for bright students. College courses were offered in high school; foreign languages were taught in elementary schools. Public and private funds were earmarked for training in science and technology. Acceleration and ability grouping were used, and efforts were made to identify gifted and talented minority students. New math and science curricula were developed, most notably the School Mathematics Study Group (SMSG) math, Physical Science Study Committee (PSSC) physics, and Biological Science Curriculum Study (BSCS) biology. In high school there was a new awareness of and concern for high scholastic standards and career mindedness. The bright and talented students were expected to take the tough courses, to ". . . fulfill their potential, and submit their developed abilities for service to the nation" (Tannenbaum, 1979).

Unfortunately, both the scare of Sputnik and the keen interest in educating gifted and talented students wore off in about five years. The awareness and concern was rekindled in the mid-1970s, however, and, while struggling in some states and districts, gifted education appears here to stay. The U.S. government and all fifty states have enacted legislation and most states are allocating funds. Many teachers and administrators nationwide and across Canada are becoming committed to gifted education. Most large school systems and many small ones are initiating new programs and services for gifted children. Researchers and materials writers are developing tests, publishing articles in new journals, and writing new materials for teaching creativity, thinking skills, computing, math, science, and writing. The movement is not uniquely North American. The July/August, 1985, and July/August, 1987, issues of *Gifted Child Today* focused on "Gifted Education Around the World," with articles describing G/T activities in mainland China, People's Republic of China, Hong Kong, Manila, South Africa, Egypt, Saudi Arabia, India, Australia, Mexico, Dominican Republic, Guam, Brazil, Russia, and Australia.

While the ball is indeed rolling, it also is true that some states have cut back on funding for gifted programs. Further, when individual school districts are faced with budget cuts, gifted programs may be first on the chopping block. Programs that are poorly run, ineffective, not well integrated with the total school programs, or that offend other teachers or parents of excluded students tend to disappear. Unfortunately, even some excellent programs have fallen victim to financial pressures.

DEFINITIONS OF GIFTEDNESS

Defining "gifted" and "talented" is an extremely important matter. It also is surprisingly complicated. The particular definition adopted by a school district will determine who is selected for the special services and training of a gifted program, and who is excluded. Further, there is continual danger that one's definition, and consequent identification methods, will discriminate against such special populations as poor, minority, handicapped, underachieving, and even female students. One's definition of gifts and talents also is tied to programming practices—opportunities should be available for different specified types of gifts and talents. Gifted education leader Renzulli (1986) noted that a definition of giftedness must (1) be based on research about characteristics of gifted individuals, (2) provide guidance in the identification process, (3) give direction and be logically related to programming practices, and (4) be capable of generating research that will test the validity of the definition.

There is no one theory-based definition of "gifted and talented" that is universally accepted, and that will fit all programs and circumstances. Further, common usage of the terms even by experts, including teachers of the gifted, is ambiguous and inconsistent. For example, it is common and acceptable to use the terms interchangeably, as when we describe the same person as a "gifted artist" or a "talented artist." Both Webster's and Random House dictionaries list *talent* as one meaning of *gift*. As another usage, some people label academic ability as "giftedness" but artistic ability as "talent," producing "academically gifted" and "artistically talented." Others will reverse this usage, giving us "academically talented" and "artistically gifted" (Cox, 1986). Renzulli (1984, 1986, 1987) and Treffinger (Treffinger and Renzulli, 1986) prefer the phrase "gifted behaviors," which can be developed in certain students at certain times and in certain circumstances, arguing that the title of "gifted" (or "not gifted") should not be bestowed on children as a result of the identification process.

Some scholars, and the general public, apparently see talent and giftedness as a continuum with giftedness at the upper end (Cox, 1986; Perrone and Pulvino, 1979). Noted Cox (1986), we speak of talented musicians, writers and scientists and the few who are truly gifted, but ". . . no one reverses this usage."

Related to this continuum definition, every program will include students who barely meet the established criteria, along with one or two others who are extraordinarily brilliant or phenomenally gifted in a particular area. No accepted label distinguishes between these two visible groups, although "extremely gifted" often is used, along with the tongue in cheek "severely gifted" or "profoundly gifted." Ronvik (1986), borrowing a term from special education, uses "low-incidence gifted" to label extraordinary students who ". . . are often neglected because they are somewhat out of place in the usual provisions for the gifted."

One's definition of gifted and talented is indeed important, yet delicate and complicated. For now, we will review definitions and categories of definitions that are relatively well known, some of which are widely accepted. While they are not in agreement, these definitions will help clarify the problem.

Five Categories of Definitions: Stankowski

As an introduction to the definition problem, Stankowski (1978) outlined five categories of definitions of "gifts" and "talents." All but the first category have been (and are) used to guide the identification process.

First, *after-the-fact* definitions emphasize prominence in one of the professions as the criterion of giftedness. The "gifted" thus are those who have shown consistently outstanding achievements in a valuable sphere of human activity.

Second, *IQ* definitions set a point on the IQ scale, and persons scoring above that point are classed as "gifted." Terman's Stanford-Binet cutoff of 140 is a classic example. The practice remains popular despite its glaring shortcomings of ignoring creative and artistic gifts and discriminating against culturally different and low socioeconomic level students. According to the Richardson Study (Wilkie, 1985), 82 percent of the school districts responding to their survey reported using IQ scores in identification, although not necessarily exclusively.

Third, *percentage* definitions set a fixed proportion of the school (or district) as "gifted." The particular percentage may be based on intelligence test scores, overall grade-point averages, or sometimes just grades in particular areas, especially math and science. The percentage figure may be a generous 15 to 20 percent or a more restrictive 1 to 5 percent.

A particularly irksome—but frequently heard—comment is that "five percent of our children are gifted!" Nature has not made the selection problem so easy. The fact is, any gift or talent is distributed according to a normal, bell-shaped curve. A specific percentage cutoff point is purely a matter of choice, usually based on available space, facilities, personnel, or the superstition that "five percent of our children are gifted."

Fourth, *talent* definitions focus on students who are outstanding in art, music, math, science, or other specific aesthetic or academic area.

Fifth, *creativity* definitions stress the significance of superior creative abilities as a main criterion of giftedness. Interestingly, while all G/T programs have implicit or explicit goals of increasing creative growth and cultivating persons who will make creative contributions to society, Torrance (1984) reported that some states do not list creativity tests as acceptable selection criteria, or else specify that creativity tests are *not* acceptable as criteria.

General Giftedness vs. Specific Talents

Some educators use the word *gifted* to describe the highly intelligent, "intellectually gifted" person and the word *talented* to refer to persons with superior skills and abilities—"talents"—in just one or a few areas, for example, art, math, science, language, or social areas. There are many variations on this "general gifts" vs. "specific talents" theme.

Cohn's (1981) model differentiates three main domains of "giftedness" each of which is subdivided into categories of "talents." *Intellectual* giftedness subdivides into quantitative, verbal, spatial, and "other specific talent dimensions." *Artistic* giftedness divides into talent in the fine arts, performing arts, and "other specific talent dimensions." *Social* giftedness breaks down into leadership talent, empathic/altruistic talent, and (you guessed it) "other specific talent dimensions."

In another variation of general gifts vs. specific talents, F. Gagne (1985) built upon Cohn's model and Renzulli's (1978, 1986; see below) three-ring definition of giftedness. Gagne concluded that "gifts" vs. "talents" should reflect the psychological distinction between *ability* vs. *performance*. That is, a gifted person is one who is distinctly above average in intellectual, creative, socioemotional, sensorimotor, and other general *ability* domains, each of which may be subdivided into specific abilities (see Figure 1.1). Talent refers to distinctly above average *performance* in fields of activities (e.g., math, music, astronomy, sculpture), the activities being "talents." Said Gagne, interests, personality traits, and environment are cata-

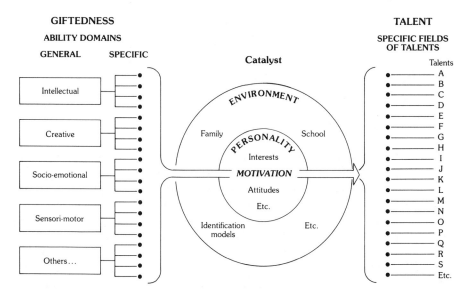

FIGURE 1.1   F. Gagne's model emphasizing gifts as abilities and talents as performances.

Reprinted by permission of the author and the National Association for Gifted Children.

lysts that orient a person toward a particular talent. Motivation, in conjunction with ability, contributes to the intensity of expression of the talent.

Note that, unlike Cohn's model, a given talent does not derive from a specific domain of giftedness. Rather, Gagne's model acknowledges that a given talent will require gifts in several domains (Figure 1.1). As another implication of Gagne's ability-performance distinction, an underachiever is classed as gifted, but not talented; he or she has the ability (gifts), but not the performances (talents).

The 1972 U.S.O.E. Definition

For many educators, the sun rises and sets with the 1972 U.S. Office of Education definition of gifted and talented (Marland, 1972). It is a multitalent approach and it is usually cited on page 1 of state plans for gifted education. It also appears in a great many written program plans prepared by individual districts or schools. It reads:

> Gifted and talented children are those identified by professionally qualified persons who by virtue of outstanding abilities are capable of high performance. These are children who require differentiated educational programs and services beyond those normally provided by the regular school program in order to realize their contribution to self and society.

Children capable of high performance include those with demonstrated achievement and/or potential in any of the following areas:

1. General intellectual ability
2. Specific academic aptitude
3. Creative or productive thinking
4. Leadership ability
5. Visual and performing arts
6. Psychomotor ability

The appeal of the U.S.O.E. definition is that it recognizes not only high general intelligence, but gifts in specific academic areas and in the arts. It further calls attention to creative, leadership, and psychomotor gifts and talents. As we will see in Chapter 4, many specific identification strategies are based on the categories of the U.S.O.E. definition. It recognizes that gifted and talented students require "differentiated educational programs and services beyond those normally provided," thus justifying the development of gifted programs. It recognizes the two fundamental aims of gifted programs: to help individual gifted and talented students develop their high potential, and to provide society with educated professionals who are creative leaders and problem solvers. By including "demonstrated achievement and/or potential ability" it takes into consideration the under-achieving student who may not be demonstrating giftedness in school.

In 1978 the U.S. Congress revised Marland's definition to read:

(The gifted and talented are)" . . . children and, whenever applicable, youth who are identified at the pre-school, elementary, or secondary level as possessing demonstrated or potential abilities that give evidence of high performance capability in areas such as intellectual, creative, specific academic or leadership ability or in the performing and visual arts, and who by reason thereof require services or activities not ordinarily provided by the school." (U.S. Congress, Educational Amendment of 1978 [P.L. 95-561, IX (A)])

The main difference between the 1972 and 1978 statements is that psychomotor ability was excluded. The reason for this change is that artistic psychomotor talents (for example, dancing, mime) could be included under performing arts, and athletically gifted students are already very well provided for. Indeed, athletic programs may be seen as almost ideal gifted programs: Special teachers (coaches) are hired; expensive equipment and space are provided; training is partly individualized; students meet with others like themselves, who encourage and reward each other for doing their best; and students even travel to other schools to meet and compete with other talented individuals and teams. Not much was lost by dropping "psychomotor ability" from Congress's definition.

Said Treffinger and Renzulli (1986) of the U.S.O.E. definition, "The categories are frequently ambiguous, undefinable, or overlapping, and are frequently adopted without regard for their actual implications for identification or programming."

The Renzulli Three-Ring Model

Based upon descriptions of gifted persons who truly make valuable contributions to society, Renzulli (1986) argues that "Gifted behavior . . . reflects an interaction among three basic clusters of human traits—these clusters being above average (but not necessarily high) general and/or specific abilities, high levels of task commitment (motivation), and high levels of creativity. Gifted and talented children are those possessing or capable of developing this composite set of traits and applying them to any potentially valuable area of human performance." As shown in Figure 1.2, the combination of the three are "brought to bear" on general and specific performance areas, resulting in gifted behaviors.

Renzulli's recommended use of the three-ring definition is in conjunction with his Revolving Door Identification Model (RDIM; Chapters 4 and 8). Within the popular RDIM, a full 15 to 20 percent of the school population is identified for a talent pool using procedures like ". . . the usual screening procedures used in more traditional identification systems" (Renzulli, 1984). Identification in the RDIM is liberal and flexible, emphasizing including rather than excluding students. Of the many students selected for the talent pool, said Renzulli, some will show or develop the necessary motivation and creativity and will self-select for independent projects in the resource room supervised by the G/T teacher-coordinator.

FIGURE 1.2 Renzulli's three-ring model. Reprinted by permission of the author.

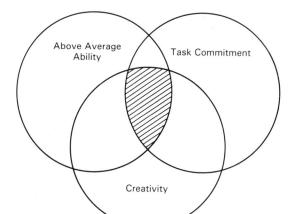

Taylor's Multiple-Talent Totem Poles

In an article entitled "How Many Types of Giftedness Can Your Program Tolerate?" Calvin Taylor described his famous totem poles (Figure 1.3). The idea is fairly straightforward: If we take the time to look, we will find that almost every student in a class is above average, if not outstanding, in some skill, ability, or knowledge area. Looking at Figure 1.3, if we use traditional academic ability (IQ, achievement) for identifying gifted students, Ann—who is at the top of the academic and creative totem poles—is the natural choice for a gifted program. However, if we look at planning (organizing, designing) talents, Randy heads the top of the totem pole. For communicating (speaking, writing) Kathy is the most talented. How do we define gifted and talented? Who should be selected to participate in a gifted education program?

Clearly, Taylor does not so much define "gifts" and "talents" as raise our awareness that most students possess special skills and talents of some variety. There is, however, a serious problem in assuming that all children are gifted. If a G/T program tried to accommodate the unique strengths and talents of all or even most children, it actually would be an enrichment

FIGURE 1.3　Taylor's (1978) Multiple Talent Totem Poles. The important point is that if you look at a large variety of gifts and talents, every child will be above average—perhaps even outstanding—in something. Who is gifted? Who is talented? Most every student? (Reprinted by permission.)

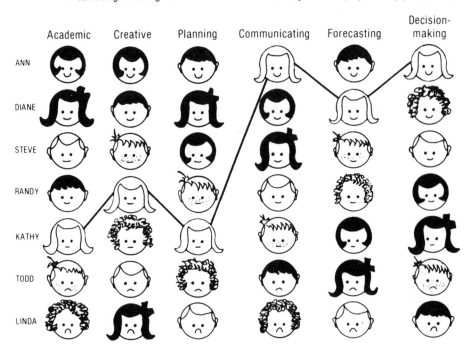

program for everyone, and would qualify only as a watered-down gifted program. Perhaps Taylor's broad definition of giftedness may be best viewed as an appropriate way to perceive, understand, and teach all children.

As a final comment on the definition challenge, we repeat that (1) there is no one final and agreed-upon definition of "gifted" and "talented," (2) the specific definition that a program accepts will determine the selection instruments and procedures, and (3) for any given program those instruments and decision criteria will actually define who is "gifted" and "talented," that is, who receives the special training and who does not.

SUMMARY

Public awareness of gifted education is increasing dramatically. Nonetheless, many gifted students remain ignored, bored, or forced to satisfy their needs outside of school.

Some parents and educators argue that gifted programs are elitist and undemocratic, and that gifted students are not the ones in need of help. The counterargument is that gifted students also deserve a "special education" commensurate with their special needs.

Society also benefits: Tomorrow's leaders are in today's schools.

Historically, ancient Sparta defined giftedness in military terms. Athenian boys attended private schools and were taught by Sophists. In Rome, both boys and girls attended first level schools, but higher education was for boys only.

Renaissance Europe rewarded its gifted artists, architects, and writers with wealth and honor.

In the seventh century, China's Tang dynasty brought child prodigies to the imperial court in order to cultivate their talents. They accepted a multiple-talent conception of giftedness, recognized that talents must be nurtured, and believed children should be educated according to their abilities.

From the 1600s into the 1800s Japan provided high level education only for Samurai children. A few private academics accepted gifted children regardless of birth.

Gifted education in early America was weak. Plantation children attended private schools. In the north, ability and wealth were needed to attend secondary school and college. Tracking was initiated in a few schools in the late nineteenth century, and special classes in the early twentieth century.

Historically, Sir Francis Galton is credited with the first significant research and writing on intelligence. He thought intelligence was related to keen senses, and so his "intelligence tests" evaluated visual and auditory acuity, reaction time, and other sensory skills. Influenced by cousin Charles Darwin, Galton concluded that intelligence was a product of natural selection and heredity. His book *Hereditary Genius* argues that genius runs in families.

Alfred Binet, invited by French officials to create a test to identify dull children, created the original prototype of the famous Stanford-Binet Intelligence Scale. He created the concept of mental age and the notion that a given child may be intellectually behind or ahead of his or her chronological age.

Lewis Terman Americanized the Binet tests, creating the Stanford-Binet scales. In the 1920s he used the Stanford-Binet to identify 1,500 gifted children—who have been tracked and studied ever since.

Over several decades prior to 1939 Leta Hollingworth worked on behalf of gifted students in the New York City area and wrote two books on gifted children and their needs.

The launching of Sputnik in 1957 triggered an American effort to improve education, particularly in the sciences and for gifted students. Unfortunately the enthusiasm disappeared after about five years.

In the mid-1970s a new, exciting and still continuing gifted-education movement began, one that included federal and state legislation, special funds, new programs, and very high interest and commitment by teachers, administrators, and educational researchers.

Defining "gifts and talents" is important because the particular definition will determine the selection of students for special programs. Poor, minority, handicapped, underachieving, and female gifted students may be discriminated against.

Renzulli noted that definitions must be based on characteristics of the gifted, guide identification, give direction to programming, and generate research to verify the definition.

There is no one universally accepted definition of "gifted" and "talented." The terms may be used interchangeably. Leaders Renzulli and Treffinger prefer the phrase "gifted behaviors," which can be developed. Some assume a continuum, with "gifted" at the high end. Extraordinary students have been labeled "severely" or "profoundly" gifted, or "low-incidence" gifted.

Stankowski's five categories of definitions included after-the-fact definitions emphasizing (usually) adult prominence, IQ cut-off definitions, percentage definitions, talent definitions, and creativity definitions.

In accord with a distinction between general gifts but specific talents, Cohn's model differentiated three domains of "giftedness" (intellectual, artistic, social), each of which subdivided into specific "talents."

F. Gagne argued that "giftedness" should refer to ability and "talent" to performance (activities), implying that an underachiever may be gifted, but not talented.

The U.S.O.E., Renzulli, and Taylor definitions are widely known and accepted, even though they are inconsistent with each other.

The 1972 U.S.O.E. definition is cited in many state plans and many individual written program plans. A multitalent definition, it includes six categories: (1) general intellectual ability, (2) specific academic aptitude, (3) creative or productive thinking, (4) leadership ability, (5) visual and performing arts, and (6) psychomotor ability. The U.S.O.E. statement cites the need for differentiated educational programs and cites the two basic goals of gifted education: to help individuals realize their potential and to provide society with high-level talent. The 1978 revision excludes psychomotor skills.

Renzulli's three-ring model emphasizes above-average general or specific ability, high task commitment (motivation), and high creativity. Within his Revolving Door Identification Model, an inclusive talent pool of 15 to 20 percent is selected according to whatever criteria a school wishes to use. Those children showing or developing creativity and motivation self-select for independent projects in a resource room.

Taylor's multiple-talent totem pole model raises the possibility that virtually all students possess special gifts and talents, if we look carefully enough.

chapter two

Characteristics of Gifted Students

Understanding characteristics of gifted children and adolescents is important. If you are a teacher, familiarity with these traits, first of all, will help you recognize and identify gifted students in your classes. You will also become better able to understand them and their strengths, weaknesses, problems, and sometimes peculiar behavior. If you are a parent, a review of characteristics of gifted children should help you judge the degree of your child's giftedness, which is a natural and necessary first step before tackling the next problem of "What do I do now?" You also may discover, to your relief, that your unusual child is not the sole member of a new species.

It is true, of course, that children differ from each other not only in size, shape, and color, but in cognitive and language abilities, interests, learning styles, motivation and energy levels, personalities, mental health and self-concepts, habits and behavior, background, and any other characteristic that one cares to look at. Especially, they differ in their patterns of educational needs. Walberg and others (1981), in reviewing childhood traits of over 200 historically eminent persons, identified some common traits (high intelligence, versatility, superior communication skills), but also found traits that were considerably different for different groups. For example, statesmen (Ben Franklin) were persuasive, popular, and economic minded; religious leaders (Martin Luther) were scholarly, ethical, and sensitive; generals (Simon Bolívar) were tall and motivated by external incentives; historians and essayists (Jean Jacques Rousseau) were persevering, intelligent, and had an absent father; poets and dramatists (Johann Wolfgang von Goethe) were neurotic, only children, and fatherless; and scientists (Isaac Newton) were single-minded, opportunistic, and had an absent mother.

The descriptions that follow, then, are "usual" characteristics, traits that have appeared and reappeared in studies of gifted children and adults. Therefore, they all will not and cannot apply to each and every gifted and talented child.

Overview

This chapter will begin with a look at the classic Terman research mentioned in Chapter 1, then turn to more recent studies and observations of the intellectual and affective traits of highly intelligent children. Following this, some recurrent personality and biographical characteristics of creative students of all ages will be reviewed. Finally, the chapter will examine two studies of the origins—environmental and hereditary—of precocity and extreme high talent. Specific characteristics of gifted and talented minority, female, economically disadvantaged, underachieving, and handicapped students will be studied in later chapters.

THE TERMAN STUDIES

Any discussion of characteristics of gifted children must begin with Terman's high-IQ gifted children (see, for example, Passow, 1981; Terman, 1981), labeled in gifted education circles as "Termites."

One of the most frequently cited findings of the Terman studies was the fact that these students were better adjusted and healthier—both physically and mentally—than average students. Now just a few decades before, Cesare Lombroso (1895), naming specific famous persons, claimed that "signs of degeneration in men of genius" included stuttering, short stature, general emaciation, sickly color, rickets (leading to club-footedness, lameness, or being hunched-back), baldness, amnesia/forgetfulness, sterility, and that awful symptom of brain degeneration—left-handedness. Lombroso's proclamation was well known and widely accepted, no doubt because it made a lot of average people feel better about being average. With scientific data to back him, Terman stressed that the myth of brilliant students being weak, unattractive, or emotionally unstable was simply not true as a predominent trend. They not only were well adjusted in childhood, but in adulthood reported greater personal adjustment, emotional stability, and self-esteem, and were professionally successful and personally content (Karamessinis, 1980; Solano, 1976a, 1976b). Statistically, they showed a below-average incidence of suicide and mental illness.

Terman and Oden (1951) summarized the main characteristics of their gifted children as follows:

> The average member of our group is a slightly better physical specimen than the average child . . .
>
> For the fields of subject matter covered in our tests, the superiority of gifted over unselected children was greater in reading, language usage, arithmetical reasoning, science, literature and the arts. In arithmetical computation, spelling and factual information about history and civics, the superiority of the gifted was somewhat less marked . . .
>
> The interests of gifted children are many-sided and spontaneous, they learn to read easily and read more and better books than the average child. At the same time, they make numerous collections, cultivate many kinds of hobbies, and acquire far more knowledge of plays and games than the average child . . .
>
> As compared with unselected children, they are less inclined to boast or to overstate their knowledge; they are more trustworthy when under temptation to cheat; their character preferences and social attitudes are more wholesome, and they score higher in a test of emotional stability . . .
>
> The deviation of the gifted subjects from the generality is in the upward direction for nearly all traits. There is no law of compensation whereby the intellectual superiority of the gifted tends to be offset by inferiorities along nonintellectual lines.

The description of Terman's Termites presents them as almost perfect children. However, while they were uniformly intelligent (IQ = 140+ in almost all cases), there was a serious bias in their selection. The 1,500 children were selected from a larger group of children who first were nominated by their teachers as "gifted," and we know that teachers are biased toward identifying as "gifted" those children who conform and who are well behaved, pleasant, attractive, and high achieving. Perhaps it is not surprising that Terman could describe their physical and mental health, along with their intellectual capability, in such glowing language. The conclusions would not necessarily apply, for example, to students who are artistically or creatively gifted or who underachieve.

It is significant that two Nobel Prize winners, Luis Alvarez and William B. Shockley, were excluded from the Terman study because their IQ scores were below 140 (Hermann and Stanley, 1983).

TRAITS OF INTELLECTUALLY GIFTED CHILDREN

Precocious Language and Thought

The overriding trait—indeed, *the* definition—of very bright students is that they are developmentally advanced in language and thought. Their intelligence test performance matches that of older children. Their mental development, or *mental age* as Binet named it, simply outstrips both their chronological age and their physical development.

Piaget (Piaget and Inhelder, 1969) tells us that children will verbalize only what they can deal with conceptually. Therefore, the accelerated improvement in speech and language reflect not only a quickly growing vocabulary and knowledge base, but rapidly improving conceptual and abstract thinking abilities as well.

Early Reading, Advanced Comprehension

Some gifted preschoolers not only talk and conceptualize at an advanced level, they may learn to read at age 4 or even 3. Some children teach themselves, and at a runaway pace. They might demand that mother or father point to each word in a book as the parent reads to the child; or the child may persistently ask, for example in a grocery store, "What does that say?" Other gifted preschoolers learn to read in a more traditional way, with mother, father, or the nursery-school teacher teaching the child to recognize letters, relate letters to sounds, recognize and pronounce words, and associate words with meanings. Whether they learn spontaneously or are taught by family members, what is most dramatic is the ease and swiftness with which they learn. Not all gifted children learn to read early or quickly—for example, Albert Einstein did not learn until he was 8—but many do.

The advanced language ability of the intellectually gifted child includes a superior comprehension skill. Therefore, the intellectually gifted child usually acquires a large working vocabulary and a large store of information about many topics. The child may grasp complex and abstract concepts and relationships that normally are learned at an older age.

Logical Thinking

Compared with the average child, the thinking processes of the gifted child are quick and logical, two traits that can disturb impatient parents and teachers. Combined with a natural curiosity and an urge to learn, the precocious child can be forever asking questions, wanting to know, and wanting to know "Why?" The bear-trap logic may not accept an abrupt "Because!" or any other incomplete or illogical response. In light of their swift and logical thinking, it is no surprise that "questioning ability," "a good understanding of cause-and-effect relationships," "convergent problem solving," "persistence" (Cox, 1926; Walberg et al., 1981), and "insight" (Davidson, 1986; Davidson and Sternberg, 1984) are frequently cited as traits of gifted children.

Early Writing, Math, Music, Art

The intellectually gifted child also may begin writing at a precocious age. This talent will result from some combination of teaching by parents, older siblings, or preschool teachers, added to the child's strong drive and mental readiness to imitate and learn. For many gifted children, advanced mathematical, musical, and artistic abilities also appear early, paralleling the verbal and conceptual skills.

The mathematically precocious child may be counting by fives and tens and adding and subtracting two-digit numbers by kindergarten. If you ask the child how he or she arrived at an answer, the child may explain with surprisingly good reasoning his or her own special way of deducing or calculating a mathematical solution. For example, one such second-grade child concluded that "There certainly must be numbers below zero because temperatures can go below zero."

Incidentally, it is not unusual for the child's slower-developing motor ability to stand in the way of some accomplishments. For example, while some young gifted children may be able to manipulate complex calculations and ideas in their heads, or even read at a fifth-grade level, they may not be able to write numbers or letters or illustrate their ideas because of immature eye-hand coordination.

Motivation, Persistence, Advanced Interests

One of the single most recurrent traits of productive gifted students and eminent adults is high motivation and persistence (Franks & Dolan, 1982; Dunn and Griggs, 1985; Renzulli, 1984, 1986). The main reason that some of Terman's students became successful and some did not was differences in their levels of motivation, due in large part to family values (Terman and Oden, 1959). Albert (1975) also stressed that a crucial trait of the geniuses he studied—eminent scientists, musicians, artists, and psychologists—was the compulsion to be productive, the ability to work hard. Even with gifted nursery-school to second-grade children, Burk (1980) found that persistence was related to both achievement and personal adjustment.

Galton (1869) himself, in his book *Hereditary Genius*, noted that natural ability included both ". . . qualities of intellect and disposition, which urge and qualify a man to perform acts that lead to reputation. I do not mean capacity without zeal, nor zeal without capacity, nor even a combination of both of them, without an adequate power of doing a great deal of very laborious work."

The high motivation and urge to learn found in many gifted children, combined with their curiosity and their advanced comprehension and logical abilities, frequently lead to surprisingly advanced interests. The nature and complexity of topics and projects tackled by enthusiastic gifted children seems unlimited. One group of gifted elementary students in Manitowish Waters, Wisconsin, conducted an environmental impact study that led the State Highway Department to move a section of a proposed freeway.

AFFECTIVE CHARACTERISTICS

Low Anxiety and Depression, Better Self-Concepts

We already noted that, on average, Terman's students were generally better adjusted both personally and socially and were emotionally stable, less neurotic, and even more trustworthy than his unselected children. Indeed, as a general rule gifted students are better adjusted and have better self-concepts than regular students (Coleman and Fults, 1982; Griggs and Dunn, 1984; Janos and Robinson, 1985). As argued by Milgram and Milgram (1976a), "Intellectual giftedness is an asset in coping with life's challenges and is associated with . . . favorable social and personal adjustment." Being selected for a gifted program does not hurt one's self-esteem either.

However, recent research on self-concepts of gifted children appears to show contradictory results, sometimes complicated by age or gender differences or by which "self" the researcher is looking at ("academic self" or "social self"). For example, Colangelo and Kelly (1983) compared scores on the *Tennessee Self-Concept Scale* of gifted students, regular students, and students with learning problems in grades 7, 8, and 9. For the overall scale, gifted students scored significantly higher than regular students, who in turn scored higher than students with learning problems. However, on closer examination the gifted students scored significantly higher only on the *academic self* subscale; on the *social self* subscale the gifted students scored about the same as the other students.

Regarding the effects of gender, Kelly and Colangelo (1984) found that gifted adolescent boys had better overall self-concepts than nongifted boys, but there were no differences in self-concepts between gifted and nongifted adolescent girls. With upper elementary students (grades 4, 5, and 6) Loeb and Jay (1987) found the reverse: Gifted girls had a more positive self-concept and higher internal locus of control than nongifted girls. Their high classroom success was congruent with ". . . a positive sense of self and feelings of control over their life space." However, there were no differences between gifted and nongifted boys in self-concept or locus of control. Explained Loeb and Jay, the intellectual orientation of gifted upper elementary boys is disturbingly inconsistent with their ideal male image of aggressiveness, self-reliance, and individualism, leading naturally to lowered self-esteem.

Some constructive suggestions for helping elementary boys included defeminization of the elementary school—more male teachers, more tolerance for independent thought and behavior, more traditionally masculine subjects (for example, mechanics, outer space), and a new definition of the "masculine ideal" that includes academic striving and excellence (Loeb and Jay, 1987).

In high school there seems to be a reversal of attitudes, with high school norms supporting a masculine achievement style, thus producing a positive self-image. The high school female, however, may experience conflict over her role as a gifted, aggressive achiever vs. her emerging identity as a woman, and her self-concept suffers (Loeb and Jay, 1987; Rodenstein, Pfleger, and Colangelo, 1977).

As with any other population, some gifted and talented students—partly because of their gifts—will have social problems and some will be anxious and depressed (Berndt, Kaiser, and Van Aalst, 1982; Gensley, 1977). According to Kester (1975), high levels of social ineptitude are not uncommon. As one might deduce, anxiety, depression, and low self-esteem reduce the academic achievement of gifted students (Milgram and Milgram, 1976a; Rimm, 1986).

Independence, Self-Confidence, Internal Control

An important set of personality characteristics of the gifted child relates to his or her typically high level of self-confidence and independence. Such an attitude is a natural outgrowth of years of favorable comparisons with less-able peers; of glowing feedback and evaluations from parents, teachers, peers, and siblings; and from the child's clear history of success in school.

The concept of high *internal control* describes the confident children or adolescents who feel responsible for their successes and failures and who feel in control of their destinies (Milgram and Milgram, 1976a; Tidwell, 1980). The child with high internal control is likely to use errors and failures constructively; he or she learns from mistakes. Importantly, the internally controlled child usually attributes failure to lack of effort, not lack of ability, and so a failure is a momentary setback that motivates the student to "try harder next time." In contrast, the externally controlled child is more likely to attribute success or failure to luck, chance, easy or difficult tasks, generous or unfair teachers, lack of sleep, a sick cat, and so on. The "external" child also is less likely to try harder after failure—since he or she does not accept responsibility for the outcome in the first place.

The generally higher levels of internal control and personal responsibility often lead gifted students to set high goals for themselves. When these goals are not met, the natural outcome is disappointment, frustration, and feelings of incompetence, ineptness, or stupidity. Parents and teachers are frequently mystified by displays of frustration and self-criticism by students who are obviously extraordinarily capable and talented. The frustration occurs not because the students are comparing their own performances with those of others, but with their own high expectations and standards.

Learning Styles

In view of the high motivation, persistence, self-confidence, independence, and high internal control of many gifted students, it is not surprising to discover that their preferred learning styles match these characteristics. In a summary statement, Griggs and Dunn (1984; see also Dunn, Bruno, and Gardiner, 1984; Dunn and Griggs, 1985) concluded that, compared with nongifted students, gifted students tend to be independent self-motivated learners more than teacher-motivated. They need and enjoy learning tasks that are unstructured and flexible, rather than the highly structured tasks needed by less able students. They prefer active participant approaches to learning, rather than spectator approaches; and they have "well-integrated perceptual strengths," meaning that they can learn through varied sensory channels, including auditory, visual, tactile, and kinesthetic. Further, they generally are more responsible, prefer a quiet learning environment, and they prefer to learn alone or with "true peers"—other gifted students—rather than with regular students (Dunn and Griggs, 1985).

Ricca (1984) compared differences between gifted and regular upper-elementary students in preferred learning conditions and activities as measured by the Dunn, Dunn, and Price (1981) *Learning Styles Inventory* and the Renzulli and Smith (1978b) *Learning Styles Inventory* (see below). For both gifted and regular students, the first choice in learning activities was teaching games and the last choice was drill and recitation. No surprise here. Between these extremes, the gifted students preferred independent study more than did the regular students, while the regular students preferred peer teaching and lecture more than did the gifted. Gifted students also preferred tactile learning, instead of visual learning, and high mobility—they wanted to get into a topic actively and physically. Further, said Ricca, preferences for flexibility and independence reflect the strong needs of gifted students for opportunities for self-determination and self-selection of learning experiences.

Griggs and Dunn (1984) and Griggs (1984) make two important points. First, within the gifted group there are large individual differences in preferred learning conditions and activities, and educators should be aware of each youngster's preferred style. Second, there are significant improvements in academic achievement, school attitudes, and behavior when students' learning styles preferences are accommodated.

The two apparently most well-developed and widely used instruments for assessing learning styles are the Dunn, Dunn and Price (1981; Dunn and Dunn, 1978) *Learning Styles Inventory* (LSI) and the Renzulli and Smith (1978b) *Learning Styles Inventory* (also LSI). The Dunn, Dunn and Price LSI assesses learning preferences in these areas: *environmental* (light, sound, temperature, design), *emotional* (motivation, persistence, responsibility, need for structure or options), *sociological* (self, peer, team, adult, varied), *physical* (time of day, need for intake, mobility, etc.), and *psychological* (global/analytical, left/right, impulsive/reflective). The Renzulli and Smith LSI evaluates, in the order of gifted students' choices found by Ricca (1984), preferences for: teaching games, independent study, programmed instruction, projects, simulation, peer teaching, discussion, lecture, and drill and recitation.

Superior Humor

The superior sense of humor of most gifted children would seem to follow quite naturally from their abilities to think quickly and see relationships, and from their general confidence and social adeptness. The humor will appear in art, creative writing, and other areas as well as in social interaction.

High Moral Thinking, Empathy, and Perspective Taking

As with language ability, moral development also is tied to intellectual development (Diessner, 1983). As a general trend, gifted students are more sensitive to values and moral issues and they intuitively understand why certain behavior is "good" and other behavior is "bad." Piaget and Inhelder (1969) explain that developmentally advanced children are less egocentric; that is, they are able to view a situation from another person's point of view. Therefore, gifted students are more likely to acknowledge the rights of others (Perrone, Karshner, and Male, 1979) and to be sensitive to the feelings and expectations of others. Bright students are less likely to steal from peers or to be abusive, and they are more likely to be fair and to empathize and sympathize with the feelings and problems of others.

Gifted children and youth also are likely to develop, refine, and internalize a system of values and a keen sense of fair play and justice at a relatively early age. This internalized value system leads to consistency in behavior and attitudes (Perrone, Karshner, and Male, 1979). The child not only is likely to be more fair, empathetic, and honest, he or she will evaluate others according to the same standards. It follows that gifted students are less likely to have behavior problems in school (Ludwig and Cullinan, 1984).

The gifted student may develop an interest in social issues, particularly those in which his or her sense of reason and justice seems to be violated. Teachers or parents may find themselves embroiled in serious discussions with gifted children about why adults litter streets and highways with beer cans and burger wrappers, why politicians cut benefits and programs for the elderly and poor, and why parents voted against enlarging the crowded school building.

Be cautioned: despite their high mental ability and high capacity for moral thought, some will turn to delinquency and crime where their talents are quickly rewarded (money, status) by an antisocial peer group (Parker, 1979).

CHARACTERISTICS OF THE CREATIVELY GIFTED

Creativity and Intelligence

The student who is intellectually gifted may or may not be creatively gifted as well. While the relationship between intelligence and creativity is a longstanding issue, a contemporary view to which the authors subscribe is the *threshold* concept (MacKinnon, 1978). According to this view, over the wide range of intellectual ability, from retardation to genius, there is generally a moderate positive correlation. The brighter children and adults tend to do more creative work and score higher on creativity tests. However, above a threshold IQ of about 120, the relationship drops to virtually nothing. Therefore, among most gifted students, creativity and intelligence may be quite independent of each other; the student with the comparatively modest 120 Stanford-Binet IQ may—or may not—show considerably more imagination and creative talent than the top scholar in the school. Reis and Renzulli (1982) found no differences in the quality of creative products produced by students in the top 5 percent in intelligence or achievement compared with students in the top 25 percent, which directly supports the threshold position.

An important implication is that if students selected for a gifted program are in the top 1 to 5 percent in intelligence, the large majority of creative students will be missed.

It is important to distinguish between creativity and intelligence, especially in relation to selecting students for the special services of a gifted and talented program. For example, when asked to nominate gifted students many teachers will quickly select the conforming, prompt, neat, and dutiful "teacher pleasers" rather than the less conforming student who is high in creativity. Also, in many classes (for example, math or science courses in the middle school) the special talents of the creatively gifted may not be required. In such circumstances the creative student will be much less visible and less likely to be nominated as "gifted," compared with the intellectually gifted student who quickly grasps the complex ideas and who usually raises his or her hand first.

Ultimately, the achievements and contributions to society of highly creative students may surpass those of the brighter, conforming grade-getters (Renzulli, 1984; 1986, Renzulli, Reis, and Smith, 1981).

Personality Traits

There is a recurrent group of traits that appears again and again in studies of the creative personality (Barron, 1969, 1978; Goertzel and Goertzel, 1962; MacKinnon, 1978; Torrance, 1981b, 1984). Of course, not all of the following characteristics will apply to all creative people. There simply are too many forms of creativity and creative people to make such a generalization. Most of the traits are not surprising; they square well with our intuitive understanding of a creative person.

Creativity consciousness.   Creative people—at least from adolescence onward when the word "creative" becomes meaningful—are consciously aware of their creativeness. They are in the habit of doing things creatively and they like being creative. If asked, they will modestly admit that, yes indeed, they probably are more creative than the average person.

Confidence, risk-taking.   The creative person also is high in self-confidence and independence and is more willing to take a creative risk. These are essential traits. The innovative person must dare to differ, make changes, stand out, challenge traditions, make waves, bend rules—and make mistakes and fail. The importance of risk-taking and its built-in likelihood of failure are reflected in a statement by Thomas J. Watson, founder and president of IBM: "The way to succeed is to double your failure rate." Interestingly, Treffinger (1983) contended that creative people may not be great risk-takers. He argued that their innovative plans and zany products are so carefully organized and thought out, with possible problems, implications, and contingency plans already taken into account, that the chances of failure are much smaller than they appear to be.

High energy, adventurousness.   Creative people typically have a very high energy level—a certain enthusiastic zest and a habit of spontaneous action. The creative person often becomes totally immersed in his or her ideas and creations, literally unable to rest until the work is complete. A related motivational trait has been called *sensation seeking* (Zuckerman, 1979) or *thrill-seeking* (Farley, 1986).

Curiosity.   The creative person has strong curiosity, a childlike sense of wonder and intrigue. He or she may have a history of taking things apart to see how they work or exploring attics, libraries, or museums, or a generally strong urge to understand the world about him or her. The curiosity frequently produces wide interests and unusual hobbies and collections.

Humor, playfulness.   As in the description of the intellectually gifted, an especially frequent trait of creative students is a good sense of humor. Humor is first cousin to the ability to take a fresh, childlike and playful approach to problems. Many discoveries, inventions, and artistic creations are the result of "fooling around" with ideas and playing with possibilities, unconstrained by well-learned habits, traditions, and conformity pressures. Both Carl Rogers and Sigmund Freud agreed that regression to a more childlike, fanciful, playful state of mind is an important feature of creative thinkers. A favorite quote is that "The creative adult is essentially a perpetual child, the tragedy is that most of us grow up" (Fabun, 1968).

Idealism and reflectiveness.   More serious traits of idealism and reflectiveness also are common. The creative person, more than the average, may ponder his role and goals in life. Their idealism and individuality may surface in antiestablishment cynicism or in dropping out of high school or college.

Alone time.   Related to reflectiveness is the common need for some privacy and alone time. The urge to create demands some time for thinking, for reflection, for solving problems, for creating.

Artistic and aesthetic interests.   Creative students usually will rate themselves high in being artistic—whether they can draw or not—and will be more conscious of artistic considerations. A considerable interest in art galleries, plays, concerts, and theatre is common.

Attraction to the novel, complex, and mysterious.   Another creative trait is the characteristic preference for complexity and attraction to the mysterious. For example, Barron (1969, 1978) found that creative individuals, similar to good artists, preferred drawings on the *Barron-Welsh Art Scale* (Welsh and Barron, 1963) that are smudgy, complex, asymmetrical, and imbalanced. Noted Martindale (1975), "Confronted with novelty, whether in design, music, or ideas, creative people get excited and involved while less creative people turn suspicious or even hostile."

There also is an interesting tendency for the creative person to be a strong believer in such mysterious matters as spirits, extrasensory perception, mental telepathy, precognition, flying saucers, and other psychic and mystical happenings (Davis, Peterson, and Farley, 1973).

Reflectiveness vs. impulsiveness. The authors' own research suggests that the characteristic of impulsiveness versus reflectiveness (Kagan, 1965) shows an interesting developmental change. Creative elementary school children tend to be more reflective in their thinking; they are more careful and meticulous in their work and decisions. However, somewhere in adolescence there frequently is a transformation to impulsiveness—the confident and adventurous spontaneity of the creative adult appears.

Other traits and some negative traits. Torrance (1981b) itemized additional traits that might help the teacher or parent recognize and understand creative students:

Likes to work by himself/herself
Is a "What if?" person
Sees relationships
Is full of ideas
Imaginative, enjoys pretending
High verbal, conversational fluency
Flexibility of ideas and thoughts
Persistent, persevering, unwilling to give up
Constructs, builds, rebuilds
Copes with several ideas at once
Irritated and bored by the routine and obvious
Goes beyond assigned tasks
Experiments with familiar objects to see if they will become something other than what they were intended to be
Enjoys telling about his/her discoveries or inventions
Finds ways of doing things differently from standard procedures
Is not afraid to try something new
Does not mind consequences of appearing different

So far, the creative personality looks pretty good. However, creative children, adolescents, and adults may show some habits and dispositions that will upset normal parents, teachers, or administrators, and other students and colleagues as well. Torrance (1962, 1981b) and Smith (1966) suggested the items below as not-uncommon characteristics of creative students. Most of these "negative traits" are related to creative students' confidence, independence, curiosity, interest in novelty, humor, and persistence. Some traits are likely to cause personal or social adjustment problems.

Indifference to common conventions and courtesies
Stubbornness
Resistance to domination
Arguments that the rest of the parade is out of step
Nonparticipation in class activities
Uncooperativeness
Capriciousness
Cynicism
Low interest in details
Sloppiness and disorganization with unimportant matters
Tendency to question laws, rules, authority in general
Egocentrism
Temperamental
Demanding
Emotional
Withdrawn
Overactive physically or mentally
Forgetfulness, absentmindedness, mind wanders
Sometimes uncommunicative
Watches windows
Won't join scouts

When stubborn Sammy or independent Elissa shows some of these upsetting characteristics, the teacher or parent might consider the possibility that the symptoms are part of a larger picture of original, energetic creativeness that may need rechanneling into constructive outlets.

True creativity is the product not only of personality traits that predispose a person to think creatively, but a constellation of creative abilities as well. Important creative abilities and ideas for strengthening them will be described in Chapters 10 and 11.

Biographical Characteristics

Biographical traits may be of two sorts: subtle and not-so-subtle. Not-so-subtle factors are simply the student's history of creative activities. Creative students and adults will have a background of creative accomplishments, such as having built things, hobbies and collections, art and handicraft projects, writing, composing, theatrical performances, scientific inventions, and so on. Such biographical facts are not highly surprising; however, they are very useful in identifying creative students.

Other biographical trends are more subtle. Schaefer (1969) discovered that creative high school students were more likely to have friends younger or older than themselves rather than the same age, and they were less interested in sports. They had lived in more than one state, and had traveled outside the US. High school girls who were good at creative writing were more likely to own a cat.

Schaefer, confirmed in studies reviewed by Somers and Yawkey (1984), also found that creative students more often had an imaginary childhood playmate. Said Somers and Yawkey, imaginary companions contribute to creativity by developing originality and elaboration and by fostering sensitivity in relationships.

According to Davis (1986), two biographical traits are especially accurate as predictors of creativeness: having had an imaginary playmate and/or participation in theatre activities.

THE ORIGINS OF HIGH TALENT AND EXTREME PRECOCITY

Heredity and environment, working together in some favorable combination, are obvious explanations for the origin of high talent. But this kind of glib answer, though accurate, tells us little. Recently, two scholars sketched in some detail just how heredity and environment, especially the latter, guide the development of extremely high levels of gifts and talents.

Parental Support and Intense Individualized Instruction: Bloom

Benjamin Bloom (1981, 1985; Bloom and Sosniak, 1981) examined the home environment and the early training of exceptional, accomplished pianists, sculptors, swimmers, tennis players, mathematicians, and research neurologists whose talents roughly represented artistic, motoric, and cognitive skill areas. Bloom discovered that the home environments and the gifted persons' parents were almost entirely responsible for nurturing the children's early interests and developing their skills to extraordinary levels.

Almost always, one or both parents had a strong interest in the particular talent and were themselves above average in the skill. In every case the parents strongly supported the children, encouraging and rewarding their interests, talents, and efforts. Importantly, the talented parent or parents served as role models, exemplifying the personality and life-style of the highly talented person. In essence, the children could not resist exploring and participating in the particular talent area; it was expected and accepted as proper.

Initially, parents themselves provided the necessary training and supervision of practice. However, at some point each child switched to a professional instructor. In many cases parent support was so strong that the family would uproot and move to another location to be closer to an outstanding teacher or better facilities. Often, the single outstanding stu-

Catherine Cox (1926), a colleague of Lewis Terman, took an approach to understanding traits of gifted persons that was quite the reverse of her famous cohort. Instead of beginning with bright children and tracking their accomplishments, she began by identifying 282 eminent persons, and then examined their biographical and personal records in order to reach conclusions regarding their intellectual and personal traits. The findings related to intelligence are most enlightening. Cox estimated their IQ scores to range from 100 to 200, with an average of 159. However, many estimated IQs were rather modest: Thirteen IQ scores fell between 100 and 110, 30 between 110 and 120, and 30 between 120 and 130. Extraordinary innate brilliance helped, but was not essential. Cox concluded that individuals who achieve eminence are likely to (1) be born of intelligent parents and raised in advantaged circumstances, (2) show precocious childhood traits and behavior that indicate unusually superior intelligence, and significantly (3) be ". . . characterized not only by high intellectual traits, but also by persistence of motive and effort, confidence in their abilities, and great strength and force of character."

In two studies, the Goertzels (Goertzel and Goertzel, 1962; Goertzel, Goertzel, and Goertzel, 1978) reviewed the family background and personal lives of some 700 adults who had achieved eminence via highly creative achievements that made a strong impact on society. A composite picture, based on recurrent traits and behavior, runs as follows:

> The eminent man or woman is likely to be the firstborn or only child in a middle-class family. . . . In these families there are rows of books on shelves, and parental expectations are high for all children . . .
>
> Children who become eminent love learning but dislike school and school teachers who try to confine them to a curriculum not designed for individual needs. They respond well to being tutored or to being left alone, and they like to go to special schools such as those that train actors, dancers, musicians, and artists . . .
>
> . . . they are more self-directed, less motivated in wanting to please than are their peers or siblings. They need and manage to find periods of isolation when they have freedom to think, to read, to write, to experiment, to paint, to play an instrument, or to explore the countryside. Sometimes this freedom can be obtained only by real or feigned illnesses; a sympathetic parent may respond to the child's need to have long free periods of concentrated effort . . .
>
> They treasure their uniqueness and find it hard to be conforming, in dress, behavior, and other ways . . . (Goertzel, Goertzel, and Goertzel, 1978, pp. 336–38).

The Goertzels and Goertzels (1962) study revealed two consistent family characteristics across all talent areas. First, the parents of all 400 creative persons in that study were highly energetic and goal-directed persons. (Although one mother was described as "somewhat lazy," her extremely high-energy husband was said to have more than compensated for her lacking.) Second, almost all of the families displayed an intense and intrinsic love for learning and achievement that was not simply attached to materialistic goals.

dent would be the central concern of the devoted instructor. During this time the student's dedication to the talent area would grow very strong—which explains his or her willingness to spend approximately fifteen hours per week in lessons and and practice.

Importantly, these students who eventually achieved extremely high levels of proficiency learned to handle failures constructively. That is, failures were learning experiences used to pinpoint problems to be solved and new skills to be mastered. In contrast, according to Bloom, among "talent dropouts" failures led to feelings of inadequacy and quitting.

Bloom (1981) contrasted the development of talent with traditional educational philosophy and methods. The four-point comparison is instructive. First, in the early years of home instruction, talent development is informal, exploratory, and similar to play; the school setting is traditionally serious, formal, and on a set schedule. Second (and most important), with talent development instruction is totally individualized, with praise and rewards based completely on individualized objectives and standards. School learning, of course, is group oriented, usually with a minimum of individualized attention, and rewards, at least to some extent, are based on group achievements. Third, the purpose of school is to provide all students with a broad basic education. Students are expected to do well in all areas and overly strong specialization is not encouraged. In talent development, the student and his or her teacher are fully mobilized toward moving the learner to higher and higher levels of accomplishment in just one specialized area. Fourth, for many students school learning is seen as devoid of meaning, something "to be suffered through." On the other hand, the purposes and meaning in talent development are quite clear, which inspires the necessary dedication and hard work.

Precocity, Available Knowledge, and Coincidence: Feldman

David Feldman (1979, 1985; Feldman & Goldsmith, 1986) reviewed the precocious talents and early achievements of such rare individuals as chess player Bobby Fisher, who became a grand master by age 15, and Wolfgang Amadeus Mozart, who composed mature works by age 10. In his research at Tufts University, Feldman also has been studying a few extremely gifted people—male chess players and music composers—all of whom were performing ". . . in his chosen field at the level of an adult professional before the age of 10." Basically, Feldman attributed such youthful accomplishments to an ". . . astonishing . . . coincidence . . . of human and cultural factors interacting across a few moments of evolutionary time."

The human component in this coincidence is the rare precocious prodigies themselves, whom Feldman described as remarkably "preorganized," highly intelligent, and quite developmentally advanced. The second component of the coincidence is the existence of a highly evolved field of knowledge that can be taught to the precocious child.

Bobby Fisher taught himself to play a fair game of chess by age 6, and from that time on he read hundreds of chess books. As with Bloom's talented people, he received intense formal instruction. Mozart too, while clearly a gifted and precocious child, grew up in a home where music was composed, played, continuously discussed, and valued. Mozart thus received considerable personal instruction, based on an existing body of knowledge, plus extensive exposure to the values and lifestyles of musicians.

Based on the observations of his precocious chess players and musicians, Feldman itemized a few conclusions regarding the prodigies and their teachers, most of which duplicate Bloom's main results.

1. The children received superb instruction.
2. To some degree, the curriculum included a history of the field. For example, the chess masters reviewed world championship games of 150 years ago. All formal music instruction, of course, includes ever-increasing exposure to classical composers.
3. The children themselves showed a passionate commitment to their field and derived a strong sense of joy from their achievements.
4. The teachers were as dedicated to the field as their students.

SUMMARY

Identifying characteristics of gifted students is important because it helps teachers and parents recognize and understand gifted children. Even though all children differ in physical, intellectual, affective, and behavioral traits, some characteristics of gifted and talented students recur frequently in the research literature.

Terman's gifted children (Stanford-Binet IQs of 140+) were better adjusted as children and adults. Compared with other children, they were better achievers and learned more easily, had more hobbies, read more books, were more trustworthy, healthier, and even better "physical specimens." However, their selection was biased due to their initial nomination by teachers prior to testing.

Bright children are developmentally advanced in language and thought. Early, rapidly improving speech reflects a growing conceptual ability and knowledge base. They may learn to read early, sometimes teaching themselves. Comprehension, retention, vocabulary, stored information, and logical abilities are also usually superior.

Writing, math, music, and artistic abilities appear early.

Motivation and persistence are common, and are important for later adult success. Gifted students' high motivation and curiosity lead to advanced interests.

Gifted students frequently show superior affective characteristics, such as lower anxiety and depression and better self-concepts. However, some G/T children will suffer from social inadequacies, anxieties, and depression, perhaps resulting in underachievement.

Research on gender differences in self-concepts has produced inconsistent results. Self-concepts of elementary age boys may be improved by "defeminizing" the elementary school.

The gifted student's history of success usually leads to high self-confidence, independence, and feelings of internal control. However, high self-expectations can lead to frustration.

Gifted students tend to have an independent, self-motivated learning style. They usually prefer unstructured and participant learning activities. Two popular inventories for assessing learning styles are the Dunn, Dunn and Price LSI and the Renzulli and Smith LSI.

Intellectually gifted students intuitively comprehend values and moral issues and are less egocentric, thus able to empathize with the rights, feelings, and problems of others. They are usually more honest and trustworthy, although some may be delinquent. Values and a sense of fairness and justice develop early, leading to consistency in attitudes and behavior and an interest in social issues.

Creativity and intelligence are different traits. They are moderately correlated, but above a threshold IQ score of about 120 the correlation disappears.

Teachers often select conforming "teacher pleasers" for gifted programs, even though creative students may ultimately make greater contributions to society. Creative students often may be less visible.

The creative personality includes high self-confidence, independence, risk taking, high energy, adventurousness, creativity consciousness, playfulness and humor, idealism, attraction to the complex and mysterious, need for alone time, and artistic and aesthetic interests.

Creative elementary school children tend to be reflective; creative adults lean toward impulsiveness.

Torrance suggested that creative students prefer working alone, see relationships, go beyond assigned tasks, and are imaginative, flexible, highly verbal, persistent, and irritated by the routine and obvious.

Some negative traits of creative children are stubbornness, uncooperativeness, egocentrism, discourteousness, indifference to conventions, and resistance to teacher domination.

A background of creative activities is an unsurprising biographical characteristic. Less expected ones include having younger or older friends, having an imaginary playmate, and much traveling.

Studying gifted pianists, swimmers, mathematicians, and others

Bloom concluded that home and parental influences were critical to high levels of talent development. Parents supported the child and modeled the appropriate personality, values, and life-style. All instruction was individualized. Student (and teacher) motivation and dedication ran high. Rather than quitting, students benefited from failures. Compared with traditional schooling, talent development is informal, individualized, specialized, and more meaningful (Bloom).

Feldman reviewed the training and personal lives of such prodigies as Bobby Fisher and Mozart, along with a few contemporary young male musicians and chess players. He stressed the coincidence of human factors (the precocious child) and cultural factors (availability of communicable knowledge). Feldman noted that the curriculum included the history of the field; in agreement with Bloom, instruction was excellent, and both students and their teachers were highly dedicated.

chapter three

Program
Planning

There are many issues and considerations in planning a program for gifted and talented students. To help structure such planning, this chapter will first look at four global areas of focus, which may be recast as why, who, what, where, when, and how questions. The main body of the chapter then will examine fifteen areas of program planning. Finally, we will look at not-uncommon attitudes and views of school board members and "other teachers," with suggestions for improving negative attitudes.

MAIN COMPONENTS OF PROGRAM PLANNING

Based in part on Treffinger's (1981, 1986a, 1986b) *Individualized Programming Planning Model,* the following are four core components of any G/T program. Program planners must attend to these components—in either a knowledgeable and systematic way or else a haphazard, hit-or-miss fashion.

1. Program philosophy and goals. Key questions:

   What is our attitude toward gifted children?
   Why are we doing this?
   What do we wish to accomplish?

2. Definition and Identification. Key questions:

   What do we mean by "gifted and talented"?
   Which categories of gifts and talents will this program serve?
   How will we select them?

3. Instruction—grouping, acceleration, and enrichment. Key questions:

   What are students' needs?
   How can we best meet those needs?
   How can we implement our instructional plans?

4. Evaluation and modification. Key questions:

   Was the program successful? How do we know?
   What did we do right?
   What did we do wrong?
   What changes shall we make?

WHY, WHO, WHAT, WHERE, WHEN, HOW QUESTIONS

As an embellishment on the above components, one can view program planning as a set of questions:

Why are we doing this? Can we prepare a defensible statement of philosophy on gifted and talented? A rationale for our general and specific goals and objectives?

Who will the program be for? Which grades? Which students? How will "gifted and talented" be defined? How will the students be identified?

Who will direct and coordinate the program? Who will serve on the school G/T committee?

What will we do? What are our goals and objectives? What sorts of grouping, acceleration, and enrichment opportunities should we provide? Which will produce the best results? Which will be the most cost-effective?

Where will we do all of this? In the regular classrooms? Special classes? A district resource room? A special school? A "school-within-a-school"? In the community?

When can the training take place? When the students finish regular assignments? On Wednesday afternoon? All day every day? After school? Saturdays? Summers?

How and *when* will we implement the plan? When can the plan begin? Can we formulate timelines for completing the planning? For beginning the identification procedures? For initiating the instructional program?

How will we evaluate gains in students' knowledge and skills? How will we evaluate the effectiveness of each program component? Each instructional activity?

INSET 3.1 A FEW CONSIDERATIONS IN PLANNING A GIFTED PROGRAM: TREFFINGER

Gifted education leader Donald Treffinger (1982b, 1986a) itemized a number of thought-provoking problems and issues related to planning a gifted program, many of which appear below. In conjunction with each problem is one or more idea-stimulating questions in the form of an IWWMW statement—"In what ways might we . . .?"

1. Gifted and talented students are present *now* in our school buildings. Pleading that we can't take action without special funds is like "waiting for Santa Claus." While extra support can be helpful, we must find ways to begin without it.

   *IWWMW initiate action for gifted programming with our own existing resources?

2. While administrators must provide the support ("clout") for gifted education, someone must also be responsible for the day-to-day tasks of program implementation, management, and monitoring.

   *IWWMW provide time and support for trained staff members to carry out daily responsibilities for gifted programming?

3. Individualized professional development, involving more than "listening to speeches on in-service day," is essential within the building.

   *IWWMW identify and respond to individual staff members' professional development interests and needs?

4. The role of "teacher" should involve more than direct services to students all day long, every day.

   *IWWMW provide opportunities for staff members to conduct professional activities not involving direct contact with students?

   *IWWMW provide our staff with more planning time and improve their planning skills?

   *IWWMW provide opportunities for staff members to confer about students' characteristics and needs?

5. Gifted programming that is blended effectively with the total school program does not "just happen." It must develop deliberately and gradually.

   *IWWMW formulate a specific plan for effective growth and change in our programming over a three- to five-year period?

6. Students and their accomplishments are the best "salespersons" for gifted programming.

   *IWWMW make our community and our educational policy-makers aware of the activities and accomplishments of our students?

7. Parents are not (necessarily) adversaries, and they often have talents to share, as well as valuable, unique data to share with us.

   *IWWMW incorporate parents' input and assistance into our gifted programming efforts?

   *IWWMW build upon the resources of existing parent organizations (e.g., PTA)?

8. You must expect obstacles and objectives to come from the least likely issues and the most unexpected sources.

   *IWWMW anticipate difficult issues, obstacles, and criticisms, and prepare to deal with them?

*IWWMW involve our critics in helping us solve problems that are of mutual concern?

*IWWMW insure that our plans will lead to action?

9. Test scores should not be used as "badges" or as "bludgeons." We should not stamp IQ scores proudly upon the student's forehead, nor allow small differences to be overblown in importance.

*IWWMW use test data intelligently, to provide a basis for instructional planning?

10. The gifted program should not merely be "fun and games," nor should it consist merely of things that should occur for many students in all classrooms.

*IWWMW provide appropriate services in the regular classroom?

*IWWMW define the unique contributions and justifications for gifted programming?

PROGRAM PLANNING: FIFTEEN AREAS

This section will describe fifteen problem areas in program planning that relate to the four main components and to the "Why, who, what, where, when, and how" questions. The fifteen areas are not sequential in the one-at-a-time sense. Many will be dealt with simultaneously in planning a G/T program. Some areas are major ones, dealing, for example, with whether there will be a program at all and, if so, the directions the program will take and the students who will be served. Other problem areas are lesser managerial or administrative matters necessary for smooth program operation. As an overview, the problem areas are listed in Table 3.1.

TABLE 3.1 Overview of Fifteen Areas in Program Planning

1. Needs Assessment
2. Preliminary Personal and Staff Education
3. Philosophy, Rationale, Goals, Objectives, and a Written Program Plan
4. Types of Gifts and Talents to be Provided for and Estimated Enrollment
5. Identification Methods and Specific Criteria
6. Specific Provisions for Identifying Female, Underachieving, Handicapped, Culturally Different, and Economically Disadvantaged Gifted Students
7. Staff Responsibilities and Assignments
8. Arranging Support Services
9. Acceleration and Enrichment Plans
10. Organizational and Administrative Design
11. Transportation Needs
12. Community Resources: Professionals and Organizations
13. In-Service Workshops, Training, and Visits
14. Budgetary Needs and Allocations
15. Program Evaluation

1. Needs Assessment

A *needs assessment* aims at determining the discrepancy between the current status of gifted education in the school or district and the desired status. All fifty states have passed legislation formally defining "giftedness" in their state (Cassidy and Johnson, 1986); they also have allocated funds for gifted programs and/or mandated that special services be provided. Therefore, for many schools and districts the former question of "*Is* there a need for a program?" has become "*What* are the needs of the gifted and talented students in the school (or district)?"

There are three excellent sources of information regarding school and district needs for a G/T program and specific student needs: *parents* of gifted and talented students, gifted *students* themselves, and *teachers* and *administrators* who have become "gifted conscious." First, many parents of gifted students have been frustrated by and vocal about the lack of specific services for their children. The authors regularly receive phone calls and letters from exasperated parents who register these types of complaints: "My third-grade daughter has a Stanford-Binet IQ of 145, but the teacher says she can't help because the superintendent is opposed to special programs for the 'haves,' and current rules do not even permit skipping a grade." "My son obviously is gifted and does wonderful and creative things at home, but in school he has become bored and lazy, and I am afraid his talent and enthusiasm are going to waste."

Second, many upper elementary and older gifted students can explain their strong special interests. Their curiosity and high energy levels also may be visible. Would they like to learn advanced computer programming? Would they like a special Saturday science or drama class? Would they be able to handle math or social studies at higher grade levels? Would they like to spend time with a professional artist, executive, or medical researcher? Would they be interested in a three-week summer education program at State University? You bet they would.

Third, another confirmation of the need for G/T programming may come from teachers and administrators who attend conferences or take courses that address the needs and problems of gifted children. With their newly found awareness, they may take an enthusiastic leadership role in helping document district needs and initiating gifted programs.

The need for a G/T program and specific student needs may be documented formally or informally, briefly or extensively depending on the size and formality of the school district and the type and source of the available information or evidence. If a school board or district administration prefers a formal and objective documentation of needs, a needs-assessment questionnaire may be distributed to parents, teachers, and perhaps students. Such a questionnaire should include two main components: (1) perceptions of what needs to be provided in the community, and (2) opinions regarding the extent to which current school programs are meeting these needs. The questionnaire will quantify the desire for differentiated educational services, the preferred directions for the services, and the extent of community support. One example of a needs-assessment questionnaire appears in Table 3.2.

Gifted children and parents of gifted children are minorities in the

TABLE 3.2 Needs-Assessment Questionnaire

Please rate the statements below in two ways. The first rating relates to the strength of a particular program as you see it in the school. The second rating refers to the way in which you think the program should be. Program need will be determined by subtracting Rating 1 from Rating 2. Programs that are presently weak but are determined to be important preferences will be set as first priorities.

Rate 1 if you STRONGLY DISAGREE with the statement.
Rate 2 if you DISAGREE SOMEWHAT with the statement.
Rate 3 if you are UNDECIDED.
Rate 4 if you AGREE SOMEWHAT with the statement.
Rate 5 if you STRONGLY AGREE with the statement.

		NOW	FUTURE
1.	In general, the needs of gifted children in the school district are being met.	1 2 3 4 5	1 2 3 4 5
2.	The attitude of most teachers toward the gifted child is positive and helpful.	1 2 3 4 5	1 2 3 4 5
3.	The program provides individualization of curriculum for gifted children.	1 2 3 4 5	1 2 3 4 5
4.	Special enrichment opportunities are provided for gifted children.	1 2 3 4 5	1 2 3 4 5
5.	Classes that teach creative and critical thinking are available.	1 2 3 4 5	1 2 3 4 5
6.	The school has appropriate guidelines for determining early entrance to kindergarten.	1 2 3 4 5	1 2 3 4 5
7.	The school has appropriate guidelines for determining subject or grade skipping	1 2 3 4 5	1 2 3 4 5
8.	The school provides for the needs of the underachieving gifted child.	1 2 3 4 5	1 2 3 4 5
9.	The special social-emotional needs of gifted children are being addressed.	1 2 3 4 5	1 2 3 4 5
10.	The special needs of the highly creative child are being met.	1 2 3 4 5	1 2 3 4 5
11.	The school provides for the needs of gifted and talented girls.	1 2 3 4 5	1 2 3 4 5
12.	The school provides for the needs of gifted and talented minority children.	1 2 3 4 5	1 2 3 4 5
13.	The school includes parents in the planning and guiding of gifted and talented children.	1 2 3 4 5	1 2 3 4 5
14.	Teacher-education opportunities in the area of gifted and talented are provided for the teaching staff.	1 2 3 4 5	1 2 3 4 5
15.	The administration supports education of the gifted and talented.	1 2 3 4 5	1 2 3 4 5

community, so one cannot expect landslide majority support for such programs. Therefore, the criteria for deciding that programs are needed should only be "sufficient" support, not necessarily strong majority support.

After a need for special services is confirmed (formally or informally), a committee of teachers, administrators, and parents can meet to discuss possible directions for gifted programs. The fifteen problem areas may provide topics for discussion. Eventually, a formal steering committee will be organized, usually appointed (on request) by a district administrator or school principal, to make concrete plans with a definite timetable. In the elementary school, the steering committee might be composed of a district coordinator; teachers from the lower, middle, and upper grades; administrators at the school and district levels; one or two school board members; the school librarian; a school psychologist or counselor; and parents (Robinson, Davis, Fiedler, and Helman, 1982). It may also be helpful to have some gifted high-school students represented; they may be able to provide important insights into the kinds of challenges which, in their experience, have been effective, ineffective, or absent.

2. Preliminary Personal and Staff Education

The goal of building a gifted education program cannot wait for several teachers and administrators to take one or two college courses in gifted education. Teachers must educate themselves and each other in the essential basics—preferably before they all make some uninformed assumptions and mistakes.

Part of a preliminary education will include becoming acquainted with the present status of gifted education in your school, district, city, and even state. One might ask such questions as:

1. What is being done at the present time?
2. What kinds of G/T services are needed?
3. Do other schools in the area have programs? What exactly are they doing?
4. What do school board members and the district superintendent think about special programs for the gifted?
5. Do existing district policies allow students to enter kindergarten early? Skip a grade? What screening procedures are in effect? What are the criteria?
6. Can high school students take college courses in person or by correspondence?
7. Is there a written district policy? A district G/T coordinator? A state G/T director?
8. What exactly does the state legislation on educating gifted children say?
9. Are other teachers interested and supportive? Are they just being agreeable, or are some willing to assume responsibility for the work?
10. Are parents or parent groups becoming restless about their ignored children?

Some of these questions can be answered with a few phone calls. Others will require lengthier exploration and thought.

People seriously interested in gifted education must acquaint themselves with any written district policies or position statements. They should read any state legislation and state plan on behalf of the gifted. The *state legislation* will at the very least (1) define gifted and talented, (2) endorse the concept of differentiated educational experiences, and usually (3) allocate funds for developing and maintaining programs. (Eventually, one can ask the State G/T Director how to apply for the funds.) A *state plan,* which is formally accepted by the superintendent or the state board of education rather than the state legislature, will also define gifted and talented and endorse providing G/T services and programs. The state plan may further itemize specific objectives related to program development, and will usually itemize training services and resources that may be used to meet those objectives.

Many state and local educational organizations sponsor one- or two-day conferences and workshops usually led by one or more experienced leaders in gifted education or related areas. For one- or two-hour workshops, chances are good that a nearby college or state education office can suggest speakers to address specific topics in gifted education.

National and state conferences are immensely informative, for example, those sponsored by the National Association for Gifted Children, the Council for Exceptional Children, the National/State Leadership Training Institute for Gifted/Talented, and by state parent groups and state educational associations. Speakers at national and state conferences will describe the workings of their programs, the pros and cons of their own identification, acceleration, and enrichment strategies, and how they coped with some of the same problems the reader will face. Several journals and magazines are also devoted to the education of gifted, talented, and creative students, especially the *Gifted Child Quarterly, Gifted Child Today, Roeper Review, Journal for the Education of the Gifted, Journal of Creative Behavior,* and *Creative Child and Adult Quarterly.*

A highly enlightening staff activity is visiting schools with successful programs. By speaking directly with involved teachers one will get an inside look at how plans are implemented and how problems are dealt with. One will also gain valuable insight into what works and what does not, tips that will help avoid common pitfalls.

3. Philosophy, Rationale, Goals, Objectives, and a Written Program Plan

A brief statement of philosophy and goals is essential because everyone (parents, teachers, administrators, the local school board) will want to know exactly what the program entails and why. The Richardson Foundation study (G/C/T, 1985) discovered, as a general trend, that districts with substantial programs tended to have a written philosophy and goal statement, along with a special G/T supervisory staff and a special budget. The written philosophy and rationale should include the reasons for the program—a "position statement" explaining why the program is necessary—plus general and, if desired, specific program objectives. An excellent guide for preparing a statement of philosophy is Kaplan's (1974) *Providing Programs for the Gifted and Talented,* which supplies examples of rationale statements and program goals. Two other fine sources of ideas are the Fall 1979 issue of the *Gifted Child Quarterly* and Joyce Juntune's (1981) book *Successful Programs for the Gifted and Talented,* both of which include summaries of many gifted programs around the country. Most of the descriptions present a brief program philosophy and list general and specific program goals. Also, a state plan, if one exists, will undoubtedly include a statement of philosophy and objectives that could be modified to fit a specific program.

A sample of the possible contents of a philosophy and goals statement appears in Appendix 3.1 at the end of this chapter. Take the time to read it now. A one-page philosophy statement for a small Wisconsin City appears in Inset 3.2.

INSET 3.2 A PHILOSOPHY OF GIFTED AND TALENTED EDUCATION

The Watertown, Wisconsin, Public School System is committed to an education program that recognizes individual student differences. Embodied in this commitment is a responsibility to talented and gifted students to help them maximize their high potential.

Gifted children differ from others in learning ability: they learn faster, have wider interests, remember more, and think with greater depth about what they learn. An education program can be designed that will more adequately meet the needs of the gifted student.

A program for gifted students should provide a comprehensively planned curriculum that utilizes within discipline and/or cross-disciplinary studies. These studies should allow for both vertical (acceleration) and horizontal (breadth and depth in a topic) movement that is educationally relevant. The program should stress higher-level thinking skills such as inquiring skills, problem solving, and creative thinking. In addition, development of self-direction, risk-taking, curiosity, imagination, and interpersonal relations should be emphasized. The program framework will allow for individual projects and peer-group interaction.

The long-range goals of this program are self-actualization for the gifted person and the development of a sense of responsibility to self, school, and society.

(Watertown, Wisconsin, School District, 1980. Reprinted by permission.)

If a statement of philosophy and goals is expanded, it can serve as a written plan for a program. A written program plan should present sufficient detail to answer any question that anyone could possibly ask about a proposed program. The written plan is often built around:

1. A definition of gifts and talents. For example, the U.S.O.E. definition is often used.
2. Philosophy and goals. This section explains why a program is necessary. Itemizing the cognitive and affective goals can be brief and general or tedious and specific.
3. Screening and identification methods. This section describes the information used (test scores, grades, teacher nominations, teacher ratings, self-nominations, and so on), the specific cutoff scores, and how the various sources of information will be combined in making final selection decisions. The identification section should also comment on provisions for identifying culturally different, economically disadvantaged, underachieving, and handicapped gifted students. This information will be scrutinized by any state or federal funding agency reading your plan.
4. Instructional programming strategies. This section outlines the curriculum model (if any) on which the program is built. Also included are the specific grouping, acceleration, and enrichment plans, along with the necessary organizational changes; subject areas of concentration and planned activities; the use of community resources; and so on.
5. Program evaluation and modification. This section outlines specific evaluation plans, both of the *formative* type, which provide continuous feedback regarding the ongoing methods and activities, and the final *summative*, did-we-succeed type at the end of the unit, the semester, or most likely, the year.

Specific sections of the written plan may deal with any of the fifteen points described in Table 3.1 and in this chapter. Two good sources of ideas for your written plan are Kaplan (1974) and Sato, Birnbaum, and LoCicero (1974).

4. Types of Gifts and Talents to Provide for and Estimated Enrollment

The topics of *types of gifts and talents* and *definitions of giftedness* are intimately related, and both belong in any statement of philosophy or written plan. The problem of specifying types of gifts and talents to be accommodated is also intimately related to the identification problem— defining who will be "in" the program—and it relates closely to the proposed program plans. Some relevant questions and considerations are: Will the program serve only bright, intellectually gifted students? Or will a multidimensional definition of gifts and talents be used, providing special opportunities to students with specific academic talents, scientific talents, creative talents, communication (speaking, writing) talents, artistic and musical talents, and perhaps others? One high-school program with which the authors are familiar arranged special training for students talented in body-and-fender work.

As for the size of the gifted population, Stanley's (e.g., 1979, 1988) original *Studies of Mathematically Precocious Youth* (SMPY) program catered to students in the top one percent in math ability. In contrast, the Renzulli, Reis, and Smith (1981; Renzulli, 1986) Revolving Door Identification Model identifies 15 to 20 percent of the school population, the talent pool, who revolve in and out of a resource room to work on special projects. Both the Stanley and the Renzulli models are widely accepted and growing in popularity. A good size for a single "pullout" or other special class is about 12 to 15 students.

If grade-skipping, taking advanced classes, or some other acceleration strategy is to be part of the plan, then fixing a number of "in" students is not as sensible as setting criteria cutoff scores that qualify *any number* of students for the acceleration. For example, standardized achievement test scores, probably already on file, are one good basis for decision making. But here is a warning: Due to random score variability, a single cutoff score should never be rigidly used to exclude students who are close to the magic cutoff number. Selection should be flexible and include subjective judgments as well as test scores.

5. Identification Methods and Specific Criteria

Issues and methods related to identifying gifted and talented students are at least sufficiently complex to merit a chapter of their own—a highly condensed chapter at that (Chapter 4). For now, we will simply mention (or repeat) a few basic considerations.

1. Identification methods must be consistent with one's definition of gifted and talented students. It is common for a stated plan to endorse the U.S.O.E. multiple-talent definition, but then use IQ scores for the selection procedure. The identification methods define exactly who is "gifted and talented" for any given program.
2. Identification methods must be coordinated with the type of program(s) one plans to implement. For example, intelligence test scores, reading and math abilities, and teacher nominations might be appropriate for selecting students for grade-skipping. Math ability would be critical for participation in an accelerated math program. If a program accommodates many types of gifts and talents, a variety of ability, achievement, motivation, and creativity tests, inventories, and nominations may be appropriate.
3. The identification methods must be defensible to the community. Parents will ask why one child was selected for a program while another (theirs) was not. Selection decisions must be clearly justifiable. Some identification methods are intelligence tests, standardized achievement tests (particularly reading and math), creativity tests and inventories; inventories assessing interests, hobbies, special needs, and past special opportunities; teacher ratings of vari-

ous characteristics (for example, academic talent, abstract thinking, creativity, motivation, leadership, organizing ability, visual or performing art talents); peer ratings of various characteristics, parent ratings and inventories, and self ratings; and work samples and products (for example, in art, music, or science).

6. Specific Provisions for Identifying Female, Underachieving, Handicapped, Culturally Different, and Economically Disadvantaged Gifted Students

We mentioned earlier that not only males and females must be fairly represented, but also economically disadvantaged, minority, and handicapped gifted students. The problem is not that these students have no gifts and talents; it is that educators do not usually look to these populations for G/T students.

Gifted underachievers may be even less visible than gifted minority, economically disadvantaged, or handicapped students. For underachieving students, their lost talent development is a personal crisis for them and a lost natural resource for humankind. More than one underachieving gifted student has become motivated toward higher educational and career achievement by the specific attention of teachers in gifted programs and, in some cases, by individual and family therapy (Rimm, 1984, 1986).

7. Staff Responsibilities and Assignments

There is a large difference between the passive acceptance or even hearty endorsement of a new gifted program versus the willingness to roll up one's sleeves and do the work. It is an essential preliminary problem to decide just who will assume responsibility for what and when.

It is not unusual to include some accountability checks, for example, by setting deadlines for obtaining certain information, preparing reports, purchasing tests or materials, conferring with administrators, and so forth. Scheduled weekly or biweekly meetings have the effect of establishing accountability—that is, getting things done.

8. Arranging Support Services

A successful program for gifted and talented students will involve experts and professionals beyond the immediate teaching staff. The school psychologist, counselors, the district or state coordinator, and outside consultants will all play important roles.

If the school psychologist is not an expert in gifted education (some are, some are not), his or her main contribution will probably be the administration and interpretation of tests. Individual intelligence tests, mainly the Stanford-Binet and the WISC-R, require a trained administrator. The psychologist might also administer and interpret interest or personality inventories such as the *Edwards Interest Inventory* or the *Kuder Preference Record* to help secondary students better understand themselves, their possible career directions, and the educational preparation necessary for various career alternatives. The school psychologist might administer and interpret personality inventories or supervise the administration of group achievement or group intelligence tests. In addition, many school psychologists are able to work with underachieving gifted students and their parents, or with gifted students with different problems. It is advisable to encourage your school psychologist to educate himself or herself in the area of giftedness by attending conferences, reading relevant books and journals, and so on.

Very few school psychologists have taken any formal coursework whatever in gifted education. If a school psychologist does have expertise in the gifted area, he or she can be helpful with all aspects of program planning and implementation.

School counselors also may or may not have expertise in gifted education. If not, the elementary school counselor will be involved in helping students cope with academic difficulties and with personal problems. The counselor can also help educate parents of gifted children regarding the child's particular talents, academic strengths and weaknesses, and personal difficulties. Importantly, the counselor can help specify the parents' role in developing the capabilities of their gifted child. For example, the counselor can recommend participation in the school's gifted program (many parents are surprisingly reluctant) and can recommend valuable summer programs such as science, art, music, language, or computer camps and workshops. As with the school psychologist, it is important that counselors learn about the special needs of gifted children. Without such additional background, they may make some shortsighted and inappropriate recommendations, for example, by stressing social adjustment and conformity instead of achievement and uniqueness.

In both the junior and senior high schools, counselors serve an invaluable function in fostering self-understanding with gifted and talented students. The educational and career counseling services of the secondary-level counselor should help steer the gifted adolescent into an educational program that is challenging and suitable to the student's college and career needs. Again, a special knowledge of personal and career needs of gifted students is mandatory for guiding them appropriately.

Planning a gifted program frequently involves a series of consultants, for example, a state or district coordinator, a university instructor with relevant experience or knowledge, a professional G/T consultant or workshop leader, or an experienced teacher-coordinator from another location. These consultants can present workshops for the entire school staff, perhaps dealing with methods of identification, alternative instructional models and strategies, program evaluation methods, problems of gifted girls, or other topics. Particularly, some might describe in colorful detail the workings and problems of their own successful program.

You may also work with consultants on a one-to-one basis, outlining strategies for:

Obtaining funds
Preparing written statements
Selecting goals and objectives
Designing relevant acceleration and enrichment activities
Selecting or creating nomination forms, rating forms, or questionnaires for identification
Insuring proper representation of different student groups
Designing program evaluation procedures
Selecting or creating instruments for program evaluation
Promoting good public relations

9. Acceleration and Enrichment Plans

Issues, details, and recommendations regarding acceleration (for example, grade-skipping, advanced classes) and enrichment (for example, resource room or Saturday programs) are elaborated in Chapters 5, 6, and 7. For now, we will simply emphasize that specific instructional plans must be designed to produce sensible, defensible, and valuable educational benefits. While this recommendation may sound obvious and trivial, as Renzulli and his colleagues (Renzulli, 1984, 1986; Renzulli and Smith, 1978a; Renzulli, Reis, and Smith, 1981) have repeated, far too many programs entertain the children with fun-and-games time fillers and interest-getters, with little attention to worthwhile, theory-based goals. For inspiration regarding valuable goals and activities, you may review the philosophy and goals ideas in Appendix 3.1 and the Curriculum for the Gifted section (Table 5.1) at the beginning of Chapter 5. Some examples of high-level goals that guide specific acceleration and enrichment plans are:

High achievement; advanced academic skills and content
Complex, abstract, theoretical thinking
Creative, critical, evaluative thinking; other thinking skills
Scientific research skills
Library research skills
Communication (speaking, writing) skills, including creative writing
Career-related content
College preparatory content
Self-awareness, affective, and humanistic principles

Each of the curriculum models outlined in Chapter 8 is based on these and other potentially valuable instructional outcomes. One or more of the models often serves as the basis for planning specific acceleration and enrichment activities.

10. Organizational and Administrative Design

Most G/T plans require some administrative reshuffling of the school organization and budget to staff the program; provide the necessary time, space, and facilities; and coordinate the G/T activities with the rest of the school schedule. If the program is district-wide or city-wide, the planning will take place partly, not entirely, at these higher levels. In addition, any program for gifted and talented students will require considerable recordkeeping by those directly involved—the teacher or teacher-coordinator, although secretaries can carry some of the burden.

For example, acceleration plans as straightforward as grade-skipping or taking college or correspondence courses will require that new types of records be created and maintained, and that student progress be monitored. Also, clear arrangements will have to be made with the local college. (University registration staff have been known to become disagreeable when an unexpected troop of grinning 15-year-olds march in to register.) A more complicated acceleration plan such as telescoping (for example, condensing three years of math or science into two) will require not only a teacher, a classroom, and a time slot, but complete coordination with the rest of the school course offerings and organization, along with creating and keeping records of student participation and success.

Enrichment plans also require attention to organizational and administrative matters. A Wednesday pullout program will require at the very least a teacher-coordinator and a resource room, plus such miscellaneous supplies and equipment as resource books, workbooks, chemistry and biology supplies, calculators, microcomputers, typewriters, art supplies, perhaps a 35-mm camera and a videocam, and so forth. Other enrichment plans, such as Saturday classes, extra classes, field trips, and mentoring programs, also will require attention to organizational, administrative, and managerial matters of staff, space, scheduling, transportation, materials, and record keeping.

If a plan is district-wide or city-wide, particularly when special schools for the gifted and talented are created or Saturday or summer programs are planned, the organizational and administrative planning is clearly more involved. It is not unusual for metropolitan areas to have several full-time G/T personnel in the central office to help plan and manage city-wide programs. However, regardless of the size and type of program, a local school staff member must be designated as having administrative responsibility for the G/T program in that school. Without a designated responsible person at whose desk the buck stops, even excellent programs will flounder and disappear.

11. Transportation Needs

Transportation plans may be simple and relatively minor, but they cannot be ignored. Transportation problems and costs must be considered for students who attend special schools, take college courses, or travel to schools with special resource-room programs. Transportation must also be considered for field trips, mentoring programs, after-school projects and clubs, summer programs, and Saturday programs.

12. Community Resources: Professionals and Organizations

Community resources, namely professional people and organizations, will be invaluable in at least three types of instructional plans and programs for the gifted: mentoring plans, enrichment-oriented field trips, and career education. Therefore, in planning a program at either the elementary or secondary level, potentially valuable community resources should be reviewed and itemized.

Mentoring plans involve the placing of gifted students with a community professional for usually a few hours each week. The professional could be in any area of the arts, science, or business. There can be no substitute for the values, attitudes, skills, job requirements, and knowledge of daily routines and life-styles acquired by gifted students in such a personal educational experience.

While mentoring plans are used almost entirely at the secondary level, using community resources for field trips and career education is useful with any age group. Some possibilities for field trips are art galleries and museums, university art, science and engineering laboratories, police and government facilities, manufacturing plants, and so forth. Engineering and computer departments seem to enjoy showing off their latest robots.

Do not forget that all students—not just the gifted—will profit from field trips in increased knowledge, better school attitudes, and perhaps raised aspirations.

Using community resources for career education would involve small-group or even individual visits with professional persons, including guided tours of their organizations. To ensure an educational benefit, the concrete plans for such a trip must include specific questions to be answered. Follow-up activities can include discussions and/or the preparation of written or oral reports on the experience.

13. In-Service Workshops, Training, and Visits

Part of the continuing education of teachers, administrators, and support staff should include a planned series of in-service workshops. These may be led by a state director of gifted programs, a district coordinator, a professional G/T consultant, or a staff member from a nearby college. Initially, the school staff should receive in-service education at the *awareness* level. The purposes of an introductory exposure are (1) to attempt to improve attitudes of teachers who believe that gifted children do not require special services and (2) to generally heighten the commitment of all teachers. Van Tassel-Baska (1986) suggested these as good awareness topics: characteristics and needs, what to do in the classroom, and general approaches to programs.

Next in order should be in-service training dealing with the *identification* of gifted children, and the teacher's role in this process. A good understanding of the selection tests, criteria, and weighting procedures—and the role of subjective judgment—may prevent some special problems later. For example, teachers should understand why Johnny, a highly creative "B" student, should be included in the program even if his tested IQ is not over 125.

The choice of other topics will vary according to the direction of the G/T program. If acceleration strategies are planned, teachers must understand both the reasons behind these strategies and the specific procedures for conducting the acceleration. If an enrichment resource program is used, all teachers should understand the curriculum of that program and how they can facilitate their own students' participation. They also must help resolve a traditional dilemma: the extent to which their students will be expected to make up missed work while in the resource room. Some in-service topics suggested by Wood and Leadbeater (1986) included definitions, characteristics, and needs of G/T students, program goals and objectives, program models and prototypes, instructional strategies, creativity, and parental involvement.

Roberts and Roberts (1986) described how in-service training can focus on any of seven stages of teacher "concerns"—that is, their perceptions, feelings, and motivations:

1. *Awareness* concerns, for example, arousing interest and explaining how G/T activities are related to other aspects of the school curriculum.
2. *Information* concerns, for example, generally explaining a program and how it meets the needs of G/T children.
3. *Personal* concerns, for example, about role expectations and conflicts with other time demands.
4. *Management* concerns, for example, scheduling, organizing activities, and ordering materials.
5. *Consequence* concerns, for example, evaluating the program and refining teachers' skills.
6. *Collaboration* concerns, for example, exchanging ideas and assisting less experienced teachers.
7. *Refocusing* concerns, for example, program changes and innovations.

Said Roberts and Roberts, resolution of the critical stage 4, management concerns, will allow teachers to proceed to the "impact concerns" of stages 5, 6, and 7.

Regardless of the specific type of program, teachers will need in-service education dealing with methods for helping gifted and talented children in the regular classroom. Also, such topics as identifying and helping minority, female, handicapped and underachieving gifted students are appropriate in every school district. In-service training on the evaluation of gifted programs will help teachers to participate in the continued improvement of the gifted and regular school program.

Weiss and Gallagher (1986) suggested that in-service training dealing with curriculum for the gifted should emphasize that a variety of learning activities and strategies should be used to reach program goals. Further, the content of the in-service training must be directly applicable to the teachers' situations and should involve demonstration and practice with new techniques.

From a survey, Tomlinson (1986), found that teachers were most interested in obtaining information concerning methods and techniques for use with gifted students at their particular grade level and/or in their subject area. Further, teachers strongly preferred group participation and hands-on experience—working through types of activities that could be used immediately with their gifted students—rather than "lecture only" approaches.

An excellent source of inspiration for planning or improving a G/T program is visiting other successful programs. It is best to visit several types of programs. These may include special schools for gifted and talented students along with schools with resource-room or pullout programs, special classes, Saturday programs, mentoring plans, telescoping plans, or whatever else you might be considering for your own school. Do not be surprised if the visits help you decide what *not* to do. You can speak with teachers regarding such matters as:

> What they are doing and how they are doing it.
>
> Who the target students are and how they were identified.
>
> What the students are specifically supposed to get out of the program (goals and objectives).
>
> Their perceptions (and evidence) of the success of their program.
>
> The difficulties they experienced and how they were resolved.
>
> The sorts of resistance they encountered from other teachers, parents, or the community.

You also might speak with the gifted and talented students in various types of programs. How do they like school? Do they like the program? What are their problems? How could the program be improved?

14. Budgetary Needs and Allocations

Many programs operate on a shoestring, using part of the regular school budget to purchase special workbooks, calculators, art supplies, or other inexpensive items. It can be done. However, to plan a proper program one should consider expenses related to some or all of the following:

A full-time or part-time teacher/coordinator—or several, in a larger district
Physical facilities
Texts and workbooks
Special equipment and supplies
Transportation costs
Tests and inventories
Secretarial services
Office supplies
Duplicating expenses
Consultant and in-service training expenses
Travel to visit other programs
Travel to state and national conferences
Services of psychologists and counselors
Evaluation expenses (a consultant; purchasing or constructing tests, rating scales or questionnaires)

Budgetary matters must be considered at the time you are planning the various identification strategies, instructional program alternatives, and needed evaluation data. From the outset, one should be concerned with cost-benefit matters. Some programs clearly cost more than others, and priorities may have to be modified in light of the available dollars. However, with creative cost-cutting many goals can be achieved relatively economically, without a large loss in interest value or educational benefit.

Finally, a search for federal, state, or private funding surely will be worthwhile. Even though funding may be scarce for "a program for gifted and talented students," requesting funds for a specific category of persons or subject matter—such as handicapped or minority gifted, computer literacy, math and science, or arts and humanities—can improve one's chances for an award or grant. Local service organizations, medical and health organizations, or local businesses or industries may be willing to provide small amounts of designated funding. Usually, a newspaper story or other publicity can be arranged to reward such contributions. Note too that chances for a financial commitment by the school district will be improved if administrators recognize that funds from other sources also are forthcoming.

15. Program Evaluation

The evaluation of gifted programs is an important and complex topic that will be discussed in more detail in Chapter 18. For now, the reader should keep in mind that good evaluation information has a direct bearing on (1) the survival and continuation of the program, (2) the continuation or improvement of budgetary allocations, and (3) the modification and improvement of the program. Evaluation is indeed important, and should be part of the program planning from the beginning. *Every* aspect of the program—the staff, the materials, the identification procedures, the acceleration and enrichment activities, and each and every goal and objective—can be evaluated regarding its effectiveness in contributing to program success.

Evaluation is of two types—first, a *formative,* ongoing process aimed at continuous modification and improvement of the program; second, a *summative,* final assessment of the overall success of the program. Both are necessary. Evaluation can be aimed at determining how well students' needs and goals were met; evaluation also is sometimes directed at assessing how well the program plan was carried out.

THE VIEW FROM THE SCHOOL BOARD

The main function of the district school board is to set policy governing school administration and programs. Because board members are either elected directly by the community or appointed by elected officials, they are accountable to the public. Whether or not school board members support providing educational services for the gifted therefore may be a political question (for example, "What will my constituency think?") as well as an educational issue. The scope of a gifted program—the number of grades and categories of gifted children served, the diversity of program alternatives and activities, the types of support services—will be affected by the support and funding by school board members.

Programs for gifted and talented students, by definition, are directed at a minority of children and adolescents. Therefore, teachers and parents must convince board members that even though gifted children are a minority, their educational needs are genuine and they must be served as part of a comprehensive educational program. How can educators and parents encourage board members to maintain a quality gifted program in a school district? The following are some suggestions for fostering support:

Keep board members educated and aware. Before board members voted for that gifted program, parents probably attended meetings and, in a positive way, showed interest in gifted education. When the G/T program is in place, that communication process must continue. Teachers or coordinators may make yearly presentations on program progress. If an oral presentation is not feasible, a short written report is helpful. Brevity is critical, since board members often are overwhelmed with reports.

Keep board members involved.   One or two board members should be included on each district or school G/T steering committee. Board members can be invited to in-service meetings, parent meetings, or student performances and shows. They also may be invited to speak at local or state parent meetings or other educational meetings.

Help board members to be accountable.   For board members to justify continued support and funding for gifted programs, they absolutely must be assured that the program is achieving its objectives. Educators therefore must keep board members informed of the effectiveness and accomplishments of the G/T program.

Encourage boards to have a written policy.   Board policy is a formalization of philosophy and should be incorporated into a formal policy manual. The written policy becomes the basis by which the school administration and teaching staff can justify decisions favorable to gifted education. An example of a written school board policy is shown in Inset 3.3.

Be patient, but not too patient.   Board members need time to gather support and plan resources for a comprehensive gifted program. Furthermore, they logically must view the gifted program in relation to the total needs of the district. At the same time, however, parents and educators must not permit board members to forget or indefinitely postpone the needs of gifted children, regardless of the stresses of educational problems and too-small budgets.

Remember that all board members should be encouraged to support gifted education.   On any school board there always will be a variety of viewpoints on gifted education. Some members will be active supporters, and it may be tempting to believe that they alone can keep programs going. It is necessary, however, to also focus one's attention on those less-willing potential supporters, those who require further convincing. Note their doubts and questions and make a special effort to personally give them the information they need to convince them that gifted education truly is legitimate, important, and a widespread national, even international movement. Even if they cannot be converted into strong supporters, the strength of their opposition might at least be reduced.

INSET 3.3 A SAMPLE SCHOOL BOARD POLICY

The Board of Education and professional staff members are dedicated to developing a comprehensive program for the identification and education of the gifted and talented child. Empathy and understanding are of paramount importance for all personnel having contact with such a child, and are basic to achievement of the district goals.

The gifted and talented child is an individual who, by virtue of outstanding abilities, is capable of high performance. This child possesses demonstrated or potential intellectual or specific academic abilities, leadership capabilities, creativity, or talent in the performing or visual arts. This child may need educational services beyond those being provided by the regular school program in order to realize his/her potential.

To provide a comprehensive program for the gifted and talented child, the Board recognizes that:

1. Early identification of the gifted and talented child is necessary to maximize the opportunities for the child's own self-realization. This shall be accomplished through the application of several criteria.
2. The educational program should provide for continuity and overlap among the elementary, junior high, and high school levels. The program should specify long-range goals for the district, with major emphasis on differentiated curriculum and programming.
3. The objectives of the educational program shall be to meet the gifted and talented child's needs, whether they be intellectual, social, physical, or emotional.
4. Active parental involvement is viewed as an integral and crucial ingredient of a quality gifted and talented program. Every effort should be made to foster parental involvement in all aspects of their child's educational program.
5. Qualified instructional and administrative personnel with appropriate knowledge, training, and experience are required to implement an effective program of education for the gifted and talented.
6. The achievement of a quality gifted and talented educational program demands the presence of a competent ancillary support staff, particularly for the early identification of the gifted or talented child.
7. The administration of the gifted and talented program shall provide leadership and coordination in developing and maintaining a comprehensive district K–12 program.
8. The placement and progress of the gifted or talented child will be continually evaluated and documented, with periodic progress reports issued to the parents of the child.

Help board members be answerable to their public. Board members will be asked by constituents why they support gifted education. They will also be given reasons why they should *not* help gifted students. In raising their awareness of the needs of the gifted, give board members the information they will require to justify to their constituents the existence and funding of special programs for the gifted. The issues they will need to debate may not always seem reasonable, but they nonetheless must be prepared with answers. Some issues to which board members often must respond are included in Inset 3.4.

INSET 3.4 SOME QUESTIONS SCHOOL BOARD MEMBERS MUST ANSWER

1. *Isn't gifted education elitist?*
RESPONSE: Gifted education only provides appropriate education for children who need a special challenge. These children come from all neighborhoods and economic backgrounds. Children from poor families often need G/T education the most because their families frequently cannot afford enrichment opportunities for them. Also, difficult financial circumstances and backgrounds sometimes prevent parents from having higher expectations for their children. If we are to keep our country a place where people can achieve regardless of their economic background, gifted education can help us. It provides a special challenge to all very bright and talented children, regardless of their cultural or economic background.

2. *We have special programs for the low-ability child and the high-ability child—but what about the average child?*
RESPONSE: Most educational programs are geared to the needs of the average child. In a real sense, most money is now spent on the average child. We agree that the average child should never be short-changed in the educational process, but neither should the gifted child.

3. *Aren't all children really gifted, so don't we need to provide for all their gifts?*
RESPONSE: In a sense, yes, all children certainly do have special gifts and talents. Some may play basketball well; some sew well; others have marvelous personal charm. The purpose of a gifted program is to provide for students' academic and creative needs not met by the regular educational program. For example, a star basketball player already has the team; the sewer has an opportunity to do excellent work in home economics courses. However, the young creative writer or poet rarely has a writing class to challenge and focus his/her skill; nor is the mathematics whiz provided with advanced or accelerated math. These students may be bored, and their talents are not challenged or strengthened. When we find special gifts and talents, we must provide opportunities to develop them.

4. *Why should we spend more money for kids who will make it anyway?*
RESPONSE: While many gifted kids will "make it anyway," it is nonetheless unfair to hold them back and make them succeed in spite of the system. More importantly, many gifted children do not "make it anyway." Their lost talent is both a personal tragedy for them and a loss to society. Studies of high school dropouts have found that between 9 and 20 percent are in the gifted IQ range—certainly many more than one would expect based on their ability, and certainly a waste.

Schools often turn off gifted children because they do not provide appropriate challenges. Further, when children become bored they sometimes use their creative energy and their giftedness in inappropriate, antisocial, and even destructive ways. They need special help and guidance.

5. *Can we afford to pay for more special education?*

RESPONSE: Gifted programs can be very inexpensive, compared to all other kinds of special education. Also, we save money in the long run by investing small amounts to help make school more meaningful. This small investment helps insure us against larger problems that can be more costly—for example, bored, apathetic, or even anti-social students, to say nothing of lost talent development.

6. *What do the rest of the kids get out of it?*

RESPONSE: Teachers who become involved in gifted education learn to stimulate creative development, to use questions effectively, to foster good self-concepts and humanistic attitudes, to individualize instruction, and other valuable concepts and skills. Much of this can be—and is—applied in the regular classroom. They become better teachers, and this benefits other children as well.

Also, when there are gifted programs in a school, it becomes apparent to all that excellence is rewarded and valued. When excellence is valued more children become motivated to achieve, and we sometimes discover giftedness where we might not have expected to find it. For example, if there has been peer pressure not to achieve, some students will hide their abilities and talents. Gifted programs encourage these children to achieve too. So while providing for the special needs of gifted children, we also encourage hard work and excellence in our schools for all children.

Support school board members who support gifted education. When school board members visibly endorse a program, they need to know there is a public "out there" supporting them. Be vocal in expressing your appreciation to board members who assist with the education you believe in. You can also help them in their campaigns, both formally and informally (for example, by telling your friends what a fine job you believe they are doing). Keeping supporters of gifted education in office will help them to provide appropriate educational opportunities in your community.

PERSPECTIVES OF OTHER TEACHERS

Not all teachers agree that gifted students truly need special services. In fact, some are downright antagonistic. However, with time and exposure some indifferent teachers come to understand the issues and concerns and will become more receptive to gifted programming. Others will never change, and progifted teachers simply have to work around them.

What are their concerns? Some will have the same reservations expressed to school board members (see Inset 3.4); others will express different problems. For example:

Some teachers will object to their brightest students leaving their classes; they will miss the contributions these students make.

Some will argue that they already are challenging the gifted children in their classrooms (sometimes they are; more often they are not).

Some will complain that the gifted program requires additional work, and they already are overworked.

Some believe that the gifted child is somehow "getting out of" required work, and will individually penalize those children by requiring makeup work or even "busy work."

If they teach a section of gifted students, some teachers will penalize them by grading on a normal curve, ignoring the fact that the students were pre-selected. A few might delight in awarding gifted children C's and D's to somehow prove the students are *not* gifted.

Some negative teachers may subtly attempt to sabotage the gifted program.

There is no secret psychological strategy to elicit the cooperation and support of every teacher. One should, however, be ready for antigifted attacks and not take them personally. If one remains positive there is a better chance of gaining converts and allies. For example, you can listen to their arguments and try to explain the unmet needs of gifted children. Negative teachers can be encouraged to take a course in gifted education or to attend a conference with you. Lend them this book. Make the assumption that they *do* care about *all* children and that with a better understanding of the issue they may develop a sincere concern for gifted children as a mistreated minority.

Fortunately, in most school districts there will be more allies than enemies. There will be many teachers who enthusiastically support the program and contribute time and ideas. There will be many who enjoy the new challenge of gifted education and the excitement of seeing new enthusiasm in energetic and talented children. Without these supporters, being a teacher of the gifted would be lonely indeed.

As a few final insights into program planning, Mosley (1982) itemized some timely recommendations ". . . which might determine whether or not the program will last one year or several." The suggestions are facetiously put into the form of "Suggestions to Ensure the Brevity of Your Gifted Program."

1. Make sure that the program always is "fun." Entertaining students is a high priority.
2. Talk about the program continuously; other teachers love to hear about your innovative program, your challenging students, and your field trips. Try also to tell parents of average children about the marvelous qualities of gifted students.
3. Try to interrupt the regular school day as much as possible, and on a regular basis. Other teachers enjoy this.

4. Emphasize that you are a "loner" and that your program is "different." You must separate yourself from the rest of the school system.
5. Avoid reading literature in the gifted education area. Because each program is different, you will learn nothing from the experiences of others.
6. Be sure to ignore professional adults in the community. They have little to offer.
7. Avoid using parents in the program. They sometimes are demanding and will only confuse matters.
8. If the program is challenged, it is easiest to concede that the program is of borderline relevance. If a response is necessary, try to use jargon and clichés, such as "high taxonomic levels," "Marland's U.S.O.E. definition," and "Renzulli's revolving door model."
9. Try to get widespread publicity for expensive activities such as field trips, so that everyone will know that the program is adequately funded.

SUMMARY

Four main components of a gifted education program are (1) program philosophy and goals, (2) definition and identification, (3) instruction (grouping, acceleration, enrichment), and (4) evaluation and modification.

One can view program planning as a series of who, what, where, when and why questions.

Fifteen problem areas in program planning are summarized as follows.

1. A needs assessment aims at determining the discrepancy between the current and the desired state of G/T education in the district. Key question: What are the needs of the gifted and talented students?
   Because gifted students are a minority, only "sufficient" (not majority) support should be needed to establish a clear need for G/T services.
   A steering committee for planning a program may consist of teachers, parents, administrators, school board members, and perhaps the librarian, school psychologist, counselor, and gifted high school students.
2. Preliminary personal and staff education, such as determining the present status of gifted education in the area and an acquaintance with state legislation and state plans, is necessary for informed planning.
3. A written statement of philosophy and rationale should explain the reasons for, and the goals and objectives of, a program. An expanded statement can serve as a written program plan.
4. The types of gifts and talents to be accommodated must be specified. This matter is related to (1) one's definition of giftedness and (2) specific identification methods.
5. Identification methods and criteria must be consistent with one's definition of giftedness and coordinated with the type of program being planned. The methods must be defensible, yet both objective and subjective.
6. Identification methods must include plans for locating gifted female, cultur-

ally different, economically disadvantaged, underachieving, and handicapped students.

7. Staff responsibilities and accountability checks (such as monthly meetings or reports) must be planned.

8. Support staff and services should include the school psychologist, school counselor, and consultants.

9. Program plans should include both acceleration and enrichment alternatives. There are many specifics to select from. They should aim at defensible goals and objectives, namely, the development of high-level skills and knowledge.

10. Any plan will require attention to the organizational and administrative design, including space allocations, record keeping, modifications to the budget, and much more. Much planning usually is at the district level.

11. Transportation needs cannot be ignored.

12. Community resources exist for enriching field trips, mentorships, or career education.

13. In-service workshops begin with general "awareness" information and proceed to the identification of the gifted or talented child and then other matters. Visits to several differing types of programs can be very informative.

14. Budgetary needs and cost-effectiveness must be considered from the outset. Some programs operate on almost nothing; others pay for teacher-coordinators plus plenty of materials and equipment. Federal, state, or private funds often can be obtained.

15. Program evaluation is important for survival and expansion. Every component of the program can be evaluated. Formative evaluations are continuous ones aimed at modification and improvement. Summative evaluations at the end of the year evaluate overall success.

School board members must be convinced that G/T students have important unmet needs. Suggestions for fostering support include keeping board members educated and involved, helping them be accountable, and changing the attitudes of nonsupportive members.

For various reasons, many teachers may not support a G/T program in a given school. One should attempt to alter their attitudes in a more positive and helpful direction.

APPENDIX 3.1 IDEAS FOR STATEMENTS OF PHILOSOPHY, RATIONALE, AND OBJECTIVES

To provide gifted and talented students with an educational environment that will provide the greatest possible development of their abilities, thus enabling them to realize their contributions to self and society.

"The gifted and talented represent a group of students whose learning style and thinking dimensions demand experiences which are outside the educational mainstream . . . (we need) an education commensurate with each child's ability to learn" (Kaplan, 1974).

To provide programs designed to help meet the psychological, social, educational, and career needs of gifted and talented students.

To assist students in becoming individuals who are able to take self-initiated action and accept responsibility for that action, and who are capable of intelligent choice, independent learning, and problem solving.

(Our program will include) " . . . administrative procedures and instructional strategies which afford intellectual acquisition, thinking practice, and self-understanding" (Kaplan, 1974).

To meet the special needs of minority gifted children.

To develop a functional procedure for identifying gifted and talented students in the school in order that they may express and develop their gifts or talents.

To provide a program that will stimulate individual interests and develop individual abilities in academic and/or talent areas.

To provide the superior learner with new and highly challenging learning experiences that are not ordinarily included in the regular classroom curriculum.

At the conclusion of their elementary school experience, students will demonstrate competency in basic skills at least equal to that of other elementary schools in the district, even though they are exposed to numerous areas of instruction not commonly found in traditional elementary school programs.

To provide opportunities that will develop self-awareness, personal strengths, and social responsibilities beyond those in the regular school program.

To provide gifted children with the opportunity to explore personal interests through independent study and community involvement.

To foster high-level thinking and self-development processes, resulting in a more complete, productive individual who is challenged by the school environment.

To provide a learning atmosphere that will enable the gifted child to develop his/her potential and exceptional abilities, particularly in the areas of decision making, planning, performing, reasoning, creating, and communicating.

To provide experiences that develop the higher operations of analyzing, synthesizing, divergent production, and evaluation.

To provide activities and experiences that will stimulate critical thinking, comprehension, competency, and creativity.

To enable those students desiring to do so to prepare for advanced placement.

To prescribe particular curricula to meet individual needs.

To encourage cross-discipline exploration.

To include strong components of basic skills, career awareness, sex-equity, and multiethnic experiences.

To develop an ability to transfer information to humanistic goals.

To develop intrinsic motivation.

To provide experiences that guide a student toward independence.

To provide gifted and talented students with a positive self-concept.

To foster awareness of self and others.

Many parents and other community leaders will be involved in the learning process.

To develop problem-solving abilities and creative thinking skills; develop research skills; strengthen individual interests; develop independent study skills; exercise communication skills in the humanities (visual, oral, and written); receive intellectual stimulation from contact with other highly motivated students; expand their learning activities to include resources available in the entire community area.

"The good of any program for the gifted should be to provide meaningful experiences in the most efficient and effective way in order to maximize learning and individual development and to minimize boredom, confusion, and frustration" (Fox, 1979).

chapter four

Identifying Gifted and Talented Students

There probably are as many different strategies and policies for identifying gifted and talented students as there are programs. Logically, if the many types of abilities, gifts, and talents are combined with the many possible measures of each—student tests, grades, and questionnaires; teacher, parent, and peer questionnaires, ratings and nominations; plus evaluations of products, performances, and perhaps motivation—the number of permutations and combinations will boggle even a gifted mind.

For example, some programs will base identification entirely upon intelligence test scores, either admitting all students who score above a certain cutoff, or else selecting the top 3 to 5 percent regardless of the particular scores. According to Cassidy and Johnson (1986), one state defines giftedness as the "top 3 percent" in intellectual ability; another as scoring two standard deviations above the mean (top 2.28 percent) in intellectual development; a third state allows for artistic and other forms of giftedness, but absolutely requires that "Persons shall be assigned to a program for the gifted when they have an IQ score of 130 or higher." Of course, these definitions intrinsically favor (or demand) an IQ identification criterion.

In the various *Talent Search* programs (for example, Cohn, 1983a; Stanley, 1988; Stanley and Benbow, 1986; Van Tassel-Baska, 1984; see Chapter 5), *Scholastic Aptitude Test-Mathematics* (SAT-M) and *Scholastic Aptitude Test-Verbal* (SAT-V) scores, which measure mathematical and verbal reasoning, respectively, are virtually the sole admission criteria.

Other programs take a multidimensional approach. As a common but minor modification of the strict IQ criterion, teachers may review IQ scores, achievement scores and grades to nominate students for a G/T program. Such nominations tend to be closely related to student grades (Richert, 1985). More serious multidimensional approaches will identify students who seem high in any one of a number of criteria, particularly the five components of the U.S.O.E. definition: general intellectual ability, specific academic talent, creativity, leadership, or talent in the visual or performing arts. Cassidy and Johnson (1986) reported that most states have adopted definitions of giftedness—which are supposed to guide identification—that are consistent with the U.S.O.E. statement.

As we will see later in this chapter, the *Kranz Talent Identification Instrument* (KTII; Kranz, 1981) assesses ten categories of gifts and talents, including most of the U.S.O.E. list. The *Baldwin Identification Matrix* (Baldwin, 1977) evaluates 11 or 12 talents, also including most of the U.S.O.E. talents. The *EBY Gifted Behavior Index* (Eby, 1984a) evaluates gifted behavior in six areas. Unlike the "either/or" U.S.O.E. and KTII approaches, ratings on the total Baldwin Matrix subtests are added to produce a single total score, which makes ranking students rather easy.

A survey of 1172 school districts by the Richardson Foundation (Wilkie, 1985) showed teacher nomination to be the most common means of identification (91 percent), followed by achievement tests (90 percent), intelligence tests (89 percent), and grades (50 percent). Self-nomination and parent nominations each were used by 6 percent of the school districts.

Overview

This chapter will first review some issues that complicate the significant—and often delicate—matter of selecting participants for a G/T program. An awareness of these issues should help the program developer design procedures that are as reasonable, fair, accurate, defensible (for example, to parents), and appropriate to the program goals as possible. We then will turn to descriptions of specific identification strategies and instruments. For each, its unique advantages and difficulties will be noted, along with suggestions for proper use and interpretation.

THOUGHTS AND ISSUES IN IDENTIFICATION

Pros and Cons of Formal Identification Methods

In her article "The Case Against Formal Identification," Davidson (1986) expressed strong frustration with all formal testing, rating, and nomination procedures, including the use of point systems and cutoffs.

Said Davidson, such procedures do not allow students actually to demonstrate their abilities in areas in which they are interested and talented (see Inset 4.1). Regarding IQ scores, Davidson noted that a student with a tested IQ of 110 may show greater giftedness in the sense of originality and thought-provoking ideas and answers than a student with a tested IQ of 140—who naturally will be selected for the program. Even creativity tests do not measure every aspect of a child's creativeness, noted Davidson, and peer, parent, and teacher nominations often are biased in favor of popular, English-speaking, middle-class students.

Davidson's three-step solution, designed to not exclude truly gifted children, included, first, setting a liberal selection quota of about 15 to 20 percent of the school, in accord with Renzulli's talent pool/revolving door

---

INSET 4.1 THE CASE AGAINST FORMAL IDENTIFICATION

The following is a condensation of a spoof by Karen Davidson (1986) that illustrates how formal testing and identification measures could inadvertently exclude truly gifted students from programs for the gifted and talented.

John loved to run and he was very good at it. He always ran the four miles down country roads from school to home. In early September John's school began a formal identification process to select students for the cross-country team.

With the peer nomination procedure, few of his fellow students had ever seen him run, and so he was nominated just once and received one point. Teachers nominated the students with the flashy jogging pants—the ones who looked like runners. One teacher saw John chase a dog and thought he was fast, and nominated him—one more point. With parent nominations, John's dad thought cross-country teams were silly, but John got two points because his dad knew he was fast.

On the *California Standardized Test of Running Skills,* a written test, John scored at the 56th percentile because he did not know such terms as "hitting the wall" and "pacing yourself." Other students had taken running lessons and scored above the 90th percentile. John earned one point.

A test of running ability partly evaluated knowledge of famous runners and muscles used in running. When John finally had a chance to run, the teacher evaluated only his form and style. He earned two more points.

John's total score in the identification procedure was seven points. With a cutoff of 15, he wasn't even close.

The moral of the story is that: "Many students who would profit from enrichment and from differentiated programs are not identified; formal identification procedures do not allow them to demonstrate their abilities in the areas in which they are most interested and able" (Davidson, 1986).

philosophy (for example, Renzulli, 1986; Renzulli and Reis, 1986). Second, and apparently despite her reservations about testing, students who score in the 90th percentile or above on intelligence, achievement, or creativity tests (according to local norms) have clear needs and should automatically be placed in the program. Third, and most importantly, Davidson recommended the increased use of *informal* parent and teacher nominations, based on observations of creativity, critical thinking, problem solving, or motivation.

Top 3 to 5 Percent or "Open Door" Identification

The traditional method for selecting students for participation in a G/T program is this: Each fall, a school screening committee reviews data from many sources for each potential candidate, for example, ability and achievement scores and nominations. The top 3 to 5 percent are selected and labeled "gifted"—and the identification process is ended for the year.

More and more, districts and individual schools are adopting Renzulli's (1984, 1986) *talent pool* strategy, part of the *Revolving Door Identification Model* (Renzulli, Reis, and Smith, 1981; Renzulli and Reis, 1986; see Chapter 8). Currently, it is the single most popular identification and programming model in the United States, Canada—and the world (Renzulli, 1987), and for good reason. With the talent pool approach, a generous, open and flexible 15 to 20 percent of the school population is identified according to ". . . general ability or any and all performance areas that might be considered high priorities in a given school's programming effort" (Renzulli, 1986, p. 76). In professional communities with large numbers of high ability students, the talent pool may consist of 25 percent or, in extraordinary neighborhoods, even 100 percent of the student body (Renzulli, 1987).

Renzulli (1987) recommends that half of the talent pool be comprised of students who score above the 92nd percentile on district-wide total language or total math achievement scores or IQ scores, if available. These will be students performing about 1½ years above grade level. The other half of the talent pool would be selected by the more informal methods of (a) teacher nominations, (b) parent, peer, or self-nominations, or (c) nominations found by sending a list of students' names to all teachers at the current and any previous school—"to protect students from this year's teacher!" (Renzulli, 1987).

From the talent pool, some students—high in motivation and creativity—self-select an intensive research, investigative, or other creative project. More specifically, informal "action information," described as ". . . the type of dynamic interactions that take place when a student becomes 'turned on' about a particular topic, area of study, issue, event, or form of creative expression," is used by teachers to recommend specific motivated students for individual work in the resource room with the teacher/coordinator. Students revolve into the resource room to work on their projects, then revolve out when the project is finished. Further, even non-talent pool students who convincingly demonstrate their interest, motivation, and creativity are allowed to pursue independent projects and become members of the talent pool.

The talent pool approach recognizes that gifted behaviors will occur in certain people, at certain times, and under certain circumstances (Renzulli, 1987). "Gifted" is not a label to be bestowed on certain students via the selection process. Rather, it is behavior to be developed ". . . in those youngsters who have the highest potential for benefitting from special education services" (Renzulli, 1986).

The main identification-related attractions of the talent pool and revolving door approach are that, most importantly, (a) more students receive the *opportunities, resources,* and *encouragement* provided in special programs—the door remains open to many children whose gifts and talents simply are not measured by tests nor easily recognized by teachers. Renzulli (e.g., 1986, 1987) has repeatedly stressed that society's most creative contributors are not always found in the "top 3 to 5 percent." In addition, with the talent pool solution (b) teachers remain concerned with identifying students for independent projects throughout the school year, not just in September; (c) charges of elitism are reduced; and (d) the difficult problem of deciding "who is and is not admissable" becomes a nonproblem. When in doubt, admit.

Disadvantaged, Minority, Handicapped, and Female Students

The identification of gifted and talented minority, economically disadvantaged, and culturally different students is an especially sensitive problem. Too often administrators claim they have "none of those children in our school." Teachers, too, are guilty of this oversight. LeRose (1977), for example, reported, "Martin Jenkins, who has conducted more studies of high IQ Black children than any one else, has commented on how frequently children with IQ's above 150 have not been spotted as outstanding by their teachers."

Culturally different learners do tend to score, on the average, about one standard deviation (15 points) lower than middle-class students on standardized intelligence tests. We repeat, "on the average." Many minority children will score extremely high in both verbal and nonverbal measures of intelligence. Nonetheless, if IQ testing is part of the selection battery, there is frequently a built-in bias against minority and economically disadvantaged children. And if your school population includes minority and culturally different students (for example, black, Chicano, Native American, Native Hawaiian, Vietnamese, immigrant), it simply will not be acceptable to produce an all-white list of children of middle-class professional people.

Issues related to minority and culturally different students will be explored in more detail in Chapter 13, along with suggestions for identification and programming. For now, we will emphasize that a multidimensional approach to identification is essential for identifying gifted and talented minority students—a procedure that looks beyond IQ scores. The quota system is one frequently used solution to the problem of ensuring racial, sexual, geographical, or economic balance in G/T programs (Hersberger and Asher, 1980; LeRose, 1978). For example, if a school contains 20 percent Tongan children, then the G/T program would contain 20 percent Tongan children.

Often we overlook gifted students among the ranks of physically or psychologically disabled (for example, learning disabled) students. Do not be shocked when ten-year-old Joe Smith, whose dyslexia prevents him from reading or writing normally, is nominated as an intellectually or artistically gifted child. Albert Einstein, Thomas Edison, Nelson Rockefeller, and other "slow learners" have had the same problems.

Regarding girls, we should be aware in our identification activities that, while times are indeed changing, cultural and social influences and perhaps parental overprotectiveness (Lois Hoffman, 1972) still may produce girls who are more dependent, more conforming, less motivated and aggressive, and less success-oriented than boys.

Biases in Ratings and Nominations

As noted earlier, there is a natural and understandable tendency for teachers to favor students who are cooperative, smiling, and anxious to please, who do their work well, neatly, and on time, and who absolutely never talk back. While "teacher pleasers" (Taylor, 1978) are a pleasure to work with, they may or may not be the most gifted and talented students in the class. However, they have a high likelihood of being perceived by teachers as "gifted," and of being nominated for participation in special programs. If teachers rate students on specific qualities such as academic talent, leadership, motivation, or sometimes even creativity, teacher pleasers again are likely to be selected. The extremely bright or the creative, curious, and questioning students, who may be stubborn, rule-breaking, egotistical, or otherwise high in nuisance value, may not be the teachers' favorites, but they sometimes are the most gifted.

Test Reliability and Validity

Reliability refers to the accuracy or consistency of a test, inventory, rating scale, or other selection procedure—the degree to which a person is likely to receive the same score or rating if he or she is assessed again, perhaps at another time. *Validity* is the degree to which a test or inventory actually measures what it is supposed to measure. Does the motivation, creativity, or leadership test truly measure these traits or abilities? Does the "total giftedness" score truly identify gifted students? Evidence for reliability and validity normally appears in manuals accompanying published tests and inventories.

When considering tests, questionnaires, rating scales, and nomination procedures for identifying gifted and talented students, one always must consider both the reliability and the validity of the test or procedure. No test, rating scale, questionnaire, or nomination procedure will have perfect reliability or perfect validity, and the usefulness of the instrument or procedure is tied very closely to its degree of reliability and validity. Sometimes, "face validity"—the degree to which a test simply looks like it should measure what it is intended to measure—will be the only information one has to go on.

Political Problems in Identification

In the real world of schools, identification of giftedness is surrounded by political and personal problems that go beyond reliability and validity. Teachers and administrators must be prepared for some controversies that surround identification. The criticisms one can expect will include everything from "Why isn't my child in the program?" to "Don't you dare identify my child as gifted," and anything in between. School board members may complain that teachers' children appear to be favored; teachers may note that offspring of administrators and board members are being selected. Some will call the selection process discriminatory and elitist; others will say it favors disadvantaged children.

NATIONAL REPORT ON IDENTIFICATION

In 1982 Susanne Richert, James Alvino, and Rebecca McDonnel completed the *National Report on Identification: Assessment and Recommendations for Comprehensive Identification of Gifted and Talented Youth,* a study commissioned by the U.S. Department of Education (Richert, 1985). The study focused on such issues as definitions adopted, principles of identification, identification instruments and procedures, and practices that screen out gifted students. The following are some capsule conclusions pertinent to identifying gifted students.

As for appropriate definitions, using the multidimensional U.S.O.E. definition (Chapter 1) was endorsed because it ". . . attempts to be comprehensive in order to be applicable in many settings . . . (and) it has the legitimacy of national law behind it" (Richert, 1985).

Some principles that should underlie identification are:

1. *Advocacy.* Identification should be designed in the best interests of all students.
2. *Defensibility.* Procedures should be based on the best available research and recommendations.
3. *Equity.* Procedures should guarantee that no one is overlooked (e.g., disadvantaged children).
4. *Pluralism.* The broadest defensible definition of giftedness should be adopted.
5. *Comprehensiveness.* As many gifted learners as possible should be identified and served.

Some common but questionable practices include:

1. Despite the common adoption of the broad U.S.O.E. definition, identification instruments tend to limit selection to academically achieving gifted students.
2. Local districts tend to seek and find white, middle-class academic achievers. Minority groups such as blacks, Hispanics, and Native Americans are underrepresented by 30 to 70 percent.
3. Identification instruments sometimes are used to identify categories of giftedness for which they were not designed. For example, achievement and intelligence tests are used interchangeably, thus confusing the categories of specific academic ability and general intellectual ability. They also are used inappropriately to identify creative and leadership talent.
4. Diagnostic tests, designed for placement within a subject area, are inappropriately used for initial screening.
5. Multiple criteria often are combined in statistically unsound ways, producing a quantitative score that obscures important indicators of high potential.
6. Despite evidence that academic performance is not highly predictive of adult giftedness, most identification procedures are limited to achievement tests, intelligence tests, grades, and teacher recommendations.

Based on these principles and problems, some recommendations were:

1. Because giftedness has many dimensions—abilities, personality factors, and environment—measures that go beyond academic achievement must be used to find students whose abilities are not indicated by tests and school performance. Both informal and formal data must be used validly.
2. Subjective procedures such as rating scales, checklists, and nominations are a legitimate part of the identification process, especially in the early nomination stage. Rating scale and checklist items should include "negative" and unexpected characteristics indicated by research.
3. Nominations by teachers, parents, peers, and students themselves are useful if the content of the nominations is clearly related to the program options and plans.
4. Data from multiple measures, such as formal tests and informal checklists, should not be combined because their purposes and results are different.

IDENTIFICATION METHODS

Intelligence Tests

Virtually every G/T program is interested in intellectual giftedness. The bottom-line instruments for confirming suspected brilliance are individual intelligence tests, particularly the *Wechsler Intelligence Scales for Children-Revised* (WISC-R) and the 1986 *Stanford-Binet Intelligence Scale, Revision IV*. Every school psychologist is qualified to administer and interpret either of these. If there is a university in your area with a graduate clinical or school psychology program, it is likely that competent graduate students would administer one of these at low cost or even free of charge.

Stanford-Binet, Revision IV. Two complaints about the "old Stanford-Binet" were, first, that it produced only one global IQ score and, second, that it was heavily loaded with items measuring verbal abilities. The new *Stanford-Binet Intelligence Scale, Revision IV,* however, handily solves both problems. It produces four subscale scores, one each for *verbal reasoning, quantitative reasoning, visual/abstract reasoning,* and *short-term memory,* along with a composite score (Silverman, 1986). The scores are no longer called "IQ scores," but "standard age scores." However, because the standard age scores still are based upon a mean of 100 and a standard deviation of 16 points, you may safely think of standard age scores as essentially the same as IQ scores.

While the subscale scores will be highly related, the profile produced by the new Stanford-Binet can provide valuable information about a student's relative intellectual strengths among the four areas. For example, the student with a rare gift in one one area (for example, quantitative reasoning) will quickly be identified by the new test.

The *Stanford-Binet, Revision IV,* produces subscale and total scores that range from −4 standard deviations (IQ = about 36) to +4 standard deviations (IQ = about 164), which covers 99.99 percent of everyone (Silverman, 1986).

WISC-R. Many school psychologists use the WISC-R, which produces a *Verbal* IQ score and a *Performance* (nonverbal) IQ score, along with the combined *Full-Scale* IQ score. Therefore, a student with spatial or mechanical gifts can be identified, not just the verbally gifted. In one recent study, Hollinger and Kosek (1986) found that a full 35 percent of their sample of gifted students (N = 26, age 6 to 15) produced significantly discrepant *Verbal* vs. *Performance* IQ scores. That is, they were much more outsanding in one area than the other. Further, a full 85 percent of the gifted students showed individual subtest scores that deviated significantly from their own average *Verbal* or *Performance* score. Examination of subtest patterns will provide insights into individual students' cognitive functioning, noted Hollinger and Kosek.

Group intelligence tests.   IQ scores from group intelligence tests are useful for identifying gifted students because they continue to be routinely administered in many school systems, and so scores may be in the office file. Some of the better-known group intelligence tests are the *Cognitive Abilities Test,* the *SRA Primary Mental Abilities Tests,* the *Henmon-Nelson Test of Mental Ability,* the *Otis-Lennon Mental Ability Test,* and the *Kuhlman-Anderson Intelligence Tests.* However, despite their comparatively low cost and convenient group administration, consider these shortcomings: Group tests tend to be less reliable and less valid than individual tests. Also, children who are not motivated will produce lower IQ scores than their informally observed ability would indicate. Group tests are mainly verbal and are highly correlated with actual school achievement; therefore, they are biased against children who are nonverbally gifted (or who speak a subcultural dialect). Because most group tests were designed to discriminate in the midsection of the bell curve, they tend to be unreliable at high IQ levels; a few chance errors may substantially lower a bright student's IQ score. Speed is an important factor in group tests, since all are timed. This is not true of individual intelligence tests.

In view of these problems, one well may question the value of group intelligence tests. However, children who score high on these tests virtually always will be capable and certainly should be included in a G/T program.

A big plus for intelligence tests, group or individual, is that they may identify underachieving students: students whose grades and classroom performance give no hint of the students' true—and unused—potential. In the negative column, if undue weight is given to intelligence test scores, students with other legitimate gifts and talents will be missed—particularly creative students, but also students with gifts in one special academic or aesthetic area, such as art, music, computers, mathematics, or even dinosaurs.

Achievement Tests

Specific academic talent is an important category of giftedness. An excellent indicator of academic talent is standardized achievement tests, such as the *Iowa Tests of Basic Skills,* the *Stanford Achievement Tests,* the *Metropolitan Achievement Tests,* the *SRA Achievement Series,* the *California Test of Basic Skills,* and the *Sequential Tests of Educational Progress* (STEP). Other good indicators of specific academic talent are teacher-made achievement tests and school grades.

Standardized tests produce scores based upon national norms (for example, grade-equivalent, percentile, or stanine scores). Consider this advantage. A teacher in an upper-middle-class neighborhood may be accustomed to very bright students who learn quickly. He or she may not realize that, compared with national norms, there are many talented and high-potential students in the class who should be participating in the district's G/T program. On the other hand, a teacher accustomed to working with slow learners may believe that a particular student is unusually able when, relative to a national comparison, the student is just slightly above average.

Two important problems should be considered relative to standardized achievement test scores. The first concerns the *grade-equivalent* score. "Grade equivalent" refers to the average score earned by children at a particular grade level on a particular test—not to the grade level at which a specific gifted child can function well in the classroom. Experienced teachers, administrators, and psychologists, as well as parents, make the faulty assumption that if a gifted fourth-grade child performs at the eighth-grade level on, say, a math achievement test, he or she could be moved into an eighth-grade classroom and perform successfully. Not so. While certainly a good math student, this child probably lacks many skills of the average eighth grader. The score is misleading and should only be used as an indication that the child needs special challenge. Further diagnostic testing would be used to determine the child's specific mathematics skills and other skill levels.

The second problem relates to the low ceiling score of typical achievement tests. For very able children, most achievement tests are not sufficiently difficult to measure their high ability, knowledge, and skill levels. A considerable number of students will score above the 95th percentile or at the ceiling grade-equivalent level; they "top out." It sometimes is incorrectly assumed that all of these children are equally talented and need a similar skill development program. In fact, after diagnostic testing with more difficult tests, a wide range of skill levels will be found among these children. (Of course, an obvious solution is to give high-potential children higher-level achievement tests in the first place.) One example of this problem comes from Stanley's (1979) SMPY program in which seventh and eighth graders who are selected to take the SAT-M must have performed above the 95th percentile on a group achievement test. The SAT-M scores for this group of "similar" children will vary between 200 and 800 on this more difficult test.

Teacher Nominations

Teacher nominations may be very informal ("Say, we're starting a new gifted program, be thinking about one or two kids you want in it!)" or quite formal, involving rating forms or checklists that will be objectively scored. Teacher nomination definitely is one of the most common identification methods, yet it can be troublesome. We already noted a tendency for some teachers to favor well-dressed, cooperative, nonhandicapped, English-speaking "teacher pleasers" who do work neatly, on time, and with no smarting off. Bright underachievers might be overlooked, along with bright disruptive students and unconventional creative ones.

With elementary students, Rimm and Davis (1976) found an inter-rater reliability coefficient of only .18 for teacher ratings of creativity, indicating that those teachers perceived creativeness quite differently. Some reliability and validity difficulties can be overcome by better acquainting teachers with characteristics of gifted students and by training them to rate and identify G/T candidates. It also is recommended that teachers get to know students well before nominating them.

One form designed by Renzulli to help structure the nomination of students for revolving door programs appears in Appendix 4.1 at the end of this chapter. Many more are available in Martinson (1974), Clasen and Robinson (1979), and Renzulli, Reis and Smith (1981). The *Kranz Talent Identification Instrument* (Kranz, 1981), also a structured teacher nomination strategy, and Renzulli's *Scales for Rating Behavioral Characteristics of Superior Students* (SRBCSS; Appendix 4.5) are discussed later. Teachers, schools, or school districts also may develop their own teacher nomination forms that help synthesize, for example, ability scores, reading and math scores, grades, parent or peer nominations, creativity, motivation, leadership, or other abilities and skills pertinent to the particular G/T program.

Creativity Tests

In some classes and with some creativity-conscious teachers, it may be easily apparent which students are highly creative and which are not. Creativity tests can be used to confirm a teacher's suspicions about the creativeness of one or more students. The tests also may be used to identify creative students whose unique talents are not visible in many classrooms.

It is important to emphasize that creativity tests are not perfect. Especially, scores from a single creativity test might be quite misleading in the sense that a student who, in fact, does extraordinarily creative work in an art or science area could produce a strictly average creativity score. Validity coefficients of published creativity tests (the correlation of test scores with another criterion of creativity, such as teacher ratings or ratings of creative products) typically range from about .25 to .40, which is moderately low. Creativity is a complex ability that can take innumerable forms. It is impossible to measure creativity exactly. The authors have repeatedly emphasized that data from creativity tests—including their own—must be combined with other information to make valid decisions regarding creativeness (Rimm and Davis, 1976). Using two criteria of creativeness is recommended (Davis, 1975, 1986). For example, a student who scores high on a creativity test and is rated as "highly creative" by a teacher is virtually certain to be a *bona fide* creative person.

Teachers who have opportunity to observe creative ideas and products may be asked to rate students' creativeness. For example, art teachers or teachers who supervise original science projects, creative writing, or drama activities are in a good position to identify creative talent.

As for creativity tests themselves, there are two main categories: divergent thinking tests and inventories that assess personality and biographical traits (Davis, 1986). Divergent thinking tests require students to think of all the ideas they can for open-ended problems, such as listing unusual uses for a newspaper or brick, imagining consequences of an unlikely event ("What would happen if people had an eye in the back of their head?"), or asking as many questions as possible about an object or event. Such tests are scored at least for ideational fluency (the number of ideas produced) and originality (uniqueness of the ideas). The *Torrance Tests of Creative Thinking* (Torrance, 1966) are the most widely used divergent-thinking tests (see Inset 4.2). They include verbal and nonverbal (figural) subtests, and are scored for *fluency, flexibility* (number of different categories of ideas or approaches to the problem), *originality,* and, with the figural tests, *elaboration* (number of additional details and embellishments). Other divergent thinking batteries are the Guilford (1967, 1977) tests, the *Monitor Test of Creative Potential* (Hoepfner and Hemenway, 1973), Williams's (1980) *Exercise in Divergent Thinking,* which is part of his *Creativity Assessment Packet* (CAP), the Wallach and Kogan (1965) tests, the Getzels and Jackson (1962) tests, and for preschool children Torrance's (1981d) *Thinking Creatively in Action and Movement.* See Davis (1986) for descriptions of published creativity tests.

In view of their extensive development and evaluation, and the standard administration and scoring procedures, the Torrance tests are the recommended divergent thinking battery. If money is a problem, the Wallach and Kogan tests and the Getzels and Jackson tests apparently may be used without charge. In the negative column, the administration and scoring of any divergent thinking test are very time-consuming.

As for inventories that assess personality and biographical information, the authors—without bias or prejudice—recommend their own *PRIDE, GIFT, GIFFI I* and *GIFFI II* instruments (Rimm and Davis, 1983). There is a stereotype of personality traits and biographical characteristics that appears again and again in studies of creative people of all ages (for example, curiosity, humor, risk taking, and a history of creative activities; see Chapter 2).

PRIDE (Preschool and Primary Interest Descriptor; Rimm, 1982) is a preschool/kindergarten inventory that parents fill out. *GIFT (Group Inventory for Finding (Creative) Talent)* consists of yes-no items in lower-, middle-, and upper-elementary school forms. *GIFFI I* and *II (Group Inventory for Finding*

INSET 4.2 TORRANCE TESTS OF CREATIVE THINKING

The *Torrance Tests of Creative Thinking* (Torrance, 1966) measure creative abilities of *fluency* (number of ideas), *flexibility* (number of different types or categories of ideas), *originality* (uniqueness), and *elaboration* (number of embellishments). Exercises similar to Torrance's subtests are presented below. Spend a few minutes on each one. Are you fluent? Flexible? Original? Are you high in elaboration?

Directions: Make a meaningful picture out of each of the nonsense forms below. Try to be original. Give each one a name.

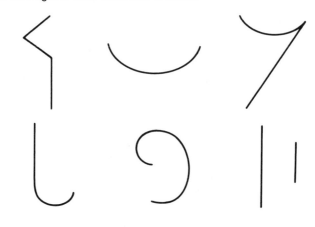

Directions: List as many unusual uses as you can for discarded rubber tires.

Reprinted by permission of Scholastic Testing Service, Inc.

Interests) are in a rating scale form designed for junior and senior high school students, respectively.

These tests have been validated in seven different countries and with many student populations, including minority, learning disabled, and gifted. The tests produce subscale scores (for example, confidence, imagination, many interests) that can be used to help understand and guide gifted children.

Two other instruments for assessing creative personality traits were designed by Williams (1980). First, his *Exercise in Divergent Feeling*, from his CAP battery, asks students in grades 3 through 12 ". . . how curious, imaginative, complex and risky they believe they are." Second, the *Williams Scale*, also a CAP test, consists of rating-scale items used by a parent or teacher to evaluate student creative abilities and traits.

Two creativity tests resembling divergent thinking tests are *Sounds and Images* and *Onomatopoeia and Images,* both part of Torrance, Khatena, and Cunnington's (1973) *Thinking Creatively with Sounds and Words. Sounds and Images* requires students to describe mental images suggested by each of four abstract sounds. *Onomatopoeia and Images* is similar except that ten image-stimulating onomatopoetic words (for example, zoom, fizzy, moan) are used instead of abstract sounds. Both tests produce a total originality score.

Parent Nominations

No one knows children and adolescents better than their own parents. For example, only the parents will know a child spoke in sentences at age two, taught him- or herself to read at age four, and drew the solar system, composed melodies, produced creative art, and asked about reasons for the Middle-East strife at age five. Unfortunately, parent nominations are not used as much as they should be. Martinson (1974) recommends that in a child's early school years, parents may be asked to provide information regarding advanced knowledge and abilities. A one-page form may simply state that the teacher is interested in planning "appropriate" educational experiences for the child, and would the parent please provide information pertaining to:

1. The child's special interests and hobbies
2. Recent books he or she has enjoyed or read
3. Special interests other than reading
4. Unusual accomplishments, past or present
5. Special talents
6. Special opportunities the child has had
7. Preferred activities when alone
8. Relationships with others
9. Special problems and/or needs

Another nomination rating form, developed by Tongue and Sperling (1976), appears in Appendix 4.2. This form evaluates precocious cognitive development (items 1–5, 9, 20), creativity (items 6, 8, 10–13), leadership (item 14), motor coordination (item 16), energy and persistence (items 7, 15, 19), and other characteristics of gifted and creative children. Using descriptions of gifted and talented students presented in Chapter 2, a teacher or G/T coordinator could tailor-make an even more suitable parent nomination inventory.

As a few cautions, some parents may not know their children well and do not follow all of the adventures and creations of their gifted child. Others, particularly nonintellectually oriented ones, may not understand their own child's precocity, gifts, or talents. Some parents overestimate their child's abilities, while others underestimate them.

Peer Nominations

Peers are very good at nominating gifted and talented classmates, and may be especially helpful in identifying culturally different gifted children (Cox and Daniel, 1983a). They know who's who. Year after year they watch Freddy and Anne finish their work first, get all the problems right, answer all of the teacher's questions correctly, volunteer to go to the board every time, and understand the most confusing issues. They also know about Freddy's and Anne's scientific and artistic accomplishments outside of school. One simple approach is to ask a few individual students, "Who's the smartest kid in the class?" "Who's the best reader?" "Who always finishes their work first?"

A more structured, but very brief, peer nomination form appears in Appendix 4.3. This form asks students to nominate which of their classmates is the brightest (items 1 and 2), the most creative (items 3 and 5), and the best leader (item 4).

Davidson (1986) suggested that students (above the lowest primary grades) may nominate each other with a form that simply says, "I believe that _____ should be placed in the gifted program because I have observed the following behaviors: _____." Said Davidson, "This type of nomination eliminates the possibility that a student may be excluded simply because some unique abilities may not be included on a standardized nomination form."

Self-Nominations

Some students have strong artistic, creative, scientific, or other interests and talents, and they want to participate in a special program—but nobody asks them. Teachers may be unaware of the talent, creativity, and high motivation. A self-nomination form used in Charlottesville, Virginia, simply asks students, "Check the area(s) in which you think you have special abilities or talents, and tell why you think you have special abilities or talents in these areas." The ten areas were general intellectual ability, math, science, social studies, language arts, reading, art, music, drama, dance, creativity, and leadership, areas based upon the U.S.O.E. definition. Self-nomination is especially recommended at the junior and senior high school levels, where peer pressures may cause youths to mask their special talents. Renzulli (1987) stated that in high school self-nomination is the *only* identification strategy he uses or recommends.

Product Evaluations

A good index of academic, artistic, creative, or scientific talent is simply the quality of work the student has done or is doing. Art teachers are in a unique position to evaluate artistic talent and creativity. Other teachers also may have an opportunity to evaluate the quality of students' poetry, science projects, electronic or computer projects, dramatic talent, photography, unusual hobbies, and so on. Such information—"face valid" reflections of gifts and talents—should be very useful in the overall identification process.

Usually, product evaluations are quite informal; the product may obviously reflect high creativity, science ability, writing skill, analysis or synthesis talent, and so on. However, if a more structured and objective product rating form is desired, Appendix 4.4 presents a form developed and used by the State of Michigan Education Department. It is helpful to use more than one rater, since teacher variation (inter-rater reliability) in judgments of creative products needs to be considered.

Rating Scales

We already have seen several rating scales in conjunction with teacher-, parent-, peer-, and self-nomination procedures and product evaluations. Renzulli (1983) developed a set of ten rating scale instruments, used by teachers, entitled *Scales for Rating Behavioral Characteristics of Superior Students* (SRBCSS). The four most widely used scales evaluate intellectual ability (learning), creativity, motivation and leadership and are reproduced in Appendix 4.5. Others assess artistic, musical, dramatic, and planning characteristics and communication-precision and communication-expressiveness.

Rimm's (1985a) *Achievement Identification Measure* (AIM), filled out by parents, consists of 77 rating-scale items designed to identify underachievement. It is, in essence, a measure of student academic motivation. The *Group Achievement Identification Measure* (GAIM; Rimm, 1985b) is virtually identical except that it is administered directly to students. Both instruments produce subscale scores of *Competition* (for example, "My child enjoys competition, win or lose"), *Responsibility* (for example, "My child seems to ask for more teacher help than most children"), *Self-Control* (for example, "My child is well behaved in school"), *Achievement Communication* (for example, "The father in the family thinks good grades are important"), and *Respect* (for example, "My child usually obeys his mother").

Kranz Talent Identification Instrument

The *Krant Talent Identification Instrument* (KTII; Kranz, 1981) is an update of Kranz's very successful *Multidimensional Screening Device* (MDSD). The KTII involves training teachers to rate all children in their classes on ten different talent dimensions, some of which are rather unusual. A frequent outcome—if not the main purpose—of the training is to raise teacher's awareness of the multidimensionality of their students. As Fiedler (1982) said, "It forces teachers to walk all the way around the kids and look at them from different perspectives."

Significantly, and uniquely, the KTII specifically aims at identifying gifted and talented children from among students who are underachievers, minority members, or poor, or whose parents are immigrants or blue-collar workers who are not education oriented.

The KTII procedure involves three main steps: (1) in-service training of the teachers, (2) the rating of every student, and (3) the final selections by a separate screening committee, based upon the ratings and other student data. "Other student data" usually will include information from the *KTII Peer Nomination Forms*, the *KTII Parent Questionnaire*, and the *KTII Pupil Questionnaire*, an interest inventory. The ten KTII talents are:

1. Visual arts talent
2. Performing arts talent
3. Creative talent
4. One-sided talent
5. Academic talent
6. Leadership and organizing talent
7. Psychomotor talent
8. Spatial and abstract thinking talent
9. Underachievement talent
10. Hidden talent

The KTII videotape and the KTII manual explain each of the talents and how they are recognized. The manual also suggests specific classroom activities and exercises that enable a teacher to observe and evaluate each type of talent.

Most of the talents need not be defined here; in fact, they almost duplicate the categories of the U.S.O.E. definition. However, (4) "one-sided talent," (9) "underachievement talent," and (10) "hidden talent" require a brief comment. One-sided talent refers to the energetic student who has maintained a long-term involvement with—and is an expert on—one particular hobby or interest. It might be photography, red-tailed hawks, the Beatles, or in Kranz's favorite example, salamanders. No matter what the topic of the class lesson or discussion—math, history, geography, spelling, social studies, or weather—the Salamander Kid can twist it into something relevant to salamanders.

Underachievement talent is not, as the name seems to suggest, a highly polished excellence in performing below one's ability. It simply refers to underachieving, the combination of high ability with low academic performance.

The most interesting of the Kranz talents is hidden talent, which comes in many forms. Primarily, it is the unusual ability to cope with school problems despite significant home difficulties. The hidden talent student may show ". . . fantastic oral ability, poetry-writing talent, or dramatic story-telling ability; the ability to think in two languages (English at school, native language at home); music and art talent; or an unusual depth of understanding" (Kranz, 1981).

Kranz recommends some specific rating methods that might well be applied to any student-rating procedures. (1) She recommends "rating vertically," that is, rating each student in the class on one particular talent before proceeding to the next talent. (2) With the KTII, a 7-point scale is used. With the exception of academic talent (talent 5), Kranz recommends awarding only one 7 for each of the talents for each class, although there many be many 6's, 5's, 4's, and so on. (3) Rate students after January, when you know them. (4) Do not rate them in subject matter areas; the ten scales are intended to be content free. Grades and achievement tests scores will provide plenty of information on specific academic talents.

As for the screening committee itself, Kranz recommends a group consisting of the principal, librarian, art teacher, music teacher, and G/T teacher. The screening committee gathers information about every child, including the ten KTII ratings, parent and peer nominations, the student interest questionnaire, and any other academic, ability, or creativity information. The screening committee, not individual teachers, will make the final decision.

Baldwin Identification Matrix

The *Baldwin Identification Matrix* (Baldwin, 1977, 1978) summarizes scores and ratings on a variety of criteria. As shown in Table 4.1, standardized intelligence and achievement test data are used for rating intelligence, reading, and math (Items 1.1–1.4). The Renzulli and Hartman (1981;

TABLE 4.1   Sample form for *Baldwin Identification Matrix*.

Area	Assessment Items	M*	S*	5	4	3	2	1	b-na	No*	RS*	Area Score (RS/N)
Cognitive	1.1 General IQ Binet	44.1	150			3						
	1.2 Stanford Reading	11.1	7			3						
	1.3 Math	11.1	8		4							
	1.4 Reading	11.2	91		4							
	1.5 Renz-Learning	22.2	28		4							
	Total Cognitive			0	12	6	0	0	0	5	18	3.6
Psychosocial	2.1 Kenz-Leadership	22.4	29					1				
	2.2 Supplemental	33.5	4		4							
	2.3 Peer Nomination	33.5	3			3						
	2.4											
	2.5											
	Total Psychosocial			0	4	3	0	1	0	3	8	2.7
Creative Prods	3.1 Art Products	33.6	7			3						
	3.2 Musical Performance	33.6	8		4							
	3.3 Supplemental	33.5	4		4							
	3.4											
	3.5											
	Total Creative Products			0	8	3	0	0	0	3	11	3.7
Psychomotor	4.1 School Assessment	33.5	4		4							
	4.2 Supplemental	33.5	5	5								
	4.3											
	4.4											
	4.5											
	Total Psychomotor			5	4	0	0	0	0	2	9	4.5
Motivation	5.1 Renz Motivation	22.1	29			3						
	5.2 Supplemental	33.5	3			3						
	5.3											
	5.4											
	5.5											
	Total Motivation			0	0	6	0	0	0	2	6	3
Creative Press	6.1 Renz Creativity	22.3	29			3						
	6.2 TTC Creativity	11.2	85%		4							
	6.3											
	6.4											
	6.5											
	Total Creative Process			0	4	3	0	0	0	2	7	3.5
	Matrix Totals		Maximum Points for this Matrix									30
			Student Total									21

Copyright © 1984 Trillium Press, Inc.

M* — Mode of Score Code

S* — Score

No* — Number of Items

RS* — Raw Score

Renzulli, 1983) *Scales for Rating Behavioral Characteristics of Superior Students* (Appendix 4.5) are used for evaluating *learning, motivation, creativity,* and *leadership* (Items 1.5, 2.1, 5.1, 6.1). The Matrix entries are added to produce a single total score, allowing students to be easily ranked. Simplicity in decision making is the main advantage of such a point system. A cutoff score may be set and any student producing a total score above that cutoff is selected, or else the top 3 or 5 percent may be chosen. In addition to the handy total score, the Baldwin Matrix also provides a profile of strengths and weaknesses for each student.

The main disadvantage of the Baldwin Matrix, and most other identification systems based on total points, is that students who are gifted or talented according to only a few criteria (for example, in a particular area) are very likely to produce mediocre total scores, and therefore will be quickly excluded despite obvious qualifications and needs. Feldhusen, Asher, and Hoover (1984) noted that a better use of the Baldwin Matrix would be to match student gifts to program goals. For example, a combination of the ratings in reading, writing, language arts, and verbal intelligence could be used to select students for a special program emphasizing the development of writing talent. Flexibility in use is recommended.

EBY Gifted Behavior Index

The *EBY Gifted Behavior Index* (Eby, 1984) is a collection of seven instruments. Six instruments evaluate gifted behaviors in these areas:

1. Verbal
2. Math/science/problem solving
3. Visual/spatial (art)
4. Social/leadership
5. Music
6. Mechanical/technical/inventiveness

The seventh scale evaluates student products, both according to the the gifted behaviors used by the student and the quality of the product itself.

Each of the seven instruments asks the teacher to evaluate gifted behaviors according to ten dimensions synthesized from a review of characteristics of giftedness:

> Perceptiveness
> Active Interaction with the Environment (enthusiasm)
> Reflectiveness
> Persistence
> Independence
> Goal Orientation
> Originality
> Productivity
> Self-Evaluation
> Communication of Findings

For each of the seven instruments, the ten traits are evaluated by statements rated on five-point scales. For example, *originality* of gifted *ver-*

bal behavior is evaluated with "Experiments with new verbal forms of expression" and "Creates unique plots, characters, story, and poetry." Apparently, each of the seven instruments can be used independently or in combination.

One attraction of the EBY scale is the emphasis on demonstrations of gifted behaviors rather than evaluations of innate ability. Inspired by Renzulli, Eby noted that gifted behavior is strongly influenced by environmental stimulation and support.

Recommendations from the National Report on Identification

The National Report on Identification (Richert, Alvino, and McDonnel, 1982; Richert, 1985), mentioned earlier, included an alphabetized list of over sixty tests, rating scales, checklists, and inventories (Table 4.2). The table includes (1) categories of giftedness assessed by each instrument, (2) appropriateness for advantaged and disadvantaged children, (3) suitable age range, and (4) appropriate stage for their use (i.e., for nominating/ identifying gifted students, assessing their abilities, or evaluating their skill development).

Final Comment

The identification procedure clearly is a crucial part of any G/T program. The procedures themselves operationally define who is "gifted" (or has the potential for gifted behavior) and who is not (or does not). It is important that the procedures be tied, on one hand, to the definition of "gifts and talents" in the original program plan. It makes little sense to publicly accept the five-part U.S.O.E. definition—and then brazenly use only IQ scores or science grades for selection. The procedures also should be tied to program purposes and goals. Said Feldhusen, Asher, and Hoover (1984), ". . . program goals will set the direction for the entire identification process."

The authors also feel compelled to reiterate some of the advantages of a liberal identification policy, such as in the talent pool/revolving door model of Renzulli (1984, 1985): More students have an opportunity to participate; identification is flexible and multidimensional; identification for independent work continues all year; motivated students self-select for independent work; uninterested, unsuccessful students do not waste resource room time and facilities; charges of elitism are reduced or eliminated; the need for painful, hard-and-fast decisions (for example, based on cutoff scores or a 3–5 percent criterion) is eliminated; and silly situations in which, due to altered identification criteria, last year's gifted student is "not gifted this year" are eliminated. There is much to be said for such a plan.

Finally, remember that "gifts and talents" extend beyond high intel-

TABLE 4.2   Alphabetical listing of instruments and recommendations for use.

INSTRUMENT	CATEGORY					POPULATION			AGE			ID STAGE		
	General Intellectual	Specific Academic	Creativity	Leadership	Visual and Performing Arts	Advantaged	Disadvantaged	Early Childhood	Grades 4-8	High School to Adult	K-12	Nomination	Assessment	Evaluation
A.S.S.E.T.S.	+	+	+		+	+		+	+			+	+	
Barron-Welsh Art Scale					+	+		+	+	+	+	+		
Biographical Inventory-Form U		+	+	+	+	+		+	+			+		
California Achievement Tests		+				+			+	+	+			
California Psychological Inventory						+		+	+			+		
Cartoon Conservation Scales	+						+	+	+			+	+	
Lattell Culture Fair Intelligence Series	+						+	+	+			+		
CIRCUS	+	+				+	+	+				+	+	
Cognitive Abilities Test	+					+		+	+	+		+	+	
Columbia Mental Maturity Scale	+					+	+	+	+			+		
Comprehensive Tests of Basic Skills		+				+			+	+	+			
Cornell Critical Thinking Tests						+				+		+		+
Creativity Assessment Packet			+			+	+	+	+			+		
Creativity Tests for Children			+			+		+	+			+		
Design Judgement Test				+	+			+	+	+		+		
Differential Aptitude Tests	+	+				+		+	+			+		+
Early School Personality Questionnaire						+	+	+				+		
Gifted and Talented Screening Form	+	+	+	+	+	+		+	+	+		+		
Goodenough-Harris Drawing Test	+					+	+	+	+	+		+		
Group Inventory for Finding Creative Talent (G.I.F.T.)			+			+		+	+			+	+	
Group Inventory for Finding Interests (G.I.F.F.I.)			+			+				+		+	+	
Guilford-Holley L Inventory						+				+		+		
GuilFord-Zimmerman Aptitude Survey	+					+				+		+		
Henmon-Nelson Tests of Mental Ability	+	+				+			+	+	+			
High School Personality Questionnaire						+			+	+		+		
Horn Art Aptitude Inventory				+	+	+				+		+		
Iowa Tests of Basic Skills		+				+		+	+	+		+	+	
Kaufman — ABC	+	+				+	+	+				+	+	
Khatena-Torrance Creative Perception Inventory			+			+		+	+			+	+	
Lorge-Thorndike Intelligence Tests	+					+	+	+	+			+		
Maier Art Judgement Tests				+	+			+	+			+		
Metropolitan Achievement Tests		+				+						+	+	
Multi-Dimensional Screening Device	+	+	+	+	+	+						+		
Musical Aptitude Profile				+	+	+		+	+	+		+	+	
Otis-Lennon Mental Ability Test	+						+					+	+	

Table 4.2 (continued)

INSTRUMENT	CATEGORY					POPULATION				AGE		ID STAGE		
	General Intellectual	Specific Academic	Creativity	Leadership	Visual and Performing Arts	Advantaged	Disadvantaged	Early Childhood	High School to Adult	Grades 4-8	K-12	Nomination	Assessment	Evaluation
Peabody Individual Achievement Test		+				+					+	+		
Pennsylvania Assessment of Creative Tendency			+			+		+	+			+		
Piers-Harris Children's Self-Concept Scale						+		+	+			+		
Preschool Talent Checklist	+	+	+	+	+	+	+	+		+		+		
Primary Measure of Music Audiation					+	+	+	+				+		
Progressive Matrices — Advanced	+					+			+			+		
Progressive Matrices — Standard	+					+						+		
Remote Associates Test						+			+			+	+	
Ross Test of Higher Cognitive Processes	+					+			+			+		+
Scales for Rating Behavioral Characteristics of Superior Students	+		+	+	+	+	+			+		+		
Seashore Measure of Musical Talents				+	+	+		+	+			+		
The Self-Concept and Motivation Inventory (SCAMIN)					+	+	+	+	+			+		
Sequential Tests of Educational Progress (STEP)		+				+		+	+	+		+		+
Short Form Test of Academic Aptitude	+	+				+		+	+	+		+		
Slosson Intelligence Test	+					+		+	+	+		+		
SOI Gifted Screening Form		+	+		+	+	+	+	+			+	+	
SOI Learning Abilities Test		+	+		+	+	+	+	+			+	+	
SRA Achievement Series		+				+					+	+	+	
Stallings' Environmentally Based Screen	+						+	+				+		
Stanford Achievement Test		+				+		+	+	+		+	+	
Stanford-Binet Intelligence Scale	+					+		+	+	+		+		
System of Multicultural Pluralistic Assessment (SOMPA)	+						+	+				+		
Tennessee Self-Concept Scale						+		+	+			+		
Test of Creative Potential			+			+		+	+			+		+
Tests of Achievement and Proficiency		+				+						+	+	
Torrance Test of Creative Thinking — Verbal			+			+			+			+		
Torrance Test of Creative Thinking			+		+					+	+	+		
Torrance Test of Creative Thinking — Figural										+	+	+		
Vane Kindergarten Test	+	+				+						+	+	
Watson-Glaser Critical Thinking Appraisal	+					+		+	+			+		+
Wechsler Intelligence Scale for Children Revised (WISC-R)	+					+		+	+	+		+		
Weschler Preschool and Primary Scale of Intelligence	+					+		+				+		

Reprinted by permission of Dr. E. Susanne Richert, Education Information and Resource Center, Sewell, NJ and *Roeper Review*.

ligence, although academic ability is an important consideration. The U.S.O.E. definition, Taylor's Totem Poles, Renzulli's rating scales, the *Kranz Talent Identification Instrument,* and the *EBY Gifted Behavior Index* all emphasize the multidimensionality of gifts and talents. Using objective scores tempered by flexibility, reasonableness, and a real concern for children is necessary and defensible. Do not permit a low test score or a teacher/child conflict to eliminate an obviously gifted child from a challenge he or she needs.

SUMMARY

There are many strategies for identifying gifted and talented students. A multidimensional approach is recommended. The most common means of identification are teacher nomination, achievement tests, intelligence tests, and grades.

Davidson argued against formal identification systems involving tests, ratings, and nominations, including point systems and cutoff scores. Davidson recommended a liberal 15 to 20 percent quota; automatic selection of students with high IQ, achievement, or creativity scores; and especially the increased use of informal parent and teacher nominations based on observations.

Another issue concerns the annual selection of 3 to 5 percent of the students as "gifted" vs. the increasingly popular 15 to 20 percent talent pool or "open door" concept. In the revolving door model, talent pool students who are motivated and creative self-select to work on independent projects.

Multidimensional criteria and a quota system will insure representation of disadvantaged and minority students. Handicapped and female students also may be overlooked in the selection process. Teachers tend to select pleasant and cooperative students, when in fact the stubborn or egotistical student may be the most gifted.

Reliability refers to the accuracy of a test (or other instrument or procedure) or the test-retest consistency. Validity is the degree to which the instrument measures what it is supposed to measure. One must consider the reliability and validity of any instrument or selection procedure.

The 1982 *National Report on Identification* endorsed the U.S.O.E. multidimensional definition of giftedness. It recommended that identification procedures be based on research, equitable, designed in the best interests of all students, based on a broad definition of giftedness, and designed to identify as many gifted learners as possible. The report identified such questionable practices as limiting selection to high-achieving students, overlooking minority students, using instruments inappropriately, and combining criteria inappropriately. The report recommended using both formal tests and informal rating and nomination procedures, and not combining the data (i.e., into a total score).

The *Stanford-Binet, Revision IV,* provides standard age scores (in place of IQ scores) for verbal reasoning, quantitative reasoning, visual/abstract reasoning, and short-term memory, plus a composite score.

The *WISC-R* produces a Verbal, Performance, and Full-Scale IQ score.

Group intelligence tests are useful, but suffer from lower reliability and validity, lower ceilings, and high verbal content. Any intelligence test will help identify underachieving students. However, too much emphasis on intelligence scores will exclude students with other gifts.

Achievement tests are good indicators of specific academic talent. However, they tend to have relatively low ceilings and therefore will not discriminate among gifted students who "top out." Grade equivalent scores do not mean that the student belongs in the grade indicated in the score.

Teacher nominations are widely used, yet among the least reliable and valid. However, teachers can be trained. Teachers also may use structured nomination and rating forms.

Creativity tests may identify creative talent that is otherwise not visible. Because of its complexity, validity coefficients for creativity tests are not high. Using two criteria of creativeness is recommended in order to accurately identify creatively gifted students.

Two main categories of creativity tests are divergent thinking tests, such as the Torrance tests, and personality/biographical inventories, such as *PRIDE, GIFT,* and *GIFFI I* and *II.*

Parents can provide valid information for identification. However, they may be unaware of their child's gifts or else overestimate their child's abilities.

Peers are good at identifying classmates who are bright, creative, good readers, and good at math.

Self-nominations are highly recommended. At the high school level, Renzulli recommends that only self-nominations be used.

Product evaluations may be informal or use structured evaluation forms.

Renzulli's most widely used rating scales allow a teacher to rate intellectual ability, creativity, motivation, and leadership.

Rimm's AIM and GAIM may be used to identify underachievement patterns.

Kranz's KTII evaluates ten talents, excluding specific academic talent. The procedure emphasizes training teachers to evaluate accurately. The KTII is designed to evaluate gifts and talents among underachieving, minority, poor, immigrant, and blue-collar children, as well as others. Most notable are her "one-sided" and "hidden" talent categories.

The *Baldwin Identification Matrix* summarizes scores and ratings on a variety of criteria, combining them into a single total score. This procedure risks overlooking students with strength in just one or a few categories.

The *EBY Gifted Behavior Index* is a rating scale instrument that a teacher may use to evaluate ten dimensions of gifted behaviors in each of seven areas.

The *National Report on Identification* includes a list of sixty instruments, with specifications for each test of the categories of giftedness assessed, appropriateness for advantaged and disadvantaged children, suitable age range, and appropriate stage in the G/T program for use.

Identification procedures must be related to one's definition of giftedness and to the goals of the program. A multidimensional approach, extending beyond intelligence scores (or grades), is recommended. Also, because of its many advantages a liberal talent pool identification procedure is endorsed.

APPENDIX 4.1 NOMINATION FORM FOR TRIAD/REVOLVING DOOR PROGRAMS

1. Student _____ Teacher _____

2. Date of Referral _____ School _____

3. Grade _____ Date of Birth _____

4. Average Grades for Current School Year

        Language Arts _____

        Social Studies _____

        Arithmatic _____

        Science _____

5. Parent Nomination (Check if appropriate): _____

6. SRBCSS Scale Total _____ 1. _____ 2. _____ 3. _____ 4. _____

7. Why do you think this student should be included in the Talent Pool? (You may wish to list examples of ideas, projects, creative endeavors, etc.)

_____

_____

_____

_____

INTERESTS
Please indicate the areas of interest that the student has displayed in your class this year. If you've noticed other specific topics (interest in dinosaurs, computers, etc.), please note this in the column entitled "Other."

	HIGH	AVERAGE	LOW		HIGH	AVERAGE	LOW
Fine Arts/Crafts				Music			
Science				Drama			
Creative Writing				Mathematics			
Social Studies				Language Arts			
Psychomotor				Other			

CURRICULAR STRENGTH AREAS
Please indicate the curricular areas in which the student has demonstrated proficiency and could possibly be considered for curriculum compacting.

        Language Arts _____   Mathematics _____

        Science _____   Social Science _____

Reprinted by permission of J. S. Renzulli.

APPENDIX 4.2 SAMPLE PARENT NOMINATION FORM AT THE EARLY CHILDHOOD LEVEL

Name of Student _____ Age _____

Address _____ School_____ Grade ___

Parent's Name _____

Instructions: In relationship to the typical child in your neighborhood, please circle a number for each item which best describes your child: 5—has this trait to a high degree; 4—has this trait more than the typical child; 3—compares with the typical child; 2—has this trait less than the typical child; 1—lacks this trait.

1. Has advanced vocabulary, expresses himself or herself well   5 4 3 2 1

2. Thinks quickly   5 4 3 2 1

3. Recalls facts easily   5 4 3 2 1

4. Wants to know how things work   5 4 3 2 1

5. Is reading (before he/she started kindergarten)   5 4 3 2 1

6. Puts unrelated ideas together in new and different ways   5 4 3 2 1

7. Becomes bored easily   5 4 3 2 1

8. Asks reasons why — questions almost everything   5 4 3 2 1

9. Likes "grown-up" things and to be with older people   5 4 3 2 1

10. Has a great deal of curiosity   5 4 3 2 1

11. Is adventurous   5 4 3 2 1

12. Has a good sense of humor   5 4 3 2 1

13. Is impulsive, acts before he/she thinks   5 4 3 2 1

14. Tends to dominate others if given the chance   5 4 3 2 1

15. Is persistent, sticks to a task   5 4 3 2 1

16. Has good physical coordination and body control   5 4 3 2 1

17. Is independent and self-sufficient in looking after himself/herself   5 4 3 2 1

18. Is aware of his/her surroundings and what is going on around him/her   5 4 3 2 1

19. Has a long attention span   5 4 3 2 1

20. Wanted to do things for himself/herself early — example: dressing and feeding himself/herself   5 4 3 2 1

Developed by the Staff of the Gifted and Talented Section, Division of Exceptional Children, North Carolina Department of Public Instruction. This instrument is part of an Identification Model developed by Cornelia Tongue and Charmian Sperling, 1976. Reprinted by permission.

APPENDIX 4.3 WHO KNOWS WHO'S WHO? PEER NOMINATION FORM

The Milwaukee Public School System created a structured peer nomination form which seems to ask: Who has a lot of information (1)? Who does school work quickly and easily (2)? Who is creative (3 and 5)? Who is a leader (4)?

You simply tally up who has the most votes in each category. A student who is outstanding in *all* categories is a good prospect for your gifted program.

Directions to Teacher

Read the following statements to your class:

1. "Each of you has been asked to assist in an information gathering survey for the Milwaukee Public Schools."
2. "Please take out a sheet of paper and a pencil."
3. "Number your paper from 1 to 5."
4. "Please answer each question that I will read with the *complete* name of one student in our class."
5. "Pick someone whom you think is the best choice and not just your friends."
6. "You can pick the same person for more than one question if you think that person is your best choice."

Questions

1. If a person from outer space wanted someone in your class to tell him about different things on earth, who do you think could tell the most?
2. What student in class can complete his or her work and still have time to take part in other activities?
3. Who says things in class that are most original, things that you never thought of before?
4. If kids didn't have to go to school, what student in your class could talk you into going?
5. Who do you think might invent or make something that no one ever made before? (This is the person you might ask to help you write a poem or play, or help you make something for a school science fair.)

APPENDIX 4.4 INSTRUMENT FOR RATING THE EXCELLENCE OF PROJECTS SUBMITTED BY STUDENTS

1. Briefly describe the product.

2. To what extent does the product represent an in-depth or superior handling of the subject?

5	4	3	2	1
To a great extent		Somewhat		To a limited extent

3. To what extent is this product of a "quality-level" beyond what one might expect of a student of this age?

5	4	3	2	1
To a great extent		Somewhat		To a limited extent

4. To what extent does the product indicate close attention to detail?

5	4	3	2	1
To a great extent		Somewhat		To a limited extent

5. To what extent is the central idea/ conception of the product beyond what a student of this age might undertake?

5	4	3	2	1
To a great extent		Somewhat		To a limited extent

6. To what extent is the product of overall excellence?

5	4	3	2	1
To a great extent		Somewhat		To a limited extent

7. List some of the criteria you used in evaluating the excellence of this product.

APPENDIX 4.5 SCALES FOR RATING BEHAVIORAL CHARACTERISTICS OF SUPERIOR STUDENTS

Name_____ Date_____

School_____ Grade_____ Age_____
Yrs.   Mos.

Teacher or person completing this form_____

How long have you known this child?   _____months

DIRECTIONS: These scales are designed to obtain teacher estimates of a
student's characteristics in the areas of learning, motivation, creativity, and leadership. The items are derived from the research literature dealing with characteristics of gifted and creative persons.
It should be pointed out that a considerable amount of individual differences can be found within this population; therefore, the profiles
are likely to vary a great deal. Each item in the scales should be
considered separately and should reflect the degree to which you have
observed the presence or absence of each characteristic. Since the
four dimensions of the instrument represent relatively different sets
of behaviors, the scores obtained from the separate scales should not
be summed to yield a total score. Please read the statements carefully
and place an X in the appropriate place according to the following
scale of values.

1. If you have seldom or never observed this characteristic
2. If you have observed this characteristic occasionally
3. If you have observed this characteristic to a considerable
    degree
4. If you have observed this characteristic almost all of the
    time

Space has been provided following each item for your comments.

SCORING: Separate scores for each of the four dimensions may be
obtained as follows:

Add the total number of X's in each column to obtain the
"Column Total."
Multiply the Column Total by the "Weight" for each column to
obtain the "Weighted Column Total."
Sum the Weighted Column Totals across to obtain the "Score"
for each dimension of the scale.
Enter the Scores below.

Learning Characteristics   _____
Motivational Characteristics _____
Creativity Characteristics   _____
Leadership Characteristics   _____

(Reprinted by permission.)

APPENDIX 4.5 (Continued)

PART I: LEARNING CHARACTERISTICS

	1*	2	3	4

1. Has unusually advanced vocabulary for age
    or grade level; uses terms in a meaningful
    way; has verbal behavior characterized by
    "richness" of expression, elaboration, and
    fluency.

2. Possesses a large storehouse of information
    about a variety of topics (beyond the usual
    interests of youngsters his or her age).

3. Has quick mastery and recall of factual
    information.

4. Has rapid insight into cause-effect
    relationships; tries to discover the how
    and why of things; asks many provocative
    questions (as distinct from information
    or factual questions); wants to know
    what makes things (or people) "tick."

5. Has a ready grasp of underlying principles
    and can quickly make valid generalizations
    about events, people, or things; looks for
    similarities and differences in events,
    people, and things.

6. Is a keen and alert observer; usually
    "sees more" or "gets more" out of a
    story, film, etc., than others.

7. Reads a great deal on his or her own; usually
    prefers adult-level books; does not avoid
    difficult material; may show a preference for
    biography, autobiography, encyclopedias, and
    atlases.

8. Tries to understand complicated material by
    separating it into its respective parts;
    reasons things out for himself or herself;
    sees logical and common sense answers.

Column Total

Weight	1	2	3	4

Weighted Column Total

TOTAL

* 1—Seldom or never
  2—Occasionally
  3—Considerably
  4—Almost always

APPENDIX 4.5 *(Continued)*

PART II: MOTIVATIONAL CHARACTERISTICS	1	2	3	4
1. Becomes absorbed and truly involved in certain topics or problems; is persistent in seeking task completion. (It is sometimes difficult to get him or her to move on to another topic.)				
2. Is easily bored with routine tasks.				
3. Needs little external motivation to follow through in work that initially excites him or her.				
4. Strives toward perfection; is self-critical; is not easily satisfied with his or her own speed or products.				
5. Prefers to work independently; requires little direction from teachers.				
6. Is interested in many "adult" problems such as religion, politics, sex, race — more than usual for age level.				
7. Often is self-assertive (sometimes even aggressive); stubborn in his or her beliefs.				
8. Likes to organize and bring structure to things, people, and situations.				
9. Is quite concerned with right and wrong, good and bad; often evaluates and passes judgment on events, people, and things.				
Column Total				
Weight	1	2	3	4
Weighted Column Total				
TOTAL				

APPENDIX 4.5 (Continued)

PART III: CREATIVITY CHARACTERISTICS	1	2	3	4
1. Displays a great deal of curiosity about many things; is constantly asking questions about anything and everything.				
2. Generates a large number of ideas or solutions to problems and questions; often offers unusual ("way out"), unique, clever responses.				
3. Is uninhibited in expressing opinion; is sometimes radical and spirited in disagreement; is tenacious.				
4. Is a high risk taker; is adventurous and speculative.				
5. Displays a good deal of intellectual playfulness; fantasizes; imagines ("I wonder what would happen if ..."); manipulates ideas (i.e., changes, elaborates upon them); is often concerned with adapting, improving, and modifying institutions, objects, and systems.				
6. Displays a keen sense of humor and sees humor in situations that may not appear to be humorous to others.				
7. Is unusually aware of his or her impulses and more open to the irrational in himself or herself (freer expression of feminine interest for boys, greater than usual amount of independence for girls); shows emotional sensitivity.				
8. Is sensitive to beauty; attends to aesthetic characteristics of things.				
9. Is nonconforming; accepts disorder; is not interested in details; is individualistic; does not fear being different.				
10. Criticizes constructively; is unwilling to accept authoritarian pronouncements without critical examination.				
Column Total				
Weight	1	2	3	4
Weighted Column Total				
TOTAL				

APPENDIX 4.5 *(Continued)*

PART IV: LEADERSHIP CHARACTERISTICS

	1	2	3	4
1. Carries responsibility well; can be counted on to do what he or she has promised and usually does it well.				
2. Is self-confident with children his or her own age as well as adults; seems comfortable when asked to show his or her work to the class.				
3. Seems to be well-liked by classmates.				
4. Is cooperative with teacher and classmates; tends to avoid bickering and is generally easy to get along with.				
5. Can express himself or herself well; has good verbal facility and is usually well understood.				
6. Adapts readily to new situations; is flexible in thought and action and does not seem disturbed when the normal routine is changed.				
7. Seems to enjoy being around other people; is sociable and prefers not to be alone.				
8. Tends to dominate others when they are around; generally directs the activity in which he or she is involved.				
9. Participates in most social activities connected with the school; can be counted on to be there if anyone is.				
10. Excels in athletic activities; is well-coordinated and enjoys all sorts of athletic games.				
Column Total				
Weight	1	2	3	4
Weighted Column Total				
TOTAL				

chapter five

Acceleration

This and many of the following chapters describe strategies and models that guide programming decisions, teaching strategies, and curriculum content. In order to provide a framework for "what to do with gifted and talented kids," Table 5.1 summarizes suggestions for program content based upon student needs. These were integrated from lists prepared by Feldhusen (1986), Feldhusen and Wyman (1980), Sato and Johnson (1978), Kaplan (1974), the National/State Leadership Training Institute for Gifted and Talented, and Davis and Rimm (1985). Read through Table 5.1 before proceeding. You likely will refer back to this table as you read the following chapters.

There are many types of programs and services designed to fit the needs summarized in Table 5.1, while at the same time accommodating the level of interest, commitment, and resources of the particular school or district. Programs may differ in (1) the categories of students served, (2) the general curriculum model(s) followed, (3) specific enrichment curricula content and program goals, (4) acceleration plans, (5) grouping and organizational arrangements, (6) instructional or delivery strategy used, (7) community professionals and resources involved, and (8) program level (national, state, district, school, or classroom; Fox, 1979).

TABLE 5.1 Curriculum for the Gifted

1. Maximum achievement in basic skills
   A. Learning activities at an appropriate level and pace
   B. Based on student needs and readiness, not grade-level appropriateness
   C. Study skills
   D. Report writing, outlining
2. Content beyond the prescribed curriculum
   A. Extends or replaces traditional curriculum; not just "more work"
   B. Content related to broad-based issues, themes, and problems
   C. Resources beyond the designated grade-level—materials, equipment, information (not just books)
   D. Learning that is interrelated with other areas; not "separate entity learning"
3. Exposure to a variety of fields of study
   A. New disciplines; interrelatedness of disciplines
   B. Various occupations—the arts, professions
   C. Access to and stimulation of reading
4. Student-selected content
   A. Based on student interests and needs
   B. In-depth learning of a self-selected topic within an area of study
5. High content complexity
   A. Working with abstract ideas and theories that require reflective, evaluative, critical, and creative thinking
   B. Working with concepts and generalizations; not just names, dates, facts, and figures
   C. Applying learning, not just parroting it
   D. Developing products that challenge existing ideas and produce "new" ideas
   E. Developing products that use new techniques, materials, and forms
6. Experience in creative thinking and problem solving (see Chapters 10 and 11)
   A. Learning creative attitudes and awarenesses
   B. Responding to open-ended problems and tasks
   C. Understanding creative people, processes, techniques
   D. Strengthening fluency, flexibility, originality, visualization, metaphorical thinking, and other creative abilities
   E. Discovery and inquiry skills
   F. Learning to seek problems (problem finding)
   G. Learning to define problems
   H. Futuristic thinking
   I. Learning things as they should be or could be, not only as they are
7. Development of thinking skills (see Chapter 12)
   A. Independent, self-directed study skills
   B. Library skills
   C. Research/scientific skills and methods
   D. Bloom's higher-level skills: application, analysis, synthesis, evaluation
   E. Critical thinking, in the sense of evaluating biases, credibility, logic, consistency
   F. Decision making, planning, organizing
8. Affective development
   A. Developing self-awareness and self-understanding; accepting one's capabilities, interests, and needs
   B. Recognizing and using one's abilities
   C. Appreciating likenesses and differences between oneself and others

(continued)

TABLE 5.1   (*Continued*)

D. Relating intellectually, artistically, and affectively with other gifted, talented, creative students
E. Moral, ethical thinking; humanitarian attitudes
9. Development of motivation
    A. Independent thinking and work
    B. Becoming self-directed, disciplined in learning
    C. Achievement motivation; internal locus of control; high-level educational and career aspirations

Overview

Dividing programming into five topics, this chapter will summarize advantages, disadvantages, and recommendations associated with several frequently used acceleration strategies. Chapter 6 will focus on grouping methods, along with some basics of educational and career counseling. Chapter 7 will review enrichment options, and Chapter 8 will summarize some main curriculum models. These five categories overlap—for example, grouping may be for the purpose of acceleration, enrichment, or counseling, and a particular curriculum model may be designed to provide specific types of enrichment activities. Nonetheless, the present five-part approach—acceleration, grouping, counseling, enrichment, and curriculum models—should help clarify what can be done in successful programs, and provide ideas for how to do it.

ACCELERATION VERSUS ENRICHMENT

Before beginning, one issue deserves space: the traditional controversy regarding the merits of acceleration versus enrichment (see for example Daurio, 1979; Passow, 1958, 1981). For example, acceleration advocate Julian Stanley (1978b) argued that ". . . most of the supplemental educational procedures called 'enrichment' and given overly glamorous titles are, even at best, potentially dangerous if not accompanied or followed by acceleration . . . in subject matter and/or grade." Stanley and Benbow (1986) referred to most kinds of enrichment as "busywork and irrelevant." In his address to the Sixth World Conference on Gifted and Talented in Hamburg, Germany, Stanley (1985a) began his speech with ". . . educational nonacceleration is an international tragedy."

On the surface, the distinction between acceleration and enrichment seems simple enough—acceleration implies moving faster through academic content, while enrichment implies richer and more varied content. Looking more closely, however, the clear distinction has very fuzzy edges. *Acceleration*, according to Fox (1979), means ". . . the adjustment of learning time to meet the individual capabilities of the students . . . leading to higher levels of abstraction, more creative thinking, and more difficult content." *Grade skipping,* for example, is a traditional acceleration method. At a 1981 "Great Debate," Van Tassel-Baska (1981b; "For Acceleration") argued that ". . . acceleration implies no more than allowing students to move at a rate with which they are comfortable and can excel, rather than holding them back to conform to a 'speed limit' set by the average learner. As for enrichment," she continued, "the term has no meaning for the gifted unless it is inextricably linked to good acceleration practices. . . ."

Speaking for the opposition, Frost (1981; "For Enrichment") pointed out that enrichment ". . . implies a supplementation of the depth, breadth, or intensity of content and process as appropriate to the students' abilities and needs . . . [and is the prevailing practice because] . . . of the diversity in meeting student needs." One example of enrichment is the popular Wednesday or Thursday afternoon *pullout* or *resource-room* plan in which ten to fifteen elementary school students meet with a G/T teacher/coordinator for special exercises, activities, and individual projects. Fox (1979) noted that enrichment may be ". . . defined as the provision of learning experiences that develop higher processes of thinking and creativity in a subject area."

Defining Acceleration and Enrichment

According to these descriptions, then, both acceleration and enrichment accommodate the high abilities and individual needs of gifted students, and both lead to depth, breadth, and the development of creativity and other high-level thinking skills. There are indeed G/T programs and activities in which the definitions of acceleration and enrichment seem overlapping and ambiguous. For example, is a special math, computer, or foreign language class in the elementary school considered "enrichment" or "acceleration"? And what of a similar course taught in high school?

There is a convenient rule-of-thumb definition that permits a reasonably clear distinction between acceleration plans versus enrichment plans: Any strategy that results in advanced placement or credit may be titled *acceleration;* strategies which supplement or go beyond standard grade-level work, but do not result in advanced placement or credit (that is, anything else) may be called *enrichment.* Thus the special foreign language or math class taught in elementary or junior high school, or a special high school drama or photography class that does not result in advanced credit or standing would be enrichment. If a junior or senior high school course or curriculum plan leads to advanced standing (for example, in math or languages), early high school graduation, or advanced standing in college, it is acceleration.

The recommendation of Fox (1979), Treffinger (1981), the Richardson Study (Cox and Daniel, 1985; Cox, Daniel, and Boston, 1985) and others—with which we totally agree—is that both enrichment and acceleration are necessary. A well-rounded, coherent G/T program will implement plans for both types of services. Gifted students should be permitted to work at their own rapid pace, accelerating through and out of primary and secondary schools. They also should have opportunities for greater variety in content, greater depth, and the development of affective, creative, scientific, and other high-level skills, that is, enrichment. In addition, they should receive educational and career counseling to help them understand themselves and make their best educational decisions.

EARLY ADMISSION TO KINDERGARTEN OR FIRST GRADE

Early admission to either kindergarten or first grade is an acceleration strategy relatively easy to administer and well supported by research (see, for example, Proctor, Black, and Feldhusen, 1986a). While the studies have varied in their criteria for selecting students and in their methods for evaluating success, the conclusions nonetheless have consistently favored early admission (Birch, 1954; Cutts and Mosely, 1957; Hobson, 1948; Reynolds, Birch, and Tuseth, 1976). Early-entering gifted children who are carefully selected for readiness perform schoolwork better and have been found to be at least as well adjusted as nonaccelerated gifted control groups.

Despite these research conclusions, teachers and administrators rarely favor admitting gifted youngsters early. Teachers' negative experiences usually stem from children who were too immature to function well in their classes. The problem is that these children typically have not been carefully screened. After several experiences with such children, teachers may incorrectly conclude that early entrance causes too many academic, personal, and social problems.

How can a school district resolve the differences between the results of multiple research projects and the typical teaching staff impressions? An early admission policy that gives careful consideration to the following variables is likely to select gifted children who will be successful despite their younger age.

Intellectual precocity.   An individual intelligence test score of 130 or more is recommended for early admission.

Eye-hand coordination.   Tests of eye-hand coordination should suggest at least average perceptual-motor skill, since problems in this area may put unnecessary stress on the early entrant who must participate in cutting, pasting, drawing, writing, and so on.

Reading readiness.   Reading is the skill most critical to early school success. Test scores should show clear readiness to read. Many gifted children are able to read prior to school entrance.

Social and emotional maturity.   Observations of the child in a preschool environment or by a psychologist will be important in determining likely school social adjustment.

Health.   A child who has a history of good health is more likely to attend school regularly and concentrate on classwork. Frequent health problems combined with a young age may put too much stress on even a very gifted child.

Gender.   Although each child must be considered individually, males do mature later than females and physical maturity is an important consideration. For this reason, it is not unusual or necessarily unfair for girls to be favored for early entrance.

School of entrance.   The average IQ in some schools may be 120 or 125, while in others the average may be 100 or less. Thus an early-entering child's intellectual ability should be considered relative to the school population. If the school has many very bright children, its regular fare is likely to provide adequate challenge. The gifted child therefore may do just as well by waiting to enter with same-age children.

Family values.   The child who is permitted to enter school early needs the support of a family that values education and academic achievement. For example, if success in team sports is an important family goal, there is a high risk of stress for the undersized accelerated boy. Hobson (1948) found that 550 early admitted youth compared favorably to nonaccelerates in general high school extracurricular activities; however, in a ten-year review of underage gifted boys he found only two who were outstanding in contact sports.

In sum, early entrance to kindergarten or first grade is definitely recommended for gifted children who are carefully screened according to the above criteria. If parents are considering early kindergarten admission for their precocious child, teachers and principals might recommend that they enroll the child in a quality nursery school. The nursery school will be helpful in providing parents and educators an opportunity to observe the child's social and cognitive adjustment in a school setting. The experience also will foster further skill development and will acquaint the child with some social and academic classroom routines.

GRADE-SKIPPING

Grade-skipping is the traditional method of accelerating precocious elementary school students. It requires no special materials or facilities, no G/T coordinator, not even a G/T program. In fact, it is extraordinarily cost-effective in moving the gifted or talented child through and out of the school system ahead of schedule. Grade-skipping may be initiated by parents who are aware that their child is one or two years ahead of the rest of the class and is bored with school and impatient with his or her peers, or by a teacher who makes the same observation. Grade-skipping or "double promotion" usually takes place in the lowest elementary grades, but sometimes in advanced grades. Some gifted children skip two or three grades (occasionally more) and enter college at age 15 or 16. Some parents become frustrated and agitated if their district does not permit grade-skipping; and many districts do not.

There are at least two major concerns regarding grade-skipping. The first is the problem of missing critical basic skills. Many teachers feel that if a child is not taught an important math or reading skill, he or she will be at a great disadvantage in later grades. They frequently predict that the child (1) will not be able to maintain good grades, (2) will see him or herself as less capable, and therefore (3) will lose school motivation. It is true that some skills are absolutely critical to the learning of later skills, and their absence could place stress on the student. However, many gifted students have acquired knowledge and skills far ahead of their grade levels, learned either independently or from an interested parent or older sibling. That is, the "missing skills" may not be missing at all. As a precaution, a series of diagnostic tests for the grade to be skipped can identify missing skills, and the motivated gifted child typically can learn these quickly, either working independently or with the help of interested adults.

The second concern, social adjustment to peers, is even more common. The concern here comes mainly from parents and teachers familiar with a gifted child who skipped a grade and experienced social problems or maladjustment. Once again we find a conflict between research conclusions and what many teachers, administrators, and parents claim. The current research-based consensus is that in most cases gifted students are quite comfortable with their *intellectual* peers—older students—and suffer no noticeable maladjustment or neuroses (for example, Brody and Benbow, 1987; Daurio, 1979; Feldhusen, Proctor, and Black, 1986; Gregory and March, 1985; Stanley, 1979, 1987, 1988; Stanley and Benbow, 1986).

Among Terman's gifted children, those who had been accelerated one or two years made *better* adjustments than those who were not (Terman and Oden, 1946). Based on a survey of former high-ability high school students, some of whom had skipped one or more high school grades or entered college early, Brody and Benbow (1987) found that accelerated students did as well or better than the others in all areas of achievement, had higher career aspirations, and attended more select colleges. There were no differences in social or emotional adjustment. Said Brody and Benbow, "This study did not reveal any harmful effects as a result of acceleration."

Reservations about grade skipping may be based on some faulty assumptions and interpretations, for example:

1. Many persons look back to their adolescence as being a difficult time for social adjustment; persons who have been accelerated may incorrectly blame these problems on their acceleration. Persons who were not accelerated might blame their problems on other factors.

2. Although many studies concluded that gifted children are better socially adjusted than typical students, other studies have found that for children with very high intelligence social adjustment is indeed a most difficult task (Hollingworth, 1942; Terman and Oden, 1947). Since these children are the ones most likely to be skipping grades, their social problems, actually related to their extremely high intelligence, may mistakenly be attributed to acceleration.

3. When outsiders observe a school child who is noticeably smaller or younger than average, based on appearance alone they may infer that the child certainly must be having social problems, even though testimony from the child him- or herself does not indicate any special problems.

To reduce the risk of problems related to grade-skipping the authors recommend the following guidelines, some of which duplicate the above recommendations for early admission to kindergarten or first grade:

1. A child should have an individually tested IQ score of 135 or higher. Feldhusen, Proctor, and Black (1986) suggest that a level of mental development above the mean for the grade he or she desires to enter also would indicate that a child is intellectually ready to skip a grade.

2. Regardless of ability, for elementary students only one grade should be skipped at a time. After the child has had several years for adjustment, there may be reason to consider skipping another grade. Older students, say age 14 or upward, who are socially and emotionally mature have successfully moved directly from *junior* high school to college (Gregory and March, 1985; Stanley and McGill, 1986).

3. Skill gaps should be diagnosed so that the child can be assisted in acquiring any missing basic skills.

4. A supportive teacher, counselor, and/or group of gifted peers should be available to help the child with social problems related to grade-skipping.

5. Parent value systems need to be considered. Especially, if families place more emphasis on athletics than academics, grade-skipping may put considerable pressure on the student who may not be big enough to compete.

6. An appraisal of the child's present intellectual and social adjustment should be considered in the decision making. If the child is not showing good social adjustment in the present grade, grade-skipping cannot be assumed to improve that adjustment. Also, continued poor adjustment in the higher grade

should not necessarily be attributed to the grade-skipping. Grade-skipping is not a cure-all, and a given child may require further guidance regardless of the grade-skipping decision.

7. Every grade-skipping decision needs to be made separately. Physical maturity, height, general emotional stability, motivation, and ability to handle challenge all should be part of the decision making. Centrally important is the gifted child's need for intellectual stimulation.

8. Feldhusen, Proctor, and Black (1986) recommend that all cases of grade-skipping be arranged on a trial basis of about six weeks. The child should be made aware that if the advancement does not go well he or she may request to be returned to the original grade. Counseling services should be available. Further, the child should not be made to feel he or she is a "failure" if the grade-skipping does not succeed.

Finally, teachers and parents too often conclude that it is simply easier to avoid making a decision that favors grade-skipping. Administratively, and in view of general inertia, they are of course correct. However, teachers and parents should recognize that keeping a highly precocious child in an unstimulating environment is also making a decision—one that communicates to the gifted child that he or she is not expected to perform up to his or her capability. That decision, says most research, is more intellectually and sometimes even socially harmful to the gifted child than the decision to skip grades. Boredom, restlessness, frustration, and disruptiveness can be replaced by enhanced motivation, improved self-concepts, and improved study habits and productivity (Hall, 1982; Karnes and Chauvin, 1982a, 1982b).

SUBJECT-SKIPPING

Grade-skipping is sometimes called *full acceleration,* and subject-skipping therefore is *partial acceleration.* Subject-skipping involves taking classes or studying particular subjects with students in higher grades. It is especially appropriate in sequential types of subject matters, particularly reading, math, and languages, but possible in other subjects as well. Subject-skipping therefore is for the student with special skills and talents primarily in a single area. The acceleration may begin in the elementary school and continue through high school.

Subject-skipping has important advantages and only one major disadvantage. On the positive side, it permits the child to be intellectually challenged in a specific area of strength while he or she continues to develop appropriate grade-level skills in other areas. It also permits the child to remain with peers to whom he or she already may be socially adjusted. Subject skipping also may be used experimentally to determine if grade-skipping would later be appropriate. Thus if the child is accelerated in his or her strongest subject, the teacher can observe the academic and social adjustment of the child in the new setting and make a more confident decision about further full acceleration.

The disadvantage of subject-skipping is the problem of continuity. Too often a particular school or teacher may be willing to accelerate a student in a single subject, such as math, but makes no overall organizational plan for continuous progress. Therefore, the child who masters three years of math in just one may suddenly discover that he or she must repeat two of them. Such repetition is likely to be more boring and damaging than moving the child through the material more slowly in the first place. However, if continuous accelerated coursework can be planned for the child, subject acceleration is an ideal approach for children with high abilities in specific areas.

EARLY ADMISSION TO JUNIOR OR SENIOR HIGH SCHOOL

This particular acceleration alternative seems not to be popular. However, for some students, the best grade to be skipped is the one just before junior or senior high school, that is, grade five or six, or grade eight or nine. From an academic perspective, the student may be ready and anxious for advanced work in the specialized and departmentalized junior or senior high school. Socially, it may be an opportune time to accelerate, since new friendships inevitably develop when students from several elementary or junior high schools meet for the first time in the new school setting.

CREDIT BY EXAMINATION

In the junior or senior high school, one cost-free mechanism for justifiable subject-skipping is credit by examination. For example, if a talented mathematics or language student feels he or she already has acquired the content of a semester course, perhaps through home study or foreign travel, the student should be allowed to "test out" of the course and, if mastery is demonstrated, receive academic credit. In addition to preventing repetition and boredom, allowing credit by examination will encourage gifted students to accept challenges, set goals, and work toward them.

As a precaution in using this option, the student should be provided with an outline of the material to be included in the test. This gives the student a fair opportunity to appraise his or her own skills and to concentrate study on those not yet mastered. Failure experienced on tests due to lack of adequate preparation, or else miscommunication about the test content, is likely to be an unpleasant experience for both the student and the school staff involved.

College credit, which permits advanced placement when the student enters college, also may be earned through examination, as in the *Advanced Placement* (AP) program described below or in the *College Level Examination Program* (CLEP; see for example, Karnes and Chauvin, 1982a; Zimmerman and Brody, 1986). Unlike the AP program, CLEP does not offer courses, just examinations. CLEP examinations for college credit are available in science, math, English (composition and literature), social sciences, business, computer science, nursing, education, psychology, and foreign languages. Most of the exams are 90 minute multiple-choice tests. A person is limited to four of these tests in one day (not many ask for more). A failed exam may be repeated after six months. The examinations are given at selected centers in the third week of every month (excluding December and February). Special administrations at more convenient locations may be requested by persons living more than 150 miles from the nearest center. The cost at the time of this writing is $35 per test. Before registering, one should check to determine if the college of one's choice will accept CLEP credits, because not all do. For additional information, write to College Board, Box 1824, Princeton, NJ 08541.

COLLEGE COURSES IN HIGH SCHOOL

Several approaches may be used for giving students the opportunity to take college courses while still in high school. With a dual enrollment program, a student may be excused from high school for part of the day to take one or more courses on the college campus. The earned college credits may be used at the particular college when he or she actually is admitted; alternatively, the credits normally can be transferred to another college of the student's choice. Importantly, the courses also should be credited toward high school graduation requirements so that the student is not burdened— punished—with double the amount of coursework.

If a sufficient number of capable high school students wish to take a particular college course, it is possible for a college professor to come to the high school to teach the course for college credit. The students will need to pay college tuition.

A highly desirable alternative, the *Advanced Placement* (AP) program, like CLEP, is conducted by the College Board. The AP program consists of college-level courses and examinations for high school students (see, for example, Zimmerman and Brody, 1986). The courses may take the form of an honors class or a strong regular class taught by a teacher following an Advanced Placement outline, or via independent study, perhaps with a tutor. Current offerings include three courses in physics, two courses each in calculus, English, Spanish, German, French, music, and studio arts, and one course in American history, European history, biology, chemistry, Latin, and art history. The courses require a full academic year to complete. AP examinations are given each spring in the third week of May. Any student may take the exams, whether or not he or she has formally participated in an AP course. The AP program thus allows credit by examination. Presently, about 650 of America's 3,000+ colleges accept AP credits. As for cost effectiveness, an entire year of college credit may be earned for about $53 per exam, ". . . at a savings ranging from $2,000 to $8,000" (Karnes and Chauvin, 1982a). The brochure *Guide to the Advanced Placement Program* is available free from College Board Publications Orders, Box 1824, Princeton, NJ, 08541. Additional information about AP programs is available from the College Board offices whose addresses are listed at the end of this chapter.

Generally, the factor most critical to the success of permitting—indeed, encouraging—high school students to accept the challenge of earning college credits is high school administrative flexibility.

CORRESPONDENCE COURSES

If a college is not accessible, and perhaps AP courses or independent study are not feasible, every major university offers correspondence courses at least at the college freshman and sophomore levels. Correspondence courses thus present valuable opportunities for the talented student who lives in a rural area or a small city or town. Correspondence courses carry full college credit. They are written by a professor and are taught by a college professor, instructor, or a qualified graduate student. Courses are available in a variety of areas, for example, college math, algebra, or statistics, or introductory psychology, educational psychology, sociology, economics, anthropology, astronomy, history, foreign languages, and others. The University of Wisconsin, Madison, even offers a correspondence course in gifted education, using this text. Correspondence courses may be taken in the summer, as a form of independent study, or as a form of enrichment in conjunction with a regular high school program. Typically, courses requiring student-teacher interaction or laboratories are not taught by mail—for example, biology, physics, or chemistry.

If the reader plans to encourage a student to take a correspondence course, it is important to realize that a considerable amount of self-motivation and independence is needed to successfully complete such a course. Students are more likely to be successful if several of them take the same course, thus permitting mutual support, stimulation, and assistance. It also is helpful if a high school faculty member can serve as an advisor for the students in case they need help understanding or interpreting the material or solving practice problems.

TELESCOPED PROGRAMS

Telescoping means, for example, collapsing three academic years' work into two, or four years of high school into three. In the junior high school, if enough talented young mathematicians are available for special classes a normal three-year math and algebra sequence might be taught at an accelerated pace in two years. It is less common, but the same telescoping can be used with other subjects, for example, by condensing three years of junior high school science into two years.

In high school, telescoping four years' work into three is almost entirely a counseling problem, assuming that district policies will permit such acceleration. The energetic and capable student, with the assistance of his or her counselor, simply cuts down on the "study hall" classes and schedules four years of high school requirements into a more compact and busier three. If three years is unrealistic for a student, a three-and-a-half year program still would permit a capable student to begin college a semester early.

EARLY ADMISSION TO COLLEGE

Many gifted and talented high school and some junior high school students are permitted to enter college early on a full-time basis (Fox, 1983; Gregory, 1984; Gregory and March, 1985; Karnes and Chauvin, 1982a, 1982b; Stanley and Benbow, 1983, 1986). In some cases high school requirements are met early, as in telescoping plans. In other cases high school requirements are flexibly waived and a qualified student simply enters college full-time without meeting all of the usual graduation requirements. With the latter plan, in view of college entrance requirements one must be sure that the particular college admissions office is agreeable to such short-cutting before plans reach an advanced stage. Some college admissions offices are not wildly enthusiastic about early entrants. Other colleges, for example, Johns Hopkins, California State University at Los Angeles, University of Wisconsin-Madison, and the University of Washington, welcome qualified senior and junior high school youth as full-time students.

As an example, after a successful pilot study the California State University at Los Angeles (CSULA) in 1983 installed a permanent Early Entrance Program—a full-time college program for junior and senior high school-aged students (Gregory, 1984; Gregory and March, 1985). Students must be at least 14 years old. They also must produce scores on the *Washington Pre-College Test* or the *Scholastic Aptitude Test* (SAT) above the 80th percentile on either the verbal or quantitative section and above the 50th percentile on the other. Students initially attend CSULA part-time, while continuing their junior or senior high school classes. Thus if the program is unsuitable, little is lost and usually some college credits are banked for future use. Students who do register full time seem to realize social and emotional benefits as well as intellectual ones (Gregory and March, 1985). The program works well.

Early admission to college, with or without graduation from high school, is an excellent way for a mature gifted student to accelerate his or her education. Unfortunately, although the authors feel that school policies should support such initiative, many high school teachers and administrators discourage early graduation and early college admission. Also, high school students who consider this approach may feel pressure to remain in high school in the form of missing opportunities for scholarships and honors and, of course, missing the social and extracurricular activities. The early college entrant should be prepared to trade some of these opportunities for the challenge of college work. If the student or his or her parents have doubts about early full-time college work, the CSULA strategy of first enrolling part-time while still in secondary school will make the decision much easier.

TALENT SEARCH AND THE STUDY OF MATHEMATICALLY PRECOCIOUS YOUTH

The best-known example of accelerating bright secondary students into college-level work is the highly successful *Talent Search* programs, which began at Johns Hopkins University in 1971 as Julian Stanley's *Studies of Mathematically Precocious Youth* (SMPY; Benbow and Stanley, 1983; Stanley, 1979, 1987, 1988; Stanley and Benbow, 1986).

The purpose of SMPY has been to locate students with extraordinarily high mathematics talent and help them develop their gift. In an Annual Mathematics Talent Search, primarily seventh-grade students are selected on the basis of high Scholastic Aptitude Test-Mathematics (SAT-M) scores. Students who score 500 or higher, which would be the 51st percentile for male college-bound high school seniors, are considered mathematically precocious (Stanley and Benbow, 1986). Seventh- and eighth-grade students with such scores reason better mathematically than 99 percent of their age-mates. Students take summer or Saturday mathematics classes, usually taught by a college professor at Johns Hopkins. According to Stanley (1982a), by working 5 to 6 hours per day, these students in three weeks can master one to two years of high school algebra and geometry. Said Stanley, many of them learn more effectively in three weeks than in a full academic year—they are working, not sleeping. By eighth grade, they are ready for calculus.

High school SMPY participants are encouraged to pursue any of a "smorgasbord" of acceleration options: (1) They may attend college part-time, earning credit for advanced placement; (2) they may earn college credit by examination in the Advanced Placement program; (3) they may skip a grade, particularly the one at the end of junior high school; (4) they may complete two or more years of mathematics in one year; (5) they may enter college early, either by early high school graduation or ". . . simply by leaving high school before completing the last grade(s) . . ." (Stanley, 1979). In every case, these students receive individual counseling regarding the educational alternatives that might be appropriate for them to pursue.

A few selected and unbiased testimonials by Stanley (1979) may be of interest: "The boredom and frustration of even the average-scoring (SMPY) contestants when incarcerated in a year-long algebra class is difficult to appreciate. Often, highly able youths themselves are not aware of the extent of their slowdown, because it has been their lot from kindergarten onward. . . . Often, they take off like rockets intellectually when allowed to do so. . . . It is clear that a large reservoir of virtually untapped mathematical reasoning ability exists all around the region. . . ."

In recent years the program has been extended in two ways. First, in 1979 Stanley created the Center for Talented Youth (CTY) at Johns Hopkins University. CTY annually surveys the entire Northeast and Middle Atlantic states, from Virginia through Maine. The CTY western Talent Search encompasses Alaska, California, Hawaii, Oregon, Washington, and western Canada (Stanley and Benbow, 1986). There also is a national search for seventh graders with SAT-Verbal (SAT-V) scores above 630 or SAT-Math (SAT-M) scores above 700.

As a second innovation, Talent Search programs accommodate verbally precocious seventh and eighth-grade students, as assessed by the SAT-V. Established Talent Search programs are sponsored by Arizona State University, University of Denver, Duke University, Northwestern University, and, of course, Johns Hopkins University.

Sanford J. Cohn's (1983a, 1983b) *Project for the Study of Academic Precocity* (PSAP) at Arizona State University is a good example of how a worthy Talent Search program can be conducted. Over 12,200 young people took part in the "1983 Western States and Canadian Provinces Talent Search." This summer program offered fourteen "rigorous academically-oriented classes" plus three Advanced Placement (AP) classes: geology, computer science (Fortran, Pascal, microcomputers), speech and debate, advanced language and composition (AP), expository writing, vocabulary development, Latin, Latin and Greek, calculus (AP), "fast mathematics," survey of social sciences, chemistry (AP), economics, mythology, and laboratory science. Admission to each class was based upon SAT scores plus a fee. For example, Computer Science-Fortran required an SAT-M score of 450 and a combined SAT-M and SAT-V score of 850, along with $190 plus books.

In addition, PSAP offered four counseling workshops plus five classes for 8- to 11-year olds (math, writing, Spanish, science, classics). The counseling workshops covered educational planning, communication skills, study skills, and career exploration.

Stanley and Benbow (1984) itemized a few benefits of SMPY participation, which presumably would apply to all Talent Search participants:

1. Increased zest for learning and life, reduced boredom in school, and better school attitudes.
2. Enhanced feelings of self-worth and accomplishment.
3. Reduced egotism and arrogance, due to the humbling effects of working for the first time with intellectual peers.
4. Far better educational preparation and thus improved qualifications for the most selective colleges.
5. Early college and graduate school admission.
6. Better graduate school and fellowship opportunities, due to better preparation, acquaintance with professors, and research skills.

In an unpublished report, Stanley added the following "Advantages of Entering College at a Younger-Than-Average Age." Highly able youths can get more academic stimulation and breadth at a good college than during their last year or two in high school. Remaining in high school, in fact, can have detrimental social and emotional consequences if such students are eager to move ahead. There is greater opportunity to interact with expert professionals. By saving one or two years of schooling, there is more time and flexibility for planning educational and other aspects of life. One also is able to enter a profession at an earlier age, allowing extra years of youthful vigorous work. Graduate and professional schools are impressed by students who graduate from college, especially an outstanding one, at a younger-than-average age. Finally, moving ahead according to one's best ability is exhilarating, motivating, and builds realistic self-confidence.

It also is true that for gifted females who would like to combine a high-level career (for example, medicine) with parenting, the saving of several years by acceleration permits family planning at a younger, less risky age for pregnancy.

After reviewing successes and some failures of mathematically precocious college entrants, Stanley and McGill (1986) recommended that early entrants should score higher on the SAT than usual college freshman—at least 625 on the SAT-V and 675 on the SAT-M.

SUMMARY

Table 5.1 is a guide for planning G/T program content, summarized in the categories of basic skills, content beyond the prescribed curriculum, exposure to a variety of fields, student-selected content, high content complexity, creative thinking and problem solving, thinking skills, affective development, and motivation.

G/T programs vary in students served, acceleration, grouping and enrichment plans, resources involved, program level, and other dimensions.

Acceleration, which speeds up learning time to match student capabilities, is defined as programming that results in advanced placement or credit; *enrichment,* which adds depth and breadth, is anything else. Both accommodate the high abilities and individual needs of gifted students. Educators have debated the merits of each. However, both are required in any well-rounded program.

With early admission to kindergarten or first grade, students are most likely to succeed if they are carefully screened. They should be intellectually precocious (recommended IQ = 130+), at least average in motor coordination, and possess adequate reading readiness, social/emotional maturity, and good health. Girls often are more mature. If a particular school already caters to very bright students, early admission may be unnecessary. Family values should emphasize academic achievement.

Grade-skipping is a good alternative. The problem of missing some essential basic skills can be solved via diagnostic tests and remedial work, if necessary. Research shows that social adjustment is usually not a problem. Acceleration is sometimes blamed for normal adolescent personal or social problems. Maladjustment due to extremely high IQ also is sometimes blamed on grade-skipping. Grade-skipping may be most successful if the student shows an IQ score of 135+, if one grade is skipped at a time, if support from a teacher, counselor, or gifted peer is available, and if intellectual and social adjustment is considered in the decision.

Subject-skipping permits the child to remain with age-mates while being challenged in a particular area of strength. Continuity with later grades probably is the only shortcoming, and one which can be provided for.

Early admission to junior or senior high school is a socially opportune time to skip a grade. The student may well be ready for the more specialized course content.

Credit by examination encourages G/T students to accept challenges and saves repetition and boredom. To be fair, an outline of the material to be covered on the test should be provided. College credit by examination may be earned in the AP program or the CLEP. Both are highly cost effective.

In a dual enrollment program, students take college courses while still in high school. Credits from college courses taken in high school should count toward high school graduation. In the AP program, students take college courses in an honors class, a fast regular class, or as independent study. With or without taking the AP courses, students may earn college credit by scoring sufficiently high in the May AP examinations.

Correspondence courses require considerable self-direction. It is therefore desirable for a group of students to take the same course and for a high school teacher or counselor to monitor progress and perhaps assist.

Telescoping involves condensing a two- or three-year course, or high school program, into fewer years.

Early college admission, or early high school graduation, is strongly recommended, despite the problem of forfeiting honors or scholarships that require attendance for the full four years. Many good students are socially and academically ready.

Stanley's Johns Hopkins University SMPY program has been remarkably successful in identifying and assisting young students, typically seventh graders, who show extraordinary math talent, that is, who score above 500 on the SAT-M. They take special summer or Saturday math classes, covering one or two years' work in a few weeks. They also may attend college part-time, earn college credit by examination, skip a grade, telescope two or more high school years of math into one, or enter college early.

The Johns Hopkins University Center for Talented Youth sponsors an ongoing national search for extraordinary seventh grade students with SAT-M scores above 700 or SAT-V scores above 630.

Talent Search programs include verbal precocity, measured by SAT-V, as well as mathematical precocity.

Benefits of SMPY and Talent Search participation include improved zest for learning, better feelings of self-worth, better educational preparation, early entrance into college and a profession, and better graduate and professional school opportunities.

Early college admission is academically stimulating, provides greater flexibility in career and life planning, permits entering a career earlier, and impresses graduate and professional schools.

College Board Offices

New York Office:
888 Seventh Ave.
New York, NY 10019
(212) 582-6210

Middle States Regional Office:
Suite 1418
1700 Market St.
Philadelphia, PA 19103
(215) 567-6555

Midwestern Regional Office:
1 American Plaza
Evanston, IL 60201
(312) 866-1700

New England Regional Office:
470 Totten Pond Rd.
Waltham, MA 02154
(617) 890-9150

Southern Regional Office:
Suite 200
17 Executive Park Dr., NE
Atlanta, GA 30329
(404) 636-9465

Southwestern Regional Office:
Suite 922
211 E. Seventh St.
Austin, TX 78701
(512) 472-0231

Denver Office:
Suite 23
2142 South High St.
Denver, CO 80210
(303) 777-4434

Western Regional Office:
800 Welch Rd.
Palo Alto, CA 94304
(415) 321-5211

chapter six

Grouping
and Counseling

Grouping is "providing various organizational structures of either long or short duration whereby students of like ability can work together" (Robinson, Davis, Fiedler, and Helman, 1982). These may include:

Full-time homogeneous classes:
    Magnet schools
    Special schools for the gifted
    Private schools
    School-within-a-school plans
    Special G/T classes in the elementary school

Full-time heterogeneous classes:
    Combined grades in a regular class
    Cluster groups of gifted students placed with regular students
    Mainstreaming in the regular class

Part-time or temporary groups:
    Pullout programs
    Resource-room plans
    Special classes
    Activity clubs
    Honors programs

There are many possible grouping plans, most of which will require a formal reorganization of the school's staff, space, and material resources. Some plans, especially magnet schools and special schools for the gifted, will require some degree of reorganization of the school system of the entire district.

Overview

In this chapter we will take a closer look at grouping options categorized under full-time homogeneous grouping, full-time heterogeneous grouping, and part-time or temporary grouping. Then we will turn to that important and often neglected component of gifted education: counseling. Too many gifted students feel alone or that they are "freakish outcasts"; many receive precious little of the educational, career, and/or personal guidance they may desperately need (Delisle, 1982).

FULL-TIME HOMOGENEOUS GROUPING

Magnet Schools

Several large cities have adopted magnet high school plans to accommodate the needs not only of gifted and talented students, but regular students seeking special training for a trade or career. A clear purpose is to make high school relevant to realistic student goals, particularly for potential dropouts who view school as prison rather than a path to economic and social success. Note that gifted students, as well as low-ability students, too often become frustrated and drop out. Boston, Cincinnati, Houston, Winston-Salem, Milwaukee, and St. Louis, for example, have magnet high schools (Cox and Daniel, 1983b). New York City has used such specialty schools for many years. All magnet schools offer specialized training in, say, the arts, math and science, business, or trade skills. A school also may be designated as a "superior abilities school." Students are bused in from all corners of the city or district to attend the high school that suits their educational and career interests. In some cases, they are placed in career-related part-time jobs so they may earn money and gain valuable experience while attending school. Such programs are indeed relevant, and they do meet students' needs. They also are known to reduce the dropout rate.

Special Schools for the Gifted

Like magnet high schools, special schools for the gifted also are typically a big-city alternative. An entire elementary or secondary school may be designated for gifted and talented youngsters. In all cases the curriculum will include both traditional academic content—based upon district guidelines and requirements—plus special enriched and accelerated training in whatever academic, artistic, scientific, or personal development areas the school chooses to emphasize.

One example of a special elementary school is the Golda Meir School in Milwaukee. Students are selected from the entire district based upon the U.S.O.E. criteria (general ability, specific academic aptitude, creativity, leadership, or visual or performing art talent), as reflected in test scores, grades, and teacher, parent, and peer nominations (Pfeil, 1978). A quota system is used to balance the school composition for sex, race, and representation from all school districts in the Milwaukee system. Because this is an elementary school, subject matter acceleration is limited so that students will not be advanced beyond grade level in particular subjects when they enter the regular junior high school.

Enrichment opportunities, however, are diverse and exciting. They include foreign language training; piano, violin, viola, and general music lessons; drama lessons from members of the Milwaukee Repertory Company; the creation of a school newspaper, aided by Milwaukee Journal reporters; field trips to Milwaukee's civic, financial, and cultural centers (between about 12 and 30 trips per student per year); "MACS Packs" (math-arts-crafts-science) which offer daily student projects; and "Lunch Bunch" involvement in games, films, reading, or just visiting. There is a Classics Club which reads above-grade level books, an Advanced Science Club, a school chorus, a Student Senate, and sometimes an infant-care class featuring a real infant—typically a student's younger brother or sister. Enthusiasm of staff and students runs extremely high. This model plan continually hosts many visitors.

An example of a special school at the secondary level, the Alabama School of Fine Arts in Birmingham offers a six-year curriculum (grades 7–12) of general academic studies (history, social studies, English, general sciences, math, and foreign languages) plus career-oriented preprofessional training in creative writing, dance, drama, music, or the visual arts. Identification and admission are based upon the student's previous academic history, an evaluation of his or her artistic training and background, an audition or other talent evaluation by a "jury board," and an interview designed to ". . . determine the degree of potential ability, the seriousness of purpose and the maturity of the student" (Juntune, 1981).

Private Schools

Achievement tends to run higher in private schools than in public schools (Coleman, 1981). Therefore, private schools can be a good alternative for an accelerated education.

Some private schools cater especially to gifted and talented students.

In Hillsborough, California, for example, the Nueva Learning Center is designed "... to provide high potential students (age 4–12 years) with opportunities for developing living skills, attitudes, and knowledge which are rarely available to them through normal learning channels ... to stimulate curiosity, encourage participation, and generate interest" (Juntune, 1981). There is training in six *R*'s (reading, writing, arithmetic, rights, respect, and responsibility), piano, ballet, math, science, and more unusual topics such as organic gardening, aviation, karate, and cross-country skiing. Responsibility, awareness, and confidence are prime goals. Student selection is based upon standardized testing (for example, the WISC-R) and interviews. Roughly following the U.S.O.E. definition, "high potential" at the Nueva Learning Center means exceptional intellectual ability, and/or high creativity, and/or special and unusual talent in some specific area (art, science, math, leadership, or physical prowess).

In Madison, Wisconsin, the Eagle School filled a strong demand for private elementary schooling for gifted children. Small classes allow close direction of work in computers, foreign languages, and innumerable special projects, along with personalized breadth and depth in the basics.

School-within-a-School

Similar to special classes for G/T students (section follows), an entire school may be organized around a school-within-a-school concept. Here, gifted and talented students from around the district attend a particular school that also accommodates regular students. For part of the day, G/T students attend special classes taught by special teachers. They mix with the rest of the students for nonacademic subjects (for example, physical education, study hall, manual arts, home economics) and for sports and social events.

Special Classes

Special classes for gifted and talented students may take several forms. First, at the elementary level all gifted students within a particular grade level, age, or age range, may be assigned to a special class. In addition to covering prescribed grade-level objectives—and usually extending beyond them—a variety of enrichment, personal development, and skill development experiences are planned. These may include thinking skills, such as creativity, analysis, synthesis, evaluation, and critical thinking, values training and other personal development activities, library and research skills, foreign languages, classic literature, typing, computer work, and others.

There are pros and cons to separating G/T elementary students into special classes. In the plus column, the students naturally benefit academically and personally from a curriculum that matches their abilities, and that tells them they have special talents. Importantly, they need to meet and interact with students like themselves, students who will accept, encourage, and challenge them. In the negative column, they may resist being separated physically and psychologically from regular students. Further, it is not unusual for other students to resent their special status and to make them feel socially uncomfortable, for example, by calling them names or by silent ostracism. Another danger, especially at the secondary level, is that teachers of special—and more difficult—classes may grade on a normal curve, thus giving "B's" and "C's" to students who could easily earn "A's" in other courses. It is not unusual for grade-conscious students to avoid "special classes" to protect their grades.

In high school there already is a variety of college preparatory classes to challenge the abilities of gifted and talented students, for example, in chemistry, physics, calculus, art, journalism, and drama. Special classes beyond these also may be created, for example, courses in college algebra, organic chemistry, advanced physics, advanced botany, creative writing, photography, or whatever else students need and the school budget will allow. If some of these can be taught in accord with Advanced Placement program guidelines they may lead to college credit, as described in Chapter 5.

Kolloff and Feldhusen (1986) described high school seminars in Indiana and Illinois that were designed for gifted students. The goals of the seminars generally included exploring abstract and complex ideas, involving students in reflective, critical, and creative thinking, and an interdisciplinary focus. For example, the Hinsdale (Illinois) Central High School honors seminar was organized as part of its English curriculum. The seminar stressed communication skills, the application of thinking skills to the study of literature, and the development of creativity in reading, writing, and speaking. The Hobart (Indiana) High School G/T seminar was team-taught, integrating mathematics, science, social studies, and English, and also included guest speakers, student presentations, discussions, and small group work. Creativity and critical thinking were stretched by analyzing and evaluating complex themes, issues, and problems of society.

FULL-TIME HETEROGENEOUS GROUPING

Multi-Age Classrooms

Frequently, a school will combine grades—say, a group of fourth-graders with a group of fifth-graders. In many cases this arrangement is an administrative convenience—the school has too many fourth and fifth graders to fit them into existing classes, but not enough to justify *two* additional classes. Therefore, "good" fourth-grade students usually are selected who might benefit from learning and interacting with children who are one chronological year older. Combining grades is a minimal form of acceleration, and is effective only if the younger students are not required to repeat similar learning experiences the following year.

Some entire elementary schools are organized according to a multi-age plan. These grouping strategies usually are not designed specifically as G/T programs. However, they lend themselves nicely to the type of individualization and cluster grouping which does accommodate G/T children. With Klausmeier's *Individually Guided Education-Multi-Unit School* (IGE-MUS) plan (Klausmeier and Goodwin, 1975; Klausmeier, Quilling, Sorenson, Way, and Glasrud, 1971), a 600-student elementary school is divided into four units of about 150 students each; for example, with students ages 4–6, 6–9, 8–10, and 10–12. Each unit is composed of a unit leader, two or three staff teachers, a first-year teacher, an intern, an instructional aide, and an instructional secretary. There is instruction with large groups, for example, a movie or demonstration for the 150 students, class-sized groups, small groups, and individuals.

The plan centers upon individualized instruction, which permits capable students to accelerate through the regular curriculum at a comfortable pace, skipping content they already know. Reading, math, and science materials have been specially written for IGE-MUS schools. The IGE plan also accommodates early entry of preschool students into school, and cluster grouping of G/T students for special assignments and projects.

Cluster Groups

There are several interpretations of *cluster groups*. To some, "cluster grouping" means placing G/T students together in a special class, either at the elementary or secondary level. Others speak of "cluster grouping" students in accelerated classes or honors classes. To still others, "cluster grouping" means putting a selected group of, say, 5 or 10 gifted students together in one regular class, along with 15 or 20 other students. We will review the latter form of cluster grouping in this section.

A cluster group of G/T students in a regular class engages in a variety of enrichment activities either individually or in small groups. For example, they might "contract" for independent learning activities such as a library research report, an independent research project, or the mastery of an advanced math, computer, science, or language-learning assignment. Alternatively, groups of three to twelve students sharing similar interests and abilities might work on a particular problem or project for a mutually agreed-upon period of time. The teacher, who normally has received some in-service training or taken coursework in gifted education, also might involve the students in exercises and activities aimed at strengthening creative and research skills or other types of high-level thinking abilities.

Kaplan (1974) itemized a number of "necessities" and "checkpoints" in planning a cluster group G/T program:

1. Developing criteria for selecting students.
2. Defining the qualifications of, and the selection process for, the teachers.
3. Clarifying the teachers' responsibilities and activities.
4. Planning the differentiated experiences for the cluster of gifted students.
5. Planning for support services and special resources, for example, counselors or computers.

The teacher will need to organize individual and small-group meetings, help students plan contracts and projects, organize field trips, and plan other educational exercises and experiences. Kaplan (1974) recommended that, with cluster grouping, the gifted students should have an opportunity to share their unique learning experiences with the total class, which reduces their isolation. The staff also, must be certain that the special activities and experiences stimulate—not penalize—students in the gifted cluster. For example, if "special learning experiences" amount to piling on more work, the students may prefer *not* to be gifted.

As an example of a cluster group plan, Project Lift of Marion, Massachusetts, places groups of five fourth-, fifth-, and sixth-grade G/T students in selected regular classes (Juntune, 1981). The goal of the program is to develop higher-level thinking skills as defined in Bloom's taxonomy: application, analysis, synthesis, and evaluation. Teachers *compact* the regular curriculum by not requiring students to study material they know and by accelerating them through material they do not know. The compacting provides time for enrichment activities, including training in creative and critical thinking and the development of research skills via independent research projects.

Mainstreaming

If a school or district has no formal G/T program, many teachers use their own ingenuity to provide special differentiated and enriched learning experiences to eager, fast-learning, creative (and perhaps bored) students. Such "mainstreaming" is very often a default plan.

D. R. Clasen (1982) itemized a number of alternatives available to the individual teacher in schools ". . . where there is minimum involvement in programming for the gifted. . . ." Specifically:

1. A student may be individually accelerated, perhaps by reading or working ahead or through the use of advanced or supplementary texts and workbooks.

2. The curriculum may otherwise be modified to permit greater depth, more complexity, or higher levels of abstraction.

3. Enrichment activities may be planned that build on or challenge the student's special skills and abilities, for example, in creative writing, photography, or computer programming.

4. Academic and perhaps career advising may be appropriate, for example, helping students understand their special capabilities and the training necessary for them to realize their full potential.

Looking specifically at helping bright math students in the regular classroom, Tucker (1982) recommended the use of (1) puzzles; (2) mental arithmetic games; (3) projects and applications—for example, computing vacation expenses or plotting data and making inferences; (4) enrichment units, which include strengthening already learned skills and learning new material; and (5) reading, particularly about mathematicians.

Hazel Feldhusen (1981; 1987) described how she accommodated gifted children in her regular classroom primarily by using teacher-developed learning centers and by individualizing instruction. For example, her classroom includes a *library center* used for individual reading or study. It is filled with commercial reading-skill materials and educational games, and includes a rocker for comfort and a typewriter for creative writing. A *math center* includes math kits, math games, a calculator (and calculator activities), and a microcomputer. Math folders or *modules* for individualized math instruction were created by cutting up math books. Said Feldhusen, "When a child finishes a module and has it corrected, he or she then gets the next module from the cabinet." A microcomputer presents fun games, logic games, math challenges, and spelling lessons.

An *art center* presents a new art project each week. A *science center* is supplied with two to five activities coordinated with each science lesson. The science center includes a record player, tape player, and film-strip viewer. The school library houses a *Learning Resource Center* that contains tapes and activities in math and language arts, all aimed at developing thinking skills. Students also use the library for research, for selecting reading, and for learning library skills.

At the heart of Feldhusen's system is the *Learning Agreement* (Figure 6.1). The chart specifies daily and weekly optional activities, plus activities that are required "musts." A self-discipline approach is used, which allows total freedom of movement and considerable decision-making regarding their self-paced learning activities. According to Feldhusen, they ". . . develop independence, self-direction, and discipline in their learning tasks."

To offer two notes on mainstreaming: First, some teachers—in concert with counselors, parents, and students themselves—use *Individualized Education Programs* (IEPs) to structure the independent work of mainstreamed gifted students (just as IEPs are used to plan the education for retarded, learning disabled, or handicapped students; see Inset 6.1).

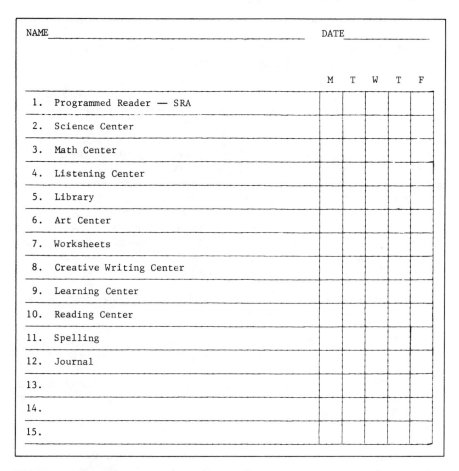

NAME_____ DATE_____

	M	T	W	T	F
1. Programmed Reader — SRA					
2. Science Center					
3. Math Center					
4. Listening Center					
5. Library					
6. Art Center					
7. Worksheets					
8. Creative Writing Center					
9. Learning Center					
10. Reading Center					
11. Spelling					
12. Journal					
13.					
14.					
15.					

FIGURE 6.1 Learning Agreement. (Reprinted by permission from H. Feldhusen, "Teaching Gifted, Creative, and Talented Students in an Individualized Classroom," *Gifted Child Quarterly* (1981), *25*, 108–111.)

Second, Treffinger (1982b) stressed that "Gifted education is becoming more concerned with meeting [all] students' needs and less concerned with developing a rationale for selecting or excluding students from various programs or activities." Treffinger itemized no less than 60 suggestions for providing better instruction for gifted and talented students in the regular classroom. Some representative examples are:

> Using pretests or mastery tests to permit students to "test out" of material they already know.
> Using individualized learning packets, programmed learning, learning modules, learning centers, and minicourses, particularly in the basics.
> Allowing uninterrupted time every day for individual or small-group projects.

INSET 6.1 USING INDIVIDUALIZED EDUCATION PROGRAMS (IEPS) WITH GIFTED AND TALENTED STUDENTS

The reader probably is aware that Public Law 94-142, the "mainstreaming law," mandated the use of an *Individualized Education Program* (IEP) for each student classified as handicapped. IEPs also serve that other variety of exceptional student, the gifted and talented, particularly when they too are mainstreamed in the regular classroom. For handicapped students, IEPs are prepared jointly ". . . by a qualified school official, by the child's teacher and parents or guardian, and if possible by the child himself. . . ." Consultants such as a psychologist, reading specialist, speech pathologist, social worker, guidance counselor, curriculum specialist, or doctor are also involved in the planning. Similar personnel can help plan IEPs for G/T students.

The IEP serves as a guide for managing the testing, placement, instruction, and procedural safeguards that each handicapped student needs (National Advisory Committee on the Handicapped, 1976; Torres, 1977). For gifted students, the IEP will include:

1. Present levels of performance, as determined by intelligence tests, achievement tests, rating scales, and informal observations and reports by teachers, parents, school psychologists, or others.
2. Annual goals, which include short-term instructional goals. These goals will dictate most of the instructional methods, learning activities, and individual projects for each student required under item 3.
3. Specific educational services to be provided, based on the needs of the individual student. These will include special teaching strategies, special equipment, individual projects and assignments, field trips, and others.
4. The extent to which the student will participate in the regular program versus special G/T classes and activities.
5. A projected date for initiation and the anticipated duration of the services.
6. Evaluation procedures and appropriate objective criteria, which may result in a review and revision of the IEP.
7. A schedule for determining whether the objectives are being achieved.

Incorporating creative thinking into subject areas.

Helping students to learn the meaning of such higher-level thinking processes as *analysis, synthesis,* and *evaluation,* and to plan independent projects around these processes.

Bringing in guest speakers to describe their careers or unusual hobbies.

Using cross-age and peer tutoring.

Helping students to understand their own strengths, interests, learning styles, and preferences, and to become sensitive to those of others.

Exploring many points of view about contemporary topics and allowing opportunity to analyze and evaluate evidence and conflicting ideas and opinions.

Helping set personal and academic goals.

As a final caution, do not permit a mainstreaming program to become camouflage for offering no program at all. If gifted and talented children are not truly involved in differentiated curriculum within their regular classrooms, one cannot say that the school is providing for their needs.

PART-TIME AND TEMPORARY GROUPING

Pullout Programs

The old standby in programming for gifted and talented students is the *pullout* program. With minor variations, elementary students are pulled out of their regular classes two to three hours per week to participate in special enrichment activities guided by a G/T teacher or district teacher/coordinator. Often, one G/T coordinator serves an entire district by conducting a pullout class in a different school each afternoon. The meeting place usually is called a *resource room* because it provides special reading material and equipment resources. As with other special classes and cluster grouping, pullout activities focus on creative development, higher thinking skills, personal development and values clarification, and independent projects.

We should mention that many knowledgeable educators oppose this strategy. Friction often develops when teachers are saddled with the dilemma of permitting students to miss important content or else forcing them to make up missed work—thus punishing them for their G/T participation (Reis, 1983). In one Wisconsin district in the author's experience, many teachers opposed a G/T pullout program for exactly that reason; their policy was to require that all missed work be made up. Other schools adopt the opposite strategy: Under the assumption that G/T kids can afford to miss some regular content, they usually are not held responsible for missed work.

Elman and Elman (1983) further noted that pullout programs (1) require the expense of an additional teacher and specialized materials and (2) involve the student for only a fraction of the school week. Moreover, (3) the regular teacher may feel undermined and resent the implication that he or she is not providing adequate instruction for gifted and talented students. Finally, (4) selecting specific students for special privileges can be detrimental to student social relationships. That is, students may not be comfortable being visibly separated from their classmates and classified as "different." Another often-voiced criticism is that such plans frequently result in too much "fun and games" and too little valuable, theory-based training; solid reasons are needed for every activity (Renzulli and Smith, 1978a).

More positively, the pullout program is a popular and often successful means of bringing G/T students together for social and intellectual support, and for the special differentiated and enriched training they deserve. When it has a well-planned, challenging, and integrated curriculum, this program can offer gifted children good opportunities for developing high-level skills.

Resource Programs and Resource Rooms

As with *cluster groups,* the phrases "resource program" and "resource room" are used rather freely. A resource room is just that, a room with special resources that ". . . provide a learning environment specifically tailored to the needs and objectives for educating the gifted and talented" (Kaplan, 1974; see Inset 6.2). Since pullout students are sent to a resource room, pullout programs are sometimes called *resource programs* or *resource-room programs.* A special class for gifted students (discussed later) might also be held in a resource room and similarly earn the label *resource program.*

The present meaning of resource program is a district-wide pullout or magnet-type plan in which students with special needs are transported to specially equipped and taught resource rooms or enrichment centers for one or two sessions per week.

One prototypic resource program is the South Windsor (Connecticut) *Project Talent* (SWEPT; Juntune, 1981). G/T students in grades 4, 5, and 6 from four schools spend one morning and one afternoon per week in a resource room. The specific morning and afternoon combination depends upon which of three units the particular student selects to explore—for instance, geology, the future, or art history—topics not ordinarily covered in elementary school. In the first phase, teachers lead students through general explorations of particular topics plus group-training experiences (for example, development of creative thinking skills and library and scientific skills). In the second, independent-study phase ". . . each student selects an issue-oriented topic and investigates it in depth." With experience, students are permitted increased freedom. A sixth-grade student, for example, might proceed directly into a research study without participating in the teacher-led phase of the resource program.

In Ankeny, Iowa, the *Ankeny Gifted and Talented Education* (AGATE) program uses city buses to transport K–9 students to a junior high school equipped with AV equipment, books, magazines, a science lab, a language corner, games, plants, a piano, and miscellaneous materials for independent projects. The enrichment curriculum has included such activities as astronomy, including building a telescope; rocketry, with student-made—and launched—rockets; film animation; journalism, resulting in a newspaper; foreign languages; American Sign Language; art; literature; theatre; photography; oceanography; and more (Juntune, 1981). Students alternate mornings and afternoons, and days of the week, to avoid missing the same activities in the same classes.

INSET 6.2 RESOURCE ROOM RESOURCES

Cecile Frey (1980) itemized materials she has found to be "absolutely essential" to the decent operation of an elementary school resource room:

A good unabridged dictionary
A copy of *Roget's Thesaurus*
Bartlett's Familiar Quotations
A biographical dictionary (Webster)
A complete atlas

In the "nice but not essential" category she recommended:

The People's Almanac
Isaac Asimov's *Biographical Encyclopedia of Science and Technology*
Mathematics Illustrated Dictionary
Any decent grammar book
The Encyclopedia of Ignorance

As for a set of encyclopedias, Frey said, "I must answer that question with a resounding 'No!'" The reason: Students rely too heavily on them and, anyway, they are (1) expensive and (2) available in the school library. However, if funds are available, and only for limited use, she recommends *The World Book* and the *Encyclopedia Britannica's Micropedia* and *Macropedia.*

The resource room also should subscribe to:

Art and Man
Literary Cavalcade
Time or *Newsweek*
Science Digest
National Geographic World
New York Times

Part-Time Special Classes

Special classes (discussed under "Full-Time Homogeneous Grouping") may also be offered as part-time or temporary options. For example, in *Project Horizon* (Seattle, Washington) elementary school G/T students are placed in specialized self-contained classes for 50–70 percent of the school day. Their differentiated experiences include independent projects, accelerated subjects, and small-group enrichment activities, all of which aim at developing creative and other high-level thinking skills.

INSET 6.3 A COMMUNITY RESOURCE CENTER

The Manchester (Connecticut) Community Resource Center was designed to allow community professionals, business persons, and educators to share their expertise with local school children, both gifted and "regular" (Plese, 1982). The Center was designed for a small, limited-budget community; it is managed, in fact, by a single part-time volunteer. The Center basically assists teachers in locating and scheduling resource persons and programs for exploratory types of enrichment experiences. Students thus are exposed to new topic areas with the goal of stimulating interest and encouraging further study in an independent or small-group project.

A key component of the plan is the resource file, a cataloged list of community persons willing to speak to a youthful audience. Ideas for resource persons were found ". . . with the guidance of blue and yellow page directories (and a list of talented friends) . . ." (Plese, 1982). While newspaper ads, direct mailings, college inter-department mail, and other assorted recruitment methods were tried, a full 85 percent of the resource persons were recruited via a personal phone call. Something worth remembering.

Even in this small community the "general file topics" included 200 specific entries, for example: architecture, banking and finance, business and careers, communications, cultures, engineering, environment, foreign languages, health and safety, history, hobbies, horticulture, insurance, law, the military, politics and government, real estate, science, social studies and social science, theatre, travel, women, and "miscellaneous." Some specific presenters included a hypnotist, a poet, a UFO specialist, and an Arabic translator. In some cases the presentation would result in a follow-up field trip to the work location of the speaker. Directories listing the resources were placed not just in school secretaries' files, but in school libraries and teachers' lounges.

The mechanics of arranging a presentation were reasonably straightforward. Teachers would phone in information regarding the topic desired, three possible dates and times, and the age and size of the class. The Center Coordinator would contact a resource person who would agree to a certain time and would specify what AV aids might be needed and what advance preparation by students (if any) is desirable.

The Resource Center has been valuable for all Manchester students. However, according to Plese (1982), it has been especially valuable to G/T programs that emphasize broad, exploratory academic and career exposure and contact with creative and productive community experts.

Additional details regarding speaker guidelines, request-confirmation forms, evaluation procedures, teachers' responsibilities, and the always necessary thank-you notes are available from Plese (1982) and the Minneapolis Public Schools.[1]

---

[1] "How to Initiate and Administer a Community Resource Volunteer Program" (1971)—Minneapolis Public Schools, 807 N.E. Broadway, Minneapolis, MN 55413.

The Wheaton-Warrenville (Illinois) district Talented and Gifted Program includes magnet-type, district-wide special classes for junior and senior high school G/T students. For example, a junior high school offers bused-in students an accelerated math class. One high school offers a specially designed Key Seminar and another a Humanities class; both classes are cross-subject, and both focus on developing high-level thinking skills.

In South Africa, eight "extracurricular centres for the gifted," essentially regional G/T offices, offer special enrichment classes outside the regular school program for gifted and talented students from preprimary through high school age (Omond, 1985). Subjects include philosophy, anthropology, paleontology, creative writing, drama, music appreciation, South African cultures, computer programming, chess, and astronomy, all taught by experts. The classes include field trips and weekend camps. As one novel and admirable feature, siblings are allowed to accompany the gifted students at some centres.

Honors programs often consist of one or more part-time special classes.

Special Interest Groups and Clubs

Most secondary schools have these, although they are rare in the elementary school. The message here is that G/T-conscious teachers can assume the leadership necessary for organizing these enriching activities for interested students. There are drama clubs, German clubs, French clubs, computer clubs, chess clubs, math clubs, and so forth. The teacher-leader can organize meetings, competitions, research projects, field trips, and meetings with community experts, and can provide career information and guidance. One also can organize mini-courses, taught either by teachers or community experts, dealing with areas such as music writing, computer programming, jewelry making, or any other academic, career, or hobby topic. Clubs and courses may meet before or after school or on Saturdays. Activities may include work with equipment not normally available; for example, a high school laboratory might be borrowed for an elementary school physics group.

COUNSELING

In addition to plans for acceleration, grouping, and enrichment, a gifted and talented program for students of any age should include a counseling component. There are three traditional counseling areas: (1) students' personal concerns and adjustment, plus the interrelated components of (2) educational and (3) career counseling. The counseling will include appraisal of students based on objective and subjective data, counseling designed to help develop self-concepts, providing information to students, helping students make educational and career decisions, and others (Kenny, 1986). Zaffrann and Colangelo (1979) caution that a good counseling program should be a *coherent* plan—one that includes goals and objectives, a rationale, methodologies geared to the objectives, and a means of evaluation. It should not consist of sporadic, hit-or-miss services aimed at testing, placement, referral, and occasional counseling sessions. As another caution, Sanborn (1979a) further noted that, in their case-by-case experience ". . . gifted and talented students differ from each other in more ways than they resemble each other . . . and counseling services require highly individualized contacts and interpretations."

One of the main purposes of counseling is to discover unique patterns of student characteristics—abilities, interests, values, and motives—and then to help students relate these characteristics to educational, career, and life-style opportunities (Sanborn, 1979a, 1979b).

Personal and Social Needs

Generally, the self-esteem of all school children is influenced by their academic achievement (Harter, 1983). It follows that gifted children—generally—will have higher self-esteem and self-confidence than regular students (Janos, Fung, and Robinson, 1985). Nonetheless, there are many potential causes of personal or social maladjustment in gifted children and adolescents. Because regular classes group students according to chronological age, not mental age, gifted students often find themselves in situations which meet neither their social nor their intellectual needs. They may develop poor social skills from their inability to find "true peers" with similar abilities, interests and needs. Many experience feelings of isolation and social frustration. They may become social outcasts in an egalitarian, democratic-minded society, discriminated against by intimidated age-mates who do not appreciate peers who are more adult in their abilities and interests, who are labeled *gifted,* and who learn and excel with little apparent effort (Sanborn, 1979a). Said one high-IQ child, "I feel too smart for them to like me" (Janos, Fung, and Robinson, 1985). Herr and Watanabe (1979) concluded that, due in part to their social isolation, many gifted children have an identity crisis regarding who and what they are, and who and what they should become.

Parents may not understand their child's gifts and talents; they may not know how to respond to talented children or how to nurture the gifts (Exum, 1983; Sanborn, 1979b). Some parents may ignore, disbelieve, resent, or be intimidated by any apparent intellectual superiority. Others will fear for the normalcy, social adjustment, or happiness of their child (Dettman and Colangelo, 1980).

In rural and economically disadvantaged areas the lack of adult models—successful, gifted adults who understand and can empathize with G/T students—adds to problems of isolation and identity. Exum (1983) recommended family counseling for gifted black students, addressing such parental concerns as loss of authority over the gifted child, the student's possible loss of respect for family and culture, the student's emotional stability, and the student's ability to interact normally with other people. Exum warned that gifted students may deliberately underachieve to return a family disrupted by giftedness to a more comfortable homeostasis.

Pulvino, Colangelo, and Zaffrann (1976) used "personal essay writing" as a means for clarifying problems, feelings, and perceptions of individual gifted students. One favorite topic, for example, is "My Place in the Future." Many gifted high school students are quite good at writing, yet may be uncomfortable talking with a counselor. Thus they may be asked to write about important personal, social, educational, or career problems, and their feelings and perceptions about those problems. The essays provide unique information for counselors to use in personal interviews and guidance. Kenny (1987b) similarly recommends creative writing to help clarify—for the counselor and the student—areas of tension, stress, or anxiety. The essays, poetry, or other assignments focus on such topics as "My Hidden Self," "Secret Dreams," "Let Me Out of Here!," "Who Am I?" "I Am Mary's Angry Feelings," "What I Do and Don't Like About Myself," "Me, Myself and I," "My Secret Hopes," and "My Future Plans"; letters of the "Dear Abby" variety addressed to "Dear Sigmund"; diaries written not to be shared; fictitious resumés based on personal, educational, and professional qualities the students hope to possess eventually; character sketches from the point of view of another person describing the student; and many others (see Kenny, 1987a, 1987b).

As a solution to problems of social isolation and lack of academic stimulation, one dependable strategy is to bring gifted students together, as in many of the grouping strategies cited earlier (Zaffran and Colangelo, 1979). Because they are experiencing many of the same problems, gifted peers offer strong understanding and social and academic support for each other. If no organized groups currently exist, a counselor may informally bring small groups together. One school district used lunch period as an opportunity for informal discussions; the weekly "sandwich seminars" allowed gifted students to discuss with each other and with a counselor such topics as peer pressure and academic challenge. While social sanctions may prevent boys from showing creativity, or girls from showing high intelligence, in groups gifted and talented peers can help each other understand their talents and recognize that it is fine—indeed, fortunate—to be different and to be bright.

Educational and Career Counseling

In the educational and career counseling of gifted and talented students, two recurring problems are: (1) multipotentiality and (2) expectations (Delisle, 1982; Culbertson, 1985).

Multipotentiality. The dilemma of multipotentiality has been described as an "embarrassment of riches" (Zaffrann and Colangelo, 1979). While some G/T students show abilities and interests in one concentrated area, the majority possess capabilities in a number of areas. Often it is extremely difficult for them to make just one or two choices from among the many possibilities. French (1959), for example, found that more high-ability students scored above the seventieth percentile in three or more areas on the *Kuder Preference Record,* an inventory that identifies different spheres of career interest. In a case known to the authors, a gifted student was confused by her results on the *Differential Aptitude Career Test*—she had scored above the ninety-fifth percentile in eight out of nine possible career areas. Such results hardly provide clear future direction.

Sanborn (1979b), using the personal-essay-writing strategy mentioned earlier, reproduced the following concerns of a twelfth-grade male: "Nothing is so simple for me that I can do a perfect job without effort, but nothing is so hard that I cannot do it. This is why it is so difficult to decide my place in the future." From a female: "There are so many things I'd like to do and be, and I'd like to try them all; where to start is the problem. . . . I'd like to be a physical therapist, a foreign correspondent, a psychiatrist, an anthropologist, a linguist, a folk singer, an espionage agent, and a social worker."

The following are two examples of further complications to the problem of multipotentiality. One extraordinarily capable student known to the authors took college courses in philosophy and computer science while in high school; both professors were duly impressed and invited her to major in their subjects. When in college, professors in literature and science similarly encouraged her to major in their areas. Another college sophomore shared his confusion about college majors and careers. He had earned a 3.9 grade-point average in engineering, political science, chemistry, calculus, history, and psychology. Making a firm career decision seemed impossible.

It is critical that a gifted student consider vocations that have potential for extensive *growth.* Too often students are attracted to careers that whet their immediate interests. Counselors should acquaint students with the kinds of careers that will be sufficiently open-ended to permit students to be continually challenged and to grow.

Expectations. The second problem, *expectations,* has many facets. First of all, career selection is seen by gifted students as highly significant—

it will be their future identity, their means of self-expression, and their philosophy of life. Career selection also is the source of many conflicts, pressures, and dilemmas. For example, some parents, keenly aware of their child's high ability, may expect great things—the highest test scores and grades, academic awards, enrollment in a prestigious university, and entrance into a status profession (Zaffrann and Colangelo, 1979). Other parents may ignore their child's special abilities and talents and expect him or her to enter the family business or work on the farm, with little or no support for the essential college education.

While parents and relatives, and even gifted students themselves, may expect high academic and career accomplishments, the student actually may prefer to spend his or her life in a totally different fashion. From a high school girl's essay: "I'd like to move to England and live in the fog with a house by the sea [and] I'd like to write books. . . . my future probably will be much different. I'll go to college for four years and major in something like math. Then I'll teach high school for awhile and get married and have a bunch of kids. . . . I'm saying to myself that this is what you should do with your life, and if I keep saying it maybe I'll start believing it."

The gifted student's own career expectations may be limited by socioeconomic status. It is therefore especially important that counselors help gifted students from economically deprived homes to aspire beyond the life-style familiar to them. In guiding these students, counselors must be innovative in searching out scholarship assistance which can make such career aspirations realistically possible. In one case, a guidance counselor helped a gifted high school student from an economically disadvantaged family discover enough scholarship aid to support her entire college education. Needless to say, this guidance counselor made a dramatic impact on the girl's life.

Final Comment

Counseling activities should be designed to assist gifted students in self-discovery—understanding themselves, their abilities, problems, motives, interests, and values. Buescher (1987) identified four categories of "critical issues" for counseling the gifted: (1) adolescent growth and development (biological, social, educational), (2) identity and adjustment (self, stress, coping strategies, costs/benefits), (3) changes in relationships (peers, parents, family structures), and (4) career paths and guidance (opportunities, strategies, obstacles).

In educational and career counseling, G/T students need help in relating their interests and abilities to specific career alternatives, and in understanding the requirements, training, life-styles, advantages, and disadvantages of various careers. Field trips, mentor programs, and work-study programs are helpful. Gifted and talented students also need to understand the commitment in time and finances, and the necessity for deferred rewards, which are required for high levels of professional training.

Further, some students will have special problems. For example, many female students may need to be convinced that a professional career and a family are not necessarily incompatible. Other students may need to understand that responsibility, effort, and following social rules are closely tied to career and life success. Many will need help arranging the resources necessary for an extended education.

Information from counseling and guidance evaluations can help teachers and other school staff understand gifted students and their abilities, problems, and educational and career needs. For example, despite their gifts, many students need help with study skills—note-taking, summarizing, studying for exams, reviewing, and test taking. Also, Perrone and Pulvino (1979) recommended that counselors and teachers become sensitive to thinking–style preferences: for example, global versus analytic, convergent versus divergent, and left-brain versus right-brain learning and thinking patterns. There are tests and evaluations to aid the counselor in understanding student abilities and interests, for example, ability tests, achievement tests, interest inventories, reading tests, personality tests, cognitive styles tests, creativity tests, work samples, observations by teachers, parents, and community leaders, and more (Pulvino, Colangelo, and Zaffrann, 1976).

While G/T students may indeed "make it on their own," systematic counseling and guidance will make the task much less painful and more sensible. It also will help those gifted and talented students who would not "make it on their own."

SUMMARY

In the category of full-time homogeneous grouping, with magnet high schools, students of various ability levels are bused to the particular school that accommodates their needs and educational/career interests. Special schools, either elementary or secondary, are devoted solely to programs that accelerate and enrich the education of gifted students. Some specialize, for example, in the fine arts. Private schools usually produce higher average achievement levels than public schools. Some private schools are totally designed for gifted and talented students. With the school-within-a-school plan, G/T students attend special classes for part of the day and mix with regular students for other (usually less academic) classes. Special classes for G/T students may be created in the elementary school or the junior or senior high school.

There are also various full-time heterogeneous grouping options:

With multi-age classrooms two grades may be combined, allowing bright younger students to learn with students at the next higher grade. Some entire schools, such as those organized under the Individually Guided Education-Multi-Unit School plan, are designed for flexible, individualized learning.

Cluster grouping, as used in this chapter, involves placing a group of five or ten gifted students in the same regular class for special assignments (for example, via contracting), independent projects and field trips. The regular curriculum may be compacted to allow time for enrichment activities.

Mainstreaming is planning special learning experiences and projects in the regular classroom. Feldhusen's model mainstreaming classroom included learning centers for art, science, reading, and creative writing, and for individualized math.

Individualized Education Programs (IEPs) may be used to individualize instruction for mainstreamed gifted students.

Treffinger itemized suggestions for providing for gifted students in the regular classroom, for example, permitting students to "test out" of material they know, using learning centers, minicourses, and independent projects, allowing them to tutor others, and helping them with goal setting.

Part-time and temporary grouping options include the following: Pullout programs, the most common elementary G/T plan, involve sending gifted students to a resource room for one or two afternoons per week for enrichment and personal development activities. One recurrent problem is dealing with missed work. Other disadvantages: The program may be expensive; it will serve students for only part of the week; teachers may feel undermined; and social relationships may be damaged.

A resource program, as used in this chapter, is a district-wide "pullout" plan in which students travel to a resource room once or twice per week for special learning activities and projects.

Special classes may be used on a part-time as well as a full-time basis. Elementary students may attend special classes for part of the day; secondary students may be bused to a district-wide special class in, say, the humanities or accelerated math. Honors programs use part-time special classes.

Special interest groups and clubs are a good outlet for students whose enthusiasm and ability exceeds the regularly offered coursework. Teachers will need to assume some organizational leadership.

Counseling is an important component of any G/T program. It may deal with personal/social concerns or educational and career decisions. Counseling should involve a coherent plan, not sporadic hit-or-miss services. The main purpose of counseling is to help students discover abilities and interests and then relate these to educational, career, and life-style opportunities.

Counseling can also help with personal and social needs. G/T students may become social outcasts, leading to identity crises. Parents may disbelieve, resent, fear, or not understand their child's gifts and talents. Family counseling can help. Personal essay writing helps counselors identify problems. Bringing gifted students together can result in academic and social support.

Educational and career counseling deals with problems such as multipotentiality. Students should be helped to rank career possibilities, favoring those open-ended ones that allow continued challenge and growth.

"Expectations" involves many subproblems. Parents may place too much achievement pressure on their children; or conversely expect them to remain in the family business or farm. Career expectations may be depressed by SES level. Counselors should help raise aspirations of gifted low-SES students, and help them locate college resources. Moreover, career expectations of parents and others may not coincide with a student's true desires; the student actually may prefer a different life-style.

Gifted students need assistance in self-discovery and guidance in educational and career planning. Buescher suggested four categories of "critical issues": biological, social and educational growth; identity and adjustment; changes in relationships; and career guidance.

Students should be helped to understand "deferred rewards" and good study habits. Females may need convincing that career and family are compatible. Gifted students do not always "make it on their own."

chapter seven

Enrichment

SELECTING WORTHWHILE ENRICHMENT ACTIVITIES

All enrichment activities should be planned and designed with "higher order" objectives in mind. One list of such objectives, designed to guide curriculum planning, was presented in Table 5.1 on page 103. As a reminder, the objectives were listed in the categories of maximum achievement in basic skills, content beyond the regular curriculum, exposure to a variety of fields of study, student-selected content, high content complexity, creative thinking and problem solving, development of thinking skills, affective development, and motivation.

Overview

In this chapter we review a variety of enrichment strategies, all of which amount to delivery methods for achieving process and content goals. *Process* goals include developing such skills as creative thinking and problem solving, critical thinking, scientific thinking, and others. The *content* is the subject matter, projects, and activities within which the processes are developed.

Enrichment strategies will include:

1. Independent study and independent projects
2. Learning centers
3. Field trips
4. Saturday programs
5. Summer programs
6. Mentors and mentorships
7. Future Problem Solving
8. Odyssey (Olympics) of the Mind
9. Junior Great Books
10. Academic Decathlon
11. Mock Court
12. Other academic competitions

Several forms of enrichment, namely, training in leadership, affective development, creative thinking, critical thinking, and other thinking skills, are sufficiently important that Chapters 9, 10, 11, and 12 are set aside for them.

INDEPENDENT STUDY AND RESEARCH PROJECTS

Independent study and research projects take place within many of the enrichment strategies in our above list, and within many of the acceleration and grouping strategies of Chapters 5 and 6. For bright and energetic students, the possibilities for independent study and independent projects are without limit. Students may work on library research, scientific research, art, drama, journalism, photography, and so on. They may work alone, in pairs, or in small groups.

Library Research Projects

A library research project must be based on strong student interest and should be student-selected. If students have difficulty selecting a topic, a brainstorming approach is one way to identify interesting possibilities. It may be best to pose a specific problem or challenge, although the nature of the initial problem may change as the project develops. For example, some questions might be "Why and how were pyramids built?" "What are the relationships between Greek and Roman gods?" "What is the evidence for Indian migration from Asia?"

In addition to the library, this type of research also might involve trips to a natural history museum, an art gallery or research laboratory, visits with or phone calls to relevant university faculty or other community (or national) experts. Students in one Wisconsin gifted program telephoned the National Aeronautics and Space Administration in Cape Canaveral to obtain answers to questions about space and rockets.

With any independent project, it is important that a *product* be produced and that the product or performance be presented to an appropriate *audience,* either students in the class or outside groups (Renzulli, 1977). A library research project could include more than a neatly typed report: It might include a student-made movie or a narrated slide show; a demonstration of some activity or skill (for example, sand painting, musket loading); a table-top demonstration (rolling 30-ton stone blocks, dinosaur models); a TV news report on the progress of a specific battle; a mini-play about mythological or historical characters; a newspaper column describing recent activities in the Spanish Inquisition; an ESP test for the class; and so on.

Most of the time the gifted student's class—G/T or otherwise—will serve as a suitable audience. However, some unusually bright students may need to prepare two reports, one simple enough for peers (or the teacher) to understand and a second full-blown one to be shared with an expert. The following case study reflects this problem.

Eric prepared a complex discussion of space travel for his sixth-grade class. His research, organization, and scientific terminology were of his usual high quality. However, his classmates greeted his enthusiastic report with boredom and teasing because of the incomprehensibility of the material. Although Eric easily could have prepared a much simpler report, it would not have allowed him an honest demonstration of what he had learned and figured out. He said that sometimes he just really wished he could be in a school where he could challenge himself yet continue to be accepted by friends. Said Eric, "Kids think I'm weird!"

Scientific Research Projects

Possibilities for scientific research are innumerable, but scientific studies will of course be limited by available equipment and resources. A few phone calls, however, could determine if, say, a physics lab in the local college might be available to supervised junior high school students.

Many elementary and junior high schools organize science fairs in which each student in the science classes creates a small scientific demonstration. Ribbons are awarded to the most elaborate, well-done, or technically competent projects, usually a "first," "second," or "third" type of rating so that all or most participants can earn a ribbon for their efforts. Projects by G/T students usually are outstanding, and their effort and ingenuity are reinforced with "first" ribbons and usually peer admiration.

With any type of research project, the teacher's main role is "the guide on the side." With elementary or secondary students, the teacher-coordinator directs the budding scientist to appropriate library or human resources for background information, helps the student clarify the problem and plan the research, aids in locating equipment and other resources and tools, and gives advice and assistance when needed.

Other Independent Projects

In addition to library and scientific research projects, individual art or handicraft projects may include drawing, painting, sculpture, silk-screen, lettering, printing, batik, pottery, ceramics, photography, weaving, or other media. Students interested in theatre and drama can research how plays are written and then write, direct, and perform in their own.

A student newspaper is an especially good independent project for a small group of students. Creating a newspaper involves interviewing people and writing stories, taking photographs, planning and designing the paper, and arranging for its printing. Students in one Wisconsin elementary school interviewed and photographed elderly people in a retirement home. They learned first-hand about local and state history and about such hobbies and skills as quilting, candle-making, tatting, and blacksmithing. Of no small importance, their appreciation and respect for the elderly increased dramatically.

LEARNING CENTERS

Learning centers were mentioned earlier in conjunction with Hazel Feldhusen's (1981, 1986) mainstreaming approach to programming. There are teacher-made learning centers; there also are commercial learning centers. The focus may be upon independent language learning, science projects and experiments, mathematics puzzles and activities, social-studies knowledge and concepts, creative writing, arts and crafts, and even music appreciation. Students—gifted and others—may self-select centers and activities, or teachers and students together may plan valuable and interesting learning center goals. Learning centers may be located in the regular classroom, someone else's classroom, the building resource room, or the district G/T resource room.[1]

The teacher should always be certain that learning center time is well spent; that is, learning center activities should meet some of the goals and purposes of enrichment itemized in Table 5.1. Be warned that learning centers also can offer time for unsupervised fooling around.

---

[1] "Learning center" sometimes is used to mean "resource center," an entire room in a school or district set aside for pullout types of learning experiences.

FIELD TRIPS

Field trips can be used as an exploratory activity, aimed at acquainting students with cultural or scientific areas or with career possibilities. Field trips can also be a source of information for students' independent projects. An entire class or a small group of interested students might visit a natural history museum, a manufacturing plant, an art gallery, planetarium, a local Greek restaurant, and so on. Some carefully written requests might earn them a tour of a major newspaper, a research laboratory, or perhaps seats at a symphony rehearsal.

Field trips are most beneficial if students have specific problems to solve, questions to answer, or post-tour projects or presentations to prepare. As Friedman and Master (1980) observed, streaking to the gift shop and cafeteria to buy postcards and potato chips is not the main intent of the trip.

Friedman and Master emphasized that in planning a successful field trip one must evaluate the materials and exhibits and the ability of the guide/educator to communicate effectively with the group. An outline of the program/tour should be planned in advance by the teacher and guide/educator. During the tour the guide should not just "lecture at" students; rather, students should be allowed to touch, respond, and question. During the tour, teacher and guide should work together to stimulate learning, with both partners commenting, contributing, and remaining open to spontaneous twists and turns in the children's interests. Students should be encouraged to discuss and evaluate during the program.

So far, the reader might correctly conclude that field trips are no different for gifted students than for typical students. Indeed, all students, regardless of ability, should have enrichment opportunities, including visits to places of artistic, historic, and scientific interest. However, if the gifted child's field trip is part of a differentiated curriculum, the preparation for the trip, the tasks of the visit, and the resulting reports or projects should be tied to knowledge goals and thinking skill development.

SATURDAY PROGRAMS

Saturday programs have the delightful advantage of permitting gifted students to meet and work with each other away from the stresses and problems of daily school requirements. Saturday programs normally take the form of a noncredit miniclass or seminar (see Kolloff and Feldhusen, 1986), covering one or a few topics and taught by volunteer teachers, college faculty, or community experts, who often are parents of the gifted children.

One model Saturday program is Feldhusen's Super Saturday plan sponsored by Purdue University (Feldhusen and Hansen, 1987; Feldhusen and Koopmans-Dayton, 1987; Feldhusen and Wyman, 1980). Feldhusen and Wyman noted that their Saturday program meets *cognitive* needs of gifted and talented youth by helping them develop thinking skills and acquire in-depth knowledge. *Affective-social* needs, specifically, motivation and an appropriate self-concept, are met via associating ". . . with intellectual and artistic peers and through identification with adult models of creatively successful individuals." *Generative* needs—needs to be producers of new ideas and products—grow out of involvement in independent investigations and creative activities.

Super Saturday offers many courses at different age levels. All courses engage students in active inquiry and/or hands-on experiences, and all are designed to foster the development of high-level thinking skills. In the spring of 1982 no less than 27 courses were available. Some examples: *Creative Thinking, Mime,* and *Exploring Space* for kindergarten and lower elementary children; *Art, French,* and *Probability and Statistics* for intermediate elementary students; *TV Production, Computers,* and *Native American Culture* for upper elementary students; and *Economics, Electrical Engineering,* and *Computers* for junior and senior high school students. Exceptionally able students in seventh grade or above can earn college credit in such courses as psychology, French, English composition, and political science.

As for the details and mechanics of the operation, parents provide transportation—from fourteen counties around Lafayette, Indiana. Parents also pay minimal registration fees and, for some courses, materials charges. Teachers are university faculty and students, public school teachers, and others in the greater Lafayette community. They must be good teachers and show energy, enthusiasm, and an interest in teaching gifted kids. Students are selected using fairly generous criteria, for example, IQ scores above 115, *or* grades in the top 10 percent, *or* evidence of artistic talents, *or,* for preschoolers, parents' statements regarding talents and abilities. The program is ". . . designed to be inclusive rather than exclusive . . ." (Feldhusen and Sokol, 1982).

SUMMER PROGRAMS

Most cities offer summer programs that are open to all students. Obviously, these may be capitalized upon by the teacher, parent, or counselor seeking enrichment opportunities for energetic and able children. In addition, many school districts and state education departments fund the planning and teaching of summer courses and workshops designed specifically for their gifted and talented children. For example, the Georgia Governor's Honors Program (GHP) brings talented and gifted teenagers together for a six-week residential (live-in) program where they take courses in communication arts, mathematics, science, social studies, visual arts, music, voice, design, executive management, theater, dance, or foreign languages (Sirmans, 1985). The students spend four hours per day, Monday through Saturday, in a major class and, because the gifted have wide interests, also a minor class.

Individual teachers or parents also can organize and/or teach summer classes for the gifted. Dermatologist and parent John Tkach (1987) described a heavy-duty physics course that he planned and taught to science-oriented children. Another of his creative efforts was a summer course covering astronomy, geology, paleontology, and evolution, including a camping trip to a dinosaur dig, tapes of Carl Sagan's *Cosmos* TV shows, and a personal letter from Sagan (Tkach, 1986).

University Sponsored Programs

Many colleges and universities offer summer programs for gifted, talented, and creative children and adolescents (see Juntune, 1986, for programs in your area). Especially noteworthy are the national Talent Search programs noted in Chapter 5. However, in view of the restrictiveness of the Talent Search programs, admission to which is based on high SAT scores, it is fortunate that there are other college-based programs with more lenient entrance requirements and lower costs.

Purdue University offers a *Super Summer Program*, modeled after their successful Super Saturday plan, and three residential summer programs that attract gifted students from throughout the midwest. The *Star* program is for gifted seventh- and eighth-grade students capable of taking highly accelerated courses in math, science, and humanities. The *Purdue Academic Leadership Seminars* (PALS) are for ninth- and tenth-grade students selected on the basis of both leadership and achievement, as recommended by teachers and counselors. PALS participants also are offered courses in math, science, and humanities. The *Purdue College Credit Program* is for ninth- through twelfth-grade students who are selected via recommendations from their schools. These students have the opportunity to earn college credit in such university courses as psychology, English composition, history, the solar system, and computers. By way of evaluation, Feldhusen noted that ". . . the students made incredible academic gains" in both content mastery and school attitudes (Van Tassel-Baska, 1983).

Various *College for Kids* and *University for Youth* plans are similar to the Purdue program in offering high-level summer enrichment for gifted and talented students, almost always in the form of mini-courses. For example, at the University of Wisconsin-Parkside (Kenosha, Wisconsin) a College for Kids plan was initiated in 1979 for children in kindergarten through fourth grade (Robinson, 1981). The purposes of this plan were, first, to provide quality enrichment experiences for gifted students and, second, to train elementary teachers to be more effective with gifted children in their regular classrooms.

With this program a parent/teacher committee was created to handle most of the preliminary conceptual planning. In addition, a paid, full-time university coordinator (starting in January) helped locate a few hundred gifted children and lots of teachers and university faculty; scheduled classrooms, laboratories, and studios; plus coped with mechanical problems of registration, scheduling, equipment, supplies, budget, and so on. The program was to last for three weeks, five half-days per week. Students were selected by sending registration brochures to parents of all students in the area already identified as "gifted" and participating in area G/T programs. Fees were $30 per child.

Interestingly, course topics were selected by the students themselves. The parent/teacher committee held a brainstorming session with the kindergarten to fourth-grade G/T children at one school. The problem: "What courses would be best for a summer enrichment program?" After narrowing an extensive list, and meeting a strict qualification of not conflicting with the regular curriculum, nine winners one year were oceanography, chemistry, astronomy, entomology, drama, photography, animation/cartooning, art, and ancient life. On the registration form, children and parents indicated their first, second, and third choices for courses. Children were assigned to two courses, with a strong effort to put everyone into their first choice.

Teachers were recruited from area school districts and were enrolled in a four-credit practicum. Their major jobs were to (1) meet the children and march them to their classes, and (2) assist the faculty in teaching or in any other way.

In accord with the Renzulli (1977) Enrichment Triad Model (Chapter 8), most children became involved in independent or small-group projects resulting in "real" products. For example, the Ancient Life class placed a time capsule in a new building; the Drama class produced, directed, and performed a play for parents and guests; and the Cartooning/Animation class produced two comic books and a 20-minute animated film.

The University of Wisconsin, Madison campus, began offering a three-week program for gifted elementary school children also titled *College for Kids* (cfk). This program, however, differed substantially from the Parkside plan (Clasen, 1982). Particularly, the Madison strategy was not to emphasize content. Rather, the goals were to (1) assist students in developing good self-concepts by helping them understand their giftedness through interaction with intellectual peers; (2) acquaint them with university activities and university life via prepared demonstrations, tours, and visitations; and (3) have them observe, learn, and practice processes of creative thinking and other thinking skills.

A complete roll-call of staff and students includes a faculty program director, a half-time program assistant employed for the calendar year, an instructor for a four-week graduate seminar taught in conjunction with cfk, 250 children in grades 4 or 5 (who, as at Parkside, are identified by area schools as "gifted"), 27 elementary school teachers (many of whom are working toward their M.S. Degrees in gifted education in the Department of Educational Psychology), and about 35 university graduate students and faculty who offer 50 one-week workshops and a half-dozen large-group "extravaganzas."

Following the morning seminar, each teacher interacts with his or her "family," a group of 10 to 12 children, both before and after their two-hour workshop or extravaganza. They discuss their experiences and practice relevant processes and skills. For example, they brainstorm solutions to some problems; they apply other creative thinking techniques; and they learn to evaluate by discussing "What was good (and bad) about today's workshop or extravaganza?" They deal with such issues as the pros and cons of being gifted, and the value of higher education.

The main agenda for the first week is the first of two five-day workshops, two hours per day, in such art and science areas as chemistry, veterinary science, TV production, photography, and university history. The second week presents a series of extravaganzas, including, for example, chemistry and physics demonstrations and lectures on astronomy and anthropology. The third week focuses on another workshop. Throughout the three weeks the teacher-leaders arrange visits to such attractions as the geology museum, veterinary school, anthropology exhibits, the historical society, a campus nuclear reactor, and the agricultural campus.

While the University of Wisconsin-Madison College for Kids plan is difficult to organize and administrate, it works very well, based upon evaluations and feedback from students, teachers, university faculty, and parents.

Music, Art, Language, and Computer Camps

Many colleges and universities have sponsored summer clinics, institutes, or camps in music, art, and drama, and many now offer computer camps as well. Some sponsor foreign language camps where students eat, sleep, swim, canoe, and communicate in Spanish, French, German, or Russian. An especially good example is the *International Language Village* sponsored by Concordia College in Moorhead, Minnesota.

Although virtually none of these camps and institutes identify themselves as "programs for the gifted," for all practical purposes they do provide a gifted program in a specific area. Students are attracted to the camp because of their talent and high interest in an area. They are expected to invest many hours of dedicated effort in acquiring specialized knowledge and skills. The students also receive stimulation and support from other students who are equally enthusiastic and talented in the same ability. For students with few peers who share their special talents, the camps are refreshing ways to meet like-minded and like-talented friends.

As a final reminder, summer programs need not be highly involved and sophisticated. We noted above that a single person, parent or teacher, can organize and teach a minicourse. A group of interested parents or educators can arrange for classes to be taught and teachers to teach them, identification methods and criteria (if any), plus publicity and registration details.

MENTORS AND MENTORSHIPS

The concept of mentoring is hardly new. In ancient Greece Mentor himself tutored Telemachus, son of Odysseus. Socrates was mentor to Plato, Plato to Aristotle, and Aristotle to Alexander the Great (Cox and Daniel, 1983b). Typically, a mentorship includes an extended relationship between a community professional and a single high school student over a period of months. However, Ellingson, Haeger, and Feldhusen (1986) described a successful mentor program for students as young as fourth grade who meet with their mentors (for example, an engineer, doctor, judge, history professor, and radio broadcaster) in groups of six. Mentors also may be invited to make presentations at the elementary or secondary school to acquaint students with career opportunities and the necessary preparation (Johnson, 1986; Reis and Burns, 1987).

The high school student in the typical mentorship may be called a protégé, intern, apprentice, or assistant. The student visits the mentor at the job site on a scheduled basis to learn first-hand the activities, responsibilities, problems, and life-style associated with the particular business, art, or profession. Students normally receive high school credit for the mentorship experience. In some cases a formal work-study plan is developed in which the student is paid for working while learning.

Edlind and Haensly (1985) summarized the main benefits of mentorships as (1) aiding career planning, (2) increasing knowledge, skills, and talents far beyond book learning, (3) establishing contacts with influential and knowledgeable persons, (4) building self-esteem and confidence, (5) developing personal ethics and sets of standards, (6) enhancing creativity, and (7) establishing a valuable and deep long-term friendship.

Noted Cox and Daniel (1983b), "Mentorship presumes a commitment on the part of the student and mentor and has as its goal the shaping of the student's life outlook." As more dramatically described by DeMott (1981), one goal of a successful mentorship is to facilitate ". . . that extraordinary inner experience in which the human creature is suddenly seized with the realization—inexplicable, incontestable—that this is what I want. This is how life could be lived!"

Describing mentors as ". . . devoted men and women lighting intellectual sparks and setting the passion for learning aflame" (J. Epstein, 1981), Mattson (1983) itemized characteristics of good mentors that are intended to help a teacher or steering committee assemble a mentor pool. While the list admittedly is idealistic, it can serve as a guide that will sensitize the teacher or committee to good "spark lighters" when they appear. The ideal mentor should possess expertise in his or her specialized field, of course. The mentor also should be high in personal integrity and have a strong interest in teaching young people. He or she should possess enthusiasm and optimism, and an "anticipation of tomorrow." Also important are tact, flexibility, and humor, all of which contribute to a desirable "acceptance of foolishness and errors." Tolerance and patience contribute to a safe and experimentally-oriented environment. Also valuable are agility, creativity, and the ability to bring the protégé to higher levels of thinking and problem solving. Good mentors should provide opportunities for students to use their gifts and abilities, to use their imaginations, and to see their own possibilities. Reis and Burns (1987) similarly recommended that a mentor be knowledgeable and enthusiastic, able to communicate with students, and able to share their methodology and inquiry skills.

In planning a mentorship program, Cox and Daniel detailed many helpful guidelines. Some of the more salient recommendations were:

1. Elicit the support of the district superintendent, the school board, and community leaders.
2. Specify the purpose of each mentorship and the role of the student.
3. Develop a clear, defensible academic credit policy. If high school credit is given, the work experience should relate directly to the course for which the credit is received.
4. Prepare written criteria for student selection based upon multiple indices, not just one.
5. Try to achieve the best mentor/student match possible. Mentors should be creative producers who will not treat the students as "go-fers."
6. Orientation seminars should be planned to acquaint students with the professional and business environments in which they will work.
7. Students should be prepared for the mentorship with related course work prior to the experience.
8. Students should be helped to develop individual goals.
9. The program must meet the academic needs of students. Students should be assigned required reading; they also should keep journals in which they analyze their activities and experiences.

FUTURE PROBLEM SOLVING

The fast-growing *Future Problem Solving* (FPS) program is an enrichment activity that can take place in a pullout, resource center, special class, or Saturday program, or with gifted students who are mainstreamed or clustered in the regular classroom. If your FPS team is good, it will travel to a state Future Problem Solving Bowl or even to the National Future Problem Solving Bowl, now held annually at Coe College, Cedar Rapids, Iowa. FPS was begun in 1975 by E. Paul Torrance at the University of Georgia (Crabbe, 1979, 1982; Torrance and Torrance, 1978; Torrance, Williams, Torrance, and Horng, 1978). It soon grew into a statewide Georgia plan, then a national program, and currently includes over 100,000 children from all over the United States and many foreign countries.

According to FPS director Anne Crabbe (1982) the objectives of the program are to help gifted children:

1. Become more aware of the future in order to deal with it actively, with feelings of optimism and the attitude that they can effect changes.
2. Become more creative; learning to go beyond the logical and obvious.
3. Develop and increase communication skills, including speaking and writing persuasively, clearly, and accurately.
4. Develop such teamwork skills as listening, respecting, understanding, and compromising.
5. Learn to use a problem-solving model and integrate it into their daily lives.
6. Develop research skills, learning how to gather information, where to go, and who to contact.

The year-long program begins with the registration of each five-student team in one of three grade-level divisions (4–6, 7–9, 10–12). The teams are sent three practice problems that they solve with this model:

1. Gathering information related to a general problem statement.
2. Identifying problems within the larger problem and selecting a main ("the big") problem to work on.
3. Generating ideas for the main problem.
4. Itemizing criteria and evaluating the ideas.
5. Preparing the best solution for presentation.

A typical problem in FPS begins with a one-page scenario that is read by the five-person team. The problem is accompanied by about twenty recent magazine and newspaper articles pertaining to the issues presented. As an example, the CANUSA problem describes a city on the Canada/USA border designed in 1987 for the "traditional" family (father, nonworking mother, and 2.5 children). Now, 30 years later, CANUSA has a population of 65,000, only 2 percent of whom are in traditional families. Using mainly the reading materials provided, students research problems of divorced families, single-parent families, retired persons, families in which mother and father both work, and couples with and without children. The general goal, of course, is to redesign the city, its schools, parks, work arrangements, etc., to meet the needs of the entire community.

Students generate at least twenty problems that may exist or arise in

CANUSA. From these, students select what they agree is the best underlying problem and brainstorm possible solutions for it. They create an evaluation matrix, with the most appropriate ideas listed vertically on the left side and criteria cross the top, which permits an objective evaluation of ideas. After the single best solution is identified, it is rewritten in essay form—the solution is carefully presented, and the outcomes and consequences of the solution are elaborated and explained.

Other future-oriented problems have dealt with underwater colonization, space exploration, garbage disposal, water shortages, illiteracy, drug abuse, child abuse, paranormal mental powers, and others.

As each problem is completed, it is sent for scoring to the state FPS organization. The first two problems are practice problems. Based on the third problem, the top 10 percent of the teams are invited to participate in the state FPS competition. For the state competition, the teams are given a topic in advance which they research. At the competition site each team is given the one-page problem scenario, then "locked" in a hotel room for two hours to prepare their problem statements and solutions according to the above five steps. The winner of each state competition is sent to the National FPS Bowl.

The intrinsic nature of the FPS activities requires teamwork and cooperation—listening, respecting, understanding, and compromising (Crabbe, 1982).

Torrance and Torrance (1978) reported student testimonials on the benefits of FPS. For example, a fifth-grade girl reported, "I learned to cooperate, to share ideas, to produce creative and clever ideas, to be excited, to learn and to work." Information on FPS is available from Future Problem Solving, Coe College, Cedar Rapids, Iowa 52402.

ODYSSEY (OLYMPICS) OF THE MIND

Like Future Problem Solving, Odyssey of the Mind (OM; formerly Olympics of the Mind) is a national program. Also like FPS, it is an excellent vehicle for teaching creative thinking and problem solving, along with self-confidence and a good self-image.

The key assumption of its founders, Ted Gourley and Sam Micklus, is that the mind can be trained and strengthened through exercise with mental games just as the body is trained with physical exercise (Gourley, 1981). OM thus was designed to combine ". . . the excitement of athletic competition with fun-filled mental gymnastics for youngsters" (Olympics of the Mind Association, 1983).

There are three age classifications, grades K–5, 6–8, and 9–12. The team will include seven students; in formal competitions only five can be "on the playing field." A "member" is one school, which registers with the

OM Association for a fee of about $50. The teacher/coach will want to purchase the books *Problems, Problems, Problems* (Micklus and Gourley, 1982) and *OMAha!* (Micklus, 1986), which supply dozens of short-term practice problems and hints for scoring well with long-term problems, and the *Odyssey of the Mind Program Handbook* (Micklus, 1985), which details competition guidelines, rules, and procedures.

The OM Association provides each member with detailed directions for preparing *long-term problems* that will require months to plan and implement prior to the regional competitions. For example, for 1988 the five long-term problems were:

Atlantis.   The team's problem is to construct the illusion of a deep-sea expedition that explores the lost city of Atlantis. The team builds and operates a submersible vessel that maneuvers into the "sea" to collect artifacts and sea samples with two remote arms operated from inside the vessel.

The Gift of Flight.   The problem is to construct six aircraft, each of which performs a specified task. For example, one aircraft, launched by pulling a string, will fly eighteen feet and break a balloon.

Straddle Structure.   A structure of balsa wood and glue must straddle an octagon, 1½ inches high and 7 inches wide, and support as much weight as possible.

It's Showtime.   The team develops a musical scene based on a play (for example, *The Emperor's New Clothes, Much Ado About Nothing*) and presents an oral summary of the play.

Comics.   The team selects one or more well-known cartoon characters and makes a large graphic cartoon, complete with captions. The team also portrays the characters in one to four humorous live performances, complete with music, a playbill, props and background set(s).

In all problems, points are awarded for "style"—the creative presentation of the problem which may include music, costumes, mime, and a sign naming the home school (or organization).

In addition to the long-term problems, students also solve *short-term* "spontaneous" problems both in practice and on the day of competition (see Micklus, 1985, 1986). For example, students might be asked to improvise with a ping pong ball ("It's a clown's nose," "It's an egg from a plastic bird"). Spontaneous problems are scored for fluency and originality, with one point for each common idea and three points for each creative idea. They learn to give creative ideas.

JUNIOR GREAT BOOKS

Another popular enrichment program is *Junior Great Books,* currently used in G/T programs in all 50 states and many foreign countries. In a two-day workshop, the Junior Great Books Foundation trains teachers to ask questions requiring interpretation of carefully selected literature. A guiding philosophy is that ". . . if you think you know the answer to a question, don't ask the question" (Will, 1986). Shared inquiry is the goal.

The Books themselves are prepared for each grade level from grade 2 through 12. They are in their original form; none have been "dumbed down." All have proven to be comprehendable, rich enough in ideas for sustained discussion of the interpretative questions, and enjoyable to read and discuss.

For further information, contact the Junior Great Books Foundation, 40 East Huron, Chicago, IL 60611.

ACADEMIC DECATHLON

Academic Decathlon is a challenging high school program that includes regional, state, and national competitions. Each team is composed of two "A," two "B," and two "C" students in grades 11 or 12. Each school competes in one of three categories based on school size. They compete in conversation skills, essay writing, formal speech, economics, language and literature, fine arts, mathematics, physical science, social studies, and a Super Quiz. The Super Quiz topic is provided in advance; in 1988 it was "The History of Flight from Daedalus to Kitty Hawk to Voyager."

For further information, contact Academic Decathlon, c/o World Book, Merchandise Mart, Chicago, IL 60654.

MOCK COURT

Mock Court (or mock trial tournament) is a plan for very talented high school students, most often those interested in a law or political career. There usually are local, regional, state, and national competitions, with the higher-level competitions held in district federal courthouses and presided over by real federal judges. Guided by a school coach, students might deal with a trial based, for example, on a drinking and driving violation. In four phases involving participation in two trials, each participant prepares an argument for the defense, a rebuttal of the prosecutor's presentation, a presentation as the prosecutor, and a rebuttal of the case for the defense. Winners of state competitions travel to Lincoln, Nebraska, for the All State

Invitational Mock Trial Tournament each May. For information, contact Mock Trial, Center for Law-Related Education, Drake University, Des Moines, IA 50311.

OTHER ACADEMIC COMPETITIONS

Andrea Williams (1986; see also Williams, 1980) described a number of academic game bowls for students in grades 1 through 12 that can be organized for district- or state-level participation. Each school can enter one or more teams, and both team and individual performances are rewarded with ribbons, certificates, and trophies. The events allow students to solve problems, apply ideas, and make intuitive leaps; strengthen written and oral communication skills; and strengthen creativity, analysis, evaluation, and leadership abilities. In addition, many participants show improved cross-sex and cross-race cooperation, better school attitudes, better coping skills, and in some big city schools, reduced absenteeism and dropping out.

The academic events themselves may be locally designed, based upon selected academic areas, content and process goals and objectives, and the target population (grade levels or interest groups). Alternatively, the competitions may be tied to national competitions, for example, Future Problem Solving, Odyssey of the Mind, National Academic Games (Box 214, Newhall, CA 91322), National Forensics League (671 E. Fond du Lac Street, Ripon, WI 54971), Computer Convention (Ronald Baillie, 3307 E. Hardies Road, Gibsonia, PA 15044), and Land of Adwin, which includes an all-day congress, Creative Problem Solving, Calcu-Solve (using calculators), and Creative Convention (Andrea Williams, 2007 Maple Leaf, Collinsville, IL 62234).

SUMMARY

Worthwhile enrichment should be guided by the types of higher-order objectives in Table 5.1, which included the categories of basic skills, content beyond the regular curriculum, exposure to a variety of fields of study, student-selected content, high complexity, creative thinking and problem solving, thinking skills, affective development, and motivation.

Enrichment strategies are delivery methods for achieving process and content goals.

Library research projects, which may include museum or laboratory visits or visits with professionals, aim at answering specific questions. Students' "reports" may take forms other than a written paper. Very bright students may prepare a simple report for their class, a more complete one for experts.

With independent science projects, the teacher plays a supportive, guiding role.

Commercial- or teacher-made learning centers can teach languages, science, math, computers, social studies, creative writing, music appreciation, and others.

Field trips are good experiences for regular and gifted students. The teacher and the guide/educator should preplan any tour. Students should be allowed to touch and question, not just be lectured at.

Feldhusen's Super Saturday is a model Saturday enrichment program that produces cognitive, affective and, generative benefits. G/T coordinators may organize Saturday minicourses for gifted students.

Regular city summer programs may be capitalized upon by parents, teachers, or counselors seeking summer enrichment activities for gifted students. Also, many school districts offer special summer courses and workshops for the gifted. The Talent Search programs offer mathematical and other accelerated and enrichment classes for extremely precocious, mainly junior high school students.

Summer programs, such as the Purdue Super Summer and summer residential programs or the University of Wisconsin College for Kids, require plenty of planning in order to recruit participants and teaching staff, and to organize the course offerings, activities, space, facilities, selection and registration procedures, and more. The programs provide marvelous opportunities for learning advanced content and subject matter skills, and for developing process skills. The programs help increase self-understanding and self-appreciation. Teachers also receive valuable training in such programs.

Music, art, language, and computer summer camps are excellent *de facto* gifted programs that teach high-level content and thinking skills. The self-confidence and peer support is invaluable for many psychologically isolated gifted students.

Mentor programs usually involve extended on-the-job, one-to-one interaction with a community professional. Students learn professional activities and problems, and the life-styles of mentors. The ideal mentor is interested in teaching and is high in integrity, enthusiasm, flexibility, humor, patience, agility, creativity, and the ability to stimulate high-level thinking and problem solving.

Planning mentorships requires clarification of the purposes of the mentorship, the role of the student, student selection criteria, the academic credit policy, optimal student/mentor matches, student goals, evaluation of the student's work, and others.

The nationally organized Future Problem Solving program, created by Paul Torrance, helps children become future-oriented and strengthens creative thinking, problem solving, communication, research, and teamwork skills. Problems are solved following a five-step model.

Odyssey of the Mind includes long-term problems, worked on during the school year, and short-term problems. OM is designed to strengthen creative problem solving and confidence.

The Junior Great Books program acquaints students with classic literature and strengthens interpretation and discussion skills.

Academic decathlon is a national high school program involving competitions in essay writing, speech, economics, language and literature, art, math, science, social studies and others. The topic for a Super Quiz is provided in advance.

Mock court, also a high school plan, requires gifted students in a first trial to present an argument for the defense and a rebuttal of the prosecutor. In a second trial the student makes a presentation as the prosecutor and rebuts the case for the defense.

Other academic game bowls and competitions may be organized for district- or state-level competition. The competitions strengthen communication skills, leadership, creativity, analysis and other thinking skills, and improve attitudes and coping skills.

chapter eight

Curriculum Models

Curriculum models help provide a theoretical framework within which specific enrichment activities may be planned. This chapter will briefly summarize eleven curriculum models, all of which have provided justifiable bases for planning differentiated experiences for G/T students. In most cases—but not all—the models and their prescriptions are quite consistent and complementary, permitting a teacher-coordinator to draw ideas from two or more curriculum models simultaneously. Some models, such as the *Revolving Door Identification Model* (Renzulli, Reis, and Smith, 1981) provide extensive details regarding program philosophy, identification, evaluation, and the specifics of carrying out the entire plan. Other models propose more general suggestions as to worthwhile skill development goals and activities, leaving it to the teacher-coordinator to fill in the details. These are the eleven models:

1. The Enrichment Triad Model (Renzulli, 1977)
2. The Revolving Door Identification Model (Renzulli, Reis, and Smith, 1981)
3. Multiple Menu Model (Renzulli, 1988)
4. Pyramid Project (Cox, Daniel, and Boston, 1985)
5. Feldhusen's Three-Stage Enrichment Model (Feldhusen and Kolloff, 1978, 1981b)

6. The Guilford/Meeker Structure of Intellect Model (Guilford, 1967, 1977; Meeker, 1969; Meeker and Meeker, 1986)
7. Treffinger's (1975) model for increasing self-directedness
8. The Autonomous Learner Model (Betts, 1985a)
9. The Williams (1970) model for developing "thinking and feeling processes"
10. The Taylor (1978) Multiple-Talent Totem Pole Model
11. The U.S.O.E. definition as a curriculum guide

ENRICHMENT TRIAD MODEL

Probably the best known curriculum guide is the *Enrichment Triad Model* originated by Joseph Renzulli (1977). The plan may be implemented with students of any age and in a variety of grouping arrangements. As an overview (see Figure 8.1), the three sequential but qualitatively different steps include: Type I enrichment, general exploratory activities designed to acquaint the student with a variety of topics and interest areas; Type II enrichment, group training activities dealing with the development of "thinking and feeling" processes—for example, creativity and research skills; and Type III enrichment, the investigation of real problems ". . . that are similar in nature to those pursued by authentic researchers or artists in particular fields" (Renzulli, 1977). Importantly, Type I and II activities are considered valuable for—and should be used with—all students. Type III activities, however, are felt to require the special creativity, ability, and energy of truly gifted students.

Type I Enrichment

The three main purposes of Type I enrichment, general exploratory activities, are (1) exposing students to topics that are not a normal part of the school's curriculum, (2) making general enrichment activities available to all interested students, and (3) inviting highly motivated students to find and pursue a later Type III independent project (Reis and Burns, 1987). Gifted students should understand that they are to explore these interest areas purposefully, with a view toward identifying ideas for further study. Some students already will have longstanding interests or hobbies which are well suited for Type III projects (photography, drama, calligraphy, and so on). In these cases, Type I activities serve mainly to expose students to new topic areas.

Resource centers should be well stocked with books, magazines, and other media dealing with a large number of topics. Appendix 8.1 at the end of this chapter, based on ideas from Renzulli (1977) and Reis and Burns (1987), lists well over 200 possibilities, some of which are categories (for example, languages, history). Topics typically are selected jointly by teachers and students and may be studied in groups or individually.

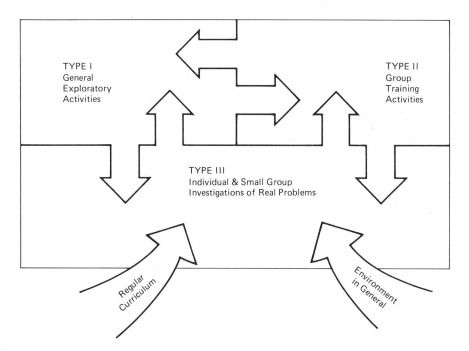

FIGURE 8.1 Renzulli's Enrichment Triad Model.

From J. S. Renzulli, *The Enrichment Triad Model: A Guide for Developing Defensible Programs for the Gifted and Talented.* Mansfield Center, Conn.: Creative Learning Press, 1977. Reprinted by permission.

Another good exploratory activity is field experiences in which gifted and talented students meet dynamic people involved in creative and problem-solving endeavors—artists, actors, engineers, museum and art gallery curators, TV show directors, business leaders, restaurant owners, and so on. This type of field trip goes beyond just visiting an art gallery or planetarium or taking a guided tour through the Schlitz Brewery. The purpose is not to "look at"—Renzulli's "museum experience"—but to *become involved with* professionals and their activities.

The design of Type I exploratory activities will require effort and ingenuity by participating teachers.

Type II Enrichment

The purpose of Type II enrichment—group training activities—is to "... promote the development of a broad range of thinking and feeling processes" (Renzulli and Reis, 1985). While these skills, abilities, attitudes, and strategies should be developed in *all* students, "... an escalation of process development should be a primary goal of programs that serve gifted and talented students" (Renzulli and Reis, 1985). Many of the skills are designed to be relevant to the advanced independent work in Type III projects. For G/T students, Renzulli and Reis especially recommended developing general and specific skills in four categories:

1. Creative thinking, problem solving, critical thinking, decision making, and affective processes such as appreciating and valuing.
2. Learning-how-to-learn skills, such as listening, observing, perceiving, note taking, outlining, interviewing and surveying, analyzing and organizing data, and other research skills.
3. Using advanced-level reference materials, including a variety of print and nonprint references, information retrieval systems, and other procedures for gaining access to advanced resources.
4. Written, oral, and visual communication skills that will be directed toward maximizing the impact of student products upon appropriate audiences.

See Renzulli and Reis (1985) for detailed lists of specific skills within each of these four categories. The development of creativity and other thinking skills are described in Chapters 10, 11, and 12.

Some affective concerns, all of which will be elaborated in Chapter 9, are helping students develop constructive, success-oriented values, especially regarding education; increasing students' awareness of others' perceptions, problems, handicaps, and points of view; helping students develop positive, achievement-oriented self-concepts; and increasing students' motivation, in part by helping them understand that they are in charge of their destinies (internal control).

Renzulli recommends that the process activities of Type II enrichment be related to students' interests and topic areas. For example, within her pet area of photography Cheryl Shutterbug might do creative, analytic, comparative, evaluative, critical, or analogical thinking activities. However, such content relevancy will not always be possible.

Incidentally, many programs for the gifted focus exclusively on the Type II kinds of process activities—creativity, thinking skills, affective development, and others. In their article entitled "Developing Defensible Programs for the Gifted and Talented," Renzulli and Smith (1978a) warn that too strong an emphasis on process activities definitely is not defensible, which brings us to Type III enrichment.

Type III Enrichment

With Type III enrichment activities, the gifted young person becomes an actual researcher investigating a real problem. Renzulli emphasizes that students should act as *producers* of knowledge, not merely consumers of information. They should not simply be asked to consult more encyclopedias, textbooks, or other already-summarized sources and then write a report. They should use raw data as their main information source, from which they draw their own conclusions.

The student should play an active part in formulating the problem, designing the research methods, and planning the final product. The teacher, as the "guide on the side," helps with clarifying the problem, designing the research, and locating materials and equipment, and recommends information sources or community experts.

Outlets for Creations

It is important for students to have audiences for their Type III products. Grown-up artists, scientists, and other professionals do not keep their work to themselves. Indeed, a good part of their motivation and satisfaction derives from at least a limited amount of publicity and public awareness of their accomplishments (Renzulli, Reis, and Smith, 1981). Gifted students also are product-oriented; they wish to hold up their accomplishments and to inform and perhaps influence a particular audience.

Local organizations such as historical societies or science or dramatic groups might be suitable audiences. Also, children's magazines and newspapers routinely publish children's writings and research summaries. Further, there may be children's art shows or science fairs that could be good outlets for the children's or adolescents' products. If such shows are not available, an energetic G/T teacher-coordinator could think about starting some. Local newspapers also like a human-interest story, and good publicity will not hurt any G/T program. Of course, as we noted in Chapter 7, the student's own class is a ready audience for products and reports that are not highly specialized or sophisticated.

As a final note, the triad model by itself continues to serve as a fine guide for curriculum planning in hundreds of programs for gifted students. However, Renzulli recommends that principles and procedures of the model be incorporated within the more comprehensive Revolving Door Identification Model.

REVOLVING DOOR IDENTIFICATION MODEL

Renzulli, Reis, and Smith (1981; see also Delisle and Renzulli, 1982; Renzulli, 1984, 1986) combined Renzulli's three-ring identification model, Enrichment Triad Model, and many other concepts into their *Revolving Door Identification Model* (RDIM). According to one reviewer, "The RDIM probably will be recognized as one of the most significant and revolutionary contributions to gifted education to date. This book is absolutely must reading for anyone who wishes to feel literate in the education of gifted and talented children and adolescents" (Davis, 1981b). At present, it is the single most popular and fastest growing programming model in existence (Renzulli, 1987), and for good reason.

The Revolving Door Identification Model actually is more than an "identification" model, it is a complete programming guide. It includes an identification philosophy and methods, a clear programming plan, and program evaluation procedures. The basic and unique thrust of the RDIM lies in the definition of who is "in" and who is "out" of a school's gifted education program. With the traditional approach, about 5 percent of the school's population is selected in the fall for participation. The selection procedure ends, the names are etched in granite, the students begin participating in the acceleration or enrichment activities, and teachers stop concerning themselves with identifying gifted students until the fall of next year. With the RDIM, about 15 to 20 percent of the school population is selected for a *talent pool*. Students are selected according to whatever criteria the school wishes to use, with the understanding that selection must be flexible and intended to include students, not exclude them (Renzulli, 1987).

All students in the talent pool receive special services—Type I and Type II enrichment activities, along with educational and career counseling and perhaps acceleration. Regular students benefit from whatever creativity, thinking skill, and affective activities—inspired by the RDIM— are brought to the regular classroom.

For students in the talent pool to work on a Type III independent project, all teachers all year must remain alert for students who show ". . . signs of interest, creativity, task commitment, and expressions of advanced ability" (Renzulli, Reis, and Smith, 1981). Note that these traits correspond to Renzulli's three-ring definition of true giftedness: high creativity, high task commitment (motivation), and above-average ability. When a talent pool student surfaces who shows or has developed the creativity and motivation and wishes to work on a project, the teacher sends a "light bulb"—an Action Information Message—to the resource-room teacher. If there is an available slot, the resource teacher meets with the regular teacher and then with the student to decide if the project is a worthwhile one that cannot be completed in the regular classroom. If accepted, the student is *revolved* into the resource room until the project is completed (a few days, weeks, or even months later), and then revolves out again to make room for another person. Experience with the RDIM shows that about 50 to 60 percent of the students in the talent pool actually work on at least one independent Type III project in the resource room each year.

One commendable feature of the RDIM is that *no* student is permanently barred from participation. Any student who shows creativity and high interest in an independent project can be nominated by a teacher, which may result in that student working in the resource room on his or her project and then becoming a bona fide member of the talent pool. In practice, many non-talent-pool students become aware of the RDIM opportunities, wish to become involved, design an independent project, and are permitted to carry it out.

The book *Revolving Door Identification Model* (Renzulli, Reis, and Smith, 1981) presents plenty of step-by-step explanations, examples, case histories, and even solutions to implementation and operating problems. There also are forms for nearly everything—nomination forms, management plans, "light bulbs," class-survey sheets, parent questionnaires, student questionnaires, teacher questionnaires, revolving-in letters (used to inform parents of their child's participation), revolving-out letters (informing parents that the project is complete), and others. Interestingly, many of the forms serve as a system of staff accountability checks, motivating everyone to do their job.

Finally, to reduce worries about not getting the RDIM "exactly right," Renzulli (1984) advised "I would like to emphasize that there is no such thing as a 'pure' Triad/RDIM program. Each school district must examine its own philosophy, resources, and administrative structure and then adopt or adapt those parts of RDIM that take into account the unique differences that exist in each local school and district."

MULTIPLE MENU MODEL

Unlike the type of learning experiences in the Triad and Revolving Door models, Renzulli's (1988) *Multiple Menu Model* focuses on ways to teach content knowledge in efficient and interesting ways. Said Renzulli, the model is a set of planning guides designed to help curriculum developers ". . . identify appropriate content or skills . . . examine various instructional sequences and activity options . . . (and) prepare a blueprint for fitting together the pieces that will allow content and process to work together in a harmonious and effective fashion."

The five planning "menus" are designed to provide guidance for designing curriculum that is consistent with the goals of gifted education.

Knowledge menu. The knowledge menu received the most attention in Renzulli's (1988) description. Rather than choices, this menu recommends a desirable sequence for teaching knowledge in a particular area.

The menu includes four subcategories or steps:

First, *location, definition, and organization* introduces the learner to ". . . the general nature of a field, the various subdivisions of knowledge within that field, and the specific mission and characteristics of any given subdivision . . . (and) . . . helps the learner see the big picture." Using a branching diagram that visually illustrates the organization of a field of study, the curriculum developer would address the purposes of a field; subareas of concentration; kinds of questions asked in subareas; sources of data; basic reference books and professional journals; major data bases; major events, persons, places, and beliefs; and insiders' humor, trivia, scandals, etc.

Second are *basic principles and functional concepts.* Basic principles are generally agreed upon truths in an area (for example, the earth orbits the sun every 365¼ days). The functional concepts largely serve as the vocabulary of a field as found in a glossary.

Third, *knowledge about specifics* refers to important facts, conventions, trends, classifications, criteria, principles and generalizations, and theories and structures that comprise a field. About 95 percent of the information in a field will be in this "warehouse of information," according to Renzulli.

Fourth, *knowledge about methodology* refers to standard investigative procedures in an area, namely, how to identify problems, state hypotheses, identify data sources, locate or construct data-gathering instruments, summarize and analyze data, draw conclusions, and report findings.

Instructional objectives/student activities menu.   The first of four subsections of the instructional objectives/student activities menu, *assimilation and retention,* refers to information input processes: listening, observing, touching, reading, manipulating, note-taking, etc. The second section of the menu, *information analysis,* suggests ". . . ways information can be processed in order to achieve greater levels of understanding," for example, classifying, ordering, gathering data, interpreting, exploring alternatives, and concluding and explaining. The third section, *information synthesis and application,* deals with the output or products of the thinking processes, for example, writing, speaking, constructing, or performing. Finally, the fourth subsection, *evaluation,* concerns review and judgment of information according to personal values or conventional standards.

Instructional strategies menu.   The instructional strategies menu itemizes teaching and learning options familiar to all teachers: drill and recitation, lecture, discussion, peer tutoring, learning center activity, simulation and role playing, learning games, and others.

Instructional sequence menu.   The instructional sequence menu deals with the organization and sequence of events that help maximize the outcomes of planned learning activities. Based on Gagne's (1974) conditions of learning model, this fixed-sequence menu includes gaining attention, informing students of objectives, relating the topic to previously learned material, presenting the material (with either passive or participative student roles), assessing performance and providing feedback, and providing opportunities for transfer and application.

Artistic modification menu. Finally, Renzulli recommends that teachers ". . . make their own creative contribution" to the lesson to increase interest and excitement. The artistic modification menu suggests sharing personal knowledge, experiences, beliefs, insiders' information, interpretations, controversies, biases or ". . . additional ways teachers might personalize the material."

Many of the components of the multiple menu model are standard good teaching practices (Davis and Thomas, 1988). However, as Renzulli states, it does ". . . direct us to consider a broad range of options, and to interrelate the many factors that must be considered when attempting to achieve balance and comprehensiveness in curriculum development." For teachers of the gifted, the Multiple Menu Model provides an organizational framework for the creative development of special curriculum in areas that are not typically covered in ordinary school programming.

PYRAMID PROJECT

The *Pyramid Project,* largely an organizational plan, grew from many of the conclusions and recommendations of the Richardson Study, a survey of existing programs (Cox, Daniel, and Boston, 1985; R. D. Feldman, 1985). Some pertinent conclusions were: Many current programs for the gifted make no provision for the brightest and most creative youngsters; rigid cutoff scores unreasonably exclude many able learners; many programs are fragmented and discontinuous; and the popular pull-out plan, found in 70 percent of all elementary gifted programs, is a ". . . part-time solution to a full-time problem" and is costly and divisive, for example, causing students to miss work they need or to make up work they do not need (Feldman, 1985).

Said Cox, the goal of the Pyramid Project is to provide appropriate instruction for all capable students of all ages, from above-average to the highly gifted, in all subjects every day (Feldman, 1985). In agreement with Renzulli (1986) that more than just 3 to 5 percent of students are "gifted," about a fourth of all students are included as "able learners."

As represented in the broad base of the pyramid in Figure 8.2, the largest numbers of able learners receive advanced material in the regular classroom, for example, using learning centers, cluster grouping, cross-grade grouping, resource room enrichment and projects, and curriculum compacting (covering material continuously and rapidly). Cox noted that classroom teachers can do the job of enrichment if they get training, support, and guidance. She recommends Renzulli's Enrichment Triad model as a good curriculum guide (Feldman, 1985).

Moving to the midsection of the pyramid, a smaller group of superior students are placed in full-time special classes. For example, honors classes

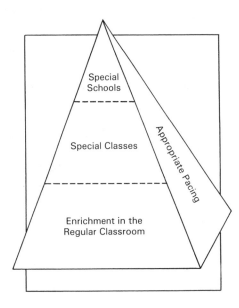

FIGURE 8.2   The Pyramid Concept.

Reprinted from *Educating Able Learners: Programs and Promising Practices* by June Cox, Neil Daniel, and Bruce O. Boston, copyright © 1985. Reprinted by permission of J. Cox, Gifted Students Institute, and the University of Texas Press.

may be created or students can participate in dual enrollment—elementary students can enroll concurrently in middle school for their strongest subjects, middle school students can enroll in high school, and high school students may take college courses.

At the top of the pyramid a still smaller number of students with even more specialized needs (for example, in science or art) are served by special magnet or residential schools.

Note that the divisions between levels are represented by dotted (not solid) lines. The divisions are thus tentative and flexible. Said Cox, "Ability is on a continuum. There is no clear break between 'gifted' and 'not gifted' and sometimes an individual moves back and forth" (Feldman, 1985).

The plan requires committees of teachers and administrators, continuous staff development, longitudinal team planning, interdisciplinary planning, special clerical help, and cooperation among parents, administrators, and teachers.

FELDHUSEN'S THREE-STAGE ENRICHMENT MODEL

Feldhusen's *three-stage enrichment model* (Feldhusen and Kolloff, 1981, 1986; Kolloff and Feldhusen, 1984) centers upon three types of instructional activities aimed at three levels of skill development. While teaching for creative development clearly is central, the training also aims at strengthening convergent problem solving, research skills and, importantly, independent learning.

Stage 1 focuses upon the development of *basic divergent and convergent thinking abilities.* The corresponding instructional activities include relatively short-term, teacher-led exercises mainly in creative thinking but also in logical and critical thinking. Some creativity exercises are, for example, listing unusual uses for trash bags, thinking of improvements for a bicycle, predicting outcomes of unlikely events (What would happen if there were no television or no McDonald's?), or ". . . designing a vehicle of the future using anything you might find in a junkyard" (Kolloff and Feldhusen, 1981). Such exercises are assumed to develop such creative abilities as ideational fluency, originality, flexibility, and elaboration, along with other relevant abilities and attitudes.

Stage 2 of the model requires *more complex creative and problem-solving activities* that (1) may extend over a longer period of time and, importantly, (2) require less teacher direction and more student initiative. Some suggested examples were learning and practicing creative-thinking techniques, such as brainstorming and the *synectics* methods (Chapter 11); working through a systematic problem-solving model (for example, defining the problem, listing ideas, evaluating ideas, implementing the solution); and working through the detective mysteries of the *Productive Thinking Program* (Covington, Crutchfield, Olton, and Davies, 1972).

Stage 3 activities aim at strengthening *independent learning abilities.* Said Feldhusen and Kolloff (1981), "Stage 3 projects should involve gifted youngsters in challenging efforts to define and clarify a problem, ambitious data gathering from books and other resources, interpretation of findings, and the development of creative ways of communicating results." Some examples of Stage 3 projects are writing haiku, short stories, or plays (which are produced), investigating alternate waste disposal systems (which one group presented to the Lafayette City Council), and researching backgrounds of community leaders (which one group presented on local radio).

Feldhusen's Stage 3 activities are designed for students with achievement levels in the sixtieth to eightieth percentile and IQs between 110 and 140. Higher-ability students, argue Feldhusen and Kolloff, might well be accelerated in grade-skipping or early admission programs, college courses in high school, or Talent Search types of advanced programs.

GUILFORD/MEEKER STRUCTURE OF INTELLECT MODEL

Guilford's (1967, 1977) structure of intellect (SOI) model has a well established niche in American theories of intelligence. The model is summarized as a cube comprised of three dimensions, *contents, products,* and *operations* (Figure 8.3). Each of 120 cells of the 1967 model represents a unique cognitive ability. Joy Paul Guilford has invested over three decades creating tests that measure each one of those 120 abilities.

As an example, the darkened slab of the model in Figure 8.3 includes the operations of *divergent production*. Somewhere in that slab will be a cell identified as the "divergent production (operation) of symbolic (content) units (product)," or just *DSU*. Some tests of DSU—or *Word Fluency*—ask the examinee to list words with the first and last letters specified (for example, R_____M); list words that include one, two, or three specified letters; or list words that rhyme with a specified word (for example, *roam*).

Mary Meeker's (1969; Meeker and Meeker, 1986; Meeker, Meeker, and Roid, 1985) curriculum model amounts to a diagnostic-prescriptive approach to evaluating and strengthening SOI abilities that she believes are

FIGURE 8.3   The Guilford (1967) Structure of Intellect Model.

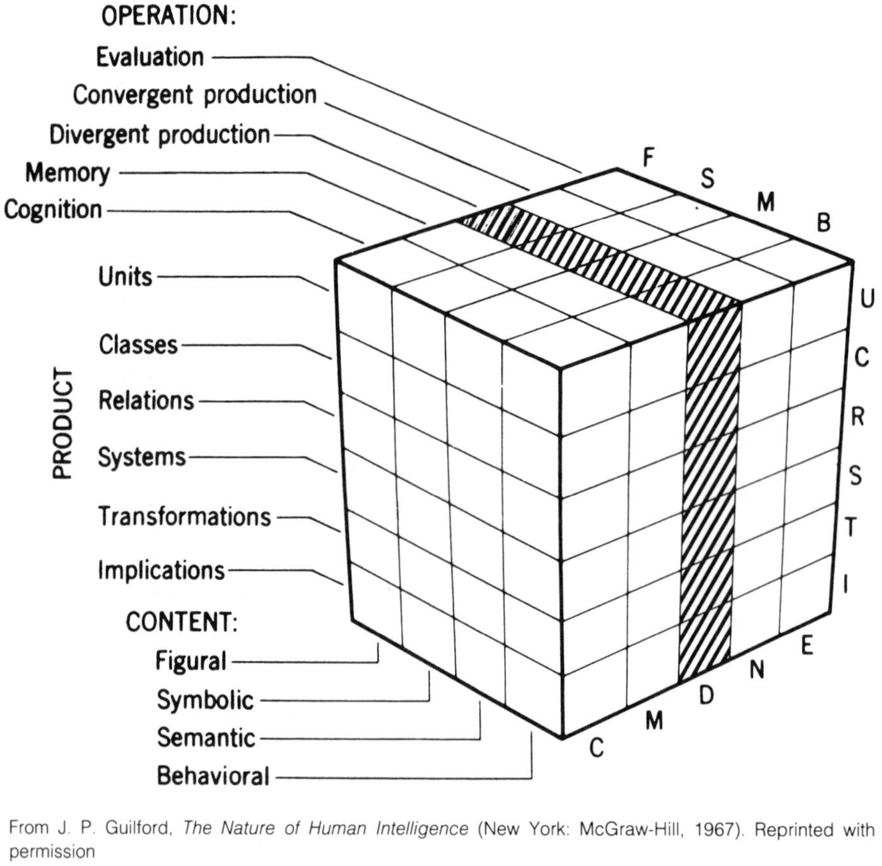

From J. P. Guilford, *The Nature of Human Intelligence* (New York: McGraw-Hill, 1967). Reprinted with permission

particularly crucial for school learning. In her own words, the "SOI design is simple":

1. Identify the abilities required for the learning of reading or arithmetic or math or requisites for any given job.
2. Test for those abilities.
3. Teach any abilities that are low, maintain those that are gifted, and develop further those that are average.
4. Compare the level of performance with and without SOI training to document the difference it can make.

Meeker's *SOI-Learning Abilities* test (SOI-LA; Meeker, Meeker, and Roid, 1985) measures 26 of Guilford's SOI abilities said to be central to reading, math, writing, creativity, and critical thinking. For example, reading readiness is said to require the abilities of Cognition of Figural Units (CFU), Memory for Semantic Systems-Visual (MSS-v), and others. Arithmetic demands such abilities as Cognition of Symbolic Systems (CSS), Memory for Symbolic Units-Auditory (MSU-a), and others. Critical thinking is said to require Evaluation of Semantic Implications (EMI), Convergent Production of Semantic Transformations (NMT), and others.

An SOI Profile, based upon the SOI-LA test—or SOI scores derived from the Stanford-Binet, WISC-R, Slosson, or *Detroit Test of Learning Abilities* (see Meeker, 1969; Meeker and Meeker, 1986)—summarizes an individual's ". . . pattern of intelligence." This pattern or profile serves to diagnose weaknesses that are remediated via individual and group tasks in five workbooks, one each for *cognition, memory, convergent production, divergent production,* and *evaluation* (Meeker, 1976). For example, brainstorming and other ideational tasks would be used for students weak in divergent production skills. Critical-thinking activities are used to strengthen both cognition and evaluation operations. After a teacher (or parent) becomes comfortable with the SOI model and the recommended tasks, he or she will be able to select other instructional materials that provide training beyond the exercises in the workbooks.

Meeker's SOI approach presents a different perspective on the conceptualization and identification of gifted and talented students, both majority and minority. Meeker (1978) argued that Anglo children, even before they enter school, have the cognitive abilities necessary for learning— for example, those itemized earlier. However, minority children from non-English-speaking, low-education, low-income families often do not. Therefore, with identification based upon intelligence tests, minority children often are excluded from participation in gifted programs. Within the multifaceted SOI theory, however, Meeker finds that non-Anglos—Native American, Hispanic American, and black students—score higher on different SOI abilities than Anglo children. Selection for program participation may be based upon these high, measured abilities.

TREFFINGER'S MODEL FOR INCREASING SELF-DIRECTEDNESS

It would seem self-evident that children, throughout their educational lives, are told what, when, how, and where to learn. Further, their learning almost always is evaluated by others. They cannot be expected to suddenly become efficient, self-initiated, and self-directed learners with little or no experience or training. Even though gifted children typically are more independent and self-directed than others, many still require help in developing the skills and attitudes necessary for independent study or research.

Donald Treffinger (1975, 1978; Treffinger and Barton, 1979; see also Treffinger, 1986) developed a seemingly logical four-step plan for teaching increasing degrees of independent, self-initiated learning. (1) In the initial teacher-directed step (*command style*), the teacher prescribes the activities for the entire class or for individual students. The working time, location, end product, and evaluation criteria also are teacher determined. (2) In the first self-directed step (*task style*), the teacher creates learning activities or project alternatives (for example, learning centers) from which students make a selection. (3) In the second self-directed step (*peer-partner style*), students assume a more active role, participating in decisions about their learning activities, goals, and evaluation. The teacher ". . . involves the pupils in creating choices and options concerning what will be learned" (Treffinger, 1975). For example, the teacher discusses with the class topics or projects for individual or group work. (4) Finally, in the *self-directed style* students are able to create the choices, make the selection, and carry out the activity—in a self-selected location over a self-selected period of time. The student also evaluates his or her own progress. Of course, the teacher is available to assist.

Students naturally differ in their abilities and experience in directing their own work. Therefore, the teacher must determine the level of self-directedness for which a student is ready. Treffinger (1975) provides checklists designed to help identify the level of help a given student requires. For example, a student would be ready for the fourth stage of self-directedness activity if (1) the student can evaluate progress mainly without teacher advice, and (2) the student can identify strengths and weaknesses in his or her own work or products using the same criteria others would use.

As some general recommendations for fostering self-directedness, Treffinger (1978) suggested:

1. Do not smother self-direction by doing things for children that they can do (or can learn to do) for themselves.
2. Develop an attitude of openness and support for self-directed learning.
3. Emphasize the interrelatedness and continuity of knowledge to help students synthesize and relate various topics and problems.
4. Provide training in problem solving and skills of inquiry and independent

research; that is, help students learn to diagnose needs, develop a plan, locate resources, carry out appropriate activities, evaluate and present the results.

5. Treat difficult situations at school or home as opportunities for independent problem solving, not as problems requiring the unilateral wisdom of an adult.

AUTONOMOUS LEARNER MODEL: BETTS

While Treffinger's model outlines four steps for increasing self-directedness, George Betts's (1985a) *Autonomous Learner Model* (ALM) is more of a total programming guide. As reflected in the title, of course, the main focus of Betts's ALM is to help students become independent, autonomous, self-directed learners. While the model originally was designed for secondary students, it may be used in elementary G/T programs. In junior or senior high school the ALM would be installed as an elective course; in the elementary school it would be incorporated into a resource room/pull-out plan with students meeting two days per week for about 2½ hours per meeting.

Said Betts (1985; Betts and Knapp, 1981), the *Autonomous Learner Model* for the gifted and talented (K–12) was designed to help students develop more positive self-concepts, comprehend their own giftedness, develop social skills, increase their knowledge in a variety of subject areas, develop their thinking, decision-making and problem-solving skills, demonstrate responsibility for their own learning in and out of school, and ultimately become responsible, creative, independent learners. Such goals square very well with purposes of G/T programs.

Space will not permit a complete explanation of the details of Betts's model; the interested reader should see Betts (1985) and Betts and Knapp (1981). As an overview, the *Autonomous Learner Model* divides into the five major dimensions summarized in Figure 8.4: Orientation, Individual Development, Enrichment Activities, Seminars, and In-Depth Study.

Orientation. The orientation dimension aims at acquainting students, teachers, administrators, and parents with central concepts in gifted education (for example, the nature of giftedness and creativity) and the specifics of the *Autonomous Learner Model* (for example, program goals, opportunities, expectations). Students learn more about themselves and what the program has to offer.

Group building and self-understanding exercises give students an opportunity to learn more about each other and themselves and about group processes. A sample exercise is "starve your vulture," best used in an overnight retreat. A "vulture" lives on two types of food—self put-downs and put-downs by others. As your vulture (who lives in your stomach) gets fat on these put-downs, your self-esteem is reduced. After the details of

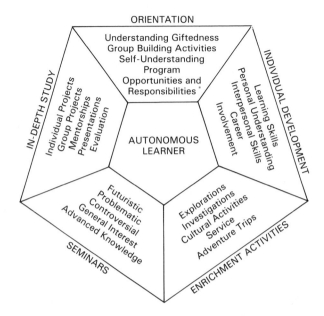

FIGURE 8.4   Autonomous Learner Model (Betts, 1985).
Reprinted by permission of the author and Autonomous Learning Publications.

vultures and put-downs are reviewed, students participate in a "Starve Your Vulture" campaign, with signs and stories about the vulture. Statistics are kept on how frequently students feed or starve their own vulture.

Individual development.   The individual development dimension of the ALM focuses more clearly on developing skills, concepts, and attitudes that promote lifelong independent, autonomous learning. As shown in Figure 8.4, four basic concerns are learning skills (for example, thinking skills and research skills), personal understanding (for example, of strengths and weaknesses), interpersonal skills (for example, communication and leadership skills), and career development (exploration).

Enrichment activities.   Betts's third dimension of enrichment activities focuses on "student-based content," that is, students decide what they want to study. Students already may have preferred topics, or "passion areas," that they wish to pursue. They also study "related passion areas" plus unrelated areas. Students may explore an area and make a presentation about it to the group; they may conduct a research-type investigation; they may participate in cultural activities, such as visiting a museum, play, concert, speech, or art display; they may perform a service, such as working with the elderly or collecting food or money for shut-ins;

or they may plan an "adventure trip," such as studying the geology and archaeology of the Grand Canyon or the cultural aspects of San Francisco.

Seminars.   The seminar dimension is designed to give each person in a small group of three to five students the opportunity to research a topic, present it in a seminar format to the rest of the group and perhaps others, and evaluate their seminar according to criteria selected by the group. Students learn to proceed through three steps of presenting general information to the audience to promote understanding of the topic; facilitating discussion of the topic to involve the audience in thinking; and bringing the discussion and activities to a close.

In-depth study.   Finally, in the fifth ALM dimension of in-depth study students pursue areas of interest in long-term individual or small-group studies. These activities resemble Renzulli Type III projects, and students decide what will be learned, what help will be necessary, what the final product will be, how it will be presented, and how the entire learning process will be evaluated.

Overall, the *Autonomous Learner Model* is a very reasonable programming guide that has been installed in many school districts in the United States and Canada. However, Betts cautioned (1985a), "Because of the newness of the ALM [it was developed in 1980], the total effectiveness is not known at this time. Research is needed. . . ."

THE WILLIAMS MODEL FOR DEVELOPING THINKING AND FEELING PROCESSES

Frank Williams (1970, 1982, 1986) developed a curriculum model that originally was intended to help teachers enrich educational programs for all students. While not designed specifically for G/T students, it is widely used in gifted programs.

The Williams approach, summarized in Figure 8.5, is based on three dimensions that may be described as *content, strategy,* and *process* (Williams, 1979). Dimension 1 is *Curriculum (Subject Matter Content),* with the six levels of art, music, science, social studies, arithmetic, and language. Dimension 2 is *Teacher Behavior (Strategies or Modes of Teaching)* and includes 18 activities and skills (defined in Table 8.1) that teachers may use to teach skills in any of the 6 content areas.

Dimension 3—containing the "thinking and feeling processes" for which Williams is famous—is called *Pupil Behaviors.* Its eight levels include the four *Cognitive (Intellective)* processes of fluency, flexibility, originality, and elaboration, plus the four *Affective (Feeling)* processes of curiosity (willingness), risk taking (courage), complexity (challenge), and imagination

**A Model for Implementing Cognitive-Affective
Behaviors in the Classroom**

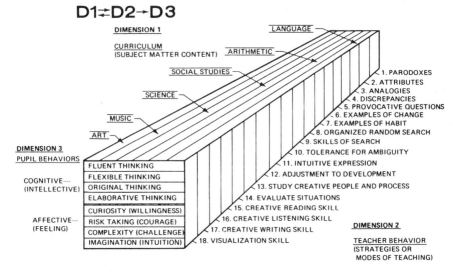

FIGURE 8.5   The Williams Model.

From F. Williams, "Classroom Ideas for Encouraging Thinking and Feeling." (Buffalo, N.Y.:
D.O.K. Publishers, Inc.).

(intuition). The "D Formula" in Figure 8.4 indicates that curriculum content (D1) interacts with teaching strategies (D2) to produce the pupil behaviors (D3).

Now with 6 subject matters, 18 teaching activities, and 8 thinking and feeling processes, there are a total of 864 (6 × 18 × 8) combinations of classroom activities. Williams (1970) outlines no fewer than 387 activities and tasks designed (1) for a specific subject matter, (2) using one of the teaching methods, and (3) intended to strengthen one of the thinking or feeling skills. Some of the learning activities are considered appropriate for several cells in the Figure 8.5 model.

The Williams Model and the Enrichment Triad Model

We mentioned earlier that G/T programming methods and strategies may be combined. Williams (1979) himself outlined how the Renzulli Enrichment Triad Model may be combined with his own curriculum model. Indeed, the two seem to complement each other very well. Said Williams, "One is a guide for what should be done, the other a multi-strategy approach for how to get it done. The Renzulli model provides direction, the Williams model yields results." The latter claim may not be an entirely unbiased one.

With just a little pencil work, Williams's 18 teaching strategies can be rearranged into Renzulli Types I and II activities good for all students, plus some Type III strategies judged by Williams to be appropriate for gifted, talented, and creative students. It's all in Table 8.1. See Williams (1979) for specific examples of Renzulli/Williams Types I, II, and III activities.

THE TAYLOR MULTIPLE-TALENT TOTEM POLE MODEL

In Chapter 1 we reviewed Taylor's (1978) *Multiple Talent Totem Poles* as a definition of giftedness, one that argues that if you look at enough talents, virtually everyone will be at least above average (if not outstanding) in something. His six totem pole talents, *academic ability, creativity, planning, communicating, forecasting,* and *decision making* (see Figure 1.2, Chapter 1), also may be used as the basis for curriculum planning. That is, one would design activities and exercises aimed at strengthening each of the six talent areas.

Eberle (1974) designed a "flip book" that explains how the teacher can prepare learning activities and questioning strategies for each of Taylor's talent areas. For example: *Communication* focuses upon teaching the communicator to (1) express him- or herself clearly and effectively in spoken, written, or artistic forms; (2) develop ideas fully and completely; (3) observe clues and analyze feelings; (4) show respect for individuality; (5) avoid being too personal or offensive; and (6) receive and understand information effectively. The teacher can have students "Summarize the story . . .," "Give an explanation for . . .," "Describe your feelings about . . .," "Have your painting express joy . . .," "Show how . . .," "Explain why . . .," and "Draw a map showing. . . ."

Planning (and organizing) strategies aim to teach students to (1) identify desired goals and outcomes; (2) understand the need for a step-by-step procedure; (3) get needed information and materials; and (4) generally formulate, design, arrange, and visualize methods or procedures. The teacher can have students "Develop a plan for . . .," "Prepare a budget for . . .," "Develop a timetable for . . .," and so on.

Forecasting (and predicting) activities try to teach students to (1) clearly perceive cause and effects; (2) view situations objectively, (3) anticipate effects and outcomes; (4) reorganize past knowledge and experience; and (5) be socially aware and sensitive to actions that would affect a situation. The teacher thus can ask students, "Foretell the outcome of a story," "Tell what you think _____ will be like in 20 years," and "Tell what would happen if. . . ."

The teaching of *decision making* (and evaluation) revolved around teaching students to (1) weigh consequences; (2) remain emotionally neu-

TABLE 8.1   Classification of Williams's Strategies Across Renzulli-type Activities

TYPE I ACTIVITIES: EXPLORATION STRATEGIES

Paradoxes	Self-contradictory statements or observations
Attributes	Inherent properties, traits or characteristics
Analogies	Similarities or situations of likeness
Discrepancies	Unknown elements or missing links
Provocative Questions	Inquiries bringing forth exploration or discovery
Examples of Change	Exploring the dynamics of things by alterations, modifications or substitutions
Examples of Habit	Sensing rigidity and habit-bound thinking

TYPE II ACTIVITIES: TRAINING STRATEGIES

Organized Random Search	Organized structure randomly leading to a production
Skills of Search	Skills of historical, descriptive, or experimental search
Study Creative People-Process	Analyze traits and study processes of eminent people
Evaluate Situations	Setting criteria, deciding, critical thinking
Creative Reading Skill	Idea generation through reading
Creative Listening Skill	Idea generation through listening
Creative Writing Skill	Self expression through writing
Visualization Skill	Expressing ideas in visual form

TYPE III ACTIVITIES: PRODUCTION STRATEGIES

Tolerance for Ambiguity	Tolerating open-ended situations without forcing closure
Intuitive Expression	Sensing inward hunches and expressing emotional feelings
Adjustment to Development	Developing from rather than adjusting to experiences or situations
Evaluate Situations	Deciding upon solutions and productions by consequences and implications
Creative Writing Skill	Self-expression through written production
Visualization Skill	Expressing ideas in visual form

Frank Williams, "Williams' Strategies to Orchestrate Renzulli's Triad," *G/C/T* (Sept.-Oct. 1979), 2–6, 10. Reprinted by permission.

tral; (3) withhold early judgment; (4) consider more than one course of action; (5) apply evaluative criteria; (6) make a decision, defend it, and act accordingly; and others. Some exercises would include asking students to "Examine all possibilities . . .," "Appraise the situation . . .," "Make a choice and justify your selection," "Support your decision . . .," "Select the best . . .," and "You be the judge, rule on the situation, and explain why."

Slichter's (1986a, 1986b, 1987) *Talents Unlimited* in-service training model also is based upon Taylor's totem poles. The plan basically acquaints teachers with Taylor's model, describes exercises for strengthening the six totem pole talents, and allows practice planning and teaching the totem pole talents. For example, *creativity* is strengthened by having students generate ideas and add details; *decision making* involves having students weigh information, make judgments, and defend decisions; *planning* involves designing the means to implement an idea, identifying needed resources, planning the steps, and pinpointing possible problems; *forecasting* involves having students make predictions about the possible causes and/or effects of various phenomena; teaching *communication* can focus on using and interpreting verbal and nonverbal forms of communication to express ideas, feelings and needs; and *academic* talent is strengthened via acquiring information and concepts to form a good knowledge base in a given topic.

THE U.S.O.E. DEFINITION AS A CURRICULUM GUIDE

Normally, the six-part U.S. Office of Education statement is used to define gifted and talented and to guide identification procedures. However, some have used the six categories as a type of curriculum guide. This general approach leaves the reader with the task of figuring out how to implement it; some categories will be easier than others. As you might guess, learning activities are planned in each of the general areas of (1) general intellectual ability, (2) specific academic talent, (3) creative thinking, (4) leadership, (5) visual and performing arts, and perhaps (6) psychomotor ability. We wish you the best of luck.

Final Comment

The thoughtful program planner should consider all of the models in this chapter, along with specific strategies for acceleration, enrichment, grouping, counseling, career education, affective development, the teaching of creativity, critical thinking and other thinking skills, and other possibilities. Select what seems to best meet the needs of the students in your district or school. There can be no single "best" program; aim for the best combination for your particular situation.

SUMMARY

Some of the ten models in the chapter make specific procedural recommendations; others make general suggestions.

The Renzulli Enrichment Triad Model includes enrichment Types I, II, and III. Type I enrichment—general exploratory activities—is intended to expose students to a variety of topics. Type II enrichment—group-training activities—tries to teach creative, critical, analytic, and evaluative thinking; good self-concepts, values, and motivation; and library and research skills. Type III enrichment consists of individual and small-group investigations of real problems. Types I and II are recommended for all students, but Type III is primarily appropriate for G/T students only.

The Revolving Door Identification Model is a complete programming guide. A talent pool consists of about 15 to 20 percent of the school population. All talent pool students receive Types I and II enrichment. Motivated talent-pool students (and sometimes others) revolve into a resource room to work on projects.

Renzulli's Multiple Menu Model is a series of five planning guides or "menus" that suggest sequences and alternatives for teaching content efficiently: a knowledge menu, instructional objectives/student activities menu, instructional strategies menu, instructional sequence menu, and an artistic modification menu.

The pyramid project is a three-level schooling plan intended to overcome many criticisms of G/T programs, especially the popular pull-out plan. Above-average students are mainstreamed in the regular classroom, more able students are placed in full-time special classes, and the most able students attend magnet or residential schools.

Feldhusen's three-stage enrichment model focuses mainly on fostering creative thinking, but also on research and independent-learning skills and positive self-concepts. Stage 1 involves short-term teacher-led exercises in creative, critical, and logical thinking. Stage 2 requires more complex thinking, such as learning creative thinking techniques. Stage 3 activities focus on independent learning by challenging students to define a problem, gather data (from books or other resources), and creatively report the findings.

The Guilford Structure of Intellect Model is a theory of intelligence based upon 120 combinations of 5 operations, 6 products, and 4 contents. Meeker uses 26 abilities from the Guilford SOI model to guide the diagnosis and remediation of specific learning abilities, particularly those related to reading, mathematics, writing, and creativity. The abilities are measured by the SOI-Learning Abilities test or by scores derived from the Binet, WISC-R, or other individual intelligence test. The SOI approach also may be used for identifying gifted minority and disadvantaged students.

Treffinger outlined four steps in increasing self-directedness. (1) The command style is totally teacher directed; (2) in the task style students select from among teacher-prepared activities; (3) the peer-partner style includes more student decisions about learning goals, activities, and evaluation; (4) in the self-directed style students create the choices, make the selections, and choose the location and the amount of working time. Some general recommendations for fostering self-directedness included encouraging self-directedness, providing training in problem solving and inquiry, and using home problems as an opportunity for independent problem solving.

Betts's Autonomous Learner Model, a relatively complete programming guide, includes the five main dimensions of orienting students and others to giftedness and to the content and purposes of the program; individual development in areas of learning skills, personal understanding, interpersonal skills, and career development; student-selected enrichment activities; seminars; and individual or small-group in-depth studies.

The Williams model includes classroom activities suggested by many combinations of subject-matter content (6 types), teaching strategies (18 types), and the 8 thinking and feeling processes themselves. Williams explains how his 18 teaching strategies may be classified according to the 3 categories of the Enrichment Triad Model.

The Taylor Multiple-Talent Totem Pole Model suggests that learning activities focus upon developing academic ability, creativity, planning/organizing, communicating, forecasting/predicting, and decision making/evaluating. Slichter's Talents Unlimited program trains teachers to teach Taylor's totem pole talents.

Similarly, the U.S.O.E. definition of gifts and talents suggests the general G/T curriculum categories of general intellectual ability, specific academic talent, creative thinking, leadership, visual and performing arts, and perhaps psychomotor ability.

There is no "best" G/T program. Each must be designed to meet the needs of particular gifted students.

APPENDIX 8.1 POSSIBLE TOPICS FOR ENRICHMENT ACTIVITIES

VISUAL ARTS, PERFORMING ARTS

Acting	Antiques
Architecture	Art history
Art appreciation	Art in various cultures
Artists	Batik

APPENDIX 8.1 (continued)

Ballet
Candle making
Cartooning
Folk art
Dance, choreography
Designing (clothes, toys, machines, etc.)
Folk music
Graphics
Leather craft
Mime, pantomime
Music composition
Musical instruments
Opera
Photography, cameras
Political satire
Print making
Radio shows
Sculpture (clay, metal, wood, etc.)
Silk screening
Television

Calligraphy
Costume design
Folk music
Dance history
Drawing
Film making (animation, drama)
Jewelry making
Macrame
Movie making
Music history
Musicians
Painting
Plays
Pottery, ceramics
Puppet making
Rug hooking
Shakespeare
Slide show making
Soft sculpture
Weaving

Theatre—dramatic production, acting techniques, dramatic literature, set design, lighting, creative dramatics, improvisational theatre, history of theatre, make-up

MATH, SCIENCE, COMPUTERS

Aeronautics
Anatomy
Animals, animal behavior
Aquarium planning
Botany
Chemistry
Computer repair
Diseases
Electricity, electronics
Engineering
Evolution
Forestry
Geology
Ichthyology

Agriculture
Archaeology
Astronomy
Biology
Brain science
Computer programming
Conservation
Ecology
Energy—solar, geothermal, tidal, wind, etc.
Fossils
Genetics
Horticulture
Marine biology

APPENDIX 8.1 *(continued)*

Math—algebra, geometry, measurement, math puzzles, statistics, probability
Microbiology
Minerology, rocks
Natural resources
Nutrition
Ornithology
Physiology
Prehistoric animals
Robots
Scientists
Space, space travel

Medicine, health
Metals
Meteorology
Microscopes
Money management
Nuclear energy
Optics, optometry
Physics
Pollution
Reptiles
Rocketry
Solar power
Veterinary science

LITERATURE, WRITING, COMMUNICATION

Broadcasting
Literature appreciation
Mythology
Play writing
Short story writing
Sports writing
Word processing

Journalism
Mysteries
Poetry writing
Public speaking
Speed reading
Typing

SOCIAL SCIENCES, CULTURE, LANGUAGE

Alcohol, drug abuse
Anthropology
Archaeology
Black history
Children, child development
Contemporary cultures
Current events
Debate
Editorial writing
Etymology
Festivals, holidays
Foreign languages
Geology
Government (U.S., foreign)

Ancient Egypt, Greece, Rome, China
Aztecs, Mayas, Incas
Careers
Civil rights
Crime, criminology, prisons
Death, dying
Divorce
Elections, voting
Famous people
Folklore
Future thinking
Geography, mapping
Handicapped people
Humor

APPENDIX 8.1 *(continued)*

History (local, state, U.S., Russian, military, etc.)

Legends, myths

Minority groups

Parapsychology, occult

Philosophy

Political cartoons

Prehistoric life

Problems of the elderly

Public opinion surveys

Social problems

Sociology

Women's rights

Law, courts

Linguistics

Newspapers

Poetry

Political science

Population problems

Presidents

Psychology, mental illness

Religion

Sign language

Travel

BUSINESS, ECONOMICS

Accounting

Banking

Economics (models, theories)

Insurance

Operating a small business

Transportation, trucking

Advertising

Careers

Finance

Law, lawyers

Stock market

MISCELLANEOUS

Bridge

Careers

Coins, stamps

Creativity

History of football

Interior decorating

Law enforcement

Running

Test taking

Bicycles, bicycling

Chess

College preparation

Gardening

Horses

Karate

Magic

Sailing

chapter nine

Affective Learning and Leadership

This chapter looks at two important goals of programs for G/T students: affective learning and leadership. *Affective learning* is a broad category that includes students' self-concepts, self-esteem, moral thinking, attitudes, values, personal adjustment, social adjustment, self-motivated learning, and such interrelated humanistic matters as self-actualization and a democratic concern for the welfare of others.

Leadership has not received much attention in gifted education, despite its inclusion as one of the five U.S. Office of Education categories of gifts and talents. In recent years several programs and strategies have emerged for clarifying the nature of leadership and specifying how leadership traits and skills can be taught to gifted and other students. Of special interest are the Karnes and Chauvin (1987) and the Richardson and Feldhusen (1986) programs reviewed later in this chapter.

AFFECTIVE LEARNING

In our early discussion of characteristics of gifted and talented children we noted that, compared with the average, G/T students are better able to understand moral issues and to be honest, truthful, and ethical. If they are moderate-to-high achievers, they are also likely to have good self-concepts, high self-esteem, and reasonably high levels of achievement needs. Nonetheless, just as we try to strengthen·the cognitive skills of students who already are cognitively superior, we also can help affectively superior students to better understand themselves and their values, to be more empathic towards others, and to generally acquire high-level values, ethics, achievement needs, and humanistic attitudes.

It also is true that some gifted students do go astray morally and legally, and many drop out of high school and college. They forfeit both their full development and self-actualization and their potential contributions to society.

The following five subsections will examine, first, the nature of the self-concept—how it is formed and how its protection can lead to subtle defensive behaviors. The next will look briefly at how the classic Kohlberg (1974) stages in moral development can serve as a guide for teaching moral and ethical thinking. The remaining sections review curriculum content and strategies for imparting constructive attitudes, awarenesses, values, and humanistic thinking, and qualities of a humanistic teacher.

THE SELF-CONCEPT

Feelings of personal competence and self-esteem are closely tied to experiences of success. For adults, there are many types of success experience that can strengthen feelings of adequacy and self-esteem—for example, job or career success, or success as a parent or church member, as a home decorator or union member, and so on. For children, however, the school setting looms very large: Feedback from schoolwork and the teacher is extremely important in telling each child whether he or she is a capable, competent, and worthwhile little person. The following are some dynamics of self-concept development:

1. Developing a healthy self-concept in school is a goal in itself. Moreover, because a student who feels capable and confident will be more motivated and will have higher academic and career aspirations, promoting good self-concepts also is a means of stimulating higher school achievement (Bloom, 1977; Davis, 1983).
2. There are many facets of the self. A person may perceive an academic self, a social self, an emotional self, and a physical self (Jordon, 1981). Gifted students sometimes have better academic selves than social selves (Ross and Parker, 1980).
3. The self-concept is organized, relatively stable, and evaluative. The evaluative component (self-esteem) relates to mental health; a person may or may not like his or her self-concept. According to Carl Rogers (1949), mentally healthy people see their actual selves as similar to their ideal selves.
    Regarding self-esteem of gifted students, Milgram and Milgram

(1976b) found that gifted students did indeed have better self-concepts than regular students. However, other researchers have found that compared with nongifted students, a large proportion of gifted students are low in self-esteem. Kanoy, Johnson, and Kanoy (1980), Whitmore (1980), and Terman and Oden (1951) confirmed that underachieving gifted students and adults have predictably worse self-concepts and lower self-esteem than high achieving gifted persons.

4. The *mirror theory* of self-concept development assumes that the self-concept is created via assessments ("reflections") from others.

5. The *self-accepting* student understands him- or herself and therefore is aware of strengths and weaknesses. This student values himself despite the weaknesses. The *self-rejecting* student considers him- or herself of little worth, and may have other symptoms of maladjustment (Shepard, 1979).

6. Academic failure implies low worth as a person and prevents students from maintaining feelings of competence. Failure after great effort is especially devastating to feelings of competence (Covington and Omelich, 1981).

7. Excuses and rationalizations, constructed to explain why the effort did not produce success, will protect the self-concept.

8. Self-esteem and pride are greatest when the student succeeds at a difficult task; the success is attributed to both high ability and high effort (Covington and Omelich, 1981).

9. Most critically, feelings of self-esteem and self-worth are a highly treasured commodity. All students are strongly motivated to protect their feelings of self-esteem.

Most often, the gifted student succeeds. The person's history of success inspires confidence in his or her abilities, a sense of responsibility for his or her actions, and feelings of control over his or her environment. When failure occurs, it typically is attributed to lack of effort, not lack of ability. Failures therefore may be used constructively to evaluate shortcomings and prepare for next time. "The person has temporarily fallen short of a goal, and has not fallen short as a person" (Covington and Beery, 1976).

Many students, however, are motivated not by strong needs to succeed, but by strong needs to avoid failure. And when failure threatens, any of several defense mechanisms may be used to ward off threats to the self-esteem.

One is *deliberate underachieving:* There will be no humiliation or destroyed self-esteem due to poor performance if the student does not really try. If the fear-of-failure student *accidentally* scores high on a test or paper there is a bonus. Doing well without trying is clear evidence of extra-high ability, thus reinforcing the underachievement pattern. In college, defensive underachieving produces the "gentleman's *C*" syndrome. An effortless *C* maintains the illusion of intellectual superiority without testing the scholar's actual abilities.

Defensive goal-setting can take several forms. A student may set a goal too high—for example, at the *A* + level—because it is no disgrace to fall short of such an impossibly high goal. Vice versa, the goal may be set too low. A low goal guarantees success, but it is a trivial and meaningless one.

We already noted that excuses can protect the delicate ego of a fear-of-failure student. Failures are attributed to external causes, not internal ones. Such students may blame anything and everything; for example, "The test was unfair," "My cat chewed up my assignment," or "I wasn't feeling well this morning." Ironically, these students may not accept credit for successes either, since success implies the ability and obligation for continued quality work.

The case history of Dan, a real-life underachiever unable to take credit for success, is instructive. Dan had been a consistent *C* student when he came to the author, Rimm, for underachievement counseling. After one quarter, his achievement had improved sufficiently to earn him a place on the honor roll. When the counselor asked Dan how he felt about his achievement, he replied, "I like it, but I guess I was just lucky." He had even thanked his English teacher for "giving" him an *A*. The counselor pointed out to Dan that he had both improved his study habits and increased the time he spent learning. He finally acknowledged, hesitantly, that there probably was some relationship between his new efforts and the improved grades.

One recommended solution to these self-defeating, self-perpetuating defense mechanisms is individualized instruction (Covington and Beery, 1976). By engaging fear-of-failure students in independent-learning assignments and projects, success is redefined in terms of meeting and exceeding one's own standards, not publicly competing with others for scarce classroom rewards and recognition. According to Covington and Beery, when students are not forced to compete they will set reachable, realistic goals, and these provide both the best challenge and the best conditions for a satisfying success.

MORAL DEVELOPMENT: THE KOHLBERG MODEL

Based upon research with the same group of 75 boys over a period of twelve years, Lawrence Kohlberg (1974, 1976) developed a model of moral thinking that has proven very valuable for (1) understanding sequential stages in moral development and (2) suggesting how to teach for moral thinking.

Kohlberg's six stages of moral development are divided into three main levels, each containing two stages. According to Kohlberg, they are true invariant stages: (1) They occur one at a time; (2) every person proceeds through the stages in the same order; (3) movement is always forward, never backward; and (4) stages are never skipped.

In both stages of the *Preconventional* level (ages 0–9) the orientation is toward the physical consequences of an action, regardless of any higher level notions of "right" or "wrong." Thus in Stage 1 obedience and good behavior are valued because they avoid punishments. This "might makes right" stage is characteristic of preschool children. In Stage 2 "right" action is that which produces rewards and satisfies one's needs or the needs of others—who will reciprocate ("You scratch my back, I'll scratch yours").

In the *Conventional* level (ages 9–15), behavior is heavily influenced by conformity pressures, strict stereotypes, social conventions and expectation, and rules and laws. Thus in Kohlberg's Stage 3 good behavior is that which pleases others or avoids disapproval, producing the "good boy-good girl" orientation. There is much conformity here. In Stage 4 right action is based upon rules and authority, "doing one's duty," and respecting the system. Laws are to be obeyed, not revised, leading to the "law and order" syndrome. Most adults, including teachers, do not rise above Conventional moral thinking.

The highly desirable *Postconventional* level includes the acceptance of universal and personal moral principles (for example, "Do unto others . . .") that are valid apart from authority. In Stage 5 right action is defined by general rights and standards which have been examined and agreed upon. Personal values and opinions present the possibility of rationally changing these rights and standards. For the chosen few, Stage 6 includes self-chosen principles and ethics based upon such universal principles and rights as justice, equality, and respect for individual differences.

Kohlberg (1974) found that children and adolescents comprehend all stages up to their own, and understand only one additional stage. Importantly, they *preferred* this next stage. A child often moves to the next stage when he or she is confronted with the appealing views of peers who are in this next stage.

In one study with 233 gifted students ages 9 to 15, Karnes and Brown (1981), using Rest's (1972) *Defining Issues Test* (DIT), found that the tendency to make Postconventional responses was positively correlated with age and with verbal intelligence scores. The authors concluded that gifted students may reach Level III (Postconventional) moral reasoning during their secondary school years, a level attained by only 10 to 15 percent of adults.

In contrast, Tan-Willman and Gutteridge (1981) found that the DIT scores of gifted 16 and 17 year olds were only slightly higher than the scores of regular students. "They are functioning predominantly on the Conventional level of moral judgment just like their age group in the general population . . . (and) the subjects' ability to reason morally is an area that needs serious and immediate attention."

As for teaching for moral development, Kohlberg suggests that a teacher might expose children to concepts just *one step higher* than their current stage, and encourage them to think at this more mature stage. Children also may be given opportunities to think about moral matters by role-playing someone who has been treated rudely or cheated. A related strategy is to discuss moral dilemmas and let children practice making moral decisions that require high-level moral thinking.

High school English teacher Joan Weber (1981) used moral dilemmas from literature to encourage higher-level moral thinking. For example, *Old Man Warner* by Dorothy Canfield describes a 93-year-old obstinate man who, despite family pressure, refuses to move in with relatives or even move closer to town. Weber asks her class, "What should the man do? Why? Would it make a difference if he lived in a big city? If he were physically ill? If he were a woman and not a man?" Literature is a rich source of personal problems and conflicts centering on moral issues and values.

Especially for gifted students, Kohlberg's six stages themselves can be good curriculum content for helping students understand moral thinking.

AN AFFECTIVE, HUMANISTIC CURRICULUM

Fantini (1981) itemized a number of suggestions for creating an affective, humanistic curriculum for children. For example:

1. Emphasize the desirability of "caring" values and behaviors as they relate to the self, to others, and to nature and the environment. Specifics might relate to clarifying values and ethics and understanding ecology, principles of health and hygiene, and related topics.
2. Students can read about and discuss difficulties of the handicapped and the elderly.
3. Students can learn about people, both common and famous, whose behavior demonstrates humanistic, caring values.
4. High school students can become involved in community service programs, working in day-care centers, hospitals, or nursing homes or other centers for the elderly. These assignments may be voluntary or mandated as a graduation requirement. They may receive course credit or recognition on their school records.
   Young children can make gifts for the elderly or the hospitalized, or perform plays or skits for the sick, elderly or handicapped.
5. There are many walk-a-thons, swim-a-thons, and so forth, aimed at raising research funds for cancer, multiple sclerosis, AIDS, heart disease, and other charitable causes. Students can participate in these.
6. Students can review social issues, for example, relating to refugees seeking asylum in America, political prisoners, military actions, migrant workers, and so on, from the perspective of humaneness.
7. To increase awareness of the environment, ecology and conservation students can participate in recycling drives and similar activities.
8. Importantly, while the above are good for all children, gifted children can initiate, plan, implement, and evaluate such social action projects, perhaps as Renzulli Type III enrichment.

MATERIALS AND STRATEGIES FOR ENCOURAGING AFFECTIVE GROWTH

Values clarification strategies are effective in helping gifted students explore their beliefs and feelings. Affective education leaders Simon, Howe, and Kirschenbaum (1972) present no fewer than 79 values clarification strategies. One of the authors' favorites, which can be modified and revised for any student population, centers on a list of attitudes and behaviors (see Table 9.1). The question is asked, "Are you someone who . . .?" and the student checks yes (A), maybe (B), or no(C)—requiring the student to decide on the spot what he or she *strongly favors,* is *neutral toward,* or is *opposed to.* Discussion follows, of course.

The traits in Table 9.1 list only a few of the hundreds of possibilities. Simon and Massey (1973) suggested that students will have a rousing time brainstorming other lists of behaviors, which could include such items as

TABLE 9.1 Are You Someone Who . . . ?

(A = yes, B = maybe, C = no)

A	B	C	Are you someone who:
			1. Likes to break the curve on an exam?
			2. Likes to stay up all night when friends visit?
			3. Will stop the car to look at a sunset?
			4. Puts things off?
			5. Will publicly show affection for another person?
			6. Will do it yourself when you feel something needs doing?
			7. Will order a new dish in a restaurant?
			8. Could accept your own sexual impotence?
			9. Could be satisfied without a college degree?
			10. Could be part of a mercy killing?
			11. Is afraid alone in the dark in a strange place?
			12. Is willing to participate in fund raising?
			13. Eats when you are worried?
			14. Can receive a gift easily?
			15. Would steal apples from an orchard?
			16. Is apt to judge someone by his or her appearance?
			17. Would let your child drink or smoke pot?
			18. Watches television soap operas?
			19. Could kill in self-defense?
			20. Needs to be alone?

"Blushes at a compliment," "Talks loudly when nervous," "Cheats on unfair tests," "Gambles on parking tickets," and so on. Adolescents will be intrigued by listing personal traits, and then responding "yes," "maybe," or "no" to the question, "I am looking for someone who is. . . ." Other values clarification strategies include writing letters to newspapers expressing views on issues, or classifying yourself as a Cadillac person or a Ford Escort person and then discussing reasons why.

The *Magic Circle* technique helps children learn ". . . why people are sometimes happy or unhappy, how to feel good about themselves, and how to get along with others" (Lefkowitz, 1975). Seven to twelve children in a circle—few enough to maintain everyone's attention—voluntarily respond to "Today's Topic," such as "I felt good when . . .," "I felt bad when . . .," "I made someone else feel good when . . .," or "Something I can do (or wish I could do) is. . . ." The teacher encourages learning and understanding with follow-up questions such as "Who can tell me why Dizzy Jones felt good on the roller coaster?" or "Why was he proud of himself?"

In his *Good Person Book: Creative Teaching of Values and Moral Thinking*, Davis (1989) describes seven strategies, with dozens of exercises for each, designed to stimulate creative thinking and at the same time:

1. Raise awareness of affective and behavioral problems.
2. Help students understand why particular values and behaviors are good and others are bad.
3. Help students empathize with people who are victimized by theft, vandalism, rudeness, bad manners, etc.
4. Help students understand that they will feel better about themselves, have more self-respect, and earn the respect of others if they decide to be "good persons."
5. Most importantly, help students clarify their own feelings and identities regarding affective matters, and make personal commitments to positive attitudes and behavior.

With the *brainstorming* approach, students might be asked: "Why is it important to be honest? List all of the ideas you can think of." "What rights do students (teachers, parents, brothers and sisters, store clerks) have? Think of all the ideas you can." "How many reasons can you think of to get as much education as you can?" Or with reverse brainstorming, "What can we do to lose friends or make people not like us?" "How many ways can you think of to show the school custodians that you are a thoughtless and crummy person?"

In *"What would happen if . . .?"* exercises, students imagine and think about consequences of hurtful behavior. For example, what would happen if everyone were a thief? If the school were vandalized every night? If nobody were friendly to anybody else? If everybody tried to hurt the feelings of everybody else? If nobody paid any attention to their health? If nobody went on to technical school or college? If we all ignored all safety rules? If everyone in the school wasted as many school supplies as they possibly could?

With *analogical thinking* students make imaginative comparisons. For example: "How is a good person like a good pizza?" "How is an honest person like a comfortable old pair of jeans?" "How is trustworthiness like a good movie?" "How are bad friends like Monopoly money?" "How is sharing like Saturday?"

The *empathy* approach requires students to imagine themselves in another role. For example, "Imagine that Nancy's parents gave her a new digital watch for her birthday. The first day she wears it to school it is stolen from her locker. How does Nancy feel? What does Nancy think about after this happens—what ideas go through her head? What will her parents think? How will they feel? What was the thief thinking about when he or she stole the watch? Was the thief thinking of Nancy's feelings? Why not?"

The *visualization* strategy is similar to the empathy approach. Students relax and shut their eyes while the teacher leads them through an episode eliciting empathy and constructive attitudes, values, and feelings. For example:

> Imagine you are a jogger . . . Today you are out jogging around the park . . . You look at the trees . . . tulips and roses . . . Birds are chirping . . . Children are swinging on the swings . . . Then a car filled with young adults passes by, and they toss out a box of empty beer bottles . . . The bottles scatter all over . . . Most of them break . . . Then you notice that lots of other soda cans, beer cans, and burger wrappers have been dumped around the park . . . Soon you see picnickers pack up their ice chest and their blanket . . . They climb into their car and drive away . . . But they left some dirty paper plates, a pork and beans can, some napkins and a potato chip bag . . . Their mess is ugly too . . . You wonder why these thoughtless people make messes that others must clear up . . . You can see that it makes the park ugly . . . that somebody else will have to clean up their garbage . . . Why can't they understand these things? . . .

Follow-up questions elicit thoughts regarding, for example: Are parks prettier or uglier when people throw their trash all over? What kind of people mess up roads and parks with trash? Are they considerate? Intelligent? Do they think about others' rights and feelings? Is it fair to leave messes for others to clean up? Are you the type of person who will mess up parks and streets with your trash?

The *questioning and discussion* approach also elicits awareness and commitment. For example, "Does a good person think about other people's feelings?" "What is wrong with stealing?" "Have you ever had anything vandalized? How did you feel? What did you think of the person who did this to you?" "Is it good to be trustworthy? Why?" "What happens to our valuable friends if we cheat them, lie to them, or treat them rudely?" "What is the opposite of courtesy?" "Which is more important, lots of money or good health? Why?" "Is it all right to be different? Or does everyone have to be exactly the same?" "Is it important to develop our talents and skills? Why?" "Is it important for others to respect us? How do we earn respect at school? At home? In the community?"

Davis's *problem-solving* approach follows just two steps. The first step is *clarifying* an affective problem, which includes helping students understand how others or themselves are hurt by bad attitudes and behavior. The teacher can ask: Why is the situation bad? Why is it wrong? Who is hurt? When does this happen? Where does it happen? Do we hurt ourselves when we do that? How? How are others in the school, family, or community affected? What would happen if everyone did this?

The second step is *finding solutions* for what can or should be done. The teacher might probe for ideas with:

> What are some examples of correct behavior? What might a helpful, thoughtful person do? What would earn us respect from others?
>
> How can we try to help others who are making mistakes like this? How can we help these people who don't understand how bad they look to others?
>
> How might we help the victims of the bad behavior?

See Davis (1989) for ideas for exercises and for further information about teaching values.

THE HUMANISTIC TEACHER

A teacher who has internalized humanistic values will be better able to communicate these values to students, both in direct teaching and by serving as a good role model. Pine and Boy (1977) listed characteristics of such a humanistic teacher. While the teacher who fully meets all of these criteria may not exist, we all might view these traits as ideals toward which we should work. The self-actualized, humanistic teacher:

1. Thinks well of him- or herself; he or she has a good self-concept.
2. Is honest and genuine; there is no conflict between the real inner person and the role-playing outer person.
3. Likes and accepts others.
4. Is a forward-growing person, continually in the process of "becoming" by learning, exploring, and changing.
5. Lives by humanistic values; is honestly concerned with the welfare of fellow humans and the improvement of human society.
6. Is sensitive and responsive to the needs and feelings of others.
7. Is creative, adventurous, risk-taking, willing to try something new, and secure enough to learn from the inevitable mistakes.
8. Has confidence in his or her feelings, intuition, decisions, and reaction.

9. Is open to the viewpoints of others, to new information and experiences, and to his or her own inner feelings.
10. Exercises control over his or her life and environment; initiates needed changes.
11. Is responsive, vibrant, and spontaneous, and tries to live optimistically and energetically.

LEADERSHIP

There is little disagreement that leadership is important for gifted and talented students, who often are labeled "tomorrow's leaders." Said Richardson and Feldhusen (1986), "Our nation's leadership is not limited to our political offices such as the President, the Congress, governors or representatives. . . . Any field of human endeavor is represented by its leaders, including the creative areas of art, music and literature . . . research, exploration, and technology require creative leadership. Each person is faced with leadership whether it be in church, schools, business, or in the home." It seems sensible that leadership training should supplement the development of other cognitive and affective skills of G/T students.

The following sections review definitions of leadership and then turn to specifics of what is taught when you "teach leadership."

As an overview, first, "definitions" of leadership typically amount to lists of traits, characteristics, and skills of leaders. Second, leadership training in the schools, when it is attempted at all, typically includes some combination of three approaches: (1) Students learn about traits of leaders, leadership styles, group dynamics, and how to be a good leader; (2) students are placed into leadership situations with the intent that on-the-job experience will strengthen leadership characteristics and skills; or (3) students receive training in component leadership skills, such as communication, creative problem solving, critical thinking, decision making, persuasion, and even understanding others' needs.

LEADERSHIP DEFINITIONS: TRAITS, CHARACTERISTICS, AND SKILLS

Different leadership traits and skills naturally are required for different leadership situations. At the same time, however, there are traits and skills that are cross-situational and that seem to characterize all leaders.

One definition of leadership is found in the Renzulli and Hartman (1981; Renzulli, 1983) leadership rating scale, reproduced in Appendix 4.5, on which teachers evaluate student leadership according to the following criteria:

1. Carries responsibility well and can be counted on to do what has been promised.
2. Is self-confident with both age-mates and adults; seems comfortable when showing personal work to the class.
3. Is well liked.
4. Is cooperative, avoids bickering, and is generally easy to get along with.
5. Can express him- or herself clearly.
6. Adapts to new situations; is flexible in thought and action and is not disturbed when the normal routine is changed.
7. Enjoys being around other people.
8. Tends to dominate; usually directs activities.
9. Participates in most school social activities; can be counted on to be there.

Plowman (1981) itemized six aspects of leadership in the form of adjectives: *charismatic, intuitive, generative, analytical, evaluative,* and *synergistic.* All of these could be considered competencies upon which a leadership curriculum could be based.

Charismatic traits include an almost mystical ability to instill others (partly by example) with a sense of mission, and to energize them to think and act to achieve objectives. *Intuitive* characteristics include the ability to sense what is about to happen via an extrapolation of current events or a keen sensitivity to subtle cues. It includes the ability to sense the needs of individuals and groups and to respond to those needs even before they are expressed. *Generative* refers to creativeness: defining problems in new ways and creating unusual ideas, processes, and courses of action. *Analytic* leadership includes seeing component parts of systems and analyzing their individual contributions. The *evaluative* involves judging the effectiveness or efficiency of activities or programs. The *synergistic* aspects ". . . are those which make the unbelievable happen"—goals are reached in half the expected time, or production is five or ten times what was expected.

Plowman (1981) also reported the results of a 1980 leadership session at the California Association for the Gifted Annual Conference in Los Angeles in which 16 traits of leadership were identified. Each trait was categorized as *cognitive* (C), *affective* (A), or *both* (B):

1. Assertive decision making (B)
2. Altruistic (B)
3. Persuasive/innovator (A)
4. Sensitivity to the needs of others (A)
5. Ability to be a facilitator (B)
6. Goal oriented (C)
7. Strong communication skills (B)
8. Integrity (A)
9. Organization ability (C)
10. Resourceful (B)

11. Risk-taker (B)
12. Charisma (A)
13. Competence (knowledge) (B)
14. Persistence ("hangs in there") (A)
15. Accepts responsibility (B)
16. Creative (B)

Only two traits were rated as *cognitive,* indicating both the importance of affective characteristics in leadership and the complexity of the traits. Each of these traits, as with the traits and "aspects" in the previous lists, could be seen as objectives or competencies of leadership curricula. That is, G/T students can be helped to understand these traits and skills, and to acquire them through practice and exercise.

LEADERSHIP TRAINING

Again, recommendations and strategies for leadership training invariably include some combination of teaching students about leadership styles, traits, and group dynamics; putting students into leadership roles; and teaching them component skills of leadership.

Magoon (1980), for example, recommended:

1. *Classroom monitorships,* in which students assume responsibility for regulating the behavior of peers (for example, in lineups), record keeping (roll taking), or other jobs (blackboard or A-V duties). Such activities teach leadership and followership, including the notion that there are menial tasks which must be carried out for the system to function.
2. *Mentorships,* in which gifted and talented students tutor peers or younger students. The mentors learn to communicate in an acceptable and challenging manner.
3. *In-school leadership projects,* identified via brainstorming, such as improving student behavior (for example, in the halls or cafeteria), improving the physical plant (classrooms, restrooms, or temperature or noise levels), or solving problems related to curriculum selection, classroom rules, safety, sanitation, etc.
4. *Community projects,* in which students take on neighborhood problems or undesirable conditions. This activity requires the development of communication skills, tact, diplomacy, and patience.
5. *Simulations,* which can involve, for example, establishing "banks" and "stores," making rules, and establishing a legal system for maintaining the rules.

Magoon (1981) also proposed that students be exposed to the "topic and content" of leadership itself. For example, training can include teaching students about leadership and followership, principles of participatory democracy, group processes, and characteristics of leaders, along with developing communication skills. Magoon's strategy is ". . . based, in part, on a leadership program that has been classroom tested with talented and gifted students for over three years with exciting results."

Plowman (1981) recommended strengthening leadership with exercises aimed at developing the component skills of critical thinking, decision making, persuading, planning, and evaluating. More complex objectives included helping students understand others' needs, exploring patterns of individual and group behavior, and showing students ways that changes are made in political, social, economic, and other spheres.

Parker (1983) suggested that leadership could be trained by strengthening the four component skills of *cognition* (especially, research, exploration, and investigative skills), *problem solving* (including creative thinking), *interpersonal communication* (including self-awareness, concern for others, cooperation, and conflict resolution), and *decision making*.

Maker's (1982) suggestions for leadership training include both practice in leading and the deliberate teaching of component skills. First, she notes that as the school year progresses, the teacher should gradually become a sideline facilitator, and the gifted and talented students should learn to become leaders. Students can be asked to teach small groups of students, a task which intrinsically requires leadership, and to take responsibility for various projects. Also, deliberate awareness-raising discussions of leadership can include listing qualities of leaders, followed by discussions of which qualities help to make leaders successful. Said Maker, the teacher also can foster discussion skills, public speaking, and group control and group dynamics skills.

Leadership Skills Development Program: Karnes and Chauvin

Karnes and Chauvin (1986, 1987) developed a two-part Leadership Skills Development Program aimed at developing important traits and skills in upper elementary and secondary students. The first part of the program centers on their *Leadership Skills Inventory* (LSI). The LSI evaluates these kinds of seemingly universal leadership traits and skills:

Fundamentals of leadership, including understanding leadership styles and terms.

Written communication, including outlining, speech writing, and report writing.

Speech communication, including defining one's view on an issue, delivering speeches, and giving constructive criticism.

Values clarification, including identifying things that one values, understanding the importance of free choice, and affirming one's choices.

Decision making, including gathering facts, analyzing the consequences of decisions, and reaching logical conclusions.

Group dynamics, including serving as group facilitator, achieving consensus, and achieving compromise.

Problem solving, including identifying problems, revising problem-solving strategies, and accepting unpopular decisions.

Personal development, including self-confidence, sensitivity, and personal grooming.

Planning, including goal setting, developing timelines, and creating evaluation strategies.

The LSI is used in several ways. It provides a profile of leadership abilities and skills for each student and for the group as a whole. It thus serves as a needs assessment instrument and guides the planning of a leadership development program based upon individual and group weaknesses. Because the results are shared with students, they learn about the nature of leadership and leadership skills, and they receive an objective assessment of their own present leadership skills. This record is used as a basis for later comparison and evaluation of progress.

The second part of the training is the *Leadership Skills Activities Handbook.* The handbook contains activities designed to strengthen each skill or trait described in every item on the LSI. Most activities are designed to be self-directed, with the teacher serving as a facilitator. For example, one LSI item reads "I am ambitious and desire success." The coordinated activity in the handbook is leading a discussion on "how the self-confident person views success." The student-leader would pose such (supplied) questions as "Are all leaders success oriented? How important is this quality to a leader?" Another LSI item is "I can describe my own style of leadership." The corresponding handbook activity asks students to describe how they would solve some fictitious problem situations.

The culminating activity for the entire Leadership Skills Development Program is the "plan for leadership." Said Karnes and Chauvin (1986), "It is a written plan whereby the student is asked to think through all the things learned about leadership and formulate a plan to put these skills into action. The individual is asked to direct activities toward a particular selected goal and formulate objectives, a timeline, and a list of resources. It is through implementation of this plan that leadership will become a reality." The Leadership Skills Development Program has been field tested, apparently with very positive results.

Leadership Education: Richardson and Feldhusen

Richardson and Feldhusen's (1986) fine book *Leadership Education* was written primarily for secondary students themselves who are participating in leadership education programs. The book presents a balanced mix of theory and principles, characteristics of leadership, guides for becoming an effective leader, plus activities and problems designed to exercise and strengthen leadership traits and skills.

By way of explaining leadership, Richardson and Feldhusen reviewed four definitions or types of leaders. The *personality* approach defines a leader as one who possesses a constellation of personality traits that are attractive to others, for example, confidence, humor, and popularity. Students with these traits often are elected to school leadership positions. Leadership as a form of *persuasion* is based on the ability to ". . . convince or inspire others to follow their directions, orders, or commands . . . to inspire people to action." Leadership as a *power relation* goes to the person with the highest rank, as in democratic government or clan leadership. Finally, a leader can be a self-directed and motivated person who *initiates action and maintains structure* when working toward group goals, as when a private citizen organizes a group to combat drug use or automobile deaths among young people.

To help students understand leadership, Richardson and Feldhusen explain that good leaders are confident and have good self-esteem. They take risks and admit mistakes. They tend to be responsible, empathic, and more assertive and extroverted than average. Good leaders also are good speakers, good listeners, and can give directions, lead discussions, and write well. They have good interpersonal skills, delegate authority, and are prepared to help others. They have good organization and planning skills; can involve group members in a task and clarify the goals and issues. They develop group cohesiveness and an atmosphere of respect, cooperation, and teamwork; refrain from harsh criticism; are fair; make decisions based on majority views; protect rights of individual members; help all members to achieve their personal goals; are good at public relations—keeping the community informed and supportive; and understand parliamentary procedures.

Students learn steps to use in leading discussions, and steps to use in brainstorming and problem solving. The authors also suggest tips for reading body language and nonverbal communication; communicating effectively; making introductions; writing letters; preparing a speech; setting and clarifying individual and group goals; planning meetings; planning work activities for the group; serving as a committee chairperson; and serving as a committee member.

Overall, the book not only provides convincing evidence that leadership can be taught, it carefully explains and provides exercises in the skills needed to improve one's leadership ability.

SUMMARY

Affective learning includes self-concepts, self-esteem, personal and social adjustment, values and moral thinking, motivation, and others.

Leadership, due to its obscure nature, largely has been ignored in gifted education. Strategies and programs for clarifying and teaching leadership have appeared recently.

High-achieving gifted students usually have good self-concepts, and gifted students usually attain higher levels of moral thinking. The self-concept is closely tied to success experiences, which makes feedback from schoolwork and the teacher extremely important for children. Academic failure implies low self-worth.

Developing good self-concepts is a goal in itself. We have many "selves" (academic, social, emotional, physical). The self-concept is organized, stable, and evaluative. Underachieving G/T students have poor self-concepts. The self-concept may be formed according to "mirrored" reflections from others. Achieving students are confident and use failures constructively.

Because self-esteem is highly valued, failure-oriented students will use defense mechanisms, such as deliberate underachieving, setting goals impossibly high or too low, setting a wide confirming interval, and attributing failures to external causes.

Individualized learning, with realistic goal-setting, is one solution to self-defeating defensive behaviors.

Kohlberg's six stages of moral development are considered true, invariant stages. In the Preconventional level, right action avoids punishment and satisfies one's needs or the needs of others (who will reciprocate). In the Conventional level, correct behavior is defined by strict social conventions. In the Postconventional level, right action is defined by universal and self-determined principles. Children understand all previous stages and one more, and prefer this next one. Research is mixed regarding whether or not gifted adolescents truly do think at the Postconventional level.

Children should be exposed to moral thinking at the next higher level. They should have opportunities to think about moral problems, for example, using moral dilemmas. Kohlberg's stages themselves can be taught.

Fantini emphasized teaching "caring" values; exposing students to problems of the elderly and handicapped, to examples of humanistic thinking, and to social issues; and involving students in community service programs, which G/T students can design and carry out.

Values clarification and the Magic Circle technique help students understand and accept positive values.

Davis's *Good Person Book* contains creativity-type exercises designed to help students understand and make commitments to positive values. Seven strategies included brainstorming, "What would happen if . . .?", analogical thinking, empathy, visualization, questionning and discussion, and problem solving.

The humanistic teacher has a good self-concept, likes others, initiates change, and is honest and genuine, forward-growing, sensitive, creative and adventurous, confident, and open to other viewpoints.

Definitions of leadership usually amount to lists of traits, characteristics, and skills of leaders. Traits that seem common to leaders, regardless of the situation, include high responsibility and confidence, being well-liked, adaptability, tendencies to dominate and direct, plus skills in communication, group dynamics, planning, persuasion, public relations, and others.

Six "aspects" of leadership (Plowman) included being charismatic, intuitive, generative (creative), analytical, evaluative, and synergistic. These and other cognitive and affective traits could be used as objectives and competencies for creating a leadership curriculum.

Leadership training includes some combination of teaching students about leadership styles, traits, and group dynamics; placing students in leadership roles; and teaching students component skills of leadership, such as communication, creative problem solving, planning, decision making, and others.

Magoon described five leadership training activities: classroom monitorships, mentorships, in-school leadership projects, community projects, and simulations.

Karnes and Chauvin's Leadership Skills Development Program included (1) using their *Leadership Skills Inventory* to assess leadership traits and skills, and then (2) prescribing leadership activities from their *Leadership Skills Activities Handbook* to strengthen each weak skill. Each student also prepares a written plan for leadership.

Richardson and Feldhusen's high school book *Leadership Education* teaches types and characteristics of leaders; steps to use in leading discussions, brainstorming, and problem solving; and many other specific leadership skills, including goal-setting, communication, and planning skills.

chapter ten

Creativity I

The Creative Person, Creative Process, and Creative Dramatics

There can be no more important topic in the education of gifted and talented children than *creativity*. Indeed, the two interrelated purposes of gifted education are (1) to help these children and adolescents develop their gifts and talents and realize their potential—that is, to help them become more self-actualized, creative individuals; and (2) to better enable them to make creative contributions to society.

Overview

This chapter and Chapter 11 are designed to help the reader better understand creativity and creative students, and to suggest ideas for stimulating creative growth. This chapter will review some basic features of creativity: (1) traits and characteristics of creative people and some important creative abilities; (2) the nature of the creative process; and (3) creative dramatics. The important topic of testing for creative potential was discussed in Chapter 4 in conjunction with identification. The relationship of creativity to intelligence was reviewed in Chapter 2. Chapter 11 will focus more specifically on teaching for creative development.

CHARACTERISTICS OF CREATIVE STUDENTS

Chapter 2 summarized recurrent personality, motivational, and biographical characteristics of creative children and adults. To briefly review, creative people are frequently high in self-confidence, independence, risk-taking, energy, enthusiasm, adventurousness, curiosity, playfulness, humor, idealism, and reflectiveness. Then tend to have artistic and aesthetic interests, to be attracted to the complex and mysterious, and to need some privacy and alone time. Most of these traits were uncovered by Frank Barron (1969) and Donald MacKinnon (1978) in their classic Berkeley studies of creative architects, writers, and mathematicians.

Further, as we also noted earlier, some traits will be troublesome to teachers. Especially, the admirable characteristics of independence and high energy, combined with the nonconformity and unconventionality intrinsic to creativeness, may lead to stubbornness, resistance to teacher (or parent) domination, uncooperativeness, indifference to accepted conventions, cynicism, too much assertiveness, sloppiness, low interest in details, a tendency to question rules and authority, forgetfulness, overactivity, uncommunicativeness, and the feeling that the rest of the parade is out of step.

The biographical traits listed earlier included some unsurprising ones, namely, a background filled with creative activities and hobbies. Frequent performances in dramatic productions is a very strong indicator of creativeness, since such performances necessarily require important creative traits (humor, energy, aesthetic interests and risk taking, for example). More subtle biographical characteristics of creativity include a background of traveling, living in more than one state, preferring friends who are younger and older, having had an imaginary playmate as a child, and a tendency to believe in psychical phemonena (and a higher than average likelihood of having psychical experiences). Naturally, not all characteristics apply to all creative students.

Many of these traits probably can be enhanced. Indeed, as we will see in the next chapter, there is every reason to believe that attitudes and personality traits can be changed to produce a more flexible, creative and self-actualized person. Participation in creativity courses often strengthens self-confidence and independence along with creative potential (Parnes, 1978); it is a chicken-egg problem as to which causes which.

Lingemann's (1982) thorough literature search for traits of creative people produced no less than 55 traits. Each trait in Table 10.1 met either of two criteria: (1) The trait was related to creativeness at a statistically significant level in at least five research studies, or (2) the trait was significantly related to creativity in three studies and mentioned as a creativity trait in two other sources (for example, in literature reviews or theories of

TABLE 10.1 **Fifty-Five Personality Characteristics Related to Creativity**

(From Lingemann. 1982. Reprinted by permission.)

Adventurous	Open
Aggressive	Open-Minded
Ambitious	Original
Assertive	Perceptive
Autonomous	Persevering
Complex	Playful
Courageous	Prefer Complexity
Curious	Questioning
Dissatisfied	Radical
Dominant	Recognition Seeking
Emotional	Reflective
Energetic	Resourceful
Excitable	Risk Taking
Experimenting	Self Aware
Expressive	Self Confident
Flexible	Self Sufficient
Humorous	Sensation Seeking
Imaginative	Sensitive/Perceptive
Impulsive	Thorough
Independent	Tolerant of Ambiguity
Individualistic	Tolerant of Disorder
Industrious	Tolerant of Incongruity
Inner-Directed	Unconcerned with Impressing Others
Internally Controlled	Unconventional
Introspective	Uninhibited
Intuitive	Varied interests
Liberal	Versatile
Non-Conforming	

creativity). Many of the traits in Table 10.1 essentially duplicate the ones presented above.

Torrance (1979) itemized other non-test indicators of creativeness in the kinesthetic and auditory areas:

Shows skillful, manipulative movement in crayon work, typing, piano playing, cooking, dressmaking, and so on

Shows quick, precise movements in mime, creative dramatics, and role playing

Works at creative movement activities for extended periods of time

Displays total bodily involvement in interpreting a poem, story, or song

Becomes intensely absorbed in creative movement or dance

Interprets songs, poems, or stories through creative movement or dance

Writes, draws, walks, and moves with rhythm and is generally highly responsive to sound stimuli

Creates music, songs, etc.

Works perseveringly at music and rhythmic activities

The characteristics listed here are intended to help the reader recognize creative children and adolescents in the classroom. The lists also might increase one's patience with the obnoxious kid who shows a few too many of the negative traits. Perhaps the creative energy, unconventionality, stubbornness, inquisitiveness, and so forth, require constructive redirection.

We also should emphasize that many academically below average students will demonstrate marvelous creative talent, for example, in art, dance, or any other area in which the student possesses special knowledge and skills.

CREATIVE ABILITIES

There are a great many intellectual abilities that contribute in one way or another to creative potential. Indeed, it would be difficult to isolate mental abilities having absolutely nothing to do with creativeness. The list below includes seemingly important creative abilities. Most have appeared elsewhere in the creativity literature, usually in Torrance's work (for example, Torrance, 1962, 1979, 1980, 1984). The first four are the classic Guilford/Torrance *fluency, flexibility, originality,* and *elaboration* abilities which are measured by the Guilford (1967) tests and the *Torrance Tests of Creative Thinking* (Torrance, 1966). Some people have mistakenly assumed that these four are a definitive and exhaustive list of creative abilities, which is not true at all.

> *Fluency.* The ability to produce many ideas in response to an open-ended problem or question. The ideas may be verbal or nonverbal (for example, mathematical, musical, and so forth). Other names are "associational fluency" or "ideational fluency."
>
> *Flexibility.* The ability to take different approaches to a problem, think of ideas in different categories, or view a situation from several perspectives.
>
> *Originality.* Uniqueness, nonconformity in thought and action.
>
> *Elaboration.* The important ability to add details to a given idea, which includes developing, embellishing, and implementing the idea.
>
> *Sensitivity to problems.* The ability to find problems, detect difficulties, detect missing information, and ask good questions (Dillon, 1982).
>
> *Problem defining.* An important capability that includes the abilities to: (1) identify the "real" problem, (2) isolate the important aspects of a problem, (3) clarify and simplify a problem, (4) identify subproblems, (5) propose alternative problem definitions, and (6) define a problem broadly. Abilities 5 and 6 both open the door to a wider variety of problem solutions.
>
> *Visualization.* The ability to fantasize and imagine, "see" things in the "mind's eye," and mentally manipulate images and ideas. According to some, this may be the single most important creative ability.

Ability to regress. The ability to think like a child, whose mind is less cluttered by habits, traditions, rules, regulations, and the firm knowledge of "how it ought to be done" and "how we've always done it"—strong barriers to creative thinking.

Analogical thinking. The ability to borrow ideas from one context and use them in another context; or the ability to borrow a solution to one problem and transfer it to another problem.

Evaluation. The very important ability to separate relevant from irrelevant considerations; to think critically; to evaluate the "goodness" or appropriateness of an idea, product, or problem solution.

Analysis. The ability to analyze details, analyze a whole into its parts.

Synthesis. The ability to see relationships, to combine parts into a workable, perhaps creative whole.

Transformation. This includes the ability to adopt something to a new use, to "see" new meanings, implications, and applications, or to creatively change one object or idea into another. Guilford (1983) considers transformation to be an extremely important creative ability.

Extend boundaries. The ability to go beyond what is usual, to use objects in new ways.

Intuition. The ability to make "intuitive leaps" or see relationships based upon little, perhaps insufficient information; the ability to "read between the lines."

Predict outcomes. The ability to foresee the results of different solution alternatives and actions.

Resist premature closure. This is another important ability, and one in which many students are deficient. It translates as deferring judgment and not jumping on the first idea that comes along.

Concentration ability. The ability to focus on a problem, free from distraction.

Logical thinking ability. The ability to separate the relevant from the irrelevant, to deduce reasonable conclusions.

Many of the thinking skills described in Chapter 12 also could be viewed as abilities important to creative problem solving, for example, considering all factors, planning, reasoning, prioritizing, recognizing the essential and nonessential, discovering relationships, making inferences, projecting consequences, and others. Further, some personality traits could be viewed as "creative abilities," for example, sense of humor, curiosity, artistic interests or talent, tolerance for ambiguity, spontaneity, and perhaps others. In addition, the 24 divergent-thinking abilities in Guilford's (1967, 1979b) *Structure of Intellect* (SOI) model, reviewed in Chapter 8, include abilities that overlap with the above list. As you may recall, Guilford's 24 abilities are combinations of four contents (figural, symbolic, semantic, and behavioral) and six products (units, classes, relations, systems, transformations, and implications). *Humor*, for example, is an SOI ability involving the "divergent production of semantic transformations" (DST). There also are innumerable learned skills and abilities in every social, scientific, business, or artistic field that are essential for creative thinking within that particular knowledge area (Keating, 1980).

THE CREATIVE PROCESS

There are several ways to view the creative process. First, the traditional approach is to describe a sequence of *stages* through which one might proceed in solving a problem creatively. Second, the creative process can be viewed as a *change in perception*—literally "seeing" new idea combinations, new relationships, new meanings, new implications, or new applications that simply were not perceived a moment before. These approaches to the creative process will be briefly summarized subsequently.

A third approach to understanding the creative process is to examine creative thinking *techniques*—strategies used by creative individuals to produce the new idea combinations and relationships that comprise creative ideas and products. This topic is postponed until Chapter 11.

Steps and Stages in the Creative Process

The Wallas model.   The best-known set of stages in the creative process is the *preparation, incubation, illumination,* and *verification* stages suggested in 1926 by Graham Wallas. The *preparation* stage includes clarifying and defining the problem, gathering relevant information, reviewing available materials, examining solution requirements, and becoming acquainted with any other relevant innuendos or implications, including previous unsuccessful solutions. This stage basically involves clarifying "the mess."

The *incubation* stage may best be viewed as a period of "preconscious," "fringe conscious," "off-conscious," or even "unconscious" activity which takes place while the thinker, perhaps deliberately, is jogging, watching TV, playing golf, eating pizza, walking along a river bank, or even napping. Guilford (1979a) suggested that incubation takes place during reflection, a pause in action, and that some people are simply more reflective than others. Many creative people keep a pad and pencil on the bedstand or a small notebook ("idea trap") in their pocket in order to jot down spontaneous ideas for incubated problems.

The third, *illumination* stage is the sudden "Eureka, I found it!" or "Aha!" experience. A solution appears, usually suddenly (although it may follow weeks of work and incubation), that seems to match the requirements of the problem.

The final *verification* stage, as the name suggests, involves checking the workability, feasibility, and/or acceptability of the illumination.

The reader may note that these stages resemble steps in the classic scientific method: state the problem, propose hypotheses, plan and conduct the research, then evaluate the results. Note also that the stages are not an invariant sequence. Some stages may be skipped or the thinker may backtrack to an earlier stage. For example, the process of defining and clarifying the problem (preparation) often leads directly to a good, illuminating idea. Or if the verification confirms that an idea will not work or will not be acceptable, the thinker may move back to either the preparation or the incubation stage.

Actually, one of the most important steps in creative thinking was ignored in the Wallas model: implementation. The idea must be developed and elaborated upon, and the solution carried out. Perhaps this step was assumed.

A two-stage model. The creative process very often, if not always, involves two fairly clear steps: A *big idea* stage and an *elaboration* stage (Davis, 1986). The big idea stage is a period of fantasy in which the creative person is looking for a new, exciting idea or problem solution. After the idea is found, perhaps using a personal creative thinking technique, the elaboration stage includes idea development, elaboration, and implementation. The artist must assemble his or her materials, do preliminary sketches, and create the final work; the novelist must create characters and plot; and the research scientist or business entrepreneur must organize the details and carry out the work necessary to implement the big idea.

The creative problem solving model. The *creative problem solving* (CPS) *model* is an extremely useful set of five stages outlined by Parnes (1981) and by Treffinger and his colleagues (Isaksen and Treffinger, 1985; Treffinger, Isaksen, and Firestien, 1982): *fact finding, problem finding, idea finding, solution finding,* and *acceptance finding*. These five steps are useful because they guide the creative process; that is, they tell you what to do at each immediate step to eventually produce one or more creative, workable solutions. Another unique feature is that each step first involves a divergent-thinking phase, in which lots of ideas (facts, problem definitions, potential solutions, evaluation criteria, implementation ideas) are generated, and then a second convergent phase in which only the most promising ideas are selected for further exploration.

The first stage, *fact finding*, involves "listing all you know about the problem or challenge" (Parnes, 1981). For example, let's say the problem is thinking of ways to stimulate creativity in an elementary school resource room G/T program. An individual or group first would list all of the facts they could think of relating to training creative thinking and perhaps to the nature of creativity and creative abilities. Parnes recommends the use of who, what, when, where, why and how questions. That is:

Who is or should be involved?
What is or is not happening?
When does this or should this happen?
Where does or doesn't this occur?
Why does it or doesn't it happen?
How does it or doesn't it occur?

The list of ideas is then convergently narrowed to a smaller number of facts that might be especially productive.

The second stage, *problem finding*, involves listing alternative problem definitions. One principle of creative problem solving is that the definition of a problem will determine the nature of the solutions. It helps to begin each statement with, "In what ways might I (we) . . . " (for example, find lists of strategies, locate someone who knows about training creativity, locate books on the topic, have someone else do it, have the kids themselves solve the problem, and so on).

One or more of the most fruitful definitions is selected for the third stage, *idea finding*. This is the divergent-thinking, brainstorming stage; ideas are freely listed for each of the problem definitions accepted in the second stage.

In the fourth stage of *solution finding*, criteria for idea evaluation are listed; for example: Will the strategy strengthen important creative abilities? Will it strengthen good creative attitudes? Will it teach usable creative thinking techniques? Will it cost too much? Will it take too much time? Are the materials available? Will the principal, other teachers accept it? Will the children cooperate? And so on. The list may be reduced to the most relevant criteria.

Sometimes, an *evaluation matrix* is prepared, with possible solutions listed on the vertical axis and the criteria across the top (see Figure 10.1). Each idea is rated according to each criteria (perhaps on a 1 to 5 scale), the rating scores are entered in the cells, and then the scores are totaled to find the "best" idea(s).

Finally, *acceptance finding* (or implementation) amounts to thinking of ". . . ways to get the best ideas into action" (Parnes, 1981).

In his inspiring book *The Magic of Your Mind*, Parnes leads the reader through problem after problem with the goal of making the five steps habitual and automatic. That is, when encountering a problem, challenge, or opportunity, one quickly would review relevant facts, identify various interpretations of the problem, generate solutions, think of criteria and evaluate the ideas, and speculate on how the solution(s) might be implemented and accepted. After 30 years as president of the Creative Education Foundation, and much experience teaching creative problem solving, learning these steps is Parnes's best recommendation for becoming a more creative problem solver and a more effective, self-actualized human being.

In the classroom, the CPS model would be used to guide a creative-thinking session that (1) improves students' understanding of the creative process, (2) exposes them to a rousing creative-thinking experience, and (3) solves a problem. With much practice with the steps, students might become habitual creative thinkers, as Parnes intended.

Parnes (1981) noted that "the five steps are a guide rather than a strict formula. Frequently, a change of sequence may be introduced into the process; and it is always advisable to provide plenty of opportunity for

	Strengthen Abilities?	Strengthen Attitudes?	Teach Techniques?	Cost Too Much?	Use Too Much Time?	Materials Available?	Principal, Teachers Accept It?	Children Cooperate?	Total Score
Use Brainstorming									
Teach Techniques									
Use Synectics									
Find Exercises									
Creative Drama									
Art, Handicrafts									
Creative Writing									
Research Projects									

FIGURE 10.1 Example of an Evaluation Matrix. Each idea is rated on a 1 (low) to 5 (high) scale according to each criterion. Total scores are then tallied.

incubation." In conversation, Parnes told the authors that people tend to use the five stages too rigidly. He suggested a star-shaped model enclosed in a circle (Figure 10.2), emphasizing that—if it helps the creative process—one may flexibly move directly from any one step to any other.

Treffinger, Isaksen and Firestein (1982) described some convergent techniques that can be used in any of the five CPS steps to aid in finding "good" facts, problem definitions, ideas, evaluation criteria (and solutions), and implementation strategies. Especially interesting are their *hits* and *hot spots*. Hits are ideas that strike the problem solver as important breakthroughs—directions to be pursued further because they could form the basis for a good solution. Groups of related hits are called hot spots. Hot spots are thus ". . . a collection of hits that center around a specific issue or relate to a similar aspect of the problem." The hot spot is given a label that paraphrases the essential meaning of this group of hits. In the convergent part of each CPS step, hits and hot spots are excellent leads for further exploration.

The CPS model may be taught to secondary students and even elementary children, as in the book *CPS for Kids* (Eberle and Stanish, 1985).

Keating's four stages in socially relevant creativity. Keating (1980) proposed that the act of producing socially relevant creative innovations involves more than just divergent thinking. His four components take ". . . a

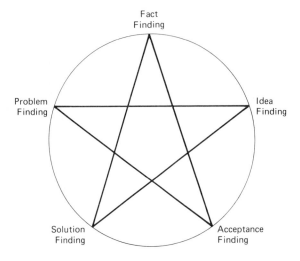

FIGURE 10.2   An alternative conception of the Creative Education Foundation Stages emphasizing that one may flexibly move from any stage to any other.

vaguely temporal sequence. . . ." Component 1, *content knowledge*, is based on the assumption that it is virtually impossible to advance beyond the status quo in a field unless one has a thorough working knowledge of the particular discipline or art form. A deep familiarity with the work of one's predecessors in any field is ". . . if not an absolute prerequisite, at least a virtually universal concomitant of creative breakthroughs."

Component 2 is *divergent thinking*, which Keating identified mainly with ideational fluency and flexibility. He considered divergent thinking to be about equal in importance to content knowledge.

Component 3 is *critical analysis*. Noted Keating, it is inacurrate to assume that critical thinking is the antithesis of creative thinking. As colorfully stated by Keating, "Critical analysis has an undeserved reputation as the tough heel on the fragile throat of creativity." Rather, ". . . some judgments must be made so that highly promising ideas may be separated from unpromising ones."

Finally, component 4, *communication skills*, assumes that an idea or artistic conception that exists only in the head of the potential creator is not "creative" in the strict sense. "Something must be made, produced, concretized in some fashion before it has a chance to succeed in contributing to the collective human experience."

An important message in Keating's "vaguely sequential components" is that programs for teaching creative thinking should not focus totally on his component 2, divergent thinking. For "real," socially relevant creative contributions, the components of background knowledge, critical thinking, and communication skills also are essential.

The Creative Process as a Change in Perception

Many creative ideas are the result of a change in perception—the usually abrupt "seeing" of new idea combinations, new relationships, new meanings, new applications, or new implications. This phenomenon occurs whether the transformation is a simple modification of a cookie recipe (perhaps substituting mint candies for chocolate chips), or an unfathomably complex discovery in mathematics, physics, medicine, or astronomy.

One simple way to illustrate the sudden perceptual change is with visual puzzles. For example, look at Figure 10.3. There is one main, meaningful figure, created in fact from a photograph. After you find this figure, try to locate: (1) a flying pig, (2) an Al Capp *Li'l Abner* character with a snaggle lower tooth, (3) a woman with her hair in a bun reclining on a sofa (she is in white). If you can find these easy (?) ones, you may proceed to (4) the Road Runner, (5) Harry Belafonte, (6) Popeye, (7) Blackbeard the Pirate, (8) a side profile of Jesus, (9) right next to Jesus a lady in a bouffant hairdo, and (10) E.T. You will find yourself exclaiming, "Oh! There it is!" or "Now I see it!" The solutions are outlined at the end of this chapter.

We do not understand this sudden perceptual change or transformation very well. In some cases it may be due simply to viewing (or thinking of) one or two stimuli and then mentally modifying them, combining them,

FIGURE 10.3   Visual Puzzle.

Reprinted with permission of Charles Scribners Sons, an imprint of Macmillan Publishing Company from *Creative Actionbook* by Sidney J. Parnes, Ruth Noller, and Angelo M. Biondi. Copyright 1976 by Charles Scribners Sons.

or otherwise detecting a new meaning or relationship. For example, a candy bar mogul, always alert for new products, may receive a sample package of macadamia nuts on an airline flight and instantly "see" a chocolate/macadamia treat. A Silicon Valley computer chip expert, upon checking his wristwatch, may suddenly visualize a baseball game or some other video game incorporated into the wristwatch. A novelist may "see" an intriguing story take shape as the result of a visit to Cuba or Beirut or from reading a description of a middle east or central America conflict.

The creative change in perception is indeed a complex, mysterious, and elusive process. Torrance (1980), for example, described the "suprarational" nature of "insight, intuition, and revelation" that happens in an instant. Said Torrance, these phenomena do not fit into the rational model of science and therefore have not been scientifically studied.

The discussion of creative thinking techniques in the next chapter will outline some unconscious creative processes that have been made conscious, knowable, and teachable. Most of these techniques are based on forcing the thinker to "see" new relationships and transformations of ideas.

CREATIVE DRAMATICS

Creative dramatics most definitely is a unique classroom activity. According to Way (1967), it is "the education of the whole person by experience." As with other creativity exercises, creative dramatics stimulates divergent thinking, imagination, and problem solving. It also may strengthen sensory awareness, concentration, control of the physical self, discovery and control of emotions, humor, self-confidence in speaking and performing, empathic and humanistic understanding of others (Davis, 1986; Davis, Helfert, and Shapiro, 1973; Way, 1967), and even critical thinking (Carelli, 1981). The reader also will discover that creative dramatics is as fun as it is beneficial. Furthermore, sessions are not difficult to lead; the two main requirements are a good sense of humor and enough energy to crank up a people machine or wade through a peanut butter swamp.

Creative dramatics activities are described in the categories of *warmups*, *movement exercises*, *sensory and body awareness exercises*, *pantomime*, and *playmaking*.

Warmup Exercises

Any creative dramatics session must begin with some simple loosening up exercises, movements that stretch a few muscles but require little or no thinking. Some suggestions are:

Holding up the ceiling.   As the leader narrates, the students strain to hold up the ceiling, slowly letting it down (to one knee), then pushing it back up into place.

Biggest thing, smallest thing.   Another easy one is to have everyone stretch his or her body into the "biggest thing" he/she possibly can. No one has any trouble guessing what the second part of the exercise is.

Stretching.   There are many ways to stretch. One strategy is to have students begin with their heads and work down, stretching then relaxing every part of the body. Vice versa, begin with the toes. Either may be done lying down.

Warmup at different speeds.   Children run in place in slow motion, then speed up until they are moving very fast. Variations include jumping, skipping, or hopping.

Movement Exercises

Circles.   The group stands in a large circle. Each participant, in turn, thinks of a way to make a circle by using his or her body. It may be a fixed or moving circle, using part or all of the body. All others must make the same circle. Names add to the fun—for example, "This is a halo circle," "This is a shoulder circle," "This is a chicken circle," "This is a Steve Martin circle." Circles will be more original if originality is clearly encouraged.

Mirrors.   Everyone needs a partner. One person becomes a mirror who mimics the movements of the partner. Roles are reversed in about three minutes.

Circus.   Each child becomes a different circus performer or animal. Variations include the leader directing what every one should be, for example, tightrope walkers, trained elephants, lion tamers, jugglers, and so forth.

People machines.   This is everyone's favorite. There are two main strategies. Students can form *groups* of six to twelve students and take 10 or 15 minutes to design and practice their machine. They are performed one at a time for the others, who try to guess what the machine is. Alternatively, with the *add-on* method an idea for a machine is agreed upon and then one person starts the action. Others add themselves. Sounds—beeps, dings, buzzes, pops, and so on—are recommended. One of the best is an old-fashioned pinball game, which can absorb fifty volunteers.

Obstacles.   With chalk, the leader draws a "start" and "finish" line on the floor, about eight feet apart. One at a time, each student makes up an imaginary obstacle that he or she must climb over (past, through, under, around) to get from start to finish. Since only one person participates at a time, it works best with small groups.

Gym workout.   Participants pantomime activities as if they were in an imaginary gym. They run in place, lift weights, roll a medicine ball, climb a rope—all at once or one at a time.

Robot walk.   Each person is a robot with a unique sound and walk. Whenever one robot touches another robot, both stop, sit down, and begin again to rise with a new sound and a new walk.

Balloon burst.   There are two main versions. First, each person is a balloon who is blown up, and up, and up. The balloon can be released and zip around the room, or else blown up until it pops. In the second version the entire group is one balloon that is blown up to the limit, then bursts.

Creative locomotion.   Have children walk like a Crooked Man, the Jolly Green Giant, Raggedy Ann, a robot, and so forth; run like a squirrel, mouse, Miss Muffett frightened by a spider, or the fattest person in the world running for a bus; jump like a kangaroo, popcorn, a jack-in-the-box; or walk through a peanut butter swamp, flypaper, a jungle, tacks, deep sand, or deep Jell-O. The leader and students call out new characters, animals, substances, surfaces, and so on.

Making letters.   Have individuals or two people shape their bodies to become alphabet letters. Others guess the letter. A small group can spell a word.

Imaginary tug-of-war.   Ask for ten volunteers (or pick them, if reluctance prevails). They are divided into two five-person teams. The leader narrates: "This side is struggling hard and seems to be winning. Now the other side is recovering. Look out! The rope broke!" Warn them to listen to the narrator, and be sure they hear the last instruction.

Sensory and Body Awareness

Trust walk (or blind walk).   This is an absolute must. Each person has a partner. The member with eyes shut, or blindfolded, is led around the room, under tables and chairs, and allowed to identify objects by touch, smell, or sound. Students walk down the hall, get a drink of water, try to read names or numbers on doors (such as "Boys"), go outside and explore trees, the sun, shade, a flower, and so on. Ask about experiences and discoveries in a follow-up discussion.

Exploring an orange. Give everyone an orange to examine closely. How does it look, feel, smell, taste? What is unique about your orange? Take the orange apart and examine and discuss the colors, patterns, and textures. Eat the orange.

Empathic vision. Ask students to inspect the room through the eyes of an artist, a fire inspector, lighting engineer, some ants. Look at today's weather from the point of view of a bicyclist, a pilot, a duck, a field mouse, a skier. Who else?

Listening. Have students sit (or lie) silently, listening first for sounds that are close, then for sounds that are far. Encourage concentration, letting sounds evoke associated images and memories. With all eyes shut, students can describe the sounds with their hands, communicating nonverbally.

Smelling. Small bottles are prepared in advance, with such familiar scents as vanilla extract, Vicks Vaporub, peanut butter, used coffee grounds, cinnamon, cloves, rubbing alcohol, lipstick, and so on. In small groups the scents are passed around and students discuss the memories thar are stimulated by each smell. The smells also can be imagined, for example, how does the smell of warm apple sauce and cinnamon make you feel?

Touching. Have students touch many surfaces, concentrating fully on the feel. Use strange objects (for example, a piece of coral) and familiar ones (for example, a piece of paper). A paper sack or box may be used to hide the objects from sight.

Pantomime

Many of the movement and sensory exercises cited thus far also include an element of pantomime (for example, circus, people machines, tug-of-war, creative locomotion). With more "serious" pantomime, students create appropriate positions, physical movements, and even eye movements as they perform in an imaginary environment. With encouragement, students can use their faces, hands, and bodies to express sadness, glee, love, fear, and so on. Pantomime can include relatively simple, short-term involvement, or else lengthier mini-plays without lines.

Some pantomime activities include:

Invisible box. Six to ten students form a circle. In turn, each person lifts the lid on an invisible box (or trunk), removes something, does something with it, then puts it back in the box and closes the lid. The action may go around the circle two or three times.

Invisible balls.   An invisible ball is passed from person to person several times around a small circle (or up and down each row in a class). As each person receives the ball, it changes size, shape, weight, smell, and so forth.

Inside-out.   Children become fish in a tank or zoo animals in cages. Others look in.

Animal pantomimes.   Each child moves to the center of the circle to pantomime his or her animal. Others guess the animal. For variety, two or three animals can act out a simple plot, for example, a cat sneaking up on a mouse; a bear looking for honey but finding bees; a bull spotting some picnickers; a squirrel and a bluejay both trying to get the same piece of bread; a rabbit and a turtle preparing for a short race. Students can think of more.

Creating an environment.   This exercise is much like an add-on people machine. Students think of and create an environment, such as a bowling alley, fishermen in a boat, a playground, ballet class, sea fish and animals, gym class, football team warming up, farm animals, an assembly line processing freshly caught salmon, and so on. The class will think of more possibilities.

Miscellaneous pantomime.   Many brief sketches may teach characterization. With no lines allowed, students pay high attention to movements and expressions. As some examples: a jolly McDonalds counterperson waiting on two or three impatient customers, a fussy person trying on hats or shoes, scared mountain climbers unable to go up or down, three stooges hanging wallpaper or performing heart surgery, a grouchy cab driver in 5 o'clock traffic getting a worried person to the airport, the President of the United States being locked out of the official airplane, and others.

Playmaking

Playmaking involves acting out stories and scenes without a script. To improve the expressiveness of movements and gestures, a sketch may be practiced without lines, that is, in pantomime. With one straightforward strategy, students are given a simple scene (plot), characters are explained, and then students improvise the action.

Way (1967) suggested that mini-plays need not be silly. They can involve, for example, miners working against time to reinforce a mine about to cave in; slow-moving astronauts assembling something on the moon; toyshop toys or museum displays coming alive at the stroke of midnight; Californians experiencing an earthquake; or witches and goblins cooking up a magic brew with improvised important ingredients. Historical episodes, folklore, mythology, fairy tales, nursery rhymes, and animal stories also present possibilities: for example, the Boston Tea Party, Columbus discovering America, Goldilocks and the Three Bears, Cinderella, and others.

A more structured playmaking strategy might run as follows. After a few warmup exercises, the leader tells a story. Then leader and students review the sequence of events—what happened first? Second? The group then discusses characterization, considering physical, emotional, and intellectual qualities (limping, slow, quick-stepping, nervous, angry, happy, excited, calm, conceited, dull-witted, scientific-minded). The play typically is broken down and worked out scene by scene. The group may first act out a scene without dialogue, to explore the movements, expressions and general believability of the characters. After improvements, it is replayed with improvised dialogue. A given scene may be replayed many times, with different students trying different roles. As noted above, ideas may be found in historical or mythological material, or in children's books, nursery rhymes, or other stories. Also, brainstorming may be used to generate plots and ideas.

For playmaking with gifted students, Carelli (1981) mentioned that the students may select the theme, assign responsibilities, plan and implement the activities, including researching the particular historical or mythological event, and evaluate both the process and the final product.

To conclude, creative dramatics is a worthwhile activity that may be used at any age level, from the elementary school pullout program to the high school drama class. By giving students a perfectly logical reason to be silly, feelings of self-consciousness and fear of failure are reduced, and confidence is built. Humor, as we noted earlier in this chapter, is a common component of creativeness, and certainly one encouraged in creative dramatics sessions.

SUMMARY

Creative students tend to be independent, risk-taking, energetic, curious, witty, idealistic, artistic, attracted to the mysterious and complex, and to need alone time.

Negative traits include stubbornness, resistence to domination, uncooperativeness, cynicism, tendencies to question rules, uncommunicativeness, and others.

Lingemann's literature search produced 55 traits of creative people.

Creative abilities include more than fluency, flexibility, originality, and elaboration. Some examples: sensitivity to problems, the ability to define a problem well, the ability to resist premature closure, and visualization, regression, analogical thinking, evaluation, analysis, synthesis, transformation, concentration, and logical-thinking abilities. Many thinking skills and personality traits may be considered creative abilities.

The creative process may be viewed, first, as stages in creative problem solving. Wallas's four stages included preparation, incubation, illumination and verification. A two-stage model included a big idea stage followed by an elaboration and development stage.

The creative problem solving model included fact-finding, problem-finding, idea-finding, solution-finding, and acceptance-finding. Treffinger's hits and hot spots aid in convergently selecting the best ideas in each step.

Keating's four components of socially relevant creativity included content knowledge, divergent thinking, critical analysis, and communication skill.

The creative process also may be viewed as a change in perception, seeing new idea combinations, new relationships, new meanings, new implications, and new applications. This sudden change in perception is not well understood, leading to speculation of suprarational thinking.

Creative dramatics seeks to strengthen divergent thinking, imagination, problem solving, and sensory awareness, as well as discovery and control of emotions and the physical self, humor, self-confidence, and empathic understanding. Five categories of activities include warm-ups, movement exercises, sensory and body awareness, pantomime, and playmaking.

Solutions to Visual Puzzle.

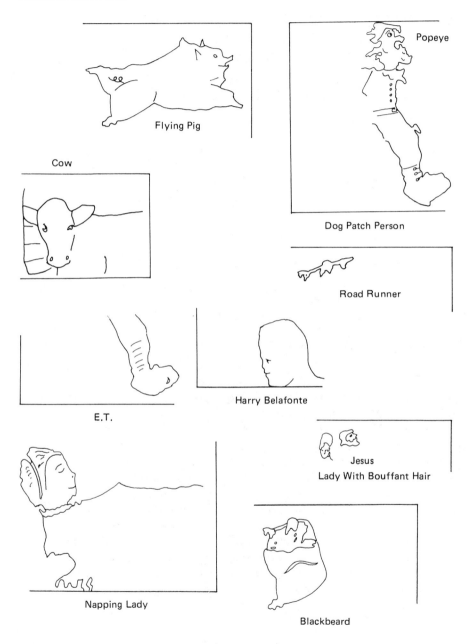

Flying Pig

Popeye

Dog Patch Person

Cow

Road Runner

E.T.

Harry Belafonte

Jesus
Lady With Bouffant Hair

Napping Lady

Blackbeard

chapter eleven

Creativity II
Teaching for Creative Growth

CAN CREATIVITY BE TAUGHT?

The authors frequently are asked a key question: Can creativity be taught or are you born with it? The answer is an unequivocal yes and yes. Some people are born with a special combination of creative genius and intelligence which, activated by high motivation and a sense of destiny, leads them to dream their dreams and implement those creations that make the world a better place. The names of da Vinci, Beethoven, Curie, Edison, Einstein, and George Washington Carver come to mind. No amount of creativity training can elevate an average person to such lofty creativeness.

Despite genetic limits, however, it is absolutely true that everyone's personal creativity can be improved. In the case of gifted and talented children, efforts to strengthen their creative abilities—and get them to use the abilities they were born with—can have visibly dramatic effects, for example, as evidenced in the marvelous products and performances in the Future Problem Solving and Odyssey of the Mind programs.

Goals of Creativity Training

What is it we want children to learn as a result of activities, exercises, and instruction in creativity? Consider the following as goals of creativity training (Davis, 1986):

1. We want students to become "creativity conscious" and to acquire creative attitudes. That is, we want them to become more aware of creativity, more likely to think creatively, and more likely to involve themselves in creative activities.
2. We want students to better understand the topic of creativity.
3. We want students to become involved in creative activities.
4. We want to strengthen creative problem solving processes.
5. We want to strengthen creative personality traits.
6. We want to help students learn creative thinking techniques of the sort used by creative people.
7. We want to strengthen students' creative abilities via practice and exercise.

Most of this chapter will elaborate on these seven points for teaching for creative growth. A final section will comment on creative teaching.

CREATIVITY CONSCIOUSNESS AND CREATIVE ATTITUDES

Increasing creativity consciousness and creative attitudes is the single most important component of teaching for creative growth. Creative attitudes are taught in every creative thinking course and program, and for good reason. To think creatively a person must be consciously aware of creativity. He or she must value creative thinking, appreciate novel and farfetched ideas, be open-minded and receptive to the zany ideas of others, be mentally set to produce creative ideas, and be willing to take creative risks, make mistakes, and even fail.

Improving creative attitudes and awarenesses probably is 90 percent of the problem of stimulating people of any age to think more creatively (Davis and Bull, 1978). Many students are capable of creative achievements. However, they do not think about creativity nor appreciate the importance of creativity for their personal growth—for developing their talents and potential, for coping successfully with their world, and for simply getting more out of life. Students also should become more aware of the importance of creative innovation in the history of civilization, and for solving society's present and future problems. Indeed, without creative innovation and creative people we still would be living in caves during our short and sick lives, and digging roots and clubbing rodents for lunch.

Creative atmosphere. The topic of creative attitudes and creativity consciousness is intimately tied to the notion of a creative atmosphere, a situation where creativity is encouraged and rewarded. Carl Rogers (1962) called it *psychological safety*, a prerequisite for creative thinking. In brainstorming it is called *deferred judgment*—the noncritical, nonevaluative and receptive atmosphere where fresh and even wild ideas may be safely proposed.

It is an ancient and honored principle of psychology that rewarded behavior will persist and become stronger, while punished or ignored behavior will disappear. A creative atmosphere rewards creative thinking and helps it become habitual.

Blocks to creativity.   Creative attitudes and predispositions may be aided by raising students awareness of blocks and barriers to creative thinking, which may be categorized as *perceptual, cultural,* and *emotional* (Davis, 1986; Simberg, 1964). With *perceptual blocks* we become accustomed to perceiving things in familiar ways, and it simply is difficult to view them in a new and creative way. As an illustration of a perceptual block, given BSAINXLEATNTEARS cross out six letters to find a meaningful word. (See footnote when you give up.[1])

Cultural blocks, as with perceptual blocks, also result from learning and habit. With cultural blocks we have the creativity-squelching effects of traditions, conformity pressures, and social expectations, which along with "fear of being different" will nip creativeness in its proverbial bud.

Conformity pressures and social expectations can take the form of idea-squelchers. The following are some favorites, condensed from a longer list by Warren (1974). You may wish to think about installing an innovative G/T program as you read these:

> It won't work . . .
> It's not in the budget . . .
> We've never done it before . . .
> We're not ready for it yet . . .
> What will parents think . . .
> We're too small for that . . .
> We have too many projects now . . .
> Somebody would have suggested it before if it were any good . . .
> You'll never sell it to the union . . .
> We can't do it under the regulations . . .
> It's not in the curriculum
> It'll mean more work . . .
> I'll bet some professor suggested that . . .

Such idea squelchers are the products of unreceptive, inflexible, and uncreative attitudes.

It is true, of course, that the human processes of socialization, education, and even healthy peer relations necessarily require a good measure of conformity. However, children and adults should realize that there is a time for conformity and a time for creativity.

[1] The solution is BANANA. What did you cross out?

Emotional blocks are the insecurities and anxieties that interfere with creative thinking. Here we find temporary states, such as job anxieties, school pressures, emotional problems, or health concerns. We also have more permanent emotional blocks, such as a chronic fear of making mistakes or failing, fear of being different, fear of rejection, fear of supervisors, timidity, poor self-concept, and other persistent anxieties.

UNDERSTANDING THE TOPIC OF CREATIVITY

Any creativity training will have more impact and make a more lasting impression if students are helped to understand the topic of creativity. There is a large body of information that contributes to this understanding (see Davis, 1986, for an overview; also Feldhusen and Treffinger, 1985; Parnes, 1981). Some main topics that could comprise lessons "about creativity" are:

> The importance of creativity to self and society
> Characteristics of creative people
> The nature of creative ideas as modifications, combinations, and analogical "connections"
> The nature of the creative process: Stages, changed perceptions, modifying, combining, analogical thinking
> Creative abilities
> Theories and definitions of creativity
> Tests of creativity and the rationale underlying them
> Creative thinking techniques

Biographies of well-known creative people provide a useful way to teach students about desirable creative characteristics, attitudes, habits, and lifestyles. The *Torrance Tests of Creative Thinking* may be used as the basis for a lesson in the meaning of *fluency, flexibility, originality,* and *elaboration* and their importance in creative thinking.

An Apple computer disk for the upper elementary grades, *Creative Thinking and Problem Solving* (Davis, 1986), teaches brainstorming, attribute listing, analogical thinking, and problem-solving steps. The important opening lesson helps students understand creativity with elaborations of such principles as: Creativity will help you live a more interesting, successful, and enjoyable life; creative people are not rigid, they see things from different points of view and are aware of pressures to conform; creative people take risks, make mistakes, play with ideas, consider lots of ideas, use techniques, think analogically, evaluate their ideas—and they *use* their talents, not waste them.

INVOLVEMENT IN CREATIVE ACTIVITIES

The most effective way to strengthen creative attitudes and abilities, along with relevant technical skills, is to involve students in creative activities.

Possibilities for creative involvement are without limit. In Appendix 8.1 we listed several hundred subtopics in art, science, theatre, etc. that would stimulate creative thinking and problem solving. We particularly recommend Future Problem Solving and Odyssey of the Mind programs, which are designed to strengthen creative thinking and problem solving.

The G/T teacher-coordinator should be continually alert for opportunities to exercise creative thinking and problem solving in content areas. Available opportunities might also be expanded. Are music, science, and art programs adequate? Are students encouraged to become involved in scientific and aesthetic activities? Are community resources and mentors being used to good advantage?

STRENGTHENING THE CREATIVE PROBLEM-SOLVING PROCESS

Chapter 10 described two ways to view the creative process: as a change in perception or as a sequence of steps. Regarding "looking at one thing and seeing something else," a teacher can use optical illusions of the type shown in Chapter 10 to help students (1) practice seeing other meanings, combinations, modifications, and transformations, and (2) understand that even simple things can be seen in different, creative ways.

As for steps and stages, we already have promoted the CPS model as an effective way to solve problems creatively. Teaching the model to any age group that can understand it and use it is a good way to "teach creativity." It would be desirable for students to practice the model until the five steps of fact finding, problem finding, idea finding, solution finding, and acceptance finding become comfortably familiar, if not habitual. That is, when confronted with a problem, opportunity or challenge, one would spontaneously review facts, look at different ways to approach (define) the problem, think of lots of ideas, think of criteria and evaluate the ideas, and think of ways to get the best ideas into action.

Creative thinking techniques, discussed below, also are creative processes that are teachable.

STRENGTHENING CREATIVE PERSONALITY TRAITS

We normally do not speak of "teaching personality traits." However, it may be sensible to recommend that teachers reward and encourage the (positive) kinds of creative traits and behaviors we reviewed in Chapters 2 and 10—confidence, independence, appropriate risk-taking, enthusiasm, adventurousness, curiosity, playfulness, humor, alone time for thinking, artistic and other aesthetic interests, and involvement in creative activities.

As we noted in Chapter 2, the main difference between people who *have* creative abilities and those who *use* their creative potential is in these affective traits that predispose people to think and behave in creative ways.

CREATIVE THINKING TECHNIQUES

Personal Techniques

Personal creative thinking techniques are methods that are developed and used, consciously and unconsciously, by every creative person regardless of the subject or content of his or her creations. This topic lies at the core of central questions such as "Where do ideas come from?" and "What is the nature of the internal creative process?" (Davis, 1981a).

Most personal techniques are analogical in nature. That is, the innovator based the idea for the creation on a news event, an historical event, or an earlier book, movie, melody, art or architecture style, invention, scientific discovery, business idea, or some other previous innovation. Indeed, whenever we hear the phrase "was inspired by . . . " or "was based upon . . . , " we can be sure that a deliberate or accidental analogical technique was used by the particular innovator.

An important point is that every one of the *standard* techniques described in the next section originated as a personal creative thinking technique—a method that some creative person used in his or her day-to-day high-level creative thinking. The standard techniques are unconscious methods made conscious, knowable, and teachable.

To present the flavor of personal creative-thinking techniques, let's look at a few familiar examples. In science, Einstein used what he called "mental experiments." For instance, he would fantasize a trip through space in an elevator at the speed of light in order to produce new perceptions, new relationships, and new ideas.

In art we find recurrent subjects and styles with every famous painter, reflecting their personal creative thinking techniques. Picasso, for example, is known for his African, harlequin, blue, and pink (rose) periods, during which his paintings were inspired by particular themes. He also deliberately disassembled faces and other pictorial elements and put them back together in more original arrangements. Paul Gauguin painted South Pacific natives in his unique style, time and again. Edgar Degas is noted for his graceful ballerinas. Renoir's trademark is his soft pastel, female subjects and still lifes. Georges Seurat used a "dot" painting style (pointillism), often with water and sailboats as subjects. His most famous painting, *Sunday Afternoon on the Island of La Grande Jatte*, inspired the Broadway musical

Sunday in the Park with George—another example of analogical thinking. Even the great Leonardo da Vinci reportedly wandered Italian streets, sketchbook in hand, to locate interesting faces for his painting *The Last Supper*. Throughout art history, ideas for paintings have been taken from mythology, the Bible, or historical events.

In music, all of Franz Liszt's *Hungarian Rhapsodies* were drawn from the folk tunes of Hungarian gypsies. Tchaikovsky, too, developed folk tunes into symphonies. Aaron Copland's marvelous *Appalachian Spring* was based on the Quaker folk tune *Simple Gifts*. Even the ever-popular *Star Spangled Banner* was based on an English drinking song.

Cartoonists continually use a deliberate analogical thinking strategy for finding ideas. In a recent political cartoon the children's TV show "Mr. Rogers' Neighborhood" became "Mr. Gorbachev's Neighborhood." Against a thick background of missiles Mr. Gorbachev's waves and grins "Hi there . . . Can you say 'friend'? . . . I'm your friend . . . Won't you be my friend? . . ." *Bloom County* analogically modified the New York subway vigilante episode into the headline "Olive-Loaf Vigilante Pummels Street Mimes—Unlicensed Luncheon Meat Was Weapon."

Columnist-humorist Art Buchwald also uses deliberate analogical thinking—borrowing ideas and concepts from one area and using them to make a humorous political comment in another. In one column he borrowed ideas from TV soap operas and used them to discuss a new "Seamy, Steamy Tale of Power and Greed—The Budget of the United States Government Fiscal Year 1984":

> I couldn't put it down. I kept turning the pages to see what government programs would be cut next. It's more frightening than *Rosemary's Baby*.
>
> You mean it's a thriller?
>
> It's more of a whodunit. Or, specifically, who's doing it to whom. It's about money and power, the struggle for survival, death and taxes and man's fate in a world he never made.
>
> Any sex?
>
> The military chapters are very sexy, particularly the love scenes between the President of the United States and the new weapons that the Pentagon has seduced him into buying.
>
> You mean the President is in bed with the military-industrial complex?
>
> All through the book! Some of the scenes are so hot that Tip O'Neill has threatened to ban the book in Boston . . .*

Toward the end of the sixteenth century, Holinshed's *Chronicles*, a history book, was published. William Shakespeare used it extensively as a source of ideas for *Macbeth, Henry IV, Henry V, Henry VI, Richard II*, and others. He drew from Plutarch's *Lives* to write *Antony and Cleopatra* and *Coriolanus*. *Troilus and Cressida* came from various accounts of the story of Troy.

* Reprinted by permission of Art Buchwald.

Contemporary writers continue to use identifiable procedures to inspire novels and movies. For example, Truman Capote used a Midwest murder as the inspiration for *In Cold Blood*. The Normandy invasion was the basis of the novel and movie *The Longest Day*; Pearl Harbor was the source of ideas for *Tora, Tora, Tora!* and *From Here to Eternity*. Another movie, *All the President's Men*, was based on Watergate. In a recent interview the screenwriter of *High Noon* confessed that the inspiration for his award-winning suspense western came from the intimidation of writers and actors in Hollywood by organized crime in the 1950s. Countless other ideas for movies and novels have been found by looking at Greek and Roman history (*I, Claudius*, for example), Biblical history (*Moses*), American history (*Gone with the Wind*), Egyptian history (*Cleopatra*), and so on.

The most successful Hollywood motion pictures to date comprise the *Star Wars* series—based partly on an effective personal creative thinking technique used by the creator George Lucas. While writing the script for *Star wars* Lucas read books on mythology. Said Lucas in a *Time* magazine interview, "I wanted *Star Wars* to have an epic quality, and so I went back to the epics." Thus we find a young man who must prove his manhood to himself and to his father; who rescues a princess in distress; who has an older and wiser mentor (actually two, Ben Kenobi and Yoda); and who battles with a villain, Darth Vader. Some western movies have been built deliberately around the same principles.

Professional comedians also use personal creative-thinking techniques, both for their unique type of humor and for their original delivery. Norm Crosby uses malapropisms: In one commercial he is "very enameled" of his light beer; he also has a "great affliction" for Johnny Carson. The comedian Don Rickles insults people, using the same insults again and again ("Shut up dummy, you're makin' a fool of yourself!").

Rodney Dangerfield's "I don't get no respect" theme makes him one of the most successful American comedians. He continually puts himself down: "When I was born the doctor told my mother, 'I did everything I could, but he's gonna' be okay.'" "I couldn't play hide-and-seek 'cause nobody wanted to find me!" "I remember when I called this girl for a date. She said, 'Sure, come on over, nobody's home.' So I went over an' nobody was home!" "Last week I went to a psychiatrist. He said 'I think you're crazy.' I said I wanted another opinion, so he said 'Okay, I think you're ugly too!'"

The list of creations and innovations produced via a personal creative thinking technique, usually analogical in nature, could be endless.

Developing Personal Creative Thinking Techniques

There are several ways students may be encouraged to develop personal creative thinking techniques. First, students should understand how even extraordinarily creative people have "found" ideas. This demystifies creativity and helps convince students that they also can legitimately build upon existing ideas without feeling "uncreative." After all, if William Shakespeare, Franz Liszt, George Lucas, and Art Buchwald can borrow plots, tunes, and ideas, so can they. Many young writers, artists, and composers are erroneously convinced that their ideas must be 100-percent original and never inspired by an outside source.

Second, some recurrent personal creative thinking techniques may be teachable. For example, some techniques include:

1. Deliberately seeking inspiration from analogically-related situations, innovations, and ideas.
2. Adapting solutions from similar types of problems, which also is analogical thinking.
3. Modifying, combining, and improving present ideas
4. Starting with the goal and working backward to deduce what is required to reach that goal
5. Beginning with an "ideal" or "perfect" solution—such as having the problem solve itself—and again working backwards to design a creative solution
6. Asking yourself how the problem will be solved 25, 100, or 200 years from now

Third, since personal creative thinking techniques develop (1) in the course of doing creative things or (2) from instruction by people who use and understand such techniques, G/T students should become involved in such inherently creative activities as art, photography, creative writing, acting, journalism, independent science, or other activities requiring creative thinking and problem solving.

Mentorships may be especially good, since they involve many hours of direct, personal work with a creative professional. Field trips lead to exposure to experts, to creative ideas, and to sophisticated elaborations and embellishments of ideas.

Visitors also can teach personal creative thinking techniques. For example, a visiting artist program can help children understand the creative processes of a professional artist or writer. School districts in some states contract with a different visiting artist or writer each school year. In this way children have a close view of, and learning experience with, a variety of artists during their school years. University and industry researchers and other creative professionals also may be invited to share their experiences related to creative discoveries and creative thinking.

STANDARD CREATIVE THINKING TECHNIQUES

There are several well-known methods for producing new ideas and new idea combinations that are taught in most university and professional creativity training courses. The strategies also may be taught to middle and high school students, and to gifted and talented elementary students. One lively workbook, *Imagination Express* (Davis and DiPego, 1973), incorporates standard creative thinking techniques into a fantasy story about a Saturday subway ride from Kansas City to Pittsburgh to Dublin to Tokyo to Santa Monica and back. It also teaches good creative attitudes and awarenesses. The workbook was written for approximately the seventh-grade level, but older students (including teachers) and younger students seem to benefit as well. The techniques of brainstorming, attribute listing, analogical thinking, and some others are taught in the upper-elementary/middle school Apple Computer disk *Creative Thinking and Problem Solving* (Davis, 1985).

It is worth repeating that every "standard" creative thinking technique began as a personal technique that some perceptive person identified, explained, and thus made conscious and teachable.

Brainstorming

In the case of brainstorming, it was Alex Osborn, cofounder of the New York advertising agency Batten, Barton, Dursten and Osborn and founder in 1954 of the Creative Education Foundation, who identified the conditions and listed the rules for brainstorming. The main principle is *deferred judgment*: Idea evaluation is postponed until later. As we mentioned earlier, deferred judgment implicitly creates a receptive, creative atmosphere and teaches good creative attitudes: receptiveness to and appreciation for novel, perhaps farfetched ideas. Osborn (1963) observed that any type of criticism or evaluation interferes with the generation of imaginative ideas, simply because you cannot do both at once. The purpose of any brainstorming session is to generate a long list of possible problem solutions.

Brainstorming is an effective procedure that may be used in the classroom for (1) teaching brainstorming as an effective creative thinking technique, (2) practicing creative thinking (thus strengthening attitudes and abilities), and/or (3) solving some pressing school problem, such as high absenteeism, messy school grounds, drug problems, traffic problems, bicycle thefts, raising money, selling play tickets, and so on. The four ground rules are quite simple:

1. **Criticism is ruled out.** This is deferred judgment, which contributes to the creative atmosphere so essential for uninhibited imaginations.
2. **Freewheeling is welcomed.** The wilder the idea the better. Seemingly preposterous ideas sometimes lead to imaginative yet workable solutions.
3. **Quantity is wanted.** This principle reflects the purpose of the session: to produce a long list of ideas, thus increasing the likelihood of finding good problem solutions.
4. **Combination and improvement are sought.** This lengthens the idea list. Actually, during the session students will spontaneously "hitch-hike" on each other's ideas, with one idea inspiring the next.

Variations on brainstorming include *reverse brainstorming*, in which new viewpoints are found by turning the problem around. For example: How can we *increase* vandalism? How can we *increase* the electric bill? How can we *stifle* creativity? How can we *decrease* morale? Reverse brainstorming quickly points out what currently is being done incorrectly, and implicitly suggests specific solutions. With *Stop-and-Go* brainstorming, short (about 10-minute) periods of brainstorming are interspersed with short periods of evaluation. This helps to keep the group on target by selecting the apparently most profitable directions. In the *Phillips 66* technique small groups of six brainstorm for six minutes, after which a member of each group reports either the best ideas or all ideas to the larger group.

It is easy to run a classroom brainstorming session. The teacher begins by discussing creativity and creative ideas, which leads to brainstorming as one method that stimulates creative thinking. Rules are discussed, a problem selected—such as "How can we turn the classroom into a foreign planet?" or "How can we raise money?"—and a volunteer scribe lists ideas on the blackboard. The teacher-leader's role is to frequently ask, "Anyone else have an idea?" Or the leader might specifically ask the quieter students if they have ideas they wish to contribute. If a serious problem (for example, messy hallways) is the focus, the leader can give the group 48 hours advance notice of the nature of the problem. Gifted and talented students can learn to organize and lead brainstorming sessions.

Idea evaluation.   Merely listing wild ideas does not represent the complete problem-solving process. Therefore, a brainstorming session may be profitably followed by an idea evaluation session. Idea evaluation would be most important if the class intended to present the school principal (or the mayor) with some blue-ribbon solutions to a real current problem. The group can brainstorm evaluation criteria, such as: Will it work? Can the school afford it? Will the community (parents, principal, mayor) go for it? Is adequate time available? Are materials available? And others. As we saw in the previous chapter, the most relevant criteria would be listed across the top of an *evaluation matrix*, the specific ideas in rows down the left side. Table 11.1 shows one evaluation matrix that was constructed to evaluate ideas brainstormed for the problem "How can we build school spirit?" The numerical row totals provide a guide to the ideas that students may wish to realistically pursue.

The use of objective criteria for the evaluation process serves many purposes. (1) It helps the class objectively evaluate ideas, of course. (2) It helps students learn to evaluate as part of the overall creative problem-solving process. (3) Evaluation requires students to consider many components of the problem. (4) The use of criteria helps prevent the evaluation from becoming a personal attack on specific children. (5) In some cases an objective evaluation can help the group explore its value system relative to

TABLE 11.1 Example of Evaluation Matrix

IDEAS	CRITERIA						
	Cost	Effect on Teachers	Educa-tional Effects	School Spirit Effect	Effect on Students	Effect on Community	Totals
Buy class sweatshirts	+3	+2	+1	+3	+3	+3	15
Establish school baseball team	−2	+2	0	+2	+2	+2	6
Start interclass competition	0	0	+1	+3	+2	0	6
Get new school building	−3	+3	+2	+3	+3	−2	6
Get rid of "hoods"	−3	0	−3	+1	−3	−3	−11

POSITIVE EFFECTS

+3 = Excellent
+2 = Good
+1 = Fair
 0 = Not Applicable

NEGATIVE EFFECTS

−1 = Slightly Negative
−2 = Somewhat Negative
−3 = Very Negative

the problem at hand. Finally, (6) idea evaluation can help children understand that thinking of "silly" and "far-fetched" ideas truly can result in good and practical solutions to problems.

Evaluation sessions may follow the use of any of the creative thinking techniques described in this section.

Attribute Listing

Robert Crawford (1978), designer of *attribute listing*, argued that, "Each time we take a step we do it by changing an attribute or a quality of something, or else by applying that same quality or attribute to some other thing." Attribute listing thus is both a *theory* of the creative process and a practical creative thinking *technique*. Following Crawford's definition, there are two forms of attribute listing: (1) attribute modifying and (2) attribute transferring. Either strategy may be used individually or with a group.

Attribute modifying.   The problem solver lists main attributes (characteristics, dimensions, parts) of a problem object, then thinks of ways to improve each attribute. For example, a group of students might invent new types of candy bars or breakfast cereals by first writing important attributes (size, shape, flavor, ingredients, color, texture, packaging, nutritional value, name, and so on) on the blackboard, and then listing specific ideas under each main attribute. Particularly good combinations may be picked out of the lists of ideas. In university design engineering courses, this strategy is called the *substitution method* of design.

In case there is any doubt that creative people actually use such a mechanical procedure, Fran Stryker used attribute listing for years to generate radio and TV episodes for his *Lone Ranger* series (Shallcross, 1981). Stryker used the attributes of *characters, goals, obstacles,* and *outcomes.* In the first column he listed specific ideas for *characters,* broadly defined to include objects and animals. *Goals* included things the character(s) wanted to become, to achieve, or to happen. *Obstacles* could be literally a brick wall or desert, but also personal characteristics such as timidity or aggressiveness. *Outcomes* could include reaching the goal, changing goals, changing personalities, or getting shot or caught. Stryker reportedly would shut his eyes, pick an idea from each column (probably several from the characters column), and then think about whether the combination would make a good episode. If not, the combination could be modified, or else it would take about three seconds to create another possibility.

A modification of Stryker's strategy was used in the computer disk *Creative Thinking and Problem Solving* (Davis, 1985) to teach children (1) the attribute listing method and (2) what components are needed for writing short stories (characters, settings, important objects, obstacles), and (3) how to create ideas for those components. Generally, the attribute listing technique is simple and it works—whether used for inventing breakfast cereals, writing short story plots, or solving any other problem in which attributes can be identified.

Attribute transferring.   Here we have a pure case of analogical thinking—transferring ideas from one context to another. We noted above how deliberate analogical thinking is used by creative persons in many aesthetic, scientific, or other areas. As one classroom application, ideas for a creative and memorable parents' night or open house might be found by borrowing ideas from a carnival or circus, Disneyland, E.T., the Wild West, a funeral parlor, McDonald's, or a *Star Wars* or *Frankenstein* movie.

Morphological Synthesis

The *morphological synthesis* technique is a simple extension of the attribute listing procedure (Allen, 1962; Davis, 1973, 1986). Specific ideas for one attribute or dimension of a problem are listed along one axis of a matrix, ideas for a second attribute are listed along the other axis. Plenty of idea combinations are found in the cells of the matrix. One sixth-grade class invented new sandwich ideas with the morphological synthesis technique (see Figure 11.1). With a third dimension (for example, type of bread) you would have a cube with three-way combinations in each cell.

A sixth grade Milwaukee class used the morphological synthesis method to generate 121 zany ideas for creative sandwiches. Can you find a tasty combination? A revolting one? If you add a third dimension, with five types of bread, how many total ideas would you have?

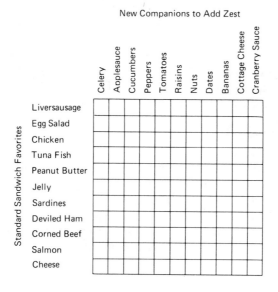

Ratings of Various Spreads

Flavor	Choices				
	1st	2nd	3rd	4th	5th
Super Goober (Peanut Butter/Cranberry)	17	2	1	0	4
Charlies Aunt (Tuna and Applesauce)	3	16	2	2	1
Irish Eyes are Smiling (Corn Beef and Cottage Cheese)	0	0	16	2	6
Cackleberry Whiz (Hard Boiled Eggs/Cheese Whiz)	1	3	2	14	4
Hawaiian Eye (Cream Cheese and Pineapple)	3	3	3	6	9

FIGURE 11.1 A Morphological Sandwich.

From *Creativity Is Forever*, second ed., by G. A. Davis (Dubuque, IA: Kendall/Hunt, 1986). Used with permission.

In fact, the method may be used with a half-dozen or so dimensions by listing ideas in columns. One recommendation is to cut the columns into strips that may be moved up or down to create the hundreds (or thousands) of possible combinations that could be found by reading horizontally.

Idea Checklists

Sometimes, one can find a *checklist* which suggests solutions for your problem. For example, the *Yellow Pages* are often used as a checklist for problems like "Who can fix my TV?" or "Where can I get a haircut?" High school counselors have used the *Yellow Pages* for career counseling ideas. A Sears or gift store catalogue may be used to solve a gift-giving problem.

Some idea checklists have been designed especially for creative problem solving (see Davis, 1973). The most popular of these is Alex Osborn's (1963) *73-idea-spurring questions* (Table 11.2). Take a few extra seconds as you read through this list and think of how a mouse trap, a back pack, a can of soda pop, or a poster advertising a school play might be improved by the suggestions on the list. Ideas will be elicited virtually involuntarily.

Synectics Methods

Synectics, taken from the Greek word *synecticos*, means the joining together of apparently unrelated elements. It was his work with creative-thinking groups that led William J. J. Gordon, originator of the synectics methods, to identify strategies that creative people use unconsciously. He made these strategies conscious and teachable in a form for adults (Gordon, 1961) and for children. His workbooks, *Making it Strange*, Books 1–4

TABLE 11.2   Osborn's "73 Idea-Spurring Questions"

Put to other uses? New ways to use as is? Other uses if modified?

Adopt? What else is like this? What other idea does this suggest? Does the past offer a parallel? What could I copy? Whom could I emulate?

Modify? New twist? Change meaning, color, motion, sound, odor, form, shape? Other changes?

Magnify? What to add? More time? Greater frequency? Stronger? Higher? Longer? Thicker? Extra value? Plus ingredient? Duplicate? Multiply? Exaggerate?

Minify? What to subtract? Smaller? Condensed? Miniature? Lower? Shorter? Lighter? Omit? Streamline? Split up? Understate?

Substitute? Who else instead? What else instead? Other ingredient? Other material? Other process? Other power? Other place? Other Approach? Other tone of voice?

Rearrange? Interchange components? Other pattern? Other layout? Other sequence? Transpose cause and effect? Change pace? Change schedule?

Reverse? Transpose positive and negative? How about opposites? Turn it backward? Turn it upside down? Reverse roles? Change shoes? Turn tables? Turn other cheek?

Combine? How about a blend, an alloy, an assortment, an ensemble? Combine units? Combine purposes? Combine appeals? Combine ideas?

(Gordon, 1974), *Teaching is Listening* (Gordon and Poze, 1972a), *Strange and Familiar* (Gordon and Poze, 1972b), The *New Art of the Possible* (Gordon and Poze, 1980), and Bob Stanish's (1977) *Sunflowering* give children first-hand experience with the fascinating synectics problem-solving methods of direct analogy, personal analogy, and fantasy analogy.

Direct analogy. With this method the person is asked to think of ways that similar problems are solved in nature by animals, birds, flowers, weeds, bugs, worms, lizards, and so on. For example, ideas for conserving energy could be found by asking how animals keep warm in winter.

In a creativity workshop for the elderly, many expressed concern for their personal safety. With a synectics approach the problem became, "How do animals, plants, birds, etc., protect themselves, and how can these ideas help the elderly?" The list included spray cans of skunk scent, slip-on fangs and claws (mildly poisonous), a compressed air can that screams, an electronic transmitter that secretly "yells" for police assistance, traveling only in groups, camouflage, or disguises (for example, wearing a police uniform), and others.

Personal analogy. Imagine you are a piece of candy sitting quietly with your candy friends on the shelf of the local drugstore. A little boy walks in, places two cents on the counter and points at you. How do you feel? What are your thoughts? Describe your experiences for the next fifteen minutes. The purpose of such exercises, similar to the "be the thing" exercises in Gordon's *Making It Strange* workbooks, is to give elementary students practice with the *personal analogy* creative thinking technique. With this strategy, new perspectives are found by becoming part of the problem, usually a problem object. What would you be like if you were a highly efficient can opener? A captivating short story? A truly exciting and valuable educational learning experience for children?

Fantasy analogy. Problem solvers think of fantastic, farfetched, perhaps ideal solutions which can lead to creative yet practical ideas. Gordon sees fantasy analogy as a type of Freudian wish fulfillment. For example, one can ask how to make the problem solve itself: How can we make the hallways keep themselves clean? How can we get parents to want to attend open house? How can we get the School Board to want to give us a new instructional materials center? Some years ago, design engineers probably asked: How can we get refrigerators to defrost themselves, make their own ice cubes? How can we get ovens to clean themselves? Automobile brakes to adjust themselves? This was employing fantasy analogy.

The synectics methods can be used in the classroom either as (1) creativity exercises or (2) material for lessons in techniques of creative thinking.

Implementation Charting

Implementation charting will help gifted children see implementation as the realistic next step in creative thinking, following the generation of ideas and the evaluative selection of one or more workable solutions. With implementation charting students are taught to prepare a chart specifying both (1) the persons responsible for implementing components of the idea(s), and (2) a completion deadline. For example, if the best idea for increasing school spirit were to sell school sweatshirts, then an implementation chart such as the one in Table 11.3 might be suitable.

Note also, there is more than one role of *evaluation* in creative problem solving. In the present example, the initial ideas were evaluated in an evaluation matrix (Table 11.1). After the idea(s) are selected and the project implemented, another evaluation must determine if the project was effective and successful and if it should be continued. Perhaps the group will be ready to implement a second idea, for example, for encouraging school spirit.

TABLE 11.3   Implementation Chart for Selling School Sweatshirts

ACTIVITY	PERSON RESPONSIBLE	TIME FOR IMPLEMEN- TATION
1. Ask permission for project	Ron	March 10
2. Design sweatshirt	Mary, Ruth	March 15–20
3. Approve design	Student Council	March 22
4. Review possible sweatshirt sellers	Barb, John	March 15–20
5. Make recommendation to Student Council	Student Council	March 22
6. Order sweatshirts	Barb, John	March 24
7. Organize student sales campaign	Tom, Mary & Allan	March 22–31
a. Posters	Bob, Andy	March 25
b. Article in school newspaper	Alice	March 25–31
c. Article in community newspaper	Allan	March 28
8. Actual beginning of sales	Tom, Mary & Allan	April 10
9. Student Sweatshirt Day	Ron, Mary & Ruth	April 12
10. Evaluation of success of project	Original Brainstorming Group	April 20

STRENGTHENING CREATIVE ABILITIES

In Chapter 10 we itemized abilities that logically underlie creativity. It is a common and reasonable strategy to try to strengthen creative abilities through practice and exercise, the same way we strengthen skills of reading, math, typing, solving chemistry problems, and shooting baskets.

We will look again at some of those abilities, noting strategies, exercises, or materials that aim at strengthening each ability. Note that most exercises not only exercise creative abilities, they also implicitly raise creativity consciousness and bend attitudes in a creative direction.

Fluency, flexibility, originality, elaboration.   Many types of questions and problems will exercise these traditional cognitive abilities underlying creativity. Students can work on these as a class, perhaps following brainstorming rules, or else individually. One of the best and most involving methods is to divide students into problem-solving teams. All teams work on the same problem and then report all or the best ideas to the entire class. Students often are surprised at the different problem interpretations, approaches, and ideas from the other groups.

Some useful types of exercises for stimulating fluency, flexibility, originality, and elaboration are as follows.

1. With "What would happen if . . . ?" exercises students list consequences for unlikely events. The events may be imaginary or potentially real. What would happen if each person had an eye in the back of his or her head? If dinosaurs roamed America? If elves stole everyone's buttons? What would America be like if the British had won the Revolutionary War? If Lincoln had remained a log splitter? If the earth shifted and Brooklyn became the North Pole? What would we do without numbers? Automobiles? Music? TV? Peanut butter? McDonald's? Football?

2. Thinking of *product improvements* is another type of open-ended question. Students may be asked to think of improvements for any product or process—pencils, desks, jogging shoes, classrooms, bicycles, pianos, school lunches, soda pop, Cracker Jacks, computers, a bathtub, and so on.

3. Thinking of *unusual uses* for common objects is probably the single oldest creativity test item; it also makes a good exercise. How might we use discarded rubber tires? A coat hanger? Empty plastic gallon milk containers? A wooden stick? A sheet of paper? Leftover and wasted cafeteria food?

4. Posing *problems and paradoxes* is intrinsically interesting and challenging. A problem may require a solution, or a puzzling situation may require a logical explanation. The problem may be realistic or fanciful. For example: How can bicycle thefts be eliminated? How can the lunch menu be improved? What can we buy for parents for Christmas/Hanukah for five dollars? How can the school (family) light bill be reduced. How can our health be improved? What can be done for Mr. Smith, a former night watchman who is 50 years old, out

of work, and has no special skills? How could we remove a stubborn elephant from the living room? How can we keep gremlins from stealing the melons from the melon patch? How can the three bears prevent burglaries?

Here are some examples of problems requiring explanations: The principal suddenly cancels recess. Why? The grass behind billboards in pastures is often lush. Why? Ten paintings were discovered missing from the art gallery, but there was no sign of a break-in. How could they have disappeared?

5. With *design problems*, students can design an ideal school, an airplane for hauling nervous kangaroos, a better lawn mower, more functional clothes, safer ways to travel, a more efficient way to serve lunch in the cafeteria, new sandwiches or other treats for McDonald's, a better mouse trap, and so on.

Looking more specifically at each ability, *fluency* can be exercised by having students list things, for example, that are round, square, sweet, sour, blue, white, made of metal, made of wood, long and slender, short and stubby, smell good, taste bad, or have sharp edges. Some *flexibility* exercises ask students to look at things from different perspectives: How does this room look to a tidy housekeeper? A hungry mouse? An alien from outer space? How does a highway look to a tire? A crow? A lost pilot? *Elaboration* exercises require the learner to build upon a basic idea, for example, developing the dog walking or cat petting machine in detail—measurements, materials, costs—or writing the short story developed from attribute listing.

Sensitivity to problems. Exercises aimed at strengthening problem sensitivity should have the learners find problems, detect difficulties, or detect missing information. Therefore, one type of exercise is having students ask questions about an ambiguous situation or even a common object. For example, what questions could you ask about clouds, Mexico, Mickey Mouse, a typewriter, the moon, or the school lunch program. Another type of problem sensitivity exercise would begin with "What don't we know about . . . ?" Or "What is wrong with . . . "

Problem defining   *Problem defining* is a complex ability. Relevant exercises would evolve around:

Identifying the real problem and simplifying and clarifying the problem. What is the basic problem here? What are we really trying to do? What really needs attention (fixing)?

Isolating important aspects of a problem. What is relevant? Essential? What should we focus on? What can we ignore?

Identifying subproblems. What problems are related to the main problem? What problems will follow from each solution?

Proposing alternative problem definitions, as in the IWWMW ("In what ways might we . . . ?") tactic of the CPS model (see Chapter 10).

Defining the problem more broadly, to open up new solution possibilities.

Visualization and imagination.   *Visualization* and *imagination* are obviously central creative abilities. Three books filled with imagination stimulation exercises are *Put Your Mother on the Ceiling* (DeMille, 1973), *Scamper*
(Eberle, 1971), and *200 Ways of Using Imagery in the Classroom* (Bagley and
Hess, 1984). All ask students to relax, shut their eyes, and visualize some
colorful narration, for example: "Now put a light bulb in each hand . . .
Hold your hands straight out to the side . . . Pretend that your light bulbs
are jet engines . . . Run down the street for a take off . . . " (Eberle, 1971).

Another exercise guaranteed to elicit visualization is a creative writing
activity suggested by Helman and Larson (1980): "Cut out headlines from
a newspaper dealing with unusual stories and have the kids make up the
stories." The familiar grocery store rags provide an endless supply of candidate headlines. As some recent winners: "Cannibals Shrink Space Alien's
Head—Dramatic Photo Inside," "5,000 Bodies Vanish from Old Ceme-
tery," "Angry Dad Sells Bratty Kids," "Two Ton Soprano Falls and
Crushes Cellist," "Mouse Hunter Shoots Himself in the Foot," "Baby Born
Talking Gives Dad Winning Lottery Numbers," and "Amazing Duck Man
Lays a Real Egg."

Analogical Thinking.   Many exercises for stimulating analogical thinking appear in the Gordon (1974), Gordon and Poze (1972a, 1972b, 1980),
and Stanish (1977) books mentioned earlier. The G/T teacher also can
make up exercises that stimulate direct analogies or personal analogies, for
example: "How is a _____ like a _____?" "What kind of
weather (animal, vegetable, car, book, fish, sport, magazine, etc.) is like
you?" "What in nature might have given somebody the idea for an um-
brella (bicycle, tin can, belt, pencil, submarine, velcro, trash masher)"?

Analysis, synthesis, evaluation.   *Analysis, synthesis,* and *evaluation,* of
course, are Bloom's (1974) higher-level thinking skills that we will see in
Chapter 12. Ideas for exercises are suggested in that chapter.

Resisting premature closure.   Most children and adults are guilty of
grabbing the first idea that presents itself. However, considering lots of
ideas and deferring judgment are two of the most basic principles of creative problem solving, principles that students should thoroughly understand. Brainstorming, with heavy emphasis on the rationale behind deferring judgment, should help with this pivotal ability (or attitude).

OTHER CREATIVITY EXERCISES

There are many other exercises that may be used to strengthen creative
abilities. Some are relatively simple divergent thinking exercises; others ask
for aesthetic products or complex solutions to difficult problems. While

some exercises may be tied to content areas, others are not. Shallcross (1981), for example, created exercises that could be integrated into specific subject matters. As some samples:

1. Sculpt something using leaves, rocks, paste, and a paper bag (art).
2. List ways to get children to enjoy brushing their teeth (health).
3. Invent a one-step "meal-in-one" (home arts).
4. Plan a mystery or soap opera series using the morphological synthesis approach (language arts).
5. Think of new ways to measure time, water, air, or height (math).
6. Have someone strike three notes on a piano. Use them as the basis for a melody (music).
7. Invent stretching exercises for joggers (physical education).
8. Brainstorm ways endangered species might be preserved (science).
9. Brainstorm ways different cultures could learn to understand each other better (social studies).

Many publishers of educational materials offer workbooks with ideas for creativity exercises and activities. One recent book by Bob Stanish (1988), *The Hearthstone Traveler*, includes instruction and exercises for poetry writing (cinquains, diamanté), creative writing, humor, analogical thinking, values, recognizing patterns in nature, idea-finding techniques (brainstorming and variations, idea checklists, attribute listing, forced combinations, synectics methods), the CPS model, idea evaluation, and more. Consider the cinquain writing strategy:

Select a title word (for example, merry-go-round).
Brainstorm words associated with the title (for example, wild horses, beasts, children, music, mirrors, ticket to ride).
Brainstorm a second list of "-ing" words descriptive of the title (for example, smiling, laughing, playing, circling, spinning, galloping, running).
Brainstorm a third list of feeling words also ending in "-ing" (for example, exciting, wondering, thrilling, mastering, owning the world, riding high).
Write the title on one line, two associated words on the second line, three "-ing" words on the third line, four feeling "-ing" words on the fourth line, and another word associated with the title on the fifth line.

As evidence that it works, the following was created on-the-spot by nonpoet Davis:

Merry-go-round
Music, wild horses
Galloping, playing, laughing
Thrilling, wondering, mastering, owning the world
Ticket to ride.

Said Stanish, such cinquain may be used to write about oneself, to capture the essence of a reading assignment or an important person one has studied, or as the conclusion to a unit of study. Try it. Some of Stanish's (1988) other exercises include:

In what ways is a clam like a galaxy?

Investigate the use of spirals in computer art, Van Gogh paintings, the human face, the horns of animals, floral patterns, religious temples.

If I were a hawk, in what ways might I assert an opinion?

Consider a starfish pattern. What could you create with this design if it had a fragrance (or pockets, wheels, legs, handles, many colors), if it were smaller (larger than a house), if it were in an automobile (aircraft), if it had wings (or a battery, one long arm), if it were made of clear plastic (or styrofoam, rubber), or if it rotated (could be thrown), etc.

Something that few people know about me is . . .

Create a humorous drawing that merges two meanings of a word (for example, horn, school, bark, sock, punch).

What kind of sound would an exclamation point (question mark, dollar sign) make?

Invent a Rube Goldberg machine, with at least five steps, to time your suntan (walk your dog, tickle an armadillo's stomach).

The possibilities for mind-stretching, ability-strengthening exercises are endless, particularly with a little searching and brainstorming by the G/T teacher.

CREATIVE TEACHING AND LEARNING

Torrance (1977b) stated that ". . . people fundamentally prefer to learn in creative ways." These ways include exploring, manipulating, questioning, experimenting, risking, testing, and modifying ideas. Said Torrance, learning creatively takes place during the processes of sensing problems, deficiencies, or gaps in information; formulating hypotheses or guesses about a problem; testing the hypotheses, revising and retesting the hypotheses; and then communicating the results. He explained that problems arouse tension, thus motivating the learner to ask questions, make guesses, and test the adequacy of the guesses, correcting errors and modifying conclusions if necessary. Further, when something is discovered we are inspired to ". . . want to tell someone about it." Creative learning, observed Torrance, is superior to "learning by authority." While creative learning strengthens such abilities as problem sensitivity, fluency, flexibility, originality, elaboration, and redefinition, learning by authority seems to strengthen primarily memory and logical reasoning (Torrance, 1977).

Some recommendations for creative teaching included the following:

Maintain high teacher enthusiasm.
Accept individual differences, for example, in preferred ways of learning, learning rates, faults, and so forth.
Permit the curriculum to be different for different pupils.
Communicate that the teacher is "for" rather than "against" the child.
Encourage and permit self-initiated projects.
Support students against peer conformity pressures.
Allow or encourage a child to achieve success in an area and in a way possible for him or her.
Respect the potential of low achievers.
Do not be blinded by intelligence test scores; they do not tell the whole story.
Do not let pressure for evaluation get the upper hand.
Encourage divergent ideas; too many "right" ideas are stifling.
Do not be afraid to wander off the teaching schedule and try something different.

Torrance (1981a, 1981c) summarized some signs that creative learning is taking place, which partly represent benefits of creative teaching and learning. These include improved motivation, alertness, curiosity, concentration, and achievement; a charged atmosphere "tingling with excitement"; the combining of activities that cut across curriculum areas, and a continuity of activities, one leading to another; improved communication of ideas and feelings; a "boldness" in ideas, drawings, stories, and so on; improved self-confidence; improved creative growth and creative expression; and importantly, a reduction of unproductive behavior, behavior problems, hostility, vandalism, and apathy, and an increase in enthusiasm about school and learning and improved career aspirations.

Creativity training and creative teaching can indeed make a difference for gifted, normal, and even troubled students.

SUMMARY

Creativity can be increased.

Goals of creativity training include increasing creativity consciousness and creative attitudes, helping students understand creativity, involving students in creative activities, strengthening creative problem-solving processes, reinforcing creative personality traits, helping students learn creative thinking techniques, and strengthening creative abilities.

Creativity consciousness and creative attitudes includes an awareness of creativity, valuing creativity, a predisposition to think creatively, a willingness to make mistakes, and others.

The notion of creative attitudes includes the creative atmosphere and blocks to creative thinking, which may be perceptual, cultural, or emotional. Conformity pressures and social expectations may take the form of idea squelchers.

Helping students understand creativity can involve lessons on the importance of creativity, characteristics of creative people, creative abilities, theories of creativity, creativity tests, creativity techniques, and the nature of creative ideas and the creative process.

Involvement in creative activities is especially valuable for developing creative skills and abilities.

The creative process may be strengthened by (1) helping students see other meanings, combinations, and transformations, perhaps using optical illusions, and (2) teaching the CPS model. Creativity techniques also are teachable creative processes.

Personality traits contributing to creativity should be reinforced, for example, confidence, appropriate risk-taking, curiosity, playfulness and humor, and artistic and aesthetic interests.

Personal creativity techniques, usually analogical, are used by every creatively productive person. Examples were cited from science, art, music, political cartooning and cartoon strips, political satire, theatre, movie-making, and comedy.

Students may be helped to develop personal creativity techniques by (1) explaining the nonmysterious techniques used by others, (2) teaching such problem-solving strategies as looking for analogically-related solutions, working backwards from an ideal goal, or asking how the problem might be solved in the future, (3) involvement in creative activities, and (4) instruction from creative professionals who use such techniques.

Standard creative thinking techniques are commonly taught in creativity courses and workshops.

Brainstorming is based on deferred judgment. Variations include reverse brainstorming, stop-and-go brainstorming, and the Phillips 66 procedure.

Students may be taught idea evaluation with an evaluation matrix.

The attribute listing technique takes two forms, (1) modifying important problem attributes, and (2) transferring attributes from one situation to another, which is analogical thinking.

Morphological synthesis, an extension of attribute listing, is a matrix approach to generating ideas.

Osborn's "73 idea spurring questions" is an idea checklist designed for creative problem solving.

Three synectics methods include direct analogy, looking for ways that similar problems have been solved in nature; personal analogy, in which ideas are found by becoming a problem object or process; and fantasy analogy, in which the thinker looks for farfetched, perhaps ideal problem solutions.

Implementation charting, basically the assigning of responsibilities and deadlines, helps students learn to follow through on their creative problem solutions.

Many exercises exist for strengthening such creative abilities as fluency, flexibility, originality, elaboration, sensitivity to problems, problem defining, visualization, analogical thinking, analysis, synthesis, evaluation, and resisting premature closure.

Shallcross suggested creativity exercises that could be integrated into subject areas.

Stanish's *The Hearthstone Traveler* includes exercises and activities involving creative writing, values development, creativity techniques, the CPS model, and many others.

According to Torrance, creative teaching and learning includes exploring, questioning, experimenting, testing ideas, and other activities. Creative learning includes sensing a problem, formulating hypotheses or guesses, testing, revising and retesting the hypotheses, and communicating the results.

Recommendations for creative teaching included high teacher enthusiasm, the acceptance of individual differences, encouraging self-initiated projects, looking beyond IQ scores, encouraging divergent thinking, and others.

Creative learning can result in improved motivation, achievement, creativity, self-confidence, school attitudes, and others.

chapter twelve

Teaching
Thinking Skills

Proponents of the thinking skills movement assume that far too much classroom learning is concerned with traditional academic knowledge and routine skills, and authoritative sources agree. For example, the *Nation At Risk* report by the National Commission on Excellence in Education (1983) recommended that thinking skills be taught in the schools.

This chapter will examine thinking skills and how they can be taught. We will describe three basic approaches to "teaching thinking": (1) strengthening intellectual abilities and skills through practice and exercise, (2) helping students learn conscious and deliberate strategies for reasoning, problem solving, and critical thinking, and (3) increasing students' understanding of their own and others' thinking. In addition, we will look at some examples of thinking skills; review the implications of Bloom's taxonomy for teaching thinking; examine the nature of critical thinking and how it may be taught; review some methods and programs for teaching thinking skills; and (4) review criteria for selecting methods and programs for thinking skills training.

INDIRECT TEACHING, DIRECT TEACHING, AND METACOGNITION

Indirect Teaching: Strengthening Abilities Through Exercise

Thinking skills may be taught in a comparatively subtle, indirect fashion by strengthening simple and complex component abilities through practice and exercise—the same way we strengthen arithmetic and typing skills. For example, a teacher may seek to strengthen classification skills by giving students plenty of practice with classification problems, including exercises with multiple classifications and subclassifications. Similarly, to teach analogical thinking a teacher might use lots of exercises of the *dog* : *cat* : : *canine* : *?* variety.

In addition to using workbook-type exercises for (indirectly) strengthening thinking skills, Arthur Costa (1986) recommended that teachers pose problems, ask questions, and have students explore paradoxes, dilemmas, and discrepancies. He also suggested that teachers try to stimulate trust, risk taking, creativity, and experimentation. Costa further recommended that teachers and other adults model the thinking skills that are desired in students. What we are calling the indirect approach was dubbed "teaching for thinking" by thinking skills expert Costa.

Direct Teaching: Knowing Why, When, and How

Many complex thinking skills may be directly taught as conscious techniques for reasoning, thinking, and dealing with problems. For example, as we will see, critical thinking may be taught by helping students to deliberately evaluate a speaker's biases, qualifications, and ability to observe; to examine whether a statement is an assumption or an opinion; and to evaluate whether conclusions necessarily follow. Creative thinking may be taught directly by helping students understand creative people and creative processes, and by teaching them when and how idea-finding techniques may be used (Davis, 1986; see Chapter 11).

One particularly noteworthy program for the direct teaching of complex thinking skills is the CoRT (Cognitive Research Trust) Thinking Program created by Edward de Bono (1973, 1983, 1985). De Bono's impressive lessons and exercises teach such thinking skills as evaluating, taking other perspectives, planning, and prioritizing as conscious and deliberate strategies. Students are helped to understand each skill and why it should be used, and to know when and how it should be applied. We will look at de Bono's high-impact strategies in a later section.

While Costa (1986) called our indirect approach "teaching *for* thinking," he referred to the direct approach as "teaching *of* thinking." Said Costa, "Most authors and developers of major cognitive curriculum projects agree that direct instruction in thinking skills is imperative." Costa is absolutely correct.

Later in this chapter we will see several plans for exercising thinking skills and abilities (indirect approach, teaching *for* thinking), and for teaching usually more complex thinking strategies (direct approach, teaching *of* thinking).

Metacognition

Metacognition, metacognitive thinking, or just metathinking refers to thinking about thinking. To the extent they are able, students should understand their thinking strategies, and they should understand why, when, and how the strategies may be used. Perhaps the de Bono CoRT strategies are prototype examples of metacognition. Students come to understand the advantages of using a particular technique; when the technique may be profitably used; and the steps involved in using it.

Other teachable aspects of metacognition include helping students to understand the sources of their own ideas, viewpoints, attitudes, and values, and also where others' ideas and values come from. For example, Barell (1984) recommended that instead of just intelligently arguing a viewpoint, students try defending the reverse position. Instead of just analyzing the theme of a literary work, students try to explain how one goes about analyzing a literary work. Students might ask themselves why they thought of a particular question, and what the question means to them personally.

Costa (1986) described three components of thinking about thinking that he called *metacognition, epistemic cognition,* and *brain functioning,* all three of which suggest worthwhile enrichment content. His "metacognition" referred to students' conscious understanding of problem solving. That is, when solving a problem students should consciously identify what is known and what needs to be known; plan a course of action before they begin; monitor themselves while executing the plan (and consciously back up to adjust the plan as needed); and evaluate their success upon completion. Other aspects of metacognition included classroom discussions of what is going on inside their heads while "thinking," and comparing different students' approaches to problems and decision making.

Costa's epistemic cognition is the study of how knowledge is produced. Here, students might learn about the lives, works, and thinking processes of famous composers, artists, philosophers, and scientists. Discussion would focus on, for example, differences and similarities between artists and scientists, creative processes used by artists, poets, and scientists, and the possible use of scientific inquiry for solving social problems.

Finally, students can learn about brain functions, for example, related to learning and memory, emotions, dreaming, and mental disorders. To these we suggest discussion of right-brain vs. left-brain thinking processes, and perhaps discussions of such thinking styles as reflectiveness vs. impulsiveness; global vs. analytic (forest vs. trees) thinking; being a morning or a night person; sensation-seeking vs. sensation-avoiding; high vs. low anxiety; and internal vs. external locus of control—which is an especially important thinking style related to achievement and career success. An internal locus of control person feels responsible for successes, failures and his or her destiny; an external locus of control person blames others for failures, attributes success to luck, and generally feels like a sock in the laundromat of life.

In the classroom, the indirect, direct, and metacognition approaches to teaching thinking may not be so neatly divided. The teaching of thinking skills often will include a combination of exercising underlying abilities; helping students to consciously analyze problems and plan steps for solving them; and helping them to metacognitively understand the reasons for the steps and for their own thinking and the thinking of others.

THINKING SKILLS

A list of thinking skills appears in Table 12.1. The list, which is not exhaustive, might help one plan a thinking skills curriculum. Most of the skills are relatively complex and could involve many other interrelated subskills. For example, skills such as "evaluation" or "deductive reasoning" could easily involve abilities to compare and contrast, interpret, consider relevance, consider implications, predict outcomes, and so on. Such complex processes as creative thinking, critical thinking, problem solving, or decision making could reasonably use any or all of the skills in Table 12.1.

In later sections we will summarize comparatively simpler skills that often are strengthened via exercises from commercially published programs and workbooks, plus many of de Bono's 50 directly taught complex thinking skills.

Nobody ever said the topic of "thinking skills" was uncomplicated.

BLOOM'S TAXONOMY OF EDUCATIONAL OBJECTIVES

When educators speak of teaching high-level thinking skills the first idea that comes to mind is the top portion of "Bloom's taxonomy," more formally entitled the *Taxonomy of Educational Objectives: Cognitive Domain* (Bloom, 1974; Bloom, Engelhart, Furst, Hill, and Krathwohl, 1956). In recent decades Bloom's taxonomy has had an international impact on education by drawing attention to the difference between "low-level" academic knowledge, which is commonly taught, and "higher-level" thinking skills— which everyone suddenly seemed to realize were rarely taught. The taxonomy was designed as a guide for the writing of instructional objectives. It therefore helps one plan a thinking skills curriculum, teaching strategies, and learning experiences. Table 12.2 lists the six main levels of the taxonomy, along with examples of learning activities at each level. Note that

TABLE 12.1   Thinking Skills

Creativity and Creative Problem Solving (Chapters 10, 11)

Critical Thinking	Evaluating bias, credibility, consistency, qualifications, recency of information Evaluating primary vs. secondary sources, inferences, validity of reasons Identifying assumptions, opinions, claims, ambiguities, missing parts of an argument, adequacy of definitions, appropriateness of conclusions
Problem Solving	Problem clarifying and defining Selecting relevant information Formulating hypotheses Identifying and evaluating alternatives Drawing conclusions
Inferential Reading	Finding main ideas Justifying interpretations Explaining authors' intentions Drawing logical inferences, implications, conclusions Relating feelings to specific content
Writing	Stating and defending an idea Sequencing appropriate information Elaborating Communicating clear relationships Expressing feelings, values Arguing persuasively, logically Developing story plots well Creating mood
Science	Identifying needed processes, information Extrapolating, interpolating Detecting reasoning errors Reading charts, graphs, tables Generating graphs from data Recognizing mathematical relationships, (e.g., in weight, distance, time)

Application	Analysis
Synthesis	Evaluation
Deductive reasoning	Inductive reasoning
Analogical thinking	Discovering relationships
Verbal reasoning	Figural/spatial reasoning
Classifying	Sequencing
Taking other points of view	Following directions
Following rules	Predicting consequences, outcomes
Analyzing assumptions	
Estimating, guessing	Planning
Setting goals and objectives	Prioritizing

(continued)

TABLE 12.1   *(Continued)*

Constructing definitions	Recognizing logical relationships
Discovering relationships	Cause-effect relationships
Part-whole relationships	Considering implications
Forming hypotheses	Making decisions
Finding errors	Evaluating generalizations
Asking questions	Comparing, contrasting
Discovering trends	Visualizing
Making inferences	Setting criteria
Ordering on salient dimensions	Measuring
Questioning	Justifying
Interpreting	

Recognizing essential, nonessential
Determining relevance and irrelevance
Recognizing assumptions, beliefs, opinions
Mnemonic learning/memory strategies
Making applications to real-life situations
Predicting outcomes based on background information
Analyzing the current situation and where you wish to end

many of the thinking skills from Table 12.1 have found their way into one category or another.

The six main levels of the taxonomy describe progressively higher levels of cognitive activity. At the knowledge and comprehension levels students deal with facts, figures, definitions, rules, categories, relationships, and theories. While the *knowledge* and *comprehension* levels naturally are necessary for all students, teachers of gifted students, especially, will want them to *apply* rules, principles, or theories; *analyze* components, relationships, hypotheses, patterns, and causes and effects; *synthesize* parts into creative solutions, plans, theories, generalizations, designs, and compositions; and *evaluate* the accuracy, value, efficiency, or utility of alternative ideas or courses of action.

As a general rule, students normally will progress from learning activities at the knowledge and comprehension levels to activities at higher levels. For example, virtually any independent or small-group research project, from creating a school newspaper or terrarium to photography or physics research, will require the acquisition and comprehension of necessary information, followed by various types of applications, analyses, syntheses, and evaluations. The latter four activities do not always need to occur in a specified order, although a final evaluation usually manages to be last.

Royer (1982) described how secondary school creative writing assignments dealing with high-interest issues and problems may be built around the taxonomic levels. For example, students may be asked to write a news article summarizing the details of an issue or problem and the activities

TABLE 12.2 Taxonomy of Educational Objectives: Cognitive Domain

Category	Examples
Knowledge	Defining terminology, symbols Recalling facts, names, examples, rules, categories Recognizing trends, causes, relationships Acquiring principles, procedures, implications, theories
Comprehension	Rephrasing definitions Illustrating meanings Interpreting relationships Drawing conclusions Demonstrating methods Inferring implications Predicting consequences
Application	Applying principles, rules, theories Organizing procedures, conclusions, effects Choosing situations, methods Restructuring processes, generalizations, phenomena
Analysis	Recognizing assumptions, patterns Deducing conclusions, hypotheses, points of view Analyzing relationships, themes, evidence, causes and effects Contrasting ideas, parts, arguments
Synthesis	Producing products, compositions Proposing objectives, means, solutions Designing plans, operations Organizing taxonomies, concepts, schemes, theories Deriving relationships, abstractions, generalizations
Evaluation	Judging accuracy, consistency, reliability Assessing errors, fallacies, predictions, means and ends Considering efficiency, utility, standards Contrasting alternatives, courses of action

From Metfessel, Michael, and Kirsner. Instrumentation of Bloom's and Krathwohl's taxonomies for the writing of educational objectives. *Psychology in the Schools* (1969), *6*, 227–310. Reprinted by permission.

surrounding it (knowledge); write a speech explaining in their own words the meaning of the issue and its implications for those involved (comprehension); write an essay explaining how, for example, a new housing code compares with a current one (application); write an argument that either attacks or defends a viewpoint on an issue (analysis); write an essay that outlines a solution for an issue (synthesis); or write a letter expressing their opinion about others' proposals on an issue (evaluation).

As another general rule, some gifted-oriented educators use the two pyramids in Figure 12.1 to point out the different emphases that should be placed upon different taxonomic levels for regular students and for gifted students (for example, Murphy, 1980). Thus the objectives and instruc-

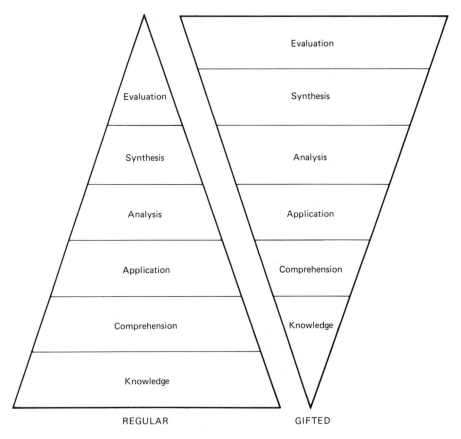

FIGURE 12.1   Based on Bloom's taxonomy, these pyramids illustrate the notion that with gifted students, more time should be invested on higher-level activities and objectives, compared with the reverse for regular students.

tional focus for regular students might emphasize knowledge and comprehension, with less attention to higher-level skills. Gifted students, who grasp information and relationships more rapidly, should invest more time and effort at the higher levels. The inverted pyramid is misleading in suggesting that evaluation should receive the absolutely largest porportion of emphasis, but you get the idea.

An important and common use of Bloom's taxonomy is as a guide for posing questions to students (Sanders, 1966; see Inset 12.1). Certainly, as a means for exercising higher-level thinking abilities, posing classroom questions at the different levels is an obvious and not-too-difficult strategy. Hunkins (1976) describes questioning at the different levels. Her key verbs for posing knowledge, comprehension, application, analysis, synthesis and evaluation questions appear in Table 12.3.

TABLE 12.3   Key Words for Questioning at Bloom's Six Taxonomic Levels

LEVEL	KEY WORDS			
Knowledge	What	Distinguish	Recall	Write
	When	Identify	Reorganize	Which
	Who	List	Show	Indicate
	Define	Name	State	Tell How
Comprehension	Compare	Distinguish	What	
	Conclude	Estimate	Fill in	
	Contrast	Explain	Give an example of	
	Demonstrate	Extend	Hypothesize	
	Differentiate	Extrapolate	Illustrate	
	Predict	Rearrange	Infer	
	Reorder	Rephrase	Relate	
	Which	Inform	Tell in Your Own Words	
Application	Apply	Build	Construct	Demonstrate
	Develop	Plan	Solve	Indicate
	Test	Choose	Show Your Work	Check Out
	Consider	How Would	Tell Us	
Analysis	Analyze	Discriminate	Relate	
	Categorize	Distinguish	Explain	
	Describe	Recognize	What Assumption	
	Classify	Support Your	What Do You	
	Compare	Indicate The		
Synthesis	Write	Suggest	Plan	
	Think of a Way	How	Formulate a Solution	
	Create	Develop	Synthesize	
	Propose a Plan	Make Up	Derive	
	Put Together	What Conclusion		
	What Would Be	What Major Hypothesis		
Evaluation	What is	Select		
	Choose	Which Would You Consider		
	Evaluate	Defend		
	Decide	Check		
	Judge	What is Most Appropriate		
	Check The	Indicate		

(From Hunkins, 1976. Reprinted by permission of the author and Allyn & Bacon, Inc.

Finally, many teachers teach the taxonomy itself to students, acquainting them with different levels of learning, thinking, and skill development. As shown in Inset 12.2, fifth-grader Monica Blanton (1982) understands the taxonomy very well.

Attention to all levels of Bloom's taxonomy, particularly the higher

INSET 12.1 BLOOM'S TAXONOMY AS A GUIDE TO CLASSROOM QUESTIONING

Sanders' (1966) book, *Classroom Questions: What Kinds,* describes how teachers can use questioning strategies to strengthen learning and skill development at all of Bloom's taxonomic levels: knowledge, comprehension, application, analysis, synthesis, and evaluation.

Knowledge questions require students to recognize or recall facts, definitions, generalizations, main points, points of view, and central issues. Some facts and definitions are ends in themselves, possessed by all literate members of a culture. Others serve as building blocks for further learning and thinking. As for which knowledge to emphasize, Sanders recommends that the teacher ask him- or herself, "What facts deserve emphasis?" and "What facts are necessary for further learning?" Examples of knowledge questions: *What is meant by "satellite"? What is the effect of the Gulf Stream upon winter weather in south Florida?*

Comprehension questions usually require students to translate information into another form (by paraphrasing or writing outlines or summaries, drawing diagrams or pictures, or making models, maps, or charts) or to interpret relationships or compare ideas. Examples: *What is the relationship between a satellite and its planet? Can you draw it? Explain in your own words the effect of the gulf stream upon southeastern coastal areas.*

Application questions require students to use knowledge, principles, generalizations and skills to solve problems. For example: *How would scientists place a satellite in orbit? In view of the effects of the gulf stream on Florida weather, how might you explain the relatively mild winters on the west coast of Oregon and Washington?*

Analysis questions can include examinations of statements and semantic meanings, interrelationships of parts, and so on. For example: *What factors could cause a satellite to crash? If you wished to become a citrus fruit grower, what geographical and weather factors would you have to consider?*

Synthesis questions can elicit creative thinking, the derivation of relationships, the formation of hypotheses, or the planning of a research project. *How would the many moons of Jupiter affect each other? How could we grow oranges in Minnesota?*

Evaluation questions implicitly or explicitly require students to establish standards or values, and then match an object or idea against those standards. Evaluation questions may require students to assess the quality of something, consider controversial or hypothetical issues, or evaluate alternate courses of action. Examples: *Is it a good idea to put so many satellites in orbit? What about the cost? Should the government help pay for orange crops lost from freezing? Why or why not?*

Asking questions is an ancient and honorable form of teaching, reviewing, and ensuring learning. With care and planning, questions can be used to teach both lower- and higher-level learning objectives.

INSET 12.2 BLOOM'S TAXONOMY REVISITED

I like your magazine very much. I read about "Bloom's Taxonomy on Bloom's Taxonomy." I am one of Alice Krueger's fifth grade students at Offerle Middle School. I'm sending in questions on *Mrs. Frisby and the Rats of NIMH* to put in *G/C/T*. I would appreciate it if you did.

Yours truly,
Monica Blanton

Mrs. Frisby and the Rats of NIMH

Knowledge—Name Mrs. Frisby's four children in order of age.

Comprehension—Restate Mrs. Frisby's first talk with Brutus the time in the rosebush.

Application—Illustrate Mrs. Frisby flying on Jeremy's back going over the river.

Analysis—Break down Mrs. Frisby's big problem and see how many little problems you can find.

Synthesis—Write a new ending to the story pretending Timothy had died.

Evaluation—Pick three animals of those six that were mentioned in the story. Try to find a new name you think would be better than the one in the book. Tell why you think your names would be better.

Source: *G/C/T* (Sept.-Oct. 1982), 22. Reprinted by permission.

levels of application, analysis, synthesis, and evaluation, will help ensure that G/T activities are not just "busy work" and time fillers.

CRITICAL THINKING

The improvement of critical thinking skills has been a classic educational objective, particularly with teachers of speech, English and social studies, and currently in programs for the gifted and talented. The reader should be warned that out in the real world the phrase "critical thinking" is used in many ways. Critical thinking has been taken to mean carping criticism ("Whatta' piece a' garbage that is!"), wholesale skepticism, thoughtful contemplation, analytic thinking (including the analysis of propaganda), reflective (not compulsive) thinking, problem solving, Bloom's evaluation level of thinking, all of Bloom's higher-level thinking skills, all important ("critical") thinking skills, careful thinking, clear thinking, logical thinking (especially!), independent thinking, along with the abilities to recognize biases, assumptions, inconsistencies, opinions, etc.

The present discussion is based upon two main definitions: critical thinking as *evaluating* and as *problem solving*.

Critical Thinking as Evaluating

Ronald R. Allen and his colleagues (Allen, Kauffeld, and O'Brien, 1968; Allen and Rott, 1969) created four programmed workbooks for teaching critical thinking based upon a definition of critical thinking as " . . . an act of evaluation based upon previously accepted standards." The definition emphasizes a logical examination of information and the avoidance of judgments based only on emotion. Allen's goal was to prepare materials that help teachers encourage critical thinking in relation to ideas and assumptions implicit in such everyday media as comic strips (for example, the far right *Orphan Annie* and the sexist *Beetle Bailey*), advertising and sales pitches, political messages, movies, and television shows.

Most of Allen's specific critical thinking abilities are worth incorporating into any thinking skills curriculum, for example:

1. The ability to appraise a speaker's testimony ("a statement issued by a source") in terms of the source's ability to accurately observe.
2. The ability to evaluate the particular biases of a source.
3. The ability to appraise the source's qualifications necessary for making an informed statement.
4. The ability to appraise whether the source is consistent with himself or herself and other sources.
5. The ability to appraise whether the source's information is the most recent available.
6. The ability to differentiate between primary—first hand—and secondary sources.
7. The ability to identify arguments based on testimony or based on reasoning.

Other of Allen's principles emphasizing critical thinking and reasoning involve:

Evaluating inferences
Evaluating reasons given for a claim
Checking the reliability and adequacy of information
Following logically valid lines of reasoning
Detecting missing parts of an argument
Discerning the relevance of objections
Recognizing appropriate conclusions

In his Cornell Project on Critical Thinking, critical thinking expert Robert Ennis (1962, 1964) compiled a number of aspects of critical thinking that also seem to stress evaluation of sources or statements. Said Ennis, students should learn to judge whether:

1. There is ambiguity or contradiction a line of reasoning.
2. Something is an assumption.
3. A statement is specific enough.
4. A conclusion necessarily follows.
5. An observation statement is reliable.
6. An inductive conclusion is warranted.
7. The (real) problem has been identified.
8. A definition is adequate.
9. A statement by an alleged authority is acceptable.

We will see in a later section that Lipman's (1976, 1981; Lipman, Sharp, and Oscanyan, 1980) *Philosophy for Children* program also includes critical thinking in the evaluation sense by teaching students to recognize inconsistent and contradictory statements, underlying assumptions, cause-effect relationships, and truth in syllogistic reasoning.

Critical Thinking as Problem Solving

To Budmen (1967), critical thinking is problem solving or an act of inquiry. He emphasized, however, that critical thinking differs from more objective scientific problem solving in that critical thinking involves values, emotions, and judgment. From this perspective, Budmen's message to teachers was that students should learn that there are problems for which there is no single solution—only alternatives and judgments. Said Budmen, "What to consider in arriving at these judgments, how to identify the alternatives and make the choices, is what the process of critical thinking is all about." He outlined four steps that could be taught.

The first step is to identify one's basic assumptions, feelings, beliefs, and values relating to an issue. This was considered ". . . the heart of the process." Second, one examines all sides of an issue. Third, one examines all possible actions and their probable results. "More than anything else, students must understand that all behavior has consequences . . . " Finally, the process requires a choice among alternatives, a decision.

Budmen stressed that a solution resulting from these steps should be the best one for the particular person. Therefore, problems best suited for the development of critical thinking should be problems without a single right answer.

Dressel and Mayhew (1954) reduced a long list of critical thinking abilities to five central ones, which also follow a problem-solving format:

1. The ability to define a problem, which includes the abilities to break complex elements into simpler, familiar and workable parts, identify central elements, and eliminate extraneous elements.
2. The ability to select pertinent information for the solution of a problem, including the ability to recognize unreliable and biased sources of informa-

tion, and information that is relevant and irrelevant to the solution of the problem.

3. The ability to recognize stated and unstated assumptions, and unsupported and irrelevant assumptions.

4. The ability to formulate relevant hypotheses, and check the hypotheses against the information and assumptions.

5. The ability to draw valid conclusions and inferences, detect logical inconsistencies, and judge the adequacy of a conclusion as a solution to the problem.

MODELS AND EXERCISES FOR TEACHING THINKING SKILLS

Thinking skills may be taught (1) as a separate course or subject, for example, in an elementary school pull-out program or a special thinking skills course in secondary school, or (2) by integrating thinking skills into the existing curriculum. A separate course could stress creativity, problem solving, critical thinking, logical thinking, analogical thinking, values clarification and moral thinking, and other skills in Table 12.1; the skills subsumed under Bloom's higher taxonomic levels (Table 12.2); and the exercising of specific skills and abilities presented in Table 12.4. Commercially available materials and programs would be extremely valuable for such a course or subject, for example, Feuerstein's (1980) *Instrumental Enrichment*, de Bono's (1973) CoRT strategies, Lipman's (1976) *Philosophy for Children* program, *Project IMPACT*, and the Midwest Publications workbooks (Harnadek, 1979; Black and Black, 1984), all of which will be reviewed later in this chapter.

The obvious problem with adding a new course or subject is cramming another subject into the full school day—and deciding what will be sacrificed in the trade. Integrating thinking skills into the existing curriculum seems most appealing to teachers and administrators. English and science, for example, may be logical places to impart thinking skills because of the natural role of analysis, reasoning, critical thinking, analogical thinking, and others (de Bono, 1983).

The following sections summarize models, strategies and exercises for teaching thinking skills. Space will not allow full descriptions, so interested readers should see the original sources for more complete information. The first two models, the de Bono (1973, 1976, 1983, 1985) CoRT approach and Lipman's *Philosophy for Children*, take a direct, conscious, metacognitive approach to skill development. That is, students fully understand that they are learning about "thinking"; they learn the meaning and purpose of each thinking skill; and they learn why, when, and how the skill should be used.

The remaining strategies, including *Project IMPACT*, Feuerstein's (1980) *Instrumental Enrichment* and the Midwest Publications workbooks, take a more indirect approach in strengthening simple and complex abilities via practice.

THE DE BONO CORT STRATEGIES

The place is Maracaibo, second largest city in Venezuela. There is a meeting of about 20 people (doctors, parents, government officials) to discuss the setting up of a new medical clinic. For three hours the arguments flow back and forth—in the usual fashion.

Suddenly, a 10-year-old boy who has been sitting quietly at the back of the room, because his mother could not leave him alone at home, approaches the table.

He suggests to the group that they "do an AGO (set the objectives), followed by an APC (outline alternatives), and then an FIP (set priorities) and, of course, an OPV (analyze other people's views). In a short while there is a plan of action.

That 10-year-old had participated in the routine thinking skills program that is now mandated by law in all Venezuelan schools (de Bono, 1985).

Edward de Bono (1973) created a delightful set of materials for the ". . . direct teaching of thinking as a skill." The CoRT program requires little or no special teacher training, is apparently enjoyable for both students and teachers, and focuses ". . . on thinking skills that help a learner to function better in his or her life outside of school, not merely to become more proficient at solving puzzles or playing games" (de Bono, 1983).

The materials were not prepared strictly for gifted children. However, the exercises seem marvelously suited to the talents of gifted children and to the goals of any G/T program.

As one example, the PMI technique is a simple and effective way to teach evaluation. Students learn that ideas, suggestions, proposals, activities, or virtually anything else may be intelligently evaluated by looking at the good points or *pluses* (P), the bad points or *minuses* (M), and points that are neither good nor bad, just *interesting* (I). Students learn the reasons (principles) behind PMI, and they practice applying the technique. The principles explain that:

By using the PMI approach one will not hastily reject an idea that initially looks bad.

Vice versa, one will not too-quickly adopt a good-looking idea that has serious but overlooked disadvantages.

Some ideas are neither good nor bad, just interesting and relevant and may lead to other ideas.

Without using a PMI, one's emotions may interfere with clear judgments.

With a PMI you pass judgment on an idea after it is explored, not before.

Small groups of fifth-grade G/T students in a College for Kids program directed by the author (Davis) did PMI's on "being gifted." They discovered they were not unique in having social problems at school, and they improved their appreciation for themselves and their high potential.

There are six sets of lessons with 10 lessons in each set, for a total of 60 lessons covering about 50 thinking skills. Many lessons teach complex skills that require the use of several previously learned skills. Some lessons use a set of nine or ten steps to *define* a particular thinking skill, *explain why and when* it is used, and present *examples* and *sample problems*. Other lessons are organized into these six sections:

1. *Introduction.* An introduction defines and explains the skill. For example, with the *Consider All Factors* (CAF) skill students learn that whenever they make a decision or choose something there are always many factors to consider. If they leave out some factors, their choice may turn out to be wrong. Further, they can try to see what factors other people have left out of their thinking.

2. *Example.* A sample problem (or statement) is presented and the skill is applied. For instance, in London a law was passed that required all new buildings to provide parking in the basement. They neglected to consider that basement parking would encourage people to drive to work, and so traffic congestion was worse than ever.

3. *Practice.* Four or five practice problems give students first-hand experience using the skill. For example, what factors are involved in choosing a hair style? What factors would you consider if interviewing someone to be a teacher?

4. *Process.* In a class or group discussion, students consider, for example, whether it is easy to leave out important factors; when it is important to consider all factors; what the difference is between a PMI and a CAF; what happens when others leave out important factors; and whether one needs to consider "all" factors or just the important ones.

5. *Principles.* Usually five sensible principles are presented, which amount to reasons for and advantages of using the skill, as illustrated in the PMI technique above. Some principles invariably duplicate information in the introductory explanation, which is fine. With the CAF strategy, five principles were:

Using a CAF is useful in choosing, planning or deciding.

It is better to consider all factors first and then select the ones that matter most.

You may have to ask someone else whether you have left out important factors.

If an important factor is left out, an answer that seems right may turn out to be wrong.

A CAF on someone else's thinking may allow you to tell them what they left out.

6. *Project.* These are additional practice problems.

CoRT thinking skills are not tied to any particular subject area. "Thinking" is taught as a subject in its own right, and as a conscious and deliberate metacognitive skill. In fact, said de Bono (1983), the thinking skills probably would be best taught in a separate class or unit. Many of the impressive CoRT thinking skills are briefly described in Inset 12.3.

INSET 12.3 CoRT THINKING SKILLS: DE BONO

Edward de Bono's (1973) CoRT thinking skills are taught in a direct, metacognitive fashion. Children consciously understand the value of each skill and when, why, and how it should be applied. The following are brief descriptions of some of the 50 CoRT thinking skills. Some skills are composed of clusters of simpler skills. The interested reader should see de Bono (1973, 1976, 1983, 1985) for details about these apparently effective and enjoyable lessons.

Thinking of good points (pluses), bad points (minuses), and interesting points of ideas, suggestions, and proposals.

Considering all factors when making choices or decisions.

Thinking of consequences (short-term, medium-term, long-term) of actions.

Thinking of goals and objectives, including seeing other people's objectives.

Planning, which includes skills of considering all factors and itemizing goals and objectives.

Prioritizing, for example, relevant factors, objectives, and consequences.

Thinking of many alternatives, possibilities, and choices, for example, in interpreting causes or in considering alternative actions.

Decision making, which requires considering the factors involved, objectives, priorities, consequences, and possible alternatives.

Seeing other points of view, which exist because other people may consider different factors, see different consequences, or have different objectives or priorities.

Selecting something according to your needs and requirements, that is, according to "best fit."

Organizing by analyzing what needs to be done, what is being done, and what is to be done next. One may need to consider all factors and think of alternatives.

Focusing on different aspects of a situation, that is, knowing when you are analyzing, considering factors, thinking of consequences, etc.

Concluding a thinking project, perhaps with ideas, an answer to a question, a problem solution, an action, or conceding an inability to solve the problem.

Recognizing opinions vs. facts as two types of evidence.

Recognizing evidence that is weak, strong, or key.

Recognizing points of agreement, disagreement, and irrelevant points.

Being right by refering to facts, authority, etc.

Supporting an argument by using value-laden words, such as right, proper, fair, sincere, or ridiculous, dishonest, devious, stupid.

Being wrong in an argument because of exaggerating, making a (e.g., factual) mistake, or by having prejudiced (fixed) ideas.

Challenging existing ways of doing things as a means of stimulating new ideas.

Improving things by identifying faults and thinking of ways to remove them.

Solving problems by thinking about problem requirements.

Recognizing information that is given vs. information that has been omitted, but is needed.

Recognizing contradictory information, which can lead to false conclusions.
Recognizing guesses based on good information ("small guesses," e.g., the
sun will rise tomorrow) vs. guesses based on little information ("big guesses,"
e.g., the final score of a future football game).
Distinguishing between ordinary emotions (e.g., anger, love, fear, sorrow) and
those concerned with one's view of oneself (ego-emotions; e.g., pride, power,
insecurity).
Understanding that values determine thinking, judgments, choices and actions.
Each of us has things we value highly, and things to which we give a low value.
And more.

PHILOSOPHY FOR CHILDREN: LIPMAN

Mathew Lipman's (Lipman, Sharp, and Oscanyan, 1980) *Philosophy for Children* program is unique in taking the form of stories in a series of upper elementary children's texts. The program claims significant results in improving reading, interpersonal relations, ethical understanding, reasoning, and critical thinking (Lipman, 1976, 1981; Weinstein and Laufman, 1981). In the stories, fictional children spend much of their time thinking about thinking, with clear explanations of good thinking and bad thinking. The idea, of course, is for the student-readers to identify with the characters and to "think along" with them. Exercises follow the stories, but the main emphasis is upon the story content and the teacher's follow-up discussions.

A few of the 30 thinking skills taught in *Philosophy for Children* are:

Cause-effect relationships. Does this statement necessarily imply a cause-effect relationship: "He threw the stone and broke the window."

Recognizing consistent and contradictory statements or ideas. For example, students can think about whether it is possible to be a true animal lover, yet still eat meat.

Identifying underlying assumptions. What is the assumption underlying a statement such as "I love your hair that way, Peg. What beauty parlor did you go to?"

Learning part-whole and whole-part relationships. Students might be asked to evaluate the truth of "If Mike's face has handsome features, Mike must have a handsome face."

Making generalizations. Students draw generalizations from sets of facts, such as "I get sick when I eat raspberries; I get sick when I eat strawberries; I get sick when I eat blackberries."

Nonreversibility. "All" statements are nonreversible: All model airplanes are toys, but not all toys are model airplanes.

Other thinking skills include creativity and understanding descriptions and explanations, universal and particular statements ("all birds are blue" vs. "This bird is blue"), hypotheses, impartiality, consistency, reasons for beliefs, alternatives, and others.

Said intelligence expert Robert Sternberg (1984) of Lipman's program, ". . . no program I am aware of is more likely to teach durable and transferable thinking skills than *Philosophy for Children*." However, Sternberg also warned that students in inner-city schools may have trouble identifying with the seemingly middle-class story characters and their types of problems. Further, poor readers or students of low-average ability or below may have trouble dealing with the program.

PROJECT IMPACT

One of the newest and most impressive thinking skills programs is the middle-school level *Project IMPACT* (*Improve Minimal Proficiencies by Activating Critical Thinking*; Orange County Department of Education, 1981; see Zinner, 1985). In her review of Project Impact, Zinner commented

> The projects' merits were tested and the results were remarkable . . . Teachers noticed improvement in students' high-level questioning abilities . . . use of vocabulary, motivation in class, attendance . . . reading and math scores . . . students enjoy the lessons so much they request them . . . teachers themselves say *IMPACT* has improved their teaching style and renewed their enthusiasm for their career as well . . . it was selected as an Exemplary/Incentive Project and a Model Staff Development Program by the California State Department of Education . . . the U.S. Department of Education ranked it first among 24 funded projects.

In a hierarchical fashion, Project *IMPACT* aims first at strengthening *enabling* skills of observing, comparing, contrasting, grouping, classifying, ordering, sequencing, patterning, and prioritizing. Next are *process* skills of analyzing facts and opinions, relevant and irrelevant information, reliable and unreliable sources, questioning, inferring meaning of statements, cause-effect relationships, generalizations, predictions, assumptions, and points of view, including prejudice. Finally, the program focuses on *operations*, including inductive and deductive reasoning and the evaluation skills of judgment and decision making.

To illustrate the reasons for the excitement, one lesson entitled "Can You Zooley" focuses on deductive reasoning. The learner studies the arrangement of the patterned drawings in Figure 12.2, which represent zoo animals and visitors. A series of questions requires the learner to analyze the information and deduce relations among the creatures. For example:

Which family is visiting the polar bears?
Which is a family of snakes?

Can You Zooley?

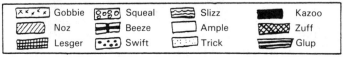

Key To Family Names

Gobbie		Squeal		Slizz		Kazoo
Noz		Beeze		Ample		Zuff
Lesger		Swift		Trick		Glup

FIGURE 12.2   "Can You Zooley?" lesson from Project IMPACT. Reprinted by permission of S. Lee Winocur, Ph.D., Center for the Teaching of Thinking, Project IMPACT.

Which family has no children?
Whose son has Mr. Crocodile just swallowed?
Which swimming family has only three sons?
Is the polar bear's cub male or female?
Which is a kangaroo?

The materials are engaging, to say the least.

INSTRUMENTAL ENRICHMENT: REUVEN FEUERSTEIN

Nicholas Hobbs (1980) said this of Feuerstein's *Instrumental Enrichment* program:

> Reven Feuerstein's *Instrumental Enrichment*, along with its companion volume, *The Dynamic Assessment of Retarded Performers*, represents an intellectual

achievement of formidable proportions. Few single works in contemporary psychology equal it in originality and ingenuity, in scope, in theoretical importance, and in potential social significance.

By way of background, Feuerstein spent several teenage years in Nazi concentration camps, later helped children and adults migrate to Israel, and studied at the University of Geneva and the Sorbonne. In Israel, ". . . a country . . . under pressure to make the most of its human potential" (Makler, 1980), he clinically evaluated the educational needs of immigrants from rural Morocco and southern France, many of whom would be classified as retarded by modern intelligence tests. Feuerstein designed his formal instructional program ". . . to change the cognitive structure of the retarded performer (who lacks adequate cognitive development) and to transform him into an autonomous, independent thinker, capable of initiating and elaborating ideas."

The cognitive functions taught in Instrumental Enrichment fall into the three categories of *input, elaboration,* and *output.*

Input.   The input (information gathering) skills include, for example, using a system or plan, describing things and events, organizing information, and being precise and accurate.

Elaboration.   Elaboration skills involve using the information that has been gathered, for example, in defining the problem, evaluating relevance of information, having a good picture of what is looked for, planning steps, looking for relationships that tie together objects, events and experiences, comparing, categorizing, thinking about possibilities, and using logic to prove things and defend your opinion.

Output.   Finally, output skills focus on expressing the solution to a problem, for example, by thinking things through before answering, and by being clear and precise in language.

Feuerstein's (1980) *Instrumental Enrichment* (FIE) program was specifically designed to correct such deficits as:

Impulsive, unplanned, unsystematic exploratory behavior in problem solving.

Impaired ability to consider two or more sources of information at once, dealing instead with data in a piecemeal fashion.

Inadequacy in recognizing the existence of a problem, and a subsequent inability to define it.

Lack of spontaneous comparison behavior.

Lack of effective strategies for hypothesis testing.

Inability to recognize the need for logical evidence.

Impaired planning ability.

Inability to relate different aspects of experience to one another.

There are 13 types of exercises, each of which is said to strengthen a number of underlying abilities. As a sample exercise:

Organization of Dots.   Students are presented with an amorphous array of dots. Their task is to identify and outline specified geometric figures, such as squares, diamonds, and stars, by connecting dots. The task, which increases in difficulty with increasing dot density and figure complexity, is said to strengthen ". . . projection of visual relationships, discrimination of form and size, constancy of form and size across changes in orientation, use of relevant information, discovery strategies, perspective, restraint of impulsivity, . . . labeling, precision and accuracy, planning, determination of starting point, systematic search and comparison to model, . . . (and) motivation" (Feuerstein, 1980).

There are exercises for classification ability; orientation in space; finding similarities and differences between objects, events or ideas; verbal and nonverbal syllogistic reasoning, including the use of sets, subsets and intersecting sets; inferring validity; finding relationships; discovering principles; choosing and processing data; and others.

Evidence for the effectiveness of the FIE program amounts to common observations and testimonials by teachers' aides and project administrators in Tennessee, Toronto, New York City, and Louisville. These people independently agreed that after Intellectual Enrichment training, children:

Used Instrumental Enrichment strategies in other subjects.

Developed problem solving strategies.

Read and used directions spontaneously.

Spontaneously corrected their own mistakes.

Increased their precision.

Became more willing to defend their own opinions on the basis of logical evidence.

Increased their tolerance of others' opinions and their listening to others.

Increased their readiness to cope with more difficult problems.

Increased the relevance and completeness of their answers.

Increased their sensitivity in social relations.

Increased their feelings of success and their self-image.

Reduced their anxiety about approaching something new; and more.

MIDWEST PUBLICATIONS THINKING SKILLS: HARNADEK AND OTHERS

Currently, one of the most broad-based approaches to strengthing thinking skills through exercise is found in over a dozen workbooks published by Midwest Publications, which of course is located in California. The workbooks by Harnadek (1977, 1978, 1979), Anderson and Haller (1975), and Black and Black (1984) include thousands of exercises intended to strengthen simple and complex thinking skills. A sample of the kinds of abilities that Harnadek and others seek to strengthen appears in Table 12.4.

The following are examples of some exercises found in the workbooks by Harnadek and others:

Analogical thinking.   Analogical reasoning skills are exercised by giving students practice in solving four-word analogy problems that basically take the classic form A : B :: C : _?_ . For example, given "*cake, bake*" and "*egg, _____,*" students complete the analogy by selecting from "*bake, fry, roast, toast.*"

Sequence problems.   Simpler forms of inductive thinking are exercised in problems that require students to induce a figural relationship among three (or four) patterns in a sequence, and then draw the next pattern in the series (Harnadek, 1979).

Verbal sequence exercises ask students to line up a sequence of four words (for example, *anxious, calm, concerned, obsessed*) in order of size, degree, or other meaningful way.

Deductive reasoning.   The thinker attempts to, for example, "match up each woman's name with her kind of work." A matrix is provided which the thinker uses, in conjunction with series of clues, to eliminate untenable possibilities and eventually find the one correct solution. Similar mind-bender exercises require the learner to figure out who is younger or taller than whom, or in Black and Black (1984) the correct order of historical events.

Classifying.   In one sense, classifying is the most basic and important of all learning and thinking skills. If we could not classify, we would be unable to cope with our complex environment. By identifying new objects or experiences as members of familiar classes, we know how to respond to them. Learning to classify amounts to learning which characteristics are common to all examples of a class, but not shared with nonexamples.

Harnadek (1977) teaches classification skills by presenting examples and nonexamples of a class. The student's job is to learn (induce) which characteristics define class membership. In these problems, examples of the class are geometric patterns assigned a nonsense name, for example, "gurnel"; each nonexample is simply "not a gurnel."

Related multiple-classification exercises in Black and Black (1984) teach students that objects simultaneously can be members of several classes, depending upon which characteristics one attends to. Other exercises in Black and Black focus on helping students learn the meanings and rela-

TABLE 12.4   A List of Some Specific Thinking Skills

FIGURAL SIMILARITIES

Matching Shapes
Combining Shapes
Matching Congruent Figures
Drawing Lines of Symmetry
Matching Congruent Solids
Combining Solids

Dividing Shapes into Equal Parts
Finding Patterns
Matching Similar Figures
Matching Volume
Recognizing Views of a Solid
Using Grids to Enlarge Figures

FIGURAL SEQUENCES

Figural Sequence Problems
Producing Reflections
Matching Pattern Pieces

Rotating Figures Problems
Paper Folding
Producing a Pattern

FIGURAL CLASSIFICATIONS

Classifying by Shape
Describing Characteristics
Matching Classes by Shape
Finding Shape Exceptions
Multiple Classifications

Classifying by Pattern
Describing Classes
Matching Classes by Pattern
Finding Pattern Exceptions
Overlapping Classes

FIGURAL ANALOGIES

Analogies—Select and Supply Problems
Describing Figural Analogies
Making up Analogies

VERBAL SIMILARITIES AND DIFFERENCES

Selecting Antonyms
Denotations

Selecting Synonyms
Connotations

VERBAL SEQUENCES

Following Directions
Completing Phrases
Similarities
True-False Tables
Describing Locations
Deductive Reasoning
Discriminating Degree of Meaning

Writing Directions
Opposites
Following Yes-No Rules
Finding Locations with Maps
Describing Directions
Time Sequences

TRANSITIVITY

Using Transitive Order
Using Yes-No Statements
Multi-Factor Deductive Reasoning

LOGICAL RELATIONSHIPS

Negation
Disjunction ("or") Rules
Cause-Effect Words

Conjunction ("and") Rules
Implication ("if then") Rules

(*continued*)

TABLE 12.4 *(Continued)*

Intervals of a Day, Year Time Zones	Schedules

FLOWCHARTING

In Problem Solving	A Sequence
A Cycle	In Planning
In Comparison Shopping	

VERBAL CLASSIFICATIONS

Parts of a Whole	Classes and Members
General to Specific	Distinguishing Relationships
Explaining Exceptions	Sorting into Word Classes
Overlapping Classes	Branching Diagrams
Diagramming Classes	
Sentences With Classes and Subclasses	

VERBAL ANALOGIES

Antonym/Synonym Analogies	Association Analogies
"Kind Of" Analogies	"Part of" Analogies
"Used to (for)"	"Degree of" Analogies
Creating Analogies	

tionships inherent in such classification-related words as "includes," "overlaps," "is separate from," and "is included in."

Exercises dealing with similarities and differences also are said to strengthen verbal classification skills (Harnadek, 1977). For example, students are asked to select which one of five words does not belong, which requires inducing a characteristic that is common to all words except one (e.g., pencil, chalk, rabbit, crayon, pen). Nothing is more frustrating than trying to write with a dull rabbit.

Verbal relationships. Many exercises help students learn verbal relationships by using antonyms, synonyms, similarities, and opposites, sometimes in verbal analogies (e.g., *cease : stop :: proceed : ?). Classification-related exercises, dealing with "includes," "overlaps," etc., and verbal sequence (ordering) exercises also are said to teach verbal relationships.

Following directions. One easily neglected thinking skill is the self-management behavior of carefully following directions. Harnadek (1979) gives students practice attending to detailed directions with tricky exercises such as:

1. In the upper right corner of your paper, write your name so that your last name is first and your first name is last.
2. Put a comma between your two names.

3. If the comma is before your first name, write "yes" in about the middle of your paper.
4. If the comma is after your last name, make a circle around the comma.
5. If the comma is before your first name and before your last name, make a star in the lower left corner of your paper.
6. If the comma is after your last name and after your first name, make a triangle in the lower right corner of your paper.
7. If your first name has less than 25 letters, draw a smiling face in the upper left corner of your paper. Otherwise, draw a smiling face below your name.
8. If your paper has a star drawn on it, write the word "good" next to the star. Otherwise, write the word "no" at the left of your name.

The reader interested in further information about the Harnadek, Anderson, and Haller, and Black and Black exercises should request a recent catalogue from Midwest Publications, Box 448, Pacific Grove, CA.

SELECTING THINKING SKILLS EXERCISES AND MATERIALS

De Bono (1983), Sternberg (1983), and Treffinger, Isaksen and McEwen (1987) itemized criteria for assessing the value and usefulness of thinking skills strategies and programs. A composite of their lists includes:

1. The program should not require extended advanced training. However, appropriate training should be readily available through workshops, seminars or printed resources.
2. A good program should be usable by teachers of varying abilities, not just gifted or highly qualified teachers.
3. The program should be robust enough to "resist damage" as it is passed from trainer to trainer, from trainer to teacher, and finally from teacher to student.
4. The program should use "parallel design," which means that if some parts are taught badly or skipped, what remains will still be usable and valuable.
5. The program should be enjoyable for teachers and children.
6. Materials should be attractive, appropriate to students' interests, and motivating.
7. Important thinking skills should be addressed; objectives should be specified.
8. The program should teach skills that help learners in their lives outside of school.
9. The program should improve metacognitive skills—understanding thinking and thinking skills.
10. Appropriate examples of practical applications of the methods and techniques should be presented.
11. Involvement should be active, not passive; experiential learning and applications are important.
12. There should be opportunities for transfer and generalization of the training.
13. The program should be assessed not only for immediate, direct effects, but also for the transferability and durability of the training.

14. It is desirable for the program to be flexible enough to accommodate individual differences, for example, in age, ability, or preferred working speed.
15. It is desirable to have individual and group activities.
16. It is desirable to be able to relate the skills to curriculum content.

As with all G/T enrichment, the program must be suited to students' needs.

SUMMARY

Thinking skills and abilities may be strengthened indirectly (teaching for thinking) via practice with classification, analogy, logical reasoning, and many other kinds of problems.

Thinking skills also may be taught directly (teaching of thinking) as conscious techniques for reasoning and solving problems.

Metacognition is thinking about thinking, that is, understanding why, when, and how problem-solving strategies should be used, and thinking about one's own thinking, the thinking of others, and sources of ideas.

Costa's "teaching about thinking" included metacognition, epistemic cognition (the study of how knowledge is produced), and brain functions.

In teaching thinking skills in the classroom, the indirect, direct, and metacognitive approaches are combined.

A list of thinking skills included creativity, critical thinking, and problem solving; skills in inferential reading, writing, and science; analogical, verbal, and figural/spatial reasoning skills; and several dozen more.

The best known higher-level thinking skills are the application, analysis, synthesis, and evaluation levels of Bloom's taxonomy. The taxonomy guides teacher questioning. Compared with regular students, gifted students should spend more time doing higher level learning activities. The taxonomy itself may be taught to all students.

"Critical thinking" is interpreted in many ways. This section explained the training of critical thinking as evaluating the biases, qualifications, and consistency of speakers, and evaluating assumptions, opinions, ambiguities, whether conclusions follow, and others. Critical thinking as problem solving included teaching students to identify assumptions and values, examine all sides of an issue, examine possible actions, and make decisions (Budmen); or else teaching students to define a problem, select pertinent information, recognize assumptions, formulate hypotheses, and draw valid conclusions (Dressel and Mayhew).

Thinking skills may be taught in a separate course or subject or, more often, integrated into the existing curriculum. Thinking may be taught as a subject in itself. It need not be tied to a specific subject.

De Bono's CoRT strategies directly teach thinking as conscious and deliberate skills independent of any subject. The PMI and CAF techniques were two of about 50 thinking skills.

Lipman's Philosophy for Children program takes the form of children's stories that teach, for example, cause-effect relations, analogical thinking, and critical thinking.

Project IMPACT was designed to strengthen enabling skills (for example, comparing, classifying), process skills (for example, analyzing facts, assumptions, cause-effect relationships), and operations (for example, reasoning, evaluating).

Feuerstein's Instrumental Enrichment program was designed to strengthen a variety of thinking skills and abilities in the categories of input, elaboration, and output via such exercises as organization of dots.

Midwest Publications produces a series of exercise-filled workbooks by Harnadek, Black and Black, and others aimed at strengthening simple and complex verbal and spatial skills (for example, analogic reasoning, classifying, cause-effect relations, and following directions).

Criteria for selecting materials and strategies emphasized usability by teachers, attractiveness and enjoyability, effectiveness in teaching important transferable skills, including metacognitive thinking, and others.

chapter thirteen

Culturally Different and Economically Disadvantaged Children
The Invisible Gifted

The scene is the principal's office in an inner-city elementary school. The principal, a black woman, is bright, determined, dedicated, and very professional; she has been carefully selected from among many competitors to lead a daring new approach to educating inner-city youngsters. Many of these children, with learning and social problems, had been written off as "nonlearners" by teachers in other schools. Today, several members of the school board who are interested in the goals and methods of this innovative "fundamental" school program interview the principal. Their questions begin with the who's, why's, and how's of this unique school. She answers that the school is based on certain fundamentals: carefully selected staff, parent involvement, basic skills, mastery learning, firm discipline, and homework.

Then a significant question:

"Ms. Jones, how will you teach your gifted students?" And the response:

"In this school we have no gifted children."

Culturally different and economically disadvantaged black, Hispanic, Native American, and white children living in large urban centers, in poor rural areas, and on Indian reservations rarely are identified or described as gifted or talented. Their formal educational needs are assumed to be only in basic skills areas; and their adjustment to school and learning almost always involves strict discipline. Their cultural or language differences plus their lack of exposure to mainstream American culture usually combine to obscure from society the gifted children among them. These gifted minority and disadvantaged children typically proceed invisibly through school until they drop out or, with luck, graduate.

Overview

Because culturally diverse and economically disadvantaged children and adolescents rarely are identified for their giftedness, they seldom are included in G/T programs. Furthermore, because their families and peers typically do not reinforce the development of their intellectual or creative talents, they are especially in need of strong school support. This chapter will discuss (1) the special needs of these children, (2) methods for identifying them, and (3) relevant programming strategies.

SPECIAL NEEDS

In 1977 Congresswoman Shirley Chisholm introduced legislation to include funding for gifted and talented minority and culturally different children within the Elementary and Secondary Education Act. She immediately was confronted with the reality of widespread misunderstanding of these students (Chisholm, 1978). She pointed out that her white colleagues did not seem to recognize the existence of *gifted* minority children, and that they assumed that all minority children were in need of academic remediation. Her black colleagues, with little apparent support, questioned her sponsorship of programs which ". . . did nothing but promote (discriminatory) IQ testing and money for affluent white children." In her keynote address before the National Forum on Minority and Disadvantaged Gifted and Talented, Chisholm (1978) lamented the failure of our educational institutions to nurture the talents of gifted disadvantaged students. She faulted American education for (1) inadequate methods for recognizing talent among culturally different children and (2) insufficient funding to provide special programs for these children.

The late 1960s and the 1970s saw the introduction of major educational and social programs to improve opportunities for minority, culturally different, and economically disadvantaged children. The Elementary and Secondary Education Act, Head Start programs, educational TV programs for children ("Sesame Street," "Electric Company"), bilingual educational funding, and court-ordered desegregation all contributed to enhancing educational preparation and opportunities. The actual educational and social impact of these investments has been both controversial and difficult to evaluate. However, some statistics are very encouraging; for example, the percentage of minority students who graduate from high school has increased dramatically. According to a 1977 U.S. Department of Commerce report, in the mid-1950s only 50 percent of black youth and less than 40 percent of Hispanic youth graduated from high school. By 1977, however, 76 percent of black and 58 percent of Hispanic students were graduating. For white students in a similar time period, graduation rates increased from just under 80 percent to 87 percent.

Another indication of a closing gap comes from an analysis of black-white achievement test scores from the National Assessment of Educational Progress. Burton and Jones (1982) found that during the 1970s, for youth tested at ages 9 and 13, the discrepancy between black and white achievement scores had become smaller in five major subjects: writing, science, mathematics, social studies, and reading. In areas where achievement had declined, it declined less for blacks than for whites. Burton and Jones concluded that efforts to provide equal educational opportunity may indeed have reduced black-white achievement differences. These important findings, demonstrating improvement in basic skills, may affect opportunities for the culturally different gifted learner in a very important way, to which we now turn.

Maslow's Hierarchy of Motivation and Rimm's Hierarchy of Cognitive Needs

In the context of teaching a badly underachieving but gifted eight-year-old Pima Indian boy, Scruggs and Cohn (1983) stated as a major implication of their work, "Ability training in skill deficit areas should be among the very highest of priorities. If the child is to function at top efficiency, that child must have the tools with which to work." To illustrate how the improvement of basic skills will aid the culturally different gifted child, it may be helpful to compare the gifted child's cognitive and creative growth with Maslow's (1954, 1968) hierarchical theory of human motivation (Figure 13.1).

In describing his hierarchy of human needs, Maslow explained that persons cannot grow toward self-actualization—the full development of one's capabilities and talents—unless lower-level needs are met first: those related to physiological needs, safety, belongingness and love, and esteem. The motivation to provide for these needs was entitled *deficiency* motivation mainly because the needs require frequent attention and, furthermore, if deficiencies in these needs are not removed, human behavior will come to resemble low-level, survival-based animal behavior. However, when the basic deficiency needs are met, *growth* motivation will direct behavior toward fulfilling higher-level needs, needs to know and understand, needs for order and beauty, and, at the pinnacle, needs for self-actualization.

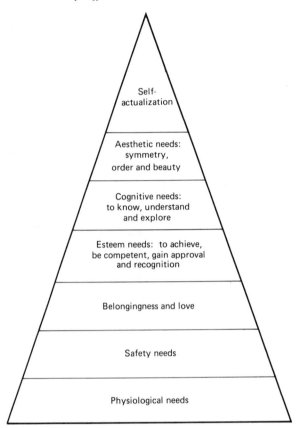

FIGURE 13.1   Maslow's Hierarchy of Needs.

Data for diagram of hierarchy of needs from *Motivation and Personality,* 3rd ed., by Abraham H. Maslow. Revised by Robert Frager et al. Copyright © 1954, 1987 by Harper & Row, Publishers, Inc. Copyright © 1970 by Abraham H. Maslow. Reprinted by permission of the publisher.

In the same way, the "three R's"—basic reading, writing, and arithmetic—sit at the base of a hierarchy of intellectual needs (Figure 13.2). These *basic skills* are prerequisite to the middle levels of the hierarchy, *knowledge and its application,* and the *analysis, synthesis, and evaluation of ideas,* which in turn are required for the top level of the hierarchy, *creative production.* All gifted and talented children should be encouraged to move toward higher levels of the hierarchy. However, they cannot achieve the higher growth levels if they have not mastered the deficiency level of basic skills. If the deficiency needs are not met, the gifted child is likely to perform as a child with average or below-average abilities and therefore will not be identified as gifted.

Two real-life examples will illustrate the dramatic effects of removing educational deficiencies on cognitive and creative growth—and the "dis-

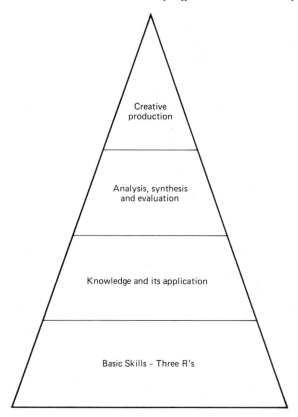

FIGURE 13.2   Rimm's Hierarchy of Cognitive Needs.

covery" of giftedness. The first example comes from the school described at the outset of this chapter. The reader will recall that the principal had indicated in her interview that no gifted children were in her school. Three years later, this same principal described with pride the artwork and creative writing of students who had won city-wide contests, as well as the drama talent and the high basic-skills achievements of her "gifted" students. These talented children were there all along; they could grow toward creativity only when deficits had been removed.

A second example comes from a fifth-grade teacher in an urban parochial school that also considered itself a "fundamental" school. The student population of this school was composed almost entirely of minority children who were relatively poor. During its initial years, this school also was assumed to have no gifted children; teaching the Three R's—and doing it well—was seen as its only mission. Within two years the faculty became aware that among these children, who had been assumed to be average or below in ability, there again were intellectually and creatively gifted children. As this teacher added creative-thinking activities to her daily lesson plans, she discovered even more gifted children.

A demonstration exercise with a group of her students made this new-found creativeness clearly visible. The students, using a technique called *random juxtaposition*, were demonstrating one type of unrehearsed creative thinking. They were to select one article from a grab bag and "tell how this article was like themselves." A black child who had been a serious behavior and learning problem before he had come to the school selected an orange from the bag. On the spot, he created this humorous comparison: "This orange is like me because its skin is tough on the outside and I am tough on the outside. When you get inside the orange, it's good and sweet and I'm good and sweet on the inside too."

These examples illustrate how reducing basic skills deficits of gifted disadvantaged youngsters was indeed the important first step to identifying these children and providing programs for them. However, meeting deficiency needs could easily become the only goal of a program for disadvantaged children and might thus prevent the discovery of the gifted and creative children in the classroom. Even when basic skills are the priority, regular opportunities for higher level thinking and divergent production should be included in the daily curriculum. It is only by providing opportunities for creative thought in the regular classroom that highly creative youngsters will be encouraged to visibly use their higher level thinking skills.

Another major problem for funded programs for disadvantaged children is that after deficient learning needs are remedied, these children are typically promoted out of the specially funded program that has served them so well and placed in a mainstream program that provides no special opportunities for developing their newly discovered abilities.

An example of one such situation comes from five years of evaluation reports of an Hispanic bilingual program in a major midwestern city. Each year the evaluator (Rimm) commended the program staff for the large gains in basic skills shown by a small proportion of the children. Each year the evaluator recommended that these fast learners be channeled into a bilingual program for gifted children. However, despite the recommendations and despite the continued needs of these youngsters, they were dropped from the program because, according to government definitions and regulations, they no longer showed basic skill deficiencies and therefore could no longer be served. Since there was little or no government money for special services for these gifted minority children, they would no longer be aided in any special way and they would be less likely to develop their higher-level cognitive abilities and move up the hierarchy of cognitive needs (Figure 13.2).

As a final comment on the needs of disadvantaged gifted students, it has been established (to no one's surprise) that early childhood experiences are critical to cognitive development and to success in school. Bronfenbrenner (1974, p. 181), for example, indicated that "while excellent early development does not guarantee lifelong excellent development, poor progress during the early years seems to be remarkably difficult to overcome." However, while a culturally impoverished childhood is hardly an asset, it does not totally prevent the later development of skills and abilities. Ogby (1981), in his cross-cultural research into the origins of human competence, concluded that early cultural deprivation does not necessarily limit the later development of skills and competencies. Said Ogby, "Given the opportunity, one does not have to be born and raised in a white middle-class home or receive 'supplementary childhood care' to become a doctor, laywer, or professor in the Western social and economic system" (p. 416).

Surely the upward mobility and career success of thousands of disadvantaged and minority persons is strong evidence for the feasibility of overcoming unfavorable early environments. This country has a strongly ingrained tradition of viewing education as the road to upward mobility. In 1912, Goddard was quoted as stating that, based on intelligence testing in the armed services, 83 percent of the Jews, 80 percent of the Hungarians, 79 percent of the Italians, and 87 percent of the Russians were "feebleminded." IQ scores soon changed dramatically to reflect the further education of these immigrant groups. Gifted programs for disadvantaged, minority, and culturally different children can provide an important, sometimes pivotal boost to the development of undiscovered potential and can help these invisible gifted children become part of tomorrow's promise.

IDENTIFICATION

As noted earlier, minority and culturally different gifted children are not easily identified. Indeed, because of cultural bias in test instruments and other identification methods, many typical procedures actually obscure students' giftedness—by "proving" these children are *not* gifted. Because actual achievement often is not outstanding, identification must be based upon superior *potential* instead of superior performance (Scruggs and Cohn, 1983). This section will review typical identification methods and evaluate their usefulness for culturally different and economically disadvantaged populations. It also will recommend other identification procedures that in some cases may be more effective.

Intelligence Tests

High intelligence test scores on either group or individual tests are one valid way to identify intellectually gifted minority youngsters. However, an average or even low IQ score may be a poor or misleading indicator of student ability if the child comes from a culturally deprived or culturally different environment.

This issue is exceedingly complex. There are frequent and continuing debates regarding *cultural bias* in mental testing and the dust is far from settled. For example, some argue that the lower average scores of minority groups are simply evidence of discriminatory test bias. From this perspective, intelligence tests ". . . have devastating labeling—and pigeon-holing— effects . . . and they are nothing more than an Anglo yardstick designed to make whites look ingenious and blacks and other minorities stupid" (Clifford, 1981; Hoffman, 1964; Zacharias, 1977). For another view, Arthur Jensen (1976), known for his "racial differences" hypothesis, argues that intelligence tests ". . . show practically no evidence of differential culture bias . . . ," by which he means that the tests do in fact predict school success for both minority and majority cultures.

In an article entitled "The Trouble With IQ Tests," physics professor Zacharias (1977) made a number of specific complaints about intelligence tests: (1) They demand an understanding of the tester's jargon, proper guessing of what the tester wants, and tolerance for boredom; (2) test items often are ambiguous, illogical, meaningless, irrelevant to what the student knows or cares about, time wasting, overprecise or not sufficiently precise, and tricky in appearance even when they contain no tricks; and (3) the tests tend to be frightening, penalizing, damaging to a student's self-image, and misleading for tracking or assigning students to grade levels. Zacharias's opinion is clear enough.

More optimistically, Thorndike and Hagen (1977) argue for the usefulness (prediction ability) of intelligence tests, but further note that (1) the tests do not determine a person's ability, they simply suggest strengths and weaknesses; (2) they describe how a person is doing at the present time; and (3) we should consider the cultural, personal, and family background in interpreting test scores. Thus controversy around this subject continues.

Educators and psychologists—whether liberal or conservative, black or white—will agree that culturally different students are more likely than the average student to have a difficult time when taking tests of *verbal ability* (vocabulary, comprehension). These tests, of course, are based upon middle-class English. The problem is that subcultural languages such as black English, (Baratz, 1974; Labov, 1974), Hawaiian pidgin, Navajo or other Native American languages are different, and so the person's linguistic structures, categories, and associations are also different. Group intelligence tests depend heavily on language ability and therefore are more likely to be biased than individually administered tests. As we saw in Chapter 4, the WISC-R separates subtests and IQ scores into verbal and performance (nonverbal) components, thereby allowing a bright child with deficient English to score high. The new Stanford-Binet similarly evaluates verbal and nonverbal abilities in its four subscores of verbal reasoning, quantitative reasoning, visual/abstract reasoning, and short-term memory. Scruggs and Cohn (1983), Kryaniuk and Das (1976), and Schubert and Cropley (1972) have commented upon the large WISC-R verbal/performance discrepancies of Native American children, due at least in part to language and cultural differences.

Witty (1978) noted that bias comes from other testing subtleties in addition to the language problem. For example, minority children may have lower expectations of success, lower test-taking motivation, and higher test-taking anxiety, particularly when the administrator is middle-class white. High anxiety is known to lower any type of human performance or test score (Weiner, 1980; Cronbach and Snow, 1977).

Despite the inadequacies often cited in regard to intelligence tests, Van Tassel-Baska (1986) maintains that the SAT-Verbal and SAT-Math tests provide a suitable basis for the identification of academically able disadvantaged students. She argues that this identification process also permits her to objectively identify students who need scholarship assistance. Nevertheless, the main problem remains: Any identification process based on the SAT or other intelligence/aptitude test will surely under-identify disadvantaged students with underdeveloped potential.

In sum, a high IQ score is convincing evidence of high intellectual ability among culturally different and poor children, just as with majority children. However, many gifted minority and economically disadvantaged children will be overlooked if intelligence tests are used as the only or the most important identification instrument. Their use is recommended, but average or low scores should be interpreted with caution, and in consideration of the language, cultural, and family background and the circumstances of testing.

Achievement Tests

Achievement tests typically are administered at regular intervals in virtually every school system, and so achievement information is readily available. However, while standardized achievement tests are highly recommended as an identification tool for most populations, with culturally different students they are plagued by exactly the same problems as intelligence tests. Therefore, while it is critical that achievement scores not be misused because of cultural bias, it certainly is reasonable to use them as one index of gifts and talents for minority children. As with IQ scores, children who produce high scores on achievement tests are showing good evidence of special kinds of giftedness. However, in culturally different populations there are likely to be gifted children who may not score high on these tests despite their giftedness. Achievement tests alone, then, are not a sufficient measure for the identification of gifted minority and poor children.

Teacher Nominations

In many instances, teacher nominations of giftedness are a highly suspect and invalid identification strategy (see Chapter 4). Nonetheless, it continues to be the most popular identification method used. For minority and poor children, the teacher nomination method creates special hazards. "Teacher pleasers," who are neat and clean, nicely dressed, who speak middle-class English, and who turn in their work neatly done and on time, are likely to be named as "gifted." Other students—poor, black, Hispanic, or Native American—are automatically "disadvantaged" by many teachers in the nomination process. Shade (1978) found that black gifted achievers, despite their giftedness, receive less praise and attention and more criticism in the classroom than their nongifted black counterparts. Clark (1983) observed that there remains the persistent attitude that gifted children are not found in certain populations.

On the other hand, a sensitive and caring teacher who is knowledgeable about characteristics of gifted children may, in fact, be the very best identifier of the culturally different gifted child. Furthermore, such a teacher may be able to guide and inspire a talented child who does not score high on any ability or achievement test. In the hands of a sensitive and aware teacher, then, the teacher nomination procedure can be a potentially important way to locate economically disadvantaged and culturally different gifted children.

The nomination procedure will be greatly improved by educating teachers regarding characteristics of gifted and talented minority children, some of which are different than usual characteristics of giftedness. For example, Gay (1978) researched common characteristics of gifted children and compared them to parallel characteristics of gifted black children. Her list of 11 characteristics stems from twenty years of teaching experience with black children and three years of teaching in a program for the gifted and talented (see Table 13.1).

The present authors might repeat an earlier warning in relation to Gay's item 11 in Table 13.1. Gifted black children may perform only at an average level in school because of socioeconomic, language, motivational, personal, or cultural handicaps. Therefore, students should be considered potentially gifted if they earn high ratings on many of the first ten characteristics, with or without actual "good" school achievement.

Swenson (1978) constructed a helpful list of characteristics of creativeness in a culturally different and socioeconomically deprived urban

TABLE 13.1   Comparative Characteristics of Giftedness

CONCEPTS FROM THE LITERATURE	MANIFESTATIONS OF GIFTED CHARACTERISTICS IN GIFTED BLACK CHILDREN
1. Keen observation	Picks up more quickly on racist attitudes and practices; may feel alienated by school at an early age.
2. Interest and ability in perceiving relationships	Seeks structure and organization in required tasks; may be slow to motivate in some abstract activities.
3. Verbal proficiency, large vocabulary, facility of expression	Many black children have large vocabularies inappropriate for the school setting; thinking in black English may hinder the facility of expression in standard English.
4. Breadth of information	Difficult to determine many areas of experimental knowledge for black children.
5. Questioning, curious, skeptical	Though some ask too many "wrong" questions, some may have been conditioned to suppress questioning behavior.
6. Critical, evaluative, possessing good judgment	Explores (in perception of relationships) better or wiser choices; reads behavioral implications.
7. Creative, inventive, original	Makes up games and activities; expresses original ideas in other ways.
8. Power of concentration, long attention span	May find some have extremely strong concentration due to persistent noise in environment; may also express displeasure at having to stop an activity.
9. Independence	Need for less supervision is especially pronounced in black gifted.
10. Diversity of interests and abilities	Frequently has artistic, musical, creative writing, psychomotor, or leadership talent in addition to global intellectual ability; may neglect school work due to other interests.
11. Academic facility and strength	Good at basic school tasks; may not have expected achievement due to inferior schooling.

From J. E. Gay, "A Proposed Plan for Identifying Black Gifted Children," *Gifted Child Quarterly*, 22 (1978), 353-59. Reprinted by permission.

school area. Her list came from information generated by 36 teachers and was based on observed original behavior related to classwork, art, and antisocial—yes, *antisocial*—behavior (see Table 13.2). Note that because teachers are accustomed to disciplining children for antisocial behavior they may overlook the creativity exhibited in such behavior (see especially items 2, 9, 18, 23, and 24 in Table 13.2).

TABLE 13.2   Characteristics of Creativity in Culturally Different Students

1.	Repeats activities so that he/she can do them differently.
2.	Invents imaginative lies.
3.	Shows that he/she sees hidden meanings, cause and effect relationships that are not obvious.
4.	Writes and illustrates stories without being asked to do so as an assignment.
5.	Utilizes free time by making up games or making something from paper and material scraps as opposed to more structured activities.
6.	Finds many answers to a situational question.
7.	Lets his/her imagination "run" when writing a story; sees more possibilities.
8.	Finds activities for spare-time work with little or no additional help.
9.	Decorates the border of his/her paper when doing an assignment.
10.	Doesn't copy other children's ideas in art.
11.	Builds and constructs things using unusual materials; uses ordinary materials in different ways.
12.	Interrelates his/her experiences and draws on them with ease in discussions.
13.	Doesn't let classroom events go unnoticed; questions them.
14.	Accomplishes things on his/her own without help.
15.	Writes poems and stories in his/her spare time.
16.	Asks unusual questions during class discussions.
17	Makes up his/her own ideas when the class does a project together.
18.	Suggests to the teacher alternate ways of doing an activity.
19.	Is willing to risk friendship to express his/her feelings or thoughts.
20.	Enthusiastic about new activities in music and art.
21.	Goes beyond what is required in class assignments; makes his/her work "fancier."
22.	Comes up with fresh, original comments or an unusual correct answer when there is more than one correct answer.
23.	Finds new ways to get attention.
24.	Tries original ways to get out of work he/she doesn't want to do.
25.	Takes the initiative when he/she wants to know something; reads or asks questions without prompting.

From J. E. Swenson, "Teacher-assessment of Creative Behavior in Disadvantaged Children, *Gifted Child Quarterly,* 22 (1978), 338-43. Reprinted by permission.

Matrix Identification Models

Matrix identification models have been developed to bring together data from a variety of sources and to specifically include variables that will help identify minority and disadvantaged gifted children. Especially, the *Kranz Talent Identification Instrument* (Kranz, 1981; see Chapter 4) was designed for the identification of culturally diverse, minority, immigrant, and poor gifted children. The *Baldwin Identification Matrix* (Baldwin, 1978, 1984; see Chapter 4) combines objective and subjective criteria and has been reported to be effective for increasing the number of black students identified for gifted programs (Dabney, 1983; Long, 1981; McBeath, Blackshear, and Smart, 1981).

Creativity Tests

Creativity tests, both divergent thinking tests and self-descriptive inventories (see Chapter 4), can be very helpful in selecting minority and culturally different children for participation in G/T programs. Specifically, they are useful in identifying highly creative children who are not motivated to achieve and who may not score high on ability or achievement tests. For both kinds of creativity tests, there has been research with minority children that supports their use.

The *Torrance Tests of Creative Thinking* (Figural Form, particularly) have been used in several research projects with minority children. For example, Solomon (1974), in an analysis of 722 test scores, found that minority children scored higher than other children in some areas of creative thinking in grades 1 and 3. At the fifth-grade level there were no significant differences between scores of minority and other children. Torrance (1971; see also Torrance, 1977b) summarized the results of 16 different studies designed to evaluate racial or socioeconomic differences in Torrance Test scores. The results varied, with some favoring the minority children and others favoring majority children, but overall his conclusions supported the notion that there is no racial or socioeconomic bias in open-ended tests of creative thinking.

The *Group Inventory for Finding (Creative) Talent (GIFT)* and the *Group Inventory For Finding Interests (GIFFI*; Rimm, Davis, and Bien, 1982) are self-report inventories that evaluate personality characteristics, attitudes, interests, and biographical information known to be associated with creativeness. Studies by Rimm and Davis (1976, 1980) indicated that *GIFT* and *GIFFI* are valid for identifying creative potential in both rural and urban socioeconomically disadvantaged populations, as well as among specific ethnic groups, including black, Hispanic, and Native American minority students.

Chambers, Barron, and Sprecher (1980) confirmed that considerable information has been collected to show that some motivational and personality characteristics are indeed related to creativeness. They used this information to help identify gifted Mexican-American elementary students, and concluded that ". . . the abilities and traits necessary for future high-level intellectual/creative contributions appear to be similar for both culturally similar and culturally different persons."

Central to the appropriate use of divergent thinking tests such as the Torrance Tests or personality/biographical inventories is the recognition that (1) scores from a single creativity test should be combined with other information, such as teacher ratings of creativity or scores on a second creativity test, in order to reach a valid decision, and (2) low creativity test scores absolutely must never be used to eliminate children from G/T programs. Creativity tests are not perfect; there simply are too many types of creativity and creative people. However, creativity tests can identify creatively gifted children, majority and minority, who may not be identified in other ways.

Parent Nominations

As indicated earlier in this text, parents typically know a lot about their children's gifts and talents. For years they may have watched their energetic children create games and stories, invent things, build things, solve problems, create humor, and produce original artwork, writing, musical compositions, mechanical gadgets, and/or scientific products. Parents also will be able to identify specific culturally valued giftedness—for example, caring for siblings and fixing dinner while waiting for Mom to come home from work—better than a person outside of the cultural system. Parents should indeed be given an opportunity to nominate their children for participation in a G/T program.

Peer Nominations

Peers of the economically deprived or culturally different gifted child usually do not place a high value on school achievement. However, they are as aware of gifts and talents among their friends and classmates as are other young people. Bernal (1978; see also Bernal, 1979), for example, noted that members of a particular ethnic group almost always can identify the "smartest" among their peers.

In order to identify unusual intellectual, creative, or leadership ability, it may be necessary to look beyond the classroom to the out-of-school cliques and crowds. One interesting approach is to meet with students named by peers as out-of-school "leaders." These leaders can explain characteristics of culturally valued giftedness within their own peer culture (Bernal, 1979; Bruch and Curry, 1978), gifts which might qualify the person for the special opportunities of a G/T program. In inner-city areas, for example, creative approaches to self-maintenance or even survival may be reasonable arenas in which to discover giftedness. Culturally valued art and music talent, which is known to peers but not expressed in the classroom, also would be important information for the identification of giftedness. Finally, the "different" or lonely child in a minority culture, even though he or she does not value intellectual pursuit, may be considered suspect for unusual talent. The child may well have special interests and talents, suppressed due to peer pressures, that should be cultivated in a G/T program.

A Quota System

One reasonable solution to minority representation in a G/T program is the quota system. A fixed percentage of culturally different children are included in a program, based upon the percentage of those students in the school or district. The quota system assumes that the *same percentage* of minority students are gifted and talented as majority students, and should therefore be included in the program regardless of comparative test scores or grades. As one might guess, this is a much debated assumption. A central issue is the fairness to majority students who are excluded and who, according to objective criteria, appear more qualified.

Kitano and Kirby (1986) agreed that a major problem with the quota system is that including some lower-scoring students from one culture group has the effect of eliminating higher-scoring students from another. As another problem, due to differing racial make-up a quota system may include a particular child in one school in the district but exclude him or her in another school, should the child move to a different neighborhood.

Despite its drawbacks, using a quota system has proven to be a successful and educationally beneficial strategy for the minority and poor children so identified (Berliner and Rosenshine, 1977; LeRose, 1978).

PROGRAMMING FOR CULTURALLY DIFFERENT GIFTED STUDENTS

Programming for culturally diverse and socioeconomically disadvantaged gifted and talented children can include any of the curriculum options for acceleration, enrichment, and grouping described in earlier chapters. However, there are important additional components of such programs that should be given special consideration: (1) maintaining ethnic identity, (2) extracurricular cultural enrichment, (3) divergent thinking curriculum, (4) counseling, (5) parent support groups, (6) development of significant models, and (7) career education. While it may not be possible to include all of these components at the outset, it is highly desirable to eventually include all of them if minority gifted children are to have an optimal opportunity to develop and use their abilities.

Maintaining Ethnic Identity

The *assimilationist* position holds that upward mobility in the United States requires conformity to the language, culture, and rules of the majority Anglo population. Assimilationists further point out that minority subcultural values prevent or at least discourage integration into the majority community, and thus limit the minority person's educational and socioeconomic opportunities (Banks, 1979). Exum (1983) noted that assimilationist attitudes of black families, who wish to succeed and be accepted in the white world, not only may be pro-white but even anti-black.

On the other hand, the *cultural pluralist* emphasizes the importance of pride in one's ethnic identity as an important part of educational and career achievement. Cultural pluralists note the close relationship of ethnic pride to the development of healthy self-concepts, and therefore consider heterogeneity and diversity to be beneficial to both individual and cultural growth.

One main arena of controversy, for example, is found in questions related to bilingual-bicultural education programs for Hispanics, Asians, and Native Americans. Assimilationists oppose such programs, indicating that they slow the process by which the culturally different child is integrated into the mainstream culture. They claim that precious time is wasted in teaching children about their heritage and in their own language. Instead, they maintain that this time should be more profitably used for teaching basic skills—in English. However, cultural pluralists argue that the positive self-concepts derived from ethnic pride are extremely important to the minority children's educational and life achievements.

The results of research studies evaluating the effects of bilingual programs on achievement in basic skills have been mixed. The Department of Educational Research and Program Development (1979) in Milwaukee and Rimm (1977) found that children in Hispanic bilingual programs showed better achievement test gains, in both Milwaukee, Wisconsin, and St. Paul, Minnesota, than Hispanic children not in the programs. However, many other school districts have found no significant measurable advantage for students involved in bilingual programs. Evaluations of bilingual education programs have not indicated a clear, unambiguous avenue for strengthening basic skills, nor a clear resolution to the assimilationist/pluralist debate.

Nonetheless, the cultural pluralist position seems innately more reasonable. People cannot totally separate themselves from their cultural backgrounds, and if they view that heritage as somehow negative or derogatory they will see themselves as second-class persons who are restricted in ability, opportunity, or both. In contrast, if a person values his or her ethnic identity, then the pride, confidence, and feelings of acceptance—all of which are basic to constructive mental health—should help motivate the person toward personal growth and achievement.

As a general principle, educators committed to providing programs for the gifted and talented necessarily support the development of diversity. That is, they intrinsically agree that each gifted child is different and therefore requires educational opportunities that fit his or her special strengths and talents. By the same reasoning, it would seem that G/T educators also should value the differences inherent in ethnic cultures, and should recognize the personal growth, mental health, and educational advantages that accompany pride in one's culture.

Banks (1979) proposed an enlightening five-stage framework for understanding ethnicity and for developing ethnic identity and pride.

Stage 1, ethnic psychological captivity.   This is a stage of negative self-concepts. Individuals in this stage have internalized the negative stereotypes about their own ethnic group. They show strong out-group identification and strive vigorously to become assimilated.

Stage 2, ethnic encapsulation.

Stage 2, ethnic encapsulation.   Interestingly, this stage most often characterizes members of the majority Anglo-American group. In this stage individuals interact only with members of their own ethnic group. Further, they believe their group is superior to other groups. Asian Americans, blacks, Hispanics, and Native Americans manage to exhibit ethnic pride without attacking Anglo-Americans; unfortunately, the reverse has not been true.

Stage 3, ethnic identity clarification.   Individuals in this stage have clarified intrapsychic conflicts about who and what they are and have developed positive attitudes toward themselves and their own ethnic group. This self-acceptance is a prerequisite to accepting and responding positively to others.

Stage 4, biethnicity.   Individuals in the biethnic stage possess a positive sense of ethnic identity and pride, but also have the skills needed to participate in another ethnic culture as well. While there is double membership in this stage, reference-group orientation—one's primary identity—is with one's own ethnic group. Importantly, there is no reference-group conflict in deciding where one's primary membership and allegiance should be—it is with one's own ethnic group.

Stage 5, multiethnicity.   Banks describes this stage as the idealized goal for all persons in a pluralistic society. Individuals at this stage are able to function within several ethnic sociocultural environments, and they understand and appreciate the variations and differences among the several cultures.

Banks's typology would appear to have direct application to the development of ethnic identity programs, with his Stage 5 as the goal of such programs. Gifted and talented children should not only acquire constructive and unprejudiced attitudes (as all children should), but should learn to function effectively within multiple sociocultural environments.

One might operationalize the Banks model, for example, by identifying the ethnic development stage in which most students in a classroom or G/T program are functioning, and then create an ethnic component designed to help those students move toward higher stages. For secondary and perhaps younger students, the Banks model itself could comprise an eye-opening part of the curriculum, one in which the "highest level of thinking" is in the multiethnic Stage 5.

If a G/T program serves students in a multicultural area, explicit objectives of the program should include the provision of multiethnic experiences and, for minority persons especially, the development of positive ethnic identity.

Extracurricular Cultural Enrichment

The cultural enrichment that comes from attending concerts, theatre, and ballet and visiting exhibitions, art galleries, and museums usually is provided by the families of middle-class gifted children. For the socioeconomically deprived child, these experiences typically are nonexistent or else limited to occasional school excursions. Exposure to the arts can be a valuable experience for economically deprived gifted children, as well as a good reinforcement for their participation in the gifted program. Importantly, such exposure would strongly reinforce students' own artistic or scientific efforts and talents.

For maximum benefit, art or science experiences should be tied to other knowledge, skill, or creative components of the G/T program. For example, historical backgrounds of particular artists, composers, or scientists would add knowledge and depth to the experiences. Also, discussions of the antecedents and idea sources of particular products or performances, or comparative evaluations of various works, would further embellish the event. "What would happen if . . . ?" or "In what other ways might we . . . ?" questions add creative and futuristic thinking to the experiences. Students also can do further research, prepare written or oral reports to the class, or write stories, newspaper columns with photos, or news reports about a person or event, and so on. Finally, as we noted earlier, field trips are the most beneficial when students are armed with specific objectives to be met and questions to be answered before they climb onto the bus.

School funding for many enrichment experiences is certain to be limited or even absent. Ideally, travel and admissions monies would be built into the original program budget. If not, local industries, businesses, or civic groups may be encouraged to fund specific trips. For the business owner, such sponsorship has the attraction of combining a small tax-deductible investment with a superb public relations opportunity (news coverage). Note also that, at least in medium to large cities, many museums, galleries, and university facilities are free, reducing expenses to bus fares and the required candy and soda pop.

Divergent Thinking Curriculum

Frasier (1987) interpreted the Rimm Hierarchy of Cognitive Needs (Davis and Rimm, 1985), described early in this chapter, as an instructional model for identification. Although the model does advocate the provision of a strong basic skills program and does make a case for increased likelihood of identification of giftedness once basic skills are mastered, it should not be assumed that a basic skill instructional model is recommended prior to the introduction of a divergent thinking and creative problem-solving curriculum. School programs for disadvantaged students that emphasize both basic skills and divergent thinking opportunities such as Creative Problem Solving (CPS; Isaksen and Treffinger, 1985; see Chapters 10 and 11) have been very effective in both identifying more gifted students and stimulating their creativity. The Rimm Hierarchy of Cognitive Needs should *not* be interpreted as a message to wait until basic needs are fulfilled before programming for higher level thinking skills. Especially among economically disadvantaged and culturally different youth opportunities for creative production are mandatory in order to motivate these gifted young people to make a strong commitment to education.

Counseling

The support that comes from an intact and secure family structure may be less available to many economically disadvantaged or culturally different students. While family problems are not unique to students in these groups, it is true that complicated and temporary marital relationships, alcohol abuse, mobility, and other forms of stress and instability are common. According to a 1981 U.S. Census, for example, 36 percent of black families are single-parent, female-headed. Health, hygiene, and nutritional values may be minimal. Peer pressure not to achieve is strong. In some difficult circumstances, and in accord with Maslow's hierarchy (Figure 13.1), survival itself takes strong precedence over educational achievement and developing gifts and talents.

Such children need shelters, persons to whom they can go when intellectual, social, developmental, and even safety and survival needs are threatened. This shelter should include an adult, an empathetic and professional counselor who understands the local economic and ethnic realities and who cares about the welfare of all children. Exum (1983) recommended that counselors in minority areas should, first, increase their knowledge about the school community, for example, by becoming acquainted with population characteristics, availability of resources, availability of public transportation, community leadership styles, and the particular types of problems that frequently come to the counselor's attention. Second, Exum noted that the counselor's credibility and trustworthiness will be enhanced if he or she becomes more visible in the community, perhaps by serving on multicultural committees and by patronizing minority businesses. A third recommendation was for counselors to be flexible in scheduling appointments—using evenings and weekends—because so many parents of minority children cannot attend counseling sessions during the regular work day. Generally, said Exum, counselors should seek to build personal relationships with minority families, because "parents are much more responsive to counselors whom they believe have a genuine personal interest in their children."

The counseling shelter also should provide a peer support group comprised of other gifted children, many of whom will share similar problems. Generally, individual and group counseling and organized peer support groups are very important for the culturally different gifted child, and should be a high priority of any G/T program in a culturally diverse area.

Parent Support Groups

Although every gifted program should encourage parent education and involvement, parents of socioeconomically deprived and culturally different children have a special and greater need. These parents will become supportive and involved only if (1) they understand their child's gifts and talents and (2) they understand the opportunities available to the gifted in our society. Further, they are more likely to assist their children and contribute to the G/T program if they do not see the program as elitist (for example, for WASPs only) or as threatening. For example, parents may resist a G/T program if they believe the program will psychologically separate them from their children or cause their children to respect them less. It may be frightening to parents with little education to learn that their child is very bright and on a track toward a middle-class education that, they believe, could alienate the child from them.

On the other hand, if the program emphasizes *positive cultural identity*, fears of alienation should be reduced. Parents also will have an avenue for relating to and making contributions to the program. Parent meetings, in which the G/T program and activities are explained and the above problems addressed, and in which parents share problems and optimism, will benefit the program and the gifted children involved.

Enhanced parenting skills should be part of parent support group activity. Shade (1978) emphasized that black children who do well in school and on achievement tests tend to have parents or guardians who engage in the following parenting behaviors:

1. The maintenance of a quality of communication that tends to stimulate the child's problem-solving ability, independence, and productivity;
2. The expression of warmth, interest, affection, and encouragement;
3. The establishment of close family ties;
4. The maintenance of some structure and order for the child;
5. The establishment of goals of performance;
6. The use of control mechanisms that include moderate amounts of praise and blame, moderate amounts of punishment, and no authoritarian tactics;
7. The giving of assistance when requested or when the need is perceived.

Shade also concluded that the parent-child interaction is more important to achievement than either family socioeconomic status or family structure.

Development of Significant Models

Chapter 14 on underachievement emphasizes the significant role of family modeling for avoiding underachievement. Shade (1983) defined *significant others* as "persons who exercise a major influence on the attitudes of individuals." She pointed out that for black youth, significant others extend beyond the immediate family to include the extended family, the media, and white society. Mother, concluded Shade, is the strongest influence upon black students' school performance (Henderson and Long, 1973; Rosenberg, 1973). Studies of occupational choice (Pallone, *et al.*, 1973) indicated that black high school girls were most influenced by their mothers, while boys were most influenced by persons holding the job to which they aspired. A study of black college freshmen by Shade (1978) found that parents ranked last in influence, while peers, teachers, counselors, friends, and siblings ranked at the top. In contrast, earlier studies of black college students showed mothers (Guren and Epps, 1966) or parents (Olsen, 1970) to have the greatest influence.

These studies again emphasize the importance of parent achievement models for academic success. They also point to an important gap: The disadvantaged black matriarchal family rarely provides a male achievement model for black adolescent boys. The message supporting education is mainly a female message. As boys move from childhood to adolescence, in order to establish their own sense of masculinity (Hetherington, 1972) they search for male conveyors of achievement and occupational aspirations.

Disadvantaged gifted boys are in almost desperate need of achievement-oriented males to serve as role models for achievement. In the absence of appropriate models, television media (Leifer, *et al.*, 1974; Fedler, 1973) and peer and street culture (Perkins, 1975) strongly influence black adolescent male youth. In one study (Bridgeman and Burbach, 1976), a videotape of black male youth being rewarded for excellence in school resulted in a significant increase in academic expectations by the black male viewers.

Providing appropriate models, particularly male models, should be considered a requirement of every gifted program for disadvantaged students. Some recommendations are included in Inset 13.1. While this Inset addresses male models, the suggestions also are applicable to providing appropriate female role models. The recommendations apply to both sexes.

INSET 13.1 SCHOOL PROGRAMS FOR ESTABLISHING MALE ACHIEVEMENT MODELS

1. Video tapes of achievement-oriented males in various careers (e.g., doctor, lawyer, professor, businessman). Men should tell about childhood experiences that fostered achievement.
2. Video tapes of a panel of minority gifted children (males and females) discussing their problems and successes in achievement. Emphasis may be placed on cultural pride and achievement.
3. Cultural intermediary (Labov & Robbins, 1969)—a young man who is achievement oriented and "streetwise" to meet with and counsel adolescent boys.
4. Speaker series—weekly talks by successful minority community persons (male and female) about their careers and their life styles.
5. Lunch seminars for small groups of students with minority community persons to talk about achievement.
6. Parenting classes for fathers only led by a male counselor or teacher who is also a parent.
7. Parenting classes for single mothers with the specific goal of assisting them in establishing appropriate minority role models.
8. General parenting classes with emphasis on the importance of appropriate role models.
9. Video and audio tapes of parenting classes for fathers only, for single parents and for general parents available for loan to parents unable to attend classes.
10. Student interview assignments with achieving adults. Collection of interviews may be assembled into a book for discussion and review.
11. Bibliography of books emphasizing the childhoods of successful minority persons. Reading assignments can be extended to include drama and videotaping.
12. Visits to college campuses including meeting with minority college students.
13. Involvement in summer and Saturday college campus enrichment programs.
14. Funding for minority teachers to spend extra personal time with minority adolescents in and out of school enrichment activities (one to one or small groups).
15. Funding for special interest mentor activities with successful adults.

Career Education

Career education is an important priority in all education. One problem for disadvantaged gifted students, however, is that "career education" traditionally focuses on occupations and careers that seem suitable or available to the majority of children in a particular school. Thus a curriculum program in a middle-class high school will feature college preparatory coursework and a professional career orientation. A high school in a minority or economically depressed area will focus on blue-collar occupations, with strong offerings in welding, machine shop, auto mechanics, and typing. There is a noticeably reduced awareness and valuing of college training and professional careers, and thus a reduced opportunity for the necessary preparation.

Career education for the gifted child in a lower-SES environment, of course, should stress the professional opportunities available and the necessary educational preparation. However, a realistic career education program also must emphasize the life-styles, values, ethics, and goals that accompany particular professional careers (Moore, 1979). To compete successfully, the disadvantaged gifted child must acquire the many subtle attitudes and skills that accompany a given profession—attitudes and skills learned at home by children of educated professional parents.

An important—indeed, crucial—component of career education is the involvement of suitable *models*. These are professional persons of similar ethnic backgrounds who have, in fact, emerged from difficult socioeconomic circumstances. They need to share their experiences, their problems, and their strategies for success with gifted young disadvantaged people. Presentations, mentorships, and on-the-job visits are good ways to provide gifted youth with a taste of career and life goals worth working for. The models also can help students understand that within the professional areas there *will* be support; and further, that once high-level positions are attained, both intrinsic and extrinsic rewards will make the educational and economic struggle worthwhile. Professional persons from disadvantaged backgrounds typically are very sensitive to the problems of culturally different and poor gifted youth and are motivated to help.

As we have seen, career education for gifted minority, economically deprived, and culturally different students usually must be *broader* than typical career education programs. While college-educated parents automatically provide good models and informal information and values to their middle-class children, it is rare for culturally different students to have such models in their immediate families or even neighborhoods. Their parents usually are not aware of the opportunities and obstacles related to a high-level professional education. Therefore, a good career education program for these students will need to provide considerable and detailed direction. For example, these young people must learn about colleges and universities that will support both their professional and their ethnic needs. They will require direction in finding scholarships or other funding assistance. They will need to learn how to prepare for entrance examinations and personal interviews. They also must be reassured about the social environment they may encounter.

The extraordinary value of a well-designed career education program for gifted disadvantaged youth is that it may guide very talented persons to become fulfilled and productive individuals, individuals who will make those "valuable contributions to self and society." However, if these gifted youth meet only dead ends and frustration and have no outlet for the development and expression of their talents, society will not only lose their positive professional contributions, but will likely be taxed (literally) by their negative contributions. Farley (1986) argued that high energy levels can be channeled either into creative and productive outlets or, in the case of many low-SES adolescents, into delinquency and self-destructiveness. Their energy, talents, and frustrations may combine into antisocial behavior—perhaps in a leadership capacity—which constitutes an obviously serious and unnecessary waste of human potential.

SUMMARY

Due to cultural and language differences, culturally and economically disadvantaged students rarely are identified as "gifted."

Some statistics indicate that educational and social programs for disadvantaged and minority students have led to reduced dropout rates and have reduced achievement differences between black and white students.

Modeled after Maslow's theory, Rimm's hierarchy of intellectual needs emphasizes that good preparation in basic skills is prerequisite to the application of knowledge, the analysis, synthesis, and evaluation of ideas, and creative production. Further, the lack of basic skills obscures the giftedness of culturally different youth. Examples demonstrated how intellectual and creative giftedness was revealed when deficiencies were removed, thus allowing the identification of culturally different gifted students. Even when skills are the priority, regular opportunities for higher level and creative thought should take place in the classroom to identify and encourage highly creative youngsters.

While early childhood experiences strongly influence later academic and career success, deprived environments do not totally prevent the development of talent.

Low IQ and achievement test scores may be misinterpreted to "prove" the absence of giftedness. Because average or below-average achievement can be common among gifted disadvantaged, identification must be based upon potential rather than actual academic performance. A high IQ score remains a valid indicator of giftedness, but an average or low score may be misleading. Cultural and family background, including language differences, and testing circumstances, such as motivation and test anxiety, must be considered.

While high achievement is good evidence of talent in particular areas, achievement test scores suffer from the same problems as intelligence test scores.

Teacher nominations may favor members of the majority culture; however, a sensitive teacher who understands characteristics of gifted students may be an excellent identifier of gifts and talents of minority students. Gay compiled a list of characteristics of gifted black children and Swenson itemized characteristics of creativity in culturally different students. Matrix identification models including the *Kranz Talent Identification Instrument* and the *Baldwin Identification Matrix* are helpful in increasing minority representation in gifted programs.

Research indicates that creativity tests, such as the *Torrance Tests of Creative Thinking* and the Rimm and Davis GIFT and GIFFI inventories, are good instruments for identifying creative disadvantaged and minority students. Parent and peer nominations also are good identification strategies.

A quota system assumes that gifts and talents exist in equal proportions in all cultural groups and assures their representation in G/T programs.

Programming options described in earlier chapters also may be used with disadvantaged and minority students. However, the following additional components of such programs should be given special consideration: (1) maintaining ethnic identity, (2) extracurricular cultural enrichment, (3) divergent thinking curriculum, (4) counseling, (5) parent support groups, (6) development of significant models, and (7) career education.

In order to support personal mental health via ethnic pride, the maintenance of ethnic identity was recommended, which is consistent with the cultural pluralist position. *Assimilationists* argue that bilingual programs interfere with the integration of culturally different children into the mainstream. *Cultural pluralists* feel that ethnic pride is central to self-esteem and educational and career success. Research on the benefits of bilingual programs is mixed.

Banks described five stages of ethnic identity. A teacher might identify students' ethnic stages and attempt to move them toward higher stages.

Extracurricular cultural enrichment is important for socioeconomically deprived and minority gifted students. Such experiences can include other knowledge, skill, and creative objectives.

School programs for disadvantaged students should emphasize a divergent thinking curriculum for identifying and stimulating gifted children in culturally diverse populations.

Troubled students need understanding, including help from a trained and empathetic counselor. Exum recommended that a counselor learn about the local community, become more visible, and be flexible in scheduling appointments. A support group of gifted peers also is beneficial.

Parents will support G/T programs if they understand the importance of the program for their child's future, and if they are not threatened by the program or its possible effects on their child. Parent meetings will aid in educating parents regarded G/T programs and will allow parents to share problems and optimism.

Career education must include not only career options and the preparation needed to attain them, but the life-styles, ethics, and goals that accompany various professions. Models—professional persons from similar disadvantaged backgrounds—are a vital component of a successful career education program.

Shade's research on the roles of significant others emphasizes the importance of achievement models for disadvantaged youth. Providing such appropriate models, particularly for males, should be considered a requirement for every gifted program for disadvantaged students.

If gifted disadvantaged and minority students are not helped to develop their skills and receive professional training, they may channel their talents into antisocial and self-destructive behavior.

chapter fourteen

Underachievement
Diagnosis and Treatment

The underachieving gifted child represents both society's greatest loss and its greatest potential resource. The child has the potential for high achievement and significant contributions, but is not using that talent in productive ways. Statistics tell us that as many as half of our gifted children do not perform up to their abilities in school (National Commission on Excellence in Education (1983). Studies of high school dropouts indicate that between 10 and 20 percent of the students who do not graduate are in the gifted range of abilities (Lajoie and Shore, 1981; Nyquist, 1973; Whitmore, 1980). Because the child's special abilities are recognized, the nonproductiveness often leads to frustration by parents, teachers, and even the child himself or herself. However, if the underachieving pattern can be reversed, the child frequently makes unusual progress in skill acquisition and in positive, productive work. In view of the child's history of underachievement, the extent of positive change after appropriate intervention usually is quite surprising.

Overview

This chapter will review characteristics, causes, and dynamics of underachievement, along with a strategy for reversing this costly syndrome.

DEFINITION AND IDENTIFICATION OF UNDERACHIEVEMENT

Underachievement is defined as a discrepancy between the child's school performance and some index of his or her actual ability, such as intelligence, achievement, or creativity scores, or observational data.

Test Scores

The chief index of actual ability is test scores. Despite all the faults and problems related to testing, despite test unreliability and measurement error, and despite all the biases that need to be considered related to low test scores, it seems apparent that children cannot score extraordinarily high on tests purely by accident. Test-taking skill alone cannot account for test scores that consistently fall two or more standard deviations above the mean, that is, above the ninety-seventh percentile. Unusually high scores then, whether on intelligence, achievement, or creativity tests, indicate special abilities or skills not apparent in the underachieving child's usual schoolwork.

Intelligence Test Scores

If a child is identified as gifted, even based on intelligence test scores alone, it is important to compare the child's *actual* school performance to the performance that would be *expected* based on those IQ scores. There are several statistical concepts that may be used in this kind of comparison, especially *grade equivalent scores, mental age* (MA) *equivalents, stanines,* and *percentiles.* For example, a third-grade child of 8 years 6 months may produce intelligence test scores in the ninth stanine (top 4 percent) or a mental age equivalent score of 10 years 2 months, but his or her usual classroom performance might range between the fourth, fifth, and sixth stanines—strictly at grade level. Any of these statistical yardsticks are satisfactory for helping to operationally define underachievement in order to identify children who need help.

A frequent error in the identification of underachievers is to use a *fixed* number of months of years below grade level as a criterion of underachievement. For example, first-grade children who are six months below their expected achievement level will have far more serious underachievement problems than eighth graders performing one full year below the expected level. For the younger children six months may represent being 50 percent behind where they should be; for the eighth-grade children one year represents only 12.5 percent behind where they would be expected to be performing. The main problem related to using a constant number of months is that younger children with underachievement problems are likely to be overlooked because the discrepancy between actual and expected achievement does not appear to be large enough in terms of actual months, even though the problem is quite serious. Since underachievement can be treated more easily when diagnosed early, it is critical to recognize this common identification error.

Achievement Test Scores

Many schools do not routinely administer group intelligence tests, but virtually all schools regularly use published (standardized) and/or teacher-made achievement tests. These provide an objective basis for determining the levels of information and skills that a child has mastered. The teacher is in the uniquely best position to compare actual school performance (for example, the quality of reports, projects, homework, math or reading proficiency, or class participation) with the achievement test scores.

The clear determination of underachievement by comparing achievement test scores with usual classroom performance is problematic and at least partly subjective. For example, if grade equivalent scores are used and a child scores three grades above average in reading achievement, this should not be interpreted to mean that the child should be reading at exactly three grade levels above the rest of the class. However, it does indicate that he or she should be reading above grade-level material comfortably. If the child seems able to read only grade-level material in class, he or she is underachieving.

Creativity Test Scores

High scores on divergent-thinking tests such as the *Torrance Tests of Creative Thinking* (Torrance, 1966) or on creative personality inventories such as GIFT and GIFFI (Davis and Rimm, 1979; Rimm, 1976; Rimm and Davis, 1980) strongly suggest that the child has talent in the area of creative and productive thinking. However, high creativity scores do not assure high achievement. On the contrary, some fairly common characteristics of creative students—such as nonconformity, resistance to teacher domination, impulsiveness, and indifference to rules—may cause the creative child serious difficulties in achieving within the classroom structure. Some highly creative students are dramatic underachievers, since their personalities and thinking styles may be quite at odds with that required for classroom success. Rimm (1987b) found that creative underachieving students often defined their identity in terms of nonconformity. Their concern for thinking and acting differently than others actually prevented them from achieving and making classroom efforts. Other creative students, however, apply their unique talents to classroom assignments and requirements and achieve at the level of students with much higher tested intelligence (Getzels and Jackson, 1962).

Children with high creativity scores but only somewhat above average IQ scores (110–130) have very high potential for making creative contributions (Rimm, 1987c; Renzulli, 1986; Renzulli, Reis, and Smith, 1981). If students in this category are not achieving at least at grade level in school, they should be identified as gifted underachievers, even though their intelligence and achievement test scores may not be in the "gifted" range.

Observation

Some underachieving gifted children do not perform well on any test due to poor test-taking habits. For example, they may not be motivated to do well. On a group test some students may answer questions randomly; on an individually administered test they may "play dumb." Teacher and parent observations provide the only basis for identifying these gifted children; there will be little or no objective evidence.

Teachers may note class behaviors, comments, or vocabulary which suggest that the child has much more intellectual, creative, or artistic potential than he or she is exhibiting in school-related work. Teachers, however, can recognize these behaviors only if they are aware of characteristics of gifted children. Teachers must remain open to the possibility of discovering giftedness in children already labeled as "average" or even "below average." Many such gifted underachievers are never discovered.

Commonly used checklists and scoring scales for gifted programs do not include traits of gifted underachievers. Hall's (1983) study of teacher identification procedures found that four gifted children described by the following statements were identified as "below average" students, although their IQ scores were above 130.

> Student A. Makes excuses for not doing assignments, doesn't take an interest in things, passive, dependent.
> Student B. Doesn't get along with others, doesn't do his work, likes to tell jokes.
> Student C. Talks too much, doesn't listen, wastes time.
> Student D. Immature, quiet, withdrawn, short interest span.

Although teacher identification of underachieving gifted children is not absolutely dependable, teachers who are aware of characteristics of both underachieving and achieving gifted students can make important observations.

Parents also are in a unique position to observe the talents and capabilities of their own gifted children, even if the children are not high achievers. Note that teachers and principals often feel threatened by parents who insist their child is "gifted." Such parents are often inappropriately described as "pushy." Educators should assure these parents that their perceptions will be given full consideration if they can provide specific examples of behaviors that would be evidence of their child's giftedness. If the anecdotal material appears reasonably convincing, further testing may indeed furnish supportive data for the parents' observations. If the anecdotal material does not suggest giftedness, the teacher or principal can explain why such behavior does not represent special talent by comparing it to anecdotal material about typical children and highly talented children.

Underachievement Test Scores

Two tests have been expressly developed for the identification of underachievement syndrome. *Achievement Identification Measure (AIM;* Rimm, 1986a) is a parent report inventory used with children in grades 1–12. *Group Achievement Identification Measure (GAIM;* Rimm, 1987a) is a self-report inventory for students in grades 5–12. Although these inventories were normed upon general and not specifically gifted populations, they are highly reliable (r = .89 and .90 for AIM and GAIM, respectively). The total score allows one to compare each student to the norm based on characteristics related to high achievement. The dimension scores, described in Table 14.1, provide information on the types of problems the children are

TABLE 14.1 Dimension Scores for *AIM* and *GAIM*

COMPETITION

    High scorers enjoy competition whether they win or lose. They are good sports and handle victories graciously. They do not give up easily.

RESPONSIBILITY

    High scorers are responsible in their home and schoolwork. They tend to be well organized and bring activities to closure. They have good study habits and understand that their efforts are related to their grades.

ACHIEVEMENT COMMUNICATION

    Children who score high are receiving clear and consistent messages from parents about the importance of learning and good grades. Their parents have communicated positive feelings about their own school experiences and there is consistency between mother and father messages of achievement.

INDEPENDENCE/DEPENDENCE

    High scorers are independent and understand the relationship between effort and outcomes. They are able to share attention at home and in the classroom.

RESPECT/DOMINANCE

    High scorers are respectful toward their parents and teachers. They are reasonably well behaved at home and school. They value education. They are not deliberately manipulative.

exhibiting. The manual which accompanies the test scores provides a guide to the interpretation and use of the scores.

AIM and *GAIM* are most useful in identifying children suspected by teachers and parents of being gifted. The tests are important as identification measures among gifted children already in programs. That is, they can uncover high-risk children with characteristics of underachievement whose superior abilities mask the problems that will appear later if not prevented. It is easier to prevent underachievement syndrome in its early stages than to cure the problem once it becomes a strong pattern (Rimm, 1986b; Whitmore, 1986).

CHARACTERISTICS OF UNDERACHIEVING GIFTED CHILDREN

Studies of gifted underachievers have identified characteristics that are typical of these children. Joanne Whitmore (1980) has summarized some of the most important traits in an identification checklist (Table 14.2). If ten or more of these characteristics are checked, she suggests this would indicate that the child should be further evaluated to determine if he or she is indeed a gifted underachiever.

Characteristics of underachievers can be categorized in three different levels in terms of their causes and visible symptoms. The primary characteristic is *low self-esteem,* which appears to be at the root of most underachievement problems. The low self-esteem seems to lead to the secondary characteristics of *academic avoidance* behaviors, which in turn produce the visible tertiary traits of *poor study habits, unmastered skills,* and *social* and *discipline problems.* However, these causes and effects are at least partly bidirectional. That is, like the chicken-egg problem, each set of characteristics tends to influence the others.

Primary Characteristic of Underachievers: Low Self-Esteem

The characteristic found most frequently and consistently among underachieving children is low self-esteem (Fine and Pitts, 1980; Rimm, 1984; Whitmore, 1980). Not believing themselves actually capable of accomplishing what their family or teachers expect of them, they may mask their low self-esteem with displays of bravado, rebellion, or with highly protective defense mechanisms (Covington and Beery, 1976; Fine and Pitts, 1980; Rimm, 1986b). For example, they may openly criticize the quality of the school or the talents of individual teachers, or else claim that they "don't care" or "didn't really try" in regard to a mediocre test score or class grade.

Related to their low self-esteem is their sense of low personal control over their own lives (Rimm, 1986b). If they fail at a task, they blame their

TABLE 14.2   A Checklist to Identify Gifted Underachievers

Observe and interact with the child over a period of at least two weeks to determine if he or she possesses the following characteristics. If the student exhibits ten or more of the listed traits, including all that are asterisked, individual intelligence testing (Stanford-Binet or WISC-R) is recommended to establish whether he or she is a gifted underachiever.

_____   *poor test performance
_____   *achieving at or below grade-level expectations in one or all of the basic skill areas: reading, language arts, mathematics
_____   *daily work frequently incomplete or poorly done
_____   *superior comprehension and retention of concepts when interested
_____   *vast gap between qualitative level of oral and written work
_____   exceptionally large repertoire of factual knowledge
_____   vitality of imagination, creative
_____   persistent dissatisfaction with work accomplished, even in art
_____   seems to avoid trying new activities to prevent imperfect performance; evidences perfectionism, self-criticism
_____   shows initiative in pursuing self-selected projects at home
_____   *has a wide range of interests and possibly special expertise in an area of investigation and research
_____   *evidences low self-esteem in tendencies to withdraw or be aggressive in the classroom
_____   does not function comfortably or constructively in a group of any size
_____   shows acute sensitivity and perceptions related to self, others, and life in general
_____   tends to set unrealistic self-expectations; goals too high or too low
_____   dislikes practice work or drill for memorization and mastery
_____   easily distracted, unable to focus attention and concentrate efforts on tasks
_____   has an indifferent or negative attitude toward school
_____   resists teacher efforts to motivate or discipline behavior in class
_____   has difficulty in peer relationships; maintains few friendships

From Joanne Whitmore, *Giftedness, Conflict, and Underachievement* (Needham Heights, MA: Allyn & Bacon, 1980). Copyright © 1980 by Allyn & Bacon, Inc. Reprinted by permission.

lack of ability; if they succeed, they may attribute their success to luck. Thus they may accept responsibility for failure, but not for success (Felton and Biggs, 1977).

This attribution process in educational achievement has been related to the original theory of *learned helplessness* earlier advanced by Seligman (1975). If a child does not see a relationship between his efforts and the outcome, he is likely to exhibit characteristics of learned helplessness and will no longer make an effort to achieve. This pattern is characteristic of many gifted underachievers. Weiner (1974, 1980) also emphasized that a child's subsequent performance will be strongly influenced by whether he or she attributes successes and failures to ability, effort, task difficulty, or luck. Especially, attributing success to *effort* leads to further effort, while attributing success to *task ease* or *luck* does not.

Secondary Characteristics of Underachievers:
Avoidance Behavior

Low self-esteem leads the underachiever to nonproductive avoidance behaviors both at school and at home, secondary characteristics of underachievement (Whitmore, 1980). For example, underachievers may avoid making a productive effort by asserting that school is irrelevant and that they see no reason to study material for which there is no use. Students may further assert that when they are really interested in learning, they can do very well. These kinds of avoidance behaviors protect underachievers from admitting the lack of self-confidence, or worse, the feared lack of ability. If they studied, they would risk *confirming* the possible shortcomings to themselves and to important others. If they do not study, they can use the nonstudying as a rationale for the failure, thus protecting their valuable feelings of self-worth (Covington and Beery, 1976).

Additional defensive avoidance behaviors that operate in a similar fashion to protect underachievers include intense interest or even leadership in out-of-school activities which are less threatening. These successes essentially compensate for academic failures.

Extreme rebellion against authority, particularly school authority, provides another route to protect the underachiever. The student seems eager to tell teachers, the principal, the superintendent, even the board of education, exactly how they ought to run the school. Faulting the school helps the underachiever avoid the responsibility of achieving by blaming the system.

Expectations of low grades and perfectionism—though apparent opposites—also serve as defense mechanisms for the underachieving child with low self-esteem. If the underachiever expects low grades, he or she lowers the risk of failure. Note that low goals are consistent with a poor self-image and low self-confidence.

On the other hand, perfectionism provides a different protection. Since perfection is unachievable, it provides the child with a ready excuse for poor performance. For example, students can assert with bravado that they set their goals higher than most people, so of course they cannot be expected to always succeed. The students thus provide a rationale for failure and do not need to label themselves as incompetent (although they may indeed feel incompetent).

By contrast, achieving children set realistic goals which are reachable, and failures are constructively used to indicate weaknesses needing attention.

Two directions of secondary characteristics have been described by Kaufmann (1986) as aggressive, hostile responses or withdrawal responses. Rimm (1986b) found underachievers to exhibit their defenses by dependency or dominance. Figure 14.1 shows these two directions. Conforming

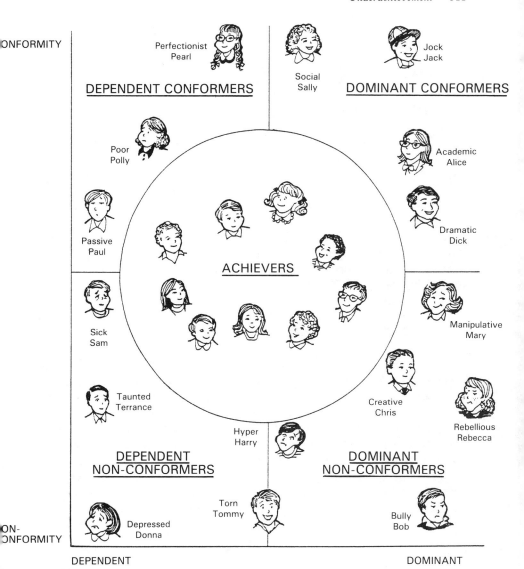

FIGURE 14.1 The Inner Circle of Achievers

underachievers differ from those in the nonconforming category in their visibility. That is, conforming dependent and dominant students have the characteristics that may lead to greater underachievement problems, but their underachievement is not obvious. Nonconforming dependent and dominant underachievers already are exhibiting serious problems. The prototypical names used in Figure 14.1, Passive Paul, Rebellious Rebecca, etc., are used to emphasize the main characteristics of these under-achievers, but any one child typically exhibits a group of these symptoms. Rimm also points out that some underachievers exhibit both dependent and dominant qualities.

Tertiary Characteristics of Underachievers

Because underachieving children avoid effort and achievement to protect their precarious self-esteem, tertiary characteristics arise which support the pattern of underachievement. These include deficient school-related skills (Fine and Pitts, 1980), poor study habits, peer acceptance problems, poor school concentration, and home and school discipline problems. It is critical to recognize that these tertiary indicators of under-achievement are the visible "tip of the iceberg," characteristics that mainly result from the secondary avoidance behaviors which protect under-achievers from the primary problem, low self-esteem and the related feelings of low personal control.

ETIOLOGIES OF UNDERACHIEVEMENT

Children are not born underachievers; there is no nature/nurture debate relative to underachievement. It is *learned* behavior, and therefore it can be unlearned. Underachievement can be taught by families, by schools, or by cultures. The last, cultural underachievement, its etiology and treatment, is discussed in Chapters 13 and 15 focusing on culturally different students and females. The following sections will describe rituals and reinforcements that maintain patterns of underachieving in the home and school. Recognizing factors that cause, support, and reward underachievers should help the reader understand the dynamics of underachievement and therefore should assist in preventing and reversing the problem.

FAMILY ETIOLOGY

When families of underachieving children are compared to families of achievers (Frazier, Passow, and Goldberg, 1958; Zilli, 1971), certain charac-teristics become apparent. Some of these characteristics are difficult to alter, but some can be easily changed by concerned parents once they are aware of the dynamics. Among the characteristics resistant to change are general poor family morale and family disruption (French, 1959) caused by death or divorce. Among those that can be changed relatively easily are parent overprotection, authoritarianism, excessive permissiveness, and in-consistencies between parents. These frequently result in manipulative rituals and parent identification problems that almost always can be recognized.

It is helpful for teachers to be familiar with "problem family" patterns, because an understanding of these patterns will help the teacher communicate with parents more effectively. Also, many family patterns which include manipulations by a child are extended by the child into the classroom. Thus a sensitivity to underachieving patterns can help the teacher avoid being manipulated by the student.

Identification and Modeling

The Terman and Oden (1947) study of underachieving gifted showed that most underachievers were boys and that the most significant characteristic of these boys was *non*identification with their father. Rimm (1984), a private practice psychologist specializing in underachieving gifted children, similarly found that underachievers frequently did not identify with the same-sexed parent. Interestingly, however, some identified very strongly with a same-sexed parent—if that parent appeared from the child's perspective to also be an underachiever or to be giving the child messages that schoolwork avoidance is acceptable.

Freud (1949) explained identification with the same-sexed parent as a product of the resolution of the *Oedipal* or *Electra* complexes. During the phallic stage of development (ages 3 to 5), said Freud, the child finds him- or herself romantically attached to the opposite-sexed parent. Recognizing that the parent already has a partner, the child sees the impossibility of the affair and resolves the issue by unconsciously identifying with the same-sexed parent. This identification purportedly causes the child to adopt the behaviors, conscience, and appropriate sex role of that parent. The three-year-old boy walking in Daddy's shoes or the girl imitating Mommy's telephone conversation is said to be evidence of the early identification process.

While conceding that it is nice for children to love their parents, contemporary social learning theorists question whether identification truly stems from the unconscious resolution of a sexual conflict. Rather, they describe identification and imitative behavior in terms of *modeling* (Meichenbaum, 1977). Research by Mussen and Rutherford (1963) and Hetherington and Frankie (1967) indicate that the parent model chosen for identification and imitation depends largely on a combination of three variables, *as perceived by the child:* (1) nurturance, (2) power, and (3) similarities between the parent and child.

The *nurturance* variable is very straightforward. The child tends to identify with, and model the behavior of, the parent who is highly nurturant. There may be an especially warm, loving relationship between the parent and a particular child or children in the family. If that parent is an underachiever, or does not stress achievement, the child may adopt similar attitudes.

The way that *power* influences identification, imitation, and underachievement is sometimes direct and at other times more complicated. In the most direct way, if one parent is definitely more powerful from the child's perspective, but does not value education or school achievement, the identifying child is not likely to perform well in school. Teachers need to be aware of this pattern because they may see only the concerned mother of an underachieving boy at parent conferences. However, it may be the *father* with whom the conference should be taking place. It is difficult to motivate a boy who identifies with his father, if the father and the boy view education as "women's work."

Some typical, more complicated power patterns that foster underachievement in children are described by Rimm (1986b) as "Father is an Ogre," "Daddy is a Dummy," "Mother is an Ogre," and "Mother is the Mouse of the House." These power patterns tend to arise because parents unintentionally compete with each other to establish their own child rearing approach as best or to feel like the "good parent." The impact of the parent rivalry for establishing oneself as the better parent is that the opposite parent is given the role of "bad" or "dumb" parent. Rimm (1986b) indicates that awareness by parents of these rituals frequently is sufficient to encourage a change in parenting approaches, and even by itself this awareness may make a major difference for underachieving gifted students.

In the first pattern, "Father is an Ogre," the father is viewed as successful and powerful, the mother as kind and caring. Often, a closer view of the home life shows a father who wears a big "No!" on his forehead. That is, he firmly prohibits many of the activities the children wish to pursue. However, the children learn to bypass his authority by appealing to their kind, sweet mother. Mother either manages to convince Dad to change his initial decision, or surreptitiously permits the children to carry out their desired activities anyway. Children quickly learn the necessary manipulative maneuvers.

The ritual worsens because as the children grow older the father begins to recognize his lack of power over his family, and he becomes more and more authoritarian as he tries to cope with his powerlessness. In response to his increasing authoritarianism, mother feels an increasing need to protect and defend her children. In desperation she invents new approaches to sabotaging her husband's power in the belief that she is doing the best thing for her children. Although girls in this family are likely to be achievement-oriented because they see their mother as powerful and positive, boys will tend to underachieve. They see no effective model in their father, who appears both hostile and powerless. They may fear and resent him, but are not likely to want to emulate him.

"Daddy is a Dummy" is a slightly different but equally disruptive ritual. This syndrome is often discovered in homes where Mother has a college education which includes courses in education and psychology. Dad has no college education or one that did not include psychology. Mother is certain that she knows the "correct" way to bring up the children which, according to her training, should include an important father role. However, whenever Dad attempts to play his parent role, Mother corrects him and explains a better way in which he can play his part. Dad feels uncomfortable and powerless in handling the children and makes every effort to withdraw, sometimes to 70 hours a week at the office. If Mother insists that he come home, the television screen becomes his escape. Sons again tend to be the underachievers in this family since they see their father as either powerless, absent, or as expressing passive-aggressive behavior. These underachieving boys often assume the same passive-aggressive posture in front of the television screen.

In the third parenting pattern, "Mommy is an Ogre," we find a disciplinarian mother and a kind, sweet, but undisciplined father. This results in at least two more poor patterns for identification. (1) If the disciplinarian mother is viewed by the children as fair and strong and supported by "kind father," this provides a weak male image for the sons, but a strong mother figure for female identification. (2) However, if the mother's discipline is overruled by the father, we have potential models for underachievement for both male and female children. The boys may identify with Father because he is viewed as powerful, but he models some characteristics and habits which make for underachievement—ignoring or violating (Mom's) rules, procrastination, and lack of discipline and perseverance. To the girls, Mother may be viewed as insignificant sound and fury, and therefore cannot become the model for an achieving daughter because of the children's perceptions of both her powerlessness and her continuous anger.

"Mother is the Mouse of the House" is the "dummy" ritual that results in rebellious adolescent daughters. It begins with a conspirational alliance between father and daughter in which daughter is often referred to as "daddy's little girl." Mother is not included in the special relationship and is treated as if she is not as intelligent as Dad. The daughter is typically a very good student in elementary school and pleases father, mother, and teacher. By fourth or fifth grade, although good achievement continues at school, an unexplainable conflict between mother and daughter begins at home. Father takes the role of mediator, or worse yet, rescuer for his daughter who has learned to convince her daddy that she is right and that mother is too controlling and overreacting. This manipulative ritual continues until adolescence when father begins to worry about teenage dangers from which he must protect his daughter. He then takes a firmer discipline position and will no longer give in to his daughter's persuasion. In frustration and surprise at her new ineffectiveness, the daughter may attempt manipulating her mother for support. Mother, impressed by the improved mother-daughter relationship, may then ally herself with her daughter. The manipulations increase and vary between mother-daughter opposed to father and father-daughter opposed to mother. Eventually and usually by high school, the parents identify the manipulations and unite in desperation to control their adolescent who seems to be pushing all limits. The adolescent, who has earlier managed to do exactly what she chose, now feels overcontrolled by her parents and rebels. Her rebellion sparks a series of punishments which increase in severity, which in turn causes more rebellion. The adolescent underachievement becomes only one of the symptoms; other, more severe behaviors, including alcohol and drug abuse, depression and/or sexual promiscuity, become the acting-out behaviors which capture adult attention. Underachievement is viewed as a minor offense in comparison.

Although these four parenting rituals may appear separately in some families, they frequently appear simultaneously within the same family. Parents may actually take "good" or "mean" roles differently for each child in the family. They may also change roles between early childhood, later childhood, and adolescence. The crucial issue for underachievement is that if children are exposed to one parent who challenges them and another parent who shelters them, they learn "to take the path of least resistance" and automatically back away from challenge, with the protection and support of the sheltering parent.

In order to prevent a child from developing an underachieving pattern, parents must compromise their points of view to avoid either overpressuring or overprotecting their children so that an appropriate and positive challenge message is issued by both parents. This permits children to accept challenge and please both parents who have thus set reasonable expectations for them.

In addition to nurturance and power, the third variable that affects identification is the *similarities* the child sees between him- or herself and a parent. This similarity provides a good basis for sex-role identification. High similarity between mother and daughter or between father and son strongly supports same-sex identification when nurturance and power of the parents are equal. However, unusual similarities in appearance, abilities, interests, or personality between boys and mothers or between girls and fathers frequently leads to cross-sex identification. Cross-sex parent identification can contribute strongly to either achievement or underachievement. Achievement motivation may be strengthened by female identification with a powerful and effective father if he is intellectually oriented, but weakened if he is not intellectually oriented. However, underachievement appears to be fostered by the cross-sex identification of sons with their mothers.

Other research has produced several findings that relate child-parent identification to achievement and underachievement. For example, Lamb (1976) and Zilli (1971) found that if father is absent from the home boys are more likely to be underachievers. Parish and Nunn (1983) discovered that males and females whose fathers left home (or died) before the age of 13 tended to be low in internal locus of control, a trait strongly related to achievement. In relation specifically to quantitative abilities, if Father is absent boys' and girls' math aptitudes and achievement are more likely to be weak (Carlsmith, 1964). However, girls and boys who identify strongly with father are more likely to have good problem solving, math, and science skills (Helson, 1971; Milton, 1957).

As we will see in Chapter 15, Rodenstein and Glickauf-Hughes (1979) found that a girl's attitude toward a career will be strongly and positively influenced by a successful working mother. However, this holds true only if there is a good family attitude toward Mother's employment and Mother's role conflict is minimal. Almquist and Angrist (1971) similarly emphasized that in order to aspire to a career, young women need good role models who can demonstrate that marriage and a career can be successfully combined.

In summary, the identification literature clearly supports the significance of identification with good parent models as an important family factor in high achievement. The lack of that identification, or the identification with a poor parent model, seems to be related to underachievement. Parents who view their own lives as interesting and successful and who model an equitable and respectful husband-wife relationship provide ideal role models for both male and female children.

Manipulative Rituals and Counteridentification

The situation in which a parent identifies with his or her child is known as *counteridentification*. The parent who counteridentifies with the child invests him- or herself in the child's activities and empathically shares efforts, successes, and failures. A familiar example of counteridentification is the vociferous father who argues desperately with the referee at the Little League baseball game as if it were he who had been unfairly called "out." Counteridentification is not always bad. Many parents vicariously enjoy seeing their children excel in sports or other talent areas, attend prestigious colleges, or travel, activities which the parents missed in their own youth.

Counteridentification has not been thoroughly explored in research, but it appears to have the potential to influence either high achievement or underachievement. The potential for positive contributions to achievement comes mainly from the parents' sharing of skills and their investment of time and resources. As mentioned in Chapter 2, Bloom (1981, 1985; Bloom and Sosniak, 1981) found that the early training of extremely talented youth included coaching by one or both parents who had a strong personal interest in the particular talent field. Bloom emphasized that the parent provided an early and influential model for the child. Based on Bloom's descriptions, it also is likely that most of the parents counteridentified with their talented child.

On the negative side, several forms of counteridentification can lead to manipulative rituals by children, supporting underachievement. Two such rituals begin with kind, empathic parents who try to be helpful to their children and try to understand their points of view. In one negative ritual rooted in counteridentification the child manipulates parents into completing his or her homework. This extremely common problem begins innocently enough. The child does not understand an assignment and goes to the parent for an explanation. The counteridentifying parent not only explains the assignment, but in order to prevent the child's "suffering" continues to work with the child. The parent explains the assignment step by step, over and over. The child soon learns that he or she needs only to briefly express confusion and the parent is brought quickly to his or her side for the evening. Together they complete the daily assignments. When father or mother does not cooperate, the child may punish the parent by failing the assignment, thus encouraging the parent to be more helpful with the next homework.

It is not surprising that as time progresses the child finds the assignments more difficult and takes longer and longer to complete the work. Not only has the child found comfortable reinforcement in the form of attention from mother or father, the child loses confidence in his or her ability to achieve independently. Since mother or father is now carrying the responsibility for much of the work, the child may no longer believe it is possible to learn the required skills.

An early manifestation of this dependent pattern in the classroom is a child seeking continuous aid from unsuspecting teachers. For example, this is the child who typically waits until instructions have been given twice and then raises his hand and innocently announces, "Ms. Jones, I just don't understand what I'm to do."

This dependent pattern sometimes has it origins in an early teacher recommendation to a parent. For example, in a primary grade a teacher may have suggested that a parent regularly help the child with homework. Teachers should be cautious in making such recommendations, and should be explicit in the kinds of help that they suggest so that this help does not lead to overdependence.

This dependent ritual is relatively easy to change if identified early, but very resistant to change in the high school years. By then, there is a sizeable gap between the student's developed skills and those necessary to succeed in high school. Furthermore, by this time the youth has little remaining confidence in his or her school-related competence.

The second maladaptive ritual that stems from counteridentification is one in which parents convey *too much power* to their gifted children and the children become aggressively manipulative. Because the children appear so bright, and because they use adult vocabulary and adult reasoning, parents find themselves interacting with them almost as adult peers long before the children have attained the wisdom to match their verbalizations (Fine and Pitts, 1980). Parents and sometimes teachers may be awed by the child's adultlike rationalizations for why they need not perform routine school tasks. To their own detriment, these children thus learn to manipulate their parents and teachers, frequently bypassing skill development because the work is "boring" or "irrelevant." Further, they may claim there is no reason to write material that they can answer orally, and they may depend on their verbal precociousness until written skills actually become deficient.

The teacher who works with dominant students must recognize that the verbally powerful child needs to be carefully led to the conclusion that he must learn and study. Opposing this child will only lead to a no-win battle, and antagonism is the likely result. Recognizing the power pattern that exists at home can help the teacher guide this child in the classroom. Whitmore (1986) described the necessary relationship as a problem-solving partnership. This alliance minimizes the potential for conflict and an adversary relationship. The adversary or competitive interaction, which occurs frequently between gifted children and their teachers, is one main cause of some teachers saying they "don't like gifted students." These gifted students will also say that particular teachers "don't like" them.

SCHOOL ETIOLOGY

The gifted child often is exposed to the "good year, bad year" syndrome. It has been estimated that at least 80 percent of the teachers in this country have had absolutely *no* exposure to teaching methods for the gifted. Some of these teachers supply most of the "bad years." However, other teachers, even without G/T training, do detect and provide for the special needs of the gifted child, creating the "good years" in school. Fortunately, not all "bad years" are devastating. Most gifted children are resilient enough to function well even in a less-than-responsive environment. However, certain personal and classroom conditions seem to create problems for the gifted child and seem to initiate or accelerate underachieving behavior patterns.

School Climate

Whitmore (1980) described classroom environments that appear to cause and support underachievement. The main characteristics she discovered were a lack of respect for the individual child, a strongly competitive climate, emphasis on outside evaluation, inflexibility and rigidity, exaggerated attention to errors and failures, an "all controlling teacher," and an unrewarding curriculum. One needs to view the school environment in relationship to the dynamics of underachievement to understand how it provides behavioral patterns and rituals that reinforce underachievement. We will look more closely at the effects of inflexible and competitive classrooms.

Inflexible classrooms. The inflexibility and rigidity that demonstrate lack of respect for the individual child provides a strong reinforcement for underachievement by the gifted child. The intellectually gifted child learns faster and integrates information more easily. The creatively gifted child thinks differently and asks frequent questions. The rigid teacher, however, adheres to an organized schedule that allows little flexibility for those who differ in speed or learning style. The gifted child quickly discovers that rapid completion of assignments usually leads to more assignments. These typically are not more challenging or more exciting, but represent "busy work" to keep the active gifted child occupied.

Initially, the gifted child may be pleased and motivated by the special treatment by the teacher. Eventually, as the child finds the busy work unchallenging and boring, he or she determines that these additional assignments are punishment for rapid work. To avoid the punishment, the child slows his or her pace and no longer completes assignments before the rest of the class. However, since the student's mind remains active and alert, he or she usually must find other diversions such as daydreaming, troublemaking, or surreptitiously reading an exciting book. In some cases the diversions become powerful reinforcers that distract the child from completing even the regular assignments, which appear dull by comparison. Consider this actual case:

> Robbie, eight years old, was a highly verbal child with an IQ in the very superior range. However, he was two years behind in mathematics and never completed his math assignments. His problem became clear after he was observed in class by the psychologist. On his lap, hidden from the teacher's view, was a book he was reading while the teacher explained the math assignment. The book was shifted to underneath the math book while students were to be doing math written work. Robbie moved further and further behind in mathematics, which was taught too slowly for his quick mind, but he read many exciting books. He was referred to the psychologist as having a "learning problem."

In addition to busy work, other ritual punishments tend to discourage the gifted child from achieving in the rigid, inflexible classroom. For example, if the gifted child responds too frequently in class or asks too many questions, he or she is not called on to speak. However, if the ignored child waves his or her hand too enthusiastically, calls out answers, or talks excitedly to a neighbor, he or she is rewarded with a scolding. The scoldings may serve either to reinforce or punish the child. If the child views them as punishment, he or she stops responding, deciding that such enthusiasm is somehow inappropriate to the school setting. If the child views the scoldings as reinforcing, he or she increases the talking out of turn and the hand waving, which become nuisances to both teachers and peers. Either way, enthusiasm for learning and thinking is diminished.

Gifted children in inflexible classrooms may adopt a variety of maladaptive behaviors that get attention (reinforcement), but contribute to underachievement. Poor handwriting, sloppy or incomplete work, not following teacher directions, noncompletion of homework, or aggressive behavior and fighting in the classroom or on the playground sometimes produce more attention and rewards in an inflexible classroom than independent thinking, questioning, enthusiasm, or the speedy completion of tasks.

Competitive classrooms. The classroom where comparative evaluation is heavily stressed and where there is extraordinary emphasis on competition is a serious problem for underachievers. The announcement to the class of grades, the comparison of students' test scores, the announced surprise expressed by a teacher when a student scores higher or lower than expected, and the continuous ranking of students all foster extreme competition within the classroom. That competition is attached to extrinsic evaluations of performance based on objective criteria that, from the perspective of the child, are viewed as the true measure of his or her competence and worth. Children who are already strong achievers and continue to find themselves at the top of the class may become even more motivated to achieve in this very competitive environment. However, even for highly motivated children too much emphasis on extrinsic rewards may detract from the intrinsic rewards of learning and creativity.

It is underachievers, of course, who are most dramatically affected by the severe competition (Covington and Beery, 1976). Underachievers, who do not have a clear sense of their own competence, are informed on a daily basis that they are not measuring up to the standards of excellence of the classroom. These children are given objective evidence of average or below-average abilities. Since competitive achievement is the only source of teacher recognition and rewards in the classroom, and since these children do not believe they are capable of attaining that recognition, they search for other classroom rewards or other evidence of personal worth, or adopt the defensive measures noted earlier in this chapter and in Chapter 9.

A highly competitive environment may be a "good year" or a "bad year" for the achieving gifted child. For the underachieving gifted child it is always a "bad year," since it provides convincing evidence of his or her own incompetence. An actual case:

Despite her IQ in the very superior range, five-year-old Bonnie's under-achievement was encouraged very early by her competitive kindergarten classroom environment. Bonnie had been a spontaneous and enthusiastic child in her nursery school class, where her teacher had described her as very bright and happily adjusted. In kindergarten she was referred to the psychologist because her mother reported that "she did not like to go to school." Her kindergarten teacher described her school performance as poor. She rarely completed her work, did not seem happy, and tended not to participate in class activities. Classroom observation revealed the competitive environment that gave Bonnie her sense of failure and motivation to slow her pace.

The child sat on the floor around the chalkboard for their letter-printing lesson. The teacher announced the letter to be printed and some children enthusiastically raised their hands. After the selected child printed the letter on the chalkboard, the children were asked if it were printed well. In chorus, they exclaimed an enthusiastic "yes" if it were and a punishing "no" if it was poorly executed. The teacher would agree or disagree with the children, pointing out the good qualities or the problems related to the printing of the letter. When Bonnie, with her hand barely raised, was selected to perform, the inadequate execution of her letter brought the "no's" that she had come to expect. Further, the "in seat" handwriting exercise that followed was carefully monitored by open teacher evaluation of each child's performance. It was not surprising to observe Bonnie's very slow performance and her non-successful efforts at the perfection which she could not achieve.

In this highly competitive kindergarten class, Bonnie already was being taught that she could not succeed in a classroom environment. Fortunately, in first grade Bonnie was placed with a supportive teacher who fostered a non-competitive environment and Bonnie developed confidence and enthusiasm again. The underachievement syndrome was reversed by a "good year."

Negative Expectations

Rosenthal and Jacobson's (1968) book *Pygmalion in the Classroom* inspired a landslide of research, much of which strongly supports the notion that a teacher's expectations can have a dramatic impact on children's self-concepts and school achievement (see Davis and Thomas, 1989, or Good and Weinstein, 1986, for reviews). The problem is that for children, teachers and school success are the major—if not the only—source of feedback concerning one's ability, competence, and worth (Covington and Beery, 1976). The teacher who sends messages of negative expectations will frequently find exactly what he or she expects: Both regular and gifted students will underachieve. As a perhaps surprising source of negative expectations, Felton and Biggs (1977) concluded that, "remediation, as it is sometimes practiced, may help the student to label herself as *stupid,* and this, in turn, may affect the teacher's attitudinal responses to that individual. This means that underachievement may be caused directly in the classroom and in the 'helping' provided there."

Not all gifted children will respond to the negative attitudes and expectations of a teacher by poor achievement. Some few may see this attitude as a special challenge and make additional efforts to meet that challenge. However, the underachieving gifted child, whose self-concept already is poor, normally will perceive the teacher's expectations of failure as a confirmation of his or her own poor self-evaluation. Another true story:

> Carla, a minority student, entered college with reasonable expectations of success. Although she had been a poor student in elementary school, hard work in senior high school showed her that she could do well. Her high school grades were very good and she felt excited about the challenge of college. Based on an English entrance examination, she was placed in a small remedial English class. Most students in the class were on probation and the English teacher made a similar assumption about Carla. When Carla came for help, it was because she worried that perhaps she did not have the ability she had only recently come to believe she had. It was the expectations communicated to her in the English class that threatened her precariously held positive assumptions about her own abilities. Fortunately, another teacher had confidence in Carla's ability and convinced her that she was indeed a very capable student, and that it would only take a small compensatory effort to learn some skills she had missed earlier in her education.
>
> It was her minority status together with some very real educational gaps that set the stereotype for negative expectations of Carla. After her confidence was restored, Carla easily learned the necessary English skills and continued college as a very successful student.

An Unrewarding Curriculum

Although the complaint from the underachieving gifted child that the school curriculum is irrelevant, dull, or unchallenging may only be a defensive avoidance ritual, it is often a real difficulty. Gifted children are particularly vulnerable to the "unrewarding curriculum" problem because of their intellectual and creative needs. Gifted children are often anxious to question, criticize, discuss, and learn beyond the levels that are appropriate for most students in the class. If the students are not challenged by the curriculum, they will find stimulation outside of the curriculum, and school will indeed be viewed as dull and boring. It is not uncommon for gifted underachievers who perform poorly in school to achieve excellence in non-school-related activities where they create their own rewarding curriculum. Consider the case of Ron:

> Ron was described as a poor reader and disinterested in school. In fourth grade he completed assignments rarely, daydreamed, performed his class work sloppily, and in general was considered a below-average student. At home he was immersed in comic books or baseball. He literally read and enjoyed thousands of comic books. As for baseball, he had easily committed to memory baseball statistics of the previous 20 years and talked knowledgeably about batting averages and pitching records that involved mathematics well beyond what he had learned in school. The same skills he seemed unable to

apply in the classroom setting were readily exhibited in his areas of true interest—comic books and baseball. A more rewarding curriculum could have brought together Ron's interests and abilities and expanded both.

Matching Efforts with Outcomes

Whitmore (1986) emphasized that gifted underachievers are not "lazy" or "unmotivated" but are merely unmotivated for schoolwork. Underachievement syndrome among gifted children may have been caused by complex family and school situations, but it nonetheless is critical to be certain that children understand the relationship between effort and outcome.

Figure 14.2 (Rimm, 1987b) illustrates how the appropriate relationship can lead either to achievement or underachievement. Quadrant 1 represents achievement. Children demonstrate appropriate effort. They have learned to work hard. They understand perseverance and have appropriate skills. Intrinsic enjoyment of challenge is part of the process and easy tasks are accomplished quickly in order that they may pursue more challenging activities. Their goals are set appropriately high, but not beyond their abilities. They continue to achieve as long as they see the relationship between effort and outcome (Rimm, 1986).

Quadrant 2 represents underachievers whose efforts are appropriate but whose goals or outcomes are set either too low or too high. In the cases of goals set too low, these children may have internalized a message from parents, society, or their peers that being "smart" is not as important as being well-adjusted or popular. Intellectual accomplishment is less valued than beauty or athletic prowess, and they do not wish to be "geeks" or "nerds." Some parents specifically promote the notion that "book learning is not as important as common sense" and that in some way they are mutually exclusive. That anti-intellectual message is more strongly delivered by parents who do not have an advanced education and may not see its value. For example, culturally disadvantaged urban and rural parents may send this message in defense of their own limited abilities and accomplishments.

The Quadrant 2 problem of goals set too high may appear in a highly competitive school environment where, despite the child's excellent intelligence and study skills, good grades are not attainable. If parents set expectations beyond children's abilities (and some do), this too will have the impact of establishing "too high" goals.

Generally, if goals are set too low children will discontinue making an appropriate effort; they have learned that it is easy to achieve those lower outcomes. If goals are set too high, they give up in desperation because they do not believe that any amount of sustained effort will make a difference in accomplishing these high-level outcomes.

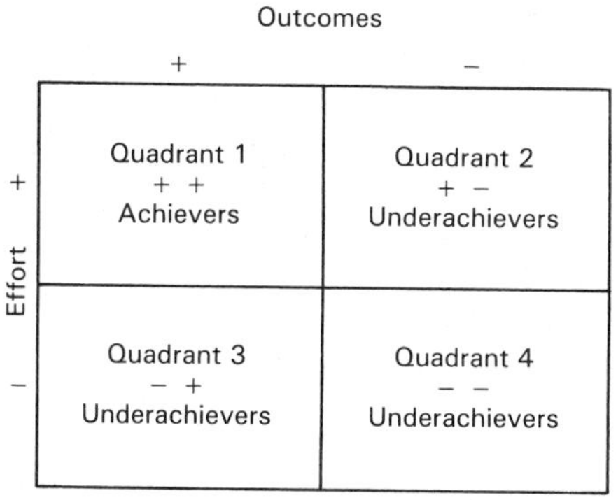

FIGURE 14.2   Relationship between Effort and Outcomes

Quadrant 3 causes underachievement syndrome when achievement otucomes are set at a reasonable level, but the process of making an effort has not been learned appropriately. That is, parents, children, and schools value good grades and school performance. Report card grades initially reflect this excellent performance, and children feel positive about school. However, activities are not sufficiently challenging, and the children learn that achievement is easy, that success is readily attainable and that learning and study should be effortless. Occasionally they may comment on boredom or lack of challenge, but as long as grades continue to be high they exhibit no problem behaviors. Unfortunately, they do not develop the good habits of perseverance, dealing with challenge, or intense study. At some point in their academic development the curriculum material becomes more complex, the student population becomes more competitive, or both. Their goals continue to be appropriately high but they have not learned the processes or efforts required to produce the expected outcomes. Some students will adjust to the additional needed effort. Others will hide behind their threatening feelings. They will worry that they are not as smart as they would like to be and they will invent or discover a whole herd of rituals and excuses that prevent them from making a good effort.

Quadrant 4 represents the most advanced stage of underachievement syndrome. It appears after children described by Quadrants 2 or 3 have not functioned as achievers for a period of time. Quadrant 4 underachievement takes place when children's efforts and skills both show deficiencies for a sufficiently long period of time that the children give up on reasonable goal setting. Teachers rarely identify these children as gifted because their intelligence or creativity are no longer exhibited in the classroom. Even parents begin to doubt their children's abilities. In conversation they may refer to the past when, they recall, their children were smart, but at this point they have given up on appropriate high-level goals and are willing to settle for their children earning a high school diploma. Quadrant 4 underachievement is most difficult to cure and may require outside therapeutic help.

THE TREATMENT OF UNDERACHIEVEMENT

As we have seen, the underachieving gifted child continues to underachieve because the home, school, and/or peer group support that underachievement. The student is not motivated to achieve, and there probably are deficiencies in skills necessary for achievement. Working below one's ability affects both immediate educational success and eventual career achievement; it is an important problem requiring attention.

While it may seem like a tall order to reverse a long-standing pattern of underachieving, Rimm's strategies have proven successful in case after case (Rimm, 1986b). She has found that the treatment of underachievement involves the collaboration of school and family in the implementation of six steps of her TRIFOCAL Model (See Figure 14.3):

1. Assessment
2. Communication
3. Changing Expectations
4. Role Model Identification
5. Correction of Deficiencies
6. Modifications of Reinforcements

FIGURE 14.3   Trifocal Model for Curing Underachievement Syndrome

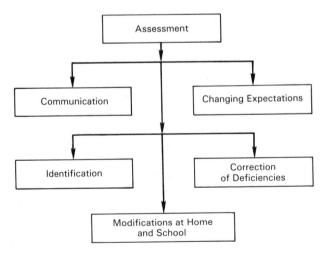

(From Rimm, 1986b)

Most of these concepts have been described in this chapter. It is important to note that to reverse underachieving patterns, all six steps must be implemented approximately simultaneously.

Biographical studies of achievers who indicate they previously had been underachievers show that all six steps usually are included in the change process. These "spontaneous changers" typically initiated their turnabout with Steps 3 or 4, the discovery of a positive model for identification or a change in expectations of important others, for example, a teacher, boyfriend, girlfriend, or spouse. These relationships, which are common in spontaneous underachievement conversion, need to be recognized as important elements in the deliberate treatment of underachievers. Parents and teachers must remain very aware of the central role they play in the implementation of the critical six steps, particularly in the areas of setting expectations and finding or becoming a good model. In addition to the use of the TRIFOCAL Model, parents and teachers should prepare to be equipped with "patience, dedication and support" (Hoffman, Wasson, & Christianson, 1985, p. 12–14.)

Step 1: Assessment of Skills, Abilities, Reinforcement Contingencies, and Types of Underachievement

The first step in the underachievement reversal process is an assessment that involves the cooperation of the school psychologist, teachers, and parents. The school psychologist should have primary involvement in this process. However, since few school districts allocate time for gifted children within the psychologist's role, it may be necessary for the guidance counselor, G/T coordinator, or classroom teacher to assume some of the responsibility. Ideally, the person should (1) have some background in measurement, (2) be sensitive to varying learning and motivational styles and problems, (3) be knowledgeable in behavioral learning theory, and (4) be aware of the special characteristics of gifted and creative children.

The *individual* intelligence test is a highly recommended first assessment instrument. That venerable IQ number has the potential to communicate important expectations related to the child's true abilities. Since the child has not been motivated, it is likely that *group* intelligence test scores have underestimated his or her intellectual potential. Also, it is characteristically difficult to score above 125 on some group intelligence tests, a serious problem for intellectually gifted students. Therefore, the WISC-R or the *Stanford-Binet* must be individually administered by the psychologist. With practice, the *Slosson Individual Intelligence Test* could be administered by a teacher or counselor. There also are other individual intelligence tests that can be administered by a psychologist to evaluate learning potential for culturally deprived, nonverbal, non-English-speaking, blind, or deaf gifted children who also may need to be individually assessed. Some of these instruments are questionable in terms of their equivalence to the most conventionally accepted tests, namely the Wechsler and Binet scales, but all provide a reasonably acceptable estimate of the child's school-related capability.

During testing the examiner must be especially aware of particular task-relevant characteristics of the child: symptoms of tension, attention to the task, perseverance at the task, responses to frustration, problem-solving approaches, defensiveness, and responses to personal encouragement by the examiner. These reflect, in miniature, approaches to educational tasks that the child very likely uses in the classroom and home environments.

Intelligence testing should be followed by individual achievement tests to clearly assess strengths and deficits in basic skills, particularly reading and math.

A creativity test or inventory, which can be administered by the teacher or psychologist, also should be part of the assessment. These produce not only a norm-referenced creativity score, but also descriptions of abilities, characteristics, and interests that are relevant to understanding the child's personality, creative potential, and learning style. The GIFT and GIFFI tests include dimension scores such as *Independence, Self-confidence,* and *Risk-taking* that provide important insights for understanding underachievement.

Either *GAIM* and/or *AIM*, which were described earlier in this chapter, can be used with children from grades 5 through 12, while *AIM* can be completed by parents of younger children. The scores will provide a description of the extent and type of the child's underachievement. Dimension scores will reveal whether the child is mainly dependent or dominant or combines a mixture of both. Scores also will permit insights regarding parent consistency in messages about achievement.

Finally, a parent interview also can be very helpful in identifying underachieving patterns unintentionally maintained at home and school. Ideally both parents should be at the interview. If only one appears, it would be important to ask about the other parent's relationship to the child. Overall, the analysis of student abilities and home and school reinforcement contingencies is critical to the second step of the underachievement modification program.

Step 2: Communication

Communication between parents and teachers is an important component of the cure for underachievers. Either a parent or the teacher may initiate the first conference, but the initiator will need to assure the other person of support rather than placing blame. If it appears to a teacher that the parents are not interested in or capable of working with the teacher, the teacher should select another child advocate person in the school with whom to work. Reversing the pattern without parent assistance is not as efficient, but it is nevertheless possible. A counselor, gifted coordinator, or resource teacher will often be an excellent advocate.

The content of the communication between parents and teachers should include a discussion of assessed abilities and achievements as well as formal and informal evaluations of the child's expressions of dependence or dominance. These are especially important in order that adults at home and at school do not fall into the trap of continuing to reinforce these problem patterns (Rimm, 1985).

Step 3: Changing the Expectations of Important Others

Parent, teacher, peer, and sibling expectations are difficult to change. As noted above, IQ scores, if higher than anticipated, are very effective in modifying expectations. Anecdotal information also can provide convincing evidence of the child's abilities. For example, a teacher convincing an adolescent or his or her parents of the child's mathematical talent can explain that the child solves problems in an unusually clever way or seems to learn math concepts more quickly than anyone else in the class. A psychologist trying to convince a teacher that a child has unusual talent can describe the unusual vocabulary or problem-solving skills that the child revealed during testing. *Specific* descriptions of unusual strengths are good evidence of giftedness.

It is very important to underachieving children that parents and teachers be able to honestly say to them that they believe in their ability to achieve (Perkins and Wicas, 1971). The expectations of these important others are basic to the personal change in self-expectations that is necessary to reverse from underachievement to high achievement. Jackson, Cleveland, and Mirenda (1975) showed in their longitudinal research with bright fourth-, fifth-, and sixth-grade underachievers that positive expectations by parents and teachers had a significant long-range effect on achievement in high school. Bloom's (1985) studies of talent development found that parents of research neurologists and mathematicians always expected their children to be very good students.

Since sibling competition frequently is a causal component of underachievement syndrome, changing the expectations of siblings is important. In the sibling rivalry that often exists, an achieving child may have assigned to a brother or sister the role of "loser" and changing that role may be threatening to the "winner." An individual and personal communication to the "winner" about the expected change is helpful. Parents should provide the assurance that the sibling's status change will not displace the achiever's role. Genetically and environmentally a "whole smart family" is not only possible, but likely. This explanation may deter the achiever from subtly trying to keep the underachiever in his or her underachieving status.

Because it is difficult to change the expectations of persons who know the child, changing the child's school environment sometimes is an effective measure. Changing schools is a drastic step to take, unless one is reasonably certain that the change will make a worthwhile difference. If extraordinarily gifted children are stifled by school environments that set only average goals and expectations, the children sometimes will change their entire achievement pattern when put in an environment that expects and values high achievement. However, for most children it is more realistic to try to change relevant expectations within the school.

Step 4: Model Identification

A critical turning point for the underachieving child is the discovery of a *model* for identification. All other treatments for underachievement dim in importance compared with strong identification with an achieving model. As noted above, Bloom's (1981, 1985; Bloom and Sosniak, 1981) biographical research with highly talented students showed that parents modeled the values and the life-styles of successful achievers in the talent area. Radin (1976) argued that the best family environment for a gifted boy is provided ". . . when a father is perceived as competent and strong, is pleased with his job, and permits his son to master tasks independently." Since this ideal situation is rarely provided for the gifted underachiever, parents and teachers need to help the student find a good model for identification.

Research on parent identification (for example, Mussen and Rutherford, 1963) indicates that the selected parent identification figure is nurturant, powerful, and shares common characteristics with the child. These same characteristics can be used to locate an appropriate achieving model for the underachieving gifted child. As a warning, however, an underachieving adolescent sometimes selects a powerful, nurturant model who shares the *underachieving* characteristics of the adolescent. This person then becomes a strong model for underachievement.

Underachieving children should be matched with an achieving person to serve as a model for them. The person selected can serve in a model capacity for more than one child. His or her actual role may be tutor, mentor, companion, teacher, parent, sibling, counselor, psychologist, minister, scout leader, doctor, and so on. However, the model should have as many of the following characteristics as possible:

1. *Nurturance.* The model must care about the child assigned. Many adults are pleased to encourage youth with whom they can counteridentify.

2. *Same sex.* Although identification with an opposite-sexed model is possible, the similarity in sex facilitates identification.

3. *Similarities to child.* These may include religion, race, interests, talents, physical disabilities, physical characteristics, socioeconomic backgrounds, specific problem experiences, or any other characteristics that will create the necessary easy rapport. When the child realizes that the model can be truly understanding, empathic, and sympathetic—because the model has experienced similar problems—rapport is more easily established and the process of identification is facilitated.

4. *Openness.* A model's willingness to share his or her own real problems in establishing him or herself as an achiever is important for encouraging communication and identification, and for motivating the underachieving child.

5. *Willingness to give time.* Achieving adults frequently have shortages of this most precious commodity. However, it is not possible to be an effective, positive model without providing time. It can be work time, play time, or talk time. Models who work on tasks with their child or play with their child can be most effective. It becomes possible for the child to see first hand such important achievement characteristics as responding to challenge, winning and losing in competition, reasoning styles, leading, communicating and relating to others, and experiencing successes and failures.

6. *Sense of positive accomplishment.* Although the model's life need not be perfect, the model must exhibit to the child the sense that his or her achievements have been personally fulfilling. Achievement involves sacrifice and postponed gratifications. The underachiever must recognize that these costs and postponements are worthwhile.

Step 5: Correcting Skill Deficiencies

The underachieving gifted child almost always has skill deficiencies as a result of inattention in class and poor work and study habits. However, because he or she is gifted, the skill deficiencies can be overcome reasonably rapidly. This is less of a problem for a very young child because the deficiencies are less likely to be extensive.

Tutoring should be goal directed with movement to a higher reading or math group or acceptance into an accelerated class the anticipated aim. It should be of specified duration, for example, weekly for two months until the child takes a proficiency test, rather than ongoing. Ideally, the tutor should be an experienced and objective adult who recognizes the child's underachievement and giftedness. Parents or siblings are not appropriate since the personal relationships are likely to cause the child additional pressure and dependency. The correction of skill deficiencies must be conducted carefully so that (1) the independent work of the underachieving child is reinforced by the tutor, (2) manipulation of the tutor by the child is avoided, and (3) the child senses the relationship between effort and the achievement outcomes. Charting progress during tutoring helps visually confirm the rapid progress to both child and tutor.

Step 6: Modification of Reinforcements at Home and School

The behavioral analysis in Step 1 will certainly identify some of the manipulative rituals discussed above in the home and school etiology sections. These behaviors need to be modified by setting important long-term goals and some short-term objectives that can ensure immediate small successes for the child both at home and at school. These successful experiences should be reinforced by rewards, anything from gold stars or extra art time to special outings with parents or money.

There are several considerations in determining the rewards to be used. First, they must be meaningful to the child. Money may seem unimportant to a six-year-old, while stars are not particularly motivating to the adolescent. They must also be within the value system and range of possibility for the givers of the rewards. Schools usually do not use money as a reward, and parents may not want to pay (bribe) their children to learn. There are, however, effective rewards within the value system of parents and within the capabilities of teachers to administer—for example, free time. The rewards should not be too large. In fact, they should be as small as possible yet effective enough to motivate behavior. They can be increased in value as necessary; but if one has already used large rewards, small rewards will no longer be effective. It is important always to supply the rewards agreed upon, and to pay them on a regular basis immediately

---

INSET 14.1 ACTIVITY CHART

ACTIVITY	MON	TUES	WED	THUR	FRI	WEEKEND
Homework						
Reading	5	X	6	4		5
Math	5	5	5	10		5
Spelling	2	X	2	X		2
Social Studies	X	2	2	X		X
Science	X	X	X	2		X
Language	2	2	X	2		X
Extra Work						
Reading	15	10	8	5		15
Writing	X	3	5	X		5
Math	X	5	X	X		X
Home Responsibilities						
Wash dishes	5	5	X	5		
Pick up bedroom	5	5	5	5		
Total	39	37	33	33		32

Instructions to Parents for Charting Activities

1. You and your child need to determine a specific minimum daily study time. Twenty minutes for first and second graders, one-half hour for third to fifth graders, one hour for sixth and seventh graders, and one and a half hours for grades 8–12 can be used as a guideline. The amount of time may vary with the child and the school. Five days a week for study are recommended.

2. The place of study should be a desk or table in the child's own room or in a quiet area away from the television and family activities.

3. Children may not watch television until study time is complete and work is reviewed.

4. Review the child's study accomplishments and points earned daily. If possible the same-sexed parent should monitor the work and review the study chart with the child.

5. A guideline for giving points is one point for each page read, two points for each page written (for example, workbook or copying material), five points for each page of math work or creative writing. The parent may add bonus points for unusual improvement in work or for especially good quality work. Points will be exchanged for tangible rewards.

6. Daily rewards should be used for very young children (stars, stickers, baseball cards). Weekly rewards are preferred by older children (trips, special privileges, money).

7. Rewards should always be paid if earned and not withdrawn based on some other inadequate behaviors.

8. Rewards should never be paid if they are not earned.

9. Clear, brief messages of praise for work well done or disappointment at work inadequately completed should be given daily by the parent.

10. Consistent and orderly monitoring of work will need to continue until the child's performance has shown consistent improvement. Eventually children will not need the external monitoring and reward system since intrinsic rewards such as satisfaction with work well done, interest in content, and positive expectations will suffice. Time needed will vary with the child's age and type of problem.

---

after the activity is successfully completed. Rewards may be based on activities completed, or based on the quality of the activity. Rewards should never be paid for incomplete work or when the work is not attempted. A sample *activity chart* appears in Inset 14.1 along with a guide for using the activity chart. Such a chart may be used to coordinate rewards with academic and nonacademic accomplishments.

Modifying reinforcement for homework and study are an important component of reversing underachievement syndrome. However, this modification by itself will not be sufficient. Dozens of other recommendations for home and school changes are described by Rimm (1986b) in her book on underachievement syndrome.

Treatment Beyond Home and School

The preceding recommendations for the treatment of underachievement at home and school are effective with many children and adolescents if the underachievement is not complicated by heavy involvement in drugs, alcohol, crime, or serious depression. However, even the adolescent who shows a long history of "complicated" underachievement also may be able to reverse the underachieving pattern, as well as the drug, crime, or other problem. In addition to the parent and educator working together, this youth is likely to need attention by a psychologist specializing in adolescent problems.

SUMMARY

Underachievement by gifted students is a great potential loss that can be reversed. It is defined as a discrepancy between students' high ability and mediocre or poor school performance.

Intelligence, achievement, and creativity scores can be used to help diagnose underachievement. If the gifted student is a poor test-taker, observation by teachers or parents is necessary for determining giftedness. Rimm researched parent and student inventories which result in scores which identify underachievers and describe the particular patterns of their problem behaviors.

Whitmore prepared a checklist of characteristics of gifted underachievers. The authors describe three levels of characteristics: (1) low self-esteem, which is the most basic; (2) defensive avoidance of threatening academic tasks; and (3) poor study habits, peer acceptance, school concentration, and discipline.

Underachievement is learned.

Gifted underachievers are less likely to identify with their same-sexed parents, unless the parents also are underachievers or do not value achievement. Freud explained identification as an unconscious product of resolving Oedipal or Electra complexes. Social learning theorists emphasize the importance of a nurturing relationship, perceived power in the parent, and similarities in child-parent characteristics.

Several parent-power patterns foster inappropriate identification and underachievement. Research shows worse male achievement for males in father-absent homes, and worse math and problem-solving skills for both sexes in such homes. Successful career mothers serve as effective models for achieving girls.

Counteridentification can lead parents to spend time with their children and reinforce the development of academic, artistic, or athletic skills. It can also lead to manipulation by children and to underachievement. If parents complete the child's homework it will encourage excessive dependence. If parents give their highly verbal children too much power, the children may manipulate their environments to avoid effort.

Teachers who recognize and provide for gifted students create their "good years"; other teachers who cannot, their "bad years." Inflexible teachers, who may pile on extra busywork, encourage underachievement. Attractive diversions also may reward underachieving.

Teachers may ignore or scold the hand-waving, question-asking gifted student, who then stops responding in class. Counterproductive behaviors, such as sloppy or incomplete work or aggressive behavior, may be rewarded by valuable teacher attention.

Heavy emphasis on competition tends to minimize intrinsic rewards of learning and creating. Competition is devastating to underachievers, whose self-concept is damaged by repeated evidence of incompetence.

Negative expectations by teachers become self-fulfilling prophecies. Remedial work also may label a student as inept.

An unrewarding curriculum prevents the gifted child from fulfilling needs to question, discuss, criticize, and so forth. Challenges may be found outside of school, for example, in hobbies or athletics.

The treatment of underachievement requires six steps: (1) assessment; (2) communication; (3) changing expectations; (4) role model identification; (5) correction of deficiencies; and (6) modifications of reinforcements.

chapter fifteen

The Cultural Underachievement of Females

The education of gifted women has been a low priority throughout history, a matter that has led to wholesale female underachievement. Many gifted girls have been, and continue to be, systematically discouraged by peers, family, and sometimes teachers and counselors from using their talent in productive ways. Stockard and Wood (1984) claimed that female under-achievement as measured by grades is a myth, since they found in student records of seventh through twelfth graders that females were less likely than males to have English and mathematics grades that were lower than would be predicted by standardized ability tests. However, the under-achievement of females is not measured or predicted by early grade and ability comparisons, but by the adult underachievement of highly intel-ligent women. Reis (1987) pointed out that the underachievement of adult women is indeed a different concept than that which is measured by grades in school and might be better defined as "what a person believes can be attained or accomplished in life." The discrepancy between the giftedness observed in girls' school achievement and their talent development in adulthood has been aptly labeled by Olshen (1987) as the "disappearance of giftedness in girls."

History shows that leading educators and psychologists had played a deliberate role in limiting educational opportunities for females. While many early educators simply ignored the education of females, some were explicit in designing education to maintain women's subservience to men.

Smith (1981) quoted one of the most influential educators of the eighteenth century, Jean Jacques Rousseau, regarding his theory for the education of "Sophie," the ideal girl.

> Women's entire education should be planned in relation to men. To please men, to be useful to them, to win their love and respect, to raise them as children, care for them as adults, counsel and console them, make their lives sweet and pleasant. These are women's duties in all ages and these are what they should be taught from childhood on.

Smith also reminds us that Sigmund Freud and Carl Gustav Jung, two illustrious leaders of early psychoanalytic psychology, described what they perceived as inferior female characteristics. Freud noted the main traits of femininity as narcissism, masochism, and passivity. Jung described the mentally healthy female as being more emotional and less rational and logical than an equally mentally healthy male.

G. Stanley Hall (1844–1924), another leading psychologist and educator, reflected Freud's views in recommending that education for women ". . . should aim at nothing but motherhood." Edward L. Thorndike, early in this century, progressed only slightly beyond Hall, suggesting that education is not likely to "harm women's health" and that some women could even be educated toward careers, provided those careers involved nurturing roles (Smith, 1981). All these quaint views both reflected and reinforced prevailing social attitudes.

Overview

This chapter will review some statistics and opinions regarding the present status of gender inequities in the work world and life satisfactions of working versus nonworking women. It also will review arguments and data regarding biological gender differences, along with information regarding the other viewpoint—that observed differences are sociocultural in origin and are maintained by mechanisms that support female underachievement. Suggestions for teaching and counseling gifted females and for reducing gender-role stereotyping, bias, and discrimination also will be itemized. Finally, we will extend the school-home model for modifying general underachievement, described in Chapter 14, to reversing underachievement patterns in gifted girls.

PRESENT STATUS OF WOMEN: WOMEN IN THE WORK FORCE

An analysis of the present status of women in the work force provides the best documentation for the argument that many gifted women are indeed functioning as underachieving adults. They often occupy gender-role stereotyped careers and occupations and receive inequitable salaries and responsibilities. Noted Jones (1978; Schwartz, 1980), only ". . . nine percent of the nation's labor force of doctoral scientists and engineers are women." Rudd and McKenry (1980) noted that 80 percent of the women in their study were involved in just 20 of 500 possible job categories. The gender-role sterotyped careers—for example, teaching, nursing, clerical work, factory work, bookkeeping, and secretarial work—were mainly low-salaried jobs and, with the exception of teaching and nursing, not considered a profession. Armstrong (1979) found that one-tenth of 1 percent of America's engineers and 2 percent of the physicists were women. Allain (1981) similarly pointed out that female college graduates earn approximately $7,000 less per year than male college graduates. In 1977 the U.S. Department of Labor reported that female college graduates earned an average of just $300 more per year than male high school dropouts. Census Bureau statistics of 1985 reported a similarly dismal picture with the average annual income of a female college graduate at $20,257, the average male high school dropout getting $19,120, and the male college graduate at $31,487 (Milwaukee Journal, July 22, 1987). Even in the higher paying professions, women earned less than men. In 1986 specific income percentage comparisons of female to male were 77 percent for lawyers, 84 percent for engineers, 78 percent for computer systems analysts, 69 percent for physicians, and 62 percent for financial managers.

A 1986 study reported in the Wisconsin State Journal (June 29, 1986) found that of 350 graduates of eastern universities, 40 percent of the men had taken scientific jobs compared to only 8 percent of the women. Education attracted 15 percent of the women and only 2 percent of the men, and 15 percent of the women and only 3 percent of the men took clerical or sales jobs.

The increase in percent of women in science and engineering is dramatic and hopeful (Farnham, 1988). However, the continued underrepresentation of women in most fields of science provides graphic proof of the underachievement of gifted women (see Figure 15.1).

These figures continue to suggest that education is less important for upward mobility and high career achievement than gender and that many talented females are indeed underachieving. Said Wolleat (1979), ". . . despite twenty or more years of formalized guidance services in most high schools, sex remains the best single predictor of who will enter many occupations . . ."

The status of women in education further documents female underachievement. Elementary and, to a lesser degree, secondary teaching have long been known as female sterotyped professions. In 1980, approximately two-thirds of all K–12 educators were female (Smith, 1981). However, the upper echelon of power in elementary and secondary education is predominantly male and again reflects dramatic achievement inequities for females: Only 15 percent of school principals are women, and just a handful of women serve as school superintendents. Leadership in teachers'

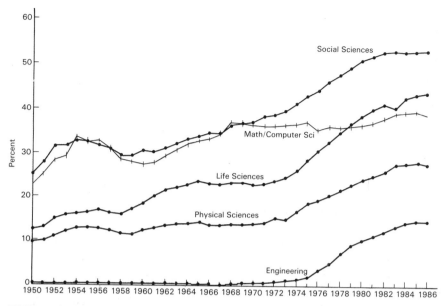

FIGURE 15.1   Percent of Science and Engineering Bachelor's Degrees Earned by Women, 1950–1986.

Reprinted by permission of the Commission on Professionals in Science and Technology.

organizations shows similar inequities, with most local, state, and national positions held by men.

Higher education has been dominated by men in numbers, rank, and salary. Most professors are men. Some 1977 U.S. Department of Health, Education and Welfare statistics reported that only at lower faculty levels, such as instructor or lecturer, do the numbers of women approach those of men. The disproportionate number of male professors is especially alarming in light of Tidball's (1973) conclusion that the number of women faculty at a given college is an excellent predictor of how many career women the college will produce.

Women also tend to be found in lower ranks and in less prestigious institutions, compared with men of similar educational preparation (Giele, 1978). Vetter and Babco (1975) reported that up to that time 60 percent of the male faculty at four-year universities were professors and associate professors, compared with only 30 percent of the female faculty. Salary inequities showed a similar pattern, with women's salaries at 78 percent of men's salaries (Kilson, 1976).

More recent statistics do not reflect great improvement. According to a 1988 National Science Foundation report, in science and engineering men are more than twice as likely as women to hold full professor rank (50 percent compared to 21 percent). Further, fewer women than men hold tenure or are in tenure-track positions.

Farnham (1988) identified a relatively recent problem for women in university settings. An increasing number of teaching assistants and post-doctoral students are foreign national males who come from cultural backgrounds that are less accepting of female professionals than is our own culture. Particularly in areas such as engineering, computer science, and physics these persons may subtly discourage females from entering these science programs.

College administration has been a virtual *no-woman's land*. A 1972 *Time* magazine article recommended, "If a woman wishes to become a college president, she is advised to become a nun." At the time, just 1 percent of college presidents were women, and virtually all of these were nuns. Frazier and Sadker (1973) reported that 100 percent of the presidents of coed universities were male, and so were 97 percent of the graduate deans, 91 percent of the deans of students, 95 percent of the admissions directors, and 96 percent of the registrars. On the positive side, as in other traditionally male professions, the number of women entering college administration is increasing. The chancellor of the entire University of Wisconsin System, for example, is a woman, as is the University of Wisconsin-Madison dean of students.

Some 1982 figures from the National Center for Educational Statistics, U.S. Department of Education, document dramatic changes in the numbers of women receiving bachelor's or professional degrees in traditionally male-dominated fields (see Table 15.1). However, except for *health professions*, the percentage of females continues to remain much lower than that of males. According to a 1988 government study, since 1983 the number of women earning Ph.D degrees in education has exceeded the number of men. Overall, while these trends are in a positive direction, they still document the underachievement of gifted women, particularly in science areas.

TABLE 15.1   Males and Females Receiving Degrees in Traditionally Male Fields in 1970–71 and 1979–80 (From the National Center for Educational Statistics)

	1970–71			1979–80		
	N	MALE	FEMALE	N	MALE	FEMALE
Bachelor's Degrees		%	%		%	%
Agriculture	12,672	96	4	22,802	70	30
Business Management	115,527	91	9	186,683	66	34
Engineering	50,046	99	1	68,893	91	9
Physical Sciences	21,502	86	14	23,410	76	24
Health Professions	25,226	23	77	63,920	18	82
Professional Degrees						
Dentistry	3,745	99	1	5,258	87	13
Medicine	8,919	91	9	14,902	77	23
Veterinary Medicine	1,252	92	8	1,835	67	33
Law	17,421	93	7	35,667	70	30

LIFE SATISFACTIONS OF WOMEN

In the postwar years, even a woman who attended college was expected to achieve life satisfaction vicariously through her husband's career. Her success was tied to his success, along with success in the wife, mother, and home manager role she would play. Qualities of being "good-looking" and "sexy" were part of her definition as a woman (Graham, 1978; Schwartz, 1980). Her primary allegiance was toward her family, while the primary allegiance of her husband was toward his career (Coser and Rokoff, 1971).

Eminent developmental psychologist Erik Erikson (1959) described the *identity crisis*—deciding who and what you are—as being resolved later for a woman than for a man, and as tied directly to marriage, her husband's career, and the birth of the first child. Identity was wrapped in the nurturing role. Adams (1971) suggested that women were caught in a "compassion trap," based on the belief that their most important function was to provide tenderness and compassion.

Note, too, that sociocultural sterotypes allowed a man to receive encouragement and support for his demanding career and professional accomplishments. However, a talented woman did not have a nurturing and supporting "wife" available, nor was anyone particularly anxious to take over home and child-rearing responsibilities for her. The 1988 book *The American Woman* reported that women in paid jobs continue to be responsible for most housework and family care.

This dramatic waste of the talents and contributions of women might be justified if women perceived themselves as fulfilled and happy in their housewife role. Surely, the nurturing of future generations is a critically important contribution to society, as is the support of men who make professional contributions. Research indicates that while some women do find high life satisfaction as homemakers, on the average life satisfaction— including self-esteem and feelings of competence—is greater for working and career women (Birnbaum, 1975). Bernard (1972), for example, found that housewives who derived their identity solely from their role as wife and mother were most likely to suffer the effects of *housewife syndrome*. This syndrome includes a sense of helplessness and hopelessness, depression, and a loss of self-esteem. The years devoted to caring for one's family seem to deprive many women of their sense of autonomy, leaving them with feelings of complete dependence. In counseling women at this stage of their lives, Rimm has found that their confidence may be so low that discussion with other adults about any topic other than child rearing may actually feel terribly threatening. On the other hand, career women usually derive much satisfaction from their work and the recognition they receive (Rodenstein and Glickauff-Hughes, 1979). Nadelson and Eisenberg (1977) reported that husbands of professional women found them to be "more stimulating" people.

A study by Holahan (1981) of life satisfactions of gifted females from

MARVIN   by **Tom Armstrong**

FIGURE 15.2 Reprinted with special permission of NAS, Inc.

Terman's research found that at a mean age of 66, career women expressed greater overall satisfaction with their lives than did homemakers and job holders. There were no significant differences between the latter two groups.

Women returning to college and the work world after five to ten years of full-time devotion to wife and child-rearing roles provide rich anecdotal material regarding the dramatic changes in their lives. The following story, shared by a young woman married to a successful physician, reveals the frustration some of these women feel.

> I had worked previous to having had my family and had received recognition and promotions for my accomplishments. When my husband completed medical school and we had our family, I reluctantly gave up my job. There were three children in rapid succession, and although I enjoyed mothering, I became more and more frustrated with my own sense of personal accomplishment. I kept telling my husband that I was anxious to return to college. One day while bathing the baby, I made the decision. I packed my suitcases and set them in the hall. When my husband came home, I simply said, "Either I return to school or I'm leaving." My husband looked strangely at me and said he hadn't realized that I wanted to go back to school, but that I certainly could. I couldn't believe his response, because I had been telling him this all year. I guess he didn't really believe me, and I had to do something really dramatic for him to hear what I was saying.

The Home-Career Conflict

Although working outside the home usually provides more self-satisfaction and life satisfaction, gifted women are caught in a very common conflict. The alternative to the *housewife syndrome* is the *working wife* or "Queen Bee" (Staines, Tavris, and Jayaratne, 1974) syndrome, a demanding superwoman role that requires women to meet the obligations of a challenging and worrisome job plus fulfill the traditional responsibilities of cleaning, shopping, cooking, laundry, and child care—and be a loving and supportive wife as well. Great mental stability is required.

Poloma (1972) interviewed 53 couples in which the wives were involved in the male-dominated professions of law, medicine, and college teaching. These woman used one or more of the following four techniques for managing the home-career conflict.

1. *They looked at the* **benefits** *of combining a career and a family, rather than the costs.* As one woman explained, "I am a better mother because I work and can expend my energies on something other than over-mothering my children."
2. *They decided in advance which role came* **first** *in the event of conflicting demands.* In virtually every case, family crises took precedence over career crises. If the baby sitter did not show up or a child got sick, the wife, not the husband, missed work that day.
3. *They* **compartmentalized** *the two roles as much as possible, keeping work and family distinct.* Few of the women brought work home with them, for example, although their husbands often did.
4. *They* **compromised.** The wives controlled the extent of their career commitment to fit the circumstances of their family lives—how the husband's work was going, his income, the ages and number of children, the husband's support (or lack of it), and so on. "When one or more of these factors is out of kilter, the wife makes the necessary adjustment to manage role strain," Poloma found.

Some women felt compelled to make unreasonable concessions. For example, a lawyer would not talk about her practice at home, so that ". . . the children would not think that her work was more important than their father's." Others expected little and asked virtually nothing of the family to help them adjust to the double demands of family and career.

For the professional woman with a family, there is no easy solution to the continous conflict of her roles. If she is committed to her career, she feels guilty for not fulfilling her nurturing commitment to her family. If she considers family first, she is criticized and feels guilty for not being sufficiently dedicated to her career.

Despite the difficulties of the double-role commitment, Birnbaum's (1975) study provides encouraging statistics for gifted young women who choose to combine *marriage and a career* or choose *careers only,* compared with becoming *housewives only.* Of the three groups, the housewives showed the lowest average self-esteem. Only 14 percent of the housewives, compared to 54 percent of the married professionals and 54 percent of the single professionals, reported "good" to "very good" self-esteem. Seventy-two percent of the housewives, compared with 36 percent of the married professionals and 73 percent of the single professionals, reported "feeling

344 *The Cultural Underachievement of Females*

lonely" fairly often. Forty-two percent of the housewives indicated that they missed challenge and creativity, compared to just 4 percent of the married professionals and none of the single professionals. Sixty-one percent of the housewives, 12 percent of the married professionals, and 58 percent of the single professionals viewed themselves as "not very attractive" to men. Interestingly, while 52 percent of the housewives considered themselves happily married, 68 percent of the married professionals rated themselves as happily married. Although the working wife syndrome will pose problems for gifted women, these figures again indicate that it beats out other alternatives in terms of personal life satisfaction.

Rodenstein and Glickauf-Hughes (1979) reported similar statistics with 201 women graduates of the University of Wisconsin, ages 24 to 35. The *single* and the *married* career women rated themselves higher in "work satisfaction" and "recognition for accomplishments" than did the *homemaker* group. Perhaps not surprisingly, while 96 percent of the homemaker and married career women indicated that children were a satisfying aspect of their lives, only 1 percent of the single career women indicated satisfaction in this area. It is noteworthy that 38 percent of the single career women planned to have children at some point in their lives; they were not rigidly locked in to a single, childless career-only life-style. They retained their flexibility and kept their options open; they could change their minds and their life-style if they wished.

In the area of science, although women are generally published less than men, there is now some documentation that marriage has an enhancing effect on scientific productivity, and parenthood does not adversely affect that productivity (Cole and Zuckerman, 1987). Among eminent female scientists, married women published more than single women and this did not change if married women had children. The most significant factor that increased the rate of publication was marriage to another scientist. Although marriage has a positive impact on scientific production for females, science unfortunately has a negative impact on marriage. Female scientists are twice as likely to be divorced as are male scientists.

As a final note, the present authors agree that society is the loser when any gifted and talented person, male or female, elects not to become a contributing professional. At the same time, it is true and acceptable that some women, gifted and "normal," do find a wife-mother-homemaker role satisfying, and free from the pressures and anxieties of job responsibilities and the career-homemaker conflict. None of the research in this section claimed that 100 percent of all housewives were unhappy and unfulfilled. Aesthetic and creative needs may be met in developing high-level homemaking and child-care skills, in artistic and creative hobbies, and in clubs and community work. It is important, however, that all young women, and especially high-potential ones, have both the encouragement and the opportunity to receive training, develop their talents, and become professionals if that is their choice. The research reviewed in this section suggests it is the best choice. The doors must remain open, and gifted females must have the support of parents, teachers, school counselors, future partners, and society.

GENDER DIFFERENCES

Comparisons of biological versus sociocultural gender differences should provide a good basis for determining the extent to which the underachievement of women can be modified. Gender differences that are biologically determined could be viewed as potentially limiting the achievements of gifted women. However, gender differences related to sociocultural norms—stereotypes, bias, and discrimination—can be changed, and the correction of these problems may be seen as freeing women to achieve equally with men.

Biological Differences

Velle (1982) reviewed research on biologically-based behavioral differences between the sexes, differences that conceivably could limit achievements of women. Although some of the research was based on animal behavior, some also involved human subjects.

Levels of physical activity.   Velle attributes high levels of male physical activity to hormonal influences in the brain during fetal development. He cited research with horses (Schafer, 1974) and monkeys (Goy and Resko, 1972). He also reminds us that castration of male domestic animals invariably produces quieter animals. His only example of actual human gender differences in activity came from research reported by Restak (1979), which showed that hyperkinesis (abnormally high levels of physical activity) is found in boys much more frequently than in girls. The hyperactivity that accompanies about 50 percent of all learning disabilities in school children is known to be largely a boys' problem (Davis, 1983).

Aggression.   Velle cited various animal studies linking the male hormone testosterone with aggression (for example, Bronson and Desjardins, 1968; Edwards, 1969). He also documented human studies (Conner, Levine, and Wertheim, 1969; Freedman, 1974; Moyer, 1974) which indicated that boys display more aggressive behavior than girls, and suggested that this is related to adolescent competitive behavior. One interesting study (Yalom, Green, and Fisk, 1973) reported the results of giving synthetic estrogen (a female hormone) to pregnant diabetic women. Their sons showed significantly less aggressive behavior at age 16, compared with same-aged boys of normal mothers and of untreated diabetic mothers.

Tomboyism.   *Adrenogenital syndrome* is an abnormal condition in girls characterized by masculinization of external genital organs. It apparently is caused by excessive androgen hormones during fetal development (Liddle, 1974). Girls with this syndrome always have corrective surgery and are raised as girls. However, despite their female socialization, most of them show characteristics usually considered masculine, such as preference for boy playmates, interest in sports and athletics, preference for boys' clothes and toys, preference for a professional career to marriage, higher physical activity levels, and a lack of interest in caring for small children, hence the nickname *tomboyism* (Money, Hampson, and Hampson, 1973; Money and Schwartz, 1978). These findings support the reality of biologically determined gender differences which, in these tomboyism cases, can override environmental and sociocultural influences.

Cerebral dominance differences.   In the past three decades, specialization of the left brain hemisphere for speech and verbal abilities and logical and sequential thinking, and the right hemisphere for spatial and other nonverbal abilities, has been continuously researched and written about. Assumptions about abilities related to gender differences based on the more specialized use of one side of the brain or the other are highly controversial and not well supported by any documented research. However, Levy-Agresti and Sperry (1968; see also Benbow and Stanley, 1980, 1981; Kolata, 1983) reported finding stronger right-hemisphere dominance for males, resulting in higher spatial abilities. Buffery and Gray (1972), in clear contradiction, argued that better male bilateral development—equal development of both sides of the brain—is responsible for the apparently superior spatial skills of males.

Levy (Kimura, 1985) theorized that differential brain pattern organizations for the sexes may be due to differences in rates of development both before and after birth, with the left hemisphere developing more quickly in girls and the right hemisphere in boys. The impact of this difference in rate would favor verbal skills in females and spatial skills in males.

If there are hemispheric differences between the sexes, no research makes it clear whether the hemisphere differences cause the differential spatial ability, or whether cultural conditions cause the differential hemispheric development. Camill Benbow (Benbow and Stanley, 1981), however, even though she would *like* to find an environment difference that has been overlooked, concluded that the superior verbal skills of girls and the superior math and spatial skills of boys are tied to differential hemispheric functions, and the difference is genetic. She reported one study in which a group of girls were specially taught spatial skills, but even that made little difference in their measured spatial ability.

Durden-Smith and DeSimone (1982) itemized some apparently biological differences between the sexes that, on balance, make females look noticeably superior—physically, psychologically, and socially. Consider these differences:

> Men are more likely to be sexual deviates or psychopaths.
>
> Women are stronger in verbal and communication abilities, but suffer more from phobias and depression.
>
> There are more males at both ends of the intellectual spectrum—retardates and geniuses.
>
> More males have heart attacks, since testosterone apparently increases cholesterol and hardening of the arteries.
>
> Girls develop faster.
>
> More males are spontaneously aborted during pregnancy, are born dead, or die in the first month of life.
>
> More males have major birth defects.
>
> Males are born less sturdy.
>
> Boys are four or five times more likely to be *autistic* (being mute or having bizarre speech) or *aphasic* (unable to produce or comprehend speech; aphasia also includes emotional and thinking disorders).
>
> Boys are much more likely to be unable to read (*dyslexia*), unable to do arithmetic (*dyscalculia*), or to have other learning disabilities.
>
> Boys are five times more likely to stutter.
>
> Males commit almost all violent crimes.
>
> Males are more prone to alcoholism.
>
> Males are more prone to schizophrenia.

We also might mention some traditional observations: Boys are more likely to be hyperactive, disruptive, and aggressive in class. Girls have better handwriting and better teeth and, when they get older, they have more hair and they live longer.

Sociocultural Differences

Although gender differences can be described and to some extent even quantified, research cannot delineate the exact extent to which specific differences are cultural versus biological in origin. However, studies of the changing role of women in society provide good documentation that many differences are indeed *not* biologically based.

The pink or blue blanket that identifies gender differences almost at birth is the first step in giving differential direction to the sexes. Next comes the infant's nursery, with pastel colors, lace, frills, and dolls for girls and bright colors, football heroes, space ships, and dump trucks for boys.

The expectations of *docility* and *conformity* for girls throughout early childhood initiate the gifted girl to her eventual underachieving role in society.

In the process of developing her *Bem Sex-Role Inventory*, Bem (1974) itemized stereotyped characteristics associated with men and women. Interestingly, characteristics considered "masculine" also are typical of successful people, for example: *aggressiveness, ambitiousness, analytical ability, assertiveness, competitiveness, leadership ability, independence,* and *self-reliance.* Characteristics in the "feminine" column included those which might be associated with mothering or, at best, a narrow range of nurturant, female-dominated occupations, for example: *affection, cheerfulness, compassion, gentleness, love of children, shyness, understanding,* and *warmth.*

Bem's gender-role stereotyped traits are further reinforced by textbooks, literature, and the media. In an analysis of one third-grade reader, Allain (1979) found that men were described as involved in 33 occupations compared with only 6 for women. Further, these occupations were clearly gender-role stereotyped, for example: doctor, minister, cowboy, inventor, and mayor for men; and teacher, princess, seamstress, and secretary for women. Children also are guided toward sex-role stereotyped books. There are "girls' books," such as *Little Women* and *Little House in the Big Woods,* and "boys' books," which include tales of mystery, adventure, risk-taking, and accomplishment (Sadker, Sadker, and Hicks, 1980).

Television, so pervasive in the lives of children, further reinforces gender-role stereotypes. Sternglanz and Serbin (1974) analyzed gender-role stereotypes of ten of the then most popular children's shows. They found half to have no female characters at all, while the others had twice as many males as females. Furthermore, females were portrayed as not making or carrying out plans; they were punished if they were too active or aggressive; and they continuously deferred to males. Male characters were highly active, aggressive, and socially dominant, and they made plans and carried them out. The Des Moines Register (December 1, 1987) reported little improvement of female television roles. Twenty percent of TV shows have no females in the cast; among the lead roles on television programs, 36 belong to males and only 7 to females.

The influence of movies and television on the aggressiveness and morals of children is an important and continuing issue. On the side of strong effects, Bandura and Walters' (1963) classic research on the effects of modeling showed that filmed models were as effective as live models in influencing physical aggressiveness in children. Even closer to the present problem, Pinegree (1978) found that five-minute commercials were effective in influencing children to accept either traditional or nontraditional roles of women.

Can gifted girls overcome the impact of families, schools, and sex-role stereotyped literature and media on their own self-perceptions? Only with high levels of awareness and some deliberate "counterconditioning."

Differences in Abilities

Jensen (1980) presented a comprehensive review of studies of differences in tested abilities. Table 15.2, adapted from Jensen, reflects the percentages of studies indicating superior performance by either sex and the percentages showing no significant gender differences. Based on these studies, there is no overwhelming support that any ability is totally and exclusively gender related. However, there is evidence that females may outperform males on tests of *verbal ability, verbal divergent thinking,* and *general intelligence,* while males may outperform females on tests of *quantitative* and *visual-spatial* abilities (Bee, 1974; Benbow and Stanley, 1980, 1981, 1983b; Block, 1976; Callahan, 1979; Maccoby and Jacklin, 1974). In addition, girls generally score higher on achievement tests, get higher grades, and as mentioned above, have fewer learning disabilities, repeat fewer grades, and cause less trouble in class (Brophy and Good, 1970; Lips and Colwill, 1978; Maccoby and Jacklin, 1974). The higher grades may be due to their acquired attitudes of dependence, conformity, and desire to please (L. W. Hoffman, 1972).

In the area of divergent thinking ability as measured by the *Torrance Tests of Creative Thinking,* Torrance (1983) found that gender differences have changed over time. In the late 1950s and early 1960s boys outperformed girls on measures of originality, and girls exceeded boys on elab-

TABLE 15.2   Numbers of Studies of Gender Differences and Their Outcomes on Various Types of Tests Published Since 1966

TYPE OF TEST	N	Significant Difference in Favor of		
		NEITHER	MALE	FEMALE
		%	%	%
General Intelligence	58	69	5	26
Verbal Ability	131	62	10	28
Quantitative Ability	35	43	46	11
Visual-Spatial (nonanalytic)	35	68	26	6
Visual-Spatial (analytic)	63	55	40	5
Reasoning (nonverbal, nonspatial)	38	69	18	13
Piagetian Tests of Conceptual Level	51	80	12	8
Divergent Thinking (verbal)	32	50	16	34
Divergent Thinking (nonverbal)	23	30	35	35

Adapted with permission of The Free Press, a division of Macmillan, Inc., from *Bias in Mental Testing* by A. R. Jensen. Copyright © 1980 by A. R. Jensen.

oration and most measures of verbal creativity (Torrance 1962, 1965). In the 1960s and 1970s gender differences began to fade out (Bruce, 1974; Torrance, 1963).

Mathematics Ability

The most prominent and heated argument related to differential abilities regards whether males have superior mathematical abilities (Armstrong, 1979; Benbow and Stanley, 1980, 1981, 1982, 1983b; National Assessment of Educational Progress, 1975; Pallas and Alexander, 1983; see also Stanley and Benbow, 1983). The math difference seems to widen over the years, becoming quite prominent by junior high school (Hilton and Berglund, 1974; Leinhardt, Seewald, and Engel, 1979; Maccoby and Jacklin, 1974). Giele (1978) and Fennema (1980), in fact, concluded that male and female math abilities are about equal in childhood, but at about age 12 or 13 boys begin to show superiority. However, a longitudinal study by Hall (1980) of 59 gifted students (29 boys and 30 girls) from preschool through grade 12 found no significant gender differences in arithmetic or spatial abilities or SAT-Math scores. She attributed her unique findings to an environmentally specific sample. The students were mainly from a university environment where many of the females' fathers were Ph.Ds, and cross-gender support for education was evident.

A male/female math comparison study in Hawaii of students in grades 4, 6, 8, and 10 (Brandon, *et al.*, 1987) found superior achievement for females over males. An analysis by ethnic background of these students further indicated that gender differences favoring girls were smaller for Caucasian students than for Japanese-American, Filipino-American and Hawaiian children.

Camilla Benbow and Julian Stanley (1980, 1981, 1982, 1983b)—basing their work on years of SAT-M, scores collected for thousands of students in Stanley's *Study of Mathematically Precocious Youth* (SMPY)—concluded that their data support a biological superiority of male math ability, which could be related to male superiority in spatial tasks. They indicated that environmental influences are not likely to so dramatically affect the "extreme absence of extraordinary female talent" among students involved in the SMPY talent search. A November 1983 Associated Press news release, based upon a recently published article in *Science* magazine (Benbow and Stanley, 1983b), noted that in the years 1980, 1981, and 1982 Benbow and Stanley found that the average SAT-Math score for 19,883 gifted seventh-grade boys was 416. For 19,937 gifted girls the average score was a noticeably lower 386. Average SAT-Verbal scores were almost identical, 367 for boys and 365 for girls. Further, boys outnumbered girls by better than 2 to 1 among those scoring above 500; by better than 4 to 1 among those who scored over 600; and by almost 13 to 1 in the group scoring 700 or higher (113 boys, 9 girls). Benbow and Stanley ". . . could not find substantial differences in attitude, background, or previous mathematical training between boys and girls." See Inset 15.1 for one possible physiological explanation of gender differences in mathematical talent.

We noted before that the superior male visual-spatial ability has been used to explain their apparently superior mathematics ability. The spatial ability-math superiority relationship is not, however, clear cut. In a male/female comparison of 77 gifted boys and 62 gifted girls, Weiner and Robinson (1986) found significantly better mathematics reasoning ability among the boys, but they did not find differences in tests of spatial relations, nor did they find spatial relationship test scores to be predictors of mathematics achievement for either girls or boys.

INSET 15.1 DOES MATH GENIUS HAVE A HORMONAL BASIS?

In recent years, Harvard Medical School neurologist Norman Geshwind has proposed that excess testosterone or unusual sensitivity to testosterone during fetal life can alter brain development (Kolata, 1983). Specifically, the right hemisphere of the brain (instead of the usual left) becomes dominant for language abilities, and the person is likely to be left-handed. Further, such individuals—mainly boys, of course—are predisposed to (1) such speech abnormalities as autism, dyslexia, or stuttering, (2) certain kinds of giftedness, particularly artistic, musical, or mathematical, and (3) disorders in the body's immune system. Said Geshwind, "If you get the mechanism adjusted just right you get superior right hemisphere talents, such as artistic, musical, or mathematical talent. But the mechanism is a bit treacherous. If you overdo it, you're going to get into trouble. It's a funny mechanism. At first, it looks like you have to deliberately produce damage to produce giftedness."

According to *Science* magazine writer Gina Kolata, Benbow and Stanley were intrigued by this possible explanation of male superiority in math talent, and promptly contacted their very best students (those who scored above 700 on the SAT-M) to see if they were left-handed or had immune system disorders. "To their surprise and delight, they find that Geshwind's predictions hold up beautifully in their group" (Kolata, 1983). Twenty percent of the mathematically talented students are left-handed, which is more than double the proportion of left-handedness in the general population. A full 60 percent have immune system disorders (allergies, asthma)—which is five times the expected rate.

When Benbow and Stanley contacted students in their list who were less mathematically talented, the students also were less likely to be left-handed or to have immune disorders.

While Geshwind agrees that the data for the precocious students "fit in perfectly, to put it bluntly," he also concedes, "There's been—understandably—an enormous degree of skepticism."

The counterarguments to a biological explanation of male math superiority mainly assert that any gender differences in mathematics ability are cultural in origin.

Cultural stereotypes.   During adolescence, when sex differences in math skills begin to become especially prominent, males and females also begin their heterosexual interests. Society encourages boys more often than girls to show superior intellectual ability to attract members of the opposite sex. However, girls, in accord with cultural stereotypes, may believe that boys do not like girls who excel in math, and therefore do not seek to develop mathematical abilities (Fox, 1977a, 1977b). Kolata (1980) emphasized the impact of cultural influences on attitudes toward math in a summary statement about the Johns Hopkins SMPY research. "Although fewer girls than boys qualify for the accelerated math courses . . . , even fewer girls enroll in them." While females who select math study achieve as well as males, few females choose to study math (Fennema and Sherman, 1978).

Unequal math training.   Based upon her review of research on mathematics learning, Fennema (1980) argued that conclusions about male superiority often have been based on studies in which the number of previous math courses has not been controlled; that is, males with more math background have been compared to females with less background. However, Fox (1981a; see also Benbow and Stanley, 1980, 1981, 1983b) emphasized that the mathematics talent searches conducted at Johns Hopkins University for the SMPY program were at grades 7 and 8, when males and females had equal math training.

Jacquelynne Parsons (1982) has argued that the spatial skills leading to strong math problem solving can be trained, and that gender differences would be removed if the training were at least equal.

Father identification.   As we saw in Chapter 14, several studies (for example, Sutton-Smith, Rosenberg, and Landy, 1968) reported that early father absence, before age 8 or 9, has a depressing effect on later math scores of both males and females. They hypothesized that children learn a mathematical problem-solving thinking style from their fathers. Helson (1971) similarly reported that creative women mathematicians and scientists tended to identify with their fathers. As noted previously, Hall (1980) attributed the strong math achievement of the gifted girls in her longitudinal study to support by fathers. Therefore it is possible that learning mathematical thinking and problem solving may take place informally in the family through the process of identification with the father. Since boys are more likely to identify with their fathers than girls, boys logically would acquire superior mathematics abilities.

Different toys.   Still another hypothesis is that gender-role stereo-typed toys improve visual-spatial abilities for boys more than for girls. Trains, model airplanes, race cars, trucks, electrical sets, Legos, Tinker Toys, and other construction toys all are more likely to be played with by boys. These toys may enhance spatial skills more than the typical dolls, tea sets, coloring books, jump ropes, and needlecraft supplied to girls.

Teacher and parent expectations.   Mathematics has been considered a male domain by both students and teachers. Ernest (1976) found in interviewing teachers that 41 percent thought boys were better at math than girls, while none thought girls were better. Since teacher expectations may affect achievement by as much as 20 percent (Brophy, 1982), the *self-fulfilling prophecy* might easily help perpetuate mathematics as a male domain.

Also rooted in cultural stereotypes and expectations, Brody and Fox (1980) found that parents of gifted boys were more likely to see a career in mathematics for their son than were parents of gifted girls.

School support.   In an analysis of schools that successfully teach math and science to girls, Casserly (1979) found that teachers in those schools were not threatened by mathematically gifted girls, that they used older females to tutor younger girls, and that they began good programs before the sixth grade—before girls come to view math as a male subject. Fox (1974) similarly found that girls were successful in a math program for the gifted when school personnel were enthusiastic and supportive of the girls.

Importance of the Math Differences Hypothesis

Differential skill in mathematics is a critical issue in relation to the professional development of gifted females. Male-dominated fields that convey high status and good financial rewards (for example, medicine, engineering, architecture, pharmacy, computer sciences, and all physical sciences) *require skill in mathematics.* Sells (1976) found that male and female applicants for admission to the University of California–Berkeley differed significantly in their math preparation. Sixty-eight percent of the females, compared with 35 percent of the males, did not qualify for college calculus. At the University of Maryland, Sells found that only 15 percent of the white females and 10 percent of the black females had the math prerequisites necessary for a mathematics or science-related major. This lack of preparation clearly prevents most females from *ever* entering many challenging and rewarding professions. Said then-President Reagan in his 1983 State of the Union address to Congress, "If a child has not acquired good mathematical training by age 16, he or she will never be able to enter the fields of engineering or science."

DIFFERENCES IN EXPECTATIONS, ACHIEVEMENT ORIENTATION, AND ASPIRATIONS

Differences in mathematical preparation creates real barriers to the entrance of females into many male-dominated professions. In addition, there are also culturally imposed gender differences that discourage females from seeking high career achievement. Family, school and peer expectations discourage a strong achievement orientation, risk-taking, independence, and self-confidence in girls. These pressures can lead to low aspirations which, in turn, result in underachievement.

Family Expectations and Identification

High educational achievement and high career aspirations begin at home. Both mother role-modeling and father expectations have a compelling influence on the achievement orientation of gifted girls.

In regard to career aspirations, many researchers (for example, Altman and Grossman, 1977; Marini, 1978; Radin, 1974; Sutherland, 1978) concluded that career modeling by mothers motivates females to have higher educational and career aspirations.

Fathers' direct expectations of their daughters also may influence female achievement. Radin and Epstein (1975) found that fathers' short- and long-term academic expectations of their daughters were positively correlated with measures of the girls' intellectual functioning. There may be a chicken-egg problem, however. That is, do higher expectations produce the higher intellectual functioning, or vice versa?

Gender-stereotyped expectations of girls—and all women—by their fathers (Lynn, 1974) and dominating fathers (Heilbrun, 1973; Heilbrun, Harrell, and Gillard, 1967; Teahan, 1963) appear to have a negative effect on girls' achievement.

Research on the comparative importance of the mother versus the father role-model for female achievement is not always consistent, nor are the dynamics uncomplicated. We noted earlier that Helson (1971) found that creative women mathematicians tended to be oldest daughters who identified with their fathers. Bardwick (1971) also emphasized the importance of girls' identification with their fathers in order to learn important achievement traits such as independence and self-esteem. Drews and Teahan (1957) and Pierce and Bowman (1960), however, concluded that mother dominance was critical in encouraging girls to become career-oriented achievers. On the other hand, some women have sought careers in a direct response to what they perceived as their mothers' "empty lives"—their mothers served as models of what *not* to do.

The influence of the media on parents may also impact on their children. Reports of the Benbow and Stanley (1980) research on gender differences in math reasoning appeared in many popular magazines and newspapers. Jacobs and Eccles (1985) discovered that parents exposed to these research findings changed their math expectations of their daughters. Compared to other mothers, mothers who read about the research appeared to expect *less* of their girls in terms of math success. The impact on fathers was not as clear cut. Previous to the media coverage fathers of girls thought their daughters had slightly less math ability than their sons; after exposure to the research news they slightly *increased* in their math expectations of their daughters. The effect of the exposure on fathers was to increase the importance of their daughters taking calculus and higher math. Apparently, although the media coverage seemed to encourage mothers to provide an easy way out for their daughters, it inspired fathers to come to their defense.

In conclusion, despite some special circumstances and exceptions, career-oriented mothers do indeed provide strong role models that, along with positive and supportive father expectations, influence educational and career achievement of gifted girls.

Peer Expectations

From early adolescence, and sometimes before, peer expectations play a very strong part in directing achievement. Because high intelligence and an achievement orientation sometimes are considered masculine characteristics, girls risk being considered "unfeminine" if they become too involved in school achievement.

Ruth Duskin Feldman, former Quiz Kid and author of the book *Whatever Happened to the Quiz Kids* (1982), shared an anecdote with the author (Rimm) that shows only a small change in peer expectations of gifted females. As a college student, she was asked by a male friend if she would rather be told she was smart or beautiful. Her response at that time was, "Beautiful—I know I'm smart!" A recent sequel to this conversation occurred in her daughter's gifted class. The teacher asked the females in the class if they would rather be beautiful or valedictorian. They all indicated they would prefer the latter. She then asked the males how they would feel about dating the class valedictorian. The boys concluded that dating the valedictorian would be fine—provided she was pretty. If peer pressure to achieve has changed for gifted girls, it has changed mainly from the female perspective. Even bright males continue to rank attractiveness ahead of intelligence.

By college age, parent attitudes toward gifted women's career choices appear less important than peer attitudes (Parsons, Frieze, and Ruble, 1978), especially those of male peers. Trigg and Perlman (1976) found that females were more likely to apply to graduate school in less traditional areas if their male friends encouraged them to do so. Horner's (1972) classic "fear of success" syndrome, in which girls suppress high achievement and success because of their fear of "failing as a female," will be discussed later. As one immediately pertinent finding, Horner found that females who received career encouragement from their male friends were less likely to experience fear of success.

School Expectations

From nursery school onward we find continuous documentation of school biases that deter an achievement orientation for females. Serbin and O'Leary (1975) compared differential treatment of boys and girls in 15 nursery school classes and recorded the following behaviors that they felt would reinforce aggressiveness, confidence, and independence in boys, but not girls. Boys were encouraged to work on their own much more often than girls. Teachers rewarded girls for being dependent by responding more when they were near, but gave similar attention to boys regardless of physical distance. All 15 teachers gave more attention to boys than girls, including more individualized instruction and more tangible and verbal rewards.

When teacher feedback is given to children, Dweck and Bush (1976; Nichols, 1979) found that poor performance often is described as "lack of ability" in girls, while similar poor performance is noted as "not working hard enough" with boys. This difference is important. If poor performance is seen by students (girls) as lack of *ability*, then increased effort will not solve the problem. However, if poor performance is interpreted as lack of *effort*, then the students (boys) will be motivated to work harder to achieve (Weiner, 1980).

Fox (1981b) interestingly noted that the "critical thought and questioning mind" of the young boy is likely to be described as "insolence" or an "argumentative nature" in a girl.

Casserly (1979) reported gender differences in willingness to take Advanced Placement courses. Although girls outnumber boys in traditionally "female" Advanced Placement courses (for example, English, Spanish, and French), girls usually take fewer Advanced Placement courses than boys in math, history, classics, German, and all sciences. In analyzing differences between schools that produce high-achieving girls and those that do not, Casserly identified two disarmingly simple factors: (1) The schools producing high-achieving girls used a tracking program that made Advanced Placement classes a natural sequence, and (2) teachers both actively recruited girls for the Advanced Placement classes and expected them to be high achievers.

School counselors have been found to possess gender stereotypes that work against female achievement. In one survey, Petro and Putman (1979) found that both male and female school counselors agreed that girls are more ". . . easily excitable in a minor crisis, easily influenced, home-oriented, passive, noncompetitive, indecisive, and easily hurt." Other evidence shows that female counselors often project their own fears of science and math into girls, cautioning them that they may not get good grades if they take difficult math and science courses (Casserly, 1979).

Counselors also suggest to girls, more often than to boys, that they need time for their social lives and/or that they should avoid courses in math and science. Quoting one counselor, ". . . there are so many fun things going on. I think they'll be busy enough and they [girls] can get into the serious work in college" (Casserly, 1979). The following quote was considered by Casserly to be representative of male counselors: "There are men with Ph.Ds in physics all over the place who can't get jobs. Why should we encourage girls?"

A study by Cooley, *et al.* (1984) compared the expectations of male and female teachers for male and female gifted students. Although male teachers are now seeing gifted females in professions that were previously closed to them, male teachers continue to view their female students in a more gender-role stereotyped manner. Male teachers saw their gifted female students as more emotional, high strung, and gullible than did female teachers and as less imaginative, less curious, less inventive, less individualistic, and less impulsive than did the female teachers. Both male and female teachers viewed the gifted male students as more competent in critical/logical thinking skills and in creative problem-solving skills than the gifted females.

From preschool to college, then, and despite improvements in recent years, many teachers and counselors by innuendo and by action discourage females from developing their talents equally with males.

Self-Expectations

Female aspirations and achievement orientations surely are changing. This change must include altered self-perceptions and self-expectations. If gifted females are to develop their talents and make their contributions to society they must acquire confidence and strong achievement needs, and they must make plans for a sound education.

Research suggests four important factors that seem to be linked to the lower self-expectations and aspirations of females: (1) a lower sense of competence, (2) a tendency to attribute failures to oneself and successes to external factors, (3) lower achievement motivation, and (4) the "fear of success" syndrome mentioned above. These undoubtedly are interrelated, and together decrease the likelihood of gifted women aspiring to challenging professions. We will examine each of the four.

Low sense of competence.   First, studies of the sense of competence among women repeatedly show that, on the average, women exhibit lower feelings of competence than do men. For example, Stake (1981) found that females tended to score lower than males in predicting their future ability to perform well in high-level careers. Addison (1981) similarly found that in evaluating their own performance females tended to underestimate their degree of success while males tended to overestimate it.

In a program in which gifted seventh- and eighth-grade students were given an opportunity for grade acceleration, only 54 percent of the girls chose acceleration, compared with 73 percent of the boys (Fox, 1977b). Said Fox, girls were less confident in trying something new and were more fearful of failure. They also experienced more problems of self-esteem—which were unrelated to actual ability—and were more fearful of peer rejection. Hall (1982) similarly reported that girls were less likely than boys to enter college early.

Maccoby and Jacklin's (1974) conclusion that boys are more intensely socialized toward competition and success provides a reasonable explanation for their developing a stronger sense of personal competence.

In a study of the social self-esteem of 260 gifted and talented female adolescents, Hollinger (1985) found that girls who had self-perceptions most similar to male gender-role stereotyped instrumentality had the greatest social self-esteem. In her study of 188 gifted male and 90 gifted female adolescents, Mills (1980) similarly found evidence of intellectual advantage for both sexes among those who showed instrumental or masculine personality characteristics.

Attributional differences.   The lower confidence that females exhibit is reflected in studies of causal attributions they make. Studies of both children and adults report a similar gender-related tendency (Deaux, 1976; Frieze, 1975; Post, 1981). Females tend to attribute their successes to hard work or to luck, but their failures to lack of ability. Males tend to follow the reverse attribution process, blaming others, bad luck, or their lack of effort for failures, but crediting their own high abilities for successes.

An extreme form of this attribution difference is found in the *imposter* phenomenon (Clance and Imes, 1978) in which women who have achieved success indicate that they do not believe they are capable of being in their position, and that their inability will somehow be discovered. It is surely an example of extremely low confidence when women who receive recognition for their achievements still are unable to attribute this success to their own ability.

Low achievement motivation.   Our third factor in female under-achievement is low achievement motivation. A basic premise of achievement motivation theory (Atkinson, 1974; McClelland, 1976) is that persons with strong needs to achieve will strive to succeed in situations requiring intelligence and leadership. The need to achieve is a highly consistent personality trait that, according to Veroff (1969; Feld, Ruhland, and Gold, 1979), begins developing as early as the second grade.

Efforts to teach achievement motivation basically encourage the learner to think as achievement-oriented individuals do; that is, to (1) value success and achievement, (2) accept moderate risks, (3) set realistic and achievable goals, and (4) feel confident that he or she can achieve these goals.

We have seen throughout this chapter that cultural stereotypes, biases, and home and school expectations have worked to reduce female independence and aggressiveness, and, consequently, their needs for high-level academic and career achievement. Achievement motivation leaders McClelland (1976) and Atkinson (1974) attribute needs for achievement to learning, rather than heredity, and point to parental influence in childhood as the crucial factor.

As an interesting historical fact, in an 873-page compilation of research into achievement motivation, a single footnote commented on achievement motivation research with women (Atkinson, 1958).

Fear of success.   As early as 1935 Margerat Mead observed that "... the achieving girl [is threatened that she] will never be chosen by a member of the opposite sex." More recent research on women's fear of success (Horner, 1972; Zinberg, 1974) suggests that in mixed sex competition, women are motivated to *avoid* success. Horner hypothesized that aggressiveness traditionally is considered a masculine characteristic. Since competitiveness or being too intellectual is not ladylike, women fear that success in the achievement domain may mean failure as a female.

In Horner's research, 90 female college students were asked to respond to the statement below with "Anne" as the character, while 88 males responded to the same statement with "John" in it:

> After first term finals Anne (John) finds herself (himself) at the top of her (his) medical school class.

The scoring of the stories showed that 90 percent of the males described rosy futures for John—but a full 65 percent of the females predicted an unhappy outcome for Anne. Anne's academic success was described as bringing her social rejection in the form of unpopularity, loneliness, lack of femininity, and low marriageability. Success in competition with males thus was seen as leading to feelings of anxiety, guilt, despair, and doubt about femininity and normalcy. Based on these sad predictions for bright women, Horner coined the phase *fear of success* and explained that this paradox in women's achievement motivation would cause many women to feel defensive about their achievements if they are successful, and sometimes will prevent them from achieving in the first place.

Lavach and Lanier (1975) discovered that Horner's fear of success was particularly prevalent among high-achieving white adolescent girls. The anxiety was aroused especially when in direct competition with males, and it increased from grades 7–9.

To be fair, we must note that in the dozens of follow-up studies of women's fear of success, the results have been inconsistent or else have demonstrated qualifying circumstances. For example, both Alper (1974) and Katz (1973) found that fear of success scores are considerably lower when the situation is less threatening. For example, when reference to "medical school" was omitted (Alper) or when it was noted that half of "Anne's" medical school classmates were women (Katz), fear of success scores dropped considerably.

EDUCATING GIFTED FEMALES

Society no doubt will continue to improve in providing a support system in which gifted women may develop their potential equally with men. Schools, however, must take a leadership role in fostering this equal development. In this section the model explored in Chapter 14, dealing with underachievement, will be used to provide some realistic guidelines that can help teachers, counselors, and parents reverse underachievement in females. That model includes the following steps:

1. Assessing skills, abilities, and home and school reinforcement contingencies
2. Improving communication between home and school
3. Changing the expectations of important others
4. Improving model identification
5. Correcting skill deficiencies
6. Modifying reinforcements at home and school

Since cultural underachievement is a more extensive problem than individual underachievement, there will be some additional special problems that educators must consider in programming for underachieving girls.

Assessing Skills, Abilities, and Reinforcement Contingencies

School district administrators, principals, teachers, counselors, and others need, at the minimum, to ask the following questions:

1. Are gender-role stereotyped books, films, and other media avoided in the classroom and library?

2. Are spatially oriented activities, such as mathematics and computer work, introduced early so that both girls and boys can begin learning these skills before peer pressures intervene?

3. Are females equally encouraged to participate in competitive activities?

4. Are counselors and teachers being educated in the opportunities for and abilities of females?

5. Are students and their parents being educated regarding the broad range of opportunities for females?

6. Are girls encouraged to take leadership roles in the school?

7. Are gifted girls encouraged to take advanced courses in all curricular areas?

8. Are students exposed to a variety of successful, professional female models?

9. Are opportunities available for assertiveness training for females?

10. Are some all-female group guidance experiences being provided, so that girls may deal with problems related to femininity, self-confidence, and an achievement orientation?

11. Are efforts being made to erase the stigma of a high achievement orientation for females?

12. Are the rewards for career achievements for females being stressed equally with those for males?

To the extent that answers to these questions reflect nonencouragement of high-level educational and career aspirations for gifted girls, changes should be made.

Communication Between Home and School

Gifted coordinators, guidance counselors, and classroom teachers may all become involved in coordinated attempts to communicate with parents about the achievement, course selection, and career expectations for gifted girls. A series of short letters to the parents of gifted students, including some specific suggestions of ways in which parents can help encourage gender equity and female talent development, may help. One example of such a letter appears in Inset 15.2. Notice that only one topic is addressed in this letter, encouraging girls to take higher-level mathematics and science courses. Other topics for brief letters could include strengthening the girl's career orientation, building confidence, the value of higher education, the role of some risk-taking in success, and perhaps even the eventual division of household chores. In each case, it is important to emphasize the rewards available to females who develop their abilities, and to encourage parents to reward girls for accepting special challenges. This is a difficult message to give parents; they have been socialized in a culture that has fostered underachievement in women, and therefore they themselves usually are guilty of reinforcing gender-role stereotypes.

INSET 15.2 CHALLENGE SENIOR HIGH SCHOOL, EVERYTOWN, WISCONSIN

Dear Mr. & Mrs. Kirkpatrick:

We would like to recommend that your daughter Sara select Calculus, Advanced Biology, and Advanced Chemistry among her courses in grade 12. Her past performances in mathematics and science suggest that she would benefit from these challenging courses. These courses are complex and do involve more homework than some other selections that she might make. As a result, some high school students, particularly females, are hesitant in selecting them for fear that they may not perform as well as they typically have performed. Mainly these students worry about a negative effect on their grade-point average or about peer pressure that may make high-level science or math courses appear to be more male related.

We hope that Sara will be encouraged to select these courses because advanced courses in science and math can provide many more career options for her. Challenge Senior High School has taken the following steps to encourage capable girls to select these difficult courses:

1. Course grades are weighted so that a "B" grade in these courses is the equivalent of 4 points or an "A" in easier courses.
2. Courses are taught by both male and female teachers who were selected based on their willingness to provide extra support and help in these challenging courses.
3. Guest lecturers from professional science and mathematics areas will provide information to students on career areas in science and mathematics.
4. Women guest lecturers will share with girls their experiences on how to combine careers and homemaking roles.
5. Students who select these courses will be eligible for Advanced Placement testing and may therefore be able to earn college credits during their senior year in high school.

You or Sara may want to chat with me further about our special program to encourage bright female students to fulfill their intellectual potential. Please don't hesitate to call me to discuss Sara's special concerns. We will also be holding a special meeting for gifted girls and their parents in early March and I hope to meet you at that time.

Sincerely yours,

Margaret Nellon

Margaret Nellon
Guidance Counselor

Changing the Expectations of Important Others

Teachers, parents, and girls themselves must acquire the expectation that females can achieve. Providing teachers, parents and gifted students with evidence of female achievement in traditionally male-dominated fields is a most effective method of changing expectations. Internship programs (in which girls work with women executives and other women professionals), career women guest speakers, and field trips to see the accomplishments of talented women all provide living evidence of female accomplishment. Local professional women's organizations, such as American Association of University Women or the local chapter of the National Organization for Women, may be pleased to cooperate with such projects.

Opportunities to hear, see and work with high-achieving women can be supplemented by reading and research projects that provide students with the opportunity to learn about achieving women and to understand the training and personality characteristics needed for high career achievement. The actual study of women's achievements in the arts, sciences, and in literature will help gifted girls, their teachers, and their families to recognize the reality of female talent and accomplishment.

Peer expectations are perhaps the most difficult area in which to effect change. One effective way to encourage peer reinforcement is to provide coeducational group meetings for gifted students, both educational and semisocial. The kind of rapport and mutual support that usually develops in such meetings encourages all gifted students to challenge themselves. Discussion in which students air their concerns (for example, regarding risk-taking or the career-homemaker conflict) may help give females the support they will need. Discussions of careers that are appropriate for all gifted students will emphasize the acceptability and desirability of female talent development. The rapport established among gifted peers can also create a more supportive and rewarding social life for gifted girls, which is an important variety of peer reinforcement.

Model Identification

Although there are fewer female models with whom gifted girls may identify—for example, women doctors, lawyers, researchers, or executives—they nonetheless can be located, even in small communities. Such persons provide the aspiring gifted girl with the assurance that it is possible for a woman to achieve a career goal and at the same time enjoy a satisfying marriage if she so chooses.

At extremely high achievement levels, however, the scarcity of female models can lead to doubly strong anxieties related to the conflict of successfully coordinating a marriage with a career requiring long, arduous preparation. The extent of this problem was recently shared by a woman

M.D./Ph.D student at Harvard Medical School. She had failed to find even one woman, either at Harvard or in her research field, who had successfully combined marriage with a career in medical research. The recognition that she was investing so much time and energy to prepare for a career-marriage role, with virtually no evidence that success was possible, left her extremely frustrated. She wanted desperately to find a model who could provide encouragement.

Educators do need to help girls locate such models. The models can share with gifted girls the experiences, rewards, frustrations, and decision-making processes that accompanied their accomplishments. In view of their own difficult experiences, they often are eager to share insights with gifted young women.

Correcting Skill Deficiencies

The skill deficiencies of gifted girls usually are found in math and science. Such deficiencies can be prevented by encouraging high school girls to take the necessary advanced courses, which will permit their eventual entry into desirable college majors and prestigious careers.

One good approach to attracting girls to advanced math classes is to encourage women teachers to teach them. Also, reasonable grading criteria, good teaching, and smaller classes that allow individual attention can make these classes more attractive to all students, and less threatening to gifted girls. Many students, male and female, avoid math classes in fear of lowering their grade-point averages, which reduces their chances for high school awards and college admission and scholarships. If advanced math course grades could be weighted such that an *A* earns 5 points instead of the usual 4, etc. gifted males and females both would be less intimidated by such courses. The greater complexity and competitiveness of these courses should justify a more lenient grading policy. Some secondary schools have successfully implemented such a grading plan.

We should note that not all areas in which females are deficient are academic. In addition to providing experiences that will help academic and creative development, teachers and counselors must ensure that gifted girls are helped in developing autonomy, self-esteem, self-confidence, a willingness to compete, leadership and assertiveness (Addison, 1979; Fox, 1981b; Navarre, 1980; Wolleat, 1979).

Changing Reinforcements at Home and School

This last step is probably the most critical one. Gifted girls are frequently reinforced for being good, perfect, pretty, and well-adjusted. None of these reinforcements helps prepare them for careers ahead. Here are some recommendations for change.

Perfectionism. Take the word *perfect* out of your vocabulary at home and at school. Each time parents and teachers tell girls that they have completed a task "perfectly" or that they are "perfect," they reinforce the pressure toward perfectionism. Fathers must be especially careful not to describe their little girls in those extreme terms. Fathers usually believe it to be a compliment that builds confidence, but girls internalize it as an expectation and an impossible pressure.

Social life. Although making friends can be positive, aloneness and independence are equally valuable. Do not make a child feel uncomfortable in independent activities. Encourage alone time. In her study of the childhoods of eminent women, Kerr (1985) found that they spent an unusual amount of time alone. She cites Gertrude Stein and Eleanor Roosevelt as examples. Most eminent women had a sense of being "different." Overemphasizing the importance of being "well adjusted" has the impact of internalizing a pressure to be popular and to make excessive compromises to please others.

Challenge. The girl who gets all *A*s and pleases everyone is not anxious to take the risk of acceleration or other extra challenge. Explain that you would rather she take the risk of doing harder work even if she is not as successful. Expect her to do more than is required and encourage her to take accelerated courses even if they are difficult. It is better to experience difficulty early and to learn to persevere and struggle than to have eight or ten years of perfect work that is easily accomplished. Pressure for perfection only prevents risk taking.

Appearance. Refuse to emphasize appearance. Whether she is pretty or not, from early on do not make a fuss about attractiveness. Reasonable neatness and cleanliness are acceptable values. Early emphasis on her beauty becomes an internalized pressure to be thin, to wear excessive makeup, and to concentrate on fashion instead of intellectual accomplishment, kindness, creativity, and other important values.

Competition. Teach little girls about realistic competition. Do not protect them from failure experiences. Do not just "let them win" at games. Teach them either to laugh at their losses or to analyze them for future learning. Even friendly insults help them to build some resilience to criticism. Do not let them use tears to attract unnecessary protection or shelter.

Careers. As a mother, if you are a career woman do not apologize for your work even if you feel guilty. Let your daughter know that you and she are better off because you have a career, not only for the money, but for the way you feel about yourself and for the independence you can permit her. If you are an educator, let girls know about the significance of your career so that they will not assume that you only work because you must have a salary. Pride in your career will inspire your daughter toward pride in establishing her own career.

Male attitudes.   Perhaps the most difficult reinforcer to change is male attitudes toward females. Convincing gifted boys to appreciate intelligent and assertive females will help prevent the pressures that girls feel about appearing too intelligent. Explaining to males that the best kind of relationships come from mutual respect rather than a perceived need to feel more intelligent than females is a critical key to supporting intelligent thinking and acting in girls. Gifted girls tend to like gifted boys, but the latter often feel threatened in the company of very bright girls. Also, the deemphasis on appearance or the "pretty girl" message to sons and male students will make for better self-actualization of both females and males.

All-girl classes or schools.   There is some evidence to suggest that some all-girl classes and all-girl schools may help some girls take leadership positions and courses they might otherwise avoid (Tidball, 1973; Tidball and Kistiakowsky, 1976). According to Higham and Navarre (1984), an all-girl environment may have a healthier impact on independence than absorption with dating and social life.

Overall, there are very difficult changes in the reinforcements which need to be made at home and school if gifted girls are to be guided to becoming gifted women.

The special problems that characterize the wide-reaching cultural underachievement of women require that all persons be enlisted in the task of changing the culture in order to support the development of women beyond their stereotyped nurturing roles. The rewards to individual women and to society will make the effort easily worthwhile.

SUMMARY

The education of gifted women historically has been largely ignored. Some early influential educators publicly specified a nurturing domestic role for women. Observations by Stockard and Wood, Reis, and Olshen seem to support the concept of a "disappearance of giftedness in girls." They excel in childhood but frequently underachieve as adults.

In the work force, women continue to be dramatically underrepresented in most traditionally male professions. Salaries also are comparatively poor.

Women are underrepresented in educational administration in elementary and secondary schools, in college teaching, and in college administration. While women's entry into "male careers" is improving, the percentage of women in these fields still is low.

Women's life satisfactions stereotypically have been tied to their husbands' career success plus success as a wife and mother. On the average, working and professional women show higher life satisfaction—greater self-esteem and greater feelings of competence—than full-time housewives.

The main problem is the home-career conflict. While there is no easy solution, some women decide in advance which role comes first (the family), compartmentalize the two roles, and often compromise to fit husband and family needs. In the area of science there is now some documentation that indicates that marriage may have an enhancing effect on scientific productivity, particularly if the woman is married to another scientist.

All gifted women should have the opportunity and encouragement to develop their talents and become professionals, if that is their choice.

Research suggests biological gender differences in levels of physical activity and aggression. Some scholars claim stronger right-hemisphere spatial abilities for males. Tomboyism, due to biological masculinization of sex organs, produces girls with many masculine interests and traits.

A list of gender differences in abilities and traits shows that, on the average, females tend to be physically, psychologically, and socially healthier. Sociocultural differences in the treatment of the sexes begin almost at birth. Differences exist in room decorations and toys and stereotyped characteristics, for example, as reflected in Bem's *Sex-Role Inventory*. Textbooks, literature, and the media, especially television, reinforce sex-role stereotypes.

Jensen's list of tested abilities showed women to be superior in verbal ability, verbal divergent thinking, and general intelligence.

The most heated debate centers on whether males have superior math ability, stemming from allegedly superior spatial abilities. Prominent in the issue are the Benbow and Stanley SAT-M statistics.

Counterarguments propose that the math differences may be due to (1) cultural stereotypes, (2) unequal math training, (3) boys' identification with father, (4) different types of toys, (5) teacher expectations, and (6) lack of school support. The issue is highly important because a lack of mathematical training will close—and is closing—permanently the doors to many high-status and well-paying male-dominated careers.

High educational and career achievements are related to family expectations. Identification with mother, especially a career mother, appears important. Fathers' expectations of their daughters also influence achievement. Gender-role stereotyped family expectations work against girls' achievement. Research shows that creative women mathematicians tend to identify with their fathers. Traits of independence and self-esteem also may be learned from fathers.

Peer attitudes and expectations often depress female achievement.

School expectations reward male independence, confidence, and aggressiveness, but reward female conformity. Likewise, female poor performance sometimes is attributed to lack of ability; male poor performance to lack of effort, leading boys to work harder.

Schools that successfully produce high-achieving girls make Advanced Placement classes a natural part of the sequence, and actively recruit girls for the Advanced Placement classes. School counselors sometimes perpetuate cultural stereotypes of male versus female traits, and often counsel girls to avoid math and science. Regarding self-expectations, women tend to have a lower sense of competence and self-esteem, attribute failure to lack of ability, and have lower achievement motivation.

Rimm's six-part model was presented as a guide for dealing with female underachievement.

chapter sixteen

The Handicapped
Gifted Child

Typically, gifted children who are handicapped are recognized for their handicap, not for their gifts and talents. Their special needs stemming from the handicaps are provided for by mandated programs in special classes and special schools funded by state and federal government. Since most handicapping conditions do not preclude or prevent giftedness, it is logical to expect that one should find among handicapped children the same percentage of gifted and talented students as in the general population. However, labeling the child as "handicapped" plus attending to the priority needs of the handicapping condition usually obscures the creative, artistic, intellectual, or scientific talents of the child. They are thus much less likely than the nonhandicapped gifted child to be identified as gifted and included in a school program that helps develop their special talents.

Overview

This chapter will explore the needs and problems of handicapped children, their identification, and some programming ideas directed toward accommodating those needs.

NEEDS OF THE HANDICAPPED GIFTED

In 1975 the U.S. Office of Education estimated that slightly more than 12 percent of all children between ages 6 and 19 were handicapped (Ysseldyke, Algozzine, and Richey, 1982). In a 1979 report it was estimated that, nationally, 7.5 percent of our children were being served by special educational programs for the handicapped. In real numbers, Gearhart and Weishahn (1976) estimated the prevalence of handicapped children between ages 5 and 18 at between six and nine million. As for *giftedness,* Schnur and Stefanich (1979), estimating a conservative 2 percent of children as gifted, calculated that 120,000 to 180,000 handicapped gifted students are in our schools. A 5 percent cutoff would raise those figures to a more realistic 300,000 to 450,000.

Public Law 94-142, the "mainstreaming law," defines *handicapped children* as

> . . . mentally retarded, hard of hearing, deaf, speech impaired, visually handicapped, seriously emotionally disturbed, orthopedically impaired or other health impaired children, or children with specific learning disabilities who by reason thereof require special education and related services.

Of these categories, it would seem that only mental retardation would preclude most forms of giftedness. Nonetheless, programs for handicapped gifted students are rare, even though state and federal funding agencies typically specify that handicapped gifted students be included in any funded G/T program. At the time Eisenberg and Epstein (1981) initiated their program they discovered that there were *no* special programs designated for handicapped gifted students in all of New York City.

Legislation clearly states that handicapped children must be served. However, Schnur and Stefanich (1979) pointed out that the handicapped gifted child may be omitted from special services (the special education class, a reading teacher, psychological services, Individualized Education Programs) if he or she is functioning reasonably well within the regular classroom. This means that, for example, an intellectually gifted child who performs at grade level, but whose achievement nonetheless is depressed by his or her handicap, would not necessarily be provided with any special services because his or her performance is equivalent to that of average classmates. To the extent that the special services would individualize evaluation and instruction, help the gifted child remediate academic weaknesses, help the child compensate for the handicapping condition, and/or develop individual talents, such special attention is lost.

It is virtually common knowledge that handicapped students have poor self-concepts, due to some amount of rejection by other students. Ironically, the labeling that is necessary to obtain funds for special services and equipment contributes to the social rejection and the poor self concept

(Hobbs, 1975). Several studies have shown that mainstreamed handicapped and emotionally disturbed children frequently are rated as the "least liked" in the classroom (Bruininks, 1978; Novak, 1974; Richardson, 1971). Burton and Hirshoren (1979) further found that the greater the severity of the problem, the greater the degree of social rejection. Bryan (1978) and Hoffman (1976) explained that some handicapped children— for example, physically handicapped or emotionally disturbed students— may visibly differ from peer group norms. Apparently, a "normal" child tends to feel that association with an atypical peer threatens the normal child's social image within his or her norm group. Sometimes, mainstreamed handicapped students are brutalized by other students, for example, by name calling or other insults, along with the social exclusion (Zigler and Muenchow, 1979). Handicapped children are under considerable stress, and strongly positive feelings of self-confidence and self-worth would indeed be surprising.

Maker (1977) suggested that gifted handicapped children themselves often are willing to accept inferior status because of their handicap, and despite their superior abilities and talents. Eisenberg and Epstein (1981) noted that even though most handicapped students do indeed have a poor self-image, in the special education room a gifted handicapped student often is a leader.

Clearly, we are dramatically underserving a segment of the population that has high potential for personal development and achievement and for making high-quality contributions to society. Among outstanding creative individuals who are handicapped, Karnes, Shwedel, and Lewis (1983) listed Ludwig van Beethoven, Thomas Edison, Helen Keller, Vincent van Gogh, and Franklin D. Roosevelt. We might add the names of contemporary musicians George Shearing, José Feliciano, Stevie Wonder, and Ray Charles, all of whom are blind; violinist Itzhak Perlman, crippled by polio; and Hollywood personality Jack Paar, former "Tonight Show" host, who stutters. Unlike most gifted handicapped persons, these people are noted for their gifts and talents, not for their disabilities.

In sum then, gifted handicapped children continue to be ignored, programs for them are lacking, and their problems are compounded by sometimes severe social problems and rock-bottom feelings of self-worth and personal integrity.

IDENTIFICATION

Identifying the gifted handicapped child usually is difficult. A major problem is that their gifts usually remain invisible to teachers and sometimes even parents. Eisenberg and Epstein (1981) described their G/T program for the handicapped in which forms for nominating handicapped gifted and talented students were sent to designated New York City schools serving a full 60,000 handicapped students. *Not one student* was nominated.

Another problem is that the handicap itself may obscure the *expression* of the special gifts and talents. For example, blindness, deafness, and some learning disabilities have the effect of slowing development and thus may result in deceptively lower IQ scores. For example, blind and deaf children, because of their sensory deficits, tend to be more concrete in their thinking, which will hardly help the abstract reasoning necessary for a high IQ score. Dyslexic children will certainly suffer on verbal components of an intelligence test, although Marx (1982) suggested that dyslexic children may have much higher than normal spatial-oriented giftedness. Other handicaps (for example, emotional disturbance or social maladjustments, orthopedic or health impairments, speech or language impairments) also can interfere with obtaining an accurate high score on an intelligence test.

In some cases then, the intelligence test—the most commonly used instrument for identifying gifted children—may add a handicap to the discovery of giftedness among already handicapped children.

A dramatic example of a case in which a handicap resulted in dependency and underachievement with the effect of obscuring giftedness is Kevin:

> Kevin, a nine-year-old fourth grader, was totally blind. He was a very good looking child and was small for his age. His disability and his young appearance invited adults to "take care of him" and do much more for him than was appropriate. Kevin's initial evaluation indicated his *WISC-R* verbal IQ score to be 109. It had been recommended that he repeat fourth grade. One year after the initial evaluation and after the dependency patterns were changed and the skills gaps were closed by tutoring, Kevin's IQ score as tested by the same unbiased tester, who had no knowledge of the treatment program, was 141. Kevin appeared to everyone to be a very bright child, but his dependent underachieving behavior related to his blindness had a major impact on the lowering of his ability scores and the initial nonidentification of his giftedness.

The *Wechsler Intelligence Scale for Children-Revised* (1974) is the most frequently used intelligence test and is often used in modified form with handicapped children. Brown (1984) suggested that other tests, which are specifically designed and normed for handicapped children, may be more appropriate. Examples of such instruments include the *Nebraska Test of Learning Aptitude* (Hiskey, 1966), used with deaf and hearing impaired children; the *Arthur Adaptation of the Leiter International Performance Scale* (Arthur, 1950) for the deaf, hearing impaired, and children with speech or language difficulties; the *Blind Learning Aptitude Test* (Newland, 1969); and *The Pictorial Test of Intelligence* (French, 1964), for children with motoric handicaps. Other tests for children with handicapping conditions are described by Bauman and Kropf (1979), Salter and Tozier (1971) and Sullivan and Vernon (1979).

Karnes (1979) reported that identifying handicapped gifted children through observation was more difficult than with "normal" children and requires a prolonged observation. Providing in-service workshops for teachers of the handicapped, which focus on characteristics of giftedness and the identification of gifted and talented children, should help the teacher identification and nomination process. Teachers who are trained to work with handicapped children rarely have training in the specific area of giftedness. Eisenberg and Epstein (1981) noted that in their search for gifted handicapped children, teachers would select conforming students, not the highly active, energetic ones. Concluded Eisenberg and Epstein, teachers definitely needed direction.

In observing possibly gifted handicapped children, one would, of course, watch for the types of characteristics and behaviors described in Chapter 2, along with an additional interesting one. As Eisenberg and Epstein described their gifted handicapped children, they ". . . understand faster, ask questions, zip through math—and they are terribly disruptive." With "normal" gifted students, disruptiveness is a trait that sometimes appears because the child is bored or frustrated in school. Because frustration and stress can be everyday matters for many handicapped gifted students, it is not surprising that *disruptiveness* can be a good indicator of giftedness with these children.

The identification procedure successfully used by Eisenberg and Epstein (1981) included IQ and achievement scores, which conveniently were already on file. They also used the Renzulli-Hartman (Renzulli, 1983) rating scales, not only the frequently used Learning, Motivation, Creativity and Leadership scales, but the less well-known Art, Music, Drama, and Communications scales as well. As noted above, when first approached via a mailing of nomination forms, not one teacher of handicapped students spontaneously nominated a single child for participation in the Eisenberg and Epstein program. However, after looking over the Renzulli-Hartman rating scales, many began *calling* (not writing) the program coordinator with the same urgent message: "Hey, I think I've got a kid for you!" The rating scales themselves served as quick in-service training for identifying gifted handicapped children.

Especially good indicators of giftedness from the Renzulli-Hartman Learning scale were:

2. Possesses a large storehouse of information about a variety of topics (beyond the usual interests of youngsters his/her age).
4. Has rapid insight into cause-effect relationships; tries to discover the how and why of things; asks many provocative questions (as distinct from information or factual questions); wants to know what makes things (or people) "tick."

6. Is a keen and alert observer; usually "sees more" or "gets more" out of a story, film, etc., than others.

Especially good items from the Motivation scale were:

1. Becomes absorbed and truly involved in certain topics or problems; is persistent in seeking task completion. (It is sometimes difficult to get him/her to move on to another topic.)
5. Prefers to work independently; requires little direction from teachers.

Eisenberg and Epstein also found peer nominations and self-nominations to be valuable; more valuable, in fact, than teacher nominations. The peers knew who were bright, creative, and fast-learning. Many handicapped students *nominated themselves* as gifted or talented, and ". . . nine out of ten were right!" In one case, a student nominated himself for the program, and shortly after had himself *decertified*—examined and taken out of the special education class.

Karnes and Shwedel (1981) created a *Talent Screening Checklist* designed especially for identifying handicapped gifted preschool youngsters. Corresponding to the U.S.O.E. definition (Marland, 1972), the checklist included the six areas of intellectual ability, specific academic talent, creativity, leadership, visual or performing art talent, and psychomotor ability. The checklist was completed by both a teacher and a parent, and if either rated the child in the top 25 percent the child was moved to the second step of the identification process. This second step involved guided observation of the child in one or more semistructured *Activities for Talent Identification* (Karnes and Shwedel, 1981). For example, a child would pick two other children and teach them to mix paint. Case conferences or a diagnostic evaluation by a psychologist were used if questions about particular children remained. Karnes and Shwedel pointed out that their identification approach minimized the risks of overlooking any truly gifted handicapped child; further, it did no harm to any participant.

To help in the identification of gifted handicapped children, Maker (1977) recommended that (1) handicapped students should be compared with others who have the same handicap, and (2) characteristics that enable the handicapped child to effectively compensate for his or her handicap should be weighted more heavily. For example, if an orthopedically impaired student cannot write, his compensating verbal and cognitive abilities should receive more weight; if a student cannot speak, his written, artistic, and creative talents should be examined.

As for creativity, the Renzulli-Hartman Creativity Scale mentioned above apparently is useful. The *PRIDE* (Rimm, 1982), *GIFT* (Rimm, 1976) and *GIFFI* (Davis and Rimm, 1980, 1982) creativity inventories have been specifically validated for use with children with learning disabilities and also should be usable with students with other handicaps.

Identification of gifted learning disabled children. As with other handicaps, gifted children with learning disabilities also may be overlooked by
typical G/T program selection procedures. They may function at or below
grade level and may exhibit deficits in cognitive ability, including long- or
short-term memory problems, visual or auditory processing weaknesses,
and/or visual-motor integration problems (Suter and Wolf, 1987). Spatial
disabilities also are common. Cognitive areas of giftedness found among
many learning disabled children are good problem-solving skills, abstract
thinking abilities, and excellent oral communication skills (Daniels, 1983;
Hadary, Cohen and Haushalter, 1979; Whitmore, 1980). Behavior problems, poor self-concepts, and dependent behaviors complicate the identification of both the giftedness and the learning disability.

Rimm (1986b) pointed out that sometimes children who are labled as
"learning disabled" in school actually are dependent underachievers. Table
16.1 includes characteristics that may help one separate children with
learning disabilities from those who are underachieving. Separating the
two categories for the purpose of differential treatment is important.

The WISC-R frequently has been used for the identification of learning disabilities. The "scatter" or differences between subtest scores (Lutey,
1977) and significant discrepancies between Verbal and Performance
scores (Kaufman, 1976a, 1976b, 1979) often are used to identify a learning
disability. While the average Verbal-Performance discrepancy is 9.7 IQ
points, Schiff, Kaufman, and Kaufman (1981) found an average Verbal-
Performance discrepancy of 18.6 points for a gifted learning disabled
group. A full 87 percent showed a higher verbal than performance score.

An examination of the case histories of 17,000 children referred to
the Temple University Reading Clinic between 1952 and 1979 produced
322 (246 boys, 76 girls) who were both gifted and learning disabled. Large
Verbal-Performance discrepancies of 15 points or more were found for
half of the gifted sample. *Similarities* (abstract verbal reasoning) and *Comprehension* (common-sense thinking) subtests were highest for these students, while *Digit Span* and *Arithmetic* were lowest. Note that the latter two
subtests require considerable concentration and attention, which often are
poor in learning disabled children (Satler, 1982).

On the affective side, one can easily imagine the confusion caused by
such extreme variability in a gifted child's capabilities and school performance. Also, because the learning disability is invisible, even though the
child may understand the cause of his or her problems, he or she may feel
shame, guilt, and other concerns (Rosner, 1985).

Fox and Brody (1983), Maker and Udall (1983), and Rosner and
Seymour (1983) all have suggested a multidimensional approach to identifying learning disabled gifted students. Such an approach might include
the WISC-R, academic tests, an informal reading inventory, teacher and
parent reports, creativity tests, and interviews with the child.

TABLE 16.1   Ways to Discriminate between Dependence and Disability

DEPENDENCE	DISABILITY
1. Child asks for explanations regularly despite differences in subject matter.	Child asks for explanations in particular subjects which are difficult.
2. Child asks for explanation of instructions regardless of style used, either auditory or visual.	Child asks for explanations of instructions only when given in one instruction style, either auditory or visual, but not both.
3. Child's questions are not specific to material but appear to be mainly to gain adult attention.	Child's questions are specific to material and once process is explained child works efficiently.
4. Child is disorganized or slow in assignments but becomes much more efficient when a meaningful reward is presented as motivation.	Child's disorganization or slow pace continues despite motivating rewards.
5. Child works only when an adult is nearby at school and/or at home.	Child works independently once process is clearly explained.
6. Individually administered measures of ability indicate that the child is capable of learning the material. Individual tests improve with testor encouragement and support. Group measures may not indicate good abilities or skills.	Both individual and group measures indicate lack of specific abilities or skills. Testor encouragement has no significant effect on scores.
7. Child exhibits "poor me" body language (tears, helplessness, pouting, copying) regularly when new work is presented. Teacher or adult attention serves to ease the symptoms.	Child exhibits "poor me" body language only with instructions or assignments in specific disability areas and accepts challenges in areas of strength.
8. Parents report whining, complaining, attention getting, temper tantrums and poor sportsmanship at home.	Although parents may find similar symptoms at home, they tend to be more sporadic than regular, particularly the whining and complaining.
9. Child's "poor me" behavior appears only with one parent and not with the other; only with some teachers and not with others. With some teachers or with the other parent the child functions fairly well independently.	Although the child's "poor me" behaviors may only appear with one parent or with solicitous teachers, performance is not adequate even when behavior is acceptable.
10. Child learns only when given one-to-one instruction but will not learn in groups even when instructional mode is varied.	Although child may learn more quickly in a one-to-one setting he/she will also learn efficiently in a group setting provided the child's disability is taken into consideration when instructions are given.

It is critical to realize that some children who are truly disabled have also become dependent. The key to distinguishing between disability and dependence is the child's response to adult support. If the child performs only with adult support when new material is presented he/she is too dependent, whether or not there is also a disability.

   Finally, as with the similarly difficult challenge of identifying gifted disadvantaged and minority children, using a *quota system* will ensure that handicapped children are examined closely for gifts and talents, and that many will be placed in programs if they show these. The identification of gifted handicapped students will continue to be difficult. However, a sensitivity to characteristics of giftedness and a willingness to look beyond the too-visible handicap will aid in the discovery of talent.

CRITICAL INGREDIENTS OF PROGRAMS FOR THE GIFTED HANDICAPPED

Programming for the gifted handicapped child may vary in type and content to the same extent as for other gifted children. It can include the same acceleration, enrichment, grouping, and counseling tactics, and with the same view toward developing the child's strengths, promoting high achievement, and enhancing creative and other high-level thinking skills. However, the program also must include some special components based on additional needs related to the handicapping condition.

   Instead of categorizing the student first as handicapped and second as gifted, the G/T program should view the child primarily as a gifted child, but one who may need some special assistance because of his or her handicap. The primary emphasis thus should be on the recognition and facilitation of the child's strengths. A secondary focus is to prevent the child's handicap from becoming a deterrent to the development and expression of his or her talent.

   Although different handicaps create different obstacles, there are a core of obstacles that appear to be critical for almost all handicapped children. It is these that we address as priorities for gifted programs that include children with handicaps.

REDUCING COMMUNICATION LIMITATIONS

Countless high-achieving handicapped college students have learned effective and socially acceptable ways to compensate for their handicapping condition. Blind students use tape recorders, study with sighted friends, and make easy arrangements to take exams orally. Severely visually impaired students will obtain (usually at government expense) head-mounted devices or other machines that magnify the pages of standard college texts. Deaf students will bring an American Sign Language interpreter to class, parking the smiling interpreter squarely next to the on-stage lecturer. Orthopedically impaired students scoot from building to building in electric wheel chairs; if they cannot write they also will use tape recorders and take exams orally. Dyslexic students pay maximum attention to lectures and illustrations, with little time devoted to frustrating printed words. On one hand, these handicapped students are admired for their courage and ingenuity. On the other, as energetic and talented individuals they simply are doing what they must do.

All handicapped persons must compensate as best they can for their limitations. In school, they must be able to perceive, respond, and express themselves; in short, they must be able to *communicate*. The regular and special education teacher must help ensure that technological aids and special training are available that will permit the handicapped gifted child not only to function "normally" in the regular class, but to develop his or her superior abilities and gifts. A short list would include wheelchairs, hearing aids, lip reading, sign language, braille training, braille texts, magnifiers, tape recorders, typewriters, artificial limbs and hands, paintbrush and pencil attachments for the head or arm, and microcomputers.

Microcomputers are presenting growing possibilities for extending the communication potential of handicapped children. For example, children who are learning disabled by reason of poor handwriting skills often do very poorly in written expression until they learn to use a word processing program on a microcomputer. Using a computer for writing assignments has the dual advantages of encouraging both fluent expression and independence. Another example of the use of microcomputers is the computerized *Versa Braille*, which permits a child to type English letters and have them translated to braille, or to type braille letters and have them translated to English.[1] Other aids and devices are continually being developed, and a teacher of the handicapped should try to stay abreast of new developments.

In many cases, gifted and talented handicapped students cannot be identified without aids that allow them to communicate. For example, in Wisconsin teachers in the Arts for the Handicapped Project (O'Connell, 1982) designed several devices that served to free physically handicapped children from some limitations of their disabilities, permitting them to express themselves through art. The strategies allowed talented artists to be identified and they were taught advanced techniques and skills.

Some communication aids, incidentally, may have the initial effect of slowing down responding, learning, and cognitive functioning. However, once the communication skill is mastered, the handicapped child will have a vastly improved potential for in-depth development, achievement, and creative expression.

The gifted handicapped child clearly needs to be provided with all possible resources to become a skilled user of substitute means of commu-

---

[1] *Versa Braille* is available from Telesensory Systems, Inc., 3408 Hillview Ave., P. O. Box 10099, Palo Alto, CA 94304.

nication. Without the use of these aids, the expression of talent is impeded and locked within. Leaders of gifted programs not only must help obtain these resources, but must interpret to the community the beneficial effects of the aids and the potential talent that can be uncovered and developed when communication barriers are lifted.

SELF-CONCEPT DEVELOPMENT

We noted earlier that rejection by others, labeling, lowered teacher expectations, and the sense of being different combine to make the handicapped gifted child feel less capable and of less worth than other children. Because a poor self-concept is a primary characteristic of underachievement, dealing with the extremely poor self-images of these children should be a primary underlying goal of a gifted program for handicapped students.

In addition to feedback from others, the self-concept also is based upon a realistic appraisal of one's own skills and achievements. Therefore, program activities should be directed not only toward helping handicapped gifted children to achieve, but toward helping them to appreciate the worth of their achievements. Further, other students should be helped to recognize the quality of the handicapped students' work.

These achievements can be evaluated according to two sets of standards. The first set of standards would be the same as applied to nonhandicapped persons, which should make it clear to all that these contributions are valuable and even superior to the average. A second set of standards acknowledges the special talent and effort needed to overcome the handicap. If handicapped gifted children have high expectations placed upon them, and if communication barriers are removed, their academic and creative achievements in the arts, literature, mathematics, science, or social studies can be as excellent as those of anyone else. And it is through the challenge of true high-level achievement that these children can realistically attain the positive self-concept they desperately need for their own personal growth.

Social Skills

Nonhandicapped children use all of their senses and their mobility to spontaneously learn social skills that permit them to be accepted by their peers. Handicapped children need to learn more concretely and specifically about the social life to which they, too, want and need to belong. This goal is indeed a challenge.

Gifted handicapped students require social activities with other bright or creative children who have similar handicaps and similar goals and interests so they will not feel alone. Peer support and peer-support groups have been recommended throughout this text as an effective solution to many self-concept and social problems of gifted students. Also, due to lack of experience, gifted handicapped children may require "social coaching" so they do not *guarantee* themselves rejection by, for example, trying to show off, forcing themselves on a group, or withdrawing completely. These are common, self-defeating coping strategies adopted unsuccessfully by many handicapped children and adolescents who so strongly wish to be "part of the group" (Halverson and Victor, 1976).

The other children in the class, too, probably will require "sensitivity training" and "values clarification" to help them empathize with the handicapped child; that is, to help them understand the problems and feelings of handicapped individuals so they will *think* before mistreating or excluding handicapped peers. Encounter-type groups—carefully monitored—which encourage open and honest communication between handicapped and nonhandicapped youth can provide an important avenue for developing social skills and social relationships of handicapped children, while providing unique sensitivity insights for the nonhandicapped child.

Classroom Tactics

Several classroom strategies may increase contact and positive feelings between different student groups. For example, mixed learning teams, which require all members to work together, have been successful in improving between-group attitudes and friendships. In Aronson's (Aronson, Blaney, Sikes, Stephan, and Snapp, 1975) *jigsaw* method mixed groups of six upper-elementary students are told that in one hour they will have a test to see how well they have learned, for example, about the life of newspaper publisher Joseph Pulitzer. Each of the six is given one paragraph covering a different aspect of Pulitzer's career. To do well, each student must read his or her own paragraph and then explain its contents to the others. Cooperation and interdependence are the only route to success. With mixed-race groups, teachers reported that changes in attitudes and self-concepts—and an improved classroom atmosphere—were very impressive.

Peer tutoring also has the effect of increasing "liking" between different students. Normal gifted students may tutor handicapped gifted students, or the handicapped students may tutor others. The handicapped students also may tutor younger children. Gartner, Kohler, and Reissman (1971) stressed that when anxious, low-esteem, low-achieving students are placed in the important and prestigious role of *teacher*, they learn new skills, feel much better about themselves, and their attitudes toward school also improve. In addition, the younger children reap educational benefits, and they learn that handicapped persons are people too.

Encouraging Independent Learning

One-to-one attention is characteristic and often necessary for educational programs for handicapped students. However, these children sometimes become too dependent upon the individual attention and the continuous positive feedback that supports their learning. Such dependence will limit the motivation and achievement of any child. Therefore, handicapped children must be encouraged to develop both intrinsic motivation, with learning and success as their own rewards, and the ability to learn independently. Further, they need both independent, self-initiated learning experiences and cooperative small-group activities in which they can serve as leaders and as equal participants.

In selecting methods by which handicapped children compensate for their handicap, attention to independence is very important. For example, the child who has a writing disability could (1) tell his or her story to a teacher, (2) dictate the story into a tape recorder, or (3) compose the story with a word processor. The first increases dependence; the latter two permit independence. Blind children (1) could have material read to them, (2) they could read the material in braille, or (3) hear it on a tape recorder. Again, the first helps keep the children dependent while the last two aid independence. Dependent help certainly is appropriate occasionally, but too much dependency can permit further crippling for the already handicapped child.

Independent, self-initiated learning and learning as part of a class group are important for *all* children, especially gifted ones who will be faced with challenging college work and complex professions. We must be innovative in providing independent learning opportunities for handicapped gifted children, just as they are provided for nonhandicapped gifted children.

HIGH-LEVEL, ABSTRACT-THINKING SKILLS

We noted earlier that limited sensory input may have the effect of depressing the development of high-level, abstract-thinking skills. Compared to persons with unimpaired senses, experiences of sensory handicapped students tend to be interpreted in a more concrete vocabulary. For handicapped children, a weakness in abstract and high-level thinking skill should not be viewed as "lack of ability," but as a deficiency that may require even more attention than with nonhandicapped gifted children.

Even more than for other gifted students, then, the gifted handicapped child must be exposed to programming methods that foster the development of such skills as *creativity, problem solving, critical thinking, classifying, generalizing, analysis, synthesis,* and *evaluation.* Encouraging such skill development is common in most gifted programs, but is doubly important for the handicapped gifted child.

An example of the introduction of abstract-thinking skills is provided by a creative problem solving (CPS) program for 16 emotionally handicapped aggressive middle school students who were not identified as gifted (Mathew, 1984). The researcher taught the youths to apply CPS to real problems. The effect of CPS training on these children was increased creativity as measured by the *Torrance Tests of Creative Thinking*. The intervention also reduced aggression significantly.

INSET 16.1 EXAMPLE OF ENRICHMENT TRIAD MODEL IN ACTION FOR LEARNING DISABLED STUDENTS (FROM BAUM, 1984)

Type I—Exposure

The students were taken to see the Lego Road Show. This is an elaborate display of Lego brick constructions of animals, buildings, and vehicles. These structures, built from thousands of Legos, were designed and built by Lego engineers. The students were overwhelmed by the exhibit and expressed a desire to become more elaborate in their own designs.

Type II—Training

We called Lego headquarters (fortunately located in our area) and arranged for consultation with an engineer. He explained to the group how designs evolved; how creative thinking skills, especially flexibility, are needed; and how principles of calculus and physics are part of the building process. Ideas basically come from experimenting with the bricks. Once the concrete structure is completed, the design is drawn. These students were delighted to hear this. So many school assignments reverse this process—"put your plan in writing before you begin."

Type III—Investigation of a Real Problem

The Lego executive in charge of marketing asked the students to design original structures for the museum display which the Lego Company was planning. The company agreed to furnish the bricks, offer technical advice, and display the product. Two boys, ages ten and twelve, eagerly accepted the challenge.

The ten-year-old designed and built an 18-wheeler truck, complete with separate tractor and trailer. The trailer was mounted on an appropriate platform and pivoted to facilitate a wide arc of movement. At the end of its two-foot long trailer was a gate that opened and closed by means of a pulley. Concern was shown by the young engineer for streamlined design for maximum function and form.

The twelve-year-old created a motorized amusement park ride. Intersecting aerial arms supported four miniature planes suspended in mid-air that revolved around its three-foot-high base. Twenty-seven revolutions comprised the ride. When asked why there were 27 revolutions, the young designer replied, "Because I set up the gears that way."

Reprinted from "Meeting the needs of learning disabled students" by Susan Baum, *Roeper Review*, 1984, 7 (1), pp. 13–19. Reprinted by permission of the author and Roeper Review.

Baum (1984) described the use of Renzulli's Enrichment Triad Model (Chapter 8) with learning disabled gifted children who displayed gifted behavior as defined by the three-ring conception of giftedness (Chapter 1). Their gifted behavior was exhibited outside of the classroom and was definitely absent within the classroom. Baum emphasized that enrichment activities should be designed to develop strengths and interests and to challenge, and not necessarily to provide remediation. Inset 16.1 describes the triad program that was successfully completed by learning disabled gifted students and which helped them to feel more motivated, challenged, and confident. The use of the enrichment triad model and the Revolving Door Identification Model (Chapter 8) are a good fit for learning disabled gifted children. A precaution for identification is that examples of creativity and task commitment may need to be discovered outside of the school environment, since learning disabled children may have lost the confidence to display these characteristics in school.

Daniels (1983) itemized the following as curriculum and remediation methods specifically for teaching learning disabled children who are gifted and talented. Note the emphasis on abstract and high-level learning objectives.

Classification	Generalizing
Levels of abstraction	Learning concepts (not "words")
Appreciating relevancy	Vocabulary, spelling
Labeling	Writing, composition
Abstracting	Punctuation, proofreading

Some relevant bibliographic resources focusing on curriculum and teaching methods for use with handicapped children appear at the end of this chapter.

PARENTING

Parenting is a critical component of any gifted program. However, parents of handicapped gifted children must deal with their child's special needs related to the handicap as well as attend to his or her giftedness. Parents of handicapped children often devote resources, time, energy, attention and patience far beyond that which is given to a normal child, which can result in advantages or, sometimes, disadvantages for the child. Consider these situations identified by Rimm in her psychology practice:

1. Intensive parental teaching of the child provided on a continuous one-to-one basis increases sensory awareness, knowledge, vocabulary, and skill development. The child will learn a great deal about his or her environment from this abundance of early teaching in the home. This obviously is an advantage.

2. Counteridentification, the parent's deriving of personal feelings of success and failure through the child's accomplishments, may cause a parent to do too much for the child. A too-helpful parent actually may rob the child of opportunities to learn skills and to build independence and self-confidence. In some cases a parent may even deny the existence of their child's handicap (for example, dyslexia, partial hearing loss). In other cases parents may use the child's handicap as an excuse for allowing the child to avoid responsibilities. Of course, the child soon learns to use the same kind of excuse to avoid unpleasant chores, for example, learning math facts. Thwarting independence and skill development is a disadvantage.

3. Manipulation by the child also can be an outcome of counteridentification. Because the parent is so anxious for their united success, the child, perhaps unconsciously, learns that he or she can easily control the parent ("I can't do it! You've got to help me!"). The manipulation skill acquired in the counteridentification process may be extended to teachers and peers. Manipulative attention-getting behaviors may take the form of overly dependent behavior, or a stubborn refusal to put forth effort in anything but the child's most preferred activities. This child and his or her parent will blame the school, the teacher, other children, and the remainder of the child's world for not helping the child to learn, instead of encouraging the child to take responsibility for his or her own learning. Manipulation, dependence, and refusal to work also are disadvantages.

4. Involvement by one parent may be so intense that it precludes the other parent from participating. For example, special skills such as using braille, American Sign Language, or special teaching procedures may need to be learned by a parent. If the second parent (usually father) has not also learned these techniques, he may be omitted from the special relationship and may finally decide that he is not a very good parent. This is particularly a problem if the child is a boy and the close parent is a mother. The alienation of the father may deprive the boy of an important male identification figure and impedes his independence and growth. The boy, as he matures, will feel both grateful to his mother for her commitment, but angry and impatient with her for his dependence on her. Neither mother nor son will understand the deterioration of what in childhood was such a strong positive relationship. Excluding one parent from close family relationships will always cause a serious problem.

A parent involvement group always should be part of a gifted program that serves handicapped students. Such a group can help parents avoid some common problems. The group also can help parents focus on their children's strengths rather than dwell on their handicaps.

The *Retrieval and Acceleration of Promising Young Handicapped and Talented* (RAPYHT) project (Karnes, Shwedel, and Lewis, 1983) is a program devoted to early education of gifted handicapped children. It includes an active and effective parent component. Noted Karnes *et al.*, parent involvement helps maintain a consistent philosophy between home and school. In

RAPYHT, parents participate in both indentification and training. The latter involves parents in helping their children compensate for their handicapping condition and develop in their areas of giftedness. Parents are encouraged to help in the classroom and are given suggested activities to be carried out with their children at home. Large-group meetings, small-group discussion sessions, individual conferences, a newsletter, and a parent library all are part of the family involvement.

Although parents should always be involved in the education of their children, the special stresses and demands of parenting gifted handicapped students requires an even closer partnership between their formal and informal educators—teachers and parents.

SUMMARY

Gifted handicapped children typically are recognized for their handicap, not their gifts. Of the estimated 6 to 9 million handicapped children (age 5 to 18), 300,000 to 450,000 could be classified as gifted. Nonetheless, there have been few G/T programs designed for the handicapped gifted. Of the many varieties of physically and psychologically handicapping conditions, perhaps only mental retardation precludes most forms of giftedness.

Too often schools fail to accommodate the handicapped gifted. If the gifted child can function reasonably well, special educational services may be withdrawn. Due largely to social rejection, handicapped students frequently have poor self-concepts.

Identification is difficult. Handicapped gifted students tend to be unseen by teachers and even parents. Also, the handicap may obscure the expression of gifts and talents. While IQ scores can be extremely useful, they may be depressed by the tendency of sensory-impaired students to think less abstractly. In-service training dealing with characteristics of giftedness and identification methods is important.

Eisenberg and Epstein successfully used IQ and achievement scores, all Renzulli-Hartman rating scales, peer nominations, and self-nominations for identification. Rimm emphasized the importance of discriminating between learning disabilities and underachievement. Maker recommended comparing handicapped students with other similarly handicapped students, and to heavily weight skills used to compensate. The Renzulli-Hartman Creativity Scale and the PRIDE, GIFT, and GIFFI inventories might be used for identifying creative giftedness.

G/T programs for handicapped gifted children can include the same acceleration, enrichment, grouping, and counseling components as other programs. Communication weaknesses must be compensated for via the use of mechanical aids and/or special training.

Developing positive self-concepts should be a main program goal of teaching the handicapped gifted. Learning to value their own superior achievements and talents should help their self-concepts. Helping other students to appreciate the achievements of handicapped gifted students also may be valuable. Peer support groups may help gifted handicapped students develop good self-concepts and social skills.

Other children probably will require sensitivity and values clarification training to help them empathize with the handicapped. Learning teams may help improve attitudes towards handicapped students.

Despite the necessity of one-to-one instruction for the handicapped gifted, the teaching of independent learning and learning in small groups also is necessary. Even more than with other gifted students, high-level abstract-thinking skills must be taught.

The great attention parents must pay to their handicapped child may result in superior learning and cognitive development. However, it can also lead to the suppression of self-confidence and independence, learning to manipulate parents, teachers, and peers, and the elimination of one parent from the family relationship.

Parent involvement groups are a critical component of a program for handicapped gifted students.

SUGGESTED READING

Visually Impaired

FUKARI, S. *How can I make what I cannot see?* New York: Van Nostrand Reinhold, 1974.

LOWENFELD, V. *The nature of creative activity.* London: Routledge and Kegan Paul, 1952.

Hearing Impaired

BRAGG, B. The human potential of human potential: Art and the deaf. *American Annals of the Deaf*, 1972, *117*, 508–511.

Other Handicaps

DANIELS, P. R. *Teaching the gifted/learning disabled child.* Rockville, Md.: Aspen, 1983.

FEINBERG, S. Creative problem-solving and the music listening experience. *Music Educators Journal*, 1974, *61*, 53–60.

GALLAGHER, P. A. Procedures for developing creativity in emotionally disturbed children. *Focus on Exceptional Children*, 1972, *4*, 1–9.

chapter seventeen

Parenting the Gifted Child

The "good parenting" any child needs is the main requirement for parenting the gifted child. However, there are some special obstacles, risks, errors, challenges, and joys that accompany being the parent of a child with unusual talents. Teachers should be sensitive to these matters in order to help guide parents of gifted children. For example: Contrary to popular belief, all parents everywhere do not believe their children are gifted. Some parents of gifted children will deny their children's special abilities in an attempt to keep them "normal" and "well-adjusted." Other parents, with the opposite attitude, seem to magnify their children's abilities and put excessive pressure on them for high achievement in all areas. This latter problem may include the tacit assumptions that (1) other children necessarily are inferior; and (2) by association, the parents also are superior. Either of these extremes, denying or magnifying giftedness, can cause problems for gifted children.

Overview

This chapter will emphasize some practical approaches to dealing with these and other special problems of parenting gifted and talented children. Although some concepts found here may apply to parenting all children, they are of special concern to parents—and therefore teachers— of gifted children.

THE "WHO'S IN CHARGE?" PROBLEM

> If God had meant gifted children to run their homes, She would have created them bigger (Rimm, 1984).

As noted briefly in Chapter 14, children who show unusual verbal and abstract-thinking ability appear to be wise and mature beyond their years, and to a degree they are. These deceptive characteristics may obscure the lack of experience and maturity that is typical of all children. It sometimes happens that devoted parents, intent on providing an ideal climate for their gifted children, fall into the trap of believing that these little beings, by virtue of their extensive vocabularies and impressive speech and logic, are capable very early of making complex decisions and setting their own goals and directions. Their interests and concerns, of course, should be considered, but parents and teachers must not abdicate responsibility for guidance.

Hollingworth (1942), in her pioneering work with gifted children, pointed out how critical it was to reach the "middle ground between arbitrary abolition of all argument and incessant argumentation." Finding that middle ground helps the child to accept the behavioral demands of adults while maintaining reasonable independence (Sebring, 1983). Ginsberg and Harrison (1977) make the following recommendation:

> . . . Discipline your gifted child when he needs disciplining. Correct him when he needs correction. Give direction when he needs direction. He should not be granted special privileges nor should unacceptable behavior be tolerated because of his intellectual gifts . . . (p. 7)

Regarding educational guidance, successful gifted achievers will usually agree that throughout their schooling they felt confident that (1) their parents and teachers were concerned and knowledgeable about an appropriate direction for their education, and that (2) following their lead was usually a wise decision.

Empowering children with adult decision-making provides power without wisdom. This can lead to formidable and continuing conflicts between gifted children and their parents as they compete for the power that parents give too early and try to recover too late. The resulting adversary mode may force adolescents to rebel too stubbornly, parents to respond too negatively, and both to lose the positive home atmosphere that can be so valuable in educating a gifted child.

PARENTING BY POSITIVE EXPECTATIONS

Parenting by *positive expectations* can be extraordinarily successful in guiding gifted children both in school and out. If high achievement, positive attitudes, and constructive behavior are expected and reinforced by parents, they will become internalized by the child, and the need for punishment usually will be negligible. How do some parents guide their children so well without punishment while others seem to need and use it so frequently?

Clear and consistent *messages*, agreed upon by both parents and transmitted to the child, are basic. In Bloom's (1985) study of talent development of concert pianists, sculptors, mathematicians, and neurologists, he found that all had in common some very clear early messages provided by parents.

> . . . parents placed great stress on achievement, on success and on doing one's best at all times . . . they were models of the "work ethic" in that they were regarded as hard workers. . . . To excell, to do one's best, to work hard, and to spend one's time constructively were emphasized over and over again (p. 510).

Parental agreement on such values as (1) the importance of study, learning, and school; (2) respect for individuality; and (3) recognition of the need for reasonable amounts of recreation and fun seem to underly a positive and achievement-oriented atmosphere. Excessive double messages and half-truths related to these matters can cause problems for children. A *double message* is two contradictory messages given by one parent, or else opposite messages sent by two parents. A *half-truth* is a message that is partly true and partly false and therefore is easily misinterpreted by the gifted child. We will look at some common and troublesome parent-to-child messages.

DOUBLE MESSAGES AND HALF-TRUTHS

The "Yes-No" Message

The parent who loses his or her temper with a young child one moment, then apologizes and begs forgiveness immediately after, is giving a confused "yes-no" message to the child. The child does not really understand if the parent approves or disapproves of the behavior. However, the child does learn that the behavior has brought an inordinate amount of valued warmth and attention. Reasonably enough, the child may increase the kind of (undesirable) behavior that produces the attention. Punishments are thus punctuated by hugs and affection, and the child, persuaded by a strong basic need for love, may *increase* the troublesome behavior in a self-perpetuating, self-accelerating negative ritual.

As a variation, confusing yes-no messages also apply to misbehavior for which the child learns to apologize—and for which he or she receives forgiveness and affection. These children learn that virtually any behavior (for example, ignoring chores, misbehavior, or poor schoolwork) is acceptable, as long as it is followed by an apology or an "I'll study and try my best next time." Gifted children who use this strategy can become facile manipulators both at home and at school. For example, after each test they fail to study for they will have an excuse and an apology that the teacher frequently believes. The same manipulation ritual learned at home is thus transferred to the classroom. The dynamics of the situation confuse parents, teachers, and the gifted children themselves.

The "That's Good, but Don't Think You're Gifted" Message

This particular message may be transmitted by parents whose primary goal is to raise children who are "well-adjusted." Their expectations include an image of their child becoming a school class officer, a team sports player (preferably a star), prom king or queen, and other forms of leadership and popularity. Their expectations specifically exclude the image of their child being seen as the "brain" or "egghead," having a too-big vocabulary, having too many intellectual interests, and being socially excluded. In an unreasonable fear that their bright child may become too involved in academics, they will prefer that the child *not* be part of a gifted program. When the child does excel in academic contests or grades, they may respond with, "That's very good, but don't think you're gifted," or "I'm glad you're interested in reading, but you need to be well-rounded. How about the soccer team?"

This child usually begins school as a successful student and quickly finds him- or herself identified as *bright*. If there is a gifted program, the child will be recommended for it. Although the teacher and the school send the child positive messages for his or her accomplishments, the parents' messages are ambiguous. In response, the child may become careless about schoolwork, and friends and playground activities take precedence. Grades and test scores begin to decline, but social leadership improves. Parents may be satisfied for a while—until in a parent-teacher conference the teacher explains that the child is not doing his or her homework and has careless study habits. Worse, he or she seems uninterested in school.

It is now time for a new message, inconsistent with the previous one. Parents now are disappointed with the laziness and poor study habits, and they may begin a withdrawal of privileges based upon grades. Popularity and leadership is suddenly a nonissue. Meanwhile, the child has lost confidence in his or her ability to achieve at a superior level, and the current skills gap may indeed make it difficult to perform well. Sports and friendships have become the highest priority—and these friends do not value "brains" and achievement.

At this point there no longer is a danger that the child will be labeled "gifted," which, of course, was the parents' initial preference. However, they are not particularly comfortable with the *underachiever* label either. The double messages of "Achievement is fine, but being well-rounded is better" and later "Popularity is fine, but you're not achieving up to your capability" can lead to both irreversible underachievement and a strained parent-child relationship.

The "Let Me Help You Make It Better" Syndrome: Counteridentification

This double message is given by a parent who places a high value on the child's giftedness and also counteridentifies with the child. As we know, in counteridentification the parent sees him- or herself in the child and, perhaps unconsciously, lives through the child's experiences as if they were the parent's own. The child's accomplishments become the parent's victories; the child's losses are the parent's defeats. Parent involvement in the child's projects goes beyond guidance and mutual interest to active participation and, all too often, taking charge of the projects.

Each accomplishment of the child typically is followed by "helpful" parent criticism. This criticism involves more than just a small suggestion; it usually changes the child's original idea and remakes it into the parent's project. The completed project may indeed be of adult quality, and in fact wins praise from teachers or wins prizes in contests. The child receives a reputation for excellence, originality, and brilliance. The parents are pleased with the child's performance and deny, even to themselves, their involvement.

Unfortunately, the child acquires feelings of doubt and ambiguity about his or her own abilities. Although delighted with the successful outcomes, the child has difficulty defining his or her own contributions. Moreover, because parental standards are so high, new projects become difficult to start. And once a project is begun, the insecure child's goal becomes perfection and the work is meticulously slow and executed too carefully. Finishing the work thus is difficult because the child feels it will never be good enough.

Goal setting may become "defensive," aimed at protecting against feelings of failure and low ability (Covington and Beery, 1976). The activities the child selects are so easy that he or she cannot fail, or else so difficult that perfectionism and high standards may be used as excuses for not completing them. The child also may manipulate parents into more and more involvement in projects and activities, and because the parents cannot bear to see their child (or themselves) fail, they are pleased with the continuous opportunity to help.

The child may become fearful that the world will discover somehow that he or she is not truly as bright as the schoolwork and IQ and achievement tests indicate. The child also might write off the purported high ability, viewing it as only the ability to get good grades, but not meaning much else in the world.

The double message that counteridentifying parents give their child is that he or she is (1) gifted, but (2) still needs much help in order to perform at an acceptably high level. Such well-meaning parents rob their child of self-confidence, spontaneity, creative thinking, and independent work. Children can only build confidence from competent personal achievement.

This theme has many variations in terms of kinds of achievement (or lack of achievement), type of parental assistance, and the type of defense mechanisms used to cope with the feelings of doubt and ambiguity. However, underlying the observed behavior is a serious *lack of self-confidence*, making the child less resilient during normal failure experiences that are part of competing and achieving. Importantly, observers of this gifted child usually cannot understand the reason for the low confidence, in view of his or her superior talents and abilities.

The "Grades Don't Count—Or Do they?" Double Message

Messages from parents about grades often are inconsistent and confusing. Calling them "double" messages is an understatement because, in any one family, the messages are likely to vary with each parent, for each child, for different subjects, and at different times. For example, Mom might strongly reinforce an *A* on a social studies test, but a week later tell the same child that his or her *C* on the next test is ". . . fine, since it's a hard subject." Furthermore, to add to the child's confusion, still other ambiguous grade messages come from teachers, peers, siblings, and even grandparents.

How can we resolve this dilemma? As parents, we know that grades are the main communicators of achievement from teachers to children and parents. Parents need to consider several important realities:

1. Grades will always be used to evaluate performance, and thus will open and close opportunity doors.
2. Children will always be able to control their own grades to some extent, but never completely. The vicissitudes of teachers and evaluators will always be part of the outcome.

3. Children should be expected to earn the best grades they are able to earn. However, if the outcome is not satisfactory after trying their best, children should look first at their own work habits to determine if they are indeed studying as efficiently as possible. At the same time, it also is fair for them to examine teacher grading styles and possible teacher biases.

4. Children should not be urged to close doors on some types of schoolwork (for example, math or science) because of less-than-outstanding grades. This point will be addressed further when we discuss the "Winning Is Everything" message.

5. If low or mediocre grades do close one door for children, they need to learn to be resilient enough to search out other opportunities and to recognize that they need not view themselves as "failures" in schoolwork. Other "open doors" can be other subjects, other years, other teachers, and other eventual careers.

6. For gifted and talented students, high grades in core academic areas are important, even if the course content is seen as "boring"; however, high grades in all courses are not equally important. Thus gifted children should be expected to get good grades in math and reading, even though they may dislike math facts or reading and language-arts workbooks.

It is certainly all right for children to receive *A*'s in physical education, but unless they plan to direct their careers toward the sports world, *B*'s and *C*'s are acceptable, and enjoyable physical activity should be a more important goal than the grade. Gifted and talented children also should be relieved of strong pressure to earn straight *A*'s in home economics, manual arts, and perhaps even art, drama, and orchestra, unless these represent a central college or career direction.

It seems important to give gifted children a message of what is *central* to their education versus what is *peripheral* (that is, primarily valuable for one's general education, cultural enrichment, or even enjoyment). This message must come from parents, since teachers of "peripheral" subjects will have different opinions.

The "Winning Is Everything" Message

Competition in school presents multiple messages that can confuse both adults and children. For gifted children, competition provides special difficulties. Gifted children usually enter school as "winners" and often continue as winners with little effort. Because of their effortless successes, there is little early challenge and they may not easily see the relationship between competitive effort and achievement. However, at some point in their school career—for some gifted children by the second grade, but for others not until college—they discover that they are effortless winners no longer.

If they do not also discover that, with effort, they can again become winners, they may adopt maladaptive coping strategies. For example, they may write themselves off as school "losers" and *mentally* drop out. That is, they may choose sports, the drama club, or mischief as their area of winning, thus competing in nonacademic, noncareer areas. They might also stop competing completely and view themselves as "average kids" who do not need to compete, who do not need to work very hard to "get by." None of these self-messages encourages the gifted child to use his or her superior abilities.

In many cases, students' self-messages are a reflection of their parent's misleading messages. One such message is to "be a winner—and if not at academics, then at sports or something else." This message encourages the gifted child to redirect the efforts from the academic classroom to the gymnasium or athletic field, where the delighted parents can cheer their child's victories. A related and equally misleading message sent by parents is, "If you can't win, you're a loser." This message causes the gifted child to accept his or her losing status as evidence of lack of ability.

Neither message helps children see that there are many levels of winning other than being "Number 1." Also, children and adolescents should learn that using their superior abilities to succeed in school will sooner or later extend their options for important lifetime winning.

Of course, achievement involves excellence, and excellence certainly can be translated by children as "winning." However, if excellence and winning are viewed by parents only as achieving "first place," their children obviously run a high risk of failure. As a consequence, they will come to view their performances that are actually successful as less than adequate, and will continue to search in frustration for areas where they may compete to win *first place*. Alternatively, they may give up the competition entirely. Gifted teenagers, we might note, are overrepresented in the ranks of high school dropouts.

The "Mom (or Dad) Is an Ogre" Message: Parent Rivalry

Even in good marriage relationships, there is often subtle competition between parents for the favor and control of children. The result, frequently, is "ogre games" (described earlier in Chapter 14) in which one parent takes for him or herself the role of "good, kind parent," leaving the spouse the role of disciplinarian—the *ogre* ("It's fine with me if you stay over at Susan's—but your mother doesn't want you to"). Gifted kids easily learn to manipulate this relationship very effectively ("Dad says it's okay, but you won't let me do anything!"). Ackerman (1980), in his recommendations for family therapy, emphasized that a coalition formed between one parent and an adolescent leads to family disequilibrium and heightened stress between the child and the other parent, thus what feels like a healthy parent-child alliance easily makes the other parent into the "ogre."

Of course, parents cannot ignore each other's opinions related to child rearing. However, as in all other components of a marriage, parents must make compromises in what they believe is good parenting, and they must support each other in their decisions. There is no one correct way for bringing up gifted children. However, if there is just one message from educational and clinical research that seems critically important to effective parenting, it is that two parents who show overt mutual respect for each other's opinions and each other's accomplishments provide ideal models for gifted children of both sexes.

What Can Parents Do?

Perhaps we first should accept the inevitable. As parents, we will not do and say what is "right" all of the time, nor do we need such absolute consistency. However, we do need to avoid a pattern of double messages that obviously causes problems for our children.

If the gifted child (or children) in the family are performing well, enjoying the expression of their talents, and growing positively in other ways, it is reasonable to assume that parents are doing their parenting job very well. Again, there is no one right way, but many. However, if the children (1) appear to be under stress, (2) are not achieving well and responsibly, (3) have serious social problems, and/or (4) have unusually difficult family relationships, one should look for a possible family pattern causing the problem. Our list of double messages and half-truths includes some common sources of such problems. When parents can clarify these messages, the results may profoundly help gifted children both in their family relationships and in the classroom.

A comment by one gifted person may be relevant (Krueger, 1978):

> My family has valued education and has strong interests in art, literature, and music. Because we are close, I've tried to emulate my parents. It is by imitating them, rather than from their telling me what to do, that I've developed a passion for learning and a compulsion to work in an organized manner. But I strongly believe that because of their love and affection, my parents gave me the self-esteem which is an essential element in constructive thinking.

COMPETITION AND PRESSURE

Competition encourages and motivates gifted children to perform to the best of their high ability, and the recognition they receive for their successes provides the motivation for continued competition. However, there are some negative side effects of extreme competitiveness. Several of these will be discussed separately.

Stress

The very competitive child may feel under continuous *stress.* Such children may exhibit symptoms of tension such as nail biting, enuresis (bed wetting), extreme sibling rivalry, loss of appetite, irritability, stomach pains, headaches, or nightmares. These problems can complicate children's lives; they also can be highly informative to parents who are aware of the potential meaning of such symptoms. Of course, every normal child exhibits these symptoms occasionally. However, continued or increased symptoms very often can be attributed to competitive stress; they are physical ways of dealing with frustrations and anxieties.

Parents and teachers should try to help the child identify specific stressors, and then restructure tasks and goals to diminish the stress. For example, the parents or teachers of a high school student can help the student decide upon a sensible and tolerable academic load that challenges his or her abilities but is not overwhelming. Extracurricular activities must be made manageable. Younger children also can find themselves under too much pressure, with plenty of homework, music lessons, Little League soccer, and trying hard to excel in all subjects and interests while simultaneously burdened with too many friends who have plenty of ideas of their own.

A subtle source of competitive stress comes from repeated adult praise which comments on being "perfect" or the "best" or the "smartest" or the "most beautiful." Such superlatives may have the impact of creating an unreasonable pressure to be perfect or the best or the most beautiful or the smartest. Adults do not intend to create pressure for children by such comments. To the contrary, their intent is to build confidence. However, if children receive too much attention based on this "first" status, it takes on a value which they may feel pressured to maintain.

Comments from adults which address effort, improvement, perseverance, good thinking, creative problem solving, kindness, sensitivity, talent, and intelligence, and which do not emphasize "best" and "first," will encourage motivation without pressure. Exaggerated praise which uses such terms as *brilliance, genius, smartest, most creative,* or *most talented* promote pressure. Although well intended, such praise may do serious harm.

In some cases children who appear to "not get anything done" also may be feeling stress. The tension may stem more from worries about inadequacy and from work undone than by the actual hard work. Here are two examples:

> Bobby, a gifted fourth-grader, complained of stomach aches which he related to worrying about the difficulty of his mathematics. He said that even while he watched TV and tried not to think about his math, he felt sick to his stomach. It was recommended that Bobby change his study habits and do his math right after school, before watching TV and worrying. The stomach

aches "miraculously" disappeared and Bobby found math to be much simpler than he thought.

Scott, a high school senior, was an exceptional student and a fine athlete. However, during the football and basketball seasons of his junior year, he suddenly began sleeping an inordinate amount (up to 36 hours at a time). All physiological problems were checked and doctors concluded that his unusual sleep was related to stress. The family and school initiated strong efforts to help Scott avoid stress. They recommended that he not be so serious in his activities and that he alert the coach if he needed to leave a game because of sleepiness. Finally, his dad took him on a special vacation to help him have fun and avoid stress. Scott slept during the entire vacation. The problem continued until it was explained to all concerned that their own anxiety levels were exacerbating Scott's anxious state. If they could back off and empower Scott to deal with his own stress by working hard, playing hard, but not expecting perfection then the sleep problems would disappear. They did.

Rimm's Law (1986b) that covers both of these cases states:

Children feel more tension when they are worrying about their work than when they are doing that work.

If parents or teachers cannot identify the source of the stress, professional help from a guidance counselor or a school or clinical psychologist may be required. It is much easier to identify and treat a stress problem early than after it leads to habitual maladaptive coping patterns for the child.

A helpful way to understand the relationship between stress and efficient performance can be demonstrated by the classic *Yerkes-Dodson law* (Hebb, 1972; Figure 17.1). This principle holds that under very low stress (or motivation, or "psychological arousal") people perform inefficiently. As the stress or arousal level increases, efficiency also increases. Performance and efficiency peak at an intermediate level, which will vary somewhat for different persons and for different tasks. As stress continues to increase after that, efficiency decreases until, at extreme tension levels, performance is completely disorganized.

Any reader can relate to this experience. At some time, probably, you studied very hard for an important and difficult examination, one which caused a great deal of stress. On examination day, you anxiously entered the classroom, stared at the examination on your desk, and for at least the first few minutes felt as if you could not recall any but the most simple ideas. Your stomach may have felt tight, and you probably felt hot or cold all over and slightly nauseous. Sometimes, the inability to perform will increase the anxiety and stress still further. Other times, one is able to calm down to a more optimal level of arousal and then perform very well.

Competitive children—and most gifted children are competitive— are more vulnerable to stress. Parents and teachers cannot deliver them

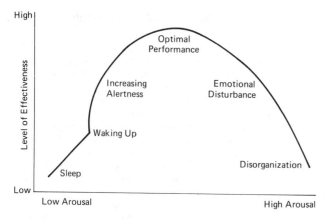

FIGURE 17.1   The Yerkes-Dodson Law Relating Stress (or Arousal) to Level of Effectiveness.

From *Textbook of Psychology*, 3rd. ed. (1972), by D. O. Hebb. Copyright © 1972 by Saunders College Publishing, a division of Holt, Rinehart and Winston Inc., reprinted by permission of the publisher.

from stress, but they can model and teach stress reduction measures. Some simple approaches to dealing with stress include regular physical exercise, recreational and "fun" activities, and especially the availability of a safe and empathic environment where children can talk openly about their pressures and anxieties. A caution, however, is that in providing that safe environment it is important that parents not counteridentify so much with the stress that their own felt anxiety actually increases the anxiety level of the children.

Webb, Meckstroth, and Tolan (1982) recommend using humor to help reduce stress. For example, parents can be melodramatic about their own "intolerable" stresses and problems—making it clear that they are laughing at themselves. Parents can also encourage the child to "think out loud" about stress by gently raising questions such as, "What is the worst thing that could happen in that situation?" and "How big a catastrophe would that be?"

In sum, parents and teachers can best help children deal with stress from competition by (1) identifying the source of the stress and then helping the student redefine priorities to reduce the stress, (2) recognizing that a moderate and manageable amount of stress is necessary for peak performance, (3) helping provide outlets or "therapy" in the form of physical and other enjoyable activities, and (4) lending an understanding, empathic, and perhaps humorous ear. These techniques can be very useful in preventing deterioration of performance due to high stress.

Failure

Gail Sheehy (1982) in her book *Pathfinders* discussed differences among adults in handling their own development crises. In comparing adults who viewed themselves as successful and who led reasonably full-filled lives versus those who saw their lives as filled with frustration and failure, she concluded that the main difference was the way in which they dealt with their *failures.* "Pathfinders," the term she used for the more satisfied persons, experienced just as many failure experiences as did the others; however, they were able to use those failures to grow and move forward. The less fulfilled persons, on the other hand, came to identify themselves as failures and remained in their less-than-satisfactory life positions.

It appears that gifted children, and perhaps all children, establish similar patterns. Children who are high achievers, creative, and success oriented, view their failures and losses as learning experiences (Covington and Beery, 1976). When failure occurs, they identify the problems, remedy the deficiencies, reset their goals, and then grow from the experiences. Failure is only a temporary setback, and they learn to attribute their failure to lack of effort, the unusual difficulty of a task, or perhaps the extraordinary skill of other competitors. As coping strategies, they may laugh at their errors, determine to work harder, and/or redesign their achievement goals. Importantly, they see themselves as falling short of a *goal,* not falling short as *persons.*

Other children, the nonpathfinders, usually take one of two main paths. Some children will persevere in the same direction, disappointed by their performance but determined to achieve that initial goal. If the goal is realistic, the renewed effort and determination may produce a satisfying success and they may feel like "winners" in the competitive game. If the goal is unrealistic, their continued efforts may fail and produce continued frustration and stress.

The other path is even more destructive. With failure, they become *failure oriented* (Covington and Beery, 1976). They come to view school as a competitive game they are incapable of winning, and so they logically decide that there is little purpose in playing. They learn to give up easily and they "get by" with a miminum of effort. The skill deficits increase, and these gifted children become underachievers who have little or no confidence in their ability to successfully compete in the school game.

To help their gifted child cope with failure, parents should first examine their own competitive style; the child may have learned maladaptive responses to failure from one or both parents. For example, parents may model an attitude of quitting too quickly if a problem gets difficult, of avoiding any type of competition, or of habitually blaming external sources for one's own shortcomings or lack of effort. A possible restructuring of parent attitudes and expectancies may, therefore, be the first item on the agenda for helping the gifted child who is not faring well in academic competition.

As another remedy, children may be taught to identify creative alternatives for their losses or failures. For example, they should recognize that normal people—even very talented ones—cannot be "Number 1" in absolutely everything, and that each has compensating areas in which they are quite outstanding. The child need not feel insecure or threatened by an occasional setback. Note, however, that a discussion of a child's failure may need to wait until after the emotional tension is reduced, to avoid defensive behaviors. Parents cannot expect rational perception or logical thinking during the immediate stress period following an upsetting defeat.

A questioning approach, rather than a lecture, may better help the child understand that (1) one cannot always win, (2) disappointment does not mean that he or she is a failure, (3) the particular experience simply was not as successful as he or she had hoped it would be, and especially (4) the central goal is to play the learning game at the student's best performance level, regardless of his or her competitive ranking.

Peripheral diversion.   It is important for parents to send a clear and direct message to their gifted child about the central role that school learning plays in their life. Indeed, if the child is to succeed academically in the way that both capitalizes on all of his or her abilities, and optimally prepares the child for higher education, then the "learning game" should be played above all others. As noted earlier, if parent messages stress that winning—regardless of the game—is all important, then winning at tennis, on the swim team, or in popularity contests may become too critical to the gifted child. A sad sight is unfulfilled adults in their twenties or thirties whose peak life achievement was election to junior class president or being star of the basketball team. Their competitive strivings helped them perform at their best, but in areas we might call peripheral. Of course, high school should not be all drudgery. However, with gifted and talented students who should be aiming at higher education and professional careers, academics should not play second fiddle to socializing or athletics.

Noncompetitive intellectual activities.   Gifted high achievers and gifted underachievers both may be highly competitive and competition conscious. In the case of the high achievers, such competitiveness is functional. For underachievers it is dysfunctional, since they may perceive themselves as "losers" in the school game and therefore stop making an effort to compete.

For both groups, however, involvement in intellectual activities that are noncompetitive can be extremely valuable. Some examples of noncompetitive intellectual activities might include individualized self-paced instruction (for example, at learning centers or with language-learning cassettes), after-school clubs or interest groups, home hobbies or interests such as computers or reading, small-group field trips, independent research projects, or creative arts or writing. For the highly competitive achiever, such activities broaden knowledge and interests, encourage the "reflective pause" necessary for creativity, and provide a comfortable respite from the more highly competitive efforts. For underachievers, noncompetitive intellectual activities entice them into playing the learning/thinking game without fear of failure. To experience the joy of intellectual discovery is a critical goal for all gifted children, and noncompetitive intellectual activities is a good route to this goal.

Sibling Problems

Sibling rivalry seems inherent in Western civilization family structure. It can be minimized and adjusted for, but it will not disappear. The underlying cause of sibling rivalry is competition for parents' attention and, sometimes, resources. With gifted children, particular sibling combinations seem to cause special complications and therefore require special handling by parents and teachers. Several of these will be described shortly.

First, however, it is important to recognize a vital underlying principal for the care and handling of all children: Each and every child in a family should be provided the most ideal opportunity for intellectual and creative development for that particular child. Individual opportunities should not be eliminated because of a misguided democratic commitment to precisely equal treatment for every child. That is, opportunities for gifted children should not be avoided or ignored simply because less able and less interested siblings cannot participate in the same activity. Other children can be offered comparably attractive—but not necessarily identical—educational or recreational opportunities. For example, if one child strongly wishes to attend a Russian-language camp or a Saturday computer class, then an alternative in music, art, swimming or tennis could be offered to a sibling who might feel cheated. Children have different abilities and different needs, and the most productive, and most fair, approach is to accommodate those differences. Treating siblings the same actually exacerbates competition as children vie for recognition of their own individuality (see Inset 17.1).

A subtle source of sibling rivalry may stem from preferential treatment of one child over the other from significant others, for example, grandparents, aunts, uncles, or neighbors. Certainly parents should ask those adults to be cautious and fair to all siblings. Sometimes this is to no avail, and parents will have to take the responsibility of monitoring fair treatment. Grandparents and important adults may continue to provide individual children with special opportunities based on age or particular interests and abilities, but not based on a favored status relationship.

Some typical sibling relationships that cause special problems for gifted children, and some suggestions for dealing with them, are outlined in the following.

INSET 17.1 A CHICKEN RIVALRY STORY

A children's book called *The Most Wonderful Egg in the World,* by Helme Heine (1983), provides a delightful vehicle for parents to deal with differences among siblings and their concerns about being best.

Dotty, Stalky and Plumy are three hens who argue about which is the most beautiful. They visit the king for his judgement. The wise king views all three and announces "What you can do is more important than what you look like" and challenges the three to produce beautiful eggs. To the producer of the most beautiful egg he offers the award of status as princess.

Dotty begins the egg laying contest by producing an egg so white and spotless and perfect that all agree it will not be surpassed. Stalky gains the sympathy of all until she produces the largest egg that any have ever seen. The sympathy is then directed toward Plumy, for surely she will not be able to compete. To everyone's surprise she produces a perfectly square egg which is surely the most unusual. The philosophical king recognizes the merit of the different excellences and awards all three with princess status. They no longer argue and go on producing wonderful eggs forever.

The king's message of the importance of the production (work) rather than appearance is the first critical family communication. Equally valuable, however, is the message that family members can excel in different ways and can all be valued for their talents without one being the "best." That makes it possible for children to understand that they can all be smart without pressure to outdo each other. They can have a "whole-smart family" without putting their brother or sister down so that they can feel smarter. Of course, the concept of many excellences without any one superlative can be generalized to their friends and classmates as well.

The gifted child with less talented siblings.   The gifted child with very high intelligence or an extraordinary special talent provides impossible competition in his or her area of giftedness for other children. The unique ability often requires an investment of an inordinate amount of time and resources to provide the special educational opportunities necessary to develop the talent and meet this child's unconventional needs. In the process, the gifted child naturally receives a large amount of attention and recognition. His or her brothers and sisters need to be able to admire the gifted sibling's success, but also recognize that a similar level of success probably is not attainable for them. They must use a different measuring stick to evaluate their own abilities, or they may fall into the trap of viewing their own real successes (and themselves) as failures. In the words of one successful and gifted "second sibling":

Once I realized that there was nothing I could do to achieve as well as my sister, I decided to stop competing with her, to do the best I could, and to realize that what I was doing was really good too.

Although this youngster came to realize that he could be successful despite his being a "second place" student, that realization was not automatic. In addition to rewarding the victories of their most gifted child, parents also must recognize and reward the success of other siblings— basing those successes on each child's abilities and efforts.

The gifted child in a family of other achieving gifted children. It is not unusual to find that all of the children in a family are gifted; this could be due to genetics, a favorable environment, positive parent and teacher expectations, or, most likely, to all of the above. It is important to recognize that each child in the family will feel increased pressure to fulfill the expectations set by preceding siblings. The first day of school for "child two," "child three," or "child four" inevitably begins with, "Oh yes, I know your sister. She was such a good student!" If the child is gifted and confident, this identification may be pleasing because he or she recognizes that the teacher has expectations that can be fulfilled. Moreover, this early recognition may quickly produce privileges and trust that otherwise would take longer to earn.

On the other hand, a less confident child may see the early identification by the teacher as a threat, since the child may worry that his or her performance may be less adequate than that of the older sibling. A sensitive teacher will quickly learn to recognize differences between siblings. Nonetheless, parents still may need to explain that "Mrs. Jones had Jimmy too, but she'll soon get to know that you're also a good worker, even though you're different than your brother."

Perhaps most important, parents of several gifted children may need to make a specific effort to ease the grade pressure for younger children. Parents should let them know that the parents understand the special pressures the children feel due to the inevitable comparisons with their siblings. The parent's "expectation message" should be that each child is expected to do the very best he or she can, and that the child's performance will be individually evaluated, not compared with the record of the older brother or sister.

The gifted child with a close-age older sibling of lesser ability. Undoubtedly, one of the most difficult relationships exists when a younger gifted child has a brother or sister of average ability (or less) who is older by just one or two years. The most typical tendency is for parents to refrain from providing appropriate enriched opportunities for the gifted child in fear of embarrassing the inevitably insecure older child. For the gifted child, this strategy produces both frustration, from the reduced opportunities for skill development, plus pressure to underarchieve and hide the high ability. The older child, of course, feels the sibling pressure anyway. In many cases, the older child also acquires lower achievement motivation due to the continual assurances that he or she is not really expected to achieve at a high level.

A better approach is to reinforce the gifted child's achievements, even if it means acceleration to the same grade as the older child. (Needless to say, it will be best if the siblings are *not* in the same classroom.) Also, parents absolutely must reinforce the older child's achievements according to that child's efforts and abilities. As the children become mature enough to discuss their differing abilities and the sense of competition they feel, open discussions of their feelings will help them deal with their sense of personal worth despite obvious differences in talent, school grades, and academic recognition.

Some parents will feel an altruistic commitment to "root for the underdog." While it's very American, this attitude can put unpleasant pressure on all children. Especially, the younger high achiever will not receive recognition at home for his or her superior achievements. In extreme cases, he or she may exhibit some of the symptoms of pressure described earlier (nail biting, nightmares, and so on), although he or she will continue to achieve. The less talented older child may become even less motivated to achieve, since he or she can earn more parent attention by not achieving. The child thus may learn to use the nonachieving behavior to manipulate and control the parents' attention.

Regardless of differences in sibling ability, it usually is better to acknowledge achievements and to reward them, relative, as we noted before, to each child's capabilities. Democratically pretending that differences do not exist, witholding important opportunities from the gifted child, or else accepting less than the best efforts from less capable children are common but unproductive responses of parents of gifted and talented children.

Generally, helping parents to deal with their children's competitive feelings—stress, failure, sibling rivalry—is a difficult problem. However, the patterns described in this section are common and recurrent ones, and the recommended solutions have proven effective again and again. The teacher should be aware of the patterns, set to recognize them, and prepared to make good recommendations to parents.

PEER PRESSURE

During early childhood, virtually all children are motivated by a desire to please parents and teachers and to be "good" children. Kohlberg (1974), in fact, titled this period the "good boy, good girl" stage in children's moral development. During these years, there is little peer pressure to distract the child from parental and school goals. Beginning usually in the preadolescent period, grades 4 or 5, however, the normal tendency to conform to peer norms and expectancies begins to exert its influence. The peer pressures become strongest and most influential in the adolescent years.

Adolescence marks the beginning of a crucial development phenomenon, the formation of a perhaps permanent *identity*—a personal knowledge of who and what one is and where one is going in life (Erikson, 1968). The youth who is changing rapidly, both physically and mentally, may have a difficult time during this "identity crisis" period. It is the structured standards of adolescent peers that often provide the needed direction, support, and strength. Close family relationships and good parent models will help to diffuse some of the ambiguity, but the necessary chore of establishing an identity separate from family ties will reduce parental influence during this period—and strengthen peer influence.

While positive relationships with parents typically are not harmful to peer relationships (Montemayor, 1984), reliance on peers for advice and acceptance can be negatively associated with closeness to parents (Kandel and Lesser, 1972). Hill (1980) suggested that continuous bickering with parents seems to propel adolescents to more dependence on and acceptance of peer norms, with rejection of parent norms. The gifted child who previously had taken pride in earning high grades now faces a difficult personal contradiction. The greatest tragedy occurs when the gifted young person mentally drops out of school, literally accepting the peer mandate that "studying is not cool." Maintaining a positive family environment helps gifted children deal with the anti-gifted peer pressure they may feel during adolescence.

> Jon came to the psychological clinic of his own volition. He felt desperately in need of help. As a junior in a highly academic high school he had little confidence that he could do anything about his problem. Although Jon's IQ score was 147, his grades were mainly C's with the exception of one D. He was no longer in accelerated courses. He wanted to go to the University of Wisconsin-Madison but no longer ranked in the top third of his class, an absolute requirement for entrance. He had been a straight A student until sixth grade. When he entered junior high school he decided that he no longer wanted to be known as a "nerd." He looked at his older brothers who were underachievers and decided that they were much more "casual." His two sisters were excellent students but they were known as nerds. He embarked on his new "casual" approach to school. His grades went down to B's at first, and then to C's. He never failed a course and was not worried until he heard about the new college entrance requirements. He then felt it might be too late to again open opportunities for the college of his choice. He may be correct.

Coleman (1961) pointed out that uncomfortable peer pressures will be reduced for scholarly adolescent boys if they can dissipate their brainy image with excellence in sports, and for girls if they have the good fortune to be pretty. Another important qualification for peer acceptance is skill in playing down one's academic ability and excellence, for example, by not using a sophisticated vocabulary, not showing high enthusiasm for high achievement, not carrying too many books at one time, and not mentioning one's large quantity of reading and studying or one's enjoyment of intellectual matters. A gifted student may continue to achieve, however.

As we have mentioned several times, probably the best way to stimulate gifted and talented students, particularly adolescents, is to help assemble a gifted cohort group. Such a group will encourage high achievement and reinforce the full use of one's talents. For example, youth symphony orchestras, high-level Saturday and summer programs in a variety of academic and art areas, special classes, and gifted-peer discussion groups help young people to value their talent and build constructive self-concepts and identities.

It also is important for parents to value and support their children's talent during this precarious period in their development, and to not add to the pressures the child already is feeling, for example, by sending messages stressing high popularity and social success. Parents will actually have to counter peer messages of popularity by pointing out that the emphasis on popularity, as a competitive form of friendship, ends at high school graduation (Rimm, 1988). They will need to point out, subtly if possible, that students who are conscientious about their studies will carry away the best scholarships and will be accepted to first-rate colleges, and that once college begins the stress on popularity is viewed as irrelevant and immature.

Finally, consider two tangentially related thoughts pertaining to peer pressures and the stresses of adolescence: First, if the gifted child has been accelerated, there is a tendency to blame difficulties of the adolescent period on the acceleration practice—"Well, skipping sixth grade just didn't work!" Maybe the acceleration was working, and the child might have been worse off without it. Second, if a gifted child is not achieving up to capacity—due entirely to an unchallenging curriculum—it is not unusual to blame anti-academic peer pressures rather than the educational deficiencies.

PARENT SUPPORT GROUPS

Since gifted children by definition are a minority, in most cases adequate educational opportunities will be provided for them only if there is a vocal and visible support group in the community. If adequate G/T programs are not available, joining or organizing a parent support group should be a top priority for concerned parents of gifted children and for teachers interested in gifted education. A fringe benefit of such visible membership is that parents make a clear statement to their children that education, cultural growth, and challenge are top priorities in family values.

A recommendation by Gina Ginsberg Riggs (1984), Executive Director of the Gifted Child Society of New Jersey, is that if parents "want to earn partner status (in education, they should) leave negative attitudes at home and concentrate on making their education partners (schools) look good at every opportunity." Also, the results of a survey of 1039 parents of gifted children (Gogel, *et al.*, 1985) showed that "parental persistence was the key factor in success in working with schools." Perhaps positive persistence and school advocacy is the best way to describe appropriate parents' roles.

Names and addresses of three national organizations are listed at the end of this chapter. These organizations can direct parents and teachers to state and local groups. They are also a source of information and have publications on giftedness and gifted education.

As a teacher of gifted children, it is critical to recognize the important role of parent groups and parent support. Teachers must not view these parents as threatening, even though they are certain to make their desires known. Parent groups can help educate individual parents regarding the problems and needs of gifted children and the educational opportunities that are—or should be—provided to them. Parent groups can also help organize enrichment activities for gifted children, such as Saturday, summer, or mentor programs. Individual parents themselves may teach special art, music, math, or computer mini-courses (for example, Tkach, 1986, 1987). Parents also can serve as the important volunteer staff—tutoring, transporting, chaperoning—which will extend the opportunities that schools can provide to gifted and talented children.

Parenting gifted and talented children is an important job, and one that teachers can help make more effective.

SOME SPECIAL FAMILY CONCERNS

Apart from our discussion thus far, some other issues related to gifted children in the family must be addressed. Teachers can also be helpful in advising parents in these areas.

Preschool Learning

Parents of very young gifted children frequently ask teachers how they can best help their children before they enter school. It is an important matter, because research evidence clearly demonstrates the strong impact of early environment on language and cognitive development.

For example, White, Kaban, and Attanucci (1979) found in their Harvard Preschool Project that "live language" directed at the child during his or her first three years was the single most critical factor in the child's later competence in cognitive, linguistic, and social areas. Morrow (1983) compared the home environments of 58 kindergarten children showing high interest in reading with the homes of 58 children showing low interest. The high-interest children came from homes with supportive literary environments. That is, the family used the public library, parents did a great deal of reading, and parents read to children frequently; there were more books in the home and, specifically, in the children's bedroom. In a study of the parenting differences between a gifted and nongifted group of middle-class children (Karnes *et al.*, 1984), the clearest difference was in the amount of time spent reading and engaging in academically-related activities with the child.

The evidence provides a clear directive to parents regarding the need for early concentrated involvement with their child for the full development of both the child's language and nonlinguistic abilities.

Language experience is probably the most critical kind of involvement. Talking to the child, reading and telling stories, rhyming and imitation, word games, children's records, and even simply listening to children all increase the children's opportunities to learn communication and attention skills. Puzzles, blocks, and construction toys help them develop small-muscle coordination, spatial abilities, and concentration skill. Large toys (tricycles, wagons, riding horses) help the development of large-muscle coordination. Many games help children learn to follow directions and cooperate. Questioning, curiosity, and independence also should be encouraged.

Moss (1983) compared the maternal teaching strategies of 14 mothers with gifted preschoolers against those of 14 mothers with nongifted children of the same age. The first group of mothers tended to structure problems and then permit their children to derive their own solutions, learning to relate parts of the task to the goal. In the second group, mothers were more directive and actually tended to provide solutions to their children rather than permitting them to arrive at their own solutions. It seems important for gifted children to gain early experience in independent thinking and problem solving.

The following are a few more preschool precautions, some *do*'s and *don't*'s in helping gifted children. First, television watching, which is basically a passive-receptive activity, should be monitored and limited. In the Morrow (1983) study mentioned earlier, the high-interest kindergarten readers came from homes in which there were rules regarding television, and in which mothers watched less television than mothers in the homes of low-interest readers. However, educational programs would be an exception to this policy.

Second, overstimulation, for example, from too many peers or too much adult talk, can confuse children and detract from active involvement, concentration, and learning. While parent communication to the child is desirable, continuous talk and long abstract lectures to children are virtually meaningless, certainly boring, and exceed children's limited attention span. For some children, endless chatter will cause them to become restless and "hyperactive"; they know they should pay attention, but they cannot. For other children, overwhelming talking by a parent has the opposite effect, preventing the child's contributions and encouraging him or her to slow down and become very quiet. They give up trying to communicate with this parent.

Third, if your child is spontaneously reading, teach the child some basic writing skills. A simple workbook that can be purchased from a local department store can be used for teaching the child to copy printing. Exercising that fine motor coordination will help a gifted child feel more evenly skilled in the classroom. Teachers often suggest leaving writing until school, but this unevenness in abilities often causes children anxiety related to their writing skills. Be sure not to pressure the child. Five minutes a day will provide sufficient practice and will help the child feel more comfortable with pencils.

Fourth, some daily "alone time" for a preschool child also is helpful. Interaction with peers and siblings is important to preschoolers, but some small amount of time each day for a child to play alone will encourage independent behavior and imagination. Creative persons of all ages seem to thrive on some amount of time alone.

All four of these precautions can help children very early to take initiative and to be active participants in their environments, rather than to receive stimulation only passively.

Early Identification and Testing

There is good evidence that supports parents' abilities to recognize their children's giftedness early. Table 17.1 (Gogel, *et al.*. 1985) summarizes the identification results of a national survey of 1039 parents of gifted children. Note that 70 percent of these children were identified accurately by parents by age three, most of those between ages one and three. Of the characteristics which caused parents to suspect giftedness, "early verbal expression" was mentioned most frequently. Other observed characteristics included an unusually long attention span, a good memory, high level of curiosity and an early demonstration of original and creative behavior.

The reliability of parents' recognition of preschool giftedness was also supported by a program at Towson State University in Baltimore, Maryland (Hanson, 1984). Parents were encouraged to enroll their children in a program for four, five, and six-year-old gifted children based on their own perceptions of the children's verbal giftedness. After enrollment these chil-

**TABLE 17.1   Percentage of Children
Identified as Gifted at Various
Ages by Parents**

PERCENTAGE	AGE
7	0–6 months
15	6–12 months
23	1–2 years
25	2–3 years
17	4–5 years
13	Later
100	

(From Gogel, *et al.,* 1985, reprinted by permission of the first author and *The Gifted Child Today* magazine.)

dren were given a battery of tests. Ninety percent of the children tested at least one year above grade level in reading and all of the five- and six-year-olds had high scores in the *Fund of Knowledge* subtests. Mathematics scores were not as consistently high, but parents had not been asked to consider math skill in their decision making.

Research certainly does confirm parents' ability to recognize giftedness in their children. Although we have no way of knowing the percentage of children who are missed by a parent identification procedure, at least we can substantiate that parents do not overidentify to the extent that teachers have often believed. In fact, studies indicate that parents usually underestimate rather than overestimate their children's giftedness (Chitwood, 1986).

If parents believe their preschool children are gifted, they might ask when and why it would be good to have them tested. Tests of preschool children are appropriate with the caution that such early tests may be somewhat unreliable. Scores can be adversely affected by many factors, including fatigue, stress, and diet (Perino and Perino, 1981). The scores should not be taken as an absolute measure of the child's ability and certainly not viewed as a limit to that ability. Tests of young children are likely to be conservative estimates of their ability since "test construction makes it virtually impossible to score at a level higher than his or her potential" (Chitwood, 1986). But they can score at a lower level. If parents are considering early entrance to school or entrance to a particular school, preschool testing can help them to make a more informed decision.

Day-Care and Nursery Schools

Day-care and nursery schools for preschool gifted children have become increasingly common as more women seek to combine careers with child rearing. The findings of previously discussed studies of the importance of language stimulation during early childhood seem to recommend a close parent-child relationship during this critical period. A day-care center on a full-time basis cannot substitute for that unique attentional experience, although part-time care may be satisfactory. A high-quality babysitter, who will talk to and interact with the child on a one-to-one basis, is a good alternative for a full-time working mother.

Attending nursery school for two or three half-days per week for a year or two before kindergarten can provide excellent language training and other forms of skill development and educational enrichment for any three- to five-year-old child. Note, however, that (1) the quality of the nursery school, (2) its sensitivity to the needs of very bright children, and (3) its encouragement of language and creative expression would be important considerations in making a selection.

The decision as to whether to place the gifted child in day-care or a nursery school is not an easy "yes" or "no" one. It must be a careful decision based on an examination of the particular needs of the child and the particular alternatives available for that child.

Nontraditional Parenting

Many gifted children are raised in single-parent families or families with other than the two traditional parents. These nontraditional families certainly can cause extra stress for parents and children. However, there are some precautions that can be followed to lessen that stress and enhance the child's adjustment.

Single-parent families.   One estimate is that a full 20 percent of today's children will spend part of their childhood in a single-parent setting. More anxiety and emotional disturbance exist for children in single-parent homes compared to children in homes that have two parents (Henderson, 1981; Hetherington, Cox, and Cox, 1982). However, there also are some positive effects.

In research reported by Cornelius and Yawkey (1985), children in single-parent families tended to have higher imaginativeness scores, had more imaginary companions, used more imaginative talk with their fantasy friends, played more imaginative games alone, and engaged in more imaginative out-of-doors games than those in two-parent families. These results were based on a group of 50 preschoolers aged four and five who were administered a 28-item *Imaginative Predisposition Interview Scale* (Yawkey, 1983). Manosevitz, Prentice, and Wilson (1973) suggested that individual imaginativeness and single-parent families reciprocally nurture each other by reason of the amounts of "empty space" preschoolers have within single-parent families.

An example of the impact of increased attention and stimulation stemming from single parenting comes from a clinical case study.

> Elizabeth was born to a teenage mother of average ability. Her father left the area immediately after he discovered the pregnancy. There was no indication of his having above average ability. Elizabeth's mother felt a great deal of guilt about the out-of-wedlock pregnancy and promised herself she would compensate Elizabeth by almost total attention. Elizabeth received extraordinary amounts of time, attention, talk, and reading to during her preschool years. In third grade her measured IQ score was 155.

Increased stimulation and attention as well as valued alone time for the child in a single-parent family can provide some advantages for giftedness and imagination. However, there are also some risks for these children and some precautions to take. Rimm (1986b) summarized these in Inset 17.2.

Multiple parent families.   When children have multiple parents living in different homes by reason of divorce or remarriage, the challenge of appropriate parenting is certainly extended. There are many books written specifically on the topic, so this brief summary will emphasize only some key risks related to giftedness. Since gifted children by reason of vocabulary and advanced reasoning appear so adultlike, the biggest problem is during a divorce one or both parents will assign them adult roles. That is, they are often treated as confidant, partner, and counselor. Initially they seem to enjoy this new adult status because they feel empowered by it. However, the risks are great. These children feel torn by their loyalty to both parents who no longer like each other. They feel insecure because of the adult responsibility given too early. They easily fall victims to manipulations and learn a manipulative style of relating to both parents. Actually, the mother who confides in her adolescent gifted child in an adult manner during the immediate pre- and post-divorce period is likely to find herself with an unmanageable adolescent. It is almost as if the teenager who has been given adult status refuses to acknowledge the parent's right to parent him or her thereafter. Even during the trauma of divorce, gifted children must reserve the right to remain children, or their social-emotional health will surely suffer. Parents going through divorce should get professional counseling for support rather than depending on their own children at this vulnerable time. Children also should have the opportunity to talk things through with a "safe" person who is not an involved member of the family strife.

SUMMARY

Some parents will deny their child's giftedness; others may exaggerate it.

INSET 17.2 SUGGESTIONS FOR SINGLE PARENTS

As a single parent are you destined to have a problem underachieving child? Of course not, but your job is more difficult. Here are some simple rules to guide you— simple only in that they are few and straightforward. In reality they are terribly difficult for single parents to negotiate. Pat yourself on the back for each successful day. You deserve it. Now the rules:

1. Find a career direction for your life to give you a sense of purpose and to build your self-confidence. Making your children your only purpose gives them power and pressure that will be too stressful for them to manage.
2. Find some adult social outlets for yourself. Don't feel guilty about enjoying yourself as an adult.
3. Find a reliable babysitter or day care center facility for your children. Consistency in care givers and surroundings is very important for young children.
4. Treat your child as a child—not a toy to be played with nor an adult to be depended on. Do not share your bed with your child (except during thunderstorms).
5. Take time (I know you have little) to enjoy your children's achievements and encourage them to take responsibilities.

Now two special rules for single mothers parenting boys.

1. Boys should have an older male to serve them as a model. Find effective role models for your boys—uncles, grandfathers, teachers, Boy Scout leaders may all be helpful to your son in learning to be comfortable with his masculinity.
2. If you do not view your children's natural father as an effective role model, absolutely do not tell your boys how much they look like and remind you of him. Also, avoid power struggles with him. If he mistreats you and shows open disrespect, your son is likely to imitate this powerful but disrespectful behavior.

These rules will sound simplistic to some and impossible to others. They may be difficult for a single parent to live by, but they are effective for parenting your children. Tape them up on your refrigerator.

(From Rimm, 1986b)

With the "Who's in Charge" problem, children are given too much adultlike decision-making power, leading to later conflicts.

Parenting by positive expectations includes expectations of high achievement, good attitudes and constructive behavior, and the minimizing of punishments, double messages, and half-truths.

Counteridentification involves parents who vicariously experience their child's successes and failures. They may criticize, correct, and take over the child's homework and projects ("Let me help you make it better"), leading to feelings of doubt, ambiguity, and low confidence. Children may become perfectionistic and defensive.

There are also many double, inconsistent messages related to grades. Children should be expected to earn the best grades they can. Even with their best efforts, however, teacher biases and other circumstances put grades beyond children's complete control. When low grades occur, G/T children should learn (1) not to close doors entirely on the subject, and/or (2) to look for alternatives: new subjects, new school years that will be better, new teachers, or other career interests.

Gifted children usually have to learn that winning at academics sooner or later will require effort. Some parents send a "Winning Is Everything" message, which may redirect efforts from academics to athletics. Children need to learn that success need not include being "Number 1."

"Ogre games" occur when one parent competes for the child's favor by being the "kind and benevolent" parent and making the other parent the disciplinarian; children then learn to play one parent against the other. Parents should support each other's decisions.

If children show symptoms of stress, underachievement, and/or have social problems, a family pattern of double messages may be the problem. Clarifying the messages for parents will help.

Competitiveness motivates high achievement. However, feelings of competitiveness that are too strong cause stress, perhaps leading to loss of appetite, enuresis, nightmares, irritability, and so forth. Parents should help gifted children and adolescents to identify sources of stress and guide them in making the burdens more manageable. A subtle source of stress may come from exaggerated and too-frequent adult praise which emphasizes superlatives and perfection.

As demonstrated in the Yerkes-Dodson law, an intermediate level of stress (arousal) produces optimal performances; stress beyond that level becomes counterproductive. Recreation, exercise, an empathic environment, and humor can help reduce stress.

Failure may be used as a learning and growing experience (by "pathfinders"), or it may lead to feelings of inadequacy (nonpathfinders). Failure will lead some children to persevere in the same direction, which may or may not produce success. Other children become "failure oriented"; they give up easily or get by with minimal effort. This attitude may be learned from parents.

Noncompetitive intellectual activities, such as individualized learning, clubs, hobbies, field trips, or independent research projects, lead to enjoyable experiences of intellectual discovery without fear of failure.

Sibling rivalry usually is due to competition for parents' attention or resources. One basic recommendation is that each child should receive individualized opportunities for creative and intellectual development; a democratic attitude of treating all children alike is counterproductive. Each child should be evaluated and reinforced for accomplishments relative to his or her own abilities and efforts. Preferential treatment by significant others such as grandparents, aunts, and uncles may exacerbate sibling rivalry.

Peer pressure, combined with adolescent identity formation, severely reduces parental influence. A disdain for academic accomplishment is a common form of peer influence that can lead to underachievement, that is, mentally dropping out. Popularity should be deemphasized by parents and explained as a competitive form of friendship which ends at high school graduation.

The gifted student can learn to downplay his or her "brainy image" but still be a high achiever. The best solution is to help assemble interest groups of gifted peers who support the gifted student's achievement orientation.

Parent support groups can lead to the creation of G/T programs, teach children that parents value education, help educate individual parents, organize enrichment activities, teach mini-courses, and assist with the G/T program.

Preschool learning is critically important for language and cognitive development. Research indicates that habits of reading and skills of independent problem solving also are acquired in the early home environment. Early identification and testing are recommended with the caution that although scores may not be reliable, they may provide guidance for decisions about early school entrance.

Excessive TV watching and parent chattering should be moderated, and some daily time alone is recommended.

A babysitter who talks and interacts with a small child may be preferable to a day-care center. A good nursery school for two or three half-days per week can be immensely valuable. Nontraditional parenting and multiple parent families may provide special problems for gifted children. Research and parenting suggestions are reviewed.

NATIONAL GIFTED AND TALENTED EDUCATIONAL ORGANIZATIONS

Council for Exceptional Children—Talented and Gifted (CEC-TAG), 1920 Association Drive, Reston, Va. 22091

Gifted Advocacy Information Network, Inc. (GAIN), 225 West Orchid Lane, Phoenix, Ariz. 85021

National Association for Gifted Children (NAGC), 4175 Lovell Road, Suite 140, Circle Pines, MN 55014 chapter eighteen

Program
Evaluation

WHY MUST PROGRAMS BE EVALUATED?

Traditionally, the systematic evaluation of gifted programs has been minimal. Developers of such programs typically feel that because they created a program in good faith, it necessarily is "successful"—besides, they prefer to spend their time planning and teaching. A second reason for the reluctance to evaluate is that "success" in teaching gifted and talented students is difficult to assess, compared with evaluating typical remedial or basic skills programs in which achievement test data provide straightforward and valid measures of the most important learning outcomes. Traxler (1987) surveyed 192 school districts having gifted programs. She found that half of these programs were not evaluated at all, and of those evaluated most did not employ trained evaluators. Teacher observation and student products were the most frequently reported measures used in evaluations. A third problem of evaluation is the risk that the evaluation results could threaten the actual program. As Cook (1986) pointed out, in schools "the primacy must be the intervention and not the evaluation." Generally, then, there has been a lack of program evaluation data pertaining to the effectiveness of G/T program components.

Overview

Although gifted programs are more difficult to evaluate than other programs, this evaluation is vital. Gifted programs come and go; the record of continuity is dismal. Therefore, if teachers and program directors hope to maintain or expand their programs, they must be able to demonstrate the success of the program to their administration, to school board members, to parents, and to state or federal funding sources. This is *accountability*. These publics will want to know who is being served by the program, how they are being served, and what beneficial effects the program is having. They also will want to know if the program is cost-effective—if the costs in time, personnel, and resources are producing optimal results. Equally important, teachers and program directors will need information allowing them to revise and improve the program. Beyond creating classroom quizzes or evaluating student papers and projects, teachers and coordinators usually have little training or experience in educational evaluation. This chapter is intended to simplify and clarify the evaluation of G/T programs and guide the teacher or coordinator in the evaluation process.

EVALUATION DESIGN: BEGIN AT THE BEGINNING

Although evaluation is the topic of the last chapter in this book, evaluation of a gifted program belongs at the very *beginning* of program planning. At the outset, when setting goals and objectives for a G/T program, one should design a methodology for measuring whether or not those objectives are reached.

"Difficult" and "Easy" Evaluations

Callahan (1986) set forth some of the difficulties which are unique to evaluations of gifted programs. She pointed out that (1) "no agreed upon standards of good programming exist within the field of gifted education and (2) many of the objectives in programs for the gifted are very complex and not easily defined."

Some examples of *difficult* objectives for evaluation are improvements in leadership, self-awareness, self-concept, decision making, reasoning, analyzing, synthesizing, evaluating, social responsibility, intrinsic motivation, critical thinking, and creative thinking. Other objectives are comparatively *easy* to evaluate. Acceleration programs, for example, provide almost self-evident evaluation data. Did students succeed in the advanced classes, the college courses, or the correpondence courses? Did the grade-skipping or the early admission to kindergarten work well for the students involved? Enrichment plans that result in a bona fide product—a school newspaper, a report of a research project, a poetry book, a dramatic production, artwork, a movie—also provide relatively easy evaluation data. Such products reflect a clear change in student skills and performances that, most likely, would not have occurred without the G/T program (Renzulli and Smith, 1979). Whether objectives are difficult or easy to measure, we nonetheless must try to evaluate every planned objective.

EVALUATION MODELS

There are many models for structuring the evaluation of education programs. Several will be summarized here, in an admittedly oversimplified fashion. In all cases, the intrigued reader will need to explore the more complete, original statements.

Provus's (1972) *discrepancy* model assumes five stages in the creation of a program. At each stage the reality of the program is compared with a standard, and any discrepancy is fed back in order to improve the program by, naturally, correcting the discrepancy. In Stage 1, *Design,* the initial program plan is compared with a set of theory-based design criteria, perhaps as defined by an outside consultant. If there is a discrepancy, the program plan is modified accordingly. In Stage 2, *Installation,* the actual reality of the program as it is implemented is compared with the design adopted in Stage 1. Again, any discrepancies between program design and installation would be used to guide changes. These changes could be in the actual installation or in the Stage 1 design criteria. In Stage 3, *Process,* the actual program activities are compared with the proposed program activities, and any discrepancies will result in corrective alternatives. Stage 3 is especially important for creating an effective, successful program. In Stage 4, *Product,* actual student products are compared with the planned ones. This is the main evaluation of program objectives. Stage 5, *Product Comparison,* involves a comparison of students' products and learning outcomes with those of other programs to determine program efficiency in the cost-benefit sense.

Part of Eash's (1972; see also Renzulli, 1975) *differential evaluation* model involves three considerations in the evaluation process: (1) *Effort*— how time is spent (that is, the program activities); (2) *Effect*—products and outcomes; and (3) *Efficiency*—the relationship of effort and resources to the quality of effects realized. As the program evolves from a newly planned, innovative program (initiatory stage), through the implementation and field testing of the program (developmental stage), to the established and stable level (integrated stage), more emphasis is placed on evaluating effects and efficiency (2 and 3).

The Renzulli and Ward (1969) DESDEG (*Diagnostic and Evaluative*

Scales for Differential Education for the Gifted) model was designed specifically for evaluating programs for gifted and talented students. It also may be used for program planning and development (Renzulli, 1975). DESDEG includes a set of five published documents corresponding to the five parts of the model. Part I is the Manual, which explains everything you ever wanted to know about DESDEG. Part II, Evaluative Scales, includes scales for evaluating each of 15 "ideally conceived educational practices" or Program Requirements, which subdivide into the five Key Features (general areas) in Table 18.1. Part III consists of Basic Information Forms, ". . . a comprehensive inventory of factual information about all aspects of a program . . . organized and keyed . . . to each of the five Key Features. . . ." These aid in the objective collection of data. Part IV is the Evaluator's Workbook, designed to aid the evaluator in handling the information derived from the Basic Information Forms and from observations. Part V is the Summary Report which (1) permits the evaluator to transfer numerical data to statistical and graphic summary sheets, and (2) aids in the creation of a summary narrative related to each Program Requirement.

It can be seen even in these sketchy outlines that the evaluation of education programs, including G/T programs, can be approached from many different viewpoints, use different strategies, and can focus on a variety of dimensions and considerations.

TABLE 18.1 The DESDEG Model

Key Feature A: Philosophy and Objectives
  Program Requirement 1: Existence and Adequacy of a Document
  Program Requirement 2: Application of the Document
Key Feature B: Student Identification and Placement
  Program Requirement 3: Validity of Conception and Adequacy of Procedures
  Program Requirement 4: Appropriateness of Relationship Between Capacity and Curriculum
Key Feature C: The Curriculum
  Program Requirement 5: Relevance of Conception
  Program Requirement 6: Comprehensiveness
  Program Requirement 7: Articulation
  Program Requirement 8: Adequacy of Instructional Facilities
Key Feature D: The Teacher
  Program Requirement 9: Selection
  Program Requirement 10: Training
Key Feature E: Program Organization and Operation
  Program Requirement 11: General Staff Orientation
  Program Requirement 12: Administrative Responsibility and Leadership
  Program Requirement 13: Functional Adequacy of the Organization
  Program Requirement 14: Financial Allocation
  Program Requirement 15: Provision for Evaluation

Joseph S. Renzulli, DESDEG Model. Reprinted by permission.

THE RIMM MODEL

Rimm's (1977) model both (1) structures program evaluation in a relatively easy-to-follow fashion, and (2) ties it to the initial program plan. To begin, summarizing a program in one picture is very helpful for conceptualizing program components and, therefore, for relating evaluation needs to those components (see Figure 18.1). The diagram demonstrates how the different parts of a program fit together and, importantly, how evaluation can help one monitor all educational *Inputs (resources),* all *Processes (activities),* and all *Outcomes (goals and objectives).* Using the model has many advantages. First, it helps us understand the relationships among educational resources, processes, and outcomes. Second, using the model helps prevent the implementation of any activity without considering its eventual *evaluation.* Third, the model helps us become more sensitive to the close rela-

FIGURE 18.1 Framework for the Evaluation and Monitoring of a Gifted Program

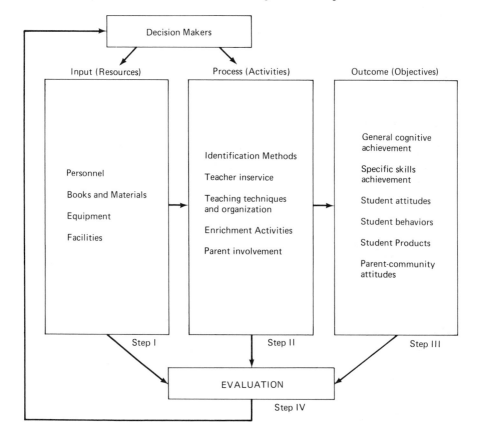

tionship of program decisions to the many student outcomes. Finally, and most importantly, the model itemizes on one page the program components that should be evaluated in regard to both (1) how well the component was implemented, and/or (2) how successfully that component helped achieve program goals.

The components within each of the three steps of the model reflect specific areas that should be evaluated. That is, each of the various types of input/resources (Step I), processes/activities (Step II), and outcomes/objectives (Step III) should be evaluated. Evaluation data (Step IV) from the components will present a comprehensive picture of the success and impact of a gifted program. This information is brought together and fed back to the decision makers who will use it for further planning—for modifying the input and process steps, which may include program expansion. Without the crucial evaluation step, there would be little clear basis for good decisions. Of course, the success of this approach depends heavily on the relevance and the clarity of the evaluation information obtained in Step IV.

The reader may wish to draw a blank framework to outline his or her own program and evaluation model and complete the diagram as this chapter is read.

Step I: *Input* represents resources. Resources typically include such program ingredients as teaching and support personnel, books, materials, equipment, and facilities. Resources may also include more specific categories such as community resource persons, specific student populations, or funding sources. Resources are the investments in the program and they usually are relatively easy to identify and list.

Step II: *Process* includes the activities of the program—everything that is planned to make the program effective. Typical categories of activities include identification procedures, teaching techniques, educational groupings, enrichment experiences, acceleration plans, teacher in-service training, and parent involvement activities. One may wish to itemize more specific curriculum activity components of the program, for example, creative-thinking instruction, creative writing, a computer mini-course, accelerated mathematics, Renzulli's (1977) enrichment triad, and so on. The list of categories of activities should be exhaustive, which means that each and every specific program activity would fit into a process category.

Step III: *Outcome* represents the goals and objectives of the gifted program. It actually may be easier to complete the list for Step III *before* completing Steps I and II. What do you expect to accomplish? What are the purposes of the program? Some ideas for program goals were listed in Chapter 3.

Note that increased academic achievement is not necessarily a central outcome of a gifted program, although it may be an objective for gifted underachievers or, for example, for an accelerated math, biology, or reading program. More frequently, increases in specific *skills* are the intended outcomes of a program, for example, creative, critical, or evaluative think-ing and independent study and research skills. Positive student *attitudes,* including self-concepts, attitudes toward education, and high career aspira-tions, are also frequently stated goals. In addition, scientific, literary, and artistic *products* are important and potentially measurable objectives. Parent and community attitudes toward the program and toward the needs of gifted children are further important outcomes to monitor.

Completing the model by inserting program components into each step should both (1) provide the reader with an overview of the entire program, and (2) assist with planning the necessary evaluations.

EVALUATING THE WRITTEN PLAN VERSUS ACTUAL ACTIVITIES

Outside persons (for example, the principal, members of the school board, the district superintendent, parents) may evaluate the results of a program strictly according to the written program plan, including the statement of philosophy, rationale, and goals (Davis, 1983). This type of evaluation is relatively easy for outsiders to conduct and requires no particular measure-ment skills; the written plans and goals are simply compared with the actual apparent activities and outcomes. The Provus (1972) *discrepancy evaluation* concept mentioned earlier is a similar approach. The outsiders may ask such questions as: Were the identification procedures sensible, effective, and fair? Were the in-service workshops held as scheduled? Were the instruc-tional strategies (grouping, acceleration, enrichment) carried out as planned? Did the planned field trips materialize? Were men-tors/professionals in the community used as planned? Did students really become independent learners, thinkers, creators, and problem solvers? Were skills of analysis, synthesis, evaluation, critical thinking, and divergent thinking really strengthened? Were the evaluation and modification pro-cedures carried out as planned?

Such questions clearly serve as a means of "checking up" on the program and its leaders, and may easily be perceived as threatening. How-ever, the intent typically is constructive.

COMPLEXITY OF EVALUATION AND AUDIENCE: A HIERARCHY

The sophistication of an evaluation will be related to the intended au-dience—the persons who are the decision makers for a particular program. These decision makers can be placed in a *hierarchy* in terms of the quantity and the quality (statistical complexity) of the information they must have to carry out their own responsibilities. The goal should be to provide the appropriate information to match the information needs of these decision makers.

Briefly, (1) students and parents will need less information than (2) teachers and program directors, who in turn need less information than (3) administrators and school board members. (4) The state department of education will require still more technical information; and (5) the federal government, with its nationally selected and highly experienced grant reviewers, will require the greatest amount and the highest technical level of information.

Table 18.2 summarizes the relationship between levels of the decision-making hierarchy, components of the program emphasized, and the persons primarily responsible for the evaluation.

The hierarchy of decision makers is based on the different purposes or uses of the program evaluation information. A student or his or her parents may need to know only if the activity is generally interesting, challenging, motivating, and beneficial in very personal terms in order to decide if the student should continue in the program. A relatively small amount of information is needed for a decision that may have an important impact upon just one student, but no particular impact on the program as a whole. The student and his or her parents, with the help of the program teacher and/or coordinator, can assess the value of the program for that student.

The teacher or program director requires quite a bit more information than students and parents in order to modify, improve, and perhaps expand the program. This function of evaluation is called *formative evaluation.* Conducted throughout the school year, it is intended to provide immediate and continuous feedback to the staff regarding program strengths

TABLE 18.2 Summary of the Relationship Between Hierarchy of Decision Making and Evaluation Plan

HIERARCHY OF DECISION MAKING	MODEL COMPONENT EMPHASIZED	STAFF RESPONSIBILITY
Individual Student or Parent	Individual Process and Outcome	Pupil, Teacher, and/or Parent
Teacher or Program Director	Process and Outcomes	Teacher, Program Director, or Administrator with some background in evaluation or independent evaluator
State or Federal Government	Input, Process, and Outcomes	Independent Evaluator with support of Program Staff

and weaknesses. The emphasis of formative evaluation will be on process (Figure 18.1); that is, on the value of various activities and experiences. Formative evaluation usually is conducted quite effectively by program staff, although observations of an independent (outside) evaluator usually add objectivity, insights, and ideas to the evaluation.

The school principal, district administrators, and members of the elected school board must decide whether to continue, change, or expand the gifted program, and hopefully not to fold it up. To make these kinds of decisions, a *summative evaluation* must be conducted. The emphasis is on *outcomes*, and so a summative evaluation is conducted at the end of a unit, project, or most often, the school year. It "sums up" program success. Administrators and school board members may expect the staff to relate program input to outcomes in order to estimate some kind of cost-effectiveness. A teacher or program director with a small amount of advanced training in evaluation and statistics sometimes can successfully conduct such an evaluation. (However, if you happen to believe that a "*t* test" is intended to compare the flavors of *teas* or is part of a golf game, it is time to call for help.) Board of education members primarily will want to know if a program has been "effective," and so the *how*'s and *why*'s of its effectiveness must be clearly and simply communicated.

Generally, local school people will feel their accountability obligation is met if one can prove that (1) the program was conducted as planned, (2) the students learned what was supposed to be taught, and (3) the process of learning was a positive one.

However, if a program is state or federally funded, a professional summative evaluation conducted by an experienced outside evaluator probably will be necessary. This evaluation typically includes a more technical, experimentally oriented evaluation. The teacher's role then becomes one of *cooperator*. The teacher need only inform the evaluator of the resources, activities, and objectives, and provide him or her with the needed data. Some test administration may be involved. Clear communication with the evaluator and full cooperation in gathering the necessary data will facilitate an accurate evaluation of the program. The outside evaluator should not be considered an adversary who is anxious to pounce on weaknesses. His or her role is to provide constructive feedback to the staff for program improvement, and to objectively report the reasonableness and effectiveness of the program plans, methods, activities, and so forth. Although the objectivity of outside evaluators may appear threatening during early program development, that same objectivity will be extraordinarily reinforcing when a program is stabilized and functioning well.

The outside evaluation may require the use of a *control group* of subjects (for example, students of similar ability in another school district where there is no program). Test scores from such a control group, when compared with scores of students in the program, would help determine if any improvements (for instance, in creativity scores, self-concept development, achievement) are actually due to the program and not due simply to maturation, the passage of time, or other educational experiences. Teacher-coordinators likely will drown in a sea of statistics if they attempt this type of evaluation on their own.

As emphasized earlier, an important first consideration for effective evaluation is outlining the evaluation design at the same time the rest of the program is planned, namely, before the program begins. Even an expert evaluator will be less able to do his or her job if the program begins without coordinating the program objectives with their eventual evaluation. Beginning a G/T program without an evaluation design is comparable to beginning one's classroom teaching without a curriculum plan. In both cases, the preplanning helps outline where you are going, how to get there, and what to do when you arrive.

In summary, no program for the gifted should be conducted without some evaluation. Whether the decision makers are students, parents, teachers, administrators, school board members, or state or federal agencies, they will want to know about the "success" and the particular "effects" of the program.

INSTRUMENT SELECTION

Some form of measurement is almost always necessary to determine the degree to which program objectives have been achieved (for example, those in the *outcome* rectangle of Figure 18.1). Ideally, in order to reach sound conclusions one should try to obtain *two* measurements of each objective, particularly the most important ones. Also, whenever possible one should use instruments—tests, questionnaires, rating forms—already available. To do a proper job of developing one's own instruments requires a considerable amount of time, and usually requires training and experience in test construction.

Besides, with a little digging a teacher-coordinator most likely will discover that the test-building work already has been done. Many instruments for assessing innumerable aspects of G/T programs are available, for example, in Renzulli (1975), Renzulli, Reis, and Smith (1981), Sjogren, Hopkins, and Gooler (1975), and the Association for the Gifted Evaluation Committee (1979).

If the same program plan is conducted in several schools or districts, the evaluation questionnaires may be shared. For example, a sample page from a parent questionnaire for a Revolving Door Identification Model (RDIM) program appears in Appendix 18.1 (Reis, 1984). Reliable and valid student and teacher questionnaires are also available for the evaluation of components of the RDIM program (see Reis, 1984; Renzulli, Reis and Smith, 1981).

For new evaluation ideas, check current journals on gifted education and creativity; they frequently describe instruments that have been recently developed and validated. Some sample instruments appear at the end of this chapter.

Tests with *norms* for different grades are desirable. Such information allows one to more easily interpret and communicate the performance of gifted students compared with students in the norm group.

Although there are indeed many different tests for review, it can happen that an instrument exactly right for a specific purpose will not be found. Do not make the mistake of using an instrument—no matter how carefully designed—that measures something other than what the program plans to teach. It is essential that the *objectives* of the program activities, on one hand, be matched with the *purposes* and the *contents* of the tests and inventories, on the other. If test purposes or contents do not match program objectives and activities, one is not very likely to find a measurable effect of the program. This simple point may seem self-evident to the sensible reader. However, it is a common error for G/T teachers and coordinators to teach one set of contents and skills (for example, creativity), yet evaluate others (for example, advanced reading)—and then be surprised and disappointed to find "no effects" or "no transfer" of the training experience. Importantly, negative evaluation findings can easily be misused; they can readily and logically be interpreted as evidence that the program was ineffective.

Pilot Testing

A program evaluator may need to *pilot* a test, that is, try it out with a few children to help decide if it is appropriate for the desired purpose. For example, suppose a program included accelerated reading or math and the evaluator wanted to determine if a particular norm-referenced test could be used to evaluate student achievement.[1] If the test is administered to two or three students and they "top out" near the maximum possible score, this would immediately signal that the test is not satisfactory. It would not assess the high achievement level of the gifted students. It may be necessary to pilot three or four tests to find an appropriate one. One strategy is to pilot several tests simultaneously with several small groups of students. This quickly provides plenty of information for test comparison and selection.

---

[1]A *norm-referenced* test is one of moderate difficulty that is designed to produce a normal, bell-curve distribution of scores—for example, a standardized achievement test.

Topping Out and Regression Toward the Mean

As discussed earlier in this book, the topping-out phenomenon is a frequent occurrence when gifted students take standardized, norm-referenced achievement tests. The tests often are not difficult enough to discriminate among nor evaluate the learning of high-achieving gifted children. If we measure improvements from pretests to post-tests but students have already achieved ceiling scores on the pretests, it will appear that the students showed no measurable improvement. In fact, there simply was no place for the scores to go. Actual progress could not be measured.

A potentially more serious problem related to using too-easy achievement tests comes from the *regression toward the mean* effect. This simply means that given a first score that is extreme (either very high or very low), by chance alone the next score is likely to "regress" toward the mean. Now if many gifted students score near the very top of a pretest, their scores on the post-test by chance alone are likely to be lower—incorrectly suggesting that participation in the special G/T activities damaged students' learning. For example, with regressed scores on a basic skills test, an audience could conclude that the gifted program is having a negative effect on the basic skills of students. They probably would attribute this damage to students missing instructional time in the regular classroom. Since pulling students out of the regular classroom often is a controversial issue in the first place, such an interpretation could be devastating to an excellent program.

TEST CONSTRUCTION

There are times when a state or federal agency will require evidence for the effectiveness of a program, but the exactly appropriate tests and measures simply do not exist. It therefore may be necessary to construct original tests or questionnaires in order to evaluate specific student skills, information, attitudes, or abilities, the effectiveness of specific program components, or even the overall quality of the total program. Technical help from an evaluation expert at a university or private consulting firm, someone experienced in evaluating G/T programs and in constructing tests, probably will be needed.

To select a consultant, contact directors of other G/T programs and state or even national leaders in gifted education to find who in the area is available and qualified. When a consultant is recommended, one can elicit opinions of his or her work from teachers and program directors for whom the consultant has provided services. One also can ask to review tests and reports the consultant has prepared for other clients.

Competitive bidding can be misleading, since there is a considerable range of quality that fixed evaluation dollars can buy. Also, a poor instrument or evaluation is worse than none at all, even if the cost is lowest. Test construction may be expensive, so be prepared. The high cost of test construction is one very good reason to use established tests, as recommended earlier.

Rating Students' Products

Artistic, literary, scientific, or other types of student prodcuts may be outcomes of a program, and although they are difficult to evaluate reliably, their quality is measurable. Product evaluation usually involves either of two approaches. With the first *gain score* approach, samples of students' work obtained at the outset of the program (pretest products) are compared with students' products at the end of the educational experience (post-test products). Gain scores may be used to evaluate products that reflect the development of such skills and abilities as art, creative writing, divergent thinking, and others.

With the second *absolute* approach, individual students' products are evaluated according to their excellence without an objective comparison with earlier products. The absolute approach would be used if science or other major projects (for example, of the Renzulli Type III variety) are evaluated for which earlier comparison products are not available.

With either the gain score or the absolute method, rating scales may be used to quantify the judgments. As two examples, Renzulli (1975) recommended the scale in Appendix 18.2, developed by the Warwick, Rhode Island, Public Schools, for evaluating the quality of visual arts products. (This art scale includes a "growth" rating, which would make no sense in a pretest. Therefore, if this scale were used to assess gain scores the "growth" item would be omitted from both the pretest and the post-test). The scale in Appendix 4.4, developed by the state of Michigan Department of Education, may be used to evaluate the excellence of virtually any type of student product.

The rating scales in Appendices 18.2 and 4.4 could serve as models for creating one's own product-rating scales. Alternatively, the following steps could be used to develop and apply original rating scales:

Step 1. Determine the evaluation criteria (for example, creativeness, technical skill) and the specific scales for rating those criteria. The criteria should come from the teaching objectives. Note the objectives reflected in each scale in Appendixes 18.2 and 4.4. As for the rating scales themselves, while Appendix 18.2 uses six-point scales, a five-point scale as in Appendix 4.4 usually is most comfortable. It is best to describe the meaning of each point on the scale. The "low," "moderate," and "high" descriptions of Appendix 18.2 and the "To a great extent," "Somewhat," and "To a limited extent" of Appendix 4.4 are very minimal descriptions. For example, a scale for evaluating the use of *humor* in creative writing might be based on the following descriptors:

"1": No use of humor.

"2": One humorous comment, which does not appear original.

"3": Two or three humorous statements or paragraphs, which do not appear original.

"4": Two or three statements or paragraphs that do appear original.

"5": Original humorous themes are skillfully integrated into the entire story.

Such scale-point descriptions will improve the accuracy (reliability) of the raters' ratings.

Step 2. Collect pretest creative products from each child in the program.   All products should be identified with code numbers so that the students' names and the date of collection will not be obvious to the raters.

Step 3. Select at least two raters.   They may be teachers or community members. Train them to use the particular scales with extra products that will not be used as "official" data. After rating several products together, use a few more extra products for the individual raters each to rate separately.

Step 4. Calculate the percentage of rater agreement.   With five-point scales, two raters should agree on at least 80 percent of the practice ratings before they begin rating the pretest and post-test products. If the raters do not agree at an 80-percent level, they need more training, including a discussion of the reasons for their disagreements.

Step 5. After interrater reliability is established, to minimize bias raters should rate all products.   This should be done without knowing the names of the children and without knowing which are pretest products and which are post-test products.

Step 6. Calculate the average pretest ratings for the group and compare them with the average post-test ratings.   If a program is effective, the average post-test rating should be higher, indicating that skill development increased since the pretest products were created. Statistics may be necessary in order to conclude that the overall increase is not due to chance. Also, as noted earlier, a control group may be necessary to prove that the improvement of the trained students was not due to the passage of time or to other educational experiences.

For information regarding the gains (or losses) of individual students, one would examine the differences between pretest and post-test ratings for each student.

Step 7. In reporting the findings, the means (and other statistics, if any) must be meaningful, reliable, and valid. If possible, include a few sample products (for example, samples of creative writing, scientific reports, photos of artwork) to illustrate the student gains. These sample products will help any audience understand the meaning of the ratings.

Classroom Observation Data

Parents, administrators, school board members, and government agencies usually like to know what happens in a gifted program, and so classroom observation data are good data to collect. A structured observation form can be developed for a program and used to describe "who is doing what with whom and when" in a very specific way. As one example, Appendix 18.3 (adapted from Rimm, 1981a) shows a structured observation form used for monitoring a reading program. The letters at the top of each column represent each of the ten students observed. Filling in a circle indicates that a student is involved in one of the activities listed in the rows. An objective observer would enter the classroom at random times of the day and observe ten randomly selected students, recording their activities on the checklist. Descriptive comment may be added to each observation to provide a richer description of the class environment.

A form such as the one in Appendix 18.3 could be adapted for use with any particular G/T program. Category headings could be modified or new ones created; each would have specific subcategories. For example, one might wish to record pupil's interest level, pupil's behavior, pupil's interactions, teacher's instructional activities, materials and equipment in use, or activities of other adults. Additional headings, each with specific subcategories, could be included depending upon the special activities of the program.

If desirable, at the end of the year summary forms can be tabulated and percentages calculated to describe the specific *type* and *extent* of the activities engaged in during that year. This summary provides objective documentation of the year's program activities. Thus if a school board member wanted to know how much time microcomputers were in use, how many students participated in the *Great Books* discussions, or what proportion of the G/T program time was spent in independent projects, exact numbers and percentages would be available to support personal observations and impressions. There is nothing quite so convincing as hard data.

Questionnaires

Activities in both the *process* and *outcomes* components of Rimm's model may be evaluated with questionnaires. While students, teachers, parents, board members, and administrators all find paperwork burdensome, the best way to find answers is to ask questions. Decision makers at all levels will want to know (and have a right to know) the effectiveness and special strengths of a program and its weaknesses as perceived by others. They also are interested in others' constructive suggestions for improving the program. If questionnaires are brief and require only that a few numbers be circled and/or a few questions be answered, most persons will respond. You can bet that those who are strongly enthusiastic and those who are most disappointed or critical will be certain to respond.

Questionnaires use various types of items. Objective items include *checklists, rating scales, rankings,* and *multiple-choice* statements. The advantages of objective items include ease of development, efficiency of administration, clear response options, easy and objective scoring, and ready quantifiability for statistical purposes. Some disadvantages include the limited nature of the response options, along with little or no information about the *reasons* for the judgments.

Because of these disadvantages, many objective questionnaires also include open-ended items. Open-ended items provide an opportunity for students, teachers, parents, principles, and even school board members to voice reasons for their opinions, as well as to contribute suggestions and potential solutions to problems. Information can indeed be rich and valuable. For formative evaluation purposes, open-ended items usually are more valuable than objective items. In the negative column, open-ended items are more time consuming for both respondents and scorers, interpretations may be ambiguous, and the answers are not readily quantifiable.

As examples of combining objective with open-ended questionnaires, Appendix 18.4 presents an example of a brief questionnaire that could be used by teacher participants in an in-service program. Appendix 18.5 shows a questionnaire that allows school board members to evaluate G/T services of a high school. Appendix 18.6 presents a nonobjective open-ended form that students could use to evaluate a learning center.

Generally, it is wise to set aside a few minutes in every program for teachers and students to complete the evaluation forms. If you create the time, persons will fill out the questionnaires on the spot; questionnaires taken home or mailed often are not returned.

DAILY LOGS

As a general principle, *log everything*. Each staff member should keep a notebook handy in which to make brief notes on daily activities. The value of the entries will far outweigh the few minutes invested each day. The kinds of information that could be logged include:

A description of activities
Preparation for the activities
Number of participants
Perceived effectiveness of the activities
Modifications for the future
Any data collected
Any anecdotal material

A personal log kept by each staff member can provide important program documentation serving at least three purposes. First and foremost, it can provide a description of the activities and accomplishments of the students, and therefore of the value of the specific learning activities and projects. Second, it can assure administration and board members that the staff member has indeed made critical contributions to the program. Third, it will serve to remind the teacher of the quantity and quality of his or her own contributions and accomplishments.

STUDENT SELF-EVALUATIONS

Student self-evaluations are important in G/T programs. Primarily, they provide individual students with a clear measure of accomplishment relative to their own goals and objectives. Positive feedback reinforces student motivation and commitment, while objectively documenting their personal progress. For program evaluators, when individual self-evaluations are combined they become important measures of student outcomes, some of which could not be obtained in any other way.

Independent self-monitoring usually can be conducted quite handily by students in junior and senior high school. Younger children also can take responsibility for self-evaluation, with a little help from their teachers. One example of a summative, end-of-the-year student self-evaluation form appears in Appendix 18.7.

PERFORMANCE CONTRACTING

Student *performance contracting* is another vehicle for individual student evaluation. Within the student contract, the teacher and the student spell out:

1. Specific *objectives*, including skills to be learned and final projects and papers to be completed.
2. The *activities* in which the student plans to engage to achieve the objectives.
3. The *deadline* by which the objectives will be completed.

4. The *materials* the student will produce (or collect) in support of his or her attainment of the objectives.

5. The *methods* and *criteria* by which the attainment of the objectives will be evaluated.

The student contract is a "study guide" for both the student and the teacher, as well as the basis for an evaluation and documentation of the student's personal performance. The emphasis of the contract should be on student responsibility, with the teacher as a facilitator. Performance contracts are a type of learning activity that encourages the independence and creativity that most gifted students thrive on. Thus individual student needs are served while providing program evaluation and accountability data.

COMMITMENT TO EVALUATION

Teachers and coordinators in gifted programs are likely to view evaluation as burdensome. Their time always is scarce, and time used for evaluation will be at the expense of time for students. It thus is very tempting simply to avoid evaluation altogether. However, skipping the evaluation process is a short-sighted decision for gifted programs—which, we repeat, have a history of being quickly cut from school, state, and federal budgets. Good evaluation is the only way to determine the most effective way to enhance the education of gifted learners. It also is the only way to prove to program sponsors and decision makers that the program has indeed accomplished its objectives.

SUMMARY

Evaluation in gifted education has been minimal. However, it is important both for demonstrating success to outsiders and for improving the program. Evaluation plans should be made at the outset of program planning.

Some objectives are difficult to evaluate, such as improvements in self-awareness, creativity, reasoning and analyzing, social responsibility, and others. Other outcomes are comparatively easy to assess, such as the success of acceleration or the improved quality of student products. Provus's discrepancy includes five steps: Design, Installation, Process (activities), Product, and Product Comparison. At each step one compares the program reality with a standard and then corrects the discrepancy.

Eash's differential evaluation focuses on three considerations, Effort (activities), Effect (products and outcomes), and Efficiency (the relationships of effort and resources to the quality of the Effects).

Renzulli's DESDEQ model included five steps corresponding to five documents, the Manual, Evaluation Scales, Basic Information Forms, Evaluator's Workbook, and the Summary Report.

Rimm's model structures the program evaluation and ties it to the initial program plan. The three steps of Input (resources), Process (activities), and Outcome (objectives), each with specific subcategories, all may be evaluated.

Increased academic achievement may or may not be a central outcome. Rather, improvements in process skills and attitudes are usual goals of G/T programs.

Audiences form a hierarchy in the quality and quantity of needed evaluation information. Students and parents need relatively little information to decide whether to continue in the program. Teachers and program directors require more information, particularly continuous, formative evaluation for program improvement. Administrators and school board members will require summative information to decide whether to continue or expand the program.

If the program is funded by state or federal sources, their decision makers will require considerable amounts of information, including test scores, some of which will involve statistical comparisons and perhaps control groups.

One should try to obtain two measurements of each important objective. It is usually easier and cheaper to locate already validated tests than to construct your own. It is important to be certain that the test measures the objectives that were the basis of the teaching. Using the wrong tests will produce negative results, creating a bad impression.

Pilot testing is advisable, for example, to cope with the topping-out problem common with gifted students. On a second testing, very high scores may regress toward the mean, creating the appearance that the program damaged, for example, basic skill development.

Ratings of student projects may use the gain-score approach; ratings of preprogram projects are compared with ratings of postprogram projects. With the absolute approach, complex projects are evaluated without a comparison to earlier projects.

In creating original rating scales, one would determine the evaluation criteria, collect pretest products, select and train at least two raters, determine rater agreement, use "blind" ratings," and compare average pretest ratings with average post-test ratings. It is desirable to include sample projects in final reports.

Classroom observation data present objective information regarding "what happens" in a gifted program.

The process (activities) and outcome (objectives) sections of Rimm's model may be evaluated with questionnaires.

Objective questionnaire items (for example, checklists, rating scales, multiple-choice questions) are easily administered and scored. They may be combined with less objective and more time-consuming—but highly imformative—open-ended questions.

Daily logs provide valuable records of activities, preparation, participants, perceived effectiveness, ideas for modifications, and anecdotal information.

Self-evaluations provide positive, motivating feedback to students. They also provide unique program evaluation data.

Performance contracting can be used to individualize instruction and to document student accomplishments.

Good evaluation is absolutely essential for program continuity and program improvement.

Revolving Door Tag Program Parent Questionnaire

Directions: Please do not sign your name to this questionnaire. No attempt will be made to identify persons completing these forms. Please return the questionnaire in the enclosed envelope within the next two or three days.

You can help to make our program better by giving careful thought to each of the questions that follow. Because of the relatively small number of persons involved in the project, each person's opinion will weigh heavily in analyzing the results. We appreciate your cooperation and assistance in helping us to evaluate this program. We suggest that you read through the entire questionnaire before you begin to answer the questions.

	YES	NO
1. Did you attend the meeting held earlier this year at which we explained the Revolving Door Tag Program?	___	___
2. Do you feel that you have been provided with enough information about the Revolving Door Identification Model in general?	___	___
3. Are you familiar with the procedures for revolving a student into the resource room?	___	___
4. Has your child been revolved into the resource room this year?	___	___
5. If the answer to Question No. 4 is yes, are you familiar with the project or topic that your child worked on while in the resource room?	___	___
6. Are you familiar with the procedures for revolving a student out of the resource room?	___	___
7. Are you familiar with a procedure we use in the TAG Program called "Curriculum Compacting"?	___	___
8. Have you been invited to visit the resource room?	___	___
9. Do you feel that you have been offered sufficient opportunity to contact the school or make an appointment to discuss your child's work in the TAG Program?	___	___
10. Has your child encountered any problems with his/her friends as a result of being involved in the TAG Program? If yes, please explain.	___	___
11. Has your child encountered any problems as a result of leaving the regular classroom to participate in the TAG resource room? If yes, please explain.	___	___
12. Has your child expressed a concern about missing work in the regular classroom or making-up assignments because he or she is out of the classroom to attend the TAG resource room?	___	___
13. Have you had any communication with your child's classroom teacher about his/her participation in the TAG Program? If yes, please describe.	___	___

APPENDIX 18.2 PROJECT GIFTED: EVALUATION SCALE FOR VISUAL ARTS

Code No. _____ Age _____ Boy/Girl _____ TOTAL SCORE _____

Evaluator _____ Position _____ Date _____

Elements	Low		Moderate		High	
	1	2	3	4	5	6
1. Creative Expression, Imagination, Uniqueness						
2. Flexibility, Appreciation, and Adaptability to Various Media						
3. Fluency, Variety or Number of Ideas						
4. Sensitivity-Composition-Design						
5. Manipulative Skills: Construction, Weaving, etc.						
6. Growth						
Column Total						
Weight	1	2	3	4	5	6
Weighted Column Total						
TOTAL SCORE						

J. S. Renzulli, *An Evaluation of Project Gifted.* Storrs, University of Connecticut, 1973. Reprinted by permission.

APPENDIX 18.3 EXAMPLE OF A STRUCTURED OBSERVATION FORM

Date _____   a.m. _____   p.m. _____   Observer _____

1. Pupil's Location

	abc	def	ghij
Desk or table	000	000	0000
Carrel	000	000	0000
Open area	000	000	0000
Materials center	000	000	0000
Other (specify):	000	000	0000

2. Instructional Content

	abc	def	ghij
Readiness	000	000	0000
Decoding skills	000	000	0000
Comprehension	000	000	0000
Enjoyment or appreciation	000	000	0000
Vocabulary	000	000	0000
Spelling	000	000	0000
Grammar	000	000	0000
Composition	000	000	0000
Oral expression	000	000	0000
School library usage	000	000	0000
Speed reading	000	000	0000
Dictionary skills	000	000	0000
Other (specify):	000	000	0000

3. Pupil's Instructional Grouping

	abc	def	ghij
Whole-class group instruction	000	000	0000
Partial-class group instruction	000	000	0000
Tutorial (one to one) instruction	000	000	0000
Independent work on individually-assigned activity	000	000	0000
Independent work on a group-assigned activity	000	000	0000
Shared work on group-assigned activity	000	000	0000
Shifting group patterns	000	000	0000

4. Instructional and Audiovisual Materials and Equipment in Use

5. Pupil's Behavior

6. Person Relating to Pupil

7. Person's Instructional Role

S. Rimm, "Evaluation of gifted programs—as easy as ABC." In R. E. Clasen et al. (eds.), *Programming for the Gifted, Talented, and Creative* (Madison: University of Wisconsin, 1981).

APPENDIX 18.4 EVALUATION FORM FOR IN-SERVICE WORKSHOPS

Workshop Title: _____CREATIVITY IN THE CLASSROOM_____

Circle the appropriate numbers below.

1. I found this program to be . . .

1	2	3	4	5
Dull		Of average Interest		Very Interesting

2. I think that what I learned today will be . . .

1	2	3	4	5
Useless		Somewhat Useful		Very Useful

3. I would like to have more inservice programs on this topic.

1	2	3	4
No, not at all	Yes, but not for a while	Yes, more this year	Other (Explain Below):

   Explanation: _____

   _____

   _____

4. The things I liked most about this inservice were: _____

   _____

   _____

   _____

5. The things I liked least about this inservice were: _____

   _____

   _____

   _____

APPENDIX 18.5 SCHOOL BOARD QUESTIONNAIRE

We suggest you read the questionnaire before you start to answer.

Please indicate the extent to which you agree or disagree with each of the following statements by circling the appropriate letter. The letters mean the following:

> SA — Strongly agree
> A — Generally agree
> U — Undecided
> D — Generally disagree
> SD — Strongly disagree

Please use the comment line if you want to explain your answer. Answer question 9 only if you have children in the high school.

1. School E High School provides a well-balanced educational program.   SA A U D SD

   Comment _____

2. This school has a good program·for able students.   SA A U D SD

   Comment _____

3. Most parents feel School E is a good school.   SA A U D SD

   Comment _____

4. The School E program is mainly for the college-bound student.   SA A U D SD

   Comment _____

5. Students at School E are receiving a good education in the basics like math, English, history, science.   SA A U D SD

   Comment _____

6. There are too many frills in the School E program.   SA A U D SD

   Comment _____

7. School E has a good extra-curricular program, i.e., athletics, music, school paper, drama, clubs, etc.   SA A U D SD

   Comment _____

8. School E should have more vocational courses.   SA A U D SD

   Comment _____

9. Most of the teachers our child has had at School E have done a good job.   SA A U D SD

   Comment _____

D. Sjogren, T. Hopkins, & D. Gooler, *Evaluation Plans and Instruments: Illustrative Cases of Gifted Program Evaluation Techniques.* Center for Instructional Research and Curriculum Evaluation, Urbana-Champaign: University of Illinois. Reprinted by permission.

APPENDIX 18.6 STUDENT EVALUATION: LEARNING CENTER PROGRAM

STUDENT EVALUATION
LEARNING CENTER PROGRAM

For the past sixteen weeks you have been attending sessions at the
_____ County Learning Center. We would like to know some
of your feelings about the program. By answering questions and
completing the following sentences, you can help us in improving
the program.

1. Which class did you like best? _____

2. Why? _____

3. Of the classes I was not in, I wish I could have taken _____

   _____

4. Why? _____

5. I wish my classes at the Learning Center were longer _____ ,

   shorter _____ , the same _____ (check one).

6. The Learning Center needs more _____

7. The class in which I learned or accomplished most was _____

   _____

8. If I could change three things about the Learning Center, I would

   a. _____

   b. _____

   c. _____

9. Has the Learning Center helped you in any way with things you do

   at school? _____

10. How? _____

11. Has the Learning Center helped you in any way with things you do

    at home? _____

12. How? _____

13. Has the Learning Center helped in any way with the way you get

    along with or feel about people? _____ . If so, how? ___

    _____

From *Florida's State Resource Manual for Gifted Child Education.* State of Florida Department
of Education, 1973. Reprinted by permission.

APPENDIX 18.7 PUPIL SELF-EVALUATION

STUDENT EVALUATION
LEARNING CENTER PROGRAM

For the past sixteen weeks you have been attending sessions at the
_____ County Learning Center. We would like to know some
of your feelings about the program. By answering questions and
completing the following sentences, you can help us in improving
the program.

1. Which class did you like best? _____

2. Why? _____

3. Of the classes I was not in, I wish I could have taken _____

   _____

4. Why? _____

5. I wish my classes at the Learning Center were longer _____,

   shorter _____, the same _____ (check one).

6. The Learning Center needs more _____

7. The class in which I learned or accomplished most was _____

   _____

8. If I could change three things about the Learning Center, I would

   a. _____

   b. _____

   c. _____

9. Has the Learning Center helped you in any way with things you do

   at school? _____

10. How? _____

11. Has the Learning Center helped you in any way with things you do

    at home? _____

12. How? _____

13. Has the Learning Center helped in any way with the way you get

    along with or feel about people? _____. If so, how? ___

    _____

R. E. Simpson, & R. A. Martinson, *Educational Program for Gifted Pupils.* Sacramento, Calif.:
California State Department of Education, 1961. Reprinted by permission.

References

ACKERMAN, N. J. (1980). The family with adolescents. In E. A. Carter & M. McGildrich (Eds.). *The family life cycle: A framework for family therapy.* New York: Gardner.

ADAMS, M. (1971). The compassion trap. In V. Gomick & B. K. Moran (Eds.), *Woman in sexist society: Studies in power and powerlessness.* New York: New American Library.

ADAMS, M. (1981). *Attribution theory and gifted females.* Presented at the CEC-TAG National Topical Conference on the Gifted and Talented Child, Orlando, FL.

ADDISON, L. (1981, December). Attribution theory and gifted females. Presented at the CEC-TAG National Topical Conference on the Gifted and Talented Child, Orlando, FL.

ALBERT, R. S. (1975). Toward a behavioral definition of genius. *American Psychologist, 30,* 140–151.

ALLAIN, V. A. (1979). Sexism in education. In T. C. Hunt (Ed.), *Society, culture, and schools: The American approach.* Garrett Park, MD: Garret Park Press.

ALLAIN, V. A. (1981). Women in education: The future. *Educational Horizons, 60,* 52–56.

ALLEN, M. S. (1962). *Morphological creativity.* Englewood Cliffs, NJ: Prentice-Hall.

ALLEN, R. R., KAUFFELD, F. J., & O'BRIEN, W. R. A. (1968). *Semiprogrammed introduction to verbal argument,* Parts 1–4. Madison, WI: Wisconsin Research and Development Center for Cognitive Learning.

ALLEN, R. R., & ROTT, R. K. (1969). *The nature of critical thinking.* Theoretical Paper No. 20. Madison, WI: University of Wisconsin, Wisconsin Research and Development Center for Cognitive Learning.

ALMQUIST, E. M., & ANGRIST, S. (1971). Role model influences in college women's career aspirations. *Merrill-Palmer Quarterly, 17,* 263–279.

ALPER, T. G. (1974). Achievement motivation in college women: A now-you-see-it-now-you-don't phenomenon. *American Psychologist, 29,* 194–203.

ALTMAN, S. L., & GROSSMAN, F. K. (1977). Women's career plans and maternal employment. *Psychology of Women Quarterly, 1*, 365–376.

ANDERSON, C., & HALLER, J. (1975). *Brain stretchers*. Book 1. Pacific Grove, CA: Midwest Publications.

ANDERSON, R. S. (1975). *Education in Japan: A century of modern development*. Washington, DC: U.S. Government Printing Office.

ANONYMOUS (1976). More divorce and less salary for women science Ph.D.'s. *New Scientist, 69*, 130.

ARMSTRONG, J. M. (1980). *Achievement and participation of women in mathematics: An overview*. Education Commission of the States. Denver, Colorado (ERIC Document Reproduction Service No. Ed 184878).

ARONSON, E., BLANEY, N., SIKES, J., STEPHAN, C., & SNAPP, M. (1975). Busing and racial tension: The jigsaw route to learning and liking. *Psychology Today, 8*(9), 43–50.

ARTHUR, G. (1950). *The Arthur adaptation of the Leiter International Performance Scale*. Chicago, IL: Stoelting.

Association for the Gifted Evaluation Committee. (1979). *Sample instruments for the evaluation of programs for the gifted and talented*. Storrs, CT: University of Connecticut.

ATKINSON, J. W. (1958). *Motives in fantasy, action, and society: A method of assessment and study*. New York: Van Nostrand.

ATKINSON, J. W. (1974). The mainsprings of achievement-oriented activity. In G. A. Davis & T. F. Warren (Eds.), *Psychology of education: New looks*. Lexington, MA: D. C. Heath.

BAGLEY, M. T., & HESS, K. K. (1984). *200 ways of using imagery in the classroom*. New York: Trillium Press.

BALDWIN, A. Y. (1977). *Baldwin identification matrix inservice kit for the identification of gifted and talented students*. East Aurora, NY: DOK Publishers.

BALDWIN, A. Y. (1978). The Baldwin identification matrix. In A. Y. Baldwin, G. H. Gear & L. J. Lucito (Eds.), *Educational planning for the gifted: Overcoming cultural, geographic, and socioeconomic barriers*. Reston, VA: Council for Exceptional Children.

BALDIN, A. Y. (1984). *The Baldwin Identification Matrix 2 for identification of the gifted and talented: A handbook for its use*. New York: Trillium Press.

BANDURA, A., & WALTERS, R. H. (1963). *Social learning and personality development*. New York: Holt.

BANKS, W. (1979). *Teaching strategies for ethnic studies*. (2nd Ed.). Boston: Allyn & Bacon.

BARATZ, J. C. (1974). Teaching reading in an urban negro school system. In G. A. Davis & T. F. Warren (Eds.), *Psychology of education: New looks*. Lexington, MA: D. C. Heath.

BARDWICK, J. M. (1971). *Psychology of women*. New York: Harper & Row.

BARELL, J. (1984). Reflective thinking and education for the gifted. *Roeper Review, 6*, 194–196.

BARRON, F. (1969). *Creative person and creative process*. New York: Holt.

BARRON, F. (1978). An eye more fantastical. In G. A. Davis & J. A. Scott (Eds.), *Training creative thinking*. Huntington, NY: Krieger.

BAUM, M. K., & KROPF, C. A. (1979). Psychological tests used with blind and visually handicapped persons. *School Psychology Digest, 8*, 257–270.

BAUMAN, S. (1984). Meeting the needs of learning disabled gifted students. *Roeper Review, 7*(1), 16–19.

BEE, H. (Ed.). (1974). *Social issues in developmental psychology*. New York: Harper & Row.

BEM, S. L. (1974). The measurement of psychological androgyny. *Journal of Consulting and Clinical Psychology, 42*, 155–162.

BENBOW, C. P. (1976). SMPY's model for teaching mathematically precocious students. In J. S. Renzulli (Ed.), *Systems and models for developing programs for the gifted and talented*. Mansfield Center, CT: Creative Learning Press.

BENBOW, C. P., & STANLEY, J. C. (1980). Sex differences in mathematical ability: Fact or artifact? *Science, 210*, 1262–1264.

BENBOW, C. P., & STANLEY, J. C. (1981). Mathematical ability: Is sex a factor? *Science, 212*, 4491.

BENBOW, C. P., & STANLEY, J. C. (1982). Intellectually talented boys and girls: Educational profiles. *Gifted Child Quarterly, 26*, 82–88.

BENBOW, C. P., & STANLEY, J. C. (1983a). Constructing educational bridges between high school and college. *Gifted Child Quarterly, 27,* 111–113.

BENBOW, C. P., & STANLEY, J. C. (1983b). Sex difference in mathematical reasoning ability: More facts. *Science, 222,* 1029–1031.

BERLINER, D. C., & ROSENSHINE, B. (1977). The acquisition of knowledge in the classroom. In R. C. Anderson, R. J. Spiro, & W. E. Montague (Eds.), *Schooling and the acquisition of knowledge.* Hillsdale, NJ: Erlbaum.

BERNAL, E. M. (1978, February). Alternative avenues of assessment of culturally different gifted. Speech presented to the Department of Educational Psychology, University of Georgia.

BERNAL, E. M. (1979). The education of the culturally different gifted. In A. H. Passow (Ed.), *The gifted and the talented.* Chicago, IL: National Society of the Study of Education.

BERNARD, J. (1972). *The future of marriage.* New York: Bantam.

BERNDT, D. J., KAISER G. F., & VAN AALST, F. (1982). Depression and self-actualization in gifted adolescents. *Journal of Clinical Psychology, 38,* 142–150.

BESTOR, A. E. (1953). *Educational wastelands.* Urbana, IL: University of Illinois Press.

BETTS, G. (1985a). *Autonomous Learner model: For the gifted and talented.* Greeley, CO; Autonomous Learning Publications and Specialists.

BETTS, G., & KNAPP, J. (1981). *Autonomous learning and the gifted: A secondary model.* In A. Arnold (Ed.), Secondary programs for the gifted. Ventura, CA: Office of the Ventura Superintendent of Schools.

BINET, A., & SIMON, T. (1905a). Methodes nouvelles pour le diagnostic du niveau intellectuel des anormaux. *L'Année Psychologique, 11,* 191–244.

BINET, A., & SIMON, T. (1905b). Sur la nécessité d'établir un diagnostic scientific des états inférierurs de l'intelligence. *L'Année Psychologique, 11,* 163–190.

BIRCH, J. W. (1954). Early school admission for mentally advanced children. *Exceptional Children, 21*(3), 84–87.

BIRNBAUM, J. A. (1975). Life patterns and self-esteem in gifted family-oriented and career-committed women. In M. T. Mednick, S. S. Tangri, & L. W. Hoffman (Eds.), *Women and achievement: Social and motivational analyses.* New York: Halsted Press.

BLACK, H., & BLACK, S. (1984). *Building thinking skills.* Pacific Grove, CA: Midwest Publications.

BLANTON, M. (1982, September/October). Blooms' taxonomy revisited. *G/C/T,* p. 22.

BLOCK, J. H. (1976). Issues, problems, and pitfalls in assessing sex differences. *Merrill-Palmer Quarterly, 22,* 283–308).

BLOOM, B. S. (1964). *Stability and change in human characteristics.* New York: John Wiley.

BLOOM, B. S. (1977). Affective outcomes of school learning. *Phi Delta Kappan, 59,* 193–198.

BLOOM, B. S. (1981). *The limits of learning.* Presented at the CEC-TAG National Topical Conference on the Gifted and Talented Child, Orlando, FL.

BLOOM, B. S. (1985). *Developing talent in young people.* New York: Ballantine Books.

BLOOM, B. S. (Ed.). (1974). *Taxonomy of educational objectives.* New York: McKay.

BLOOM, B. S., & SOSNIAK, L. A. (1981). Talent development vs. schooling. *Educational leadership, 39,* 86–94.

BLOOM, B. S., ENGLEHART, M. D., FURST, E. J., HILL, W. H., & KRATHWOHL, D. R. (1956). *Taxonomy of educational objectives, handbook I: Cognitive domain.* New York: Longmans Green.

BRANDON, P. R., NEWTON, B. J., & HAMMOND, O. W. (1987). Children's mathematics achievement in Hawaii: Sex differences favoring girls. *American Educational Research Journal, 24*(3), 437–461.

BRIDGEMENT, B., & BURBACH, H. (1976). Effects of black and white peer models on academic expectations and actual performance of fifth-grade students. *Journal of Experimental Education, 45,* 9–12.

BRODY, L., & FOX, L. H. An accelerative intervention program for mathematically gifted girls. In L. H. Fox, L. Brody, & D. Tobin (Eds.), *Women and the mathematical mystique.* Baltimore, MD: Johns Hopkins University Press.

BRODY, L., & BENBOW, C. P. (1987). Accelerative strategies: How effective are they for the gifted? *Gifted Child Quarterly, 31,* 105–110.

BRONFENBRENNER, U. (1974). Developmental research and public policy and the ecology of childhood. *Child Development, 45,* 1–5.

BRONSON, F. H., & DESJARDINS, C. (1968). Aggression in adult mice: Modification by neonatal injection of gonadal hormones. *Science, 161,* 705–706.

BROPHY, J. E. (1982, April). Research on the self-fulfilling prophecy and teacher expectations. Presented at the American Educational Research Association, New York.

BROWN, S. W. (1984). The use of WISC-R subtest scatter in the identification of intellectually gifted handicapped children: An inappropriate task? *Roeper Review, 7*(1).

BRUCE, P. (1974). Reactions of preadolescent girls to science tasks. *Journal of Psychology, 86,* 303–308.

BRUCH, C. B., & CURRY, J. A. (1978). Personal Learnings: A current synthesis on the culturally different gifted. *Gifted Child Quarterly, 22,* 313–321.

BRUININKS, V. L. (1978). Peer status and personality characteristics of learning disabled and nondisabled students. *Journal of Learning Disabilities, 11,* 484–489.

BRYAN, T. (1978). Social relationships and verbal interactions of learning disabled children. *Journal of Learning Disabilities, 2,* 107–115.

BUDMEN, K. O. (1967). What do you think, Teacher? Critical thinking, a partnership in learning. *Peabody Journal of Education, 45,* 2–5.

BUESCHER, T. M. (1987). Counseling gifted adolescents: A curriculum model for students, parents, and professionals. *Gifted Child Quarterly, 31,* 90–94.

BUFFERY, A. W. H., & GRAY, J. A. (1972). Sex differences in the development of spatial and linguistic skills. In C. Ounsted & D. C. Taylor (Eds.), *General Differences: Their ontogeny and significance.* Baltimore, MD: Williams & Wilkins.

BURK, E. A. (1980). *Relationship of temperamental traits to achievement and adjustment in gifted children.* Ann Arbor, MI: University Microfilms International.

BUROS, O. K. (1982). *Mental measurements yearbook.* Highland Park, NJ: Gryphon Press.

BURTON, N. W., & JONES, L. V. (1982). Recent trends in achievement levels of black and white youth. *Educational Researcher, 10,* 10–14.

BURTON, T. A., & HIRSHOREN, A. (1979). Some further thoughts and clarification on the education of severely and profoundly retarded children. *Exceptional Children, 45,* 618–625.

CALLAHAN, C. M. (1979). The gifted and talented woman. In A. H. Passow (Ed.), *The gifted and the talented.* Chicago: National Society for the Study of Education.

CALLAHAN, C. M. (1986). Asking the right questions: The central issue in evaluating programs for the gifted and talented. *Gifted Child Quarterly, 30*(1), 38–42.

CARELLI, A. O. (1981). Creative dramatics for the gifted: A multi-disciplinary approach. *Roeper Review, 5*(2), 29–31.

CARELLI, A. O. (1982, Nov./Dec.) Sex equity and the gifted. *G/C/T,* pp. 2–7.

CARLSMITH, L. (1964). Effect of early father absence on scholastic aptitude. *Harvard Educational Review, 34,* 3–21.

CASSERLY, P. L. (1979). Helping able young women take math and science seriously in school. In N. Colangelo & R. T. Zaffrann (Eds.), *New voices in counseling the gifted.* Dubuque, IA: Kendall/Hunt.

CASSIDY, J., & JOHNSON, N. (1986, November/December). Federal and state definitions of giftedness: Then and now. *Gifted Child Today,* 15–21.

CHAMBERS, J. A., BARRON, F., & SPRECHER, J. W. (1980). Identifying gifted Mexican-American students. *Gifted Child Quarterly, 24,* 123–128.

CHISHOLM, S. (1978, November/December). Address at the National Forum on the Culturally Disadvantaged Gifted Youth. *G/C/T,* 2–4, 40–41.

CHITWOOD, D. G. (1986). Guiding parents seeking testing. *Roeper Review, 8*(3), 177–179.

CLANCE, P. R., & IMES, S. A. (1978). The imposter phenomenon in high achieving women: Dynamics and therapeutic intervention. *Psychotherapy: Theory, Research and Practice, 15*(3), 241–245.

CLARK, B. (1983). *Growing up gifted* (2nd ed.). Columbus, OH: Charles E. Merrill.

CLASEN, D. R. (1982). *Meeting the rage to know: College for kids, an innovative enrichment program for gifted elementary children.* (Unpublished report), Madison, WI: University of Wisconsin, Department of Educational Psychology.

CLASEN, R. E., & ROBINSON, B. (Eds.). (1979). *Simple gifts.* Madison, WI: University of Wisconsin-Extension.

CLIFFORD, M. M. (1981). *Practicing educational psychology.* Boston: Houghton Mifflin, 1981.

COHN, S. J. (1981). What is giftedness? A multidimensional approach. In A. H. Kramer (Ed.), *Gifted children: Challenging their potential.* New York: Trillium Press.

COHN, S. J. (1983a). Talent searches: A national and international effort. *Chronical of Academic and Artistic Precocity, 2,* 1–3.

COHN, S. J. (1983b). *Summer classes sponsored by the Project for the Study of Academic Precocity.* Tempe, AZ: Arizona State University, Department of Special Education.

COLANGELO, N., & KELLY, K. R. (1983). A study of student, parent, and teacher attitudes toward gifted programs and gifted students. *Gifted Child Quarterly, 27,* 107–110.

COLE, J. R., & ZUCKERMAN, H. (1987, June). Motherhood and science do mix. *Psychology Today,* 57.

COLEMAN, J. M., & FULTS, B. A. (1982). Self-concept and the gifted classroom: The role of social comparisons. *Gifted Child Quarterly, 26,* 116–120.

COLEMAN, J. S. (1961). *The adolescent society.* New York: The Free Press.

COLEMAN, J. S. (1981, April). *Public and private schools.* Invited address to the American Educational Research Association, Los Angeles, CA.

CONNER, R. S., LEVINE, S., & WERTHEIM, G. S. (1969). Hormonal determinants of aggressive behavior. *Annals of the New York Academy of Science, 159,* 760–776.

COOK, T. D. (1986). Using evaluation and research theory to improve programs in applied settings: An interview with Thomas D. Cook by Thomas M. Buescher. *Journal for the Education of the Gifted, 9*(3), 169–179.

COOLEY, D., CHAUVIN, J. C., & KARNES, F. A. (1984). Gifted females: A comparison of attitudes by male and female teachers. *Roeper Review,* 6(3) 164–167.

CORNELIUS, G. M., & YAWKEY, T. D. (1985). Imaginativeness in preschoolers and single parent families. *The Journal of Creative Behavior, 19,* 56–66.

COSER, R. L., & ROKOFF, G. (1971). Women in the occupational world: Social disrup-tion and conflict. *Social Problems, 18,* 535–554.

COSTA, A. L. (1984). Thinking: How do we know students are getting better at it? *Roeper Review, 6,* 191–193.

COSTA, A. L. (1986). Teaching for, of, and about thinking. In A. L. Costa (Ed.), *Developing minds: A resource book for teaching thinking.* Washington, D.C.: National Assessment of Educational Progress.

COVINGTON, M. V., & BEERY, R. G. (1976). *Self-worth and school learning.* New York: Holt.

COVINGTON, M. V., & OMELICH, C. L. (1979). It's best to be able and virtuous too: Student and teacher evaluative responses to successful effort. *Journal of Educational Psychology, 71,* 688–700.

COVINGTON, M. V., CRUTCHFIELD, R. S., OLTON, R. M., & DAVIES, L. (1972). *Productive thinking program.* Columbus, OH: Charles E. Merrill.

COX, C. M. (1926). *The early mental traits of three hundred geniuses. Volume II: Genetic studies of genius.* Stanford, CA: Stanford University Press.

COX, J. (1986). The Richardson Study: Results and recommendations. In J. Van Tassel-Baska (Ed.), *The Richardson Study: A catalyst for policy change in gifted education.* Evanston, IL: Northwestern University.

COX, J., & DANIEL, N. (1983a, November/December). Identification: Special problems and special populations. *G/C/T,* 54–61.

COX, J., & DANIEL, N. (1983b, September/October). The role of the mentor. *G/C/T,* 54–61.

COX, J., & DANIEL, N. (1983c, May/June). Specialized schools for high ability students. *G/C/T,* 2–9.

COX, J., & DANIEL, N. (1985, March/April). The Richardson survey concludes. *G/C/T,* 33–36.

COX, J., DANIEL, N., & BOSTON, B. A. (1985). *Educating able learners: Programs and promising practices.* Austin, TX: University of Texas Press.

CRABBE, A. B. (1979, November/December). The 1979 future problem solving bowl. *G/C/T,* 15–16.

CRABBE, A. B. (1982). Creating a brighter future: An update on the future problem solving problem. *Journal for the Education of the Gifted, 5,* 2–9.

CRAWFORD, R. P. (1978). The techniques of creative thinking. In G. A. Davis & J. A. Scott (Eds.), *Training creative thinking*. Melbourne, FL: Krieger.

CRONBACH, L. J., & SNOW, R. E. (1977). *Aptitude and instructional methods*. New York: Irving Publishers.

CULBERTSON, S. (1985, May/June). Career guidance for the gifted. *G/C/T*, 16–17.

DABNEY, M. (1983, July). *Perspectives and directive in assessment of the black child*. Paper presented at the meeting of the Council for Exceptional Children, Atlanta, GA.

DANIELS, P. R. (1983). *Teaching the gifted/learning disabled child*. Rockville, MD: Aspen.

DAURIO, S. P. (1979). Educational enrichment vs. acceleration: A review of the literature. In W. C. George, S. J. Cohn, & J. C. Stanley (Eds.), *Acceleration and enrichment: Strategies for educating the gifted*. Baltimore, MD: Study of Mathematically Precocious Youth, Johns Hopkins University.

DAVIDSON, J. E. (1986). The role of insight in giftedness. In R. J. Sternberg & J. E. Davidson (Eds.), *Conceptions of giftedness*. Cambridge, MA: Cambridge University Press.

DAVIDSON, J. E., & STERNBERG, R. J. (1984). The role of insight in intellectual giftedness. *Gifted Child Quarterly, 28*, 58–64.

DAVIDSON, K. (1986). The case against formal identification. *Gifted Child Today, 9*(6), 7–11.

DAVIS, G. A. (1973). *Psychology of problem solving: Theory and practice*. New York: Basic Books.

DAVIS, G. A. (1975). In frumious pursuit of the creative person. *Journal of Creative Behavior, 9*, 75–87.

DAVIS, G. A. (1981a). Personal creative thinking techniques. *Gifted Child Quarterly, 25*, 99–101.

DAVIS, G. A. (1981b). Review of the Revolving Door Identification Model. *Gifted Child Quarterly, 25*, 185–186.

DAVIS, G. A. (1982). A model for teaching for creative development. *Roeper Review, 5*(2), 27–29.

DAVIS, G. A. (1983). *Educational Psychology: Theory and practice*. New York: Random House.

DAVIS, G. A. (1985). *Creative thinking and problem solving*. (Apple computer disk and manual). Buffalo, NY: Bearly Limited.

DAVIS, G. A. (1986). *Creativity is forever* (2nd ed.). Dubuque, IA: Kendall/Hunt.

DAVIS, G. A. (1987). What to teach when you teach creativity. *Gifted Child Today, 10*, 7–19.

DAVIS, G. A. (1989). *Good person book: Creative teaching of values and moral thinking*. East Aurora, NY: DOK.

DAVIS, G. A., & BULL, K. S. (1978). Strengthening affective components of creativity in a college course. *Journal of Educational Psychology, 70*, 833–836.

DAVIS, G. A., & DIPEGO, G. (1973). *Imagination express: Saturday subway ride*. East Aurora, NY: DOK.

DAVIS, G. A., HELFERT, C. J., & SHAPIRO, G. R.(1973). Let's be an ice cream machine!: Creative dramatics. *Journal of Creative Behavior, 7*, 37–48.

DAVIS, G. A., PETERSON, J. M., & FARLEY, F. H. (1973). Attitudes, motivation, sensation seeking, and belief in ESP as predictors of real creative behavior. *Journal of Creative Behavior, 8*, 31–39.

DAVIS, G. A., & RIMM, S. (1979). Identification and counseling of creatively gifted. In N. Colangelo & R. T. Zaffrann, (Eds.), *New voices in counseling the gifted*. Dubuque, IA: Kendall/Hunt.

DAVIS, G. A., & RIMM, S. (1980). *GIFFI II: Group inventory for finding interests*. Watertown, WI: Educational Assessment Service.

DAVIS, G. A., & RIMM, S. (1982). Group inventory for finding interests (GIFFI) I and II: Instruments for identifying creative potential in the junior and senior high school. *Journal of Creative Behavior, 16*, 50–57.

DAVIS, G. A., & RIMM, S. B. (1985). *Education of the gifted and talented*. Englewood Cliffs, NJ: Prentice Hall.

DAVIS, G. A., & THOMAS, M. A. (1989). *Effective schools and effective teachers*. Needham Heights, MA: Allyn & Bacon.

DEAUX, K. (1976). Ahh, she was just lucky. *Psychology Today, 10*, 70.

DEBONO, E. (1973). *CoRT Thinking*. Elmsford, NY: Pergamon.

DEBONO, E. (1976). *Teaching thinking*. London: Maurice Temple Smith.

DEBONO, E. (1980). *Opportunities*. New York: Penguin.

DEBONO, E. (1983). The direct teaching of thinking as a skill. *Phi Delta Kappan, 64*, 703–708.

DeBono, E. (1985, September). Partnerships of the mind: Teaching society to think. *ProEducation,* 56–58.

Delisle, J. R., & Renzulli, J. S. (1982). The revolving door identification and programming model: Correlates of creative production. *Gifted Child Quarterly, 26,* 89–95.

DeMille, R. (1973). *Put your mother on the ceiling.* New York: Viking/Compass.

DeMott, B. (1981). Mind-expanding teachers. *Psychology Today, 4,* 110–119.

Department of Educational Research and Program Development. (1979). *ESEA Title VII bilingual/bicultural educational program, 1978–1979.* Milwaukee, WI: Milwaukee Public Schools.

Dettman, D. F., & Colangelo, N. (1980). A functional model for counseling parents of the gifted. *Gifted Child Quarterly, 24,* 158–161.

Diessner, R. (1983, May/June) The relationship between cognitive abilities and moral development. *G/C/T,* 15–17.

Dressel, P. L., & Mayhew, L. B. (1954). *General education: Explorations in evaluation.* Washington, DC: American Council on Education.

Drews, E., & Teahan, J. (1957). Parental attitudes and academic achievement. *Journal of Clinical Psychology, 13,* 328–332.

Dunn, R., Bruno, A., & Gardiner, B. (1984). Put a cap on your gifted program. *Gifted Child Quarterly, 28,* 70–72.

Dunn, R., & Dunn, K. (1978). *Teaching students through their individual learning styles.* Reston, VA: Reston Publishing Division of Prentice Hall.

Dunn, R., Dunn, K., & Price, G. E. (1981). *Learning style inventory.* Lawrence, KS: Price Systems.

Dunn, R., & Griggs, S. (1985, November/December). Teaching and counseling gifted students with their learning styles preferences: Two case studies. *G/C/T,* 40–43.

Durden-Smith, J., & DeSimone, D. (1982, November). Is there a superior sex? *Readers Digest,* 263–270.

Dweck, C. S., & Bush, E. S. (1976). Sex differences in learned helplessness: I. Differential debilitation with peer and adult evaluators. *Developmental Psychology, 12,* 147–156.

Eash, M. (1972). *Issues in evaluation and accountability in special programs for gifted and talented children.* Chicago: University of Illinois-Chicago Circle.

Eberle, B. (1971). *Scamper.* East Aurora, NY: DOK.

Eberle, B. (1974). *Classroom cues: A flip book for cultivating multiple talent.* East Aurora, NY: DOK.

Eberle, B., & Stanish, B. (1985). *CPS for kids.* Carthage, IL: Good Apple.

Eby, J. W. (1984). *Administration manual for the EBY gifted behavior index.* Crystal Lake, IL: Gifted Behavior Research and Development Center.

Edlind, E. P., & Haensly, P. A. (1985). Gifts of mentorships. *Gifted Child Quarterly, 29,* 55–60.

Edwards, D. A. (1969). Early androgen stimulation and aggressive behavior in male and female mice. *Physiological Behavior, 4,* 333–338.

Eisenberg, D., & Epstein, E. (1981, December). *The discovery and development of giftedness in handicapped children.* Paper presented at the CEC-TAG National Topical Conference on the Gifted and Talented Child, Orlando, FL.

Ellingson, M., Haeger, W., & Feldhusen, J. F. (1986, March/April). The Purdue mentor program. *G/C/T,* 2–5.

Elman, L. L., & Elman, D. (1983, January/February). Mainstreaming the gifted: An approach that works. *G/C/T,* 45–46.

Ennis, R. H. (1962). A concept of critical thinking: A proposed basis for research in the teaching and evaluation of critical thinking ability. *Harvard Educational Review, 32,* 83.

Ennis, R. H. (1964). *Critical thinking readiness in grades 1–12: Phase I. Deductive reasoning in adolescence.* Project No. 1680, School of Education, Cornell University.

Epstein, J. (1981). *Portraits of great teachers.* New York: Basic Books.

Erikson, E. H. (1959). *Identity and the life cycle: Selected papers by Erik H. Erikson.* New York: International Universities Press.

Erikson, E. H. (1968). *Identity: Youth and crisis.* New York: Norton.

Ernest, J. (1976). Mathematics and sex. *American Mathematical Monthly, 83,* 595–614.

Exum, H. (1983). Key issues in family counseling with gifted and talented black students. *Roeper Review, 5*(3), 28–31.

Fabun, D. (1968). *You and creativity.* New York: Macmillan.

FANTINI, M. D. (1981). A caring curriculum for gifted children. *Roeper Review, 3*(4), 3–4.

FARLEY, F. H. (1986, May). The big T in personality. *Psychology Today,* 47–52.

FARMER, H. S., & BOHN, M. J. (1970). Home career conflict reduction and the level of career interest in women. *Journal of Counseling Psychology, 17,* 228–232.

FARNHAM, P. (1988, February). Women in science: Numbers have improved, but problems remain. *Federation Journal Public Affairs,* Federation of American Societies for Experimental Biology, 171.

FEDLER, F. (1973). The mass media and minority groups. *Journalism Quarterly, 50,* 109–117.

FELD, S., RUHLAND, D., & GOLD, M. (1979). Developmental changes in achievement motivation. *Merrill-Palmer Quarterly, 25,* 43–60.

FELDHUSEN, H. J. (1981). Teaching gifted, creative, and talented students in an individualized classroom. *Gifted Child Quarterly, 25,* 108–111.

FELDHUSEN, H. J. (1986). *Individualized teaching of gifted children in regular classrooms.* East Aurora, NY: DOK.

FELDHUSEN, J. F. (1986). A new conception of giftedness and programming for the gifted. *Illinois Council for the Gifted Journal, 5,* 2–6.

FELDHUSEN, J. F., ASHER, J. W., & HOOVER, S. M. (1984). Problems in the identification of giftedness, talent, or ability. *Gifted Child Quarterly, 28,* 149–151.

FELDHUSEN, J. F., & HANSEN, J. (1987). Selecting and training teaches to work with the gifted in a Saturday Program. *Gifted International, 4*(1), 82–94.

FELDHUSEN, J. F., & KOLLOFF, P. B. (1981). A three-stage model for gifted education. In R. E. Clasen, B. Robinson, D. R. Clasen, & G. Libster (Eds.), *Programming for the gifted, talented and creative: Models and methods.* Madison, WI: University of Wisconsin-Extension.

FELDHUSEN, J. F., & KOLLOFF, P. B. (1986). The Purdue three-stage enrichment model for gifted education at the elementary level. In J. S. Renzulli (Ed.), *Systems and models for developing programs for the gifted and talented.* Mansfield Center, CT: Creative Learning Press.

FELDHUSEN, J. F., & KOOPMANS-DAYTON, J. D. (1987). Meeting special needs of the gifted through Saturday programs. *Gifted International, 4*(2), 89–101.

FELDHUSEN, J. F., PROCTOR, T. B., & BLACK, K. N. (1986). Guidelines for grade advancement of precocious children. *Roeper Review, 9*(1), 25–27.

FELDHUSEN, J. F., & SOKOL, L. (1982). Extraschool programming to meet the needs of gifted youth: Super Saturday. *Gifted Child Quarterly, 26,* 51–56.

FELDHUSEN, J. F., & TREFFINGER, D. J. (1985). *Creative thinking and problem solving in gifted education* (3rd ed.). Dubuque, IA: Kendall/Hunt.

FELDHUSEN, J. F., & WYMAN, A. R. (1980). Super Saturday: Design and implementation of Purdue's special program for gifted children. *Gifted Child Quarterly, 24.* 15–21.

FELDMAN, D. H. (1979). The mysterious case of extreme giftedness. In A. H. Passow (Ed.), *The gifted and the talented.* Chicago: National Society for the Study of Education.

FELDMAN, D. H. (1986). Giftedness as a developmentalist sees it. In R. J. Sternberg & J. E. Davidson (Eds.), *Conceptions of giftedness.* Cambridge, MA: Cambridge University press.

FELDMAN, D. H., & GOLDSMITH, L. T. (1986). *Nature's gambit; Child prodigies and the development of human potential.* New York: Basic Books.

FELDMAN, R. D. (1982). *Whatever Happened to the Quiz Kids?* Chicago: Chicago Review Press.

FELDMAN, R. D. (1985, October). The pyramid project: Do we have the answer for the gifted? *Instructor,* 62–65.

FELTON, G. S., & BIGGS, B. E. (1977). *Up from underachievement.* Springfield, IL Charles C. Thomas.

FENNEMA, E. (1980). Sex-related differences in mathematics achievement: Where and why. In L. H. Fox, L. Brody, & D. Tobin (Eds.), *Women and the mathematical mystique.* Baltimore, MD: Johns Hopkins University Press.

FENNEMA, E., & SHERMAN, J. A. (1978). Sex-related differences in mathematics achievement and related factors: A further study. *Journal for Research in Mathematics Education, 9,* 189–203.

FEUERSTEIN, R. (1980). *Instrumental enrichment: An intervention program for cognitive modifiability.* Baltimore, MD: University Park Press.

FIEDLER, E. D. (1982, October). *The Kranz Talent Identification instrument.* Speech presented at the Wisconsin Council on Gifted and Talented, Madison, WI.

FINE, M. J., & PITTS, R. (1980). Intervention with underachieving gifted children: Rationale and strategies. *Gifted Child Quarterly, 24,* 51–55.

First Official U.S. Education Mission to the USSR. (1959). *Soviet commitment to education, Bulletin 1959, No. 16.* Washington, DC: Office of Education, Department of Health, Education, and Welfare.

FITZGERALD, L. F., & CRITES, J. O. (1980). Toward a career psychology of women: What do we know? What do we need to know? *Journal of Counseling Psychology, 27,* 44–62.

FOX, L. H. (1974). Facilitating the development of mathematical talent in young women. Unpublished Ph.D. thesis, Johns Hopkins University.

FOX, L. H. (1977a). The effects of sex-role socialization on mathematics participation and achievement. In J. Shoemaker (Ed.), *Women and mathematics: Research perspectives for change.* Papers in Education and Work, No. 8, Washington, DC: National Institute of Education, U.S. Department of Health, Education and Welfare.

FOX, L. H. (1977b). Sex differences: Implications for program planning for the academically gifted. In J. C. Stanley, W. C. George, and C. H. Solano (Eds.), *The gifted and the creative: A fifty-year perspective.* Baltimore, MD: Johns Hopkins University Press.

FOX, L. H. (1979). Programs for the gifted and talented: An overview. In A. H. Passow (Ed.), *The gifted and talented.* Chicago: National Society for the Study of Education.

FOX, L. H. (1981a, February). Mathematically able girls: A special challenge. *Arithmetic Teacher,* 22–23.

FOX, L. H. (1981b, March/April). Preparing gifted girls for future leadership roles. *G/C/T,* 7–11.

FOX, L. H. (1981c). Identification of the academically gifted. *American Psychologist, 36,* 1103–1111.

FOX, L. H. (1983). Bridging the transition from high school to college. *Chronical of Academic and Artistic Precocity, 2,* 4.

FOX, L. H., & BRODY, L. (1983). Models for identifying giftedness: Issues related to the learning-disabled child. In L. H. Fox, L. Brody & D. Tobin (Eds.), *Learning disabled gifted children.* Boston: University Park Press.

FRANKS, B., & DOLAN, L. (1982). Affective characteristics of gifted children: Educational implications. *Gifted Child Quarterly, 26,* 172–178.

FRASIER, M. M. (1987). The identification of gifted black students: Developing new perspectives. *Journal for the Education of the Gifted,* 155–180.

FRAZIER, A., PASSOW, A. H., & GOLDBERG, M. L. (1958). Curriculum research; Study of underachieving gifted. *Educational Leadership, 16,* 121–125.

FRAZIER, N., & SADKER, M. P. (1973). *Sexism in school and society.* New York: Harper & Row.

FREEDMAN, D. G. (1974). *Human infancy: An evolutionary perspective.* Hillsdale, NJ: Erlbaum.

FRENCH, J. I. (1964). *Pictorial test of intelligence.* Boston: Houghton Mifflin.

FRENCH, J. L. (1959). *Educating the gifted: A book of readings.* New York: Holt.

FREUD, S. (1949). *An outline of psychoanalysis.* New York: Norton.

FREY, C. (1980, May/June). The resource room. *G/C/T,* 26–27.

FRIEDMAN, J. M., & MASTER, D. (1980). School and museum: A partnership for learning. *Gifted Child Quarterly, 25,* 42–48.

FRIEZE, I. H. (1975). Women's expectations for and causal attributions of success and failure. In M. T. Mednick, S. S. Tangri, & L. W. Hoffman (Eds.), *Women and achievement: Social and motivational analyses.* New York: Halsted.

FROST, D. (1981, December). *The great debates: For enrichment.* Presented at the CEC-TAG National Topical Conference on the Gifted and Talented Child, Orlando, FL.

GAGE, N. L., & BERLINER, D. C. (1984). *Educational psychology* (3rd ed.). Chicago: Rand McNally.

GAGNE, F. (1985). Giftedness and Talent: Reexamining a reexamination of the definitions. *Gifted Child Quarterly, 29,* 103–112.

GAGNE, R. M. (1974). *Essentials of learning for instruction.* New York: Holt.

GALTON, F. (1869). *Hereditary Genius.* London: Macmillan.

GARTNER, A., KOHLER, M., & REISSMAN, F. (1971). *Children teach children.* New York: Harper & Row.

GAY, J. E. (1978). A proposed plan for identifying black gifted children. *22,* 353–357.

GEARHEART, B. R., & WEISHAHN, M. W. (1976). *The handicapped child in the regular classroom.* St. Louis, MO: Mosby.

GENSLEY, J. (1977). The gifted child in the affective domain. *Gifted Child Quarterly, 21,* 448–449.

GETZELS, J. W., & DILLON J. T. (1973). The nature of giftedness and the education of the gifted. In R. M. Travers (Ed.), *Second handbook of research in training.* Chicago: Rand-McNally.

GETZELS, J. W., & JACKSON, P. W. (1962). *Creativity and intelligence.* New York: Wiley.

GIELE, J. Z. (1978). *Women and the future: Changing sex roles in modern America.* New York: Free Press.

GINSBERG, G., & HARRISON, C. H. (1977). *How to help your gifted child.* New York: Monarch Press.

GOERTZEL, M. G., GOERTZEL, V., & GOERTZEL, T. G. (1978). *300 eminent personalities.* San Francisco: Jossey-Bass, 1978.

GOERTZEL, V., & GOERTZEL, M. G. (1962). *Cradles of eminence.* Boston: Little, Brown.

GOGEL, E. M., McCUMSEY, J., & HEWETT, G. (1985, November/December). What parents are saying. *G/C/T,* 7–9.

GOOD, H. G. (1960). *A history of western education* (2nd ed.). New York: Macmillan.

GOOD, T. L., & WEINSTEIN, R. S. (1986). Teacher expectations: A framework for exploring classrooms. In K. K. Zumwalt (Ed.), *Improving teaching: 1986 ASCD yearbook.* Alexandria, VA: Association for Supervision and Curriculum Development.

GORDON, W. J. J. (1961). *Synectics.* New York: Harper & Row.

GORDON, W. J. J. (1974). *Making is strange.* Books 1–4. New York: Harper & Row.

GORDON, W. J. J., & POZE, T. (1972a). *Teaching is listening.* Cambridge, MA: SES Associates.

GORDON, W. J. J., & POZE, T. (1972b). *Strange and familiar.* Cambridge, MA: SES Associates.

GORDON W. J. J., & POZE T. (1980). *The new art of the possible.* Cambridge, MA: Porpoise Books.

GOURLEY, T. J. (1981). Adapting the varsity sports model to nonpsychomotor gifted students. *Gifted Child Quarterly, 25,* 164–166.

GOY, R. W., & RESKO, J. A. (1972). Gonadal hormones and behavior of normal and pseudohermaphroditic nonhuman female primates. *Recent Progress in Hormone Research, 28,* 707–733.

GRAHAM, P. A. (1978). Expansion and inclusion: A history of women in American higher education. *Signs, 3,* 759–773.

GREGORY, E. H. (1984). Search for exceptional academic achievement at California State University, Los Angeles. *Gifted Child Quarterly, 28,* 21–24.

GREGORY, E. H., & MARCH, E. (1985). Early entrance program at California State University, Los Angeles. *Gifted Child Quarterly, 29,* 83–86.

GRIGGS, S. (1984). Counseling the gifted and talented based on learning styles. *Exceptional Children, 50,* 429–432.

GRIGGS, S., & DUNN, R. (1984). Selected case studies of the learning style preferences of gifted students. *Gifted Child Quarterly, 28,* 115–119.

GUILFORD, J. P. (1967). *The nature of human intelligence.* New York: McGraw-Hill.

GUILFORD, J. P. (1977). *Way beyond the IQ.* Buffalo, NY: Creative Education Foundation.

GURIN, P., & EPPS, E. (1966). Some characteristics of students from poverty backgrounds attending predominantly Negro colleges in the deep south. *Social Forces, 45,* 27–39.

HADARY, D., COHEN, S., & HAUSHALTER, R. (1979). Out of darkness and silence. *Science and Children, 16,* 40–41.

HAGEN, E. (1980). *Identification of the gifted.* New York: Teachers College Press.

HALL, E. G. (1980). Sex differences in IQ development for intellectual gifted students. *Roeper Review, 2(3),* 25–28.

HALL, E. G. (1982, November/December). Accelerating gifted girls. *G/C/T,* 49–50.

HALL, E. G. (1983). Recognizing gifted underachievers. *Roeper Review, 5(4),* 23–25.

HALVERSON, C., & VICTOR, J. (1976). Minor physical anomalies and problem behavior in elementary school children. *Child Development, 47,* 281–285.

HANSON, I. (1984). A comparison between parent identification of young bright children and subsequent testing. *Roeper Review*, 7(1), 44–45.

HARNADEK, A. (1977). *Basic Thinking skills: Analogies—B.* Pacific Grove, CA: Midwest Publications.

HARNADEK, A. (1978). *Mind benders B1: Deductive thinking skills.* Pacific Grove, CA: Midwest Publications.

HARNADEK, A. (1979). *Inference-B: Inductive thinking skills.* Pacific Grove, CA: Midwest Publications.

HARTER, S. (1983). Developmental perspectives on the self-system. In P. Mussen (Ed.), *Handbook of Child psychology* (Vol. 3). New York: Wiley.

HEBB, D. O. (1972). *Textbook of psychology* (3rd Ed.). Philadelphia, PA: W. B. Saunders.

HEILBURN, A. B. (1973). *Aversive maternal control.* New York: Wiley.

HEILBRUN, A. B., HARRELL, S. N., & GILLARD, B. J. (1967). Perceived child-rearing attitudes of fathers and cognitive control in daughters. *Journal of Genetic Psychology, 111,* 29–40.

HEINE, H. (1983). *The most wonderful egg in the world.* New York: Alladin Books, Macmillan Publishing Company.

HELMAN, I. B., & LARSON, S. G. (1980). *Now what do I do?* East Aurora, NY: DOK.

HELSON, R. (1971). Women mathematicians and the creative personality. *Journal of Consulting and Clinical Psychology, 36,* 210–211, 217–220.

HENDERSON, E. H., & LONG, B. H. (1973). Personal-social correlates of academic success among disadvantaged school beginners. *Journal of School Psychology, 9,* 101–113.

HENDERSON, R. W. (1981). *Parent-child interaction: Theory, research and prospects.* New York: Academic Press.

HERMANN, K. E., & STANLEY, J. C. (1983, November/December). An exchange: Thoughts on nonrational precocity. *G/C/T,* 30–36.

HERR, E. L., & WATANABE, A. (1979). Counseling the gifted about career development. In N. Colangelo & R. T. Zaffrann (Eds.), *New voices in counseling the gifted.* Dubuque, IA: Kendall/Hunt.

HERSBERGER, J., & ASHER, W. (1980). Comment on "A Quota System for Gifted Minority Children." *Gifted Child Quarterly, 24,* 26.

HETHERINGTON, E. M. (1972). Effects of father-absence on personality development in adolescent daughters. *Developmental Psychology, 7,* 313–326.

HETHERINGTON, E. M., COX, J., & COX R. (1982). Effects of divorce on parents and children. In Lamb, M. E. (Ed.), *Nontraditional families: Parenting and child development.* Hillsdale, NJ: Lawrence Erlbaum.

HETHERINGTON, E. M., & FRANKIE, G. (1967). Effects of parental dominance, warmth and conflict on imitation in children. *Journal of Personality and Social Psychology, 6,* 119–125.

HIGHAM, S. J., & NAVARRE, J. (1984). Gifted Adolescent females require differential treatment. *Journal for the Education of the Gifted, 8*(1), 43–58.

HILL, J. P.(1980). The family. In M. Johnson (Ed.), *Toward adolescence: The middle school years.* (Seventh-ninth Yearbook of the National Society for the Study of Education.) Chicago: University of Chicago Press.

HILTON, T. L., & BERGLUND, G. W. (1974). Sex differences in mathematics achievement—a longitudinal study. *Journal of Educational Research, 67,* 231–237.

HISKEY, M. (1966). Hiskey-Nebraska test of learning aptitude. Lincoln, NE: Union College Press.

HOBBS, N. (Ed.). (1975). *Issues in the classification of the children.* Volume 2. San Francisco: Jossey-Bass.

HOBBS, N. (1980). Feuerstein's instrumental enrichment: Teaching intelligence to adolescents. *Educational Leadership, 38,* 566–568.

HOBSON, J. R. (1948). Mental age as a workable criterion for school admission. *Elementary School Journal, 48,* 213–321.

HOEPFNER, R., & HEMENWAY, J. (1973). *Test of creative potential.* Hollywood, CA: Monitor.

HOFFMAN, B. (1964). *The tyranny of testing.* New York: Collier Books.

HOFFMAN, E. (1976). Children's perceptions of their emotionally disturbed peers. *Dissertation Abstracts, 37,* 952.

HOFFMAN, J. L., WASSON, F. R., & CHRISTIANSON, B. P. (1985, May/June). Personal development for the gifted underachiever. *G/C/T,* 12–14.

HOFFMAN, L. W. (1972). Early childhood experiences and women's achievement motives. *Journal of Social Issues, 28*(2), 129–156.

HOFFMAN, L. W. (1974). Fear of success in males and females. *Journal of Consulting and Clinical Psychology, 42,* 353–358.

HOLAHAN, C. K. (1981). Lifetime achievement patterns, retirement and life satisfaction of gifted aged women. *Journal of Gerontology, 36,* 741–749.

HOLLINGER, C. L. (1985). The stability of self perceptions of instrumental and expressive traits and social self esteem among gifted and talented female adolescents. *Journal for the Education of the Gifted, 8*(1), 107–126.

HOLLINGER, C. L., & KOSEK, S. (1986). Beyond the use of full scale IQ scores. *Gifted Child Quarterly, 30,* 74–77.

HOLLINGWORTH, L. S. (1926). *Gifted children: Their nature and nurture.* New York: Macmillan.

HOLLINGWORTH, L. S. (1942). *Children above 180 IQ Stanford-Binet: Origin and development.* New York: World Book Co.

HORNER, M. S. (1972). Toward an understanding of achievement related conflicts in women. *Journal of Social Issues, 28,* 155–175.

HUNKINS, F. P. (1976). *Involving students in questioning.* Boston: Allyn & Bacon.

ISAKSEN, S., & TREFFINGER, D. (1985). *Creative problem solving: The basic course.* Buffalo, NY: Bearly Limited.

ISAKSEN, S. G., & TREFFINGER, D. J. (1985). *Creative problem solving: The basic course.* Buffalo, NY: Bearly Limited.

JACKSON, R. M., CLEVELAND, J. C., & MIRENDA, P. F. (1975). The longitudinal effects of early identification and counseling of underachievers. *Journal of School Psychology, 13,* 119–128.

JACOBS, J. E., & ECCLES, J. S. (1985, March). Gender differences in math ability: The impact of media reports on parents. *Educational Researcher,* 20–25.

JANOS, P. M., FUNG, H. C., & ROBINSON, N. M. (1985). Self-concepts, self-esteem, and peer relations among gifted children who feel "different." *Gifted Child Quarterly, 29,* 78–82.

JANOS, P. M., & ROBINSON, N. M. (1985). The performance of students in a program of radical acceleration at the university level. *Gifted Child Quarterly, 29,* 175–179.

JENSEN, A. R. (1969). How much can we boost IQ and scholastic achievement? *Harvard Educational Review, 39,* 1–123.

JENSEN, A. R., (1976). Test bias and construct validity. *Phi Delta Kappan, 58,* 340–346.

JENSEN, A. R. (1980). *Bias in mental testing.* New York: Free Press.

JOHNSON, B. (Ed.). (1977). *A new general of leadership: Education for the gifted and talented.* Bethesda, MD: ERIC Reproduction Services (ED 145601).

JOHNSON, T. (1986, January/February). Creating a speakers bureau. *G/C/T,* 18–19.

JONES, J. L. (1978). Women in science. *USA Today, 107,* 4.

JORDON, T. J. (1981). Self-concepts, motivation, and academic achievement of black adolescents. *Journal of Educational Psychology, 73.* 509–517.

JUNTUNE, J. (1981). *Successful programs for the gifted and talented.* Circle Pines, MN: National Association for Gifted Children.

JUNTUNE, J. (1986). *Summer opportunities for the gifted.* Circle Pines, MN: National Association for Gifted Children.

KAGAN, J. (1965). Impulsive and reflective children: Significance of conceptual tempo. In J. D. Krumboltz (Ed.), *Learning and the educational process.* Chicago: Rand McNally.

KANDEL, D. B. & LASSER, G. S. (1972). *Youth in two worlds.* San Francisco: Jossey-Bass.

KANOY, R. C., JOHNSON, B. W., & KANOY, K. W. (1980). Locus of control and self-concept in achieving bright elementary students. *Psychology in the Schools, 17,* 395–399.

KAPLAN, S. N. (1974). *Providing programs for the gifted and talented.* Ventura, CA: Office of the Ventura County Superintendent of Schools.

KARAMESSINIS, N. P. (1980, May/June). Personality and perceptions of the gifted. *G/C/T,* 11–13.

KARNES, F. A., & BROWN, K. E. (1981). Moral development and the gifted: An initial investigation. *Roeper Review, 3*(4), 8–10.

KARNES, F. A., & CHAUVIN, J. C. (1982a, September/October). Almost everything that parents and teachers of gifted secondary school students should know about early college enrollment and college credit by examination. *G/C/T,* 39–42.

KARNES, F. A., & CHAUVIN, J. C. (1982b). A survey of early admission policies for younger than average students: Implications for gifted youth. *Gifted Child Quarterly, 26,* 68–73.

KARNES, F. A., & CHAUVIN, J. C. (1987). *Leadership skills development program: Leadership skills inventory and leadership skills activities handbook.* East Aurora, NY: DOK.

KARNES, M. B. (1979). Young handicapped children can be gifted and talented. *Journal for the Education of the Gifted, 2,* 157–172.

KARNES, M. B., & SCHWEDEL, A. M. (1981). *RAPYHT Project: Activities for talent identification.* Mimiograph. Urbana, IL: University of Illinois, Institute for Child Behavior and Development.

KARNES, M. B., SHWEDEL, A. M., & LEWIS, G. F. (1983). Long-term effects of early programming for the gifted/talented handicapped. *Journal for the Education of the Gifted, 6,* 266–276.

KARNES, M. B., SHWEDEL, A. M., & STEENBERG, D. (1984). Styles of parenting among parents of young gifted children. *Roeper Review, 6*(4), 232–235.

KATZ, M. L. (1973). *Female motive to avoid success: A psychological barrier or a response to deviancy.* Princeton, NJ: Educational Testing Service.

KAUFMAN, A. S. (1976a). A new approach to the interpretation of test scatter on the WISC-R. *Journal of Learning Disabilities, 9,* 160–168.

KAUFMAN, A. S. (1976b). Verbal-performance IQ discrepancies on the WISC-R. *Journal of Consulting and Clinical Psychology, 44,* 739–744.

KAUFMAN, A. S. (1979). *Intelligence testing with the WISC-R.* New York: Wiley-Interscience.

KAUFMANN, F. (1986). *Helping the muskrat guard his musk: A new look at underachievement.* Bossier City, LA: Bossier Parish School Board.

KEATING, D. P. (1980). Four faces of creativity: The continuing plight of the intellectually underserved. *Gifted Child Quarterly, 24,* 56–61.

KELLY, K. R., & COLANGELO, N. (1984). Academic and social self-concepts of gifted, general, and special students. *Exceptional Children, 50*(6), 551–554.

KENNY, A. (1986, July/August). Counseling and gifted, creative, and talented: Guidance for the gifted. *G/C/T,* 33–37.

KENNY, A. (1987a, May/June). Counseling the gifted, creative, and talented: An arts activities approach. *G/C/T,* 33–37.

KENNY, A. (1987b). Counseling the gifted, creative, and talented: Creative writing and poetry therapy. *Gifted Child Today, 49*(2), 33–37.

KERR, B. A. (1985). Smart girls, gifted women: Special guidance concerns. *Roeper Review, 8*(1), 30–33.

KESTER, E. S. (1975). The affective domain: A dialog not a monolog. *Creative Child and Adult Quarterly, 24,* 56–61.

KILSON, M. (1976). The status of women in higher education. *Signal, 4,* 935–942.

KIMURA, D. (1985, November). Male brain, female brain: The hidden difference. *Psychology Today,* 50–58.

KITANO, M. K., & KIRBY, D. (1986). *Gifted education: A comprehensive view.* Boston, Little, Brown.

KLAUSMEIER, H. J., & GOODWIN, W. (1975). *Learning and human abilities* (4th ed.). New York: Harper & Row, 1975.

KLAUSMEIER, H. J., QUILLING, M. R., SORENSON, J. S., WAY, R. S., & GLASRUD, G. R. (1971). *Individually guided education and the multi-unit elementary school: Guidelines for implementation.* Madison, WI: Research and Development Center for Cognitive learning.

KOHLBERG, L. (1969). *Stages in the development of moral thought and action.* New York: Holt.

KOHLBERG, L. (1974). The child as moral philosopher. In G. A. Davis & T. F. Warren (Eds.), *Psychology of Education: New looks.* Lexington, MA: D. C. Heath.

KOHLBERG, L. (1976). Moral states and moralization: The cognitive developmental approach. In T. Lickona (Ed.), *Moral development and behavior.* New York: Holt, Rinehart, & Winston.

KOLATA, G. B. (1983). Math genius may have hormonal basis. *Science, 222,* 1312.

KOLATA, G. B. (1980). Math and sex: Are girls born with less ability? *Science, 210,* 1234–1235.

KOLLOFF, P. B., & FELDHUSEN, J. F. (1981). PACE (Program for Academic and Creative Enrichment): An application of the Purdue three-stage model. In R. E. Clasen, B. Robinson, D. R. Clasen, & G. Libster (Eds.), *Programming for the gifted, talented and creative: Models and methods.* Madison, WI: University of Wisconsin-Extension.

KOLLOFF, P. B., & FELDHUSEN, J. F. (1984). The effects of enrichment on self-concept and creative thinking. *Gifted Child Quarterly, 28,* 53–57.

KOLLOFF, P. B., & FELDHUSEN, J. F. (1986). Seminar: An instructional approach for gifted students. *Gifted Child Today, 9*(5), 2–7.

KRANZ, B. (1981). *Kranz talent identification instrument.* Moorhead, MN: Moorhead State College.

KRUEGER, M. L. (1978). *On being gifted.* New York: Walker & Company.

KRYANIUK, L. W., & DAS, J. P. (1976). Cognitive strategies in native children: Analysis and intervention. *Alberta Journal of Educational Research, 22,* 271–280.

LABOV, W. (1974). Academic ignorance and black intelligence. In G. A. Davis & T. F. Warren (Eds.), *Psychology of education: New Looks.* Lexington, MA: D. C. Heath.

LAJOIE, S. P., & SHORE, B. M. (1981). Three myths? The over-representation of the gifted among dropouts, delinquents and suicides. *Gifted Child Quarterly, 25,* 138–141.

LAMB, M. E. (1976). *The role of the father in child development.* New York: Wiley.

LAVACH, J. F., & LANIER, H. B. (1975). The motive to avoid success in 7th, 8th, 9th and 10th grade high-achieving girls. *Journal of Educational Research, 68,* 216–218.

LEFKOWITZ, W. (1975). Communication grows in a "Magic Circle." In D. A. Read & S. B. Simon (Eds.), *Humanistic education sourcebook.* Englewood Cliffs, NJ: Prentice Hall.

LEIFER, A., NEAL, G., & GRAVES, S. (1974). Children's television: More than more entertainment. *Harvard Educational Revue, 44,* 1213–1245.

LEINHARDT, G., SEEWALD, A. M., & ENGEL, M. (1979). Learning what's taught: Sex difference in instruction. *Journal of Educational Psychology, 71,* 432–439.

LEROSE, B. (1977). *The lighthouse design: A model for educating children.* Racine, WI: Racine Unified School District.

LEROSE, B. (1978). A quota system for gifted minority children: A viable solution. *Gifted Child Quarterly, 22,* 394–403.

LEVY-AGRESTI, J., & SPERRY, R. W. (1968). Differential perceptual capacities in major and minor hemispheres. *Proceedings of the National Academy of Sciences, 61.*

LINGEMANN, L. S. (1982). Assessing creativity from a diagnostic perspective: The creative attribute profile. Unpublished Ph.D. Thesis, University of Wisconsin, Madison.

LIPMAN, M. (1976), Philosophy for children. *Metaphilosophy, 7*(1), 17–39.

LIPMAN, M. (1981). What is different about the education of the gifted? *Roeper Review, 4*(1), 19–20.

LIPMAN, M., SHARP, A. M., & OSCANYAN, F. S. (1980). *Philosophy in the classroom* (2nd ed.). Philadelphia: Temple University Press.

LIPS, H. M., & COLWILL, N. L. (1978). *The psychology of sex differences.* Englewood Cliffs, NJ: Prentice Hall.

LOEB, R. C., & JAY, G. (1987). Self-concept in gifted children: Differential impact in boys and girls. *Gifted Child Quarterly, 31,* 9–14.

LOMBROSO, C. (1985). *The man of genius.* London: Scribner's.

LONG, R. (1981, April). *An approach to a defensible non-discriminatory identification model for the gifted.* Paper presented at the meeting of the Council for Exceptional Children. New York, NY.

LUDWIG, G., & CULLINAN, D. (1984). Behavior problems of gifted and nongifted elementary girls and boys. *Gifted Child Quarterly, 28,* 37–39.

LUTEY, C. (1977). *Individual intelligence testing: A manual and sourcebook* (2nd ed.). Greeley, CO: Carol I. Lutey Publishing.

LYNN, D. B. (1974). *The father: His role in child development.* Monterey, CA: Brooks/Cole.

MACCOBY, E. E., & JACKLIN, C. (1974). *Psychology of sex differences.* Stanford, CA: Stanford University Press.

MACKINNON, D. W. (1978). Educating for creativity: A modern myth? In G. A. Davis & J. A. Scott (Eds.), *Training creative thinking.* Melbourne, FL: Krieger.

MAGOON, R. A. (1980, March/April). Developing leadership skills in the gifted, creative, and talented. *G/C/T,* 40–43.

MAGOON, R. A. (1981). A proposed model for leadership development. *Roeper Review, 3*(3), 7–9.

MAKER, C. J. (1977). *Providing programs for the handicapped gifted.* Reston, VA: Council for Exceptional Children.

MAKER, C. J., & UDALL, A. (1983). A pilot program for elementary-age learning disabled/gifted students. In L. Fox, L. Brody

& D. Tobin (Eds.), *Learning disabled gifted children.* Baltimore: University Park Press.

MAKLER, S. J. (1980). On instrumental enrichment: A conversation with Frances Link. *Educational Leadership, 38,* 569–571, 582.

MANOSEVITZ, M., PRENTICE, N. M., & WILSON, F. (1973). Individual and family correlates of imaginary play companions in preschool children. *Developmental Psychology, 8*(1), 72–79.

MARINI, M. M. (1978). Sex differences in the determination of adolescent aspirations: A review of Research. *Sex Roles: A Journal of Research, 4,* 723–754.

MARLAND, S. P., JR. (1972). *Education of the gifted and talented, Volume 1. Report to the Congress of the United States by the U. S. Commissioner of Education.* Washington, D.C.: U.S. Government Printing Office.

MARTINDALE, C. (1975). What makes a person different? *Psychology Today, 9*(7), 44–50.

MARTINSON, R. A. (1974). *The identification of the gifted and talented.* Ventura, CA: Office of the Ventura County Superintendent of Schools.

MARX, J. L. (1982). Autoimmunity in left-handers. *Science, 217,* 141–142, 144.

MASLOW, A. H. (1954). *Motivation and personality.* New York: Harper & Row.

MASLOW, A. H. (1968). *Toward a psychology of being* (2nd ed.). Princeton, NJ: Van Nostrand.

MASLOW, A. H. (1971). *The farther reaches of human nature.* New York: Viking Press.

MATHEW, S. T. (1984). A creative problem-solving (CPS) program for emotionally handicapped children to reduce aggression. *Journal of Creative Behavior, 18,* 278.

MATTSON, B. D. (1983, March/April). Mentors for the gifted and talented: Whom to seek and where to look. *G/C/T,* 10–11.

McBEATH, M., BLACKSHEAR, P., & SMART, L. (1981, August). *Identifying low income, minority gifted and talented youngsters.* Paper presented at the annual meeting of the American Psychological Association, Los Angeles, CA.

McCLELLAND, D. C. (1965). Toward a theory of motive acquisition. *American Psychologist, 29,* 321–333.

McCLELLAND, D. C. (1976). *The achieving society.* New York: Irvington.

McCLELLAND, D. C., ATKINSON, J. W., CLARK, R. A., & LOWELL, E. I. (1953). *The achievement motive.* New York: Appleton.

MEAD, M. (1935). Sex and achievement. *Forum, 94,* 302.

MEEKER, M. N. (1969). *The structure of intellect: Its interpretation and uses.* Columbus, OH: Charles E. Merrill.

MEEKER, M. N. (1976). *Basic teaching comprehension skills workbook.* Books 1–5. El Segundo, CA: SOI Institute.

MEEKER, M. N. (1978). Nondiscriminatory testing procedures to assess giftedness in Black, Chicano, Navajo and Anglo children. In A. Baldwin, G. Gear, & L. Lucito (Eds.), *Educational planning for the gifted.* Reston, VA: Council for Exceptional children.

MEEKER, M. N., & MEEKER, R. (1986). The SOI system for gifted education. In J. S. Renzulli (Ed.), *Systems and models for developing programs for the gifted and talented.* Mansfield Center, CT: Creative Learning Press.

MEEKER, M. N., MEEKER, R., & ROID, G. (1985). *Structure-of-intellect learning abilities test (SOI-LA).* Los Angeles: Western Psychological Services.

MEICHENBAUM, D. H. (1977). *Cognitive-behavior modification.* New York: Plenum.

METFESSEL, N. S., MICHAEL, W. B., & KIRSNER, D. A. (1969). Instrumentation of Bloom's and Krathwohl's taxonomies for the writing of educational objectives. *Psychology in the Schools, 6,* 227–231.

MEYER, A. E. (1965). *An educational history of the western world.* New York: McGraw-Hill.

MICKLUS, S. (1985). *Odyssey of the mind program handbook.* Glassboro, NJ: Creative Competitions.

MICKLUS, S. (1986). *OMAha!* Glassboro, NJ: Creative Competitions.

MICKLUS, S., & GOURLEY, T. (1982). *Problems, problems, problems.* Glassboro, NJ: Creative Competitions.

MILGRAM, R. M., & MILGRAM, N. A. (1967a). Personality characteristics of gifted Israeli children. *Journal of Genetic Psychology, 125,* 185–192.

MILGRAM, R. M., & MILGRAM, N. A. (1976b). Self-concept as a function of intelligence and creativity in gifted Israeli children. *Psychology in the Schools, 13,* 91–96.

MILLS, C. (1980). Sex-role-related personality correlates of intellectual abilities in adolescents. *Roeper Review, 2*(3), 29–31.

MILTON, G. A. (1957). The effects of sex-role identification upon problem-solving skill. *Journal of Abnormal and Social Psychology, 55*, 208–212.

MONEY, J., HAMPSON, J. G., & HAMPSON, J. L. (1973). Hermaphroditism: Recommendations concerning assignment of sex, change of sex, and psychological management. *Bulletin of Johns Hopkins University Hospital, 97*, 284–300.

MONEY, J., & SCHWARTZ, M. (1978). Biosocial determinants of gender identity differentiation and development. In J. B. Hutchinson (Ed.), *Biological determinants of sexual behavior.* New York: Wiley.

MONTEMAYER, R. (1984). Changes in parent and peer relationships between childhood and adolescence: A research agenda for gifted adolescents. *Journal for the Education of the Gifted, 8*(1), 9–23.

MOORE, B. A. (1979). A model career education program for gifted disadvantaged students. *Roeper Review, 2*(2), 20–22.

MORROW, L. (1983, April). *Home and school correlates of early interest in literature.* Paper presented at the American Educational Research Association, Montreal.

MOSLEY, J. H. (1982, November/December). Ten suggestions to insure the brevity of your gifted program. *G/C/T, 46.*

MOSS, E. S. (1983, April). Mothers and gifted preschoolers-teaching and learning strategies. Paper presented at the American Educational Research Association, Montreal.

MOYER, K. E. (1974). Sex differences in aggression. In R. C. Friedman, R. M. Richart, & R. L. Vande Weile (Eds.), *Sex difference in behavior.* New York: Wiley.

MURPHY, S. (1980, March/April). Programming for the academically gifted: The Hard Day's Night model. *G/C/T*, 20–21.

MUSSEN, P. H., & RUTHERFORD, E. (1963). Parent-child relations and parental personality in relation to young children's sex-role preferences. *Child Development, 34*, 589–607.

NADELSON, T., & EISENBERG, L. (1977). On being married to a professional woman. *American Journal of Psychiatry, 134*, 1071–1076.

National Advisory Committee on the Handicapped. (1976). *The unfinished revolution:* *Education for the handicapped.* Washington, DC: U.S. Government Printing Office.

National Assessment of Educational Progress. (1982). *Reading, thinking, and writing.* Denver, CO: National Assessment of Educational Progress.

National Assessment of Educational Progress. (1975). *Male-Female achievement in eight learning areas: A compilation of selected assessment results.* Denver, CO: Educational Commission of the States.

National Commission on Excellence in Education. (1983). *A nation at risk: The imperative for educational reform.* Washington, D.C.: U.S. Government Printing Office.

NEWLAND, T. E. (1969). *Manual for the blind learning aptitude test: Experimental edition.* Urbana, IL: Newland.

NEWLAND, T. E. (1976). *The gifted in socioeducational perspective.* Englewood Cliffs, NJ: Prentice Hall.

NICHOLS, J. G. (1979). Development of perception of own attainment and causal attribution for success and failure in reading. *Journal of Educational Psychology, 71*, 94–99.

NOVAK, D. (1974). Children's reactions to emotional disturbance in imaginary peers. *Journal of Consulting and Clinical Psychology, 42.*

NYQUIST, E., (1973). *The gifted: The invisibly handicapped, or there is no heavier burden than a great potential.* Paper presented at the National Conference on the Gifted, Albany, NY.

O'CONNELL, B. (1982). *Arts for the handicapped, ESEA Title IV-C Model Sites Project.* Sheboygan, WI: Wisconsin Department of Public Instruction.

OGBY, J. U. (1981). Origins of human competence: A cultural-ecological perspective. *Child Development, 52*, 413–429.

OLSEN, H. (1970). A comparison of academic self-concept, significant others of black and black pre-college students. *Child Study Journal, 1*, 28–32.

OLSHEN, S. R. (1987). The disappearance of giftedness in girls: An intervention strategy. *Roeper Review, 9*(4), 251–254.

Olympics of the Mind Association. (1983). *What is Olympics of the Mind?* Glassboro, NJ: OM Association.

OMOND, J. (1985, July/August). Extracurricular centres for the gifted in South Africa. *G/C/T*, 36–37.

Orange County Department of Education. (1984). *Project IMPACT.* Costa Mesa, CA: Orange County Department of Education.

OSBORN, A. F. (1963). *Applied imagination* (3rd ed.). New York: Scribner's 1963.

PALLAS, A. M., & ALEXANDER, K. L. (1983). Sex differences in quantitative SAT performance: New evidence on the differential coursework hypothesis. *American Educational Research Journal, 20,* 165–182.

PALLONE, N., RICHARD, F., & HURLEY, R. (1973). Further data on key influencers of occupational expectations of minority youth. *Journal of Counselling Psychology, 20,* 484–486.

PARISH, T. S., & NUNN, G. D. (1983, April). *Locus of control as a function of family type and age at onset of father absence.* Paper presented at the American Educational Research Association, Montreal.

PARKER, J. (1983, September/October). The leadership training model. *G/C/T,* 8–13.

PARKER, M. (1979, September/October). Bright kids in trouble with the law. *G/C/T,* 62–63.

PARNES, S. J. (1978). Can creativity be increased? In G. A. Davis & J. A. Scott (Eds.), *Training creative thinking.* Melbourne, FL: Krieger.

PARNES, S. J. (1981). *The magic of your mind.* Buffalo, NY: Creative Education Foundation.

PARSONS, J. (1982, April). *Women and mathematics: Synthesis of recent research.* Paper presented at the American Educational Research Association, New York.

PARSONS, J., FRIEZE, I. H., & RUBLE, D. M. (1978). Intrapsychic factors influencing career aspirations in college women. *Sex Roles: A Journal of Research, 4,* 337–348.

PASSOW, A. H. (1981). The nature of giftedness and talent. *Gifted Child Quarterly, 25,* 5–10.

PASSOW, A. H. (1987). Curriculum for the gifted. *Gifted Child Today, 10*(2), 15–16.

PERINO, S. C., & PERINO, J. (1981). *Parenting the gifted—developing the promise.* New York: R. R. Bowker Company.

PERKINS, E. (1975). *Home is a dirty street: The social oppression of black children.* Chicago: Third World Press.

PERKINS, J. A., & WICAS, E. A. (1971). Group counseling bright underachievers and their mothers. *Journal of Counseling Psychology, 18,* 273–278.

PERRONE, P. A., KARSHNER, W. W., & MALE, R. A. (1979). Identification of talented students. In N. Colangelo & R. T. Zaffrann (Eds.), *New voices in counseling the gifted,* Dubuque, IA: Kendall/Hunt.

PERRONE, P. A., & PULVINO, C. J. (1979). New directions in the guidance of the gifted and talented. In J. C. Gowan, J. Khatena, & E. P. Torrance (Eds.), *Educating the ablest* (2nd ed.). Chicago: Peacock.

PETRO, C. S., & PUTNAM, B. A. (1979). Sex-role stereotypes: Issues of attitudinal changes. *Signs, 5,* 1–4.

PFEIL, M. P. (1978, March). Fourth Street School's new claim to fame. *American Education,* 10–13.

PIAGET, J., & INHELDER, B. (1969). *The psychology of the child.* (H. Weaver trans.) New York: Basic Books.

PIERCE, J. W., & BOWMAN, P. (1960). Motivation patterns of superior high school students. *Cooperative Research Monograph No. 2,* 33–36.

PINE, G. J., & BOY, A. V. (1977). *Learner-centered teaching: A humanistic view.* Denver, CO: Love Publishing Co.

PINEGREE, S. (1978). The effects of nonsexist television commercials and perceptions of reality on children's attitudes about women. *Psychology of Women Quarterly, 2,* 262–277.

PLESE, S. (1982). An application of triad for gifted enrichment: The organization of a community resource center. *Roeper Review, 5*(2), 5–8.

PLOWMAN, P. D. (1981). Training extraordinary leaders. *Roeper Review, 3*(3), 13–16.

POLOMA, M. M. (1972). Role conflict and the married professional woman. In C. Safilios-Rothchild (Ed.), *Toward a sociology of women.* Lexington, MA: Xerox College Publishing.

POST, R. D. (1981). Causal explanations of male and female academic performance as a function of sex-role biases. *Sex Roles, 7,* 691–698.

PROCTOR, T. B., BLACK, K. N., & FELDHUSEN, J. F. (1986). Early admission of selected children to elementary school: A review of the research literature. *Journal of Educational Research, 80*(2), 70–76.

PROVUS, M. M. (1972). *Discrepancy evaluation.* Berkeley, CA: McCutchan.

PULVINO, C. J. (1974). Observed maternal behavior with four-year-old boys and girls in lower-class families. *Child Development, 45,* 1126–1131.

PULVINO, C. J. (1976). The role of the father in cognitive, academic and intellectual development. In M. E. Lamb (Ed.), *The role of the father in child development.* New York: Wiley.

PULVINO, C. J., COLANGELO, N., & ZAFFRANN, R. T. (1976). *Laboratory counseling programs.* Madison, WI: Department of Counseling and Guidance, University of Wisconsin.

PULVINO, C. J., & EPSTEIN, A. (1975, April). *Observed paternal behavior and the intellectual functioning of pre-school boys and girls.* Paper presented at the Society for Research in Child Development, Denver, CO.

RADIN, N. (1974). Observed maternal behavior with four-year-old boys and girls in lower-class families. *Child Development, 45,* 1126–1131.

RADIN, N. (1976). The role of the father in cognitive, affective and intellectual development. In M. E. Lamb (ed.), *The role of the father in child development.* New York: Wiley.

RADIN, N., & EPSTEIN, A. (1975). Observed paternal behavior and the intellectual functioning of preschool boys and girls. Paper presented at the Society for Research in Child Development, Denver, CO.

REIS, S. M. (1983). Creating ownership in gifted and talented programs. *Roeper Review, 5*(4), 20–23.

REIS, S. M. (1984). Avoiding the testing trap: Using alternative assessment instruments to evaluate programs for the gifted. *Journal for the Education of the Gifted, 7*(1), 45–59.

REIS, S. M. (1987). We can't change what we don't recognize: Understanding the special needs of gifted females. *Gifted Child Quarterly, 31,* 83–89.

REIS, S. M., & BURNS, D. E. (1987). A schoolwide enrichment team invites you to read about methods for promoting community and faculty involvement in a gifted education program. *Gifted Child Today, 49*(2), 27–32.

REIS, S. M., & RENZULLI, J. S. (1982). A case for a broadened conception of giftedness. *Phi Delta Kappan, 63,* 619–620.

REIS, S. M., & RENZULLI, J. S. (1986). The secondary triad model. In J. S. Renzulli (Ed.), *Systems and models for developing programs for the gifted and talented.* Mansfield Center, CT: Creative Learning Press.

RENZULLI, J. S. (1975). *A guidebook for evaluating programs for the gifted and talented.* Ventura, CA: Office of the Ventura County Superintendent of Schools.

RENZULLI, J. S. (1977). *The enrichment triad model: A guide for developing defensible programs for the gifted and talented.* Mansfield, CT: Creative Learning Press.

RENZULLI, J. S. (1978). What makes giftedness? Reexamining a definition. *Phi Delta Kappan, 60,* 180–184.

RENZULLI, J. S. (1983, September/October). Rating the behavioral characteristics of superior students. *G/C/T,* 30–35.

RENZULLI, J. S. (1984). The triad-revolving door system: A research-based approach to identification and programming for the gifted and talented. *Gifted Child Quarterly, 28,* 163–171.

RENZULLI, J. S. (1986). The three-ring conception of giftedness: A developmental model for creative productivity. In R. J. Sternberg & J. E. Davidson (Eds.), *Conceptions of Giftedness.* Cambridge, MA: Cambridge University Press.

RENZULLI, J. S. (1987, April). *The triad/revolving door model.* Workshop presented in Madison, Wisconsin.

RENZULLI, J. S. (1988). *The multiple menu model for developing differentiated curriculum for the gifted and talented.* Unpublished manuscript, Bureau of Educational Research, University of Connecticut, Storrs, CT.

RENZULLI, J. S., & HARTMAN, R. K. (1981). Scale for rating the behavioral characteristics of superior students. In W. B. Barbe & J. S. Renzulli (Eds.), *Psychology and education of the gifted* (3rd ed.). New York: Irvington.

RENZULLI, J. S., & REIS, S. M. (1985, March/April). Scope and sequence approach to process development. *G/C/T,* 2–6.

RENZULLI, J. S., & REIS, S. M. (1986). The enrichment triad/revolving door model: A schoolwide plan for the development of creative productivity. In J. S. Renzulli (Ed.), *Systems and models for developing programs for the gifted and talented.* Mansfield Center, CT: Creative Learning Press.

RENZULLI, J. S., REIS, S. M., & SMITH, L. H. (1981). *The revolving door identification model*. Mansfield, CT: Creative Learning Press.

RENZULLI, J. S., & SMITH, L. H. (1978a). Developing defensible programs for the gifted and talented. *Journal of Creative Behavior, 12*, 21–29, 51.

RENZULLI, J. S., & SMITH, L. H. (1978b). *Learning styles inventory*. Mansfield Center, CT: Creative Learning Press.

RENZULLI, J. S., & SMITH, L. H. (1979). Issues and procedures in evaluating gifted programs. In A. H. Passow (Ed.), *The gifted and the talented*. Chicago: National Society for the Study of Education.

RENZULLI, J. S., & WARD, V. S. (1969). *Diagnostic and evaluative scales for differential education for the gifted*. Storrs, CT: University of Connecticut.

REST, J. (1972). *Defining issues test*. Minneapolis, MN: University of Minnesota.

RESTAK, R. (1979). *The brain: The last frontier*. New York: Doubleday.

REYNOLDS, M. C., BIRCH, J. W., & TUSETH, A. A. (1976). Research on early admissions. In W. Dennis & M. Dennis (Eds.), *The intellectually gifted: An overview*. New York: Grune & Stratton.

RICCA, J. (1984). Learning styles and preferred instructional strategies of gifted students. *Gifted Child Quarterly, 28*, 121–126.

RICHARDSON, S. (1971). Handicap, appearance, and stigma. *Social Science and Medicine, 5*, 621–28.

RICHARDSON, W. B., & FELDHUSEN, J. F. (1986). *Leadership education: Developing skills for youth*. New York: Trillium Press.

RICHERT, E. S. (1985). Identification of gifted students: An update. *Roeper Review, 8*(2), 68–72.

RICHERT, E. S., ALVINO, J. J., & McDONNEL, R. C. (1982). *National report on identification: Assessment and recommendations for comprehensive identification of gifted and talented youth*. Washington, D.C.: Educational Information Resource Center, U.S. Department of Education.

RIGGS, G. G. (1984). Parent power: Wanted for organization. *Gifted Child Quarterly, 28*, 111–114.

RIMM, S. B. (1976). GIFT: *Group inventory for finding creative talent*. Watertown, WI: Educational Assessment Service.

RIMM, S. B. (1977, Fall). A comprehensive framework for total educational evaluation. Forward, *Journal of the Wisconsin Association for Supervision and Curriculum Development*, 9–18.

RIMM, S. B. (1980, September/October). Congratulations Miss Smithersteen, you have proved that Amy isn't gifted. *G/C/T*, 22–24.

RIMM, S. B. (1981a). Evaluation of gifted programs—as easy as ABC. In R. E. Clasen, B. Robinson, D. R. Clasen, & G. Libster (Eds.), *Programming for the gifted, talented and creative: Models and methods*. Madison, WI: University of Wisconsin-Extension.

RIMM, S. B. (1982). *PRIDE: Preschool interest descriptor*. Watertown, WI: Educational Assessment Service.

RIMM, S. B. (1983, March/April). Identifying creativity, Part 1. *G/C/T*, 34–37.

RIMM, S. B. (1984, January/February). If God had meant gifted children to run our homes, she would have created them bigger. *G/C/T*, 26–29.

RIMM, S. B. (1985, September). How to reach the underachiever. *Instructor Magazine*, 73–76.

RIMM, S. B. (1986a). *AIM: Achievement identification measure*. Watertown, WI: Educational Assessment Service.

RIMM, S. B. (1986b). *Underachievement Syndrome: Causes and Cures*. Watertown, WI: Apple Publishing Company.

RIMM, S. B. (1987a). *GAIM: Group achievement identification measure*. Watertown, WI: Educational Assessment Service.

RIMM, S. B. (1987b, January/February). Marching to the beat of a different drummer. *Gifted Child Today*, 2–6.

RIMM, S. B. (1987c, November/December). Why do bright children underachieve? The Pressures they feel. *Gifted Chid Today*, 30–36.

RIMM, S. B. (1988). Popularity ends at grade twelve. *Gifted Child Today*.

RIMM, S. B., & DAVIS, G. A. (1976). GIFT: An instrument for the identification of creativity. *Journal of Creative Behavior, 10*, 178–182.

RIMM, S. B., & DAVIS, G. A. (1979). *GIFFI I: Group inventory for finding interests*. Watertown, WI: Educational Assessment Service.

RIMM, S. B., & DAVIS, G. A. (1980). Five years of international research with GIFT: An instrument for the identification of creativity. *Journal of Creative Behavior, 14,* 35–36.

RIMM, S. B., & DAVIS, G. A. (1983, September/October). Identifying creativity, Part II. *G/C/T,* 19–23.

RIMM, S. B., DAVIS, G. A., & BIEN, Y. (1982). Identifying creativity: A characteristics approach. *Gifted Child Quarterly, 26,* 165–171.

ROBERTS, J. L., & ROBERTS, R. (1986). Differentiating inservice through teacher concerns about education for the gifted. *Gifted Child Quarterly, 30,* 107–109.

ROBINSON, B. (1981). College for kids: The anatomy of a summer enrichment program for K–4 gifted children at the University of Wisconsin-Parkside. In R. E. Clasen, B. Robinson, D. R. Clasen, & G. Libster (Eds.), *Programming for the gifted, talented and creative: Models and methods.* Madison, WI: University of Wisconsin-Extension.

ROBINSON, B., DAVIS, G. A., FIEDLER, E. D., & HELMAN, I. B. (1982). *Education of the gifted and talented: A primer.* Madison, WI: Wisconsin Department of Public Instruction.

RODENSTEIN, J. M., & GLICKAUF-HUGHES, C. (1979). Career and lifestyle determinants of gifted women. In N. Colangelo & R. T. Zaffrann (Eds.), *New voices in counseling the gifted.* Dubuque, IA: Kendall/Hunt.

RODENSTEIN, J., PFLEGER, L., & COLANGELO, N. (1977). Career development needs of the gifted: Special considerations for gifted women. *Gifted Child Quarterly, 20,* 340–347.

ROGERS, C. R. (1949). A coordinated research in psychotherapy: A non-objective introduction. *Journal of Consulting Psychology, 13,* 49–51.

ROGERS, C. R. (1962). Toward a theory of creativity. In S. J. Parnes & H. F. Harding (Eds.), *A source book for creative thinking.* New York: Scribner's.

RONVIK, R. W. (1986). Policy issues in the Richardson Study; A local practitioner's perspective. In J. Van Tassel-Baska (Ed.), *The Richardson Study: A catalyst for policy change in gifted education.* Evanston, IL: Northwestern University.

ROSENBERG, M. (1973). Which significant others? *American Behavioral Scientist,* 829–859.

ROSENTHAL, R. J., & JACOBSON, L. (1968). *Pygmalion in the classroom.* New York: Holt.

ROSNER, S. (1985, May/June). Guidelines for developing effective programs for gifted children with special learning disabilities. *G/C/T,* 55–58.

ROSNER, S., & SEYMOUR, J. (1983). The gifted child with a learning disability: Clinical evidence. In L. Fox, L. Brody, & D. Tobin (Eds.), *Learning Disabled/Gifted Children.* Baltimore: University Park Press.

ROSS, A., & PARKER, H. (1980). Academic and social self-concepts of the academically gifted. *Exceptional Children, 47,* 6–10.

ROYER, R. (1982, January/February). Creative writing assignment for the gifted. *G/C/T,* 29–30.

RUDD, N. A., & MCKENRY, P. C. (1980). Working women: Issues and implications. *Journal of Home Economics, 72*(4), 26–29.

RUHLAND, D., GOLD, M., & FELD, S. (1978). Role problems and the relationship of achievement to performance. *Journal of Educational Psychology, 70,* 950–959.

SADKER, M. P., SADKER, D. M., & HICKS, T. The one-percent solution? Sexism in teacher education texts. *Phi Delta Kappan, 61,* 550–553.

SALTER, J., & TOZIER, L. (1971). A review of intelligence test modifications used with the cerebral palsied and other handicapped groups. *Journal of Special Education, 4,* 391–398.

SANBORN, M. (1979a). Career development: Problems of gifted and talented students. In N. Colangelo & R. T. Zaffrann (Eds.), *New voices in counseling the gifted.* Dubuque, IA: Kendall/Hunt.

SANBORN, M. (1979b). Differential counseling needs of the gifted and talented. In N. Colangelo & R. T. Zaffrann (Eds.), *New voices in counseling the gifted.* Dubuque, IA: Kendall/Hunt.

SANDERS, N. M. (1966). *Classroom questions: What kinds?* New York: Harper & Row.

SATLER, M. (1982). *Assessment of children's intelligence and special abilities* (2nd ed.). Boston: Allyn and Bacon.

SATO, I. S., BIRNBAUM, M. & LoCICERO, J. E. (1974). *Developing a written plan for the education of gifted and talented students.* Ventura, CA: Office of the Ventura County Superintendent of Schools.

SATO, I. S., & JOHNSON, B. (1978). Multifaceted training meets multidimensionally gifted. *Journal of Creative Behavior, 12,* 63–71.

SCHAEFER, C. E. (1969). Imaginary companions and creative adolescents. *Developmental Psychology, 1,* 747–749.

SCHAEFER, C. M. (1970). *Biographical inventory-creativity.* San Diego: Educational and Industrial Testing Service.

SCHAFER, M. (1974). *Die sprache des pferdes.* Munich: Nymfenburger Verlagshandlung.

SCHIFF, M. M., KAUFMAN, A. S., & KAUFMAN, N. L. (1981). Scatter analysis of WISC-R profiles for learning disabled children with superior intelligence. *Journal of Learning Disabilities, 14,* 400–404.

SCHNUR, J. O., & STEFANICH, G. P. (1979). Science for the handicapped gifted child. *Roeper Review, 2*(2), 26–28.

SCHUBERT, J., & CROPLEY, A. J. (1972). Verbal regulation of behavior and IQ in Canadian Indian and white children. *Developmental Psychology, 7,* 295–301.

SCHWARTZ, L. L. (1980). Advocacy for the neglected gifted: Females. *Gifted Child Quarterly, 24,* 113–117.

SCHWARTZ, L. L. (1975, Spring). Women and their achievement motivation. *Pennsylvania Personnel and Guidance Association Journal,* 11–16.

SCRUGGS, T. E., COHN, S. J. (1983). A university-based summer program for a highly able but poorly achieving Indian child. *Gifted Child Quarterly, 27,* 90–93.

SEBRING, A. D. (1983). Parental factors on the social and emotional adjustment of the gifted. *Roeper Review, 6*(2), 97–99.

SELIGMAN, M. E. P. (1975). *Helplessness: On depression, development and death.* San Francisco: Freeman.

SELLS, L. W. (1976). Mathematics, minorities, and women. *ASA Footnotes, 4*(1), 1, 3.

SERBIN, L., & O'LEARY, D. K. (1975). How nursery schools teach girls to shut up. *Psychology Today, 9*(12), 56–58.

SHADE, B. J. (1978, April). Social-psychological characteristics of achieving black children. *The Negro Educational Review, 29*(2), 80–86.

SHADE, B. J. (1983). The social success of black youth. The impact of significant others. *Journal of Black Studies, 14*(2), 137–150.

SHALLCROSS, D. J. (1981). *Teaching creative behavior.* Englewood Cliffs, NJ: Prentice-Hall.

SHAVER, P., & FREEDMAN, J. (1976). Your pursuit of happiness. *Psychology Today, 10*(8), 26–32.

SHEEHY, G. (1982). *Pathfinders.* New York: Bantam Books.

SHEPARD, L. A. (1979). The evaluative component of the self-concept construct. *Journal of Educational Research, 16,* 139–160.

SILVERMAN, L. K. (1986). An interview with Elizabeth Hagen: Giftedness, intelligence and the new Stanford-Binet. *Roeper Review, 8*(3), 168–171.

SIMBERG, A. L. (1964). *Creativity at work.* Boston: Industrial Education Institute.

SIMON, S. B., HOWE, L., & KIRSCHENBAUM, H. (1972). *Value clarification: A handbook of practical strategies for teachers and students.* New York: Hart.

SIMON, S. B., & MASSEY, S. (1973). Values clarification. *Educational Leadership, 31,* 738–739.

SIRMANS, R. (1985, September/October). The Georgia Governor's Honors Program. *G/C/T,* 34.

SJOGREN, D., HOPKINS, T., & GOOLER, D. (1975). *Evaluation plans and instruments: Illustrative cases of gifted program evaluation techniques.* Champaign, IL: Center for Instructional Research and Curriculum Evaluation, University of Illinois.

SLICHTER, C. L. (1986a). Talents unlimited: An inservice education model for teaching thinking skills. *Gifted Child Quarterly, 30,* 119–123.

SLICHTER, C. L. (1986b). Talents unlimited: applying the multiple-talent approach in mainstream and gifted programs. In J. S. Renzulli (Ed.), *Systems and models for developing programs for the gifted and talented.* Mansfield Center, CT: Creative Learning Press.

SLICHTER, C. L. (1987). Thinking skills instruction for classrooms. *Gifted Child Today, 49,* 2–7.

SMITH, J. M. (1966). *Setting conditions for creative teaching in the elementary school.* Boston: Allyn & Bacon.

SMITH, L. G. (1981). Centuries of educational inequities. *Educational Horizons, 60,* 4–10.

SOLANO, C. (1976a). *Precocity and adult failure.* Paper presented at the National Association for Gifted Children.

SOLANO, C. (1976b). *Teacher and pupil stereotypes of gifted boys and girls.* Paper presented at the American Psychological Association, Washington, D.C.

SOLOMON, A. O. (1974). Analysis of creative thinking of disadvantaged children. *Journal of Creative Behavior, 8,* 293–295.

SOMERS, J. V., & YAWKEY, T. D. (1984). Imaginary play companions: Contributions to creativity and intellectual abilities of young children. *Journal of Creative Behavior, 18,* 77–89.

STAINES, G., TAVRIS, C., & JAYARATNE, C. (1974). The Queen Bee syndrome. *Psychology Today, 7*(8), 55–60.

STAKE, J. E. (1981). The educator's role in fostering female career aspirations. *Journal of NAWDAC,* 3–10.

STANISH, B. (1977). *Sunflowering.* Carthage, IL: Good Apple.

STANISH, B. (1988). *The hearthstone traveler.* Carthage, IL: Good Apple.

STANKOWSKI, W. M. (1978). Definition. In R. E. Clasen & B. Robinson (Eds.), *Simple gifts.* Madison, WI: University of Wisconsin-Extension.

STANLEY, J. C. (1977). Rationale of the studies of mathematically precocious youth (SMPY) during its first five years of promoting educational acceleration. In J. C. Stanley, W. C. Solano, & C. H. George (Eds.), *The gifted and the creative: A fifty-year perspective.* Baltimore, MD: Johns Hopkins University Press.

STANLEY, J. C. (1978a). Concern for intellectually talented youths: How it originated and fluctuated. In R. E. Clasen & B. Robinson (Eds.), *Simple gifts.* Madison, WI: University of Wisconsin-Extension.

STANLEY, J. C. (1978b). Identifying and nurturing the intellectually gifted. In R. E. Clasen & B. Robinson (Eds.), *Simple gifts.* Madison, WI: Univeristy of Wisconsin-Extension.

STANLEY, J. C. (1979). The study and facilitation of talent for mathematics. In A. H. Passow (Ed.), *The gifted and the talented.* Chicago: National Society for the Study of Education.

STANLEY, J. C. (1985, August). *Fostering use of mathematical talent in the USA: SMPY's rationale.* Keynote address at the Sixth World conference on Gifted and Talented Children, Hamburg, Germany.

STANLEY, J. C. (1987). Making the IMO team: The power of early identification and encouragement. *Gifted Child Today, 10*(2), 22–23.

STANLEY, J. C. (1988). Some characteristics of SMPY's "700-800 on SAT-M before age 13" group: Youths who reason extremely well mathematically. *Gifted Child Quarterly, 32,* 205–209.

STANLEY, J. C., & BENBOW, C. P. (1983). Educating mathematically precocious youths: Twelve policy recommendations. *Educational Researcher, 11*(5), 4–9.

STANLEY, J. C., & BENBOW, C. P. (1986). Extremely young college graduates: Evidence of their success. *College and University, 58,* 361–371.

STANLEY, J. C., & McGILL, A. M. (1986). More about "young entrants to college: How did they fare?" *Gifted Child Quarterly, 30,* 70–73.

STERNBERG, R. J. (1983). Criteria for intellectual skills training. *Educational Research, 12,* 6–13.

STERNBERG, R. J. (1984). How can we teach intelligence? *Educational Leadership, 42,* 38–48.

STERNGLANZ, S. H., & SERBIN, L. A. (1974). Sex-role stereotyping in children's television programs. *Developmental Psychology, 10,* 710–715.

STOCKARD, J., & WOOD, J. W. (1984). The myth of female underachievement: A reexamination of sex differences in academic underachievement. *American Educational Research Journal, 21,* 825–838.

SULLIVAN, P. M., & VERNON, M. (1979). Psychological assessment of hearing impaired children. *School Psychology Digest, 8,* 271–290.

SUTER, D. P., & WOLF, J. S. (1987). Issues in the identification and programming of the gifted/learning disabled child. *Journal for the Education of the Gifted, 10*(3), 227–237.

SUTHERLAND, S. L. (1978). The unambitious female: Women's low professional aspirations. *Signs: Journal of Women in Culture and Society, 3,* 774–794.

SUTTON-SMITH, B., ROSENBERG, B. G., & LANDY, F. (1968). Father-absence effects in families of different sibling compositions. *Child Development, 39,* 1213–1221.

SWENSON, E. V. (1978). Teacher-assessment of creative behavior in disadvantaged children. *Gifted Child Quarterly, 22,* 338–343.

TAN-WILLMAN, C., & GUTTERIDGE, D. (1981). Creative thinking and moral reasoning of academically gifted secondary school adolescents. *Gifted Child Quarterly, 25,* 149–153.

TANNENBAUM, A. J. (1979). Pre-Sputnik to post-Watergate concern about the gifted. In A. H. Passow (Ed.), *The gifted and the talented.* Chicago: National Society for the Study of Education.

TAYLOR, C. W. (1978). How many types of giftedness can your program tolerate? *Journal of Creative Behavior, 12,* 39–51.

TEAHAN, J. E. (1963). Parental attitudes and college success. *Journal of Educational Psychology, 54,* 104–109.

TERMAN, L. M. (1930). *Genetic studies of genius.* Palo Alto: Stanford University Press.

TERMAN, L. M. (1981). The discovery and encouragement of exceptional talent. In W. B. Barbe & J. S. Renzulli (Eds.), *Psychology and education of the gifted* (3rd ed.). New York: Irvington.

TERMAN, L. M., & ODEN, M. H. (1925). *Genetic studies of genius: Mental and physical traits of a thousand gifted children.* Stanford, CA: Stanford University Press.

TERMAN, L. M., & ODEN, M. H. (1947). *Genetic studies of genius: The gifted child grows up.* Stanford, CA: Stanford University Press.

THORNDIKE, R. S., & HAGEN, E. P. (1977). *Management and evaluation in psychology and education.* New York: Wiley.

TIDBALL, M. E. (1973). Perspective on academic women and affirmative action. *Educational Records, 54,* 130–135.

TIDBALL, M. E., & KISTIAKOWSKY, V. (1976). Baccalaureate origins of American scientists and scholars. *Science, 193,* 747–752.

TIDWELL R. (1980). Gifted students' self-image as a function of identification procedure, race, and sex. *Journal of Pediatric Psychology, 5*(1), 57–69.

TKACH, J. R. (1986, March/April). What to do with a gifted kid this summer. *G/C/T,* 24–25.

TKACH, J. R. (1987). What to do with a gifted kid this summer. *Gifted Child Today, 10*(3), 6–8.

TOMLINSON, S. (1986). A survey of participant expectations for inservice in education of the gifted. *Gifted Child Quarterly, 30,* 110–113.

TONGUE, C., & SPERLING, C. (1976). *Parent nomination form.* Raleigh, NC: North Carolina Department of Public Instruction.

TORRANCE, E. P. (1962). *Guiding creative talent.* Englewood Cliffs, NJ: Prentice Hall.

TORRANCE, E. P. (1963). *Education and the creative potential.* Minneapolis, MN: University of Minnesota Press.

TORRANCE, E. P. (1965). *Rewarding creative behavior.* Englewood Cliffs, NJ: Prentice Hall.

TORRANCE, E. P. (1966). *Torrance tests of creative thinking.* Bensenville, IL: Scholastic Testing Service.

TORRANCE, E. P. (1971). Are the Torrance tests of creative thinking biased against or in favor of disadvantaged groups? *Gifted Child Quarterly, 15,* 75–81.

TORRANCE, E. P. (1976). Future careers for gifted and talented students. *Gifted Child Quarterly, 20,* 142–156.

TORRANCE, E. P. (1977). *Creativity in the classroom.* Washington, DC: National Educational Association.

TORRANCE, E. P. (1979). *The search for satori and creativity.* Buffalo, NY: Creative Education Foundation.

TORRANCE, E. P. (1980). Assessing the further reaches of creative potential. *Journal of Creative Behavior, 14,* 1–19.

TORRANCE, E. P. (1981a). Creative teaching makes a difference. In J. C. Gowan, J. Khatena, & E. P. Torrance (Eds.), *Creativity: Its educational implications* (2nd ed.). Dubuque, IA: Kendall/Hunt.

TORRANCE, E. P. (1981b). Non-test ways of identifying the creatively gifted. In J. C. Gowan, J. Khatena, & E. P. Torrance (Eds.), *Creativity: Its educational implications* (2nd ed.). Dubuque, IA: Kendall/Hunt.

TORRANCE, E. P. (1981c). Sociodrama as a creative problem-solving approach to studying the future. In J. C. Gowan, J. Khatena, & E. P. Torrance (Eds.), *Creativity: Its educational implications* (2nd ed.). Dubuque, IA: Kendall/Hunt.

TORRANCE, E. P. (1982). *Thinking creatively in action and movement.* Bensenville, IL: Scholastic Testing Service.

TORRANCE, E. P. (1983). Status of creative women: Past, present, future. *Creative Child and Adult Quarterly, 8*(3), 135–144.

TORRANCE, E. P. (1984). Teaching gifted and creative learners. In M. Wittrock (Ed.), *Handbook of research on teaching* (3rd ed.). Chicago: Rand-McNally.

TORRANCE, E. P., KHATENA, J., & CUNNINGTON, B. F. (1973). *Thinking creatively with sounds and words.* Bensenville, IL: Scholastic Testing Service.

TORRANCE, E. P., & TORRANCE, J. P. (1978). The 1977–78 future problem-solving program: Interscholastic competition and curriculum project. *Journal of Creative Behavior, 12*, 87–89.

TORRANCE, E. P., WILLIAMS, S. E., TORRANCE, J. P., & HORNG, R. (1978). *Handbook for training future problem-solving teams.* Athens, GA: Georgia Studies of Creative Behavior, University of Georgia.

TORRES, S. (1977). *A primer on individualized education programs for handicapped children.* Reston, VA: Council for Exceptional Children.

TRAXLER, M. A. (1987). Gifted education program evaluation: A national review. *Journal for the Education of the Gifted, 10*(2), 107–113.

TREFFINGER, D. J. (1975). Teaching for self-directed learning: A priority of the gifted and talented. *Gifted Child Quarterly, 19*, 46–59.

TREFFINGER, D. J. (1978). Guidelines for encouraging independence and self-direction among gifted students. *Journal of Creative Behavior, 12*, 14–20.

TREFFINGER, D. J. (1981). *Blending gifted education wtih the total school program.* Honeoye, NY: Center for Creative Learning.

TREFFINGER, D. J. (1982a). Demythologizing gifted education: An editorial essay. *Gifted Child Quarterly, 26*, 3–8.

TREFFINGER, D. J. (1982b). Gifted students, regular students: Sixty ingredients for a better blend. *Elementary School Journal, 82*, 267–273.

TREFFINGER, D. J. (1983, April). *Creativity: Celebrating the vision.* Speech presented at the Third Annual Midwest Conference on Gifted and Talented Children, Milwaukee, WI.

TREFFINGER, D. J. (1986a). *Blending gifted education with the total school program* (2nd ed.). East Aurora, NY: DOK.

TREFFINGER, D. J. (1986b). Fostering effective, independent learning through individualized programming. In J. S. Renzulli (Ed.), *Systems and models for developing programs for the gifted and talented.* Mansfield Center, CT: Creative Learning Press.

TREFFINGER, D. J., & BARTON, B. L. (1979, January/February). Fostering independent learning. *G/C/T*, 3–6.

TREFFINGER, D. J., ISAKSEN, S. G., & FIRESTIEN, R. L. (1982). *Handbook of creative learning* (Vol. 1). Williamsville, NY: Center for Creative Learning.

TREFFINGER, D. J., ISAKSEN, S. G., & McEWEN, P. (1987). *Checklist for preparing for evaluating thinking skills instructional programs.* Honeoye, NY: Center for Creative Learning.

TREFFINGER, D. J., & RENZULLI, J. S. (1986). Giftedness as potential for creative productivity: Transcending IQ scores. *Roeper Review, 8*(3), 150–154.

TRIGG, L. J., & PERLMAN, D. (1976). Social influences on women's pursuit of a non-traditional career. *Psychology of Women Quarterly, 1*(2), 138–150.

TSUIN-CHEN, O. (1961). Some facts and ideas about talent and genius in Chinese history. In G. Z. E. Bereday & J. A. Lauwerys (Eds.), *Concepts of excellence in education: The yearbook of education.* New York: Harcourt, Brace & World.

TUCKER, B. F. (1982). Providing for the mathematically gifted child in the regular classroom. *Roeper Review, 4*(4), 11–12.

VAN TASSEL-BASKA, J. (1981a). Review of the revolving door identification model. *Gifted Child Quarterly, 25*, 187–188.

VAN TASSEL-BASKA, J. (1981b, December). *The great debates: For acceleration.* CEC/TAG National Topical Conference on the Gifted and Talented Child, Orlando, FL.

VAN TASSEL-BASKA, J. (1983). Purdue offers summer programs. *Midwest Talent Search Quarterly, 1*(1), 11.

VAN TASSEL-BASKA, J. (1984). The talent search as an identification model. *Gifted Child Quarterly, 28*, 172–176.

VAN TASSEL-BASKA, J. (1986). Lessons from the history of inservice in Illinois: Effective staff development in the education of gifted students. *Gifted Child Quarterly, 30*, 124–126.

VELLE, W. (1982). Sex hormones and behavior in animals and man. *Perspectives in Biology and Medicine, 25*, 295–315.

VEROFF, J. (1969). Social comparison and the development of achievement motivation. In C. P. Smith (Ed.), *Achievement-related motives in children.* New York: Russel Sage Foundation.

VETTER, B. M., & BABCO, E. L. (1975). *Professional women and minorities: A manpower data resource service.* Washington, D.C.: Scientific Manpower Commission.

WALBERG, H. J., TSAI, S., WEINSTEIN, T., GABRIEL, C. L., RASHER, S. P., ROSE-CRANS, T., ROVAI, E., IDE, J., TRUJILLO, M., & VUKOSAVICH, P. (1981). Childhood traits and environmental conditions of highly eminent adults. *Gifted Child Quarterly, 25,* 103–107.

WALLACH, M. A. (1970). Creativity. In P. H. Mussen (Ed.), *Carmichael's manual of child psychology* (3rd ed.). New York: Wiley.

WALLACH, M. A., & KOGAN, N. (1965). *Modes of thinking in young children.* New York: Holt.

WALLAS, G. (1926). *The art of thought.* New York: Harcourt, Brace, & World.

WARMINGTON, E. H. (1961). Ability and genius in ancient Greece and Rome. In G. Z. G. Bereday & J. A. Lauwerys (Eds.), *Concepts of excellence in education: The yearbook of education.* New York: Harcourt, Brace, & World.

WARREN, T. F. (1974). How to squelch ideas. In G. A. Davis & T. F. Warren (Eds.), *Psychology of education: New looks.* Lexington, MA: D. C. Heath.

WAY, B. (1967). *Development through drama.* London: Longman.

WEBB, J. T., MECKSTROTH, E. A., & TOLAN, S. S. (1982). *Guilding the gifted child.* Columbus, OH. Psychology Publishing Company.

WEBER, J. (1981). Moral dilemmas in the classroom. *Roeper Review, 3*(4), 11–13.

WECHSLER, D. (1974). *The Wechsler intelligence scale for children-revised.* New York: Psychological Corporation.

WEINER, B. (1974). *Achievement motivation and attribution theory.* Morristown, NJ: General Learning Press.

WEINER, B. (1980). *Human motivation.* New York: Holt.

WEINER, N. C., & ROBINSON, S. E. (1986). Cognitive abilities, personality and gender differences in math achievement of gifted adolescents. *Gifted Child Quarterly, 30*(2), 83–87.

WEINSTEIN, J., & LAUFMAN, L. (1981). The fourth R: Reasoning. *Roeper Review, 4*(1), 20–22.

WEISS, P., & GALLAGHER, J. J. (1983, November/December). Parental expectations for the gifted children. *G/C/T, 2–6.*

WEISS, P., & GALLAGHER. J. J. (1986). Project TARGET: A needs assessment approach to gifted inservice. *Gifted Child Quarterly, 30,* 114–118.

WELSH, G. S., & BARRON, F. (1963). *Barron-Welsh art scale.* Palo Alto, CA: Consulting Psychologists Press.

WHITE, B. L., KABAN, B. T., & ATTANUCCI, J. S. (1979). *The origins of human competence: Final report of the Harvard Preschool Project.* Lexington, MA: D. C. Heath.

WHITMORE, J. R. (1980). *Giftedness, conflict, and underachievement.* Boston: Allyn & Bacon.

WHITMORE, J. R., (1986). Understanding a lack of motivation to excel. *Gifted Child Quarterly, 30*(2), 66–69.

WILKIE, V. (1985, January/February). Richardson Study Q's and A's. *G/C/T, 2–9.*

WILL, H. (1986, January/February). Junior great books. *G/C/T, 6–7.*

WILLIAMS, A. T. (1980, March/April). Academic game bowls: Competition for the gifted and talented. *G/C/T, 10–12.*

WILLIAMS, A. T. (1986, January/February). Academic game bowls as a teaching/learning tool. *G/C/T, 2–5.*

WILLIAMS, F. E. (1970). *Classroom ideas for encouraging thinking and feeling.* Buffalo, NY: DOK Publishers.

WILLIAMS, F. E. (1979, September/October). Williams' strategies to orchestrate Renzulli's triad. *G/C/T, 2–6,* 10.

WILLIAMS, F. E. (1980). *Creativity assessment packet.* East Aurora, NY: DOK Publishers.

WILLIAMS, F. E. (1982). *Classroom ideas for encouraging thinking and feeling* (Vol. 2). East Aurora, NY: DOK Publishers.

WILLIAMS, F. E. (1986). The cognitive-affective interaction model for enriching gifted programs. In J. S. Renzulli (Ed.), *Systems and models for developing programs for the gifted and talented.* Mansfield Center, CT: Creative Learning Press.

WITTY, P. A. (1978). Equal educational opportunity for gifted minority group children: Promise or possibility? *Gifted Child Quarterly, 22,* 344–351.

WOLLEAT, P. L. (1979). Guiding the career development of gifted females. In N. Colangelo and R. T. Zaffrann (Eds.), *New voices in counseling the gifted.* Dubuque, IA: Kendall/Hunt.

WOOD, S., & LEADBEATER, P. (1986). Stages of entry for target groups participating in gifted program inservice and staff development. *Gifted Child Quarterly, 30*, 127–130.

YALOM, I. D., GREEN, R., & FISK, N. (1973). Prenatal exposure to female hormones: Effect on psychosexual development in boys. *Archives of General Psychiatry, 28*, 554–561.

YAWKEY, T. D. (1983). Imaginative predisposition interview scale: Test and administration manual. Unpublished Report, University Park, PA: Pennsylvania State University.

YSSELDYKE, J. E., ALGOZZINE, B., & RICHEY, L. (1982). Judgment under uncertainty: How many children are handicapped? *Exceptional Children, 48*, 531–534.

ZACHARIAS, J. R. (1977). The trouble with IQ tests. In P. L. Houts (Ed.), *The myth of measurability*. New York: Hart.

ZAFFRANN, R. T., & COLANGELO, N. (1979). Counseling with gifted and talented students. In N. Colangelo and R. T. Zaffrann (Eds.), *New voices in counseling the gifted*. Dubuque, IA: Kendall/Hunt.

ZIGLER, E., & MUENCHOW, S. (1979). Mainstreaming: The proof is in the implementation. *American Psychologist, 34*, 993–996.

ZILLI, M. G. (1971). Reasons why the gifted adolescent underachieves and some of the implications of guidance and counseling to this problem. *Gifted Child Quarterly, 15*, 279–292.

ZIMMERMAN, W. E., & BRODY, L. E. (1986, March/April). Part-time college for gifted high school students. *G/C/T*, 32–33.

ZINBERG, D. (1974). College: When the future becomes the present. In R. B. Kundsin (Ed.), *Women and success: The anatomy of achievement*. New York: William Morrow.

ZINNER, J. (1985, June). Thinking makes an IMPACT. *Thrust*, 30–32.

ZUCKERMAN, M. (1979). *Sensation seeking: Beyond the optimal level of arousal*. Hillsdale, NJ: Erlbaum.

Author Index

Subject Index